P/ Wilkins
1975.

1&2 CORINTHIANS

A COMMENTARY ON

1&2 CORINTHIANS

Charles Hodge

THE BANNER OF TRUTH TRUST

THE BANNER OF TRUTH TRUST
3 Murrayfield Road, Edinburgh EH12 6EL
P.O. Box 652, Carlisle, Pennsylvania 17013

*

1 Corinthians first published 1857
Reprinted by the Banner of Truth Trust 1958, 1960 & 1964
2 Corinthians first published 1859
Reprinted by the Banner of Truth Trust 1959 & 1963
Both works reprinted in one volume 1974
ISBN 0 85151 185 6

*

Printed by offset lithography in Great Britain
by Billing & Sons Limited, Guildford and London

1 CORINTHIANS

INTRODUCTION.

§ 1. CORINTH.

THE Grecian Peloponnesus is connected with the continent by an isthmus from four to six miles wide. On this isthmus stood the city of Corinth. A rocky eminence, called the Acrocorinthus, rises from the plain almost perpendicularly, to the height of two thousand feet above the level of the sea, and is sufficiently broad at the summit for a town of considerable size. From the top of this abrupt hill the eye reaches towards the east over the expanse of the Ægean Sea, with its numerous islands; and westward, towards the Ionian Sea, a prospect scarcely less inviting was presented. Looking towards the north, the eye rests on the mountains of Attica on the one hand, and north-eastern Greece on the other; the Acropolis of Athens being clearly visible at a distance of forty-five miles. As early as the days of Homer, Corinth was an important city. Its position made it, in a military point of view, the key of the Peloponnesus; and its command of a port on two seas made it the centre of commerce between Asia and Europe. The supremacy enjoyed by one Grecian State after another, had at last fallen to the lot of Corinth. It became the chief city of Greece, not only in authority, but in wealth, magnificence, literature, the arts, and in luxury. It was characteristic of the place, that while the temple of Minerva crowned the Acropolis of Athens, the Acrocorinthus was the site of the temple of Venus. Of all the cities of the ancient world it was most notorious for licentiousness. It was entirely destroyed by the Roman consul Mummius, 120 years B.C., its inhabitants were dispersed, and the conqueror carried with him to Rome the richest spoils that ever graced the triumph of a Roman general. For a century after this event it lay in ruins, serving only as a quarry whence the Roman patricians gathered marble for their palaces. Julius Cæsar, recognizing the military and commercial importance of the position, determined to rebuild it, and for that purpose sent thither a colony consisting principally of freed men. This accounts for the predominance of Latin names which we meet with in connection with the Christians of this city. Erastus, Phoebe, and Sosthenes are Greek names ; but Gaius, Quintus, Fortunatus, Crispus, Justus, Achaicus, are of Roman origin. This colony, however, was little more than the nucleus of the new city. Merchants flocked thither from all parts of Greece ; Jews also were attracted by the facilities of commerce ; wealth, art, literature, and luxury revived. The Isthmian games were again celebrated under the presidency of the city. It was made the capital of Achaia, which, as a Roman province, included the greater part of Greece. Under the fostering care of Augustus, Corinth regained much of its ancient splendour, and during the century which had nearly elapsed since its restoration, before it was visited by the Apostle Paul, it had reached a pre-eminence which made it the glory of Greece. It was at this time under the rule of the Proconsul Gallio, the brother of Seneca,—a man distinguished for integrity and mildness. His brother says of him : *Nemo enim mortalium uni tam dulcis est, quam hic omnibus.* His refusal to entertain the frivolous charges brought by the Jews against Paul (Acts 18, 14–16), is in keeping with the character given of him by his contemporaries. He was one of the victims of the cruelty of Nero.*

---

* Several monographs, proceeding from German scholars, are devoted to the description and history of Corinth : Wilchen's " Rerum Corinthiarum specimen

§ 2. Paul's Labours in Corinth.

As Corinth was not only the political capital of Greece, but the seat of its commercial and intellectual life; the place of concourse for the people not only of the neighbouring cities, but of nations; a source whence influences of all kinds emanated in every direction, it was specially important for the diffusion of the gospel. Paul, therefore, leaving Athens, which he had visited in his second missionary journey, went alone to Corinth, where he was soon after joined by Silas and Timotheus, who came from Macedonia. (Acts 18, 5.) A stranger in this great city, and without the means of support, he associated himself with Aquila, a Jew lately come from Italy, in consequence of the edict of Claudius banishing the Jews from Rome. While living in the house of Aquila, and working with him at his trade of tent-making, Paul attended the synagogue every Sabbath, and "persuaded the Jews and Greeks." But "when they opposed themselves and blasphemed, he shook his raiment, and said unto them, Your blood be upon your own heads; I am clean: henceforth I will go unto the Gentiles. And he departed thence, and went into a certain man's house, named Justus, one who worshipped God, and whose house joined hard to the synagogue. And Crispus, the chief ruler of the synagogue, believed on the Lord, with all his house; and many of the Corinthians hearing it believed, and were baptized. Then spake the Lord to Paul by night, by a vision, Be not afraid, but speak, and hold not thy peace: for I am with thee, and no man shall set on thee to hurt thee; for I have much people in this city. And he continued there a year and six months, teaching the word of God

ad illustrationem utriusque Epistolæ Paulinæ." 1747. Barth's "Corinthiorum Commercia et Mercaturae particula." Berlin, 1844. A very interesting chapter in Conybeare and Howson's Life and Epistles of Paul is devoted to this subject. Vol. 1: ch. 12. See also Winer's Real Wörterbuch. and Arnold's Epistles of Paul to the Corinthians.

among them." (Acts 18, 1–11.) The success of Paul aroused the enmity of the Jews, who determined to arraign him before the Roman governor. As soon as the governor ascertained the nature of the charge, he refused to listen to it, and dismissed the accusers from the judgment-seat with evident displeasure, which encouraged the bystanders to beat the Jews. Thus the opposers of the apostle were ignominiously defeated. After remaining some time longer in Corinth, he sailed from Cenchrea, the eastern port of the city, to Ephesus, with Aquila and Priscilla. Leaving his friends in that city, he sailed to Cæsarea, and thence went up to Jerusalem. After remaining a short time in the Holy City, he went to Antioch, and thence, through Phrygia and Galatia, again to Ephesus. Shortly after Paul left Ephesus the first time, Apollos, an Alexandrian Jew, having been more fully instructed in the doctrine of Christ by Aquila and Priscilla, went to Corinth, and there "mightily convinced the Jews, and that publicly, shewing by the Scripture that Jesus was the Christ." (Acts 18, 24–28.) It is altogether probable, considering the constant commercial intercourse between Corinth and Ephesus, that the apostle had frequent opportunities of hearing of the state of the Corinthian church during his three years' residence in the latter city. The information which he received led him, as is generally supposed, to write a letter no longer extant, exhorting them "not to keep company with fornicators." (See 1 Cor. 5, 9.) Not satisfied with this effort to correct an alarming evil, he seems himself to have made them a brief visit. No record is indeed found in the Acts of his having been to Corinth more than once before the date of this epistle; but there are several passages in his second epistle which can hardly be understood otherwise than as implying an intermediate visit. In 2 Cor. 12, 14 he says, "Behold, the third time I am ready to come to you." This may indeed mean that for the third time he had prepared to go to Corinth; but this the context does not suggest, and would really amount to nothing. It was not how often he had purposed to visit them, but how often he had actually made the journey, which was the point on which stress is laid. In ch. 13, 1 he says, "This is the third time I am coming to you," which is still more explicit. In ch. 2, 1 he says, "I determined I would not come again to you in heaviness." This supposes that he had already made them one sorrowful visit, *i.e.*, one in which he had been obliged to cause sorrow, as well as to experience it. See also ch. 12, 21, and 13, 2, where further allusion seems to be made to a second visit. Notwithstanding his frequent injunctions, the state of things in Corinth seemed to be getting worse. The apostle therefore determined to send Timothy and Erastus to them. (1 Cor. 4, 17. Acts 19, 22.) Whether Timothy reached Corinth at this time is doubtful; and it would seem from 1 Cor. 16, 10, that the apostle himself feared that he might not be able to accomplish all that had been appointed him in Macedonia, and yet get to Corinth before the arrival of this letter. After the departure of Timothy, Paul received such intelligence from the household of Chloe, and from a letter addressed to him by the Corinthians themselves (1 Cor. 7, 1), that he determined at once to write to them.

§ 3. STATE OF THE CHURCH IN CORINTH.

The state of the church in Corinth may be partially inferred from the character and circumstances of the people, but with certainty only from the contents of this and the following epistles. As remarked above, the population of the city was more than ordinarily heterogeneous. The descendants of the colonists sent by Julius Cæsar, the Greeks who were attracted to the principal city of their own country, Jews and strangers from all parts of the Roman Empire, were here congregated. The predominant character of the people was doubtless Gre-

cian. The majority of the converts to Christianity were probably Greeks, as distinguished from Jews. (See ch. 12, 1.)
In all ages the Greeks were distinguished by their fondness
for speculation, their vanity and love of pleasure, and their
party spirit. A church composed of people of these characteristics, with a large infusion of Jewish converts, educated
in the midst of refined heathenism, surrounded by all the
incentives to indulgence, taught to consider pleasure, if not
the chief good, yet in any form a good, plied on every hand
by philosophers and false teachers, might be expected to exhibit the very characteristics which in this epistle are brought
so clearly into view.

Their party spirit. "One said I am of Paul, another I am
of Apollos; another I of Cephas, another I of Christ." Much
ingenuity and learning have been expended in determining
the nature of these party divisions. What may be considered
as more or less satisfactorily determined is,—1. That there
were factions in the church of Corinth which called themselves by the names above mentioned, and therefore that the
names themselves give a clew to the character of the parties.
The idea that the names of Paul, Apollos, and Cephas, are
used figuratively, when other teachers were really intended,
is so unnatural, and has so little to sustain it, that it is now
almost universally repudiated. 2. There can be little doubt
that those who called themselves by the name of Paul, or
made themselves his partisans, were in the main the Gentile
converts,—men brought up free from the bondage of the
Mosaic law, and free from the influence of Jewish ideas
and usages. They were disposed to press to extremes the
liberty of the gospel, to regard as indifferent things in themselves sinful, and to treat without respect the scruples of the
weak. 3. The intimate relations which subsisted between
Paul and Apollos, as indicated in these epistles, authorizes
the inference that it was not on doctrinal grounds that the
followers of the latter differed from those of the former. It

is probable that those who objected to Paul that he did not preach with the "wisdom of words," were those attracted by the eloquence of Apollos. 4. It is scarcely less certain that those who said, "We are of Peter," were the Judaizers, as Peter was specially the apostle of the circumcision. There is no evidence, however, from this epistle, that the leaders of this party had attempted to introduce into Corinth the observance of the Jewish law. But they were determined opponents of the Apostle Paul. They had come to Corinth with letters of commendation (2 Cor. 2, 1). They were Hebrews (2 Cor. 11, 22); they professed to be ministers of Christ (ch. 11, 23); they were false apostles (ch. 11, 13); the ministers of Satan, handling the word of God deceitfully. These men, as is evident from the defence which the apostle makes of his divine commission (1 Cor. 9, 1–3. 2 Cor. 12, 11, 12), called in question his apostleship, probably on the ground that he was not of the original twelve. On this ground, also, to give themselves the greater authority, they claimed to be disciples of Peter, who was the first of the apostles. They also accused Paul of inconstancy and insincerity (2 Cor. 1, 17–24). In short, they stirred up against him all the elements of discord which they could find in a congregation composed of such incongruous materials. 5. With regard to those who said, We are of Christ, only two things are certain. First, that they were as much to blame as the other parties. It was in no Christian spirit that they set up their claim to be of Christ. And secondly, that they assumed to have some relation to Christ, which they denied to others. Whether it was because they had seen and heard him, or because they claimed connection with "James, the brother of the Lord," or because they were the only genuine Christians, inasmuch as through some other channel than the apostles, they had derived, as they pretended, their knowledge of the gospel, is a matter of conjecture. Billroth and Baur regard this class as identical with the followers of Peter, who claimed

to be of Christ, because Paul was no apostle, and therefore
his disciples were not "of Christ." According to this view
there were only two, instead of four, parties in Corinth—the
followers of Paul and Apollos belonging to one class. This,
however, does violence to the plain meaning of the passage
in 1 Cor. 1, 12. These neutrals were probably the worst class
in the congregation, as is commonly the case with those who
claim to be Christians to the exclusion of all others.

Another great evil in the Corinthian church was the violation of the seventh commandment in various forms. Educated as we are under the light of the gospel, in which the
turpitude of such sins is clearly revealed, it is impossible for
us to appreciate correctly the state of feeling in Corinth on
this subject. Even by heathen philosophers offences of this
kind were regarded as scarcely deserving of censure, and by
the public sentiment of the community they were considered
altogether indifferent. They were in fact so associated with
their religious rites and festivals as to lose their character as
immoralities. With such previous training, and under the
influence of such a public sentiment, and surrounded by all
incitements and facilities to evil, it is surely not a matter of
surprise that many of the Corinthians should take the ground
that things of this class belonged to the same category with
questions of food (1 Cor. 6, 12). It is certain, from numerous passages in these epistles, that the church of Corinth
was not only very remiss in the exercise of discipline for such
matters, but also that the evil was widely extended.

Another indication of the latitudinarian spirit of one portion of the church, was their conduct in reference to the
sacrificial offerings and feasts of the heathen. They had
been accustomed not only freely to eat meat which had been
offered in sacrifice to idols, but to attend the feasts held in
the temples. As they were told as Christians that the distinction between clean and unclean meats was abolished, and
that the gods of the heathen were nothing, they insisted on

their right to continue in their accustomed habits. This gave rise to great scandal. The stricter portion of the church, whether Jews or Gentiles, regarded all use of sacrificial meat as involving in some form connection with idolatry. This, therefore, was one of the questions of conscience which was answered differently by different parties, and no doubt contributed to promote the divisions existing among them.

The turbulent and independent spirit of the people also was conspicuously manifested in their public assemblies. Instead of following the instructions of the apostles and the usages of the church, they converted the Lord's Supper into a disorderly common meal; in violation of the public sentiment and the custom of all the churches, they allowed women to appear unveiled in their congregations and to speak in public; and in the spirit of emulation and ostentation they exercised their gifts of prophecy and speaking with tongues, without regard to order or edification. Besides all this, under the influence probably of the heathen philosophy, some among them denied the doctrine of the resurrection, and thus subverted the very foundation of the gospel.

Such is the picture presented in this epistle of one of the most flourishing churches of the apostolic age, drawn, not by an enemy, but by the apostle himself. With all this, however, there were not only many pure and exemplary members of the church, but much faith and piety even in those who were more or less chargeable with these disorders. Paul, therefore, addressed them as sanctified in Christ Jesus, thanks God for the grace which he had bestowed upon them, and expresses his confidence that God would preserve them blameless until the day of the Lord Jesus. This shows us how the gospel works in heathen lands. It is like leaven hid in a measure of meal. It is long before the whole mass is leavened. It does not transform the character of men or the state of society in a moment; but it keeps up a continual conflict with evil until it is finally overcome.

§ 4. DATE.—CONTENTS OF THE EPISTLE.

The date of this epistle is determined by its contents. It was evidently written from Ephesus towards the close of Paul's protracted sojourn in that city. He tells the Corinthians that he was to visit Macedonia, and would then come to Corinth, but that he must tarry in Ephesus till Pentecost (ch. 16, 5–8.) Compare also v. 19, which agrees with the account given in Acts 19, 20. 20, 1, 2. After the uproar excited by Demetrius, Paul, as we learn from these passages, did go to Macedonia, and then to Greece; and thence, with the contributions of the saints, to Jerusalem. Accordingly, in his epistle to the Romans, written from Corinth, he says, "Now I go unto Jerusalem to minister to the saints. For it hath pleased them of Macedonia and of Achaia to make a certain contribution for the poor saints which are in Jerusalem." (Rom. 15, 25, 26.) These and other data seem to fix the date of the epistle about the year 57, or five years after his first visit to Corinth. There are no indications of a later date, unless any one should find it hard to believe that Paul had already suffered all that is recorded in 2 Cor. 11, 23–28. Five times he had received of the Jews forty stripes save one, thrice he had been beaten with rods, once he was stoned, thrice he had suffered shipwreck, a day and a night he had been in the deep. These and the other dangers there enumerated seem enough to fill a lifetime. But this only shows how small a part of the labours and sufferings of the apostles is recorded in the Acts. It furnishes no sufficient reason for referring this epistle to a later period of the apostle's career.

As this epistle was written to correct the various disorders which had arisen in the Corinthian church after the apostle's departure, and to meet the calumnies and objections of the false teachers by whom the peace of the church had been disturbed, and his own authority called in question, its contents are to a corresponding degree diversified. The apostle begins with the assertion of his Divine commission, and with the usual salutation, 1, 1–3. Then follows the general introduction to the epistle, commendatory and conciliatory in its tone and intention, 1, 4–9. He then introduces the subject of the party divisions by which the church was disturbed, and showed how inconsistent they were with the relation which believers bear to Christ and to each other; and how careful he had been to avoid all appearance of desiring to be a party leader among them. He had even abstained from baptizing lest any should say he baptized in his own name, 1, 10–16. He had baptized only a few among them, for his business was to preach rather than to baptize.

As one class of his opponents directed their attacks against his want of philosophy and rhetorical refinement as a preacher, he for a time leaves the subject of their party contentions, and addresses himself to these objections. He tells them that he did not preach the wisdom of this world, because God had pronounced it to be folly, because all experience proved it to be inefficacious to bring men to the knowledge of God, because God had determined to save men by the preaching of Christ as crucified, because their history showed that it was not the wise who embraced the gospel, but God so administered his grace as to force all men to acknowledge that it was of him, and not of themselves, that they became united to Christ, and thereby partakers of the true wisdom, as well as of righteousness, holiness, and redemption, 1, 17–31. Such being the case, he had come among them, not with the self-confidence of a philosopher, but as a simple witness to bear testimony to the fact that the Son of God had died for our redemption. Under a deep sense of his insufficiency, he spoke to them with fear and trembling, relying for success not on his own powers of persuasion, but wholly on the power with which the Holy Spirit accompanied the truth; knowing that the true foundation of faith was not argument, but the witness of the Spirit with and by the truth, 2, 1–5. Howbeit, although he repudiated human wisdom, the gospel which he preached was the true wisdom, a system of truth which God had made known, which was far above the power of man to discover, but which the Spirit of God had revealed. This Divine wisdom he preached not in the words which the rhetorician prescribed, but which the Holy Ghost dictated. Both the truths which he taught, and the words which he used in communicating that truth, were taught by the Holy Ghost. If any man neglected what was thus presented, the fault was neither in the doctrines taught, nor in the mode in which they were exhibited, but in the objector. The things of the Spirit must be spiritually discerned, 2, 6–16.

After this defence of his mode of preaching, the apostle resumes the subject of their divisions. He had preached to them in as high a strain as they were able to bear. They were but babes in Christ, and had to be fed with milk. That they were in this low stage of the Christian life was manifest from their contentions, 3, 1–4. As these contentions had reference to their religious teachers, Paul endeavours to correct the evil by showing what ministers really are. First, he says, they are mere instruments,—servants; men sent to deliver a message or perform a given work; not the authors of the system of truth which they taught. All authority and efficiency are in God. Secondly, ministers are one. They teach the same doctrine, they have the same object, and stand in the same relation to God. Thirdly, every one will have to answer for his work. If he attempt to lay any other foundation than Christ, he is not a Christian minister. If on that foundation he builds with sound doctrine, he shall receive a reward; if with false doctrine, he shall be punished. Fourthly, human wisdom in this matter must be renounced. A man must become a fool in order to be truly wise. Fifthly, such being the relation of ministers to the church, the people should not place their confidence in them, or regard themselves as belonging to their ministers, since all things were subordinate to the people of God, ministers as well as other things, 3, 5–20. Sixthly, ministers being stewards, whose office it is to dispense the truth of God, fidelity on their part is the great thing to be demanded. So far as he was himself concerned, it was a small matter what they thought of his fidelity, as the only final judge was the Lord. The true character of the ministerial office he had illustrated by a reference to himself and Apollos, that they might learn to estimate ministers aright, and not contend about them. He then contrasts himself, as suffering, labouring, and despised, with the false teachers and their followers, and exhorts the Corinthians to be followers of him, and intimates his apprehension that he would have to come to them with a rod, 4, 1–21. This is the end of that portion of the epistle which relates to the divisions existing in the church.

The second evil which it was the design of this epistle to correct, was the remissness of the Corinthians in the exercise of church discipline. Fornication was not only tolerated, but they allowed a man who had married his father's wife to retain his standing in the church. Paul here interferes, and in the exercise of his apostolical authority, not only pronounces on this incestuous person a sentence of excommunication, but delivers him to Satan, 5, 1–5. He enforces on the church the general duty to exclude immoral members from their communion, 5, 6–13.

Thirdly, the practice which some of them had introduced of going to law before heathen magistrates, he severely condemns, 6, 1–11. Fourthly, the principle that all things are lawful, which the apostle had often uttered in reference to the ceremonial distinction between clean and unclean meats, some of the Corinthians had perverted as an argument to prove that fornication is a matter of indifference. The apostle shows the fallacy of this argument, and assures them that no sin is so great a desecration of the body, or more fatal to its union with Christ, and participation of the benefits of redemption, 6, 12–20.

Fifthly, marriage was another subject about which the minds of the Corinthians were disturbed, and on which they sought the advice of the apostle. They wished him to tell them whether marriage was obligatory, or lawful, or expedient; whether divorce or separation was allowable; and especially, whether a Christian could consistently remain in the conjugal relation with a heathen. All these questions are answered in the seventh chapter, in which the apostle lays down the principles which are applicable to all cases of conscience in reference to that subject, 7, 1–40.

Sixthly: Surrounded as the Corinthians were by idolatry, whose institutions pervaded all the relations of society, it became a question how far Christians might conform to the usages connected with heathen worship. The most important question was, whether it was lawful to eat meat which had been offered in sacrifice to idols. On this point Paul agreed in principle with those who took the affirmative side in this controversy. He admitted that the idols were nothing, and that what was offered them was nothing, *i.e.*, received no new character from its having been a sacrifice, and that the use of it involved no communion with idolatry. A regard, however, to the spiritual welfare of others, should lead them to abstain from the use of such meat under circumstances which might encourage others to act against their own convictions, 8, 1–13.

In exhorting them to exercise self-denial for the benefit of others, Paul urged them to nothing which he was not himself willing to do. Although he enjoyed all the liberty which belongs to other Christians, and had all the rights belonging to ministers or apostles, he had abstained from claiming them whenever the good of the church required. For example, although entitled on all the grounds of justice, usage, and of divine appointment, to be supported by those to whom he preached, he had sustained himself by the labour of his own hands; and so far as the Corinthians were concerned, he was determined still to do so. He was determined that his enemies in Corinth should not have the slightest pretext for accusing him of preaching the gospel from mercenary motives, 9, 1–18. This, however, was not a solitary instance. In all things indifferent he had accommodated himself to Jews and Gentiles, to the strong and to the weak. He had exercised the self-denial and self-control which every combatant in the ancient games was obliged to submit to who hoped to win the prize, 9, 19–27. What he did, other Christians must do. The history of the church shows that the want of such self-denial was fatal even to those who were the most highly favoured. The ancient Israelites had been delivered out of Egypt by the direct and manifest intervention of God; they had been miraculously guided and miraculously fed in the wilderness, and yet the great majority perished. Their experience should be a warning to the Corinthians not to be overcome by similar temptations, and especially to be on their guard against idolatry, 10, 1–13. Their danger in this respect was very great. They knew that the Grecian deities were imaginary beings; they knew that things offered to those deities had no contaminating power; they knew that it was, under some circumstances, lawful to eat meat which had been thus offered; they were, therefore, in danger of being led to eat it under circumstances which would render them guilty of idolatry. As they were constantly exposed to have such meat set before them, it became a matter of the highest importance to know when it might, and when it might not be eaten with impunity. The general principle which the apostle lays down on this subject is, that all participation in the religious services of a people, brings us into communion with them as worshippers, and therefore with the objects of their worship. Consequently, to eat of heathen sacrifices under circumstances which gave a religious character to the act, was idolatry. It is not necessary that they themselves should view the matter in this light. They might worship idols, and incur the guilt and penalty of idolatry, without knowing or suspecting that they did so. To prove this, he appealed to their own convictions. They knew that all who came to the Lord's table did thereby join in the worship of Christ; and that all who attended the altars of the Jews, and eat of the sacrifices, did thereby unite in the worship of Jehovah. By parity of reasoning, those who took part in the religious festivals of the heathen, joined in the worship of idols. And, although the idols were nothing, still the worship of them was apostacy from God, and the worship of devils, 10, 14–22. On the other hand, to eat of these sacrifices under circumstances which precluded the idea of a religious service, was a matter of indifference. Therefore, if meat offered to idols was exposed for sale in the market, or met with at private tables, it might be eaten with impunity, 10, 23–33.

Seventhly : Grave abuses had been introduced into the celebration of public worship at Corinth. The women spoke in public unveiled; the Lord's Supper was degraded into a common meal; and the use of spiritual gifts gave rise to great disorder. With regard to the first of these abuses, the apostle teaches that, as by the divine constitution the woman is subordinate to the man, and as the veil was the conventional symbol of that subordination, for a woman to appear in public unveiled, was to renounce her position, and to forfeit the respect due to her sex, 8, 1-16. As to the Lord's Supper, it seems probable that it was, in Corinth at least, connected with an ordinary meal, in which all the Christians met at a common table. For this meal each one brought what provisions he was able to contribute. Instead, however, of its being a feast of brotherly love, the rich ate by themselves, and left their poorer brethren no part in the feast. To correct this abuse, destructive of the whole intent of the sacrament, the apostle reminds his readers that he had communicated to them the account of the original institution of the ordinance, as he himself had received it of the Lord. According to that institution, it was designed not to satisfy hunger, but to commemorate the death of Christ. It was therefore a religious service of a peculiarly solemn character. The bread and wine being the appointed symbols of his body and blood, to eat and drink in a careless, irreverent manner, making no distinctions between the consecrated elements and ordinary food, was to be guilty of the body and blood of the Lord, 11, 17–34.

With regard to spiritual gifts, the apostle, after reminding the Corinthians that the possession of these gifts was one of the distinctive marks of their Christian, as distinguished from their heathen state, teaches that all these extraordinary manifestations of the Holy Ghost have a common origin; that they were all given, not for the exaltation of those who received them, but for the edification of the church, and that they were distributed according to the good pleasure of God. He illustrates all these points by a reference to the human body. As the body is one, being animated by one soul, so the church is one, being animated by one Spirit. And as the vital principle manifests itself in different forms in the different members of the body, for the common good; and as the different members have their office assigned to them by God, and are mutually dependent, being bound together as a common life, so that one part cannot be injured or honoured, without all sharing in the joy or sorrow, so it is in the church. There should, therefore, be no discontent or envy on the part of those who have subordinate gifts, and no pride or ostentation on the part of those more highly favoured ; especially as the more showy gifts were not the most useful. So far, therefore, as their gifts were objects of desire, they should seek those which were the most useful, 12, 1–31.

There was, however, one thing more important than any of these gifts, and without which all others, whether faith, knowledge, or the power to work miracles, would be of no avail; and that is Love. The love which renders its possessor meek, kind, humble, disinterested, forbearing, and enduring. This is the highest grace, which is to endure when all these extraordinary endowments have passed away, 13, 1–13. The two gifts which were most conspicuous in the church of Corinth, were those of prophecy, and the gift of speaking in foreign tongues. The latter being the more wonderful, and exciting more admiration than the other, was unduly coveted and ostentatiously exercised. The apostle shows that it was very subordinate to the gift of prophecy, because the prophets were inspired to communicate, in an intelligible manner, divine truth to the edification of the church. Whereas, their speaking with tongues, where the language they used was not understood, could only edify themselves, 14, 1–40.

Eighthly: Certain persons in Corinth denied the Resurrection. Whatever were the grounds on which this doctrine was rejected, the apostle shows that its denial involved the destruction of the gospel, for if the dead cannot rise, Christ is not risen; and if Christ be not risen, we have no Saviour. He therefore proves, first, the fact of the resurrection of Christ, and then shows that his resurrection secures that of his people, 15, 1–36; and finally, that the objection that material bodies, such as we now have, are unsuitable to the future state, is founded on the false assumption, that matter cannot be so refined as to furnish material for bodies adapted to the soul in its highest state of existence, 15, 36–58. The sixteenth chapter is devoted to directions relative to the collection for the poor, and to certain admonitions and salutations.

§ 5. Importance of this Epistle.

Paul's relation to the church in Corinth was in some respects peculiar. He was not only the founder of the congregation, but he continued in the closest relation to it. It excited his solicitude, called for the wisest management, tried his patience and forbearance, rewarded him at times by signal evidence of affection and obedience, and filled him with hopes of its extended and healthful influence. His love for that church was therefore of special intensity. It was analogous to that of a father for a promising son beset with temptations, whose character combined great excellencies with great defects. The epistles to the Corinthians, therefore, reveal to us more of the personal character of the apostle than any of his other letters. They show him to us as a man, as a pastor, as a counsellor, as in conflict not only with heretics, but with personal enemies. They reveal his wisdom, his zeal, his forbearance, his liberality of principle and practice in all matters of indifference, his strictness in all matters of right and wrong, his humility, and perhaps above all, his unwearied activity and wonderful endurance.

There is another consideration which gives a special interest to these epistles. They show more clearly than any other portion of the New Testament, Christianity in conflict with heathenism. We see what method Paul adopted in founding the church in the midst of a refined and corrupt people; how he answered questions of conscience arising out of the relations of Christians to the heathen around them. The cases may never occur again, but the principles involved in their decision are of perpetual obligation, and serve as lights to the church in all ages. Principles relating to church discipline, to social relations and intercourse, to public worship, the nature of the church, and of the sacraments, are here unfolded, not in an abstract form, so much as in their application. These epistles, therefore, in reference to all practical measures in the establishment of the church among the heathen, and in its conduct in Christian lands, are among the most important portions of the word of God.

I. CORINTHIANS.

CHAPTER I.

Introduction to the Epistle. Vs. 1–9.

PAUL declares himself to be a divinely appointed messenger of Christ, v. 1. In this character he addresses the church at Corinth, as those who were sanctified in Christ, and called to be saints. He includes in his salutation all the worshippers of Christ in that vicinity, v. 2; and invokes upon them the blessings of grace and peace, v. 3.

The introduction is as usual commendatory. He thanks God for the favour shown to the Corinthians; for the various gifts by which the gospel had been confirmed among them, and by which they were placed on a full equality with the most favoured churches, vs. 4–7. He expresses his confidence, founded on the fidelity of God, that they would be preserved from apostasy until the day of the Lord, vs. 8, 9.

1. Paul, called (to be) an apostle of Jesus Christ through the will of God, and Sosthenes (our) brother.

Paul, so called after his conversion and the commencement of his labours among the Gentiles. His Jewish name was Saul. It was common for the Jews to bear one name among their own people, and another among foreigners.

Called (*to be*) *an apostle*, that is, appointed an apostle. The apostleship being an office, it could not be assumed at pleasure. Appointment by competent authority was absolutely indispensable. The word *apostle* means literally *a messenger*, and then *a missionary*, or one sent to preach the gospel. In its strict official sense it is applied only to the immediate messengers of Christ, the infallible teachers of his religion and founders of his church. In calling himself an apostle Paul claims divine authority derived immediately from Christ.

By the will of God, that is, by divine authority. Paul was made an apostle neither by popular election, nor by consecration by those who were apostles before him; but by immediate appointment from God. On this point, see his explicit declaration, Gal. 1, 1.

And Sosthenes (*our*) *brother*. In the Greek it is *the* brother. He was a brother well known to the Corinthians, and probably one of the messengers sent by them to the apostle, or whom they knew to be with him. In Acts 18, 17 a man by this name is mentioned as the ruler of the synagogue in Corinth, and a leader of those who arraigned Paul before the judgment seat of Gallio. This identity of name is not a sufficient proof that the person was the same, especially as the name was a common one. The companions of the apostles, whom he associates with himself in his salutations to the churches, are not thereby placed in the position of equality of office and authority with the apostle. On the contrary, they are uniformly distinguished in these respects from the writer of the epistles. Thus it is "Paul *the apostle*," but "Sosthenes *the brother ;*" or, "Paul the apostle and Timothy the brother," Col. 1, 1, and elsewhere. They are associated in the salutation, not in the epistle. Very probably Sosthenes was the amanuensis of Paul in this instance, and Timothy in others.

2. Unto the church of God which is at Corinth, to them that are sanctified in Christ Jesus, called (to be) saints, with all that in every place call upon the name of Jesus Christ our Lord, both theirs and ours.

To the church of God. The word *church* is used in Scripture as a collective term for the people of God, considered as called out from the world. Sometimes it means the whole number of God's people, as when it is said, Christ loved the church and gave himself for it, Eph. 5, 25. Sometimes it means the people of God as a class, as when Paul said, he persecuted the church of God, Gal. 1, 13. Sometimes it means the professing Christians of any one place, as when mention is made of the church in Jerusalem, Antioch, or Corinth. Any number, however small, of professing Christians collectively considered may be called a church. Hence we hear of the church in the house of Philemon, and in the house of Aquila and Priscilla, Rom. 16, 5. It is called the church *of God*, because it belongs to him. He selects and calls its members, and, according to Acts, 20, 28, it is his, because he has bought it with his blood.

To them that are sanctified in Christ Jesus. This is explanatory of the preceding clauses, and teaches us the nature of the church. It consists of the sanctified. The word (ἁγιάζω) translated *to sanctify*, means *to cleanse*. And as sin is presented under the twofold aspect of guilt and pollution, to sanctify, or to cleanse from sin, may mean either to expiate guilt by an atonement, or to renew by the Holy Ghost. It is used for expiation by sacrifice in Heb. 2, 11. 10, 14. 13, 12, and elsewhere. The word also means to render sacred by consecrating any person or thing to the service of God. In the present case all these ideas may be united. The church consists of those whose guilt is expiated, who are inwardly holy, and who are consecrated to God as his peculiar people.

In Christ Jesus, that is, in virtue of union with him. It is only in him that we are partakers of these inestimable blessings. It is because we are in him as our head and representative, that we are justified by his righteousness; and it is because we are in him as a branch is in the vine, that we are purified by his Spirit.

Called (to be) saints, that is, by the effectual call of the Holy Spirit constituted saints. "The called" always mean the effectually called as distinguished from the merely externally invited. *Saints.* The original word (ἅγιος) sometimes signifies *sacred*, set apart to a holy use. In this sense the temple, the altar, the priests, the prophets, and the whole theocratic people, are called holy. In the New Testament the word is commonly expressive of inward purity, or consecration of the soul to God. Believers are saints in both senses of the word; they are inwardly renewed, and outwardly consecrated. It is not to be inferred from the fact that the apostle addresses all the nominal Christians in Corinth as saints and as sanctified in Christ Jesus, that they were all true believers, or that those terms express nothing more than external consecration. Men are uniformly addressed in Scripture according to their profession. If they profess to be saints, they are called saints; if they profess to be believers, they are called believers; and if they profess to be members of the church, they are addressed as really belonging to it. This passage teaches also, as Calvin remarks, the useful lesson that a body may be very corrupt both as to doctrine and practice, as such corruptions undoubtedly prevailed even in Corinth, and yet it may be properly recognized as a church of God. *Locus diligenter observandus, ne requiramus in hoc mundo ecclesiam omni ruga et macula carentem: aut protinus abdicemus hoc titulo quemvis coetum in quo non omnia votis nostris respondeant.*

With all that in every place call on the name of Jesus Christ our Lord. To call upon the name of any one is to invoke his aid. It is properly used for religious invocation. Compare Acts 9, 14, 21, and 22, 16. Rom. 10, 12, 13. 2 Tim. 2, 22. To call upon the name of Jesus Christ our Lord, is to invoke his aid as Christ, the Messiah predicted by the prophets, and as our almighty and sovereign possessor and ruler. It is in that sense Jesus is Lord. All power in heaven and earth has been committed unto him; and he died and rose again that he might be the Lord of the dead and of the living; that is, that he might acquire that peculiar right of possession in his people which arises from his having purchased them with his blood. To call upon the name of Jesus as Lord is therefore to worship him. It is to look to him for that help which God only can give. All Christians, therefore, are the worshippers of Christ. And every sincere worshipper of Christ is a true Christian. The phrase expresses not so much an individual act of invocation, as an habitual state of mind and its appropriate expression.

It might at first view appear from this clause that this epistle was addressed not only to the church in Corinth, but to all the worshippers of Christ. This would make it a catholic, or general epistle, which it is not. To get over this difficulty some explain the connection thus: 'Called to be saints together with all who call upon the name of Christ:' that is, the Corinthians as well as all other worshippers of Christ were called to be saints. A reference to 2 Cor. 1, 1 suggests a better explanation. It is there said, "To the church of God which is at Corinth with all the saints which are in all Achaia." The same limitation must be supplied here. This epistle was addressed not only to the Christians in Corinth, but also to all their brethren in the province of which Corinth was the capital.

Theirs and ours. These words admit of two connections. They may be connected with the word Lord, 'Their Lord and ours.' There were certain persons in Corinth who claimed a peculiar relation to Christ, and said, "We are of Christ;" to whom Paul said, "If any trust to himself that he is Christ's, let him of himself think this again, as he is Christ's, so are we Christ's," 2 Cor. 10, 7. It is possible that he may have intended at the very opening of his epistle, to rebuke this exclusive spirit, and to remind his readers that Christ is the common Lord of all who call upon him. The position of the words however renders it more natural to understand the apostle to mean, "in every place, theirs and ours." If this be the true construction, then the sense may be, 'In every place of worship theirs and ours.' This interpretation supposes that the divisions known to exist in Corinth had led to the separation of the people into different worshipping assemblies. There is, however, not only no evidence that such external separation had occurred, but clear evidence in ch. 11, 18 to the contrary. Others understand the sense to be, 'In every place, theirs and ours,' i. e. 'where they are, and where I am.' This supposes the epistle to be general. A third interpretation has been proposed. The epistle is addressed to all Christians in Corinth and Achaia, wherever they might be. Every place is at once theirs and ours. Their place of abode, and my place of labour.

3. Grace (be) unto you, and peace from God our Father, and (from) the Lord Jesus Christ.

Grace is favour, and *peace* its fruits. The former includes all that is comprehended in the love of God as exercised towards sinners; and the latter all the benefits which flow from that love. All good, therefore, whether providential or spiritual, whether temporal or eternal, is comprehended in these terms: justification, adoption and sanctification, with all the benefits which either accompany or flow from them.

These infinite blessings suppose an infinite source; and as they are sought no less from Christ than from God the Father, Christ must be a divine person. It is to be remarked that God is called our *Father*, and Christ our *Lord*. God as God has not only created us, but renewed and adopted us. God in Christ has redeemed us. He is our owner and sovereign, to whom our allegiance is immediately due; who reigns in and rules over us, defending us from all his and our enemies. This is the peculiar form which piety assumes under the gospel. All Christians regard God as their Father and Christ as their Lord. His person they love, his voice they obey, and in his protection they trust.

4. I thank my God always on your behalf, for the grace of God which is given you by Jesus Christ.

Paul expresses his gratitude for *the grace of God* given to the Corinthians. The word *grace*, as just remarked, means favour, and then the blessings of which that favour is the source; just as we use the word *favour* sometimes for a disposition of the mind, and sometimes for gifts; as when we speak of receiving favours. The latter is the sense of the word in this place.

By Christ Jesus, or rather, *in* Christ Jesus. This limits and explains the kind of favours to which the apostle refers. He renders thanks for those gifts which God had bestowed upon them in virtue of their union with Christ. The fruits of the Spirit are the blessings referred to. These inward spiritual benefits are as much gifts as health or prosperity, and are, therefore, as properly the grounds of gratitude. All virtues are graces, gifts of the grace of God.

5. That in every thing ye are enriched by him, in all utterance, and (in) all knowledge.

This verse is explanatory of the preceding. Paul gives thanks for the grace which they had received, i. e. that in every thing they were enriched. *In every thing* (ἐν παντί), in every respect they were richly endowed with the gifts of the Spirit. *In all utterance and in all knowledge;* that is, with all the gifts of utterance and knowledge. Some were prophets, some were teachers, some had the gift of tongues. These were different forms of the gift of utterance. *In all know-*

ledge, that is, in every kind and degree of religious knowledge. This interpretation gives a good sense, and is the one very generally adopted. The word (λόγος) translated *utterance,* may however be taken in the sense of *doctrine,* and the word (γνῶσις) translated *knowledge,* in the sense of *insight.* The meaning would then be, that the church in Corinth was richly endowed with divine truth, and with clear apprehension or understanding of the doctrines which they had been taught. They were second to no other church either as to doctrinal knowledge or spiritual discernment. Λόγος, according to this view, is the truth preached; γνῶσις, the truth apprehended.— MEYER.

6. Even as the testimony of Christ was confirmed in you.

Even as, i. e. because, inasmuch as. They were thus enriched, because the testimony of Christ, that is, the gospel, was confirmed among them. The gospel is called the 'testimony of Christ,' either because it is the testimony concerning God and divine things, which Christ bore; or because it is the testimony which the apostles bore concerning Christ. Either explanation is agreeable to the analogy of the Scripture. Christ is called the true witness; and is said to have borne witness of the truth. Compare John 3, 11. 32. 33. 8, 13. 14. On the other hand, the apostles are frequently called the witnesses of Christ, and are said to have borne testimony concerning him. The gospel, therefore, is, in one view, the testimony which Christ bore; and, in another, the testimony which the apostles bore concerning him. The former is the higher, and therefore, the better sense. It is good to contemplate the gospel as that system of truth which the eternal Logos, or Revealer, has made known.

Was confirmed in you. This may mean either, was firmly established among you; or was firmly established in your faith. The gospel was demonstrated by the Holy Spirit to be true, and was firmly settled in their conviction. This firm faith was then, as it is now, the necessary condition of the enjoyment of the blessings by which the gospel is attended. Therefore the apostle adds,

7. So that ye come behind in no gift; waiting for the coming of our Lord Jesus Christ.

Such was their strength of faith that the gifts of the Spirit were bestowed upon them as abundantly as upon any other church. This connection of faith with the divine blessing is often presented in Scripture. Our Lord said to the father who sought his aid in behalf of his demoniac child, "If thou canst believe, all things are possible to him that believeth," Mark 9, 23. And on another occasion, "According to thy faith be it unto thee," Matt. 9, 29. In his own country, it is said, he did not many mighty works "because of their unbelief," Matt. 13, 58. The Holy Ghost, therefore, confers on men his gifts in proportion to their faith. The word (χάρισμα) *gift*, is used both for the ordinary and extraordinary gifts of the Spirit; most frequently for the latter. Here it includes both classes. The Corinthians had not only the inward gifts of repentance, faith and knowledge, but also those of miracles, of healing, of speaking with tongues, of prophecy, in rich abundance. No church was superior to them in these respects. The extraordinary gifts, however, seem to be principally intended. Paul's commendation has reference to their wisdom, knowledge and miraculous gifts, rather than to their spiritual graces. Much as he found to censure in their state and conduct, he freely acknowledged their flourishing condition in many points of view.

Waiting the coming of our Lord Jesus Christ. Waiting (ἀπεκδεχομένους) *patiently* expecting, comp. 1 Pet. 3, 20, or expecting with desire, i. e. longing for. Comp. Rom. 8, 19. 20. 23. The object of this patient and earnest expectation of believers is the *coming* (ἀποκάλυψιν) i. e. *the revelation of our Lord Jesus Christ*. The second advent of Christ, so clearly predicted by himself and by his apostles, connected as it is with the promise of the resurrection of his people and the consummation of his kingdom, was the object of longing expectation to all the early Christians. So great is the glory connected with that event that Paul, in Rom. 8, 18–23, not only represents all present afflictions as trifling in comparison, but describes the whole creation as looking forward to it with earnest expectation. Comp. Phil. 3, 20. Tit. 2, 13. So general was this expectation that Christians were characterized as those "who love his appearing," 2 Tim. 4, 8, and as those "who wait for him," Heb. 9, 28. Why is it that this longing for the coming of Christ is awakened in the hearts of his people? The apostle answers this question by saying that the "first fruits of the Spirit" enjoyed by believers in this life

are an earnest, that is, a foretaste and pledge, of those blessings which they are to receive in their fulness at the second
advent. The Spirit, therefore, awakens desire for that event.
See Rom. 8, 23. Eph. 1, 14. The same truth is here implied.
The Corinthians had received largely the gifts of the Spirit:
the consequence was they waited with patience and desire for
the revelation of Christ, when they should enter on that inheritance of which those gifts are the foretaste and pledge.
If the second coming of Christ is to Christians of the present
day less an object of desire than it was to their brethren during the apostolic age, it must be because they think the Lord
is "slack concerning his promise," and forget that with him a
thousand years is as one day.

8. Who shall also confirm you unto the end, (that
ye may be) blameless in the day of our Lord Jesus
Christ.

Who most naturally refers to God as its antecedent, because he is the prominent subject in the context; and because
the reference to Christ would make the apostle say 'Christ
shall confirm unto the day of Christ;' and because in the
following verse, God is expressly mentioned. 'Because God
is faithful, he will confirm you,' is the clear meaning of the
passage. Besides, vocation and perseverance are, in the work
of redemption, specially referred to the Father.
Shall also confirm you. God had not only enriched them
with the gifts of the Spirit, but he would *also* confirm them.
The one was an assurance of the other. Those to whom God
gives the renewing influence of the Spirit, he thereby pledges
himself to save; for "the first fruits of the Spirit" are, as just
remarked, of the nature of a pledge. They are an earnest, as
the apostle says, of the future inheritance, Eph. 1, 14. 2 Cor.
1, 21. 22. *Shall confirm* (βεβαιώσει) i. e. shall make steadfast,
preserve from falling. The word is used in reference to persons and things. God is said to confirm his promises, when
he fulfils them, or so acts as to prevent their failing, see Rom.
15, 8, or when he demonstrates their truth, Mark 16, 20. He
is said to confirm his people when he renders them steadfast
in the belief and obedience of the truth, 2 Cor. 1, 21. *Unto
the end*, may mean the end of life, or the end of this dispensation, i. e. to the end of the period which was to precede the
advent of Christ; or it may be understood indefinitely as we

use the expression "final perseverance." *Unblamable*, i. e. not arraigned or accused. He is unblamable against whom no accusation can be brought. In this sense it is said "a bishop must be blameless," Titus 1, 6. 7. God will confirm his people so that when the day of judgment comes, which is the day of our Lord Jesus, i. e. the day of his second advent, they shall stand before him blameless, not chargeable with apostasy or any other sin. They are to be 'holy and without blame.' Compare 1 Thess. 5, 23. When we remember on the one hand how great is our guilt, and on the other, how great is our danger from without and from within, we feel that nothing but the righteousness of Christ and the power of God can secure our being preserved and presented blameless in the day of the Lord Jesus.

9. God (is) faithful, by whom ye were called unto the fellowship of his Son Jesus Christ our Lord.

God is faithful, one in whom we may confide; one who will fulfil all his promises. The apostle's confidence in the steadfastness and final perseverance of believers was founded neither on the strength of their purpose to persevere, nor on any assumption that the principle of religion in their hearts was indestructible, but simply on the fidelity of God. If God has promised to give certain persons to his Son as his inheritance, to deliver them from sin and condemnation and to make them partakers of eternal life, it is certain he will not allow them to perish. This is plain enough, but how did the apostle know that those to whom he wrote were included in the number of those given to Christ, and that the fidelity of God was pledged to their salvation? It was because they were *called*. Whom he calls, them he also justifies; and whom he justifies them he also glorifies, Rom. 8, 30. The *call* intended is the effectual call of the Holy Spirit, by which the soul is renewed and translated from the kingdom of darkness into the kingdom of light. The only evidence of election is therefore vocation, and the only evidence of vocation, is holiness of heart and life, for we are called *into the fellowship of his Son Jesus Christ our Lord*. Compare again Rom. 8, 29, where believers are said to be "predestinated to be conformed to the image of his Son." To this they are effectually called. They are made like Christ. *Fellowship* includes union and communion. The original word (κοινωνία) signifies participation, as in 10, 16, "participation of the blood of Christ," 2 Cor. 13, 13, "participation of the Holy Ghost." We are called to be partakers of Christ; partakers of his life, as members of his body; and therefore, partakers of his character, of his sufferings here and of his glory hereafter. This last idea is made specially prominent. Believers are called to be partakers of the glory of Christ, Rom. 8, 17. 23. 2 Thess. 2, 14. It is because believers are thus partakers of Christ, that the apostle was assured they could never perish. The person with whom believers are thus intimately united, is *the Son of God*, of the same nature, being the same in substance and equal in power and glory. He is also *Jesus*, a man; consequently he is both God and man, in two distinct natures, and one person. This incarnate God, the Saviour, is *the Christ*, of whom the Old Testament says and promises so much. He is also *our Lord*, we belong to him; he is our possessor, our sovereign, our protector. How can they apostatize and perish who stand in this relation to the eternal Son of God?

Of the Divisions in the Church of Corinth. Vs. 10–16.

As one of the principal objects of this epistle was to correct the evils which had arisen in the church of Corinth, the apostle adverts, first, to the divisions which there existed. He exhorts the members of that church to unity, v. 10. The reason of that exhortation was the information which he had received concerning their dissensions. v. 11. These divisions arose from their ranging themselves under different religious teachers as party leaders, v. 12. The sin and folly of such divisions are manifest, in the first place, because Christ is incapable of division. As there is one head, there can be but one body. As there is but one Christ, there can be but one church. And in the second place, because religious teachers are not centres of unity to the church. They had not redeemed it, nor did its members profess allegiance to them in baptism, v. 13. These divisions, therefore, arose, on the one hand, from a forgetfulness of the common relation which all Christians bear to Christ; and, on the other, from a misapprehension of the relation in which believers stand to their religious teachers. Paul expresses his gratitude that he had not given any occasion for such misapprehension. He had baptized so few among them, that no man could suspect him of a desire to make himself the head of the church or the leader of a party, vs. 14–16.

10. Now I beseech you, brethren, by the name of our Lord Jesus Christ, that ye all speak the same thing, and that there be no divisions among you, but (that) ye be perfectly joined together in the same mind and in the same judgment.

There is but one exhortation in this verse, which is expressed first in general terms, "that ye all say the same thing;" and is then explained in the negative form, "that there be no divisions among you;" and then positively, "that ye be perfectly joined together."

By the name of our Lord Jesus Christ, i. e. out of regard to Christ, Rom. 12, 1. 15, 30. 2 Thess. 4, 12. Their reverence and love of Christ, and regard for his authority as their Lord, should induce them to yield obedience to the apostle's exhortation. It was not out of respect to him, but out of regard to Christ they should obey. This renders obedience easy and elevating. *To say the same thing* (τὸ αὐτὸ λέγειν) is a phrase of frequent occurrence to express agreement. It may be so understood here, and then the following clauses are explanatory. Or, it may be understood in reference to v. 12, of outward profession. 'Do not say I am of Paul, and I of Apollos, but all say the same thing.' The former explanation appears the more natural.

And that there be no divisions among you, literally, *schisms*. The word (σχίσμα) means, 1. *A rent*, as in a garment, Matt. 9, 16. 2. Difference of opinion, John 7, 43. 3. Alienation of feeling, or inward separation. 4. In its ecclesiastical sense, it is an unauthorized separation from the church. The schisms which existed in Corinth were not of the nature of hostile sects refusing communion with each other, but such as may exist in the bosom of the same church, consisting in alienation of feeling and party strifes.

But (that) ye be perfectly joined together. The original word (καταρτίζω) means *to repair*, or *to mend*, Matt. 4, 21, *to reduce to place*, as a dislocated limb; *to render complete*, or *perfect* (ἄρτιος); then figuratively, *to restore* or *set right* those in error; *to prepare, to render perfect.* Hence in this place the sense may be, 'That ye be perfect,' as the Vulgate renders it; or, 'that ye be united,' as in our translation; or, 'that ye be reduced to order.' The context shows that the idea of union is what the apostle intended. They were not to be divided, but united. This union was to be both *in mind* and *in judgment* (νοῦς and γνώμη). The former term may refer either to the intellect or feelings. The latter in the New Testament always means judgment or opinion. When the words are united, the former is most naturally understood of feeling, a sense in which the word *mind* is often used by us. The unity which Paul desired was a union in faith and love. Considering the relation in which Christians stand to each other as the members of Christ, dissensions among them are as inconsistent with their character, as conflict between the members of the human body.

11. For it hath been declared unto me of you, my brethren, by them (which are of the house) of Chloe, that there are contentions among you.

This verse contains the reason of the foregoing exhortation. He urges them to union because he had heard they were divided. *By those of Chloe*, whether the persons referred to were the children or domestics of Chloe is left undetermined. Chloe was a Christian woman well known to the Corinthians; whether a member of the church in Corinth whose people had come to Ephesus where Paul was; or an Ephesian whose family had been to Corinth, and learned the state of things there, is a matter of conjecture. All Paul wished was to assure the Corinthians that he had sufficient evidence of the existence of contentions among them. This word (ἔριδες) *strifes, wranglings*, explains the nature of the schisms referred to in the preceding verse. These strifes, as appears from what follows, were about their religious teachers.

12. Now this I say, that every one of you saith, I am of Paul; and I of Apollos; and I of Cephas; and I of Christ.

This explains the nature of these contentions. In almost all the apostolic churches there were contentions between the Jewish and Gentile converts. As Paul was the apostle of the Gentiles, and Peter of the Jews, Gal. 2, 8, it is probable that the converts from among the Gentiles claimed Paul as their leader; and the Jewish converts appealed to the authority of Peter. It is plain from the contents of this and of the following epistle, that these contentions were fomented by false teachers, 2 Cor. 11, 13; that these teachers were Hebrews, 2 Cor. 11, 22, and that they endeavoured to undermine the authority of Paul as an apostle. The two principal parties in Corinth, therefore, were Gentiles calling themselves the disciples of Paul, and Jews claiming to be the followers of Peter. The Gentile converts, however, were not united among themselves. While some said, we are of Paul; others said, we are of Apollos. As Apollos was an Alexandrian Jew, distinguished for literary culture and eloquence, it is probable that the more highly educated among the Corinthian Christians were his peculiar followers. Apollos is a shortened form of Apollonius, as Silas is of Silvanus. The first governor of Egypt appointed by Alexander bore that name; and probably on that account it became in that country so exceedingly common. As the Judaizers objected to Paul that he was not an apostle, these followers of Apollos undervalued him as a preacher. He was neither a philosopher nor a rhetorician after the Grecian school. We shall find the apostle defending himself against both these classes of objections. Who those were who said, we are of Christ, it is not so easy to determine. It is plain that they were as much to blame as the other parties mentioned. They must therefore have claimed some peculiar relation to Christ which they denied to their fellow believers, 2 Cor. 10, 7. Whether this exclusive claim was founded, as some suppose, on the fact that they had themselves seen and heard Christ; or whether they asserted their superior and more intimate relation to him on some other ground, is altogether uncertain. It would appear from the frequency with which Paul speaks of certain persons in Corinth " glorying in the flesh," and " in appearance," that this party claimed some peculiar external relation to Christ, and that their views of him were " carnal," or worldly.

13. Is Christ divided? was Paul crucified for you? or were ye baptized in the name of Paul?

The grounds of our allegiance to Christ are, first, that he is the Christ, the Son of the living God; second, that he hath redeemed us; third, that we are consecrated to him in baptism. All these grounds are peculiar to Christ. To no other being in the universe do believers stand in the relation which they all sustain to their common Lord. As, therefore, there is but one Christ, but one redeemer, but one baptism,

Christians cannot be divided without violating the bond which binds them to Christ and to one another.

Is Christ divided? Of course the answer must be in the negative. As Christ is incapable of division, as there can be but one Christ, the church cannot be divided. It is contrary to its nature to be split into hostile parties, just as it is contrary to the nature of a family to be thus divided. As the head is one, so are the members.

Was Paul crucified for you? Did Paul redeem you? Were you purchased by his blood, so as to belong to him? If not, then you are not his, and it is wrong to say, We are Paul's. Believers bear no such relation even to inspired teachers, as to justify their being called by their names. They are called Christians, because they are the worshippers of Christ, because they belong to him, and because they are consecrated to him.

Or were ye baptized in the name of Paul? (εἰς τὸ ὄνομα), literally, *unto the name*, i. e. in reference to Paul, so that he should be the object of your faith and the one whose name you were to confess. By baptism we are brought into the number of the disciples and followers of him into whose name, or in reference to whom, we are baptized. As, therefore, all Christians are baptized unto Christ, and not unto the apostles, much less any uninspired teacher, it is Christ whom they should confess, and by his name they should be called.

14. 15. I thank God that I baptized none of you, but Crispus and Gaius; lest any should say that I had baptized in mine own name.

Although it was the duty of the apostles to baptize, Matt. 28, 19, yet Paul rejoiced that it had so happened that he had administered that ordinance to only a few persons in Corinth, as thus all pretext that he was making disciples to himself, was taken away. Paul did not consider this a matter of chance, but of providential direction, and, therefore, a cause of gratitude. Crispus was the chief ruler of the synagogue in Corinth, whose conversion is recorded in Acts 18, 8. Gaius is mentioned in Rom. 16, 23, as the host of the apostle.

16. And I baptized also the household of Stephanas; besides I know not whether I baptized any other.

Stephanas was one of the three messengers sent to inform the apostle of the state of the church in Corinth, and to deliver the letter to which reference is made, ch. 7, 1, comp. 16, 15. 17. Paul says he baptized the *household* or family of Stephanas. Under the old dispensation, whenever any one professed Judaism or entered into covenant with God as one of his people, all his children and dependents, that is, all to whom he stood in a representative relation, were included in the covenant and received circumcision as its sign. In like manner under the gospel, when a Jew or Gentile joined the Christian church, his children received baptism and were recognized as members of the Christian church. Compare Acts 16, 15 and 33.

Besides I know not whether I baptized any other. The nature of inspiration is to be learnt from the declarations of the Scriptures and from the facts therein recorded. From these sources we learn that it was an influence which rendered its recipients infallible, but it did not render them omniscient. They were preserved from asserting error, but they were not enabled either to know or to remember all things.

Paul's defence of his manner of preaching. Vs. 17–31.

The apostle having been led to mention incidentally that he had baptized very few persons in Corinth, assigns as the reason of that fact that his great official duty was to preach the gospel. This naturally led him to speak of the manner of preaching. It was one of the objections urged against him that he did not preach " with the wisdom of words," that is, that he did not preach the doctrines taught by human reason, which he calls the wisdom of the world. Through the remainder of this, and the whole of the following chapter, he assigns his reasons for thus renouncing the wisdom of the world,—and resumes the subject of the divisions existing in the church of Corinth at the beginning of the third chapter. 1. His first reason for not teaching human wisdom is that God had pronounced all such wisdom to be folly, vs. 19. 20. 2. Experience had proved the insufficiency of human wisdom to lead men to a saving knowledge of God, v. 21. 3. God had ordained the gospel to be the great means of salvation, vs. 21–25. 4. The experience of the Corinthians themselves showed that it was not wisdom nor any other human distinction that secured the salvation of men. Human wisdom could neither discover the method of salvation, nor secure compliance with its terms when revealed. They were in Christ (i. e. converted), not because they were wiser, better, or more distinguished than others, but simply because God had chosen or called them, vs. 26–30. The design of God in all this was to humble men so that he who glories should glory in the Lord. v. 31.

17. For Christ sent me not to baptize, but to preach the gospel: not with wisdom of words, lest the cross of Christ should be made of none effect.

For indicates the connection. 'I baptized few, *for* I was not sent to baptize, but to preach.' The commission was, "Go ye into all the world, and preach the gospel to every creature." This does not mean that baptism was not included, but it does mean that baptizing was very inferior to preaching It is subordinated in the very form of the commission, "Go ye therefore, *make disciples* of all nations, baptizing them," &c. The main thing was to make disciples; recognizing them as such by baptism was subordinate, though commanded. Baptism was a work which the apostles seem to have generally left to others, Acts 10, 48. During the apostolic age, and in the apostolic form of religion, truth stood immeasurably above external rites. The apostasy of the church consisted in making rites more important than truth. The apostle's manner of speaking of baptism in this connection as subordinate to preaching is, therefore, a wonder to those who are disposed unduly to exalt the sacraments, as may be seen in Olshausen's remarks on vs. 13–16. We must not infer from this that baptism is of little importance, or that it may be safely neglected. Although Paul controverted the Jewish doctrine that circumcision secured salvation and was necessary to its attainment, he nevertheless admitted that its advantages were great every way, Rom. 3, 2. And in the Old Testament it is expressly said that the uncircumcised man-child should be cut off from the people, i. e. deprived of the benefits of the theocracy. While therefore it is unscriptural to make baptism essential to salvation or a certain means of regeneration, it is nevertheless a dangerous act of disobedience to undervalue or neglect it.

His preaching Paul describes by saying it was "not with the wisdom of words," (οὐκ ἐν σοφίᾳ λόγου). So far as the signification of these words is concerned, the meaning may be, 1. Not with skilful discourse, that is, eloquence. 2. Or, not with philosophical discourse, that is, not in an abstract or

speculative manner, so that the truth taught should be presented in a philosophical form.   According to this view the
doctrine taught would still be the gospel, but the thing rejected and condemned would be merely the philosophical
mode of exhibiting it.   3. The meaning may be, not with a
discourse characterized by wisdom; that is, the contents of
which was human wisdom, instead of truths revealed by God.
The context is in favour of the interpretation last mentioned.
In this whole connection the apostle contrasts two kinds of
wisdom.   The one he describes as the wisdom of the world,
the wisdom of men, or of the rulers of the world.   By this he
means human wisdom, that which has a human origin.   This
he pronounces to be folly, and declares it to be entirely inefficacious in the salvation of men.   The other kind of wisdom,
he calls the wisdom of God, i. e. derived from God; the hidden wisdom, consisting in truths which human reason never
could discover.   The former he repudiates.   He says, he did
not come to preach the teachings of human reason, but the
testimony of God.   He was among them in the character, not
of a philosopher, but of a witness.   As in what follows the
apostle argues to prove that human wisdom is folly and cannot save men, and gives that as the reason why he came
preaching the doctrine of the cross, it seems plain that this is
the meaning of the passage before us.   'Christ sent me to
preach, not with wise discourse, that is, not with human wisdom—not as a philosopher, but as a witness.'   His preaching
therefore was the simple exhibition of the truth which God
had revealed.

Lest the cross of Christ should be made of none effect, i. e.
rendered powerless and inoperative.   If Paul in preaching
had either substituted human wisdom for the doctrine of the
cross, or had so presented that doctrine as to turn it into a
philosophy, his preaching would have been powerless.   It
would lose its divine element and become nothing more than
human wisdom.   Whatever obscures the cross deprives the
gospel of its power.

18. For the preaching of the cross is to them that
perish, foolishness; but unto us which are saved, it is
the power of God.

The preaching of the cross, or, *the doctrine* (ὁ λόγος) of the
cross, that is, the doctrine of salvation through the crucifixion

of the Son of God as a sacrifice for the sins of men. This doctrine, though to one class, viz., *those who are lost*, i. e. those certainly to perish, *foolishness ;* yet to another class, viz., *those certainly to be saved*, it is the power of God. That is, it is that through which *the power of God* is manifested and exercised, and therefore it is divinely efficacious. All the hearers of the gospel are divided into two classes. To the one, the doctrine of salvation through a crucified Redeemer appears absurd. They are called "the lost," not only because they are certainly to perish, but also because they are in a lost state while out of Christ, John 3, 18. To the other, this doctrine is divinely efficacious in producing peace and holiness. These are called "the saved," not only because they are certainly to be saved, but also because they are now in a state of salvation. Compare 2 Cor. 2, 15.

This verse contains the reason why Christ sent the apostle to preach, and why he preached the doctrine of the cross, and not human wisdom. That reason is, because the doctrine of the cross alone is effectual to salvation. This proposition he proceeds to establish by a series of arguments designed to prove that the wisdom of the world cannot save men. His first argument is derived from the express declaration of the word of God to this effect.

19. For it is written, I will destroy the wisdom of the wise, and will bring to nothing the understanding of the prudent.

This is not to be considered as the citation of any one particular passage of the Old Testament, so much as an appeal to a doctrine therein clearly revealed. In a multitude of passages, and in various forms, God had taught by his prophets the insufficiency of human reason to lead men to the knowledge of the way of salvation. In Isaiah 29, 14. nearly the same words are used, but with a more limited application. "The wisdom of the wise," and "the understanding of the prudent," are parallel expressions for the same thing.

20. Where (is) the wise? where (is) the scribe? where (is) the disputer of this world? hath not God made foolish the wisdom of this world?

This is a challenge to the wise of every class and of every

nation to disprove what he had said. It was too plain to be
denied that God had made foolish the wisdom of this world,
i. e. he had showed it to be foolish, and dealt with it as such.
Among the Jews there were three classes of learned men, distinguished by terms corresponding to those which the apostle
here uses. It is not probable, however, that Paul refers to
that classification, because he is not speaking specially of the
Jews. The first term (σοφός), *wise man*, is probably to be
taken in a general sense including that of the two following
words. 'Where is the wise, whether Jewish scribe or Grecian
sophist?' The word *scribe* is the common designation of the
learned class among the Jews. It was originally applied to
the secretaries whose business it was to prepare and issue de-
crees in the name of the king (2 Sam. 8, 17. 20, 25. 2 Kings
12, 10. 19, 2). Afterwards, and especially in the New Testament, it was used as the designation of those learned in the
law, who were charged not only with its transcription, but
also with its exposition, and at times with its administration.
The same title was given in many of the Asiatic states to the
magistrate who presided over the senate, took charge of the
laws, and who read them when necessary to the people, Acts
19, 35.

Where is the disputer? (συζητητής) *inquirer, questioner,
sophist;* the appropriate designation of the Grecian philosopher. *Of this world,* or *age.* This qualification belongs to
all the preceding terms. 'Where is the wise of this world,
whether *scribe* or *sophist?*'

**21. For after that in the wisdom of God the world
by wisdom knew not God, it pleased God by the foolishness of preaching to save them that believe.**

This and the following verses contain the apostle's second
argument in proof of the insufficiency of human wisdom. The
argument is this: experience having shown the insufficiency
of human wisdom, God set it aside, and declared it to be
worthless, by adopting the foolishness of preaching as the
means of salvation. This argument therefore includes two
distinct proofs. First, that derived from experience; and
secondly, that derived from God's having appointed the gospel, as distinguished from human wisdom, to be the means of
saving men.

For after that. It is to be remarked that the word *for* in

Paul's writings very often refers to something implied but not expressed in the context; most commonly it refers to the answer to a preceding question. It is so here. 'Hath not God made foolish the wisdom of this world? *He has*, for, &c.' *After that* (ἐπειδή) properly, *since*. This particle, though in the Greek writers generally used of time, in the New Testament is almost uniformly used in a causal sense. This is its meaning here. 'For, *inasmuch as*, or *because*.'

In the wisdom of God. This means either, in the wise ordination of God, or, in the midst of the manifestation of the wisdom of God. If the former interpretation be adopted, the meaning is, that it was a manifestation of divine wisdom to leave the world for four thousand years to test the power of human wisdom, that thus its insufficiency might be clearly demonstrated. The latter interpretation is generally adopted, and gives a better sense. 'In the wisdom of God, that is, although surrounded by the manifestations of the divine wisdom in creation and providence, man failed to attain any saving knowledge of God.' *The world by (its* τῆς) *wisdom knew not God.* This is not inconsistent with Rom. 1, 20, where the apostle says, God's eternal power and Godhead are clearly seen, being understood by the things that are made. In this latter passage Paul speaks of the revelation which God had made of himself; in the former, of the use which men had made of that revelation. The revelation was clear, but men, through their imbecility and perverseness, did not comprehend it. In the midst of light they continued blind. The fault was in them, and not in the revelation. They did not like to retain God in their knowledge, Rom. 1, 28. Besides, sometimes the knowledge of God, in Scripture, means that speculative knowledge which human reason is adequate to derive from the works of God, and which renders their idolatry inexcusable; at other times, it means saving knowledge. Hence it is perfectly consistent to say in the former sense, that men by wisdom may attain the knowledge of God; and, in the latter sense, that they cannot attain that knowledge. Paul is here speaking of the knowledge which is connected with salvation. Such knowledge the world by wisdom had failed to secure. Therefore, *it pleased God by the foolishness of preaching to save them that believe.* "The foolishness of preaching" means the preaching of foolishness, that is, the cross. The doctrine of the cross was foolishness in the estimation of men. God thus put to shame all human wisdom by making a doctrine which the wise of this world regarded as absurd the means of salvation. This passage in its connection clearly teaches two great truths; first, that the cross, or the doctrine of Christ crucified, is the substance of the gospel, that in which its vitality and power consist; and secondly, that it is the preaching, or public proclamation (κήρυγμα) of that doctrine which is the great means of salvation. To this all other means, however important, are either preparatory or subordinate. It is to be remembered, however, that *preaching*, in the Scriptural sense of the term, includes the inculcation of the truth, whether to an individual or to a multitude—whether by the road side, or in the school, or lecture-room, or the pulpit. Philip, as he rode in the chariot with the eunuch, "preached to him Jesus," Acts 8, 35.

22. 23. For the Jews require a sign, and the Greeks seek after wisdom ; but we preach Christ crucified, unto the Jews a stumbling-block, and unto the Greeks foolishness.

This passage is parallel to the preceding. ' *Since* the world by wisdom knew not God, it pleased God by the foolishness of preaching to save them that believe—and *since* the Jews ask a sign and the Greeks seek wisdom, we preach, &c.' That is, since human reason in all its developments, Jewish or Grecian, had failed, we preach Christ.

The Jews require, or, *ask* (αἰτοῦσι) *a sign.** This was characteristic of the Jews. They required external supernatural evidence as the ground of their faith. Their constant demand was, "What sign showest thou?" Matt. 12, 39. Mark 8, 11. John 6, 30. To this disposition our Saviour referred when he said, "A wicked and adulterous generation seeketh after a sign, and there shall no sign be given to it, but the sign of the prophet Jonas," Matt. 16, 4. *The Greeks*, on the other hand, *seek after wisdom*. They required rational evidence. They would receive nothing as true which they could not understand, and see the rational grounds of. These are types of permanent classes of men.

But we preach Christ crucified. This doctrine met the

* Instead of σημεῖον, *a sign*, the MSS., A. B. C. D. E. F. G., besides many others of later date, read σημεῖα, *signs*, which almost all the modern editors adopt.

demands of neither class. It satisfied neither the expectations
of the Jews, nor the requirements of the Greeks. On the
contrary, it was to the Jews *a stumbling-block*. They had
anticipated in the Messiah a glorious temporal prince, who
should deliver and exalt their nation. To present to them
one crucified as a malefactor as their Messiah, was the greatest possible insult. He was to them, therefore, a stone of
stumbling and a rock of offence, Rom. 9, 33. 1 Pet. 2, 8. To
the Greeks this doctrine was foolishness. Nothing in the apprehension of rationalists can be more absurd than that the
blood of the cross can remove sin, promote virtue, and secure
salvation; or that the preaching of that doctrine is to convert
the world.

24. But unto them which are called, both Jews and
Greeks, Christ the power of God, and the wisdom of
God.

The called (κλητοί) always mean the effectually called, as
distinguished from those who are merely externally invited.
There is a twofold call of the gospel; the one external by the
word; the other internal by the Spirit. The subjects of the
latter are designated "the called," Rom. 1, 7. 8, 28. Jude 1.
Rev. 17, 14. compare Isaiah 48, 12. The Jews desired an exhibition of power; the Greeks sought wisdom: both are found
in Christ, and in the highest degree. He is the power of God
and the wisdom of God. In his person and work there is the
highest possible manifestation both of the divine power and
of the divine wisdom. And those who are called not only
see, but experience this. The doctrine of Christ crucified
produces effects on them which nothing short of divine power
can accomplish. And it reveals and imparts to them the true
wisdom. It makes them divinely wise; it makes them holy;
it makes them righteous; and it makes them blessed. It
does infinitely more than human wisdom could ever conceive,
much less accomplish. It has already changed the state of
the intelligent universe, and is to be the central point of influence throughout eternity. This is the doctrine which the
wise of this world wish to see ignored or obscured in behalf
of their speculations. Just as the heathen exchange the true
God for birds and beasts and creeping things, and think themselves profound.

25. Because the foolishness of God is wiser than men, and the weakness of God is stronger than men.

This is a confirmation of what precedes. The gospel is thus efficacious, *because* the lowest manifestation of divine wisdom exceeds the highest results of the wisdom of men; and the lowest exercise of God's power is more effectual than all human strength. Or, instead of taking the verse in this general sense, *the foolishness of God*, may mean the gospel. The meaning then is, 'The doctrine of the cross, though regarded as absurd and powerless, has more of power and wisdom than any thing which ever proceeded from man.'

26. For ye see your calling, brethren, how that not many wise men after the flesh, not many mighty, not many noble (are called).

The connection is not with the preceding verse but with the whole preceding context. The apostle introduces a new argument in proof of the uselessness of human wisdom. The argument is derived from their religious experience. 'You see, brethren, it is not the wise who are called.'

Your calling (κλῆσις) does not mean mode of life, profession, or station, as the word *vocation* often does with us. The Greek word is never used in this sense in the New Testament, unless 1 Cor. 7, 20 be an exception. It always refers to the call of God by his word and Spirit. It is to be so understood here. 'You see, brethren, your conversion, that not many wise are converted.' In this sense we speak of "effectual *calling*."

Wise after the flesh, i. e. wise with human wisdom. *Flesh* in Scripture often means human nature. There are two kinds of wisdom, the one human, the other divine. There are, therefore, two classes of wise men; those possessing the wisdom which is from men, and those who have the wisdom which comes from God. Few of the former class become Christians; therefore it is not by wisdom that men find out God, which is what the apostle designs to prove.

Not many mighty, i. e. *the great* (οἱ δυνατοί, those having δύναμις, in the sense of power and authority). The opposite class is designated as the weak or uninfluential, see Acts 25, 5. *Not many noble*, i. e. well-born. The converts to Christianity were not in general from the higher ranks in society.

The things which elevate man in the world, knowledge, influence, rank, are not the things which lead to God and salvation. As there is no verb in the original to agree with these nominatives, "the wise," "the mighty," "the noble," we may either supply the simple substantive verb *are*: 'You see your calling, not many of you are wise, or mighty, or noble;' or, we may supply, as in our version, the word *called*, 'not many wise are called;' or, the word *chosen*, 'not many wise are chosen, for God hath chosen, &c.' The sense remains the same. Human distinctions are insignificant and inefficacious in the sight of God, who is sovereign in the distribution of his grace.

27. But God hath chosen the foolish things of the world to confound the wise, and God hath chosen the weak things of the world to confound the things which are mighty.

In this and the following verses the apostle asserts affirmatively what he had just stated negatively, 'God does not choose the wise, but he chooses the foolish.'

The foolish things of the world, (τὰ μωρὰ τοῦ κόσμου) *the foolish portion of mankind.* In this and in the following clauses the neuter is used although persons are intended, because the reference is indefinite. God hath chosen the foolish, the weak, the insignificant, &c. *Hath chosen.* It is implied in this form of expression, which is repeated for the sake of emphasis, that as, on the one hand, the wise and the great were not chosen on account of their wisdom or greatness, so, on the other, the foolish and the weak were not chosen on account of their want of wisdom or greatness. God chose whom he pleased. He chose the ignorant *that he might confound* the wise; and the weak, *that he might confound* the mighty. That is, that he might put them to shame, by convincing them of the little value of the things on which they prided themselves, and by exalting over them those whom they despised.

28. And base things of the world, and things which are despised, hath God chosen, (yea) and things which are not, to bring to nought things that are;

The base things, i. e. the base, the ignoble (τὰ ἀγενῆ), those without family, as opposed to the noble. *Things which are despised*, i. e. men in low condition, whom the rich and noble look upon with contempt. *Things which are not*, (τὰ μὴ ὄντα,) those who are entirely overlooked as though they had no existence. There is a climax here. God has chosen not only plebeians, but of the plebeians those who were objects of contempt, and even those below contempt, too insignificant to be noticed at all. These, and such as these, does God choose to make kings and priests unto himself. *To bring to nought*, (καταργήσῃ), literally, *that he might bring to nought*. This is a stronger term than that used in the preceding verse, and here specially appropriate. God brings to nothing *the things that are* (τὰ ὄντα), i. e. those who make their existence known and felt, as opposed to those who are nothing. It is apparent from the dispensations of grace, that knowledge, rank, and power do not attract the favour of God, or secure for their possessors any pre-eminence or preference before him. This should render the exalted humble, and the humble content.

29. That no flesh should glory in his presence.

The design of God in thus dealing with men, calling the ignorant rather than the wise, the lowly instead of the great, is that no man should boast before him. No one can stand in his sight and attribute his conversion or salvation to his own wisdom, or birth, or station, or to any thing else by which he is favourably distinguished from his fellow-men.

30. But of him are ye in Christ Jesus, who of God is made unto us wisdom, and righteousness, and sanctification and redemption.

To be *in Christ Jesus* is to be united to him, 1. Representatively, as we were in Adam, Rom. 5, 12–21. 1 Cor. 15, 22. 2. Vitally, as a branch is in the vine, or a member in the body, John 15, 1–7. 3. Consciously and voluntarily by faith, Rom. 8, 1, *et passim*. Of this union with Christ, the apostle teaches us here, first, its origin, and secondly, its effects. As to its origin, it is of God. *Of him ye are in Christ Jesus.* It is (ἐξ αὐτοῦ) of him as the efficient cause. It is to be referred to him alone that ye are in Christ. Your conversion or saving union with Christ is not due to yourselves; it is not because you are wiser, or better, or more diligent than others that you are thus distinguished. This which is the turning point in theology, and therefore in religion, is here most explicitly asserted. And it is not only asserted, but it is declared to be the purpose of God to make it apparent, and to force all men to acknowledge it. He so dispenses his grace as to make men see with regard to others, and to acknowledge with regard to themselves, that the fact that they are in Christ, or true Christians, is due to him and not to themselves. The effects of this union, as here stated, are, that Christ is *of God* (ἀπὸ Θεοῦ), as the author, made unto us, 1. Wisdom. Christ is the true wisdom. He is the Logos, the Revealer, in whom dwells all the fulness of the Godhead, and all the treasures of wisdom and knowledge. No man knoweth the Father but the Son, and he to whom the Son shall reveal him, John 1, 18. Union with him, therefore, makes the believer truly wise. It secures the knowledge of God, whose glory is revealed in the face of Christ, and whom to know is eternal life. All true religious knowledge is derived from Christ, and it is only those who submit to his teaching who are wise unto salvation.

2. The second effect of union with Christ, is righteousness and sanctification (δικαιοσύνη τε καὶ ἁγιασμός); these are intimately united (τε καί) as different aspects of the same thing. *Righteousness* is that which satisfies the demands of the law as a rule of justification; *sanctification*, or holiness, is that which satisfies the law as a rule of duty. Christ is both to us. He is our righteousness, because by his obedience and death he has fully satisfied the demands of justice, so that we are "the righteousness of God in him," 2 Cor. 5, 21. When we stand before the judgment-seat of God, Christ is our righteousness. He answers for us; he presents his own infinite merit as the all-sufficient reason for our justification. Rom. 3, 21. 22. 5, 19. Phil. 3, 9. He is also our *sanctification*. His Spirit dwells in all his people as the Spirit of holiness, so that they are transformed into his likeness from glory to glory. Wherever the Spirit dwells there are the fruits of the Spirit. Acts 26, 18. Rom. 8, 9. 10. Gal. 5, 22. Eph. 2, 5. 10.

3. The third effect is *redemption*, i. e. deliverance from evil. This term sometimes includes all the benefits received from Christ. When he is called our Redeemer he is presented as our deliverer from guilt, from hell, from sin, from the power of Satan, from the grave. But when redemption is distinguished from justification and sanctification, it refers to the final deliverance from evil. The "day of redemption" is the day when the work of Christ shall be consummated in the

perfect salvation of his people as to soul and body. Rom. 8,
23. Eph. 1, 14. 4, 30. Heb. 9, 12.

Those, then, who are in Christ have divine wisdom or the saving knowledge of God and of divine things; they have a righteousness which secures their justification. There is no condemnation to those that are in Christ Jesus, Rom. 8, 1. They are
renewed after the image of God, and shall finally be presented
without spot or blemish before the presence of his glory. And
they are partakers of eternal redemption or full deliverance
from all the evils of sin, and are introduced into the glorious
liberty of the children of God. These infinite blessings can be
obtained only through Christ. Union with him is the necessary, and the only necessary, condition of our participation of
these blessings. And our union with Christ is of God. It is
not of ourselves, by our own wisdom, goodness, or strength,
but solely by his grace; and therefore must be sought as an
unmerited favour.

31. That, according as it is written, He that glorieth, let him glory in the Lord.

That, i. e. *in order that.* The design of God in making
wisdom, righteousness, sanctification, and redemption dependent on union with Christ, and union with Christ dependent,
not on our merit, but on his own good pleasure, is that we
should glory only in him; that is, that our confidence should
be in him and not in ourselves, and that all the glory of our
salvation should be ascribed to him and not to us. Such being the design of God in the work of redemption, it is obvious
we must conform to it in order to be saved. We must seek
wisdom, righteousness, sanctification, and redemption only in
Christ; and we must seek union with Christ as an undeserved
favour.

The passage quoted is probably Jeremiah 9, 23. 24, the
sense of which is condensed. In quoting the Old Testament
the apostle frequently cites the words as they stand, without
so modifying them as to make them grammatically cohere
with the context. As in the Septuagint, which he quotes, the
imperative mood is used, the apostle here retains it, and instead of saying, 'In order that he who glories *should glory* in
the Lord,' he says 'That, He that glories *let him glory* in the
Lord.' Comp. 2, 9. Rom. 15, 3.

CHAPTER II

Continues his defence of his mode of preaching. In vs. 1–5 he shows that he
acted on the principles set forth in the preceding paragraph. In vs. 6–9
he shows that the gospel is the true wisdom. The source of this knowledge, as externally revealed and as spiritually apprehended, is the Holy
Spirit, vs. 10–16.

Continuation of his defence of his mode of preaching
Vs. 1–16.

As GOD had determined to save men not by human wisdom
but by the gospel, Paul, when he appeared in Corinth, came
neither as an orator nor as a philosopher, but simply as a witness, vs. 1, 2. He had no confidence in himself, but relied for
success exclusively on the demonstration of the Spirit, vs. 3,
4. The true foundation of faith is not reason, but the testimony of God, v. 5.

Though what he preached was not the wisdom of men, it
was the wisdom of God, undiscoverable by human reason, vs.
6–9. The revealer of this divine wisdom is the Holy Ghost,
he alone being competent to make this revelation, because he
only knows the secret purposes of God, vs. 10–12. In communicating the knowledge thus derived from the Spirit, the
apostle used words taught by the Spirit, v. 13. Though the
knowledge communicated was divine, and although communicated in appropriate language, it was not received by the
natural man, because the things of the Spirit can be discerned
only by the spiritual, vs. 14–16.

1. And I, brethren, when I came to you, came not
with excellency of speech or of wisdom, declaring unto
you the testimony of God.

And I, i. e. *accordingly I.* 'In accordance with the clearly revealed purpose of God to reject the wisdom of the world
and to make the cross the means of salvation.'
Excellency of speech or of wisdom. As speech and wisdom (λόγος and σοφία) are here distinguished, the former
probably refers to the manner or form, and the latter to the
matter of his preaching. It was neither as a rhetorician nor
as a philosopher that he appeared among them. This clause

may be connected either with the word *came*, 'I came not with excellency of speech;' or with the word *declaring*, 'I came not declaring with excellency of speech, &c.' The former mode is generally preferred, not only because of the position of the words in the sentence, but also because of the sense. Paul does not mean to say merely that he did not declare the testimony of God in a rhetorical or philosophical manner; but that what he declared was not the wisdom of men, but the revelation of God.

The testimony of God may mean either the testimony which Paul bore concerning God, or God's own testimony, i. e. what God had revealed and testified to be true. "The testimony of God" is, in this sense, the gospel, as in 2 Tim. 1, 8. The latter interpretation best suits the connection, as throughout these chapters Paul contrasts what reason teaches with what God teaches. He did not appear as a teacher of human wisdom, but as announcing what God had revealed.

2. For I determined not to know any thing* among you, save Jesus Christ, and him crucified.

For is confirmatory. 'I came not with excellency of speech or of wisdom, *for* I determined, &c.' The negative particle in this sentence may be connected either with the word *to know*, 'I determined *not* to know;' or with the word *determined*, 'I did not determine, i. e. I had no intention or purpose.' The position of the words (οὐ γὰρ ἔκρινα) is in favour of the latter interpretation. The meaning in either case is the same.

Jesus Christ, and him crucified. Paul's only design in going to Corinth was to preach Christ; and Christ not as a teacher, or as an example, or as a perfect man, or as a new starting point in the development of the race—all this would be mere philosophy; but Christ *as crucified*, i. e. as dying for our sins. Christ as a propitiation was the burden of Paul's preaching. It has been well remarked that *Jesus Christ* refers to the person of Christ, and *him crucified*, to his work; which constitute the sum of the gospel.

3. And I was with you in weakness, and in fear, and in much trembling.

* The common text here is τοῦ εἰδέναι τὶ. The τοῦ is omitted in the MSS., A, B. C. D. E. F. G. The reading adopted in the recent editions is τὶ εἰδέναι.

I came to you, ἐγενόμην πρὸς ὑμᾶς, I came to you and was with you, see John 1, 2. The weakness of which he here speaks was not bodily weakness; for although he elsewhere speaks of himself as weak in body, 2 Cor. 10, 10, and as suffering under bodily infirmity, Gal. 4, 14, yet here the whole context shows he refers to his state of mind. It was not in the consciousness of strength, self-confident and self-relying, that he appeared among them, but as oppressed with a sense of his weakness and insufficiency. He had a work to do which he felt to be entirely above his powers.

In fear and trembling, i. e. in anxiety, or solicitude of mind arising out of a sense of his insufficiency, and of the infinite importance of his work, 2 Cor. 7, 15. Phil. 2, 12. Eph. 6, 5.

4. And my speech and my preaching (was) not with enticing words of man's wisdom, but in demonstration of the Spirit and of power.

My speech and preaching (λόγος and κήρυγμα). If these terms are to be distinguished, the former may refer to his private, and the latter to his public instructions; or, the former is general, including all modes of address, and the latter specific, limited to public discourse. 'My instructions in general, and my public preaching in particular.' Both terms, however, may designate the same thing under different aspects.

His mode of preaching is described, first, negatively, and then positively. It was *not* with the enticing words of man's wisdom, i. e. the persuasive words which human wisdom would suggest. In his endeavours to bring men to the obedience of the faith, he did not rely upon his own skill in argument or persuasion. This is the negative statement. Positively, his preaching was *in* (or *with*, ἐν; the preposition is the same in both clauses, though rendered by our translators in the former, *with*, and in the latter, *in*) *the demonstration of the Spirit and of power*. This may mean, 'The demonstration of the powerful Spirit;' or, 'The demonstration of the Spirit and of (miraculous) power;' referring to the twofold evidence or proof of the gospel, viz., the internal influence of the Spirit, and the external evidence of miracles. The word (δύναμις), rendered *power*, often means miraculous power, but as such cannot be its meaning in the following verse, it is not probable it was intended to have that sense here. The phrase probably means 'The demonstration of which the Spirit is the author, and which is characterized by power;' so that the sense is, *the powerful demonstration of the Spirit.*

Demonstration (ἀπόδειξις) *setting forth*, exhibition of proof. Paul relied, therefore, for success, not on his skill in argument or persuasion, nor upon any of the resources of human wisdom, but on the testimony which the Spirit bore to the truth. The Holy Ghost demonstrated the gospel to be true.

5. That your faith should not stand in the wisdom of men, but in the power of God.

That, i. e. *in order that.* The design of the apostle in acting as stated in the preceding verse, was that the faith of his hearers might not rest upon human reason, but on the testimony of God. It might have been easy for him to argue the Corinthians into a conviction of the truth of the Gospel, by appealing to its superiority to heathenism and to the evidence of its divine origin afforded by prophecy and miracles. He might have exhibited the folly of idolatry, and the absurdity of pagan rites and ceremonies, and convinced them of the historical truth of Christianity. The conviction thus produced would be rational and important; but it would not be saving faith. Faith founded on such evidence is merely speculative. The true foundation of faith, or rather, the foundation of true faith, is *the power of God.* This is explained by what he had before called "the demonstration of the Spirit." That exercise of divine power, therefore, to which he refers as the ground of faith, is the powerful operation of the Spirit, bearing witness with and by the truth in our hearts. A faith which is founded on the authority of the church, or upon arguments addressed to the understanding, or even on the moral power of the truth as it affects the natural conscience, such as Felix had, is unstable and inoperative. But a faith founded on the demonstration of the Spirit is abiding, infallible, and works by love and purifies the heart.

In these verses, therefore, we are taught, 1. That the proper method to convert men in any community, Christian or Pagan, is to preach or set forth the truth concerning the person and work of Christ. Whatever other means are used must be subordinate and auxiliary, designed to remove obstacles, and to gain access for the truth to the mind, just as the ground is cleared of weeds and brambles in order to prepare it for the precious seed. 2. The proper state of mind in which to preach the gospel is the opposite of self-confidence or care-lessness. The gospel should be preached with a sense of weakness and with great anxiety and solicitude. 3. The suc-cess of the gospel does not depend on the skill of the preacher, but on the demonstration of the Spirit. 4. The foundation of saving faith is not reason, i. e. not arguments addressed to the understanding, but the power of God as exerted with and by the truth upon the heart.

6. Howbeit we speak wisdom among them that are perfect: yet not the wisdom of this world, nor of the princes of this world, that come to nought.

Paul had in the preceding chapter, vs. 17–31, asserted the insufficiency of human wisdom, and in vs. 1–5 of this chapter, he had said he was not a teacher of human wisdom. Was it to be inferred from this that he despised knowledge, that he was an illiterate contemner of letters, or that he taught nonsense ? Far from it ; he taught the highest wisdom. It is plain from this whole discussion, that by the wisdom of the world, Paul means that knowledge of God and divine things which men derive from reason. It is also plain that what he says of the worthlessness of that knowledge has reference to it as a means of salvation. The objection urged against him was, that he did not teach philosophy. His answer is, philosophy cannot save men. Whatever may be its value within its own sphere and for its own ends, it is worse than useless as a substitute for the gospel. He was not for banishing philosophy from the schools, but from the pulpit. Let the dead bury the dead ; but do not let them pretend to impart life.

Howbeit, nevertheless, i. e. ' although we do not teach hu-man wisdom, we teach the true wisdom.' *Among them that are perfect* (ἐν τοῖς τελείοις), i. e. the mature, the full-grown, the competent. The ἐν here is not redundant as though the sense were *to* the perfect ; but has its proper force *among.* Among one class of men the doctrine which he preached was regarded as foolishness, but among another it was seen to be divine wis-dom. Who are meant by the perfect ? There are two an-swers to this question. Some say they were the advanced or mature Christians as distinguished from the babes in Christ. Others say, they were believers as opposed to unbelievers ; those taught by the Spirit and thus enabled to understand the truth, as opposed to the unrenewed. According to this view, Paul means to say that the gospel, although foolishness to the Greek, was the highest wisdom in the estimation of the truly enlightened. In favour of this view of the passage, and in opposition to the other, it may be argued, 1. That those who regarded Paul's doctrine as foolishness were not the babes in Christ, but the unrenewed, "the wise of this world;" consequently those to whom it was wisdom were not advanced Christians, but believers as such. Throughout the whole context, the opposition is between "the called" or converted, and the unconverted, and not between one class of believers and another class. 2. If "the perfect" here means advanced Christians as distinguished from babes in Christ, then the wisdom which Paul preached was not the gospel as such, but its higher doctrines. But this cannot be, because it is the doctrine of the cross, of Christ crucified, which he declares to be the power of God and the wisdom of God, 1, 24. And the description given in the following part of this chapter of the wisdom here intended, refers not to the higher doctrines of the gospel but to the gospel itself. The contrast is between the wisdom of the world and the wisdom of God, and not between the rudimental and the higher doctrines of the gospel. Besides, what are these higher doctrines which Paul preached only to the élite of the church? No one knows. Some say one thing, and some another. But there are no higher doctrines than those taught in this epistle and in those to the Romans and Ephesians, all addressed to the mass of the people. The New Testament makes no distinction between (πίστις and γνῶσις) higher and lower doctrines. It does indeed speak of a distinction between milk and strong meat, but that is a distinction, not between kinds of doctrine, but between one mode of instruction and another. In catechisms designed for children the church pours out all the treasures of her knowledge, but in the form of milk, i. e. in a form adapted to the weakest capacities. For all these reasons we conclude that by "the perfect" the apostle means the competent, the people of God as distinguished from the men of the world; and by wisdom, not any higher doctrines, but the simple gospel, which is the wisdom of God as distinguished from the wisdom of men.

The apostle describes this wisdom, first negatively, by saying it is not *the wisdom of this world*, or, *wisdom not of this world*, i. e. it belongs not to the world, and is not attained by the men of the world. *Nor of the princes of this world.* This designation includes all who take the first rank among men; men of influence, whether for their wisdom, birth, or power. He does not refer exclusively to magistrates, or princes, in the restricted sense of that term. This seems plain from the connection, and from what follows in v. 8. *Who come to nought,* i. e. whom it is God's purpose to confound, as taught above, 1, 28.

7. But we speak the wisdom of God in a mystery, (even) the hidden (wisdom), which God ordained before the world unto our glory.

Having in v. 6 stated what this wisdom is not, he here states what it is. It is, first, the wisdom of God; secondly, it is mysterious, or hidden; thirdly, it is a system of truth which God from eternity had determined to reveal for the salvation of his people. In other words, it is the revelation of the counsels of eternity in reference to the redemption of man.

The wisdom of God, i. e. the wisdom derived from God; which he has revealed, as distinguished from any form of knowledge of human origin. *In a mystery.* The word mystery always means something into which men must be initiated; something undiscoverable by human reason. Whether its being undiscoverable arises from its lying in the future, or because hid in the unrevealed purposes of God, or from its own nature as beyond our comprehension, is not determined by the signification of the word, but is to be learned from the context. The most natural connection of the words here is with what precedes, " wisdom in a mystery," for mysterious, or hidden wisdom, as is immediately explained by what follows. As there is no connecting article (between σοφίαν and μυστηρίῳ) in the original, some prefer connecting this clause with the verb. 'We speak in a mystery,' i. e. as declaring a mystery or matter of revelation.

Which God *before the world* (πρὸ τῶν αἰώνων), *before the ages,* i. e. before time, or from eternity, *preordained to our glory*—predetermined in reference to our glory. The word *glory* is often used for all the benefits of salvation. It includes all the excellence and blessedness which Christ has secured for his people, Rom. 5, 2. The idea that the scheme of redemption, which the apostle here calls the wisdom of God, was from eternity formed in the divine mind, far out of the reach of human penetration, and has under the gospel been made known for the salvation of men, is one often presented by the apostle, Rom. 16, 25. 26. Eph. 3, 9.

8. Which none of the princes of this world knew : for had they known (it), they would not have crucified the Lord of glory.

Which refers to *wisdom*, and not to *glory ;* because the former, and not the latter, is the subject of discourse. 'Which wisdom none of the princes, i. e. the great men, of this world knew.' The reference is here principally to the rulers of the Jews, the authors of the crucifixion of Christ, and the representatives of the class to which they belonged. It was the world in its princes who rejected Christ.

Lord of glory is a title of divinity. It means, possessor of divine excellence. "Who is the King of glory ? The LORD of hosts, he is the King of glory," Ps. 24, 10. Acts 7, 2. James 2, 1. Eph. 1, 17. The person crucified, therefore, was a divine person. Hence the deed was evidence of inconceivable blindness and wickedness. It was one that could only be done through ignorance. "And now, brethren," said the apostle Peter to the Jews, "I wot that through ignorance ye did it, as *did* also your rulers," Acts 3, 17. The fact that the princes of this world were so blind as not to see that Christ was the Lord of glory, Paul cites as proof of their ignorance of the wisdom of God. Had they known the one, they would have known the other.

This passage illustrates a very important principle or usage of Scripture. We see that the person of Christ may be designated from his divine nature, when what is affirmed of him is true only of his human nature. The Lord of glory was crucified; the Son of God was born of a woman; he who was equal with God humbled himself to be obedient unto death. In like manner we speak of the birth or death of a man without meaning that the soul is born or dies; and the Scriptures speak of the birth and death of the Son of God, without meaning that the divine nature is subject to these changes. It is also plain that to predicate ignorance, subjection, suffering, death, or any other limitation of the Son of God, is no more inconsistent with the divinity of the person so designated, than to predicate birth and death of a man, is inconsistent with the immateriality and immortality of the human soul.

Whatever is true either of the soul or body may be predicated
of a man as a person; and whatever is true of either the divine or human nature of Christ may be predicated of Christ
as a person. We need not hesitate therefore to say with Paul,
the Lord of glory was crucified; or even, in accordance with
the received text in Acts 20, 28, "God purchased the church
with his blood." The person who died was truly God, although the divine nature no more died than the soul of man
does when the breath leaves his body.

9. But as it is written, Eye hath not seen, nor ear
heard, neither have entered into the heart of man, the
things which God hath prepared for them that love
him.

The meaning of this verse is plain, although there are several difficulties connected with it. Paul had said, he preached
the hidden wisdom of God, which none of the princes of this
world knew;·he taught what no eye hath seen, nor ear heard,
nor heart conceived. That is, he preached truth undiscoverable by human reason. *To enter into the heart* means to occur
to the mind. Compare in the Hebrew, Isaiah 65, 17.

The first difficulty connected with this verse is a grammatical one, which does not appear in our version because of
the freedom of the translation. Literally the passage reads,
'What no eye saw, and no ear heard, and no heart conceived,
what God has prepared for those who love him—.' The sentence is incomplete. This difficulty may be met either by a
reference to the usage referred to in the note on the last verse
of the preceding chapter, v. 31, the custom of the apostles to
quote passages from the Old Testament without weaving them
grammatically into their own discourses. Or, we may supply,
as many do, the word (λαλοῦμεν) '*we speak* what God hath
prepared for those who love him.' Or this verse may be connected with what follows: 'What eye hath not seen— what
(namely) God hath prepared for his people, he hath revealed
to us by his Spirit.'—The first of these explanations is generally adopted and is the most satisfactory.

The second difficulty relates to the passage quoted. As the
formula, "As it is written," is never used by the apostles except
in the citation of the canonical books of the Old Testament, it
cannot be admitted that Paul intended to quote either some
book now lost, or some apocryphal writing. If it be assumed

that he intended to quote Isaiah 64, 4, the difficulty is twofold, first, the language or words are different, and secondly, the sense is different. Isaiah 64, 4, (or 3 in the Hebrew) as literally translated by Dr. J. A. Alexander, is: "And from eternity they have not heard, they have not perceived by the ear, the eye hath not seen, a God beside thee (who) will do for (one) waiting for him." The idea is, that men had never known any other God than Jehovah who did, or could do, what he threatened to do. The Septuagint expresses the same idea. The meaning in Isaiah as connected with what precedes, seems to be that the reason why such fearful things as had been predicted were to be expected from Jehovah is, that he alone had proved himself able to perform them. To get over this difficulty some propose a different interpretation of the passage in the prophet. By connecting it with what follows, and by taking the word *God* in the vocative, the sense may be, 'From eternity they have not heard, nor perceived by the ear, eye hath not seen, O God, without thee, (i. e. without a revelation) what he, (or, by change of person) what thou hast prepared for those that wait for thee.' This is the version given in the Vulgate, and brings the passage into harmony with the apostle's quotation.

Others, assuming the first-mentioned interpretation of the passage in Isaiah to be the true one, consider the apostle as using scriptural language without intending to give the sense of the original. This we often do, and it is not unfrequently done in the New Testament, Rom. 10, 18. *As it is written* is not, in this case, the form of quotation, but is rather equivalent to saying, 'To use the language of Scripture.'

A third explanation of this difficulty is, that the apostle did not intend to quote any one passage of scripture, but to appeal to its authority for a clearly revealed truth. It is certainly taught in the Old Testament that the human mind cannot penetrate into the counsels of God; his purposes can only be known by a supernatural revelation. This is the truth for which the apostle cites the authority of the Old Testament. There is, therefore, not the slightest ground for imputing failure of memory, or an erroneous interpretation to the inspired apostle.

10. But God hath revealed (them) unto us by his Spirit: for the Spirit searcheth all things, yea, the deep things of God.

What was undiscoverable by human reason, God hath revealed by his Spirit. *Unto us,* i. e. unto those to whom this revelation, was made, viz. " the holy apostles and prophets," Eph. 3, 5. This revelation was made by the Spirit, *for* he alone is competent to make it ; for he alone searches the deep things of God. *Searches,* i. e. explores, accurately and thoroughly knows. The word does not express the process of investigation, but rather its results, viz., profound knowledge. Thus God is said to search the hearts of the children of men, to intimate that there is nothing in man that escapes his notice, Rom. 8, 27. Rev. 2, 23. So there is nothing in God unknown to the Spirit. *The deep things,* i. e. depths of God, the inmost recesses, as it were, of his being, perfections and purposes. The Spirit, therefore, is fully competent to reveal that wisdom which had for ages been hid in God. This passage proves at once the personality and the divinity of the Holy Ghost. His personality, because intelligent activity is ascribed to him ; he *searches ;* his divinity, because omniscience is ascribed to him ; he knows all that God knows.

11. For what man knoweth the things of a man, save the spirit of man which is in him? even so the things of God knoweth no man, but the Spirit of God.

This verse is designed to illustrate two points: First, as no one knows the thoughts of a man but the man himself, so no one knows the thoughts of God, but God himself. Therefore no one but a divine person is competent to make a revelation of the thoughts and purposes of God. Second, as every man does know his own thoughts, so the Spirit of God knows the thoughts of God. His knowledge of what is in God is analogous to that which we have of the contents of our own consciousness. The analogies of scripture, however, are not to be pressed beyond the point which they are intended to illustrate. The point to be illustrated here is, the knowledge of the Spirit. He knows what is in God, as we know what is in ourselves. It is not to be inferred from this that the Spirit of God bears in other points the same relation to God, that our spirits do to us.

12. Now we have received, not the spirit of the world, but the Spirit which is of God ; that we might know the things that are freely given to us of God.

The apostle had set forth two sources of knowledge, the one, human; the other, divine; the one, the informing principle which is in man; the other, the informing principle which is of God. And he asserts that the source of that wisdom or knowledge which he communicated, was not the former, but the latter. It was not human reason, but the Spirit of God. *The spirit of the world* does not here mean a worldly disposition or temper; but *spirit* is that which knows and teaches. The spirit of the world is therefore a periphrase for reason, which is the principle of knowledge in men. When Paul says he had not received that spirit, he means that human reason was not the source of the knowledge which he communicated. *The Spirit which is of God*, is the Holy Spirit as proceeding from him and sent by him as the instructor of men. *To receive* the Spirit is to be the subject of his influence. It, therefore, depends upon the context and on the nature of the influences spoken of, who are intended by those who receive the Spirit. Here the whole connection shows that the apostle is speaking of revelation and inspiration; and therefore *we* must mean *we apostles*, (or Paul himself,) and not we Christians.

That, i. e. in order that, *we might know the things freely given to us of God*, i. e. the things graciously revealed by God. This clause does not refer to inward spiritual blessings now enjoyed by believers, nor to the future blessedness of the saints, except so far as these are included in the general subject of Paul's preaching. The connection is with v. 10. 'What human reason could not discover, God hath revealed to us apostles, in order that we might know what he has thus graciously communicated.' The subject is the wisdom of God, the gospel, as distinguished from the wisdom of the world. This is clear both from what precedes and from what follows.

13. Which things also we speak, not in the words which man's wisdom teacheth, but which the Holy Ghost teacheth ; comparing spiritual things with spiritual.

Which things ; the things revealed by the Spirit. We *also* speak. We do not only know, we also communicate the things which God has revealed. How is this done ? What language did the apostle use in communicating what he had received by divine revelation ? He answers, according to his

usual method, first, negatively; and then, positively. It was
not done "in the words which man's wisdom teacheth." This
includes two things. The words used by the apostle were
neither such as the skill of the rhetorician would suggest, nor
such as his own mind, uninfluenced by the Spirit of God, suggested. The affirmative statement is, that the words used
were taught by the Holy Ghost. This is verbal inspiration,
or the doctrine that the writers of the Scriptures were controlled by the Spirit of God in the choice of the words which
they employed in communicating divine truth. This has been
stigmatized as "the mechanical theory of inspiration," degrading the sacred penmen into mere machines. It is objected
to this doctrine that it leaves the diversity of style which
marks the different portions of the Bible, unaccounted for.
But, if God can control the thoughts of a man without making
him a machine, why cannot he control his language? And
why may he not render each writer, whether poetical or
prosaic, whether polished or rude, whether aphoristic or
logical, infallible in the use of his characteristic style? If the
language of the Bible be not inspired, then we have the truth
communicated through the discolouring and distorting medium
of human imperfection. Paul's direct assertion is that the
words which he used, were taught by the Holy Ghost.

Comparing spiritual things with spiritual; or rather,
joining spiritual things to spiritual words, or, explaining the
things of the Spirit in the words of the Spirit. For the use of
συγκρίνειν in the sense of *interpreting* or *explaining,* see Gen.
40, 8. 16. 41, 12. 15. Dan. 5, 12. in the LXX. This interpretation is demanded by the connection. The apostle had said
that the truths which he taught were revealed by the Spirit;
and that the words which he used were taught by the Spirit,
which he sums up by saying, he explained spiritual things in
spiritual words. This view of the passage is perfectly consistent with the signification of the words. The original word
(συγκρίνω) means not only mentally to combine and hence to
compare, but also to join together; and also to explain. It
is used in the Septuagint to express the act of interpreting
dreams or enigmas. The clause in question may, therefore,
be translated either, *combining spiritual things with spiritual
words;* or, *explaining* the one by the other. Besides, the
word *spiritual* (πνευματικοῖς), which has no substantive connected with it, most naturally agrees with *words* (λόγοις) understood, which immediately precedes.

The other interpretation, *comparing spiritual things with spiritual*, whether it means comparing the Old Testament with the New, as some say; or, as others understand it, comparing one portion of the Spirit's teaching with another, is inconsistent with the context. Much less can be said in favour of a third interpretation of this clause adopted by many, who understand the apostle to say, he explains spiritual things to spiritual *persons*. This anticipates what follows.

14. But the natural man receiveth not the things of the Spirit of God; for they are foolishness unto him: neither can he know (them), because they are spiritually discerned.

Although *the things of the Spirit*, that is, the truths of his word, are so clearly revealed; and although they have been communicated in language taught by the Spirit, yet, by a certain class of men, they are rejected. That is, they are not believed, appreciated, and obeyed. This class of men is called *natural*. The meaning of this term cannot be determined by the mere signification of the word (ψυχικός), for it signifies both sensual (i. e. under the influence of the lower animal principles of our nature), and also *natural*, i. e. under the influence of what belongs to the nature of man as it now exists, as distinguished from the Spirit of God. Many commentators say that the (ψυχικοί) *natural* are the sensual, and the opposite class the (πνευματικοί) *spiritual* are the intellectual, the rational, those under the influence of the (πνεῦμα) *spirit* in the sense of the higher, as distinguished from the lower, principles of our nature. According to this view, Paul means to say, that although sensual men do not receive the things of the Spirit, intellectual men do. This interpretation, however, cannot be correct. 1. Because it gives a meaning to the passage not only inconsistent with the direct assertion of the apostle, but opposed to the whole drift and design of his argument. He not only declares that it was not the wise, the refined and cultivated who received the gospel—but his whole object is to prove that the reason of man, or man in the highest development of his nature, can neither discover "the things of the Spirit," nor receive them when revealed. It is of God, and not because of their superior culture or refinement, that men are in Christ, 1, 30. These things are hid from the wise and prudent, and revealed unto babes, Matt. 11, 25. 2. Because the word *spiritual*, when used in the New Testament of persons, never means *intellectual*. It always means one under the influence of the Holy Spirit. It therefore must have that meaning here. 3. The very distinction designed to be expressed here and elsewhere by the terms natural and spiritual, is that between nature and grace, between the natural and supernatural, James 3, 15. Jude 19. 4. The reason assigned why the natural man does not receive the things of the Spirit, viz., because "they are spiritually discerned," does not mean ' because they are rationally discerned,' and therefore it is not the want of due cultivation of the reason that characterizes the natural man, but the want of the Spirit. By *natural man*, therefore, we must understand the unrenewed man ; the man under the influence of human nature, as distinguished from those who are under the influence of the Holy Spirit. The natural or unrenewed man does not *receive* the things of the Spirit. As the things which the Holy Ghost has revealed address themselves not only to the intellect as true, but to the conscience as obligatory and to the affections as excellent and lovely, not to receive them, is not to recognize, in our inward experience, their truth, authority, and excellence.

For they are foolishness unto them. The word (μωρός) *foolish*, as an adjective, means in Greek, *dull, insipid, tasteless ;* as a substantive, one that is dull, or stupid ; that is, one on whom truth, duty and excellence do not produce their proper effect. *Foolishness* (μωρία) is that which is to us absurd, insipid, powerless. When, therefore, it is said that the things of the Spirit are foolishness to the natural man, it means that they are to him absurd, insipid and distasteful.

And he cannot know them. *To know* is to discern the nature of any thing, whether as true, or good, or beautiful. This is in accordance with the constant usage of scripture. To know God is to discern his truth and excellence ; to know the truth is to apprehend it as true and good. The wise are the good, that is, those who discern the truth and excellence of divine things. The fools are the wicked, those who are insensible to truth and goodness. What, therefore, the apostle here affirms of the natural or unrenewed man is, that he cannot discern the truth, excellence, or beauty of divine things. He cannot do it. It is not simply that he does not do it ; or that he will not do it, but he cannot. We do not say of a clown that he will not discern the truth, excellence, and beauty of a poem. The difficulty is not merely in his will but in his whole inward state. The thing is foolishness to him. So the scriptures do not say of the natural man merely that he will not discern the things of the Spirit, because the difficulty in his case is not in the will alone, but in his whole inward state. He cannot know them. And the reason is,

Because they are spiritually discerned. That is, because they are discerned through the Spirit. Therefore those who have not the Spirit cannot discern them. If the effect of sin on the human soul is to make it blind to the truth, excellence and beauty of divine things; if, as the apostle asserts, the natural, or unrenewed, man is in such a state that the things of the Spirit are foolishness to him, absurd, insipid and distasteful, then it follows that he can discern them only through the Spirit. His inward state must be changed by the influence of the Spirit before he can apprehend the truth and excellence of the gospel. There must be congeniality between the perceiver and the thing perceived. Only the pure in heart can see God. If our gospel be hid, says the apostle, it is hid tc them that are lost. The only hope of the unrenewed, therefore, is in doing as the blind did in the days of Christ. They must go to him for spiritual discernment; and those who go to him he will in no wise cast out.

15. But he that is spiritual judgeth all things, yet he himself is judged of no man.

To judge here means to discern, to appreciate, and thus pass judgment upon. As the original word is the same in this as in the preceding verse, there is no good reason why the translation should vary. The spiritual man discerns the things which are spiritually discerned, though he himself is not discerned or properly appreciated by any natural man. The *all things* here spoken of are limited by the context to the things of the Spirit. It is not of the officers of the church only, nor of the church collectively, but of each and every man in whom the Holy Spirit dwells, that the apostle affirms this ability to discern the truth, excellence and beauty of divine things. It is as impossible that one man should discern for another what is true and good, as that one man should see for another. We must see for ourselves or not at all. The right of private judgment in matters of religion, is inseparable from the indwelling of the Spirit. Those who can

see, have the right to see. It is the office of the Holy Spirit
to reveal the truth, to open our eyes to discern it in its true
nature, and to feel its power. It is on this demonstration of
the Spirit, as taught above, that saving faith is founded. And
as this demonstration is granted to every one who has the
Spirit, the faith of the Christian is founded neither on the
wisdom of men nor on the authority of the church, and is
subject to neither.

Yet he himself is judged of no man. This again is limited by the context. He is appreciated by no man who has
not the Spirit. Paul afterwards says it was to him a smal.
matter to be judged by man's judgment, 4, 3. He is not
here speaking of the legitimate subjection of the believer to
his brethren; for he elsewhere teaches that those who have
the Spirit may sit in judgment on those who profess to be
spiritual, and determine how far they are really led by the
Spirit. And he gives the rule by which that judgment is to
be directed, 5, 9–12. 12, 3. Gal. 1, 8. If any man profess to
be spiritual, and yet does what the Spirit in his word forbids,
or denies what the Spirit teaches, we know that he deceives
himself, and that the truth is not in him. We must try the
spirits, whether they be of God. This is true, and is perfectly
consistent with what the apostle here says, which only means
that the spiritual man cannot be discerned or estimated aright
by those who are not spiritual.

16. For who hath known the mind of the Lord,
that he may instruct him? But we have the mind of
Christ.

This is a confirmation of what precedes. No one can
judge a spiritual man, for that would be to judge the Lord.
The Lord had revealed certain doctrines. The spiritual discern those doctrines to be true. For any man to pronounce
them false, and to judge those who held them, supposes he is
able to teach the Lord. As no one can do this, no one can
judge those who have the mind of Christ, that is, those whom
Christ by his Spirit has taught the truth. Syllogistically
stated, the argument would stand thus: No one can instruct
the Lord. We have the mind of the Lord. Therefore no one
can instruct or judge us. The first member of this syllogism
is expressed in the language of Isaiah 40, 15, according to
the Septuagint. The philosophers of Greece and the scribes

among the Jews had sat in judgment upon Paul, and pronounced his preaching foolishness. He tells them they were
not competent judges. The natural man cannot discern the
things of the Spirit, and is incompetent to judge those whom
the Spirit has taught. As what we teach is the mind of the
Lord, to condemn our doctrine, or to judge us as the teachers of those doctrines, is to condemn the Lord.

What in the Old Testament is said of Jehovah is often in
the New Testament applied to Christ. This is the case here.
Who hath known the mind of the Lord? means, who hath
known the mind of Jehovah? *We have the mind of Christ*,
therefore, means, we have the mind of Jehovah. What is
true of the one is true of the other. The same person who is
revealed in the New Testament as the Son of God, was revealed of old as Jehovah. This teaches how firm a foundation
the believer has for his faith, and how impossible it is for any
one taught by the Spirit to give up his convictions to the authority of men.

CHAPTER III.

Transition from the defence of his mode of preaching to the subject of their
divisions, vs. 1–5. The true relation of ministers to the church as servants, and not party leaders, vs. 7–23.

*Reproof of the Corinthians for their dissensions about their
religious teachers.* Vs. 1–23.

THE apostle resumes the subject of the contentions in the
church of Corinth. He passes to that subject from the defence of his mode of preaching by a natural association. One
of the objections against him was, that his preaching was too
simple. He answers, he could not make it otherwise, because
they were mere babes in Christ. The proof of their being in
this infantile or carnal state was that strifes and divisions existed among them; one saying, I am of Paul; and another, I am
of Apollos, vs. 1–4.

As their dissensions had reference to their religious teachers, the apostle endeavours to correct the evil by presenting

the ministerial office in its true light.   1. Ministers were not heads of schools or rival sects as were the Grecian philosophers, but mere servants, without any authority or power of their own.   One may plant, and another water, but the whole increase is of God, vs. 5–7.   2. Ministers are one.   They have one master and one work.   They may have different departments in that great work, but they are like fellow-labourers on the same farm, or fellow-builders on the same temple, vs. 8. 9.   3. In the discharge of their respective duties they incur a great responsibility.   If they attempt to build up the temple of God with the rubbish of their own wisdom, they will be severely punished. If they employ the materials which God has furnished, they will be rewarded, vs. 10–15.   4. It is because the church is the temple of God, that ministers will be held to this strict account for the doctrines which they preach, and for the way in which they execute their office, vs. 16. 17.   5. No minister need deceive himself in this matter.   He cannot preach a higher wisdom than the wisdom of God; and to learn that wisdom he must renounce his own, vs. 18–20.   6. Therefore the people should not place their confidence in ministers, who belong to the church, and not the church to them.   To the interests and consummation of the church, all things, visible and invisible, are made subservient, vs. 21–23.

1. And I, brethren, could not speak unto you as unto spiritual, but as unto carnal,* (even) as unto babes in Christ.

There were two classes of opponents of the apostle in Corinth.   The false teachers, some of whom he denounces as anti-Christian, and others he speaks of as only errorists; and secondly, those members of the church whom these false teachers had seduced.   As against the false teachers and the unconverted Jews and Greeks he upheld the simple gospel as higher than the wisdom of the world.   His only answer to their objection that he did not preach with " the wisdom of words," was that the wisdom of the world was foolishness with

---

* Instead of σαρκικοῖς, *unto carnal*, Griesbach, Tischendorf and others read σαρκίνοις, *to those made of flesh*, comp. 2 Cor. 3, 3.   The latter term, used in a moral sense, would be stronger than the former, as indicating the very nature as carnal.   In all the places in the New Testament where the form σάρκινος appears, except in 2 Cor. 3, 3, the reading is doubtful.   Rom. 7, 14. Heb. 7, 16, and here.

God. To the objection, as urged by believers, that his preaching was too elementary, he answered, it was adapted to their
state. He could only speak to them as to children.

They were *babes in Christ*, that is, children in Christian
knowledge and experience. This idea he expresses by saying
they were not *spiritual* but *carnal*. Now as all Christians
are spiritual, in the sense in which that term is used in the
preceding chapter, to say that men are not spiritual in that
sense, would be to say they are not Christians. Here, however, the apostle tells those whom he admits to be Christians,
and whom he calls brethren, that they are not spiritual. He
must use the word therefore in a modified sense. This is a
very common usage. When we predicate spirituality of a
Christian as compared to other Christians, we mean that he is
eminently spiritual. But when the distinction is between
Christians and the world, then every Christian is said to be
spiritual. In like manner we speak of some Christians as
worldly or carnal, without intending to deny that they are
Christians. It is obvious that the apostle uses the terms here
in the same manner. He is not speaking of Christians as distinguished from the world, but of one class of Christians as
distinguished from another.

2. I have fed you with milk and not with meat;
for hitherto ye were not able (to bear it), neither yet
now are ye able.

As they were children, he had treated them accordingly.
He *had fed them with milk ;* literally, 'I gave you milk to
drink and not meat.' A concise form of expression. What
is the distinction which the apostle here makes between milk
and meat? It is evidently not the distinction between the
wisdom of the world and the wisdom of God. Paul did not
preach the wisdom of the world to babes in Christ, and the
wisdom of God to advanced Christians. Neither does he
sanction any thing of the nature of the *Disciplina Arcani*, or
doctrine of the hidden essence of Christianity, which was introduced in later times. For the sake either of conciliating
the heathen, or of preventing beginners from forming false
notions of the gospel, it became common deliberately to conceal the truth. This is the foundation of the doctrine of re
serve, as it is called, which the Romish church has so exten-

sively practised and taught, inculcating a blind faith, and keeping the people in ignorance. Neither is the distinction that which also extensively prevailed in the early church after the age of the apostles, between truth as the object of faith and truth as the object of knowledge. This is a distinction true in itself, but as then understood, it meant nothing less than the difference between the doctrines of the Bible and the speculations of men. Philosophers of our own, and of every other age, have been willing to allow the people the truth as presented in the Scriptures, provided they themselves were allowed to explain them away into philosophical formulas. The true nature of the distinction is to be learnt partly from the import of the figure, and partly from parallel passages. The import of the figure leads to the conclusion that the difference is rather in the mode of instruction, than in the things taught. The same truth in one form is milk, in another form strong meat. "Christ," says Calvin, "is milk for babes, and strong meat for men." Every doctrine which can be taught to theologians, is taught to children. We teach a child that God is a Spirit, every where present and knowing all things; and he understands it. We tell him that Christ is God and man in two distinct natures and one person for ever. This to the child is milk, but it contains food for angels. The truth expressed in these propositions may be expanded indefinitely, and furnish nourishment for the highest intellects to eternity. The difference between milk and strong meat, according to this view, is simply the difference between the more or less perfect development of the things taught. This view is confirmed by those passages in which the same distinction is made. Thus in Hebrews 5, 11–14, the apostle speaks of his readers as having need of milk and not of strong meat. The reference is there to the distinction between the simple doctrine of the priesthood of Christ and the full development of that doctrine. The important truth is that there are not two sets of doctrine, a higher and a lower form of faith, one for the learned and the other for the unlearned; there is no part of the gospel which we are authorized to keep back from the people. Every thing which God has revealed is to be taught to every one just so fast and so far as he has the capacity to receive it.

3. For ye are yet carnal: for whereas (there is)

among you envying, and strife, and divisions, are ye not
carnal, and walk as men?

Their unfitness to receive any other nourishment than that
adapted to children, is proved by their being carnal; and their
being carnal is proved by the divisions existing among them.
Ye are yet carnal, i. e. under the influence of the flesh, or corrupt nature. They were imperfectly sanctified. Even Paul
said of himself, ' I am carnal.' This term therefore may be
applied even to the most advanced Christians. Its definite
meaning depends on the context.

The existence among them of the evils mentioned was
proof of their low religious state. Of these evils the first was
envying (ζῆλος). The word means zeal, fervid feeling. Whether
good or bad, and of what particular kind depends on the connection. Here *party spirit* would seem to be the special evil
intended. This gives rise to *strife* (ἔρις), and that again to
divisions (διχοστασία), literally, *standing apart;* here not sects,
but parties. If these things are among you, asks the apostle,
are ye not carnal, *and walk as men?* 'To walk as men' is to
be guided by principles which belong to men, as distinguished
from the Spirit of God. The doctrine that human nature is corrupt, and that all holiness in man is due to the influence of the
Spirit, is taken for granted every where in the Bible. Therefore "the world" means the wicked or the unrenewed; to be
worldly, or to act after the manner of men, is to act wickedly.

The description here given of the state of the church of
Corinth is not inconsistent with the commendations bestowed
upon it in the beginning of the first chapter. Viewed in comparison with the heathen around them, or even with other
churches, the Corinthians deserved the praise there given
them. But judged by the standard of the gospel, or of their
privileges, they deserved the censures which the apostle so
faithfully administers. Besides, in addressing the same
church, the apostle has sometimes one class of its members in
view, and sometimes another. He therefore sometimes speaks
as if they were all Jews, at other times as though they were
all Gentiles; sometimes as though they were weak and nar-
row-minded, and sometimes as if they were latitudinarian—
one time he addresses them as if they were in a high state of
piety, and at another, as if they were in a very low state.
His language is to be limited in its application to those for
whom the context in any case may show it was intended.

4. For while one saith, I am of Paul; and another, I (am) of Apollos; are ye not carnal?

This confirms the fact that there were such divisions among them as proved them to be governed by unholy feelings, and also explains the nature of those divisions. There were in Corinth, as appears from 1, 12, more parties than two; but the apostle confines himself to those here mentioned, because throughout the whole discussion he has had reference to the opposition of the Grecian element in the church; and because from the intimate relation between himself and Apollos, he could speak of him as freely as he did of himself. As the party spirit which disturbed the peace of the Corinthian church arose from wrong views of the relation of ministers to the church, the apostle endeavours to correct the evil by presenting that relation in its true light.

5. Who then is Paul, and who is Apollos, but ministers by whom ye believed, even as the Lord gave to every man?

This passage may read, 'Who then is Paul, and who is Apollos?' ministers by whom ye believed,' &c. Ministers are mere instruments in the hands of God. The doctrines which they preach are not their own discoveries, and the power which renders their preaching successful is not in them. They are nothing; and therefore it is an entire perversion of their relation to the church to make them the heads of parties. In the oldest MSS. the name of Apollos stands first; and some of them have τί instead of τίς. '*What* then is Apollos, and *what* is Paul.' Both these emendations are adopted by the later editors.

Paul and Apollos, men of the highest office and of the highest gifts, are *ministers* (διάκονοι) *waiters, attendants, servants;* so called not from their relation to God merely, as those who serve him, but also because of their relation to the church, whose they are, to whom they belong, and whom they serve.

By whom, i. e. by whose instrumentality, *ye are believers,* or, *became believers.* The design of the ministry is to bring men to "the obedience of faith," Rom. 1, 5. It is appointed for that end by God himself, and therefore it is of the greatest importance and value. This Paul does not deny. He admits, and often urges the necessity of the office for the extension and edification of the church, Eph. 4, 11–16. The people, therefore, are bound to regard the ministry as a divine institution, and to value its services; but preachers are not to be regarded as party leaders, or as lords over God's heritage.

Even as the Lord gave to every man; literally, *to each one,* i. e. to each minister. They are all servants, and each has his appointed work to perform, Rom. 12, 3. *The Lord* here probably refers to God, though elsewhere the appointment of ministers and the distribution of their various gifts are referred to Christ. Here, however, vs. 9. 10, the reference is to God. In scripture the same act is sometimes referred to one, and sometimes to another of the persons in the Trinity, because they are one God.

6. I have planted, Apollos watered : but God gave the increase.

This illustrates two points; first, the diversity of service on the part of ministers, spoken of in v. 5, one plants and another waters; and secondly, the entirely subordinate and instrumental character of their service. As in nature, planting and watering are not the efficient causes of vegetation ; so in the church, ministerial acts are not the efficient causes of grace. In both cases all the efficiency is of God. And as in nature, planting and watering by human instrumentality, are not the necessary conditions of vegetation, so neither are ministerial acts the necessary conditions of faith. On the other hand, however, as the work of the husbandman is the ordinary and appointed means of securing a harvest, so the work of the ministry is the ordinary means of conversion.

7. So then, neither is he that planteth any thing, neither he that watereth : but God that giveth the increase.

This is the conclusion. Ministers are nothing. They are the instruments in the hands of God. He only is to be looked up to as the source of truth, of strength, or of success. To him is to be referred all the good ministers may be the instruments of effecting. If this be so, if ministers are thus inefficient, why should any one say, I am of Paul ? as though Paul would save him ; or, as though a mere instrument could forgive sin or impart grace.

8. Now he that planteth and he that watereth are one : and every man shall receive his own reward, according to his own labour.

Are one. Ministers have the same office ; they have the same work, they stand in the same relation to God and to his Church. They are fellow-labourers. To array the one against the other, is, therefore, inconsistent with their relation to each other and to the people whom they serve.

Every man shall receive his own reward. Diversity and unity is the law of all God's works. Ministers are one, yet they have different gifts, different services to perform. One plants and another waters, and they have different rewards.

According to his own labour. The rule of reward is not the talents or gifts, nor the success of ministers, but their labours. This brings the humblest on a level with the most exalted ; the least successful with the most highly favoured. The faithful, laborious minister or missionary who labours in obscurity and without apparent fruit, will meet a reward far beyond that of those who, with less self-denial and effort, are made the instruments of great results. Corinth was the field of labour of a multitude of teachers, some faithful, and some unfaithful ; some laborious, and others indolent and self-indulgent. Each would have to answer for himself, and would receive a reward proportioned to his fidelity and self-denial.

9. For we are labourers together with God : ye are God's husbandry, (ye are) God's building.

For we are labourers together with God. This is at once the reason why ministers are one, and why they are to be rewarded according to their labours. They are one because they are all co-workers with God in the same great enterprise ; and they are to be rewarded according to their labour, because that is the rule according to which labourers are rewarded. The propriety of this representation is apparent, because the church is God's *husbandry*, or farm, which he renders fruitful by the light of truth and the dew of his grace, and on which his servants labour. This is a familiar scriptural illustration, as the church is often called the vineyard of the Lord, in which his ministers are labourers. A labourer who does not labour is a contradiction ; and a minister who is not a worker cannot expect a labourer's reward. *Ye are God's building.* A still more frequent figure; as the church is so often compared to a temple which is in the course of erection, and of which ministers are the builders, Eph. 2, 20–22. 1 Pet. 2, 5. Union and fidelity in labour are required of those engaged in tilling the same farm, or in the erection of the same building; and they are no less required in those engaged in cultivating the vineyard of the Lord, or in erecting his temple. The apostle drops the former, and carries out the latter figure.

10. According to the grace of God which is given unto me, as a wise master-builder, I have laid the foundation, and another buildeth thereon. But let every man take heed how he buildeth thereupon.

According to the grace of God given unto me. Paul often speaks of his apostolic office as *a grace* or favour which he had received of God, but here, as in 15, 10, the reference is more general. By *the grace of God* he means all the gifts and influences of the Spirit, which not only qualified him for his work, but rendered him so laborious and faithful. Here, as elsewhere, he attributes to God all he was, and all that he was enabled to accomplish.

As a wise master-builder. *Wise* (σοφός), i. e. skilful. The word is familiarly used of artificers. Paul was not only a labourer, but an (ἀρχιτέκτων) *architect.* To him was revealed the whole plan of the building, and he was inspired to develope that plan, and to prescribe the way in which it should be carried out. He laid *the foundation.* The same idea as was expressed above by saying, "I have planted, Apollos watered." He began the work in Corinth. Those who came after him were to carry on the edifice which he had commenced. The building must be erected upon the foundation and according to it. And, therefore, he adds, *Let every man* (i. e. every builder) *take heed how he buildeth thereupon.* In the whole context he is speaking of ministers, and therefore this clause must be considered as a warning addressed to them. They are to take heed *how,* i. e. with what materials, they carried on the building of this holy temple. Fidelity as well as diligence is required in a minister. No matter how laborious he may be, unless he employs the proper materials, he will lose his reward. Nothing but truth can be safely used in the development of Christian character, or in building up the

Church. To mix the wisdom of men with the wisdom of God in this work, is, as the apostle afterwards says, like using alternate layers of straw and marble in the erection of a temple. Let no man deceive himself in this matter. He will prove himself a fool, if he attempts to substitute philosophy for the gospel in the work of saving men.

11. For other foundation can no man lay than that is laid, which is Jesus Christ.

For, others can only carry on the work already begun, for the foundation cannot be changed. The foundation of the church is Christ. Is. 28, 16. Acts 4, 11. Eph. 2, 20. 1 Pet. 2, 6. This may be understood either of the person or of the doctrine of Christ. In either way the sense is good. Christ, as the incarnate Son of God, according to one scriptural figure, is the head of the church which is his body, that is, he is the source of its life ; according to another figure, he is its foundation or corner-stone, because on him all the members of the church, considered as a temple, rest for salvation. On the other hand, however, it is also true that the doctrine concerning Christ, is the fundamental doctrine of the gospel. We may, therefore, understand the apostle to say, that the work of the ministry is to build up the church on the foundation which *God* has laid in the person and work of Christ. There can be no other ground of confidence for the justification, sanctification, and salvation of men. Or we may understand him to say, that the work of those who followed him in Corinth was simply to build on the foundation which *he* had laid, in preaching the doctrine of Christ and him crucified, for there can be no other foundation of the church than that doctrine. The former interpretation, which is adopted by many distinguished commentators, is more in accordance with the common representations of Scripture which speak of God having constituted Christ the corner-stone of the church. It is also perhaps more in accordance with the form of expression here used. Jesus Christ himself is the foundation, which was already laid. The second interpretation, however, is certainly more consistent with the context. In v. 10 Paul says, *he* had laid the foundation. This can only mean that he had in Corinth taught the doctrine concerning the person and work of Christ. This is the only sense in which he can be said to have laid that foundation *which is Jesus Christ*. Besides, the whole passage has reference to doctrine. Paul had preached the truth; those who came after him must take heed what they preached.

12. 13. Now, if any man build upon this foundation gold, silver, precious stones, wood, hay, stubble; every man's work shall be made manifest : for the day shall declare it, because it shall be revealed by fire ; and the fire shall try every man's work, of what sort it is.

In consistency with the context, gold, silver and precious stones, can only mean truth; and wood, hay and stubble, error. If by the foundation which Paul had laid were intended the first converts in Corinth, then the above terms would naturally be understood of good and bad members of the church. The sense would then be, 'I laid the foundation of the church in Corinth by receiving true believers to its communion; let others take heed with what kind of members they build up the church.' But as the foundation which Paul laid is expressly declared to be Jesus Christ, or the truth concerning his person and work, the words above mentioned must refer to true and false doctrines. 'I have laid the foundation of Christ crucified ; do you take heed with what kind of doctrine you carry on the work.' Besides, the whole discussion has reference to preachers and their duties. *Precious stones* here mean stones valuable for building, such as granite and marble. Gold and silver were extensively employed in adorning ancient temples, and are therefore appropriately used as the symbols of pure doctrine. Wood, hay, and stubble are the perishable materials out of which ordinary houses were built, but not temples. Wood for the doors and posts ; *hay*, (χόρτος,) dried *grass* mixed with mud for the walls; and *straw*, (καλάμη,) for the roof. These materials, unsuitable for the temdle of God, are appropriate symbols of false doctrines.

Every man's work shall be made (or, *become*) *manifest.* In this life it may be disputed whether a man's doctrines are true or false. He may have great confidence in their truth, and set himself above his brethren and even above the Bible. But his work hereafter will appear in its true character. *For the day shall declare it. The day* does not mean indefinitely *time,* 'Time shall declare it;' nor the day of tribulation; nor the day of light and knowledge as distinguished from the present ignorance; but the great day, the day of judgment, or, as it is so often called, the day of the Lord. That day shall make manifest the truth or falsehood of the doctrines taught, *because it is* (i. e. is certainly to be) *revealed by fire ;* literally, *in* or *with* fire (ἐν πυρί). In 2 Thess. 1, 8, it is said, "The Lord Jesus shall be revealed in flaming fire," i. e. in the midst of flaming fire. Fire is the constant symbol of trial and judgment. The meaning therefore is, that the day of the Lord will be a day of severe trial. Every work will then be subjected to a test which nothing impure can stand. The context shows that the word *day*, and not *work*, is the nominative to *revealed*. 'The day of judgment shall declare every man's work, because that day shall be revealed with fire.'

And the fire shall try every man's work of what sort it is. The figure is that of a building on which many workmen are engaged. Some use proper materials, others wood, hay and stubble. The building is to be subjected to the test of fire. The wood, hay and stubble will be burnt up; only the solid materials will stand. False doctrine can no more stand the test of the day of judgment, than hay or stubble can stand a raging conflagration.

14. 15. If any man's work abide which he hath built thereupon, he shall receive a reward. If any man's work shall be burned, he shall suffer loss : but he himself shall be saved ; yet so as by fire.

This is an amplification of what precedes. If the materials employed by a spiritual builder stand the test of the day of judgment, he shall receive the reward of a faithful servant. *Which he hath built thereupon*, i. e. upon the foundation. Comp. v. 12. *If any man's work shall be burned* (κατακαήσεται for κατακαυθήσεται) ; that is, if the materials used by any builder shall not stand the test of that day, *he shall suffer loss* (ζημιωθήσεται, see 2 Cor. 7, 9. Phil. 3, 8). That is, he will lose his reward.

But he himself shall be saved. Just as a man who has built his house of combustible materials, though he may escape when the fire comes, his property is lost, and all his labour comes to nothing. The apostle is here speaking of those teachers who, although they retain the fundamental doctrines of the gospel, yet combine them with error. This is plain from v. 12, "If any man shall build on this foundation." It is not enough, therefore, that a minister hold fast to fundamental truth ; he must take heed what he teaches in connection with that truth.   If he mingles with it the wood, hay and stubble of his own philosophy, he will find himself a loser on the day of judgment.   Many of the Fathers understand σωθήσεται here in the sense of *shall be preserved*.   His work shall be consumed, but he himself shall be kept alive in the midst of the fire.   It is not then the salvation, but the final perdition of the false teacher that the passage teaches.   This, however, is contrary to the uniform meaning of the word in the New Testament. The common interpretation is therefore to be preferred.

Yet so as by fire, i. e. with difficulty.   Comp. 1 Pet. 3, 20. Jude 23. Zech. 3, 2.   He will just escape with his life, as a man is rescued from a burning building.   His salvation will not only be effected with difficulty, but it will be attended with great loss.   He will occupy a lower place in the kingdom of heaven than he would have done.   Romanists found their doctrine of purgatory on tradition rather than on Scripture. They are glad, however, to avail themselves of any semblance of scriptural support, and therefore appeal to this passage to prove that men are saved through fire.   But, 1. Paul is here speaking of ministers and of their doctrines, and not of be- lievers in general.   2. The fire of which he speaks is not a state of trial preceding the judgment, but the judgment itself. 3. The fire is that in the midst of which Jesus Christ is to ap- pear.   4. Paul does not say, the man is to be saved by being purified by fire, but simply ' with difficulty,' as the expression " so as by fire " familiarly means.

16. Know ye not that ye are the temple of God, and (that) the Spirit of God dwelleth in you ?

The apostle justifies the representation given above of the responsibility of ministers.   The unfaithful builders deserve to be thus punished, because they are engaged in the erection of no ordinary building.   They are not raising up a house for themselves, to be constructed of what materials and on what- ever plan may suit their taste.   They are building the temple of God.   This truth the Corinthians seem to have forgotten, for they regarded their teachers as men allowed to preach their own speculations, and valued them according to their proficiency in " the wisdom of words."   He, therefore, asks them, " Know ye not that ye are the temple of God ? "   See 6, 19. 2 Cor. 6,

16. Eph. 2, 21. A temple is a house in which God dwells; and therefore, it is added, *and that the Spirit of God dwelleth in you.* This indwelling of the Spirit constitutes each believer, every separate church, and the Church collectively the temple of God. As in the Jewish temple, in its inmost recess, the Shechinah, or glory of God, was constantly present, and conferred on the building its awe-inspiring power, and rendered any profanation of it a direct offence to God; so does the Holy Spirit dwell in the Church, the profanation of which by false doctrine is therefore sacrilege.

17. If any man defile the temple of God, him shall God destroy: for the temple of God is holy, which (temple) ye are.

The word translated *defile* in the first clause of this verse, is the same as that rendered *destroy* in the second clause. It (φθείρω) has the general meaning *to bring into a worse state.* In the LXX. as well as in the New Testament it means *to mar.* The passage may, therefore, be rendered, 'If any man injure the temple of God, him will God injure.' The temple cannot be injured with impunity. Under the old dispensation the penalty for defiling the sanctuary was either death, Lev. 15, 31, or excision from the people, Num. 19, 20. God is not less jealous of his spiritual temple, than he was of the typical temple, built of wood and stone by the hands of men. Ministers injure the souls of men and injure the church when they preach false doctrine, and therefore they defile the temple of God, and will certainly be punished.

For the temple of God is holy, i. e. sacred; something which cannot be violated with impunity. In this sense every thing consecrated to God is holy, and especially any place or person in which he dwells. *Which (temple) ye are.* As the word for temple is not in the text (which reads οἵτινές ἐστε ὑμεῖς) the reference may be to the word *holy.* 'The temple is holy, which ye also are.' The same reason exists why the church cannot be defiled or injured, that there is that the temple could not be profaned. Both are sacred. The view given in our version is commonly preferred.

18. Let no man deceive himself. If any man

among you seemeth to be wise in this world, let him
become a fool, that he may be wise.

Let no man deceive himself. 'Let no man doubt the truth
of what I have said of the worthlessness of human wisdom,
and of the danger of substituting it for the wisdom of God.
If he does, he will find himself mistaken.'

If any man among you seemeth to be wise, (δοκεῖ σοφὸς
εἶναι), thinks himself to be wise. *In this world* may be connected with the word *wise,* 'wise with the wisdom of this
world.' Or, it may be connected with the whole preceding
clause. 'If any imagines he is wise among you, in this world.'
The former explanation is more in keeping with the whole
context. "Wise in this world" is equivalent to "wise after
the flesh," 1, 26.

Let him become a fool, that he may be (or, *become*) *wise.*
Let him renounce his own wisdom in order that he may receive the wisdom of God. We must be empty in order to be
filled. We must renounce our own righteousness, in order to
be clothed in the righteousness of Christ. We must renounce
our own strength, in order to be made strong. We must renounce our own wisdom, in order to be truly wise. This is
a universal law. And it is perfectly reasonable. We are
only required to recognize that to be true, which is true.
We would not be required to renounce our own righteousness, strength, or wisdom, if they were really what they assume to be. It is simply because they are in fact worthless,
that we are called upon so to regard them.

19. 20. For the wisdom of this world is foolishness
with God. For it is written, He taketh the wise in their
own craftiness. And again, The Lord knoweth the
thoughts of the wise, that they are vain.

We must renounce our own wisdom because it is folly.
The infinite mind sees that to be folly which we children think
to be wisdom. There are two senses in which this is true, or
in which wisdom may be said to be folly. Even truth or true
knowledge becomes folly, if employed to accomplish an end
for which it is not adapted. If a man attempts to make men
holy or happy; if he undertakes to convert the world, by
mathematics, or metaphysics, or moral philosophy, he is foolish,
and his wisdom, as a means to that end, is folly. He must

renounce all dependence on those means if he would accomplish that end. But in the second place, much that passes for wisdom among men is in itself, and not merely as a means to an end, foolishness. Both these ideas are evidently comprehended in the apostle's statement. He means to say that human knowledge is entirely inadequate to save men; because that end can only be accomplished by the gospel. And he means also to brand as folly the speculations of men about "the deep things of God."

In proof of the assertion that the wisdom of men is foolishness with God, he quotes two passages of Scripture. The first is from Job 5, 13, the second is from Ps. 94, 11. The former is a fragment of a sentence containing in the Greek no verb. Our translation renders the participle (ὁ δρασσόμενος) as though it were a verb. Those passages clearly express the same sentiment which the apostle had uttered. They declare the impotency and insufficiency of human wisdom.

21. Therefore let no one glory in men : for all things are yours.

To glory in any person or thing is to trust in him or it as the ground of confidence, or as the source of honour or blessedness. It is to regard ourselves as blessed because of our relation to it. Thus men are said to glory in the Lord, or in the cross; because God, or Christ as crucified, is regarded as the ground of confidence and the source of blessedness. Others are said to glory in the flesh, in the law, or even in themselves. The apostle having shown that ministers are mere servants, nothing in themselves, and that the wisdom of the world is foolishness with God, draws from these premises the inference that they are not the ground of the believer's confidence. The Corinthians did glory in men, when they said, I am of Paul, I of Apollos, and I of Cephas. They forgot their own dignity when they regarded as masters those who were their servants.

For all things are yours. The amplification of these words, given in the next verse, shows that they are to be taken in their widest sense. The universe is yours. How unworthy then is it, that you should glory in men. Paul often appeals to the dignity and destiny of the church as a motive to right action. " Know ye not that the saints shall judge the world ? " 6, 2. There are two senses in which the declaration, " All

things are yours," may be understood. It means that all
things are designed to promote the interests of the church.
The consummation of the work of redemption is the great end
to which all things are directed, and to which they are to be
made subservient. And secondly, the church is the heir of
the world, Rom. 4, 13. All things are given to Christ as the
head of the church, and to the church in him. For his people
are to reign with him, Rom. 8, 17, and the glory which the
Father gave him, he gives them, John 17, 22. The church,
which is to be thus exalted, is not any external society with
its hierarchy, nor is it the body of poor, imperfect believers as
they now are, who for their own good are despised and down-
trodden. But it is the consummated church to be formed out
of materials now so unpromising. The people of God, how
ever, should not be unmindful of their high destiny, nor act
unworthily of it.

**22. Whether Paul, or Apollos, or Cephas, or the
world, or life, or death, or things present, or things to
come ; all are yours ;**

This is the amplification of the preceding verse. In the
" all things " there mentioned are included, 1. The ministry,
which belongs to the church and is designed for its edification.
The church does not belong to the ministry, as a kingdom
belongs to a king, but the reverse. 2. The world (κόσμος) in
its widest sense. The present order of things is maintained
and directed to the promotion of the great work of redemption. 3. Life and death. This means not merely that the
question whether the people of God live or die, is determined
with reference to their own good; but also that life and death
are dispensed and administered so as best to fulfil the designs
of God in reference to the church. The greatest men of the
world, kings, statesmen and heroes, ministers, individual believers and unbelievers, live or die just as best subserves the
interests of Christ's kingdom. 4. Things present and things
to come, i. e. the present and the future. It is no temporary
subjection of all things to the church which is intended. The
plan of God contemplates the permanent exaltation of the
redeemed.

23. And ye are Christ's : and Christ (is) God's.

As all things are subject to the church and belong to it,

the church itself can be subject and belong to none but Christ. In him, therefore, only can it glory.

Christ is God's. As the church is subject only to Christ, so Christ is subject only to God. The Scriptures speak of a threefold subordination of Christ. 1. A subordination as to the mode of subsistence and operation, of the second, to the first person in the Trinity; which is perfectly consistent with their identity of substance, and equality in power and glory. 2. The voluntary subordination of the Son in his humbling himself to be found in fashion as a man, and becoming obedient unto death, and therefore subject to the limitations and infirmities of our nature. 3. The economical or official subjection of the theanthropos. That is, the subordination of the incarnate Son of God, in the work of redemption and as the head of the church. He that is by nature equal with God becomes, as it were, officially subject to him. The passages the most directly parallel with the one before us are 11, 3, and 15, 28, but in Phil. 2, 6–11. Heb. 1, 3, and in many other passages, the same truth is taught.

CHAPTER IV.

Deduction from the preceding discussion, teaching the proper light in which the people should regard the ministry, vs. 1–6. Contrast between the apostles and the false teachers, vs. 6–21.

Ministers, as stewards, should be faithful, as Paul had proved himself to be, vs. 1–21.

IT follows, from what was said in the preceding chapter, that the people should regard their ministers as the servants of Christ, and dispensers of the truths which God had revealed, v. 1. The most important qualification of a dispenser is fidelity, v. 2. It is a small matter how men may estimate the fidelity of ministers. The only competent judge is the Lord; and, therefore, to his judgment the decision of that question should be referred, vs. 3–6.

What the apostle had said of himself and of Apollos, in the foregoing exhibition of the true nature of the ministerial office, was intended to apply to all ministers, that the people should not estimate them unduly, and that all emulous contentions might be avoided, vs. 6, 7. The false teachers in Corinth, and the people under their influence, considered themselves to be in a high state of religious prosperity, and were disposed to self-indulgence, v. 8. The apostles were in a very different condition, at least as to their external circumstances. They were despised, afflicted, and persecuted; while their adversaries were honoured, prosperous, and caressed, vs. 9–13. Paul presented this contrast not to mortify, but to admonish his readers, v. 14. He, if any one, had a right to admonish them, for he was their spiritual father, v. 15. They should therefore imitate him; and, to that end, he had sent Timothy to remind them of his instructions and example, vs. 16. 17. He himself intended soon to visit Corinth; and it depended on them whether he should come with a rod, or in the spirit of meekness, vs. 18–21.

1. Let a man so account of us, as of the ministers of Christ, and stewards of the mysteries of God.

This is the conclusion or deduction from the preceding discussion. Ministers are the servants of Christ, and stewards of God. *Let a man*, i. e. every one. *Account of us*, (λογι-ζέσθω) let him think of us, or regard us as being. *The ministers of Christ.* Literally the word (ὑπηρέτης) means *an under-rower*, or common sailor; and then, subordinate servant of any kind. It is generally and properly used of menials, or of those of the lower class of servants. This is not always the case, but here the idea of entire subjection is to be retained. Ministers are the mere servants of Christ; they have no authority of their own; their whole business is to do what they are commanded.

And stewards of the mysteries of God. Stewards (οἰκονό-μοι) were generally slaves appointed as managers or overseers. It was their business to direct the affairs of the household, and dispense the provisions. It is *as dispensers* ministers are here called *stewards*. They are to dispense *the mysteries of God*, that is, the truths which God had revealed, and which, as being undiscoverable by human reason, are called mysteries, into the knowledge of which men must be initiated. *Mysteries* here do not mean the sacraments. The word is never used in reference to either baptism or the Lord's Supper in the New

Testament. And such a reference in this case is forbidden by the whole context. In the second chapter, the mystery which Paul speaks of is declared to be the gospel considered as a revelation of God. In the Romish church, the principal function of ministers is to dispense the sacraments to which they are assumed to have the power, in virtue of the grace of orders, to give supernatural power. In the apostolic church they were regarded as the dispensers of the truth. This verse, therefore, contains two important truths: Ministers have no arbitrary or discretionary authority in the church. Neither have they any supernatural power, such as is attributed to them in the Romish church. Their authority is merely ministerial, limited by the commands of Christ, and, therefore, to be judged by the standard of those commands, which are known to the whole church. And secondly, they are not, like Aristotle or Plato, the originators of their own doctrines, or the teachers of the doctrines of other men, but simply the dispensers of the truths which God has revealed.

2. Moreover, it is required in stewards, that a man be found faithful.

Moreover, (ὃ δὲ λοιπόν) *but what remains is ; as to the rest.* Instead of the words just mentioned Lachmann and Tischendorf adopt the reading ὧδε, *here*, i. e. in the earth, or, in this matter. The most ancient MSS. are in favour of this reading, and the sense is good. The great requisite for the discharge of the office of a steward is fidelity. As he is a servant he must be faithful to his master; as he is a dispenser, he must be faithful to those subject to his oversight. He must not neglect to dispense to them their food; neither may he adulterate it, or substitute any thing in the place of that which is given them to distribute. The application of this to the case of ministers is plain. The great thing required of them is fidelity. Fidelity to Christ as servants; not arrogating to themselves any other than ministerial power, or venturing to go beyond his commands. Fidelity also to the people, not failing to dispense to them the truths which God has revealed, nor mixing those truths with their own speculations, much less substituting for those doctrines human knowledge or wisdom.

3. But with me it is a very small thing that I

should be judged of you, or of man's judgment: yea, I judge not mine own self.

Fidelity to duty supposes responsibility to some one. As ministers are required to be faithful, who is to judge of their fidelity? Paul says, so far as he was concerned, it was not the Corinthians, not the world, not himself—but, as he adds in the next verse, the Lord.

But with me, (ἐμοὶ δέ); *to me,* i. e. in my estimation. *It is a very small thing* (εἰς ἐλάχιστόν ἐστι), *it amounts to nothing.* "That I should be judged of you." This does not refer to the judicial judgment of the church, but simply to the opinions which the Corinthians entertained of Paul. It mattered little to him whether they thought him faithful or unfaithful. His responsibility was not to them. They had not sent him they had not told him what doctrines to preach. He was not their steward, but the steward of God. *Or of man's judgment* (ὑπὸ ανθρωπίνης ἡμέρας) literally, *by human day.* As 'the day of the Lord' means the day of God's judgment, so 'the day of men' means the day of man's judgment. The sense is obvious, though the expression no where else occurs. The apostle, although denying his responsibility to the Corinthians, or to any human tribunal for his fidelity as a minister of Christ, does not mean to assert that he was his own judge. He therefore adds, "I judge not my own self." Many men think themselves faithful, who are most unfaithful. It is not enough that our own conscience does not condemn us. Conscience is a partial, and often an unenlightened judge. We may justify ourselves, and be at last condemned by God. But, if our heart condemn us, how can we stand before him who knows all things?

4. For I know nothing by myself; yet am I not hereby justified: but he that judgeth me is the Lord.

For I know nothing by myself, (οὐδὲν γὰρ ἐμαυτῷ σύνοιδα) *I am conscious of nothing.* That is, my conscience does not accuse me of any thing. Paul is speaking of his fidelity as a steward. He says, he was not his own judge, for though his conscience did not accuse him of want of ministerial fidelity, that did not justify him. *I am not thereby justified.* That is, I am not thereby acquitted. My judgment of myself is not final. The only impartial, competent, and final judge is the

Lord. This interpretation of the verse is suited to the meaning of the words and to the connection, and has the sanction of general approbation. The connection indicated by *for* is between what precedes and the latter part of the verse, 'I judge not myself, *for* he that judgeth me is the Lord.' It need hardly be remarked, that when Paul says, he was conscious of nothing wrong, the declaration is to be limited by the connection. He speaks of himself elsewhere as the chief of sinners, which is perfectly consistent with his saying that his conscience acquitted him of failure in fidelity as a minister. The clause, *I am not hereby justified*, must also be explained in reference to the connection. He is not speaking of the doctrine of justification; and, therefore, is not to be understood to say, 'My justification is not thereby secured.' That is, he does not mean to say that ministerial fidelity is not the ground of his justification. This would be entirely out of keeping with the context. All he means is, that the question whether he was faithful, was one not to be decided by his conscience, but by the Lord. *Lord* here evidently means Christ, who is therefore a higher judge than conscience. As a moral agent, as a believer, and as a minister, Paul felt himself accountable to Christ. This inward allegiance of the conscience is the highest form of worship. The Lord Jesus was to the apostle the object of all those sentiments and feelings which terminate on God. And he must be so to us, or we are not Christians; because, what makes a man a Christian, is to feel and act towards Christ as God.

5. Therefore judge nothing before the time, until the Lord come, who both will bring to light the hidden things of darkness, and will make manifest the counsels of the hearts: and then shall every man have praise of God.

As the Lord is the only judge, we must wait for his appearance, and neither assume his prerogative, nor anticipate his decision. *Judge nothing before the time* (καιρός), i. e. the appropriate, or appointed time. What time is intended is intimated in the next clause. *Until the Lord come*, (ἕως ἂν ἔλθῃ, shall have come,) i. e. until the second advent of Christ, which in the New Testament is constantly represented as contemporaneous with the resurrection of the dead and the general

judgment. He is to come for judgment, Matt. 24, 30. 46.
2 Pet. 3, 4. 12. Jude 14. Rev. 1, 7. The reason why the
coming of the Lord is the appropriate time for judgment is,
that he will then do what cannot be done before, or by any
creature. *He will bring to light* (shed light upon) *the secret
things of darkness ;* that is, things which are now hidden in
darkness. This includes acts which are now unknown, and
those principles of action which lie concealed in the recesses
of the heart, where no human eye can reach them. This is all
the context requires. In other connections the secret things,
or the works of darkness, means *wicked works ;* works done
in the dark to avoid detection; or works which spring from
moral darkness, Eph. 5, 11. But the apostle is here speaking
of the reason why judgment should be deferred until the coming of Christ. The reason is that he alone can bring to light
the secret acts and motives of men. These secret works and
motives, and not merely outward acts, are the grounds of
judgment. Whether a man is faithful in preaching the gospel depends upon his motives; for some preached Christ of
contention, Phil. 1, 16. This view of the passage is confirmed
by the explanatory clause which follows, *and will make manifest the counsels of the hearts.* The former expression is general, this is special. The ' counsels of the heart' are included
in the ' secret things of darkness.' He who sheds light on the
secret things of darkness not only reveals acts done in secret,
but makes manifest the counsels of the heart. What a work
is here ascribed to the Lord Jesus! He will bring to light
the secret acts and hidden motives of every human being.
He will exercise the prerogative of judging the heart and conscience ; a prerogative which none but an omniscient being
can rightfully claim or possibly exercise. It is therefore in
Scripture always spoken of as peculiar to God, Ps. 26, 2. Jer.
11, 20. 20, 12. Rev. 2, 23. Paul appealed from the fallible
judgment of short-sighted men, to the infallible judgment of
his omniscient Lord.

And then ; not before, because not until then will the full
truth be known. *Shall every man have praise* (ἔπαινος, much
praise, applause, a loud and clear acclaim of commendation;
Well done, thou good and faithful servant!) The reason why
Paul uses the word *praise*, and not the general term *recompense*, probably is, that he is throughout the passage speaking
of himself. The Corinthians had sat in judgment on his fidelity. He tells them that neither they nor he could competently

decide whether he was faithful, or not. The Lord was the
only judge. When he comes, the truth will be known, and
then there shall be praise. He knew there was laid up for him
a crown of righteousness, which the Lord the righteous judge
would give him in that day, 2 Tim. 4, 8. Still, as what is
true of him is true of others, he expresses himself in general
terms. Then shall *every man* have praise. That is, every
faithful servant. Praise *of God*, i. e. from God. He is the
ultimate source of all good. He is in Christ; and Christ is in
God. The Theanthropos, as final judge, is the representative
of the Godhead, so that his decisions and awards are the decisions and awards of God. As remarked above, 2, 15, what
the apostle says of his independence of human judgment, and
his command not to anticipate the judgment of the Lord, is
consistent with his frequent recognition of the right and duty
of the church to sit in judgment on the qualifications of her own
members. He is here speaking of the heart. The church
cannot judge the heart. Whether a man is sincere or in-
sincere in his professions, whether his experience is genuine
or spurious, God only can decide. The church can only judge
of what is outward. If any man profess to be holy, and yet
is immoral, the church is bound to reject him, as Paul clearly
teaches in a following chapter. Or if he profess to be a Christian, and yet rejects Christianity, or any of its essential doctrines, he cannot be received, Tit. 3, 10. But "the counsels
of the heart" the Searcher of hearts only can judge.

6. And these things, brethren, I have in a figure
transferred to myself and (to) Apollos for your sakes;
that ye might learn in us not to think (of men) above
that which is written, that no one of you be puffed up
for one against another.

These things refers to what was said in the preceding
chapter of preachers, especially to what is said from 3, 5, and
onwards. These things he had *in a figure transferred to himself and Apollos.* That is, instead of teaching in an abstract,
general form, that ministers were mere servants, he had
presented the truth in a concrete form, saying that he and
Apollos were servants, mere instruments in the hand of God.
This was the ($\mu\epsilon\tau\alpha\sigma\chi\eta\mu\alpha\tau\iota\sigma\mu\acute{o}\varsigma$), the change of form which he
had adopted. He did this, he says, that they might learn *in*

us, i. e. by what I have said of Apollos and myself, *not to think above that which is written.* That is, not to estimate ministers above the scriptural standard. As Paul had been treating of this subject, *above that which is written,* might seem naturally to refer to what he himself had just written. But as the phrase always elsewhere refers to the Old Testament, which were the *writings* recognized as of divine authority, such is probably the reference here. He does not appeal to any one passage, but to the doctrine taught in the Scriptures concerning ministers of religion. The Corinthians were not to think of their ministers more highly than the Bible authorized them to think. Comp. Jer. 9, 23, 24. The particle (ἵνα), rendered *that,* has its ordinary force, *in order that,* although the following verb (φυσιοῦσθε,) is in the indicative, a combination which occurs nowhere else except in Gal. 4, 17. The connection is with the preceding clause, 'That ye may learn to think correctly, *in order that,*' &c.

That no one be puffed up for one against another ; literally, *that ye be not puffed up one for one against another.* This admits of two interpretations. It may mean, 'That ye be not inflated one on account of one teacher, and against another.' The Corinthians were proud of their connection one with one teacher, and another with another. And this led to the strifes and divisions which existed among them. Paul taught them that ministers were servants, in order that they might not thus contend about them. This, although it gives a good sense, is neither consistent with the structure of the passage nor with what follows. The meaning is, 'Be not puffed up one above another,' (εἰς ὑπὲρ τοῦ ἑνός), comp. in the Greek 1 Thess. 5, 11. The followers of Apollos exalted themselves over those of Paul, and those of Paul over those of Cephas. One exalted himself above another and against him. He not only thought himself better than his brother, but assumed a hostile attitude towards him. This view is confirmed by the next verse, which is directed against the self-conceit of the Corinthians and not against their zeal for their teachers.

7. For who maketh thee to differ (from another)? and what hast thou that thou didst not receive ? Now if thou didst receive (it), why dost thou glory, as if thou hadst not received (it) ?

Who maketh thee to differ ? This may mean either, 'Who

thinks you are better than others?' Your superiority over
your brethren is mere self-conceit and inflation. The difference between you is only imaginary. Or, it may mean, 'Who
is the author of this superiority?' Admitting you to be as
superior to others as you imagine, to whom are you indebted
for it? According to the latter explanation the verse contains but one argument against their pride, viz., that all distinguishing advantages are derived from God. According to
the former, there are two distinct considerations urged: first,
that they had no ground for thinking themselves better than
others; and second, if they had any superiority it was due not
themselves, but to God. So that in either case their inflation
was absurd and unchristian. It is here assumed that every
thing, whether natural or gracious, by which one man is favourably distinguished from another, is due to God; and being thus due to him and not to the possessor, is a cause of
gratitude, but not of self-complacency or of self-applause.
This is true even of those things which are acquired by great
self-denial and exertion. Paul was as much self-formed as any
man ever was, and yet he said, By the grace of God I am
what I am.

8. Now ye are full, now ye are rich, ye have reigned
as kings without us : and I would to God ye did reign,
that we also might reign with you.

Having, says Calvin, repressed their self-conceit, he here
derides it. That the passage is ironical, and even sarcastic,
cannot be denied. This is not the only instance in which
these weapons are used by the inspired writers. The prophets
especially employ them freely in their endeavours to convince
the people of the folly of trusting to idols. The propriety of
the use of weapons so dangerous depends on the occasion and
the motive. If the thing assailed be both wicked and foolish,
and if the motive be, not the desire to give pain, but to convince and to convert, their use is justified by Scriptural examples. There is an evident climax in the verse. Ye are not
only full, but more than full; ye are rich, you have more than
enough; and ye are not only rich, ye are as kings. *Now* (ἤδη)
already. 'You have reached the goal of perfection very quick;
and that *without us.* You have left us poor apostles far behind you.' The reference is to the benefits of redemption.
Paul represents the Corinthians as thinking that they had al-

ready attained the full blessedness of the Messiah's reign; that they had already attained, and were already perfect. He therefore adds, *I would ye did reign.* 'I would that the con· summation of Christ's kingdom had really come, for then I would share with you in its glories.' *I would to God* is a translation not authorized, or at least not demanded, by the original, ὄφελον, which in the later Greek, and in the New Testament, is a particle of wishing or an interjection; *would that, O that.* So the Greek phrase (μὴ γένοιτο) so often rendered in our version, "God forbid!" is simply an expression of aversion, "Let it not be." The Scriptures do not countenance such appeals to God as seem to have been common when our version was made.

9. For I think that God hath set forth us the apostles last, as it were appointed to death : for we are made a spectacle unto the world, and to angels, and to men.

For. 'I would that the consummation were really come, *for* we apostles are now very far from being treated as kings.' *God hath set forth,* i. e. publicly exhibited. He has made us conspicuous as the last, the lowest, the most afflicted of men. The original does not admit of the translation proposed by many, *us the last apostles,* i. e. those last appointed—referring to himself, who was, as he says, born out of due time. The emphasis, from the collocation of the words, is thrown on *apostles* and not on *last.* What follows is explanatory. *As appointed unto death.* This does not merely mean that they were exhibited as men daily exposed to death; which indeed was true, 15, 30. 31. 2 Cor. 1, 8. 9. 11, 23; but also that they were treated as men condemned to death, that is, as convicts, men to whom all comforts were denied. '*We have become a spectacle* (θέατρον, literally, *a theatre;* here metonymically, *a show* exhibited in a theatre) to the universe (κόσμῳ), as well to angels, as to men.' Such were the sufferings of the apostles that men and angels gazed on them with wonder, as people gaze on a spectacle in a theatre. The word *angels* when used without qualification always means good angels, and must be so understood here.

10. We (are) fools for Christ's sake, but ye (are) wise in Christ; we (are) weak, but ye (are) strong; ye (are) honourable, but we (are) despised.

In amplification of what he had just said, he contrasts, in this and the following verses, his situation with theirs. There are two things included in these contrasts. The opinion which the Corinthians entertained, and that which was entertained by others. *We are fools on account of Christ ;* our devotion to the cause of Christ is such that you and others regard us as fools; *ye are wise in Christ ;* your union with Christ is such that you regard yourselves and are regarded by others as wise. *We are weak,* we feel ourselves to be so, and are so considered; *ye are strong,* you so regard yourselves, and are so regarded. *You are honoured,* you are objects of respect, we of contempt. All this doubtless has special, though not exclusive, reference to the false teachers, whose state in Corinth he contrasts with his own.

11. Even unto this present hour we both hunger, and thirst, and are naked, and are buffeted, and have no certain dwelling-place ;

That a man should freely subject himself to hunger, thirst, and nakedness, and submit to be buffeted, and homeless, for no selfish purpose, but simply to preach Christ, was indeed, in the eyes of the world, foolishness. The fact that Paul gladly submitted to all these afflictions, presented his case in glaring contrast with that of his opposers in Corinth, who exposed themselves to no such sufferings out of zeal for Christ.

12. 13. And labour, working with our own hands. Being reviled, we bless ; being persecuted, we suffer it ; being defamed, we entreat : we are made as the filth of the world, (and are) the off-scouring of all things unto this day.

Working with our own hands. The apostle, in a subsequent chapter, proves at length his right, and that of other ministers to an adequate support from the church. But he did not avail himself of that right in Corinth, 9, 15.

Being reviled (λοιδορούμενοι), being railed at, or made the object of scurrility. *We bless,* i. e. we speak well of, or *implore good upon.* We return abuse with kind words, or, with good wishes and prayers. *Being persecuted.* As the former term refers to injurious words, this refers to injurious acts.

We suffer it, i. e. we patiently submit to it without resistance or complaint. *Being defamed*, i. e. having evil deeds or motives ascribed to us. *We entreat* (παρακαλοῦμεν), we exhort. That is, we endeavour to meet with kindness such injurious imputations, instead of repelling them with anger and indignation. In all this the apostle followed the example of his divine master, who when he was reviled, reviled not again; when he suffered, he threatened not, but committed himself to him who judgeth righteously, 1 Peter 2, 23.

We are made as the filth of the earth, or rather of the world (κόσμου). That is, we are regarded as the filthiest of mankind. And *the off-scouring of all things*, or of all men. That is, as the refuse of society. The words (περικάθαρμα and περίψημα) rendered *filth* and *off-scouring*, signify, the former, what is carried off by rinsing, and the latter, what is scraped off. They both express the general idea of refuse. This is all the context demands or suggests. The apostle sums up all he had previously said, by saying, 'We are regarded as the dregs or refuse of the world.' As both of these words, however, and especially the former, are used of victims chosen from the lowest class of the people, who in times of calamity were offered in sacrifice to the gods, it is very generally assumed that Paul here refers to that custom; and means to say that he was regarded as one of those who were considered only fit to be put to death for the good of others. This brings out the same idea in a different form. It is not probable, however, that any such allusion is here intended; because the custom was not so common as to be familiar to his readers generally, and because the word commonly used for such sacrifices was not περικάθαρμα, which Paul uses, but κάθαρμα. In Prov. 21, 18, however, it is said, The wicked is a ransom (περικάθαρμα) for the righteous. Paul certainly did not consider himself or his sufferings as a propitiation for other men. The point of comparison, if there be any allusion to the custom in question, is to the vileness of such victims, which were always chosen from the worthless and despised. This and other passages of Paul's writings (comp. 2 Cor. 11, 23–27) present in a very strong light the indignities and sufferings which he endured in the service of Christ, and may well put us to shame, as well as the self-satisfied and self-indulgent Corinthians. What are we doing for him for whom Paul did and suffered so much?

14. I write not these things to shame you, but as my beloved sons I warn (you).

Not as shaming you (ἐντρέπων) *write I these things.* The word used signifies to invert, to turn round, or back; and then, generally, to move, and especially to move to shame. It may be rendered here, 'I write not these things as moving you,' i. e. to work upon your feelings. The use of the word in 2 Thess. 3, 14, and Tit. 2, 8, is in favour of the common interpretation. Paul's object in drawing such a contrast between their case and his, was not to mortify them; but as his beloved sons, i. e. out of love to them as his sons, he says, *I warn you.* The word (νουθετέω) is that generally used to express parental admonition and instruction. His design was to bring the truth to their minds, and let them see what they really were, as contrasted with what they imagined themselves to be.

15. For though ye have ten thousand instructors in Christ, yet (have ye) not many fathers : for in Christ Jesus I have begotten you through the gospel.

Paul was entitled to admonish them as sons, for he was their spiritual father. The words *in Christ* are not connected with *instructors*, as though the sense were, 'instructors who are in Christ,' i. e. Christian instructors. The position of the words in the original show that they belong to the verb. 'Though ye may have in Christ, i. e. in reference to Christ, or as Christians, many teachers, ye have not many fathers.' The pedagogues (παιδαγωγοί) among the Greeks were usually slaves, who were the constant attendants, rather than the teachers, of the boys of a family. They had, however, the charge of their education, and therefore the word is used in the New Testament for instructors. Paul contrasts his relation to the Corinthians as their spiritual father, with that of their other teachers. The point of the contrast is not that he loved them, and they did not; or that they were disposed to arrogate too much authority, and he was not; but simply, that he was the means of their conversion, and they were not. His relation to them preceded theirs and was more intimate and tender.

He was their father, "*for* in Christ Jesus he had begotten them." That is, in virtue of his union to Christ, as his apostle and minister. In himself he could do nothing. It was only as an instrument in the hand of Christ that he was successful in bringing them to the obedience of faith. Comp. Gal. 2. 8. *By the gospel*, i. e. by means of the gospel. There are three agencies in the conversion of men. The efficiency is in Christ by his Spirit; the administrative agency is in preachers; the instrumental in the word. What God has joined together, let not man put asunder. We cannot do without the first and the third, and ought not to attempt to do without the second. For though multitudes are converted by the Spirit through the word, without any ministerial intervention, just as grain springs up here and there without a husbandman, yet it is the ordinance of God that the harvest of souls should be gathered by workmen appointed for that purpose.

16. Wherefore, I beseech you, be ye followers of me.

Wherefore, i. e. because I am your father. *Be ye followers* (μιμηταί, literally, *imitators*) *of me*. He does not exhort them to become his followers or partisans, instead of being the followers of Apollos or of Cephas. But as he had spoken of himself as being humble, self-denying and self-sacrificing in the cause of Christ, he beseeches them to follow his example. In 11, 1 he says, " Be ye imitators of me, as I am of Christ." Comp. 1 Thess. 1, 6. 2, 14. Eph. 5, 1.

17. For this cause have I sent unto you Timotheus, who is my beloved son, and faithful in the Lord, who shall bring you into remembrance of my ways which be in Christ, as I teach every where in every church.

For this cause, that is, to secure your imitating my example. This end, Timothy, whom he commends as his son, and as faithful, was to accomplish by vindicating the apostle from the aspersions which had been cast upon him, by reminding the Corinthians of his conduct and teaching as a minister of Christ. Nothing more was necessary than to appeal to their own knowledge of what Paul had been among them. *My son ;* not only the object of my love, but my child ; one whom I have begotten through the gospel. This is implied from the use of the word in v. 14. Comp. 1 Tim. 1, 2, where he speaks of him as " his own son in the faith." The fact that Timothy stood in this endearing relation to Paul, was a reason for his sending him, and also a reason why they should receive him with confidence. He was, however, not only Paul's son, but *faithful in the Lord*. And this was a further reason both for his mission and for their regard and confidence. *Faithful in the Lord* means faithful in the service of Christ, or as a Christian. The words *in the Lord* admit of being connected with the word *son*, so as to give the sense, " My faithful son in the Lord."

The work which Timothy was to do was to remind the Corinthians of what they seem to have forgotten, viz., of Paul's *ways which were in Christ, how he taught*, &c. The latter clause limits and explains the former. It was not so much his *ways* or deportment in general, as his character and conduct as a teacher, which were to be brought to mind. This, however, included his consistency, his zeal, humility and fidelity. It is evident from 2 Cor. 1, 17–20 that inconsistency and instability both as to his doctrines and plans, was one of the objections urged against Paul in Corinth, as in other places, comp. Gal. 5, 11. *My ways which be in Christ*, means the ways which I follow in the service of Christ. It was his official conduct as an apostle and teacher which Timothy was to bring to their recollection. *As* (καθώς), in the sense of *how*. Acts 15, 14. 3 John 3. He is to remind you *as*, i. e. how, I teach *every where in every church*. Paul's doctrine and mode of teaching were every where the same. And to this fact Timothy was to bear testimony, and thus vindicate him from the aspersions of his enemies.

18. Now some are puffed up, as though I would not come to you.

His sending Timothy was not to be considered as any indication that he himself did not intend to visit Corinth, as some in their pride and self-confidence supposed. It appears from numerous passages in this and the following epistle, that the false teachers in Corinth in various ways endeavoured to undermine Paul's authority. They called in question his apostleship, 9, 1–3. 2 Cor. 12, 12 ; they accused him of lightness, or instability, 2 Cor. 1, 17 ; they represented him as weak in person and contemptible in speech, 2 Cor. 10, 10. These were the persons who *were puffed up*, that is, so conceited as to their own importance, and as to the effect of their injurious representations respecting the apostle, as to give out that he

was afraid to come to Corinth, and therefore sent Timothy in
his place.

19. But I will come to you shortly, if the Lord
will, and will know, not the speech of them which are
puffed up, but the power.

In opposition to this boasting of his opponents, Paul declares his purpose soon to visit Corinth, *if the Lord* (i. e.
Christ) *will.* Comp. 16, 7, and Acts 16, 7. This is a recognition both of the providential and spiritual government of
Christ. It supposes the external circumstances, and the
inward state of the apostle, his purposes and convictions of
duty, to be determined by the providence and Spirit of Christ.
Thus constantly did Paul live in communion with Christ as
his God, submitting to him and trusting to him at all times.
*And will know not the speech but the power of those who
are puffed up.* That is, not what they can say, but what they
can do. By *power* (δύναμις) some understand miraculous
power, which does not suit the context. Others confine it to
spiritual power, that is, the power derived from the Spirit.
The word is sometimes used for the essential power, or true
nature and efficacy of a thing. And this sense best suits the
antithesis between *speech* and *power.* Paul meant to put to
the test, not what these men could say, but what they really
were and did; that is, their true character and efficiency.
Comp. 1 Thess. 1, 5. 2 Tim. 3, 5. "Having the form of god-
liness, but denying the power (δύναμιν) thereof," i. e. its real
nature and efficacy.

20. For the kingdom of God (is) not in word, but
in power.

The idea expressed by the phrase "kingdom of God," in
the New Testament, is very comprehensive and manifold, and
therefore indefinite. The two senses under which most, if not
all, its applications may be comprehended are, 1. The royal
authority or dominion exercised by God or Christ; and 2.
Those over whom that authority extends, or who recognize
and submit to it. In the former sense, the word (βασιλεία)
kingdom is used in such expressions as, Thy kingdom come
Of his kingdom there is no end, The sceptre of his kingdom,
&c., &c. In such expressions as, To enter the kingdom of

God; The children, or members of the kingdom, the phrase means the community over which God reigns, whether in this world, or in the world to come. In the former sense the meaning is equivalent to the reign of God. Hence to say, Thy kingdom come, and to say, May God reign, is the same thing. Now as God reigns in the hearts of his people—as well as in the church, and in heaven—so this inward spiritual dominion is called the kingdom of God. In this sense the passage, "the kingdom of God is within you," may be understood; and also Rom. 14, 17, "The kingdom of God is not meat and drink, but righteousness and peace, and joy in the Holy Ghost;" which is equivalent to saying that true religion does not consist in external observances, but in inward graces. This is the form of the idea which seems best suited to the passage before us. 'God's reign, his dominion in the heart, or true religion, does not consist in professions, but in reality.' The word *power* is to be taken in the same sense here as in v. 19. Paul says, 'I will know, not what these men say, but what they really are; *for* the kingdom of God (or religion) does not consist in what is apparent and outward, but in what is inward and real.' It is not a semblance, but a reality.

21. **What will ye? shall I come unto you with a rod, or in love, and (in) the spirit of meekness?**

Paul, so far from being afraid to go to Corinth, as his enemies imagined, was prepared to go there with authority. He was their spiritual father and ruler. He had the right and the ability to punish them. It depended on themselves in what character he should appear among them; whether as a punisher or as a comforter—whether in the exercise of discipline, or as a kind and tender parent. The preposition (ἐν) rendered *with* in the first clause, is the same as that rendered *in* in those which follow. It has the same force in them all. It means *furnished with*, *attended by*. That is, it marks the attending circumstances. The expression "spirit of meekness" is commonly understood to mean a meek or gentle spirit or disposition of mind. As, however, the word spirit, when connected with an abstract noun, always refers to the Holy Spirit, as in the phrases Spirit of truth, Spirit of wisdom, Spirit of adoption, Spirit of love, of fear, or of glory, it should be so understood here. Paul asks whether he should come with severity, or filled with the Spirit as the author of meekness. It is plain from this, as from numerous other passages, that the apostles exercised the right of discipline over all the churches; they could receive into the communion of the church, or excommunicate from it, at their discretion. This prerogative was inseparable from their infallibility as the messengers of Christ, sent to establish and to administer his kingdom. The following chapter furnishes a notable instance of the exercise of this authority.

CHAPTER V.

The case of the incestuous member of the church, vs. 1–5. Exhortation to purity, and to fidelity in discipline, vs. 6–13.

Reproof for retaining an unworthy member in the church.
Vs. 1–13.

THE second evil in the church of Corinth, to which Paul directs his attention, is allowing a man guilty of incest to remain in its communion. He says it was generally reported that fornication was tolerated among them, and even such fornication as was not heard of among the heathen, v. 1. He reproves them for being inflated, instead of being humbled and penitent, and excommunicating the offender, v. 2. As they had neglected their duty, he determined, in the name of Christ, and as spiritually present in their assembly, to deliver the man guilty of incest to Satan, vs. 3–5. He exhorts to purity, in language borrowed from the Mosaic law respecting the passover. As during the feast of the passover all leaven was to be removed from the habitations of the Hebrews, so the Christian's life should be a perpetual paschal feast, all malice and hypocrisy being banished from the hearts and from the assemblies of believers, vs. 6–8. He corrects or guards against a misapprehension of his command not to associate with the immoral. He shows that the command had reference to church communion, and not to social intercourse; and therefore was limited in its application to members of the church. Those out of the church, it was neither his nor their prerogative to judge. They must be left to the judgment of God, vs. 9–13.

1. It is reported commonly (that there is) fornication among you, and such fornication as is not so much as named among the Gentiles, that one should have his father's wife.

Having dismissed the subject of the divisions in the church of Corinth, he takes up the case of the incestuous member of that church. *It is reported commonly* (ὅλως ἀκούεται). This may mean what our translation expresses, viz., it was a matter of notoriety that fornication existed among them. Ὅλως may have the force of *omnino*, 'nothing is heard of among you except, &c.' Or it may mean, 'In general, fornication is heard of among you.' That is, it was a common thing that fornication was heard of; implying that the offence, in different forms, more or less prevailed. This is the less surprising, considering how little sins of that class were condemned among the heathen, and how notorious Corinth was for its licentiousness. To change the moral sentiments of a community is a difficult and gradual work. The New Testament furnishes sad evidence, that Jewish and Gentile converts brought into the church many of the errors of their former belief and practice. The word *fornication* (πορνεία) is used in a comprehensive sense, including all violations of the seventh commandment. Here a particular case is distinguished as peculiarly atrocious. The offence was that a man had married his step-mother. His *father's wife* is a Scriptural periphrase for step-mother, Lev. 18, 8. That it was a case of marriage is to be inferred from the uniform use of the phrase *to have a woman* in the New Testament, which always means, to marry. Matt. 14, 4. 22, 28. 1 Cor. 7, 2. 29. Besides, although the connection continued, the offence is spoken of as past, vs. 2. 3. Such a marriage Paul says was unheard of among the Gentiles, that is, it was regarded by them with abhorrence. Cicero, *pro Cluent.* 5, 6. speaks of such a connection as an incredible crime, and as, with one exception, unheard of. It is probable from 2 Cor. 7, 12, that the father of the offender was still alive. The crime, however, was not adultery, but incest; for otherwise the apostle would not have spoken of it as an unheard of offence, and made the atrocity of it to arise out of the relation of the woman to the offender's father. We have here therefore a clear recognition of the perpetual obligation of the Levitical law concerning marriage. The Scriptures are a perfect rule of duty; and, therefore, if they do not prohibit marriage

between near relatives, such marriages are not sins in the
sight of God. To deny, therefore, the permanency of the law
recorded in Lev. 18, is not only to go contrary to the authority of the apostle, but also to teach that there is for Christians
no such crime as incest.

2. And ye are puffed up, and have not rather
mourned, that he that hath done this deed might be
taken away from among you.

They were puffed up, i. e. elated with the conceit of their
good estate, notwithstanding they were tolerating in their
communion a crime which even the heathen abhorred. Some
have endeavoured to account for the occurrence of such an
offence, and for the remissness of the church in relation to it,
by supposing that both the offender and the church acted on
the principle taught by many of the Jews, that all bonds of
relationship were dissolved by conversion. The proselyte to
Judaism became a new creature. He received a new name.
His father was no longer his father, or his mother his mother.
The Rabbins therefore taught that a proselyte might lawfully
marry any of his nearest kindred. It is possible that such a
notion may have partially prevailed among the Jewish portion
of the church; but not very probable, 1. Because of its absurdity; 2. Because its prevalence among the Jews was only
after their reprobation as a people; 3. Because the wiser class
of the Jews themselves condemned it. It is more probable,
if the crime was defended at all, it was on the principle that
the Scriptures and nature condemn intermarriages on the
ground only of consanguinity and not also of affinity. A principle opposed to Leviticus 18, and to what the apostle here
teaches.

And have not rather mourned (ἐπενθήσατε), i. e. grieved
for yourselves. Your condition, instead of filling you with
pride, should humble you and make you sad. *That* (ἵνα), not
so that, but *in order that*, as expressing the design which the
apostle contemplated in their humiliation and sorrow. Comp.
John 11, 15. 'I would that ye were grieved and sorry for
yourselves, *in order that* he who had done this deed might be
taken away.' The ἵνα may depend on a word implied. 'Ye
have not mourned, *desiring* that, &c.' Chrysostom says the
idea is, that they should have acted as they would have done
had a pestilence appeared among them which called for

mourning and supplication in order that it might be removed.
It is a right inherent in every society, and necessary for its
existence, to judge of the qualification of its own members;
to receive those whom it judges worthy, and to exclude the
unworthy. This right is here clearly recognized as belonging
to the church. It is also clear from this passage that this
right belongs to each particular church or congregation. The
power was vested in the church of Corinth, and not in some
officer presiding over that church. The bishop or pastor was
not reproved for neglect of discipline; but the church itself,
in its organized capacity.

3–5. For I verily, as absent in body, but present in
spirit, have judged already, as though I were present,
(concerning) him that hath so done this deed, in the
name of our Lord Jesus Christ; when ye are gathered
together, and my spirit, with the power of our Lord
Jesus Christ, to deliver such an one unto Satan for the
destruction of the flesh, that the spirit may be saved in
the day of the Lord Jesus.

These verses constitute one sentence, and must be taken
together in order to be understood. The construction of the
principal clauses is plain. Paul says, 'I have determined to
deliver this man unto Satan.' All the rest is subordinate and
circumstantial. The connection of the subordinate clauses is
doubtful. Perhaps the best interpretation of the whole passage is the following : 'I, though absent as to the body, yet
present as to the spirit, have determined as though present, in
the name of the Lord Jesus, ye being gathered together, and
my spirit being with you, with the power (i. e. clothed or
armed with the power) of our Lord Jesus Christ, to deliver
this man to Satan.' There was to be a meeting of the church,
where Paul, spiritually present, would, in the name of Christ,
and in the exercise of the miraculous power with which he
was invested, deliver the offender to the power of Satan. The
connection with what precedes is indicated by the particle *for*.
'I would ye were in a state of mind to remove this offender,
for I have determined to cut him off.' I *verily* (μέν), or I *at
least*. 'Whatever you do or leave undone, I *at least* will do
my duty.' *Absent in body, but present in spirit.* Neither
Paul's capacity nor his authority to judge, nor his power to

execute his judgment, depended on his bodily presence. He was present in spirit. This does not mean simply that he was present in mind, as thinking of them and interested in their welfare; but it was a presence of knowledge, authority, and power. *Have judged already.* That is, without waiting either for your decision in the matter, or until I can be personally present with you.

Him that hath so done this deed. This is one of the clauses, the construction of which is doubtful. Our translators insert the word *concerning*, which has nothing to answer to it in the text, unless it be considered a part of the translation of the preceding verb, (κέκρικα,) *I have judged concerning*, i. e. 'I have judged or passed sentence upon him.' This, however, creates embarrassment in the explanation of the fifth verse. The best explanation is to make this clause the object of the verb *to deliver*, in v. 5. 'I have already determined to deliver him who did this deed.' As, however, so much intervenes between the object and the verb, the object (*such an one*) is repeated in v. 5.

In the name of Christ, means by the authority of Christ, acting as his representative. The phrase includes, on the one hand, the denial that the thing done was done in virtue of his own authority; and on the other, the claim of the right to act as the organ and agent of Christ. This clause may be connected with what follows. 'Ye being gathered in the name of Christ.' Against this construction, however, it may be urged, 1. That the words would in that case most naturally have been differently placed. That is, it would be more natural to say; 'Assembled in the name of Christ,' than 'In the name of Christ assembled.' 2. It is a common formula for expressing apostolical authority, to say, 'In the name of Christ.' 3. The sense and parallelism of the clauses are better if these words are connected with the main verb, 'I have determined in the name of Christ to deliver,' &c. Paul was acting in the consciousness of the authority received from Christ. Compare 2 Thess. 3, 6. Acts 16, 18. *When ye are gathered together, and my spirit.* The church was to be convened, and Paul spiritually present. The sentence was not to be passed or executed in secret, but openly. It was to have the solemnity of a judicial proceeding, and, therefore, the people were convened, though they were merely spectators. *With the power of our Lord Jesus Christ.* This may be connected with the immediately preceding words, 'My spirit invested with the power of Christ being present.' Or with what follows, 'I have determined to deliver such an one with the power of Christ to Satan.' The sense is substantially the same. The sentence was to be passed and carried into effect in the name of Christ and by his power.

To deliver such an one unto Satan. There have from the earliest times been two prevalent interpretations of this expression. According to one view, it means simply excommunication; according to the other, it includes a miraculous subjection of the person to the power of Satan. Those who regard it as merely excommunication, say that "to deliver to Satan" answers to "might be taken away from you," in v. 2, and therefore means the same thing. The Corinthians had neglected to excommunicate this offender, and Paul says he had determined to do it. Besides, it is argued that excommunication is properly expressed by the phrase "to deliver to Satan," because, as the world is the kingdom of Satan, to cast a man out of the church, was to cast him from the kingdom of Christ into the kingdom of Satan. Comp. Col. 1, 13. In favour of the idea of something more than excommunication, it may be argued, 1. That it is clearly revealed in scripture, that bodily evils are often inflicted on men by the agency of Satan. 2. That the apostles were invested with the power of miraculously inflicting such evils, Acts 5, 1–11. 13, 9–11. 2 Cor. 10, 8. 13, 10. 3. That in 1 Tim. 1, 20, the same formula occurs probably in the same sense. Paul there says, he had delivered Hymeneus and Alexander unto Satan, that they might learn not to blaspheme. 4. There is no evidence that the Jews of that age ever expressed excommunication by this phrase, and therefore it would not, in all probability, be understood by Paul's readers in that sense. 5. Excommunication would not have the effect of destroying the flesh, in the sense in which that expression is used in the following clause. Most commentators, therefore, agree in understanding the apostle to threaten the infliction of some bodily evil, when he speaks of delivering this offender to Satan. *For the destruction of the flesh.* This is by many understood to mean, for the destruction of his corrupt nature, so that the end contemplated is merely a moral one. But as *flesh* here stands opposed to *spirit*, it most naturally means the body. 'The man was delivered to Satan that his body might be afflicted, in order that his soul might be saved.' *In the day of the Lord Jesus.* That is, the day when the Lord Jesus shall come the

second time without sin unto salvation. It appears from
2 Cor. 7, 9–12, that this solemn exercise of the judicial power
of the apostle, had its appropriate effect. It led the offender
himself, and the whole church, to sincere and deep repentance.

6. Your glorying (is) not good. Know ye not
that a little leaven leaveneth the whole lump?

Your boasting, (καύχημα,) ground of boasting. You have
no good reason to boast of your religious state; on the contrary, you have abundant reason to be alarmed. *Know ye
not;* do ye not consider the obvious and certain danger of
this evil spreading? *A little leaven leaveneth the whole lump.*
This proverbial expression is not here intended to express the
idea that one corrupt member of the church depraves the
whole, because, in the following verses, in which the figure is
carried out, the leaven is not *a person*, but *sin*. The idea,
therefore, is, that it is the nature of evil to diffuse itself. This
is true with regard to individuals and communities. A single
sin, however secret, when indulged, diffuses its corrupting influence over the whole soul; it depraves the conscience; it
alienates from God; it strengthens all other principles of evil,
while it destroys the efficacy of the means of grace and the
disposition to use them. It is no less true of any community,
that any one tolerated evil deteriorates its whole moral sense.

7. Purge out therefore the old leaven, that ye may
be a new lump, as ye are unleavened. For even Christ
our passover is sacrificed for us :

Purge out the old leaven is an exhortation to purity, as the
old leaven is afterwards said to be malice and wickedness.
This leaven is said to be *old*, because in the present apostate
state of our nature, what is old is evil. Hence, the *old* man
is a scriptural designation of our corrupt nature. *That ye
may be a new lump*. *New*, i. e. pure—as the *new* man is the
renewed nature. *As ye are unleavened*. Leaven in this connection is a figurative expression for sin. To say, therefore,
that they were unleavened, is to say that they were holy.
This was their normal state—as Christians. A Christian is a
new or holy man. The argument, therefore, is drawn from
the acknowledged fact that Christians, as such, are holy.
'Purge out the leaven of wickedness, that ye may be pure,

for believers are holy.' *For even*, (καὶ γάρ,) or, *for also*. This is a second reason why they should be pure; *for Christ our passover is slain for us*. *Is slain ;* rather, *is sacrificed*, as θύω means *to kill and offer in sacrifice*, or, to slay as a victim. When the paschal lamb was slain, the Hebrews were required to purge out all leaven from their houses, Ex. 12, 15. The death of Christ imposes a similar obligation on us to purge out the leaven of sin. Christ is our passover, not because he was slain on the day on which the paschal lamb was offered, but because he does for us what the paschal lamb did for the Hebrews. As the blood of that lamb sprinkled on the door-posts secured exemption from the stroke of the destroying angel, so the blood of Christ secures exemption from the stroke of divine justice. Christ was slain *for us*, in the same sense that the passover was slain for the Hebrews. It was a vicarious death. As Christ died to redeem us from all iniquity, it is not only contrary to the design of his death, but a proof that we are not interested in its benefits, if we live in sin. Our passover, viz., Christ. The words ὑπὲρ ἡμῶν, (*for us*), are omitted in all the older manuscripts, and are not necessary to the sense.

8. Therefore let us keep the feast, not with old leaven, neither with the leaven of malice and wickedness ; but with the unleavened (bread) of sincerity and truth.

Let us *therefore* keep the feast. That is, since our passover Christ is slain, let us keep the feast. This is not an exhortation to keep the Jewish passover—because the whole context is figurative, and because the death of Christ is no reason why the Corinthians should keep the Jewish passover. Christians are nowhere exhorted to observe the festivals of the old dispensation. Neither is the feast referred to the Lord's Supper. There is nothing in the connection to suggest a reference to that ordinance. A feast was a portion of time consecrated to God. *To keep the feast* means, 'Let your whole lives be as a sacred festival, i. e. consecrated to God.' As a feast lasting seven days was connected with the slaying of the paschal lamb; so a life of consecration to God should be connected with the death of our passover—Christ. This feast is not to be celebrated with the *old* or corrupt leaven, which is explained to mean *the leaven of malice and wicked-*

ness. Πονηρία, wickedness, is a stronger word than κακία, *badness.* Any one who does wrong is κακός, *bad;* but he who does evil with delight and with persistency, is πονηρός. Hence Satan is called ὁ πονηρός, "The evil one." *But with the unleavened bread of sincerity and truth.* Sincerity and truth are the unleavened bread with which the Christian's life-long feast should be celebrated. *Sincerity*, (εἰλικρίνεια,) is *purity*, transparent clearness; something through which the sun may shine without revealing any flaw. *Truth* is in scripture far more than veracity. In its subjective sense, it means that inward state which answers to the truth; that moral condition which is conformed to the law and character of God.

9. I wrote unto you in an epistle not to company with fornicators :

This may be understood to refer to what he had written above in this epistle. Comp. Rom. 16, 22. 1 Thess. 5, 27. Col. 4, 16, where *the* epistle, ἡ ἐπιστολή, means the epistle he was then writing. Calvin, Beza, and almost all the modern commentators, understand it to refer to an epistle no longer extant. This is obviously the more natural interpretation, first, because the words (ἐν τῇ ἐπιστολῇ), *in the epistle*, would otherwise be altogether unnecessary. And, secondly, because this epistle does not contain the general direction not to company with fornicators; which, it would seem from what follows, the Corinthians had misunderstood. There is, indeed, a natural indisposition in Christians to admit that any of the inspired writings are lost. But nothing is more natural than the assumption that the apostles wrote many short letters, not intended as pastoral epistles designed for the church in all ages, but simply to answer some question, or to give some direction relative to the peculiar circumstances of some individual or congregation. 'I wrote to you in the epistle,' naturally means here as in 2 Cor. 7, 8, the epistle which you have already received, and not the one which he was then writing; and it is not wise to depart from the natural meaning of the words simply to avoid a conclusion we are unwilling to admit. The church has all the inspired writings which God designed for her edification; and we should be therewith content. *Not to company with*, (μὴ συναναμίγνυσθαι), not to be mixed up together with. That is, not to associate with. See 2 Thess. 3, 14. This may have reference either to social intercourse or to church communion. This indefinite command Paul explains, first, by stating that he did not mean to forbid social intercourse; and then saying he did intend to prohibit Christian fellowship with the wicked.

10. Yet not altogether with the fornicators of this world, or with the covetous, or extortioners, or with idolaters ; for then must ye needs go out of the world.

Not altogether. This limits the prohibition. The apostle did not intend to prohibit all intercourse with the fornicators of this world. This would be an impossibility; while in the world we must have more or less intercourse with the men of the world. Or, the words (οὐ πάντως), *not altogether*, may be connected with the words *I wrote*, in the sense of *by no means.* Comp. Rom. 3, 9. ' I *by no means* wrote to you not to associate with the wicked.' This, although perhaps the more common explanation, does not give so good a sense. It is not so much a positive denial of having so written, as a limitation of the application of his command, that the apostle designs to give. *The world* means mankind as distinguished from the church, Gal. 4, 3. Eph. 2, 2. Col. 2, 8. The prohibition, such as it was, was not limited to any one class of the immoral; it included all classes. The *covetous ;* those who will have more (πλεονέκτης) ; and especially those who defraud for the sake of gain. In the Scriptures the controlling love of gain is spoken of as a sin specially heinous in the sight of God. It is called idolatry, Eph. 5, 5, because wealth becomes the object supremely loved and sought. The man, therefore, who sacrifices duty to the acquisition of wealth; who makes gain the great object of his pursuit, is a covetous man. He cannot be a Christian, and should not, according to the apostle, be recognized as such.

Or with extortioners, i. e. the ravenous; those who exact what is not justly due to them, or more than is justly due. The sin is not confined to exactions by force or open robbery, but to all undue exactions. The man who takes advantage of another's poverty, or of his necessities, to secure exorbitant gain, is an extortioner. *Or with idolaters*, those who either professedly worship false gods, or who do what, in its own nature, and in the common judgment of men, amounts to such worship. This is said to be the earliest known instance of the use of the word εἰδωλολάτρης ; it is never used in the LXX, although εἴδωλον is constantly employed in that version in the sense of *false gods*. *For then ye must needs go out of the world.* This is the reason why the apostle did not prohibit all intercourse with wicked men. We should have to seek another world to live in.

11. But now I have written unto you not to keep company, if any man that is called a brother be a fornicator, or covetous, or an idolater, or a railer, or a drunkard, or an extortioner ; with such an one no not to eat.

But now (νυνὶ δέ). If taken in the ordinary sense, these particles refer to time. 'In the former epistle I wrote to you so and so, *but now* I write to you, &c.' They may have an inferential sense—*therefore*. 'Since ye cannot go out of the world, *therefore* I wrote unto you.' The apostle is explaining the meaning of what he had written. 'I did not write this, but I wrote, i. e. I meant, this.' This explanation best suits the context, and agrees better with the force of the tense (ἔγραψα) here used ; for although the aorist of this verb is used in the epistolary style in reference to the letter in the process of writing, it is not used to express what is about to be written. The command is not to associate with any one who is *called a brother*, and yet is a fornicator, or covetous, or an idolater, or a railer (slanderer), or a drunkard, or an extortioner. A man in professing to be a Christian professes to renounce all these sins ; if he does not act consistently with his profession, he is not to be recognized as a Christian. We are not to do any thing which would sanction the assumption that the offences here referred to are tolerated by the gospel. It may appear strange that Paul should assume that any one calling himself a Christian could be an idolater. By idolatry, however, he understands not merely the intentional and conscious worship of false gods, but doing any thing which, according to the common judgment of men, expresses such worship. Thus eating sacrifices within the precincts of a temple was an act of heathen worship, as much as partaking of the Lord's supper is an act of Christian worship. And yet some of the Corinthians did not hesitate to eat of heathen sacrifices under those circumstances, 10, 14–22. The principle laid down by the apostle is, that to join in the religious rites of any people is to join in their worship, whether we so intend it or not.

With such an one no not to eat. This does not refer to the
Lord's supper, which is never designated as a meal. The
meaning is, that we are not to recognize such a man in any
way as a Christian, even by eating with him. It is not the act
of eating with such persons that is forbidden. Our Lord eat
with publicans and sinners, but he did not thereby recognize
them as his followers. So we may eat with such persons as
are here described, provided we do not thereby recognize
their Christian character. This is not a command to enforce
the sentence of excommunication pronounced by the church,
by a denial of all social intercourse with the excommunicated.
The command is simply that we are not, in any way, to recognize openly wicked men as Christians. This passage, therefore, affords no plea for the tyranny of Romanists in refusing
all the necessaries of life to those whom they cast out of the
church.

12. For what have I to do to judge them also that
are without ? do not ye judge them that are within ?

Those without ; those out of the church. Mark 4, 11.
Col. 4, 5. 1 Thess. 4, 12. The command of the apostle had
reference only to those within the church, *for* it was not his
prerogative to judge those that are without. The Corinthians
acted on the same principle. They confined church discipline
to church members, and therefore should not have understood
his injunction not to company with the wicked to apply to
others than to those within the church.

13. But them that are without God judgeth.
Therefore put away from among yourselves that wicked
person.

God, and not the church, is the judge of those who are
without. The verb may be accented so as to express either
the present or the future. God judges (κρίνει) ; or, God will
judge (κρινεῖ). The present gives the better sense, as expressing the divine prerogative, and not merely the assurance of a
future judgment. *Therefore put away,* literally, according to
the common text (καὶ ἐξαρεῖτε), *and ye shall put away ;* which
seems to have been borrowed from Deut. 24, 7. The better
reading is (ἐξάρατε) *put away.* It is a simple imperative injunction, or necessary application of the principle of Christian

communion just laid down. This passage is not inconsistent
with the interpretation given to verses 3–5. In consequence
of their neglect of duty, Paul determined to deliver the incestuous member of the Corinthian church to Satan. He calls
upon them to recognize the validity of that sentence, and to
carry it into effect. The sentence was pronounced; they, so
far as it involved their communion, were to execute it.

<hr>

CHAPTER VI.

This chapter consists of two distinct paragraphs. The first, vs. 1–11, relates
to lawsuits before heathen magistrates. The second, vs. 12–20, to the
abuse which some had made of the principle, "All things are lawful."

On going to law before the heathen. Vs. 1–11.

PAUL expresses surprise that any Christian should prosecute
a fellow Christian before a heathen judge, v. 1. If Christians
are destined to judge the world, and even angels, they may
surely settle among themselves their worldly affairs, vs. 2. 3.
If they had such suits, must they appoint those whom the
church could not esteem to decide them? Was there not one
man among themselves able to act as a judge? vs. 4–6. It
was a great evil that they had such lawsuits. It would be
better to submit to injustice, v. 7. Instead, however, of submitting to wrong, they committed it, v. 8. He solemnly assures them that the unjust, or rapacious, or corrupt should
not inherit the kingdom of God, vs. 9. 10. They had been
such, but as Christians they were washed from these defile-
ments, and justified through Christ and by his Spirit, v. 11.

1. Dare any of you, having a matter against another, go to law before the unjust, and not before the
saints?

The third evil in the church of Corinth which the apostle
endeavours to correct, was the prosecuting legal suits before
heathen judges. There was no necessity for this practice.
The Roman laws allowed the Jews to settle their disputes

about property by arbitration among themselves. And the early Christians, who were not distinguished as a distinct class from the Jews, had no doubt the same privilege. It is not necessary, however, to assume that the apostle has reference here to that privilege. It was enough that these civil suits might be arranged without the disgraceful spectacle of Christian suing Christian before heathen magistrates. The Rabbins say, "It is a statute which binds all Israelites, that if one Israelite has a cause against another, it must not be prosecuted before the Gentiles." *Eisenmenger's* Entdeckt. Judenth. ii. p. 427.

Dare any of you? Is any one so bold as thus to shock the Christian sense of propriety? *Having a matter.* The Greek phrase (πρᾶγμα ἔχειν) means *to have a suit,* which is obviously the sense here intended. *To go to law before the unjust.* It is plain that by the *unjust* are meant the heathen. But why are they so called? As the terms holy and righteous are often used in a technical sense to designate the professed people of God without reference to personal character; so the terms sinners and unjust are used to designate the heathen as distinguished from the people of God. The Jews as a class were holy, and the Gentiles were unholy; though many of the latter were morally much better than many of the former. In Gal. 2, 15, Paul says to Peter, "We are by nature Jews, and not sinners of the Gentiles;" meaning thereby simply that they were not Gentiles. The reason why the heathen as such are called the unjust, or sinners, is that according to the Scriptures the denial of the true God, and the worship of idols, is the greatest unrighteousness; and therefore the heathen, because heathen, are called the unrighteous. The word *unjust* is too limited a word to answer fully to the Greek term (ἄδικος), which in its scriptural sense means *wicked,* not conformed to the law of God. In this verse the opposite term, *saints,* or *the holy,* designates Christians as a class; and, therefore, the *unjust* must mean the heathen as a class. The complaint against the Corinthians was not that they went to law before unjust judges, but that they appealed to heathen judges. It is true their being heathen proved them to be unrighteous in the scriptural sense of the term; but it was not their moral character, so much as their religious status, that was the ground of the complaint. It was indeed not to be expected that men governed by heathen laws and principles of morals, would be as fair and just as those governed by

Christian principles; but what Paul complained of was, not
that the Corinthians could not get justice at the hands of
heathen magistrates, but that they acted unworthily of their
dignity as Christians in seeking justice from such a source.
Paul himself appealed to Cesar. It was, therefore, no sin in
his eyes to seek justice from a heathen judge, when it could
not otherwise be obtained. But it was a sin and a disgrace
in his estimation for Christians to appeal to heathen magistrates to settle disputes among themselves.

2. Do ye not know that the saints shall judge the
world? and if the world shall be judged by you, are ye
unworthy to judge the smallest matters?

Do you not know? a form of expression often used by the
apostle when he wishes to bring to mind some important truth,
which his readers knew but disregarded. It was a conceded
point, one which entered into the common faith of Christians,
that the saints are to judge the world. *The saints* (οἱ ἅγιοι),
the people of God, who are called saints because separated
from the world and consecrated to his service. Those, therefore, who are of the world and devoted to its pursuits, are not
saints. *The saints shall judge the world.* This does not
mean that the time would come when Christians would become magistrates; nor that the conduct of the saints would
condemn the world, as it is said the Queen of the South would
condemn those who refused to listen to the words of Christ,
Matt. 12, 42. The context and spirit of the passage require
that it should be understood of the future and final judgment.
Saints are said to sit in judgment on that great day for two
reasons; first, because Christ, who is to be the judge, is the
head and representative of his people, in whom they reign
and judge. The exaltation and dominion of Christ are their
exaltation and dominion. This is the constant representation
of Scripture, Eph. 2, 6. In Heb. 2, 5–9 the declaration that
all things are subject to man, is said to be fulfilled in all things
being made subject to Christ. Secondly, because his people
are to be associated with Christ in his dominion. They are
joint heirs with him, Rom. 8, 17. If we suffer, we shall reign
with him, 2 Tim. 2, 12. In Dan. 7, 22 it was predicted that
judgment (the right and power to judge) should be given to
the saints of the Most High. Comp. Matt. 19, 28. Luke 22,

30. Rev. 2, 26. 27. If then, asks the apostle, such a destiny as this awaits you, are ye unfit to decide the smallest matters? *If the world* (mankind) *shall be judged by you* (ἐν ὑμῖν), i. e. before you as judges. *Are ye unworthy* (ἀνάξιοι), i. e. of too little weight or value, having neither the requisite dignity nor ability. Unworthy *of the smallest matters.* The word (κρι-τήριον), here rendered *matters,* in the sense of causes, or matters for judgment, means, 1. A criterion or test; a rule of judgment. 2. A tribunal or place of judgment, and then, the court or assembled judges. Ex. 21, 6. Judges 5, 10. Dan. 7, 10, and in the New Testament, James 2, 6. 3. The trial, i. e. the process of judgment. 4. The cause itself, or matters to be tried. This last sense is doubtful, although it is generally adopted here because it suits so well the fourth verse, where the same word occurs. The second sense would suit this verse. 'If ye are to sit with Christ on the seat of universal judgment, are ye unworthy of the lowest judgment seats.' But the fourth verse is in favour of the explanation adopted in our version. 'Are ye unfit for the least causes?'

3. Know ye not that we shall judge angels? how much more things that pertain to this life?

As, according to Scripture, only the fallen angels are to be judged in the last day, most commentators suppose the word must here be restricted to that class. Not only men, but fallen angels are to stand before that tribunal on which Christ and his church shall sit in judgment. If agreeably to the constant usage of the Scriptures, according to which (as remarked above, 4, 9) the word when unqualified means good angels, it be understood of that class here, then the explanation is probably to be sought in the comprehensive sense of the word to judge. As kings were always judges, and as the administration of justice was one of the principal functions of their office, hence to rule and to judge are in Scripture often convertible terms. To judge Israel, and to rule Israel, mean the same thing. And in Matt. 19, 28, "sitting on twelve thrones judging the twelve tribes of Israel," means presiding over the twelve tribes. So in the case before us, "Know ye not that we shall judge angels?" may mean, 'Know ye not that we are to be exalted above the angels, and preside over them; shall we not then preside over earthly things?' This explanation avoids the difficulty of supposing that the good angels are to be called into judgment;

and is consistent with what the Bible teaches of the subordination of angels to Christ, and to the church in him.

4. If then ye have judgments of things pertaining to this life, set them to judge who are least esteemed in the church.

Paul laments that there were litigations among them ; but if they could not be avoided, Christians should act in reference to them in a manner consistent with their high destiny. Here the word (κριτήρια), rendered judgments, seems so naturally to mean *causes*, things to be tried, that that sense of the word is almost universally assumed. It may, however, mean *trials, judicial processes ;* which is more in accordance with the established use of the words. *Set them to judge who are least esteemed in the church.* The original admits of this translation. If the passage be so rendered, then it has a sarcastic tone. 'Set your least esteemed members to decide such matters.' It may, however, be read interrogatively, 'Do ye set as judges those least esteemed in (i. e. by) the church (that is, the heathen) ? ' This translation is generally preferred as best in keeping with the context. The sentence is emphatic. 'Those despised (see 1, 28) by the church,— those do you set to judge ? ' It is an expression of surprise at their acting so unworthily of their high calling.

5. I speak to your shame. Is it so, that there is not a wise man among you ? no, not one that shall be able to judge between his brethren ?

I speak to your shame. That is, I desire to produce in you a sense of shame. This may refer either to what precedes or to what follows. It was adapted to make them ashamed that they had acted so unworthily of their dignity as Christians ; and it was no less disgraceful to them to suppose that there was not in the church a single man fit to act as arbitrator. *Who shall be able.* The future here expresses what should or may happen. *Between his brethren ;* literally, *between his brother ;* i. e. between his complaining brother and him against whom the complaint was brought.

6. But brother goeth to law with brother, and that before the unbelievers.

Instead of referring the matter to the arbitration of a judicious brother, ye *go to law*, and that before unbelievers. There are here two grounds of complaint. First, that they went to law (κρίνεσθαι) instead of resorting to arbitration (διακρῖναι). Secondly, that they made unbelievers their judges. By *unbelievers* are to be understood the heathen. In this connection the heathen are designated under one aspect, the unjust; under another, the despised; and under a third, the unbelieving, i. e. not Christians—but, as the implication in this particular case is, pagans. *And that* (καὶ τοῦτο), a form of expression often used when particular stress is to be laid on the circumstance indicated.

7. Now therefore there is utterly a fault among you, because ye go to law one with another. Why do ye not rather take wrong? Why do ye not rather (suffer yourselves to) be defrauded?

Now therefore (ἤδη μὲν οὖν), *already indeed therefore*. That is, these lawsuits are already, or in themselves (ὅλως), an evil irrespective of their being conducted before heathen judges. The word ἥττημα does not so properly mean *fault* as loss or evil. It is a loss or evil to you to have these litigations. See Rom. 11, 12, where the rejection of the Jews is called their (ἥττημα) loss. *Why do you not*, &c. That is, why, instead of going to law with your brethren, do you not rather submit to injustice and robbery? This is a clear intimation that, under the circumstances in which the Corinthians were placed, it was wrong to go to law, even to protect themselves from injury. That this is not to be regarded as a general rule of Christian conduct is plain, because, under the old dispensation, God appointed judges for the administration of justice; and because Paul himself did not hesitate to appeal to Cesar to protect himself from the injustice of his countrymen.

8. Nay, ye do wrong, and defraud, and that (your) brethren.

Instead of having reached that state of perfection in which

ye can patiently submit to injustice, ye are yourselves unjust
and fraudulent. This must have been the case with some of
them, otherwise there would be no occasion for these lawsuits.
Their offence was aggravated, because their own brethren
were the object of their unjust exactions.

9. 10. Know ye not that the unrighteous shall not
inherit the kingdom of God?   Be not deceived : neither fornicators, nor idolaters, nor adulterers, nor effem-
inate, nor abusers of themselves with mankind, nor
thieves, nor covetous, nor drunkards, nor revilers, nor
extortioners, shall inherit the kingdom of God.

The tendency to divorce religion from morality has mani
fested itself in all ages of the world, and under all forms of
religion.   The pagan, the Jew, the Mohammedan, the nominal Christian, have all been exact in the performance of religious services, and zealous in the assertion and defence of
what they regarded as religious truth, while unrestrained in
the indulgence of every evil passion.   This arises from looking upon religion as an outward service, and God as a being
to be feared and propitiated, but not to be loved and obeyed.
According to the gospel, all moral duties are religious services ; and piety is the conformity of the soul to the image
and will of God.   So that to be religious and yet immoral is,
according to the Christian system, as palpable a contradiction
as to be good and wicked.   It is evident that among the members of the Corinthian church, there were some who retained
their pagan notion of religion, and who professed Christianity
as a system of doctrine and as a form of worship, but not as a
rule of life.   All such persons the apostle warned of their fatal
mistake.   He assures them that no immoral man,—no man
who allows himself the indulgence of any known sin, can be
saved.   This is one of the first principles of the gospel, and
therefore the apostle asks, *Know ye not that the unrighteous
shall not inherit the kingdom of God?*   Are ye Christians at
all, and yet ignorant of this first principle of the religion you
profess ?   The *unrighteous* in this immediate connection,
means the *unjust ;* those who violate the principles of justice
in their dealings with their fellow-men.   It is not the unjust
alone, however, who are to be thus debarred from the Re-

deemer's kingdom—but also those who break any of the commandments of God, as this and other passages of Scripture distinctly teach.

Believers are, in the Bible, often called heirs. Their inheritance is a kingdom; that kingdom which God has established, and which is to be consummated in heaven, Luke 12,
32. Matt. 24, 34, &c. &c. From this inheritance all the immoral, no matter how zealous they may be in the profession
of the truth, or how assiduous in the performance of religious
services, shall be excluded. Let it also be remembered that
immorality, according to the Bible, does not consist exclusively
in outward sins, but also in sins of the heart; as covetousness,
malice, envy, pride, and such like, Gal. 5, 21. No wonder
that the disciples, on a certain occasion, asked their master,
Lord, are there few that be saved? or that the Lord answered
them by saying, " Strait is the gate, and narrow is the way
that leadeth unto life, and few there be that find it," Luke 13, 24.

11. And such were some of you : but ye are
washed, but ye are sanctified, but ye are justified in
the name of the Lord Jesus, and by the Spirit of our
God.

And such were some of you. This is understood by many
as equivalent to *Such were you.* The word (τινές) being redundant, or the idea being, ' Some were impure, some drunkards, some violent, &c., or ταυτά τινες being taken together as
equivalent to τοιοῦτοι. The natural explanation is, that the
apostle designedly avoided charging the gross immoralities
just referred to upon all the Corinthian Christians in their
previous condition. With regard to the three terms which
follow, *washed, sanctified, justified,* they may be taken, as by
Calvin and others, to express the same idea under different
aspects. That idea is, that they had been converted, or completely changed. They had put off the old man, and put on
the new man. Their sins, considered as filth, had been washed
away; considered as pollution, they had been purged or purified; considered as guilt, they had been covered with the
righteousness of God, Rom. 1, 17. The majority of commentators take the several terms separately, each expressing a
distinct idea. In what precise sense each of these words is to
be understood, becomes, then, somewhat doubtful.

But ye are washed. The word here used (ἀπελούσασθε) is in the middle voice, and therefore may be rendered, *ye have washed yourselves*, or, *permitted yourselves to be washed;* or, as the majority of commentators prefer, on account of the following passives, *ye were washed.* This use of the First Aorist Middle in a passive sense is very unusual, but not unauthorized; see 1 Cor. 10, 2. It does not seem to be of much moment whether the word be taken here as active or as passive, for the same thing may be expressed in either form. Men are called upon to wash away their sins, Acts 22, 16; to put off the old man, etc. and to put on the new man, Eph. 4, 22. 24; although the change expressed by these terms is elsewhere referred to God. The reason of this is, that a human and a divine agency are combined in the effects thus produced. We work our own salvation, while God works in us, Phil. 2, 12. 13. With equal propriety, therefore, Paul might say to the Corinthians, 'Ye washed yourselves;' or, 'Ye were washed.' *To wash* means to purify, and is frequently used in Scripture to express moral or spiritual purification. Is. 1, 16, "Wash ye, make you clean." Ps. 51, 7, "Wash me, and I shall be whiter than snow." Jer. 4, 14. In these and many other passages the word expresses general purification, without exclusive reference to guilt or to pollution. There is no reason why it should not be taken in this general sense here, and the phrase be rendered, either, 'Ye have purified yourselves,' or, 'Ye are purified.' The reference which so many assume to baptism, does not seem to be authorized by any thing in the context.

But ye are sanctified. This clause is either an amplification of the preceding one, expressing one aspect or effect of the washing spoken of, viz., their holiness; or, it is to be understood of their separation and consecration. 'Ye have not only been purified, but also set apart as a peculiar people.' In Scripture, any thing is said to be sanctified that is devoted to the service of God. Thus, God blessed the seventh day and sanctified it, Gen. 2, 3. Moses sanctified the people, Ex. 19, 14, &c. &c.

But ye are justified. As to justify in Scripture always means to pronounce righteous, or to declare just in the sight of the law, it must be so understood here. The Corinthians had not only been purified and consecrated, but also justified, ι. e. clothed in the righteousness of Christ, and on that account accepted as righteous in the sight of God. They were

therefore under the highest possible obligation not to relapse into their former state of pollution and condemnation.

*In the name of the Lord Jesus, and by the Spirit of our
God.* These clauses are not to be restricted to the preceding
word, as though the meaning were, 'Ye have been justified
in the name of the Lord Jesus, and by the Spirit of our God.'
They belong equally to all three of the preceding terms. The
believers were indebted for the great change which they had
experienced; for their washing, sanctification, and justification, to Christ and to the Holy Ghost. The Spirit had applied to them the redemption purchased by Christ. *In the
name of the Lord Jesus.* "The name of God," or "of Christ,"
is often a periphrase for God or Christ himself. To call upon
the name of God is to call on God. To baptize unto the name
of Christ, and to baptize unto Christ, are interchanged as
synonymous expressions. So here, to be justified or sanctified
in the name of Christ, means simply by Christ; see John 20,
31, "That believing ye might have life through his name."
Acts 10, 43, "That through his name whoso believeth in him
might have remission of sins." Though these forms of expression are substantially the same as to their import, yet
the "name of God" means not strictly God himself, but God
as known and worshipped. The Holy Ghost is called *the Spirit of our God;* that is, the Spirit of our reconciled God and
Father, by whom that Spirit is sent in fulfilment of the promise of the Father to the Son. Christ hath redeemed us from
the curse of the law in order that we might receive the promise of the Spirit, Gal. 3, 13. 14.

Abuse of the principle of Christian liberty. Vs. 12–20.

The principle of Christian liberty, or the doctrine that
"all things are lawful," is to be limited in its application to
things indifferent; first, by considerations of expediency; and
secondly, by regard to our own spiritual freedom, v. 12. From
that principle it is legitimate to infer, because of the adapta-
tion of the stomach to food, that all things suited for food are
lawful. The one is obviously designed for the other, during
the temporary condition of the present life. But no such application of the principle is allowable in the case of fornication; because the body is not designed for that end, but
belongs to the Lord, with whom it stands in an indissoluble
connection, so that he who raised him up will also raise up our

bodies, vs. 13. 14. It is because of this intimate relation of our bodies to Christ as his members, that fornication is so great a crime, inconsistent with our union to him as partakers of his Spirit, vs. 15–17. It is, in a peculiar manner, a sin against the body, destructive of its very nature, v. 18. The body is a temple in which the Spirit dwells, but it ceases to be such if profaned by licentiousness, v. 19. Believers must remember that they, even their bodies, are the objects of redemption, having been purchased by the blood of Christ, and therefore they should be devoted to his glory, v. 20.

12. All things are lawful unto me, but all things are not expedient: all things are lawful for me, but I will not be brought under the power of any.

Having in the preceding paragraph declared that the immoral cannot inherit the kingdom of God, and having given special prominence to sins against the seventh commandment, the Apostle comes in this paragraph to consider the ground on which the violations of that commandment were defended or palliated. That ground was a gross perversion of the principle of Christian liberty. Paul was accustomed to say in reference to the ceremonial or positive enactments of the Jewish law, and especially in reference to the distinction between clean and unclean meats, " All things are lawful to me." As the Greeks and Romans generally regarded fornication as belonging to the class of things indifferent, that is, not immoral in themselves ; it is not surprising that some of the Corinthians educated in that belief should retain and act on the principle even after their profession of Christianity. They reasoned from analogy. As it is right to eat all kinds of food which are adapted to the stomach, so it is right to gratify any other natural propensity. Paul's answer to this argument is twofold. He first shows that the principle of Christian liberty in things indifferent is to be restricted in its application ; and secondly, that there is no analogy between the cases mentioned. Food is a thing indifferent ; whereas fornication is in its own nature a profanation and a crime.

The first limitation to which the principle " all things are lawful " is subject in its application to things indifferent, is expediency. All lawful things are not expedient. It is both absurd and wicked to do any thing which is injurious to ourselves or others, simply because it is not in its own nature sinful. This principle of expediency the Apostle enforces at length in Rom. 14, 15–23, and 1 Cor. 8, 7–13, and 10, 23–33. The second limitation of our liberty in the use of things indifferent, is self-respect. Because it is lawful to eat, that is no reason why I should make myself a slave to my appetite. "I will not," says Paul, "be brought under the power of any thing." I will not make myself its slave. It is of great importance to the moral health of the soul that it should preserve its self-control, and not be in subjection to any appetite or desire, however innocent that desire in itself may be. This is a scriptural rule which Christians often violate. They are slaves to certain forms of indulgence, which they defend on the ground that they are not in themselves wrong; forgetting that it is wrong to be in bondage to any appetite or habit.

13. Meats for the belly, and the belly for meats : but God shall destroy both it and them. Now the body (is) not for fornication, but for the Lord ; and the Lord for the body.

Meats for the belly, and the belly for meats. The one is evidently adapted and designed for the other. It is a legitimate inference from this constitution that it is lawful to eat, and to eat every thing adapted for food. But this is a mere temporary arrangement. *God will destroy both it and them.* The time shall come when men shall no more be sustained by food, but shall be as the angels of God. The fact that the present constitution of the body is temporary, is a proof that meats belong to the class of things indifferent. They can have no influence on the eternal destiny of the body. This is not true with regard to fornication. The body was never designed for promiscuous concubinage. And such a use of it is inconsistent with the design of its creation and with its future destiny.

The body is for the Lord ; and the Lord for the body. The one stands in an intimate relation to the other. The body is designed to be a member of Christ, and the dwelling-place of his Spirit. And he so regards it ; redeeming it with his blood, uniting it to himself as a member of his mystical body, making it an instrument of righteousness unto holiness. With this design of the body the sin in question is absolutely incompatible, and destructive of the relation which the body sustains to the Lord.

14. And God hath both raised up the Lord, and will also raise up us by his own power.

The destiny of the body being what is stated in the preceding verse, it is not to perish, but is to share in the resurrection of Christ. "He who raised Christ from the dead shall also quicken our mortal bodies by his Spirit that dwelleth in us," * Rom. 8. 11. This verse is parallel to the second clause of v. 13. Of the stomach and meats, it is said, God will destroy both it and them; of the Lord and the body it is said, As he raised up the one, he will also raise up the other. The cases, therefore, are widely different. The relation between our organs of digestion and food is temporary; the relation between Christ and the body is permanent. What concerns the former relation is a matter of indifference; what concerns the other touches the groundwork of our nature and the design for which we were created. On this destiny of the body compare 15, 15. 20. 35–56. Phil. 3, 21. Rom. 8, 11. 2 Cor. 4, 14. 1 Thess. 4, 14.

15. 16. Know ye not that your bodies are the members of Christ? shall I then take the members of Christ, and make (them) the members of an harlot? God forbid. What! know ye not that he which is joined to an harlot is one body? for two, saith he, shall be one flesh.

The design of these verses is to establish two points. First, that the relation between our bodies and Christ is of the intimate and vital character which had just been stated. And second, that the sin in question was inconsistent with that relation, and incompatible with it.

Know ye not that your bodies are the members of Christ? This is a conceded and familiar point of Christian doctrine, one with which they were supposed to be acquainted; and which proved all that the Apostle had said of the relation be-

---

* Instead of the future ἐξεγερεῖ, *will raise up*, Lachmann and Tischendorf after A. D. read ἐξεγείρει, *he raises up*. Meyer after B. 67, prefers ἐξήγειρε, *he raised up*. According to this last reading the resurrection of believers is represented as involved in that of Christ. As they died when he died, so they rose when he rose. The common text however is the best supported, and gives a good sense.

tween the body and Christ. Our bodies are the members of Christ, because they belong to him, being included in the redemption effected by his blood; and also because they are so united to him as to be partakers of his life. It is one of the prominent doctrines of the Bible that the union between Christ and his people includes a community of life; and it is clearly taught that this life pertains to the body as well as to the soul, Rom. 8, 6–11. Eph. 2, 6. 7. 5, 30. This is the truth which the Apostle recalls to the minds of the Corinthians, and makes it the ground of his indignant condemnation of the sin of which he is speaking. That fornication is incompatible with the relation of the bodies of believers to Christ, arises out of the peculiar nature of that sin. The parties to it become partakers of a common life. Whether we can understand this or not, it is the doctrine of the Bible. Therefore as we cannot be partakers of the life of Christ, and of the life of Belial, so neither can our bodies be the members of Christ, and at the same time have a common life with " one who is a sinner," in the scriptural sense of that phrase.

17. But he that is joined unto the Lord is one spirit.

That is, has one Spirit with him. This does not mean has the same disposition or state of mind, but the same principle of life, v. 12, the Holy Spirit. The Holy Spirit is given without measure unto Christ, and from him is communicated to all his people who are thereby brought into a common life with him, Rom. 8, 9. 10. 1 Cor. 12, 13. John 17, 21. 23. Eph. 4, 4. 5, 30. This being the case, it imposes the highest conceivable obligation not to act inconsistently with this intimate and exalting relationship.

18. Flee fornication. Every sin that a man doeth, is without the body; but he that committeth fornication, sinneth against his own body.

This does not teach that fornication is greater than any other sin; but it does teach that it is altogether peculiar in its effects upon the body; not so much in its physical as in its moral and spiritual effects. The idea runs through the Bible that there is something mysterious in the commerce of the sexes, and in the effects which flow from it. Every other sin,

however degrading and ruinous to the health, even drunkenness, is external to the body, that is, external to its life. But
fornication, involving as it does a community of life, is a sin
against the body itself, because incompatible, as the Apostle
had just taught, with the design of its creation, and with its
immortal destiny.

19. What ! know ye not that your body is the temple of the Holy Ghost (which is) in you, which ye have
of God, and ye are not your own ?

There are two things characteristic of a temple. First, it
is sacred as a dwelling-place of God, and therefore cannot be
profaned with impunity. Second, the proprietorship of a
temple is not in man, but in God. Both these things are true
of the believer's body. It is a temple because the Holy
Ghost dwells in it ; and because it is not his own. It belongs
to God. As it is a temple of the Holy Ghost, it cannot be profaned without incurring great and peculiar guilt. And as it
belongs in a peculiar sense to God, it is not at our own disposal. It can only be used for the purposes for which he designed it.

20. For ye are bought with a price : therefore
glorify God in your body, and in your spirit, which are
God's.*

Ye are bought. The verb is in the past tense, ἠγοράσθητε,
ye were bought, i. e. delivered by purchase. The deliverance
of men from the power and condemnation of sin was not
effected by power or by truth, but by a ransom. We were
justly held in bondage. We were under the penalty of the
law, and until that penalty was satisfied, we could not be delivered. The blood of Christ is our ransom, because it met
all the demands of justice.

The proprietorship in believers asserted at the close of the
preceding verse, does not arise from creation or preservation,
but from redemption. ' Ye are not your own, for ye are
bought with a price,' Rom. 6, 17. Gal. 3, 13. Eph. 3, 13. Acts

* The last clause of this verse is omitted by all the modern editors from
Griesbach down. They are not found in the MSS. A. B. C. D. E. F. G., nor
in several of the ancient versions.

20, 28. The price of redemption is the blood of Christ, Matt.
20, 28. Rom. 3, 24. Eph. 1, 7. 1 Pet. 1, 18. 19, and every where
where the subject is spoken of in Scripture. *Therefore*, i. e.
because redeemed, and because redeemed at such a price;
glorify God, i. e. honour him, and so act as to cause him to
be honoured by others. *In your body* as a temple consecrated to his worship, and employed only in his service.

The following words, *and in your spirit, which are God's*,
may have been added, because the body alone is not the object
of redemption, and therefore the obligation of the redeemed
to be devoted to the service of God pertains also to the soul.
As however these words are not found in the great majority
of the oldest manuscripts, most modern editors omit them.

------ •••• ------

CHAPTER VII.

Instructions relative to marriage, vs. 1–17. The Gospel was not designed to
   interfere with the ordinary relations of men, vs. 18–24. Concerning virgins and widows, 25–40.

Instructions concerning marriage and other social relations.
Vs. 1–24.

THE Corinthians had written to the Apostle, seeking his advice in reference to the state of things in their church. It
appears from this chapter that one of the subjects about which
they were in difficulty, and respecting which they sought direction, was marriage. On this subject the Apostle tells them,
1st. That, as they were situated, marriage was inexpedient to
them. But as a general law every man should have his own
wife, and every woman her own husband, vs. 1. 2. 2d. That
the obligation of the parties to the marriage covenant is mutual; the one therefore has no right to desert the other.
Temporary separation, for the purpose of devotion, is allowable; but nothing more, vs. 3–5. 3d. What he had said
either in reference to marriage or temporary separation, was
not to be considered as any thing more than advice. He
could only tell them what, under the circumstances, was expedient; each one must act according to the grace given to him,

vs. 6–9.   4th. With regard to the married the Lord had already taught that divorce was unlawful; the husband could not put away his wife, nor the wife her husband, vs. 10. 11.   5th. As to the case not specially contemplated in our Lord's instructions, where one of the parties was a Christian and the other a Jew or Pagan, the Apostle teaches, first, that if the unbelieving party is willing to remain in the marriage relation, it should not be dissolved.   Secondly, that if the unbeliever departed, and refused to continue in the marriage connection, the marriage contract was thereby dissolved, and the believing party was at liberty, vs. 12–15.   6th. Such separations, however, are, if possible, to be avoided, because the gospel is a gospel of peace.   It was not designed to break up any of the lawful relations of life.   As a general rule, therefore, every man should continue in the same condition in which he was called.   If a man was called being circumcised, his becoming a Christian did not impose upon him the obligation to become uncircumcised; and if called being uncircumcised, he was not required to be circumcised.   In like manner, if a slave is called to be a Christian, he may remain a slave, because every slave is the Lord's free man, and every free man is the Lord's slave.   These social distinctions do not affect our relation to Christ.   Redemption, in raising all to the relation of slaves to Christ, that is, making them all his property, has raised them into a sphere where all earthly distinctions are insignificant. Therefore, let every man abide in the relation wherein he was called, vs. 16–24.

1. Now concerning the things whereof ye wrote unto me : (It is) good for a man not to touch a woman.

It is evident that there was a diversity of opinion on the subject of marriage among the Corinthian Christians.   Probably some of them of Jewish origin thought it obligatory, while other members of the church thought it undesirable, if not wrong.   Paul says, It is good for a man not to marry. The word *good* (καλόν) here means expedient, profitable, as it does frequently elsewhere, Matt. 17, 4. 18, 8. 9. 1 Cor. 9, 15. That the Apostle does not mean to teach either that marriage is morally an evil as compared with celibacy, or that as a general rule it is inexpedient, is evident. 1. Because in the following verse he declares directly the reverse. 2. Because in

v. 26 he expressly states that "the present distress," or the peculiar circumstances of trial and difficulty in which the Christians of that day were placed, was the ground of his advice on this subject. 3. Because in 1 Tim. 4, 3, he specifies "forbidding to marry" as one of the signs of the great apostasy which he predicted was to occur. 4. Because marriage is a divine institution, having its foundation in the nature of man, and therefore must be a good. God accordingly declared, "It is not good for man to be alone," i. e. to be unmarried, Gen. 2, 18. Paul cannot be understood in a sense which would make him directly contradict the word of God. 5. Because throughout the Scriptures marriage is spoken of as honourable, Heb. 13, 4, and is used to illustrate the relation between God and his people, and between Christ and his church. 6. Because all experience teaches that it is, as a general rule, necessary to the full development of the character of the individual, and absolutely essential to the virtue and the well-being of society. To depreciate marriage would be to go contrary both to nature and revelation, and such depreciation has never failed to be attended by the most injurious consequences to the church and to the world. If, therefore, Scripture is to be interpreted by Scripture, we must understand the Apostle as intending to say: 'Considering your peculiar circumstances, it is expedient for you not to marry.'

2. Nevertheless, (to avoid) fornication, let every man have his own wife, and let every woman have her own husband.

As a general rule, says the Apostle, let every man have his own wife, and every woman her own husband. Whatever exceptions there may be to this rule in particular cases, or in peculiar conditions of society or of the church, the rule itself stands. There is undoubtedly an increase of worldly care and anxiety connected with marriage, and therefore it may be expedient for those to remain single to whom freedom from such cares is specially important. This however does not alter the great law of God, that it is not good for man to be alone. Celibacy is to be the exception, not the rule.

3–5. Let the husband render unto the wife due

benevolence : * and likewise also the wife unto the husband.   The wife hath not power of her own body, but
the husband : and likewise also the husband hath not
power of his own body, but the wife.   Defraud ye not
one the other, except (it be) with consent for a time,
that ye may give yourselves to fasting and prayer ; and
come together again, that Satan tempt you not for your
incontinency.

There is abundant evidence in the New Testament of the
early manifestation of those principles of asceticism which
soon produced such wide-spread effects, and which to so great
a degree modified the reigning spirit of the church.   The idea
that marriage was a less holy state than celibacy, naturally
led to the conclusion that married persons ought to separate ,
and it soon came to be regarded as an evidence of eminent
spirituality when such separation was final.   The Apostle
teaches that neither party has the right to separate from the
other ; that no separation is to be allowed which is not with
mutual consent, for a limited time, for the purpose of special
devotion, and with the definite intention of reunion.   Nothing
can be more foreign to the mind of the Apostle than the
spirit which filled the monasteries and convents of the mediæval
church.

6. 7. But I speak this by permission, (and) not
of commandment.   For I would that all men were
even as I myself.   But every man hath his proper
gift of God, one after this manner, and another after
that.

The reference of the word *this* in v. 6, is a matter of doubt.
Some refer it to the immediately preceding clause, ' Your
coming together again I speak of as permitted, not as commanded.'   But that clause is an entirely subordinate one ; and
the sense thus given to the passage is not consistent with the

---

* Instead of ὀφειλομένην εὔνοιαν of the received text, A. B. C. D. E. F. G.
have the simpler reading, ὀφειλήν, which most editors adopt.   The same authorities omit the words τῇ νηστείᾳ καί, in the latter part of the passage.

context. It was not a matter permitted, but commanded that husbands and wives should live together. Others refer it to the whole of v. 5. ' Your separating yourselves only by consent and for a limited time for the purpose of devotion, is a matter of permission, not of command ; you may separate for other purposes and for an unlimited time.' But to this also it is an obvious objection, that it conflicts with the mandatory character of vs. 3. 4, and with the meaning of v. 5 itself; for that verse has not the form of a command. The reference to the 5th verse may be made under a different aspect. ' What I have said of your separating by consent for a season, is a matter of permission, not of command.' But this is not consistent with the reason assigned in the next verse. The most natural reference is to v. 2, and to what follows. His saying, ' Let every man have his own wife and every woman her own husband, and let them remember their mutual obligations,' was permissive and not a matter of command. Marriage, in other words, is permitted, not commanded. *For* I would that all were as I am. The sense is not materially different, if with many editors we read θέλω δέ instead of θέλω γάρ. ' Marriage is not commanded, but I would,' etc. The Apostle did not take sides with the extreme Jewish party, who regarded marriage as obligatory. He admitted the expediency of all remaining single in those times of persecution to whom God had given the requisite grace.

8. 9. I say therefore to the unmarried and widows, It is good for them if they abide even as I. But if they cannot contain, let them marry : for it is better to marry than to burn.

This is the application of the principle laid down in v. 1 to the Corinthians. ' I say to the unmarried and to the widows among you, it is well not to marry.' *The unmarried* is not to be limited to *widowers*, as is commonly done on account of the word *widows* following, because the word does not admit of that limitation ; and because the word *married* in the following verse includes all classes. ' To the unmarried, and specially to widows, I say so ; to the married I say so.'

If these verses and others of like import, are to be understood of men generally, and not of men in the peculiar circumstances of the early Christians, then it must be admitted that Paul depreciates marriage, and that he represents it as scarcely having any higher end than the sexual intercourse of brutes. This cannot be his meaning; not only because it is contrary to Scripture, but also because Paul elsewhere, Eph. 5, 22–33, represents marriage as a most ennobling spiritual union; which raises a man out of himself and makes him live for another; a union so elevated and refining as to render it the fit symbol of that bond between Christ and his people, by which they are exalted to the full perfection of their being. Marriage, according to Paul, does for man in the sphere of nature, what union with Christ does for him in the sphere of grace. The truth is that the apostle writes to the Corinthians as he would do to an army about to enter on a most unequal conflict in an enemy's country, and for a protracted period. He tells them, 'This is no time for you to think of marriage. You have a right to marry. And in general it is best that all men should marry. But in your circumstances marriage can only lead to embarrassment and increase of suffering.' This is the only view of the matter by which we can reconcile the apostle with himself, or with the truth of Scripture and of fact. This must therefore be borne in mind in the interpretation of this whole chapter.

10. 11. And unto the married I command, (yet) not I, but the Lord, Let not the wife depart from (her) husband : But and if she depart, let her remain unmarried, or be reconciled to (her) husband : and let not the husband put away (his) wife.

The first part of the 11th verse is a parenthesis, the construction goes on with the last clause. To the married I command, 'Let not the wife depart from her husband; and let not the husband put away his wife.' The distinction which he here and in v. 12 makes between his commands and those of the Lord, is not a distinction between what is inspired and what is not; nor is it a distinction between what Paul taught and what the Scriptures teach as Calvin understands it; but *Lord* here evidently refers to Christ; and the distinction intended is between what Christ had taught while on earth, and what Paul by his Spirit was inspired to teach. He tells the Corinthians that so far as the matter of divorce was concerned, they had no need to apply to him for instruction; Christ had already taught that the marriage bond could not be dissolved at the option of the parties. The wife had no right to leave her husband; nor had the husband the right to repudiate his wife. But although the marriage bond cannot be dissolved by any human authority, because it is, in virtue of the law of God, a covenant for life between one man and one woman; yet it can be annulled, not rightfully indeed, but still effectually. Adultery annuls it, because it is a breach of the specific contract involved in marriage. And so does, for the same reason, wilful desertion, as the apostle teaches in a following verse. This is the Protestant doctrine concerning divorce, founded on the nature of marriage and on the explicit instructions of our Lord, Matt. 5, 32. 19, 3–9. Mark 10, 2–12. Luke 16, 18. According to this doctrine nothing but adultery or wilful desertion is a legitimate ground of divorce, first, because the Scriptures allow of no other grounds; and secondly, because incompatibility of temper, cruelty, disease, crime, and other things of like kind, which human laws often make the occasion for divorce, are not in their nature a destruction of the marriage covenant. Romanists teach that divorce *a vinculo matrimonii*, where both parties were baptized, is never allowable. As this rule is contrary to Scripture, it is found injurious in practice; and therefore it is evaded by declaring marriages on frivolous grounds void *ab initio;* or by granting separation without dissolution of the marriage tie, for reasons not sanctioned by Scripture. The plain doctrine of the passage before us, as well as other portions of the word of God, is that marriage is an indissoluble covenant between one man and one woman for life, admitting neither of polygamy nor of divorce. If the covenant be annulled, it can only be by the sinful act of one of the parties.

But and if she depart. The law of Christ is that she should not depart; but if in violation of that law, or if from necessity she be obliged to depart, she has but two things to choose between,—she must remain unmarried, or she must be reconciled to her husband. This is not intended as an exception to the law, but it contemplates a case which may occur in despite of the law. ' In case a woman has actually departed, with or without just cause, then she must remain unmarried, or be reconciled to her husband.' There are cases undoubtedly which justify a woman in leaving her husband, which do not justify divorce. Just as there are cases which justify a child leaving, or being removed from, the custody of a parent. The apostle teaches, however, that in such cases of separation, the parties must remain unmarried.

12. 13. But to the rest speak I, not the Lord: If any brother hath a wife that believeth not, and she be pleased to dwell with him, let him not put her away. And the woman which hath an husband that believeth not, and if he be pleased to dwell with her, let her not leave him.

But to the rest; i. e. to those married persons not contemplated in the preceding class. The context makes it clear, that the distinction between the two classes was, that in the former, both parties were Christians; and in the latter, one was a Christian, and the other a Jew or heathen. With regard to these mixed marriages our Lord had given no specific command; therefore Paul says, I speak, not the Lord. The rule which the apostle lays down is, that such marriages are lawful, and therefore there is no obligation on the Christian party to dissolve the connection. And if he is not bound to do it, he has no right to do it. If, therefore, the unbelieving party consent (συνευδοκεῖ) to remain, the marriage may not be dissolved. The Christian husband is forbidden to repudiate (ἀφιέναι) his heathen wife; and the Christian wife is forbidden to repudiate her heathen husband. The same word is used in both cases, because, by the laws both of the Greeks and of the Romans, the woman as well as the man, had, on legal grounds, the right of divorce. Having said that these mixed marriages might be lawfully continued, he proceeds to remove the scruples which the Christian party might entertain on that point. He shows there is nothing unholy in such a connection.

14. For the unbelieving husband is sanctified by the wife, and the unbelieving wife is sanctified by the husband : else were your children unclean ; but now are they holy.

The proof that such marriages may properly be continued, is, that the unbelieving party is sanctified by the believing; and the proof that such is the fact, is, that by common consent their children are holy; which could not be, unless the

marriages whence they sprang were holy; or unless the principle that intimate communion with the holy renders holy,
were a correct principle.

The assertion of the apostle is, that the unbelieving husband or wife is sanctified in virtue of the marriage relation
with a believer. We have already seen that the word (ἁγιά-
ζειν), *to sanctify*, means, 1. To cleanse. 2. To render morally
pure. 3. To consecrate, to regard as sacred, and hence, to
reverence or to hallow. Examples of the use of the word in
the third general sense just mentioned, are to be found in
all parts of Scripture. Any person or thing consecrated to
God, or employed in his service, is said to be sanctified. Thus,
particular days appropriated to his service, the temple, its
utensils, the sacrifices, the priests, the whole theocratical people, are called holy. Persons or things not thus consecrated
are called profane, common, or unclean. To transfer any person or thing from this latter class to the former, is to sanctify
him or it. "What God hath cleansed (or sanctified), that
call not thou common," Acts 10, 15. Every creature of God
is good, and is to be received with thanksgiving, "For it is
sanctified by the word of God and prayer," 1 Tim. 4, 5. This
use of the word is specially frequent in application to persons
and communities. The Hebrew people were sanctified (i. e.
consecrated), by being selected from other nations and devoted to the service of the true God. They were, therefore,
constantly called holy. All who joined them, or who were
intimately connected with them, became in the same sense,
holy. Their children were holy; so were their wives. "If
the first-fruits be holy, the lump is also holy; and if the root
be holy, so are also the branches," Rom. 11, 16. That is, if
the parents be holy, so are also the children. Any child, the
circumstances of whose birth secured it a place within the
pale of the theocracy, or commonwealth of Israel, was, according to the constant usage of Scripture, said to be holy. In
none of these cases does the word express any subjective or
inward change. A lamb consecrated as a sacrifice, and therefore holy, did not differ in its nature from any other lamb.
The priests or people, holy in the sense of set apart to the
service of God, were in their inward state the same as other
men. Children born within the theocracy, and therefore holy,
were none the less conceived in sin, and brought forth in iniquity. They were by nature the children of wrath, even as
others, Eph. 2, 3. When, therefore, it is said that the unbe-

lieving husband is sanctified by the believing wife, and the
unbelieving wife by the believing husband, the meaning is,
not that they are rendered inwardly holy, nor that they are
brought under a sanctifying influence, but that they were
sanctified by their intimate union with a believer, just as the
temple sanctified the gold connected with it; or the altar the
gift laid upon it, Matt. 23, 17. 19. The sacrifice in itself was
merely a part of the body of a lamb, laid upon the altar,
though its internal nature remained the same, it became something sacred. Thus, the pagan husband, in virtue of his union
with a Christian wife, although he remained a pagan, was
sanctified; he assumed a new relation; he was set apart to
the service of God, as the guardian of one of his chosen ones,
and as the parent of children who, in virtue of their believing
mother, were children of the covenant.

That this is so, the apostle proves from the fact, that if the
parents are holy, the children are holy; if the parents are unclean, the children are unclean. This is saying literally what
is expressed figuratively in Rom. 11, 16. "If the root be
holy, so are the branches." It will be remembered that the
words *holy* and *unclean*, do not in this connection express
moral character, but are equivalent to *sacred* and *profane*.
Those within the covenant are sacred, those without are profane, i. e. not consecrated to God. There are two views which
may be taken of the apostle's argument in this verse. The
most natural, and hence the most generally adopted view is
this: 'The children of these mixed marriages are universally
recognised as holy, that is, as belonging to the church. If
this be correct, which no one disputes, the marriages themselves must be consistent with the laws of God. The unbelieving must be sanctified by the believing partner. Otherwise, your children would be unclean, i. e. born out of the
pale of the church.' To this it is indeed objected by several
modern commentators, that it takes for granted that the
Corinthians had no scruples about the church-standing of the
children of these mixed marriages. But this, it is said, is very
improbable so soon after the establishment of the church,
when cases of the kind must have been comparatively few.
The principle in question, however, was not a new one, to be
then first determined by Christian usage. It was, at least, as
old as the Jewish economy; and familiar wherever Jewish
laws and the facts of the Jewish history, were known. Paul
circumcised Timothy, whose father was a Greek, while his

mother was a Jewess, because he knew that his countrymen
regarded circumcision in such cases as obligatory, Acts 16,
1–3. The apostle constantly assumes that his readers were
familiar with the principles and facts of the Old Testament
economy. Comp. 10, 1–13.

The other view of the argument is this: 'If, as you admit, the children of believers be holy, why should not the
husband or the wife of a believer be holy. The conjugal relation is as intimate as the parental. If the one relation secures this sacredness, so must the other. If the husband be
not sanctified by his believing wife, children are not sanctified
by believing parents.' This, however, supposes a change in
the persons addressed. Paul is speaking to persons involved
in these mixed marriages. *Your* children naturally means
the children of you who have unbelieving husbands or wives.
Whereas this explanation supposes *your* to refer to Christians
generally. In either way, however, this passage recognises as
universally conceded the great scriptural principle, that the
children of believers are holy. They are holy in the same
sense in which the Jews were holy. They are included in the
church, and have a right to be so regarded. The child of a
Jewish parent had a right to circumcision, and to all the privileges of the theocracy. So the child of a Christian parent
has a right to baptism and to all the privileges of the church,
so long as he is represented by his parent; that is, until he
arrives at the period of life when he is entitled and bound to
act for himself. Then his relation to the church depends
upon his own act. The church is the same in all ages. And
it is most instructive to observe how the writers of the New
Testament quietly take for granted that the great principles
which underlie the old dispensation, are still in force under
the new. The children of Jews were treated as Jews; and the
children of Christians, Paul assumes as a thing no one would
dispute, are to be treated as Christians. Some modern German writers find in this passage a proof that infant baptism
was unknown in the apostolic church. They say that Paul
could not attribute the holiness of children to their parentage,
if they were baptized—because their consecration would then
be due to that rite, and not to their descent. This is strange
reasoning. The truth is, that they were baptized not to make
them holy, but because they were holy. The Jewish child
was circumcised because he was a Jew, and not to make him
one. The Rabbins say: Peregrina si proselyta fuerit et cum

ea filia ejus — si concepta fuerit et nata in sanctitate, est ut
filia Israelita per omnia. See WETSTEIN *in loc.* To be born
in holiness (i. e. within the church) was necessary in order to
the child being regarded as an Israelite. So Christian children are not made holy by baptism, but they are baptized because they are holy.

**15. But if the unbelieving depart, let him depart.
A brother or a sister is not under bondage in such
(cases) : but God hath called us to peace.**

The command in the preceding verse was founded on the
assumption, that the unbelieving party consented to remain
in the marriage relation. If the unbeliever refused thus to
remain, the believer was then free. The believer was not to
repudiate the unbelieving husband or wife; but if the unbeliever broke up the marriage, the Christian partner was thereby liberated from the contract. This is the interpretation
which Protestants have almost universally given to this verse.
It is a passage of great importance, because it is the foundation of the Protestant doctrine that wilful desertion is a legitimate ground of divorce. And such is certainly the natural
sense of the passage. The question before the apostle was,
'What is to be done in the case of these mixed marriages?'
His answer is, 'Let not the believer put away the unbeliever,
for Christ has forbidden a man to put away his wife for any
cause except that of adultery, Matt. 5, 32. But if the unbeliever breaks up the marriage, the believer is no longer bound.'
There is no conflict here between Christ's command and Paul's
instructions. Both say, a man cannot put away his wife (nor
of course a wife her husband) on account of difference of religion, or for any other reason but the one above specified.
The apostle only adds that if the believing party be, without
just cause, put away, he or she is free.

A brother or sister is not in bondage (οὐ δεδούλωται, equivalent to οὐ δέδεται, v. 39), i. e. *is not bound;* if the unbeliever
consent to remain, the believer is bound; if the unbeliever
will not consent, the believer is not bound. In the one case
the marriage contract binds him; in the other case it does
not bind him. This seems to be the simple meaning of the
passage. Others understand the apostle as saying that the
believer is not bound to continue the marriage—that is, is
under no obligation to live with a partner who is unwilling to

live with him. But the one part of the verse should be allowed to explain the other. An obligation which is said to exist in one case, Paul denies exists in another. If the unbeliever is willing to remain, the believer is bound by the marriage contract; but if she be unwilling, he is not bound.

But God hath called us in peace (ἐν εἰρήνῃ, i. e. ὥστε εἶναι ἐν εἰρήνῃ). Peace is the state in which the called should live. The gospel was not designed to break up families or to separate husbands and wives. Therefore, though the believer is free if deserted by his unbelieving partner, the separation should be avoided if possible. Let them live together if they can; and let all proper means be taken to bring the unbelieving party to a sense of duty, and to induce him to fulfil the marriage covenant. This is the common view of the meaning of this clause. Others understand it in a directly opposite sense, viz., as assigning a reason why the separation should take place, or at least why the attempt to detain an unwilling husband or wife should not be pressed too far. 'As God hath called us to live in peace, it is contrary to the nature of our vocation to keep up these ill-assorted connections.' This, however, is contrary to the whole animus of the apostle. He is evidently labouring throughout these verses to prevent all unnecessary disruptions of social ties.

16. For what knowest thou, O wife, whether thou shalt save (thy) husband? or how knowest thou, O man, whether thou shalt save (thy) wife?

The meaning of this verse depends on the interpretation given to the preceding. If Paul there said, 'Your call to live in peace forbids the continuance of the marriage relation with an unwilling husband or wife;' then this verse must give a further reason why (supposing one of the parties to be unwilling) such marriages should not be continued. That reason is, the utter uncertainty of any spiritual good flowing from them. 'Why persist in keeping up the connection, when, O wife, you know not whether you can save your husband?' If, however, the common interpretation of v. 15 be adopted, then the meaning is, 'Live in peace if possible, for how knowest thou whether thou shalt not save thy husband?' &c. We have here, therefore, an additional reason for avoiding separation in the case supposed. Compare 2 Sam. 12, 22. Joel 2, 14. Jonah 3, 9, in the Septuagint, where the phrase τίς οἶδεν εἰ, *who knows if*, is used to express hope. So here the idea is, 'Who knows, O wife, but that thou shalt save thy husband?'

17. But as God hath distributed to every man, as the Lord hath called every one,* so let him walk. And so ordain I in all churches.

Paul was not only averse to breaking up the conjugal relation, but it was a general ordinance of his that men should remain in the same social position after becoming Christians, which they had occupied before. We can very imperfectly appreciate the effect produced by the first promulgation of the gospel. The signs and wonders, and diverse miracles and gifts of the Holy Ghost by which it was attended; the perfect equality of men which it announced; the glorious promises which it contained; the insignificancy and ephemeral character which it ascribed to every thing earthly; and the certainty of the second coming of Christ which it predicted, produced a ferment in the minds of men such as was never experienced either before or since. It is not surprising, therefore, that men were in many instances disposed to break loose from their social ties; wives to forsake their unbelieving husbands, or husbands their wives; slaves to renounce the authority of their masters, or subjects the dominion of their sovereigns. This was an evil which called for repression. Paul endeavoured to convince his readers that their relation to Christ was compatible with any social relation or position. It mattered not whether they were circumcised or uncircumcised, bond or free, married to a Christian or married to a Gentile, their fellowship with Christ remained the same. Their conversion to Christianity involved, therefore, no necessity of breaking asunder their social ties. The gospel was not a revolutionary, disorganizing element; but one which was designed to eliminate what is evil, and to exalt and purify what is in itself indifferent.

As God (or *the Lord*) *hath distributed to every man*, i. e. whatever lot in life God has assigned any man. *As the Lord* (or *God*) *hath called every man*, i. e. whatever condition or station a man occupied when called by the word and Spirit of God, let him remain in it. His conversion, at least, does not

---

* The MSS., A. B. C. D. E. F. G., read ὁ κύριος with ἐμέρισε, and ὁ θεός with κέκληκεν.

render any change necessary. The principal difficulty with regard to this verse does not appear in our version. The words (εἰ μή), rendered *but* at the beginning of the verse, mean *except* or *unless*, and this meaning they have so uniformly that many commentators insist that they must be so rendered here. Some of them say the meaning is, 'What do you know *except* this, that every man should remain in the condition in which he was called?' But in this way the verse does not cohere with the preceding one. 'How knowest thou, O man, whether thou shalt save thy wife? *except* let every man remain as he was called.' This every one feels to be intolerably harsh. It would be better with others, to supply something at the beginning of the verse. 'What is to be done *except*.' 'Do not favour the separation of husbands and wives on account of difference in religion. God has called us to peace. The wife may save her husband, and the husband his wife. *What then is to be done*, except to remain in the condition in which you were called.' Others get over the difficulty by separating the εἰ and μή and connecting the latter with a verb understood. 'How knowest thou, O man, but that thou shalt save thy wife? If not, i. e. if thou shalt not save her, still the principle holds good that every man should remain in the state in which he was called.' This gives a good sense, but it would require εἰ δὲ μή. As it is undeniable that the Greek of the New Testament, especially in the use of the particles, is in a measure conformed to the usage of the Hebrew, a freer use of these particles is allowable, when the context requires it, than is common in classic writers. Most commentators therefore render the words in question as our translators have done. *And so I ordain in all the churches.* That is, this is the rule or order which I lay down in all churches. The apostles, in virtue of their plenary inspiration, were authorized not only to teach the doctrines of the gospel, but also to regulate all matters relating to practice.

18. Is any man called being circumcised? let him not become uncircumcised. Is any called in uncircumcision? let him not be circumcised.

This is the first application of the principle just laid down. Let every man remain as he is, circumcised or uncircumcised. The Jews were wont, when they abandoned their religion, to endeavour to obliterate the mark of circumcision. The Juda-

izers were disposed to insist on the circumcision of the Gentile
converts. Both were wrong. Paul's command is that they
should remain as they were. Instead of the interrogative form
adopted in our version, the preferable translation is, " One was
called (ἐκλήθη) being circumcised ; let him not become uncircumcised. Another was called in uncircumcision ; let him not
be circumcised." *To call*, throughout the doctrinal portions
of the New Testament, is to convert, to call effectually.

19. Circumcision is nothing, and uncircumcision is nothing, but the keeping of the commandments of God.

This is the reason why they should be treated with indifference. *They are nothing ;* they have no influence either
favourable or unfavourable on our relation to God. No man
is either the better or worse for being either circumcised or
uncircumcised. The gospel has raised men above all such
things. The question to be asked is not whether a man is
circumcised or uncircumcised ; but whether he keeps the commandments of God. The things, therefore, about which the
Christian ought to be solicitous, are not such external matters,
which have no influence on his spiritual state, but conformity
in heart and life to the revealed will of God. Rom. 2, 25. 29.
Gal. 5, 6. " In Christ Jesus neither circumcision availeth any
thing (is of any worth), nor uncircumcision ; but faith which
worketh by love." 'Faith that worketh by love,' and 'keeping the commandments of God,' are the same thing. They
express the idea of holiness of heart and life under different
aspects.

20. Let every man abide in the same calling where-in he was called.

This is a repetition of the sentiment contained in v. 17,
which is again repeated in v. 24. The word calling (κλῆσις),
always in the New Testament means the call of God, that efficacious operation of his Spirit by which men are brought into
the kingdom of Christ. It is hard, however, to make it bear
that sense here. The meaning is plain enough. 'As he was
called, so let him remain.' But this is the idea detached
from the form in which it is here expressed. The great majority of commentators agree in giving the word in this place
the sense of *vocation*, as we use that word when we speak of

the vocation of a mechanic or of a farmer. In whatever station or condition a man is called, therein let him remain. This of course is not intended to prohibit a man's endeavouring to better his condition. If he be a labourer when converted, he is not required always to remain a labourer. The meaning of the apostle evidently is, that no man should desire to change his status in life simply because he had become a Christian; as though he could not be a Christian and yet remain as he was. The gospel is just as well suited to men in one vocation as in another, and its blessings can be enjoyed in all their fulness equally in any condition of life. This is illustrated by an extreme case in the following verse.

21. Art thou called (being) a servant? care not for it: but if thou mayest be made free, use (it) rather.

Here again the general sense is plain. A man's being a slave, so far as his being a Christian is concerned, is a matter of no account. It need give him no concern. The interpretation of the latter part of the verse is somewhat doubtful. According to most of the Fathers the meaning is, 'Care not for being a slave; but even if you can be free, prefer to remain as you are.' This interpretation is adopted by several of the modern German commentators. It is urged in its favour that the original demands it. Paul does not say *but if* (ἀλλ᾽ εἰ), but, *but if even* (ἀλλ᾽ εἰ καί). 'Care not for your slavery; but if even you can be free, use it rather;' or, 'although (εἰ καί) thou canst be free, &c.' The English version overlooks the καί. Besides, it is said the common interpretation is in conflict with the context. The very thing the apostle has in view is to urge his readers to remain in the condition in which they were called. 'Art thou called being circumcised, remain circumcised; art thou called being free, remain free; art thou called being a slave, remain a slave.' There is not much force in this argument; because, as before remarked, Paul's object is not to exhort men not to improve their condition, but simply not to allow their social relations to disturb them; or imagine that their becoming Christians rendered it necessary to change those relations. He could, with perfect consistency with the context, say to the slave, 'Let not your being a slave give you any concern; but if you can become free, choose freedom rather than slavery.' A third argument urged in favour of the interpretation above mentioned, is that it is more

consistent with the spirit of the apostle, with his exalted views
of the equality of all men in Christ, and with his expectation
that all earthly distinctions would soon be swept away. The
advice to slaves to avail themselves of the opportunity to become free, it is said, would be trivial in the estimation of one
who believed that those slaves might, at any moment, be exalted to be kings and priests to God. It must be admitted
that this interpretation is plausible. It is not, however, demanded either by the language used, or by the context. The
conjunction (καί), overlooked in our version, may be rendered
also. 'Wast thou called being a slave? care not for it; but
if also (i. e. in addition to your being called) thou canst become
free, use it rather.' Luther, Calvin, Beza, and the great body
of commentators from their day to this, understand the apostle to say that liberty was to be chosen if the opportunity to
become free were offered. That the context does not conflict
with this view of the passage, which our translators evidently
adopted, has already been shown.

22. For he that is called in the Lord, (being) a
servant, is the Lord's freeman: likewise also he that is
called, (being) free, is Christ's servant.

The connection is with the first, not with the last clause of
v. 21. 'Care not for your bondage, *for*,' &c. *He that is
called in the Lord;* or, as the words stand, 'The slave called
in the Lord.' That is, the converted slave. *Is the Lord's
freeman,* i. e. is one whom the Lord has redeemed. The possession of that liberty with which Christ makes his people
free, is so great a blessing, that all other things, even the condition of slavery, are comparatively of no account. Paul, in
Rom. 8, 18–23, says that the afflictions of this life are not
worthy to be compared with the glorious liberty of the sons
of God, towards which the whole creation, now subject to
vanity, looks with longing expectation. A man need care
little about his external condition in this world, who is freed
from the bondage of Satan, the curse of the law, the dominion
of sin, and who is made a child and heir of God; that is, who
is conformed to the image of his Son, and made a partaker of
his exaltation and kingdom. *Likewise also he that is called,
being free, is the Lord's servant* (i. e. slave, δοῦλος). The distinction between master and slave is obliterated. To be the
Lord's freeman, and to be the Lord's slave, are the same thing.

The Lord's freeman is one whom the Lord has redeemed from Satan, and made his own; and the Lord's slave is also one whom Christ has purchased for himself. So that master and slave stand on the same level before Christ. Comp. Eph. 6, 9.

23. Ye are bought with a price; be not ye the servants of men.

Ye (i. e. all Christians, bond and free,) *were bought with a price.* That is, purchased by Christ with his most precious blood, 1 Pet. 1, 18. 19. Ye belong to him; ye are his slaves, and should therefore act accordingly; and not be *the slaves of men.* The slave of one master cannot be the slave of another. One who is redeemed by Christ, who feels that he belongs to him, that his will is the supreme rule of action, and who performs all his duties, not as a man-pleaser, but as doing service as to the Lord, and not to men, Eph. 6, 6. 7, is inwardly free, whatever his external relations may be. This verse is a proper sequel to the preceding one. The apostle had exhorted all believers, even slaves, to be contented with their external condition. As a motive to such contentment, he had said they were all equally the subjects of redemption. They all belonged to Christ. To him their allegiance was due. They, therefore, whether bond or free, should act in obedience to him, and not in obedience to men. There is a very important sense in which even slaves are forbidden to be the servants of men—that is, they are not to be men-pleasers, but in all things should act from a sense of duty to God.

24. Brethren, let every man, wherein he is called, therein abide with God.

That is, as all these external relations are of no account, and especially, as a man may be a slave and yet a freeman, let every man be contented with the station which God has assigned him in this life. *With God* (παρὰ θεῷ); near him, perpetually mindful of his presence and favour. In other words, in communion with God. This would secure their contentment and happiness. They would find his favour to be life, and his loving-kindness to be better than life. To live near to God is, therefore, the apostle's prescription both for peace and holiness.

Of Virgins and Widows. Vs. 25–40.

In this portion of the chapter the apostle treats principally of the marriage of virgins—including, however, the young of both sexes. On this subject he says he was not authorized to speak with authority, but simply to advise, v. 25. His advice was, on account of the impending troubles, that they should not marry, vs. 26. 27. It was not wrong to marry, but it would expose them to greater suffering, v. 28. Besides, they should consider the transitory nature of all earthly ties. The fashion of the world was passing away, vs. 29–31. Still further, a single life was freer from worldly cares. The unmarried could consecrate themselves without distraction to the service of the Lord, vs. 32–35. To parents he says, that, if circumstances render it desirable, they might without hesitation give their daughters in marriage, v. 36. But if they were free to act on their own judgment, his advice was to keep them unmarried, vs. 37. 38. Marriage can only be dissolved by death. After the death of her husband, a woman is at liberty to marry again; but she should intermarry only with a Christian; and in Paul's judgment, her happiness would be promoted by remaining single, vs. 39. 40.

25. Now concerning virgins I have no commandment of the Lord: yet I give my judgment, as one that hath obtained mercy of the Lord to be faithful.

Now (δέ, *but,*) serves to resume the connection broken off by the preceding digression. 'But to resume my subject,' which in this chapter is marriage. *Concerning virgins,* (παρ-θένοι.) The word properly means *maidens,* though as an adjective it is used of both sexes, Rev. 14, 4. *I have no commandment of the Lord.* That is, neither Christ himself, nor the Spirit of Christ, by whom Paul was guided, had commissioned him to do any thing more than to counsel these persons. He was inspired, or led by the Spirit, in this matter, not to command, but to advise. His advice, however, was worthy of great deference. It was not merely the counsel of a wise and experienced man; but of one who had obtained mercy of the Lord to be *faithful,* i. e. worthy of confidence, one who could be trusted. This is a sense the word (πιστός) often has, as in the expressions, "faithful saying," "faithful witness." Paul felt himself indebted to the mercy of Christ

for those inward graces and qualities which entitled him to
the confidence of his readers. He recognised Christ as the
giver of those gifts, and himself as undeserving of them. Had
he been left to himself, instead of being the wise, disinterested, and faithful counsellor of Christians, he would have
been a blaspheming persecutor. Philosophy would teach us
that moral excellence must be self-acquired. The Bible teaches us that it is the gift of God; and being the gift of Christ,
Christ must be God. As such, Paul blessed him for having
been so merciful to him as to convert him, and bring him to
the knowledge and obedience of the truth.

26. I suppose therefore that this is good for the
present distress, (I say,) that (it is) good for a man so
to be.

I suppose therefore, (νομίζω οὖν,) i. e. *I think then. The
being so,* i. e. as you are, unmarried, is *good,* in the sense of
expedient. There is a slight grammatical inaccuracy, or
change of construction, in this verse. ' I think then this to
be expedient on account of the coming necessity; that is, I
think that it is expedient for a man so to be.' Paul here expressly states the ground of his opinion that it was inexpedient for his readers to marry. It was on account of *the present
distress,* (ἐνεστῶσαν ἀνάγκην,) the distress standing near, whether
actually present, or impending, depends on the context, Luke
21, 23. 2 Cor. 6, 4. 10, 12. 1 Thess. 3, 7. In the present case
it was probably not so much the troubles in which Christians
were then actually involved, as those which the apostle saw to
be hanging over them, which he refers to. The Scriptures
clearly predicted that the coming of Christ was to be preceded
and attended by great commotions and calamities. These
predictions had reference both to his first and second advent.
The insight even of inspired men into the future was very imperfect. The ancient prophets searched diligently into the
meaning of their own predictions, 1 Pet. 1, 10–12, and the
apostles knew little of the times and seasons, Acts 1, 7. They
knew that great calamities were to come on the earth, but how
or when it was not given to them clearly to see. The awful
desolation which was soon to fall upon Jerusalem and on the
whole Jewish race, and which could not but involve more or
less the Christians also, and the inevitable struggles and persecutions which, according to our Lord's predictions, his fol-

lowers were to encounter, were surely enough to create a deep
impression on the apostle's mind, and to make him solicitous
to prepare his brethren for the coming storm. It is not necessary, therefore, to assume, as is so often done, that the apostle
anticipated the second advent of Christ during that generation, and that he refers to the calamities which were to precede that event. Such expectation would not, indeed, be incompatible with his inspiration. It was revealed to him that
Christ was to come the second time ; and that he was to come
as a thief in the night. He might, therefore, naturally look
for it at any time. We know, however, that in the case of
Paul at least, it was revealed, that the second advent was not
to occur before the national conversion of the Jews, Rom. 11,
25 ; or before the great apostasy and rise of the man of sin,
2 Thess. 2, 2. 3. Still, he knew not when those events might
occur, and therefore he knew not when Christ would come.
It was not, however, to the calamities which are to precede
the second advent, to which Paul here refers, but rather to
those which it was predicted should attend the introduction
of the gospel.

**27. Art thou bound unto a wife? seek not to be
loosed. Art thou loosed from a wife? seek not a wife.**

Marriage, in the present circumstances of the church, will
prove a burden. Although this fact will not justify the dissolution of any marriage, it should dissuade Christians from getting married.

**28. But and if thou marry, thou hast not sinned;
and if a virgin marry, she hath not sinned. Nevertheless such shall have trouble in the flesh: but I spare
you.**

If thou marry, or, 'If thou shalt have married, thou didst
not sin; and *if a virgin shall have married*, she did not sin.'
Marriage is inexpedient, not sinful. It is not because there
is any thing wrong in getting married that Paul dissuades
from it, but because *such shall have trouble* (θλίψις, suffering)
in the flesh ; that is, external, as opposed to inward or spiritual afflictions. The reference is to the afflictions which must
attend marriage in times of trouble. The word *flesh* is often
used in this sense for what is external. John 6, 63. Eph. 6, 5.

2 Cor. 11, 18. *But I spare you.* The design of my dissuading you from marriage is to spare you these sufferings.

29–31. But this I say, brethren, the time (is) short ; it remaineth, that both they that have wives be as though they had none ; and they that weep, as though they wept not ; and they that rejoice, as though they rejoiced not ; and they that buy, as though they possessed not ; and they that use this world, as not abusing (it) : for the fashion of this world passeth away.

'This is another reason why you should not marry. You will soon have to leave your wives. It is nothing relating to your permanent and eternal interests which I urged you to forego, but only something which pertains to the fleeting relations of this changing world.'

But this I say, i. e. This I would have you bear in mind, as giving force to my advice. *The time*, i. e. the appointed time (καιρός, not χρόνος) *is short* (συνεσταλμένος). The verb properly means to *roll* or *wind up*, Acts 5, 6, then to *contract* or *shorten*. 'The time is shortened.' Comp. Matt. 24, 22. Mark 13, 20, where the idea is the same, though the word used is different. This interpretation is on the whole preferable to another almost equally common. 'The time is calamitous ;' for this use of the word, however, no certain authority can be given. The words rendered, *it remaineth*, properly belong to the preceding clause. The meaning is not, 'It remaineth *that*,' but 'The time *henceforth* (τὸ λοιπόν) is short.' That is, the allotted time is brief. *That* does not depend on *This I say*, as though the sense were 'I say *that* ;' but on what immediately precedes. 'The time is shortened *in order that*, &c.' It is the design of God in allowing us but a brief period in this world, or in this state, that we should set lightly by all earthly things ; that those who have wives should be as though they had them not, and those that weep, as though they wept not ; those who rejoice, as though they rejoiced not ; those who buy, as though they possessed not ; those using the world, as though they used it not.' We should set our affections on things above, and not on the things on the earth. Col. 3, 2. The clause rendered 'they that use this world as not abusing it,' is properly so translated, as καταχράομαι means *to use over-much*. The only reason for preferring the other translation is the analogy of the other passages. Either version is consistent with the usage of the word. *For the fashion of this world passeth away*, i. e. is in the act of passing away. *The fashion* (σχῆμα), the external form, the essence as it appears, the present state of things. The figure is derived from the scenes of a theatre, in the actual process of change. The fact that the present condition of the world is not to last long, and that our participation in its joys and sorrows is to be so short-lived, is the reason which the apostle urges why we should not be wedded to earthly things.

32. 33. **But I would have you without carefulness. He that is unmarried careth for the things that belong to the Lord, how he may please the Lord : but he that is married careth for the things that are of the world, how he may please (his) wife.**

This is the third reason why Paul wished the early Christians to remain unmarried. The first was, the increased suffering marriage would probably bring with it. The second was, the transitory nature of all earthly things. And the third is, the comparative freedom from care connected with a single life. The unmarried man may devote himself to the things of the Lord, i. e. to the service of Christ. Having no family to provide for and to protect in times of distress and persecution, he is less encumbered with worldly cares. Christ, and not his wife is, or may be, the great object of his solicitude.

34. **There is difference (also) between a wife and a virgin. The unmarried woman careth for the things of the Lord, that she may be holy both in body and in spirit : but she that is married careth for the things of the world, how she may please (her) husband.**

What is true of men is true also of women. *There is a difference between a wife and a virgin.* The difference is, that the virgin may devote her whole time to the Lord ; the wife must be involved in worldly cares for the sake of her husband. The Greek literally rendered is, *Divided is a wife and a virgin.* Their interests are diverse. The one has a husband to divide her attention; the other is free from such distraction. The reading adopted by Lachmann and Rückert modifies the sense of this passage, and relieves some of its difficulties. They connect μεμέρισται with the preceding sentence, 'He that is married careth for the things of the world, how he may please his wife, and is divided, i. e. distracted between the service of the Lord and his social duties.' In the following clause they read 'ἡ γυνὴ ἡ ἄγαμος καὶ ἡ παρθένος ἡ ἄγαμος, the unmarried woman and the virgin care for the things of the Lord.' Jerome pronounces in favour of this reading, which he says he found in his Greek MSS., and it is also adopted by Calvin. The common text, however, is generally preferred. The virgin cares for the things of the Lord, *that she may be holy both in body and in spirit.* That is, that she be consecrated as to body and spirit. The word *holy* has the sense here that it has in v. 14, and so often elsewhere. It is not in purity and spirituality that the virgin is said to have the advantage of the wife; but in freedom from distracting cares. In v. 14, even the unbelieving husband or wife is said to be sanctified or made holy. And it is in the same general sense of consecration, that holiness is here predicated of virgins as distinguished from wives. It would be to impugn a divine ordinance, and to contradict all experience, to say that married women, because married, are less holy than the unmarried. Paul advances no such idea.

35. And this I speak for your own profit; not that I may cast a snare upon you, but for that which is comely, and that ye may attend upon the Lord without distraction.

The object of the apostle was their advantage. In urging them to remain single, he had no intention "to cast a snare upon them," i. e. to restrain their liberty. Or the meaning of the figure is, 'I do not wish to raise scruples, to make you afraid to move lest you fall into a snare.' The former explanation, however, is preferable. An animal ensnared was confined; it had no liberty of action. Paul did not wish to bring his readers into that state. They were perfectly free to do as they pleased. There was no moral obligation upon them to remain single; no superior holiness in celibacy. He was only saying what in his judgment would be most to their advantage under existing circumstances. That is, as he expresses it, his design was to promote what was *becoming and proper* in them; that is, to promote assiduous, undistracted devotion to the Lord. In other words, that they might be free from any thing to divert their minds from the service of the Lord. The literal translation is, 'For devotion to the Lord without distraction.' Every where the apostle is careful to show that celibacy was preferred merely on the grounds of expediency, and not on the ground of its being a higher state of virtue. All assumption or imposition of vows of celibacy, is a restriction of the liberty which the apostle was solicitous not to invade. Such vows are a snare; and those who take them are like an animal in a net.

36. But if any man think that he behaveth himself uncomely toward his virgin, if she pass the flower of (her) age, and need so require, let him do what he will, he sinneth not : let them marry.

This and the following verse are addressed to fathers, for with them, according to the usage both of Jews and Greeks, rested the disposal of the daughters of the family. Though the apostle regarded marriage at that time as inexpedient, he tells fathers that they were perfectly free to exercise their own judgment in giving their daughters in marriage, or keeping them single. *If any man* (i. e. any father) *thinketh he behaveth himself uncomely towards his virgin.* The word (ἀσχημονέω) may be taken either actively or passively. The meaning may therefore be, 'If any father think he exposes himself to disgrace by keeping his daughter unmarried ;' as it was considered a reproach to be unmarried. Or, 'If he think that he exposes her to disgrace.' The latter interpretation is to be preferred because agreeable to the common use of the word, and because it is required by the preposition (ἐπί), which indicates the object of the action of the verb. *If she pass the flower of her age.* This is one of the conditions of the case on which Paul gives his advice. The daughter must be of full age ; and secondly, there must be some reason why in her case marriage is necessary : *if need so require.* The daughter's happiness may be involved. Under these circumstances the father may *do what he will ; he does not sin* in giving his daughter in marriage, and, therefore, *let them* (i. e. the parties) *marry.* In all cases of indifference, where no moral principle is concerned, our conduct must be regulated by a wise consideration of circumstances. But where a thing is in its own nature either right or wrong, there is no room for discretion.

37. Nevertheless he that standeth steadfast in his heart, having no necessity, but hath power over his own will, and hath so decreed in his heart that he will keep his virgin, doeth well.

He that standeth steadfast in his heart, i. e. whose judgment is settled and firm, being fully persuaded of the inexpediency of his daughter's marrying. *Having no necessity,* i. e. being controlled by no external necessity; nothing, in other words, rendering it necessary for him to act contrary to his own judgment. *But hath power over his own will,* i. e. is able to act as he pleases, or according to his judgment. *And hath so decreed in his heart,* i. e. has fully made up his mind, *to keep his virgin,* i. e. to keep his daughter unmarried; he doeth well.

38. So then he that giveth (her) in marriage doeth well; but he that giveth (her) not in marriage doeth better.

As there is no sin in marriage, and no superior virtue in celibacy, it is a mere question of expediency, to be determined by the circumstances of each particular case. All Paul says is that, other things being equal, it is *better* (i. e. wiser) not to marry than to marry; on account, as he before said, of impending calamities.

39. The wife is bound by the law as long as her husband liveth; but if her husband be dead, she is at liberty to be married to whom she will; only in the Lord.

The uniform doctrine of the New Testament is, that marriage is a contract for life, between one man and one woman, indissoluble by the will of the parties or by any human authority; but that the death of either party leaves the survivor free to contract another marriage. See Rom. 7, 1–3. Such being the doctrine of the Bible, no civil or ecclesiastical body can rightfully establish a different rule, or prescribe another or (as they pretend) a higher rule of morality. All attempts to be better than the Bible, on this or any other subject, only render men worse. Paul, therefore, teaches that a woman on the death of her husband, is free to marry whom she will— *only in the Lord.* There are two ways in which this restriction may be understood. First, that she should marry only one who is in the Lord, i. e. a Christian. Though mixed marriages between Christians and Jews or Gentiles should not, when formed, be broken up (as taught above, vs. 12–15); yet no such marriage ought to be contracted. Or, secondly, the phrase may be taken adverbially as expressing manner, *as becomes those who are in the Lord,* i. e. in a Christian manner. She is to marry as becomes a Christian. This interpretation includes the other. Compare Rom. 16, 2. 22. Eph. 6, 1, &c. The former explanation is the more simple and natural.

40. But she is happier if she so abide, after my judgment : and I think also that I have the Spirit of God.

Happier, freer from exposure to suffering, v. 28 ; and freer from worldly care, v. 32. *After my judgment;* it was an opinion founded, as he says, on the peculiar circumstances of the time, and not intended to bind the conscience or to interfere with the liberty of others, v. 35. Nevertheless, it was the opinion of a holy and inspired man, and therefore entitled to the greatest deference. *To have the Spirit,* means to be under the influence of the Spirit ; whether as a Christian or as an apostle, depends on the context. The meaning here clearly is, that the apostle was led by the Spirit to give the advice in question ; so that his advice is, so to speak, the advice of the Spirit. But is not the advice of the Spirit obligatory ? Certainly, if he meant it to be so ; but if he meant simply to lay down a general rule of expediency, and to leave every one to judge of its application to his or her peculiar case, then it leaves all concerned free. It would cease to be advice if men could not act contrary to it, without irreverence or disobedience. *I think* (δοκῶ) *I have,* is only, agreeably to Greek usage, an urbane way of saying *I have,* comp. Gal. 2, 6. 1 Cor. 12, 22. Paul was in no doubt of his being an organ of the Holy Ghost. *I also,* i. e. I as well as others. This is generally considered as referring (somewhat ironically) to the false pretenders in Corinth. 'I think I have the Spirit of God as well as those among you who make such high pretensions.'

———•••———

CHAPTER VIII.

Eating of sacrifices offered to idols is not in itself wrong, vs. 1–7. But it should be avoided if it gave offence, vs. 8–13.

On eating of sacrifices. Vs. 1–13.

THE second subject on which the Corinthians had requested the advice of the apostle was the lawfulness of eating of the sacrifices offered to idols. To the discussion of that question in its different aspects the eighth, ninth and tenth chapters of this epistle are principally devoted. At the council of Jerusalem it was decided by the apostles, elders and brethren, that the Gentile converts should abstain "from meat offered to idols, from blood, and from things strangled, and from fornication," Acts 15, 29; and this decree was referred to the Holy Ghost as its author, v. 28. Yet Paul, though present in that council, not only does not refer to it, but goes directly against it. That decree forbade the eating of meat offered to idols; Paul, in ch. 10, tells the Corinthians that when exposed for sale in the market, or found on private tables, they might eat it without scruple. These facts do not prove any discrepancy between the apostles gathered in Jerusalem and Paul; nor that the decisions of that council were not obligatory on the church. They only serve to explain the true intent and meaning of those decisions. They show, 1. That there was no permanent moral ground for the prohibition of meat offered to idols. 2. That the ground of the prohibition being expediency, it was of necessity temporary and limited. It had reference to Christians in the midst of those to whom eating such meat was an abomination. It, therefore, ceased to be binding whenever and wherever the grounds of the prohibition did not exist. It is analogous to Paul's condemnation of women appearing in church without a veil. The decisions of that council, therefore, were no barrier to Paul's discussing the question on its merits. In this chapter the subject is viewed in two aspects; first, considered in itself; and secondly, in its bearing on the weaker or less enlightened class of Christians. Most of the questions which disturbed the early church had their origin in the conflicting prepossessions and prejudices of the Jewish and Gentile converts; or at least, of the more and less enlightened of the Christian converts. For it is probable that many of those who had been educated as heathen belonged to the class of weaker brethren. As a body, however, the Gentiles were disposed to latitudinarianism; and the Jews to superstitious scrupulousness. So far as general principles were concerned, Paul sided with the Gentile party. Their views about meats and drinks, and holy days, and ceremonies were derived from the apostle himself, and were therefore approved by him. But the spirit and practice of this party he severely condemns. Thus, in the present instance, he admits that an idol is nothing; that a sacrifice is nothing; that all enlightened Christians know this; that, consequently, eating of the heathen sacrifices was a matter of indifference, it made a man neither better nor worse; and yet eating of them might be, and in their case it was, sinful; because injurious to their weaker brethren. He begins the chapter with the admission, therefore, that all enlightened Christians have knowledge. He reminds them, however, that there is something higher than knowledge; that knowledge without love is, after all, only another form of ignorance. The main thing to be known is not apprehended, vs. 1–3. He admits, however, that Christians know that the gods of the heathen are vanities and lies, that there is but one only, the living and true God, v. 4. For although the heathen acknowledge a whole hierarchy of deities, celestial and terrestrial, Christians acknowledge but one God and one Mediator, v. 6. All this is admitted. It is, however, nevertheless true that many Christians, though they know that there is but one God, yet are not persuaded that the heathen deities are nothing, and therefore they stand in awe of them, and could not help believing that eating of sacrifices offered to idols was an act of worship, or in some way defiling, v. 7. The apostle also admits the second principle relied upon by the Gentile converts, viz., that meat does not commend us to God, that it can have no influence on our spiritual state, v. 8. It is not enough, however, that an act should be in its own nature in-

different to justify us in performing it. If our doing what·is
in itself innocent be the occasion of leading others into sin, it
is for that reason sinful for us, v. 9. If, therefore, a weak
brother should be led, against the convictions of his own mind,
to join his stronger brethren in eating such sacrifices, he would
bring himself into condemnation. It was, therefore, a breach
of charity and a sin against Christ, to eat of the heathen
sacrifices under circumstances which emboldened others to
sin, vs. 10–12. The apostle avows his own determination
never to eat meat at all, if by so doing he should cause his
brethren to sin, v. 13.

1. Now as touching things offered unto idols, we
know that we all have knowledge. Knowledge puffeth
up, but charity edifieth.

The idolatry of the Greeks and Romans pervaded their
whole life. Their social intercourse, their feasts, the administration of justice, the public amusements, the offices and honours of the government, were all more or less connected with
religious services. Christians, therefore, were constantly exposed to the danger of being involved in some idolatrous
homage without even knowing it. This gave rise to numerous and perplexing questions of conscience, which were often
decided differently by different classes of Christians. One of
the most perplexing of these questions related to the use of
things offered to idols. Some had no scruples on this point;
others thought it sinful to eat of such sacrifices under any circumstances. This was a question which it was necessary to
have authoritatively settled, because it came up every day for
decision. The victims offered in sacrifices were usually divided
into three parts. One was consumed on the altar, another
was given to the priest, and a third was retained by the offerer.
The portion given to the priest, if not needed for himself, was
sent to the market. The portion retained by the offerer was
either eaten at his own table, or within the precincts of the
temple. The Christians, therefore, if they bought meat in the
market, or if invited to the houses of their heathen friends, or
to the festivals in the temples, were liable to have these sacrifices placed before them. The two grounds on which the
more liberal of them defended the use of such meat, were,
first, that the idols were nothing, they were not really gods;
and secondly, that meat cannot commend us to God. Both

these principles are true, and therefore the apostle concedes
them, but at the same time corrects the practical inferences
which the Gentile converts drew from them.   There were
really two distinct questions relating to this subject.   The
first was, whether eating such sacrifices was lawful ? the other,
whether it was lawful to eat them within the precincts of the
temple ?   The apostle does not distinguish these questions
until the tenth chapter.   Here he speaks of the subject only
in its general aspects.

Now as touching things offered unto idols. Literally, *But,
concerning idol-sacrifices.* The particle (δέ,) *but,* serves to introduce a new topic.   As the fourth verse begins, *concerning
therefore the eating things offered to idols,* the intervening
words are a logical parenthesis.   This parenthesis may begin
immediately after the word *idols,* or after the word *knowledge,* so that the first two clauses of the verse are connected.
"But concerning idol-sacrifices, we know we all have knowledge."   This claim to knowledge, though a claim of the
Corinthians, and the ground on which they defended the eating of those sacrifices, is not put forward as a point to be contested.   The apostle adopts it, or makes it his own, and then
proceeds to qualify and limit it, precisely as he did with the
aphorism, "All things are lawful," in 6, 12; see also 10, 23.
The subject of the two verbs *know* and *have* in this verse are
not necessarily the same.   The sense may be: 'I know we all
have knowledge.'   The knowledge intended is determined by
the context.   It is the knowledge concerning idols.   In this
verse Paul says, "We all have knowledge;" but in v. 7, he
says, "This knowledge is not in all."   This apparent contradiction may be explained by supposing, what is perfectly
natural, that the apostle has reference to different classes of
persons in the two passages.   In v. 1 he may intend himself
and his followers. *We all,* that is, all the stronger or more
enlightened class of believers.   Whereas, in v. 7, he may refer
to Christians generally, including the strong and weak. 'This
knowledge is not in all, for the weak have it not.'   Or the distinction may be between theoretical and practical knowledge.
All Christians admit, as a matter of theory, that an idol is
nothing, but this knowledge is not in all believers practical
and controlling.   This also is natural and satisfactory.   It is
analogous to the statements of this same apostle in reference
to the heathen.   In Rom. 1, 23, he says, 'They know God,'
but in 1 Cor. 1, 21, he says, they 'know not God.'   These

statements are perfectly consistent, because the word *know* has different senses. There is a sense in which all men know God ; they all, from the constitution of their nature, and from the works of God, know that there is a being on whom they are dependent, and to whom they are responsible. But this is not the knowledge of God which is said to be " eternal life." It is therefore perfectly consistent to attribute the former knowledge to the heathen, though he denies to them the latter. So here it is consistent to say that all Christians have a theoretical knowledge of the truth that there is but one God, and that idols are nothing, and yet say that this knowledge is not practical and controlling in all. It is one of the great beauties of the Scriptures, that the sacred writers in the calm consciousness of truth, in the use of popular, as distinguished from philosophical language, affirm and deny the same verbal proposition, assured that the consistency and intent of their statements will make their way to the heart and conscience. That the apostle is here speaking of theoretical, as distinguished from true, practical knowledge, is plain from what he says of it. *It puffeth up.* The Greek word here used (φυσιόω,) is, in the New Testament, employed in the sense of the word (φυσάω,) which means *to blow, to fill with wind, to inflate ;* and then, *to render vain and conceited.* Mere theoretical or speculative knowledge, that is, knowledge divorced from love, tends to inflate the mind, i. e. renders it vain and conceited. It is a great mistake, therefore, to suppose that mere knowledge, without religion, elevates and refines men, or can purify society. It is essential, but it is insufficient.

Charity edifieth. *Charity* is an inadequate and unhappy translation of the Greek word (ἀγάπη), because, agreeably to its Latin derivation, it properly means the feeling which arises from the perception of the wants and sufferings of others, and the consequent desire to relieve them. *Love* (ἀγάπη, a word peculiar to Hellenistic Greek,) is much more comprehensive than this, not only because it may have God for its object, but also because, when exercised towards men it includes complacency and delight as well as benevolence. It is of this comprehensive virtue the apostle treats at length in the thirteenth chapter of this epistle, and of which he here says, *it edifies.* It does not terminate on itself, as knowledge does, but goes out of itself, and seeks its happiness in another, and lives and acts for others. It is, therefore, something incomparably higher than knowledge, when the two are separated and distinguished.

2. And if any man think that he knoweth any thing, he knoweth nothing yet as he ought to know.

The knowledge which puffs up is not true knowledge. One is constantly astonished at the profound remarks which every where occur in the sacred writings ; remarks which do not directly refer to the mysteries of the gospel, but philosophical remarks ; that is, such as reveal the deepest insight into the nature of man and the workings of his constitution. Philosophy and theology are inseparably connected. The former is an element of the latter. A system of philosophy might be constructed by collecting and classifying the aphorisms of the Bible. And the reason why the philosophy which underlies Augustinianism has stood as a rock in the ocean, while other systems rise and fall like waves around it, is, that it is derived from the word of God, and not from the speculations of men. The relation between the cognitive and emotional faculties is one of the most difficult problems in philosophy. In many systems they are regarded as distinct. Paul here teaches, that with regard to a large class of objects, knowledge without feeling is nothing ; it supposes the most essential characteristics of the object to be unperceived. And in the following verse he teaches that love is the highest form of knowledge. To know God is to love him ; and to love him is to know him. Love is intelligent, and knowledge is emotional. Hence the apostle says, If a man thinketh that he knoweth any thing ; that is, if he is proud or conceited, he is ignorant. He does not apprehend the true nature of the objects which he pretends to know. He does not see their vastness, their complexity, their majesty and excellence. These are the attributes of religious truths which are the most essential, and without the apprehension of which they cannot be known.

3. But if any man love God, the same is known of him.

To love is to know and to be known. Compare 1 John 4, 7. 8, "Every one that loveth is born of God, and knoweth God ; he that loveth not, knoweth not God, for God is love."

This is the precise sentiment of the text. Love is essential to knowledge. He that loves God, knows God. The apostle in this connection interchanges love of the brethren and the love of God, because the love of the brethren is only one of the forms in which the love of God manifests itself. When he said, "Love edifieth," he meant love to the brethren, and without that love, he says, there can be no true knowledge; but if a man love God, (which includes love to the brethren,) *the same is known of him.* What is meant by this last expression, is not easy to determine. *To be known of God* may, according to scriptural usage, mean, 1. To be selected or approved by him, Exod. 33, 12. 17. Nahum 1, 7. Matt. 7, 23. 2. To be recognized as belonging to a particular class. So here, the sense may be, 'Is recognized by him as one of his disciples, or as one of his children. 3. To be the object of God's knowledge; but what this can mean in this connection, unless it include the idea of approbation, it is not easy to see. 4. According to others, the word (ἔγνωσται) is to be taken in a Hophal sense—'has been caused to know.' 'If any man loves God, the same has by him been brought to the true knowledge.' This view certainly suits the context. 'If a man is without love, he has not true knowledge; but if he love God, he has the right kind of knowledge.' The later grammarians deny that the passive form of Greek verbs ever has a causative sense analogous to the Hophal of Hebrew verbs. But as intransitive verbs in Greek often have a causative signification, (see Matt. 5, 45. 28, 19. 2 Cor. 2, 14,) it is not unreasonable that the passive form should be so used, if the context require it. In Gal. 4, 9, Paul says, "If after that ye have known God, or rather are known of God;" where the sense may be, 'or rather have been taught of God.' Whether the general principle be admitted or not, that the passive of Greek verbs can have this causative force, it is not improbable that Paul assumed that the particular verb γινώσκειν might mean *cognoscere facere,* (i. e. *to teach,*) a sense attributed to it by Stephanus in his Thesaurus; and if so, the passive as here used may mean, *was taught.* It is to be noticed, that it is only this verb that he appears to use in this way. If, however, this interpretation be rejected, as is done by the majority of modern commentators, as contrary to Greek usage, the first explanation given above gives a good sense. 'If any love God, the same is approved of him, i. e. is recognised as having the right kind of knowledge.'

4. As concerning therefore the eating of those
things that are offered in sacrifice unto idols, we know
that an idol (is) nothing in the world, and that (there
is) none other God but one.

Concerning then. The particle (οὖν,) *then* serves to resume the subject of v. 1 after the interruption occasioned by
the preceding parenthesis. For the general expression in v. 1,
" Concerning idol-sacrifices," we have here the more definite
one, " Concerning *the eating* of idol-sacrifices ;" which was the
point in dispute. To determine whether it was proper to eat
of these sacrifices, it must be determined, first, what an idol
is ; and secondly, what effect the eating would have. As to
the former, Paul says, there is no idol, (or an idol is nothing ;)
and as to the latter, that the eating could have no effect on
our religious state ; it could make us neither better nor worse,
v. 8. From this it follows, that eating or not eating is a mat
ter of indifference. Nevertheless, if our eating causes others
to sin, we ought not to eat. It is worthy of remark that the
apostle, in answering questions of conscience, does not give a
categorical reply, but gives the reason for his decision. So
here ; and in ch. 11 he does not simply say it was wrong for
Grecian women to appear in public unveiled, but he unfolds
the principles valid for all time, on which the decision of that
particular question rested.

As to the question, What is an idol ? it is obvious that the
word (εἴδωλον, *image*,) is used metonymically for the deity
which the image was intended to represent. It is of such
deity, or rather of the heathen gods generally, the apostle
here speaks. His words are, " We know that οὐδὲν εἴδωλον ἐν
κόσμῳ," which may mean, either, *an idol is nothing in the
world ;* or, *there is no idol in the world*, i. e. *the universe.* If
the former version be adopted, the sense may be, either,
' these deities are nonentities,' they have no existence ; or,
they are powerless, they have no influence over the affairs of
men. In favour of that translation is the analogy of Scripture.
In the Old Testament the gods of the heathen are frequently
said to be nothing, vanities, lies, &c., Is. 41, 24. 44, 8. 9. Jer.
10, 14. Ps. 115, 4. 8. So the Rabbis also said, Noverant
utique Israelitae, idolum nihil esse, *Sanhdr.* 63. 2. But this
explanation is not suitable here. As οὐδεὶς θεός in the next
clause means *there is no God*, οὐδὲν εἴδωλον must mean, *there is
no idol.* This does not mean that the heathen gods are either

nonentities or powerless, for in 10, 19 Paul says they are demons. But it means, there are no such beings in the universe as the heathen conceived their gods to be. There was no Jupiter, Juno, or Mars. *There is no God*, no real divine being but one. The objects of heathen worship were neither what the heathen took them to be, nor were they gods in the true sense of that term.

5. For though there be that are called gods, whether in heaven or in earth, as there be gods many, and lords many,

This verse admits of two interpretations. It is commonly understood to mean, that although there are many imaginary gods in heaven and earth, i. e. beings whom the heathen regard as divinities, yet in fact there is but one God. When he says, there *are* many gods and many lords, he is to be understood to mean that such is the fact in the mythology of the heathen. A large number of commentators, however, understand the passage thus: 'There is but one true God; for although it be admitted that there are many beings called gods, as in fact there are gods many and lords many, yet to us there is but one.' The apostle concedes that, in the wide sense of the term, there are many gods and lords; and, therefore, if it should be admitted (what he does not admit) that the whole hierarchy of divinities, as conceived of by the heathen, actually existed, it is nevertheless true that there is but one God, the creator and end of all things. In favour of this interpretation is the usage of the O. T. Deut. 10, 17, "The Lord your God is God of gods and Lord of lords." Jos. 22, 22. Dan. 2, 47. Ps. 136, 2. 3. These passages show that the words *god* and *lord* are applied in a wide sense to other beings than to the true God. 2. The position and force of the words are in favour of this view. They mean, *Sunt qui dii dicuntur;* there *are* powers and beings who are called gods, as *there are* gods many, and lords many. To make this mean, there are *in the estimation of the heathen* many gods, is to insert something which is not in the text. 3. In 10, 19. 20, the apostle asserts that the objects of heathen worship are real and powerful beings. 4. The apparent contradiction between saying, *there is no idol in the world*, and saying, *there are many gods*, is easily removed. The meaning is, 'There is no such being in the universe as Jupiter or Mars; for although there is a multitude of supernatural beings, called gods and lords, not only by the heathen, but also in Scripture, yet there are no such beings as those which the heathen imagine.' The whole heathen mythology is a fable, the work of the imagination. There are no such gods in existence, though there are demons in abundance, of various ranks and powers, called gods. There are two things which the apostle means to deny. 1. The existence of such beings as the heathen conceived their gods to be. 2. That the supernatural beings who do really exist, and who are called gods, are really divine. They are mere creatures.

6. But to us (there is but) one God, the Father, of whom (are) all things, and we in him ; and one Lord Jesus Christ, by whom (are) all things, and we by him.

Though there are many creatures called gods, there is but one true God, the creator of all things. *To us*, i. e. to Christians. *There is one God*, i. e. only one being who is eternal, self-existing and almighty. This one God is, first, *the Father ;* not the first person of the Trinity, but our father. The word does not here express the relation of the first to the second person in the Godhead, but the relation of God as such to us as his children. When we say, " Our Father who art in heaven," the word Father designates the Supreme Being, the Triune Jehovah. Secondly, of this one God it is said, *of him are all things.* He, the one God, is the source of the whole universe, and all that it contains. He created all things by the word of his power. All other beings are his creatures. Thirdly, *we are to him.* He is our end ; for his glory we were created and redeemed. Our version rendering the words εἰς αὐτόν, *in him*, is an unnecessary departure from their proper meaning.

As there is but one divine Being, so there is but one Lord, i. e. one administrator of the universe, into whose hands all power in heaven and earth has been committed, and who is the only mediator between God and man. This one Lord is *Jesus Christ*, Jesus the Messiah, the historical person, born in Bethlehem and crucified on Calvary. Of this one Lord it is said, first, *all things are by him.* The *all things* in this clause must be coextensive with the all things in the preceding one, i. e. the universe. Comp. Eph. 3, 9. Col. 1, 16. Heb. 1, 2. The universe was created *through* Jesus Christ, i. e. the energy of the one God was exercised *through* the Logos, who became flesh, assuming our nature into personal union with himself, and is therefore called Jesus Christ. This passage affords a striking illustration of the fact that the person of Christ may be denominated from his human nature, when what is affirmed of him is true only of his divine nature. He is here called Jesus Christ, though the work of creation attributed to him was the work of the Logos. Secondly, it is said of this one Lord, that *we are by him*. This does not mean we were created by him; for we Christians are included in the *all things*. It would be tautological to say, He created all things, and he created us. The meaning is, we as Christians (not, we as creatures, for that had been said before), we as the children of God are by him. We were redeemed by him; we are brought unto God by him.

7. Howbeit (there is) not in every man that knowledge: for some with conscience of the idol unto this hour eat (it) as a thing offered unto an idol; and their conscience being weak is defiled.

The context shows that (ἡ γνῶσις), *the* knowledge, means the particular kind of knowledge of which he had been speaking, viz. the knowledge that there is no idol in the world, or that the gods of the heathen are imaginary beings. Though the weaker believers knew that there is but one true God, they were still not fully persuaded that the gods of the heathen had no existence. *With conscience of an idol.* The word συνείδησις unites the meanings of our words *conscience* and *consciousness*, being sometimes the one and sometimes the other. Here the former meaning is better suited to the context. *Conscience of an idol* means a conscience under the influence of an idol; as in 1 Pet. 2, 19 *conscience of God* means a conscience under the influence of God.* The moral judgments and feelings of the persons referred to, were still influenced by the apprehension that the heathen gods might be real beings. *Unto this hour.* The words (ἕως ἄρτι) *until*

---

* Instead of συνειδήσει the MSS. A. B. 17. 46, and the Coptic, Ethiopic and Syrian versions read συνηθείᾳ, which reading is adopted by Lachmann and Tischendorf. The meaning would then be '*through custom of an idol*,' i. e. from being long accustomed to believe that there were such beings. The great weight of authority, however, is in favour of the common reading.

now, in the common Text stand after the word for *idol;* most modern editors of the Greek Testament, on the authority of the older MSS., place them before that word. In the one position, they naturally qualify the word *to eat;* '*until now they eat*,' i. e. they continue to eat. In the other, they qualify the word *conscience; with a conscience still under the influence of an idol*, which gives a better sense. Having this persuasion, or at least this apprehension of the reality of the idol, they eat the sacrifice as a sacrifice. That is, they do not regard it as ordinary meat, but as something which had a religious character and influence, from the fact of its having been offered in sacrifice. Hence *their conscience being weak was defiled.* A *weak* conscience is one which either regards as wrong what is not in fact so; or one which is not clear and decided in its judgments. According to the Scriptures, "whatever is not of faith is sin," Rom. 14, 23; therefore whatever a man does, thinking it is wrong, or doubtful whether it be wrong or not, to him it is sin. Thus the man who eats an idol-sacrifice, uncertain whether he is doing right or not, defiles his conscience. The conscience is said to be defiled, either when it approves or cherishes sin, or when it is burdened by a sense of guilt. The latter form of pollution is that here intended. The man who acts in the way supposed feels guilty, and is really guilty.

8. But meat commendeth us not to God: for neither, if we eat, are we the better; neither, if we eat not, are we the worse.

This verse is analogous to v. 1, in so far that it contains a principle adopted by the apostle as his own, which the Corinthians urged to justify their latitudinarian practice with regard to these sacrifices. It is not introduced as an objection, or as a point to be contested, but as an admitted truth, the application of which is to be regulated by other principles no less true. It is admitted that meat does not *commend us to God.* Literally, does not cause us to stand near to God; which involves the idea expressed in our version. *For* eating makes us neither better nor worse. It neither causes us to excel (περισσεύειν) nor to come behind (ὑστερεῖν).

There is another view of the bearing of this passage which has much to commend it, and which has many advocates. It is regarded as assigning a reason why the strong should have respect to the weak. 'If meat were a matter of importance, if it really commended us to God, there would be a valid reason why you should eat these sacrifices. But as it is a matter of indifference, you should not cause your brethren to offend.' This would be a natural interpretation if the caution which follows were introduced as an inference. That is, if the apostle had said, 'Eating is a matter of indifference, *therefore* you should use your liberty with due regard to your brethren. His language, however, is, 'Meat does not commend us to God; it makes us neither better nor worse; *but* take heed how you use your liberty.' It is evidently a concession limited by what follows; comp. 6, 12, "All things are lawful, *but* all things are not expedient;" see also 10, 23.

9. But take heed lest by any means this liberty of yours become a stumblingblock to them that are weak.

Admitting you have the right to eat of these sacrifices, take care lest your eating become an occasion of sin to your weaker brethren. *Your liberty.* The word (ἐξουσία) means, 1. Ability or power. 2. Lawful power or right. 3. Author ity; 'Who gave thee this authority?' 4. Power over others, dominion or rule. Here the second sense is the one in which the word is to be taken. *Stumblingblock,* (πρόσκομμα,) elsewhere rendered *offence*, in a moral sense is that which is an occasion to sin, or which causes men to fall. In the same sense the word (σκάνδαλον, literally, *a trap-stick,*) *scandal* is used, Luke 17, 1. Rom. 14, 13. 1 John 2, 10. *The weak* are the doubting, the undecided, those "not having knowledge," as is implied in the next verse.

10. For if any man see thee which hast knowledge sit at meat in the idol's temple, shall not the conscience of him which is weak be emboldened to eat those things which are offered to idols;

This verse is designed to show how eating these sacrifices might be an occasion of sin to others. *For* serves to introduce the illustration. *See thee having knowledge.* This is the description of the strong. They were those whose views were clear and their convictions decided. *Sit at meat,* (κατακείμενον,) literally, *lying down*, according to the ancient custom of reclining on a couch at table. The word ἀνάκειμαι, *to lie up*, is also used, as the couches were usually higher than the table. *In the idol's temple.* In the tenth chapter the apostle teaches, that as eating of things offered to idols was a matter of indifference, there was no harm in buying such meat in the market, or in partaking of it at a private table ; but that to eat it within the precincts of the temple was an act of idolatry, and brought them into communion with demons, and therefore utterly broke off their connection with Christ. Here he views the matter simply under the aspect of *an offence*, or in reference to its effect on the weaker brethren, and therefore says nothing of the sinfulness of the act in itself. In like manner, in the eleventh chapter, speaking of it as a matter of decorum, he simply condemns women speaking in church *unveiled*, as though he had no objection to their speaking in public ; but in the fourteenth chapter he condemns the thing itself, and not merely the manner of doing it. *Shall not the conscience of him being weak* (i. e. being uncertain whether he was doing right or wrong,) *be emboldened ;* literally, *be edified*. This must either be understood ironically, which is out of keeping with the whole tone of the passage, or the word must be taken in the sense of *built up, carried forward* to the point (εἰς) of eating of the idol-sacrifices. That is, he might be led to do what his conscience secretly condemned.

11. And through thy knowledge shall the weak brother perish, for whom Christ died ?

That is, shall your knowledge be the occasion of the perdition of a weak brother ? There are three forms in which the apostle expresses the consequence of doing what the conscience is not satisfied is right. In v. 7 he says, the conscience is defiled ; here, he says, the man perishes or is lost ; in Rom. 14, 23, he says, "He that doubteth is damned (condemned) if he eat." All these forms of expression amount to the same thing. Guilt, condemnation and perdition are connected. The one implies the other. Whatever brings guilt on the conscience exposes to condemnation, and condemnation is perdition.

For whom Christ died. There is great power and pathos in these words. Shall we, for the sake of eating one kind of meat rather than another, endanger the salvation of those for whom the eternal Son of God laid down his life ? The infinite distance between Christ and us, and the almost infinite distance between his sufferings and the trifling self-denial required at our hands, give to the apostle's appeal a force the Christian heart cannot resist. The language of Paul in this verse seems to assume that those may perish for whom Christ died. It belongs, therefore, to the same category as those numerous passages which make the same assumption with regard to the elect. If the latter are consistent with the certainty of the salvation of all the elect, then this passage is consistent with the certainty of the salvation of those for whom Christ specifically died. It was absolutely certain that none of Paul's companions in shipwreck was on that occasion to lose his life, because the salvation of the whole company had been predicted and promised ; and yet the apostle said that if the sailors were allowed to take away the boats, those left on board could not be saved. This appeal secured the ac complishment of the promise. So God's telling the elect that if they apostatize they shall perish, prevents their apostasy. And in like manner, the Bible teaching that those for whom Christ died shall perish if they violate their conscience, prevents their transgressing, or brings them to repentance. God's purposes embrace the means as well as the end. If the means fail, the end will fail. He secures the end by securing the means. It is just as certain that those for whom Christ died shall be saved, as that the elect shall be saved. Yet in both cases the event is spoken of as conditional. There is not only a possibility, but an absolute certainty of their perishing if they fall away. But this is precisely what God has promised to prevent. This passage, therefore, is perfectly consistent with those numerous passages which teach that Christ's death secures the salvation of all those who were given to him in the covenant of redemption. There is, however, a sense in which it is scriptural to say that Christ died for all men. This is very different from saying that he died *equally* for all men, or that his death had no other reference to those who are saved than it had to those who are lost. To die *for one* is to die for his benefit. As Christ's death has benefited the whole world, prolonged the probation of men, secured for them innumerable blessings, provided a righteousness sufficient and suitable for all, it may be said that he died for all. And in reference to this obvious truth the language of the apostle, should any prefer this interpretation, may be understood, 'Why should we destroy one for whose benefit Christ laid down his life?'

All this is perfectly consistent with the great scriptural truth that Christ came into the world to save his people, that his death renders certain the salvation of all those whom the Father hath given him, and therefore that he died not only *for* them but *in their place*, and on the condition that they should never die.

12. But when ye sin so against the brethren, and wound their weak conscience, ye sin against Christ.

We sin against our brethren when we wound their weak conscience. The one phrase explains the other. To wound a man's conscience is to give it the pain of remorse. When we bring on him a sense of guilt we inflict on him the greatest evil in our power; not only because a wounded spirit is worse than a wounded body; but also because a sense of guilt alienates us from God and brings us under the power of Satan. He who thus sins against his brother, *sins against Christ*. This is true in two senses. An injury done to a child is an injury to the parent, both because proper regard for the parent would prevent one from injuring his child; and also because the parent suffers in the child. They are so united that the injury of the one is the injury of the other. So also it is a manifestation of want of love to Christ, an insult and injury to him, to injure his people; and moreover, he and they are so united that whatever of good or evil is done to them is done also to him. "Inasmuch as ye have done it unto one of the least of these my brethren, ye have done it unto me," Matt. 25, 40. If we believed this aright it would render us very careful not to wound our fellow Christians, and make us also feel it to be an honour to relieve their wants.

13. Wherefore, if meat make my brother to offend, I will eat no flesh while the world standeth, lest I make my brother to offend.

The word σκανδαλίζω means either to offend, or to cause to offend. That is, either to provoke, or to cause to sin. The English word is also used in both these senses. Matt. 17, 27, "That we may not offend them," i. e. provoke them. Matt. 5, 29, "If thy eye offend thee," i. e. cause thee to sin; and Matt. 18, 6, "Whoso shall offend (i. e. cause to sin) one of these little ones which believe in me, it were better for him that a mill-stone were hanged about his neck, and that he were drowned in the depth of the sea." This last quoted passage shows how serious a matter our Lord considers it to lead even the weakest Christian into sin. It is still worse to lead him into error, for error is the mother of many sins. It shows also how great an evil sin is, and justifies the strong language of the apostle that he would never eat flesh rather than cause his brother to offend. It is morally obligatory, therefore, to abstain from indulging in things indifferent, when the use of them is the occasion of sin to others. This is a principle the application of which must be left to every man's conscience in the fear of God. No rule of conduct, founded on expediency, can be enforced by church discipline. It was right in Paul to refuse to eat flesh for fear of causing others to offend; but he could not have been justly exposed to discipline, had he seen fit to eat it. He circumcised Timothy, and refused to circumcise Titus. Whenever a thing is right or wrong according to circumstances, every man must have the right to judge of those circumstances.

---•••---

CHAPTER IX.

The apostle illustrates the duty of foregoing the exercise of our rights for the good of others, by a reference to his giving up his undoubted right to be supported by the church, vs. 1–18. He shows that in other ways he accommodated himself to the opinions and prejudices of others, 19–23. He reminds his readers that nothing good or great could be attained without self-denial, vs. 24–27.

The right of ministers to an adequate maintenance. The necessity of self-denial. Vs. 1–27.

HAVING in the preceding chapter urged on the strong the duty of foregoing the use of their rights for the sake of their weaker brethren, the apostle shows how he had acted on that principle. He was an apostle, and therefore had all the rights of an apostle. His apostleship was abundantly clear, because he had seen the Lord Jesus and was his immediate messenger; and his divine mission had been confirmed, at least among the Corinthians, beyond dispute. They were the seal of his apostleship, vs. 1–3. Being an apostle, he had the same right to be supported and to have his family supported, had he chosen to marry, as Peter or any other apostle, vs. 4–6. This right to adequate support he proves, First, from the principle which lies at the foundation of society, that the laborer is worthy of his reward, v. 7. Secondly, from the fact that this principle is recognized in the Old Testament, even in its application to brutes, vs. 8–10. Thirdly, from the principles of commutative justice, v. 11. Fourthly, from the fact that the Corinthians recognized this right in the case of other teachers, v. 12. Fifthly, from the universal recognition of the principle among all nations. Those who served the temple were supported from the temple, v. 13. Sixthly, from the express ordinance of Christ, who had ordained that those who preached the gospel should live by the gospel, v. 14. This undoubted right Paul had not availed himself of, and he was determined, especially at Corinth, not to avail himself of it in the future. By so doing he cut off occasion to question his motives, and gave himself a ground of confidence in resisting his opponents which he was determined not to relinquish, vs. 15–18. This was not, however, the only case in which he abstained from the exercise of his rights for the good of others. He accommodated himself to Jews and Gentiles in every thing indifferent, that he might gain the more, vs. 19–23. Such self-denial the heathen exercised to gain a corruptible crown—should not Christians do as much to gain a crown that is incorruptible? Without self-denial and effort the prize of their high calling could never be attained, vs. 24–27.

1. Am I not an apostle? am I not free? * have I not seen Jesus Christ our Lord? are not ye my work in the Lord?

The order of the first two of these questions is reversed by most editors on satisfactory external and internal evidence. *Am I not free?* That is, am I not a Christian, invested with all the liberties wherewith Christ has made his people free? Am I not as free as any other believer to regulate my conduct according to my own convictions of what is right; free from

* The MS. A. B., the great majority of the ancient versions, and many of the Fathers put ἐλεύθερος before ἀπόστολος, which is the natural order of the words, and which, after Griesbach, has been adopted by almost all editors.

any obligation to conform to the opinions or prejudices of other men? This, however, is a freedom which I have not availed myself of. Nay more, *Am I not an apostle?* Be sides the rights which belong to all Christians, have I not all the prerogatives of an apostle? Am I not on a level with the chief of the apostles? Who of them can show a better title to the office? There were three kinds of evidence of the apostleship. 1. The immediate commission from Christ in the sight of witnesses, or otherwise confirmed. 2. Signs and wonders, and mighty deeds, 2 Cor. 12, 12. 3. The success of their ministry. No man could be an apostle who had not seen the Lord Jesus after his resurrection, because that was one of the essential facts of which they were to be the witnesses, Acts 1, 22. Neither could any man be an apostle who did not receive his knowledge of the gospel by immediate revelation from Christ, for the apostles were the witnesses also of his doctrines, Acts 1, 8. 10, 39. 22, 15. Gal. 1, 12. The necessity of this immediate mission and independent knowledge is insisted upon at length in the epistle to the Galatians. In proof of his apostleship Paul here appeals only to two sources of evidence; first, to his having seen the Lord Jesus; and second, to the success of his ministry. *Ye are my work in the Lord.* That is, either, you in the Lord, your being in the Lord (i. e. your conversion), is my work; or, the words (ἐν κυρίῳ) may mean *by the Lord,* i. e. by his co-operation. The former explanation is to be preferred, as the apostle's object is to state in what sense they were his work. It was as being in the Lord. The connection of this verse, and of the whole chapter, with what precedes is obvious. His design is to show that he had himself acted on the principle which he urged on others. Neither as a Christian nor as an apostle had he insisted upon his rights, without regard to the prejudices of others or the good of the church.

2. If I be not an apostle unto others, yet doubtless I am to you : for the seal of mine apostleship are ye in the Lord.

If to others, i. e. in the estimation of others, *I be not an apostle, surely I am to you.* Whatever pretence others may have to question my apostleship, you certainly can have none; *for the seal of my apostleship are ye in the Lord.* Your conversion is the seal of God to my commission. The conversion of men is a divine work, and those by whom it is accomplished are thereby authenticated as divine messengers. It is as much the work of God as a miracle, and therefore, when duly authenticated, has the same effect as an evidence of a divine commission. This, although valid evidence, and as such adduced by the apostle, is nevertheless very liable to be abused. First, because much which passes for conversion is spurious; and secondly, because the evidence of success is often urged in behalf of the errors of preachers, when that success is due to the truth which they preach. Still there are cases when the success is of such a character, so undeniable and so great, as to supersede the necessity of any other evidence of a divine call. Such was the case with the apostles, with the reformers, and with many of our modern missionaries.

3. Mine answer to them that do examine me is this :

That is, what precedes, and not what follows; for what follows is no answer to those who called his apostleship in question. Both the words here used, (ἀνακρίνω) *to examine*, and (ἀπολογία), *apology*, or *answer*, are forensic terms. Paul means that when any of his opponents undertook to question him, as it were, judicially, as to his apostleship, he answered, 'I have seen the Lord Jesus, and he has set his seal to my commission by the success with which he has crowned my labours.' This answer satisfied Peter, James and John, who gave to Paul the right hand of fellowship, seeing that to him had been committed the apostleship unto the Gentiles, Gal. 2, 8. 9.

4. Have we not power to eat and drink ?

Power here as above, 8, 9, means *right*. Have we not the right to eat and drink? This, taken by itself, might mean, 'Have we not the same right that others have as to meats and drinks? All distinctions on this subject are abolished as much for us as for others. Are we not free?' The context shows, however, clearly that such is not the apostle's meaning. The right in question is that which he goes on to establish. It is the right to abstain from working, and of being supported by the church. Having proved his apostleship, he proves his right to be supported, and then shows that he had not availed himself of that right. He could, therefore, with the greater freedom urge the Corinthians to forego their right to eat of things offered to idols for the sake of their weaker brethren

5. Have we not power to lead about a sister, a wife, as well as other apostles, and (as) the brethren of the Lord, and Cephas?

This is an amplification of the preceding verse. *Have we not the power*, i. e. the right. *To lead about*, a form of expression chosen because the apostles were not stationary ministers, each with his own parish or diocese, but were constantly travelling from place to place. *A sister*, i. e. a Christian woman. *A wife*, this determines the relation which this travelling companion sustained. It is as much as saying, 'A sister who is a wife.' Many of the Fathers explain this passage as referring to the custom of rich women attending the apostles on their journeys in order to minister to their support. In this interpretation they are followed by many Romanists in order to avoid the sanction which the ordinary and only legitimate interpretation gives to the marriage of the clergy. *As other apostles;* literally, "*the* other apostles." This does not necessarily imply that all the other apostles were married; but the implication is that as a body they were married men. Olshausen and others understand the apostle, in the vs. 4–6, as asserting his liberty as to three points; 1. As to meats, 'Have I not the same liberty that you claim as to eating and drinking?' 2. As to marriage, 'Have I not the right to marry?' 3. As to support. But this introduces more into the text than the connection warrants. There is no question about the right of marriage alluded to in the context; and what follows is a defence neither of his liberty to disregard the Jewish laws about meats and drinks, nor of his right to be married.

And the brethren of the Lord. Whether these were the children of Joseph and Mary, or the children of Mary, the sister of our Lord's mother, is a point very difficult to determine. Tradition, or the general voice of the church, is greatly in favour of the latter opinion. The former, however, is probably the opinion embraced by a majority of modern commentators. The discussion of this question belongs properly to the evangelical history.* The following passages may be compared on this subject: Matt. 1, 25. 12, 46. 13, 55. Luke

---

* The question is discussed by Neander, in his Planting of the Church, p. 554; by Winer, in Real Wörterbuch, under the head of Jacobus; by Prof. Schaf, who has devoted to it a volume; and by many other writers, ancient and modern.

2, 7. John 2, 12. Acts 1, 14. Gal. 1, 19. *And Cephas ;* this is the name by which Peter is called whenever he is mentioned by Paul, except in the epistle to the Galatians ; and Lachmann reads Cephas instead of Peter in Gal. 1, 18. 2, 9. 10. 14, leaving Gal. 2, 8. 9 the only exception. That Peter was married is clear from Matt. 8, 14. Mark 1, 30.

6. Or I only and Barnabas, have we not power to forbear working ?

The power to forbear working ; literally, *the right of not working.* 'Is there any reason why I and Barnabas should be the only exceptions to the rule that preachers of the word are to be supported by the churches?' From this it appears that Barnabas, while the apostle's missionary companion, followed his example in working with his own hands, that he might make the gospel of Christ without charge. Paul proceeds to demonstrate the right in question, not on grounds peculiar to the apostles or to that particular age of the church; but on grounds applicable to all ministers and to all ages. His first argument is from the universally recognized principle that labour is entitled to reward. This principle is illustrated in the following verse.

7. Who goeth a warfare any time at his own charges? who planteth a vineyard, and eateth not of the fruit thereof? or who feedeth a flock, and eateth not of the milk of the flock ?

Here are three illustrations, taken from the common occu pations of men, of the principle in question. The soldier, the agriculturist, the shepherd, all live by their labour ; why should not the minister? His work is as engrossing, as laborious, and as useful as theirs; why should not it meet with a similar recompense? *Who goeth to war,* i. e. who serves in war, as a soldier, *at his own charges* (ἰδίοις ὀψωνίοις), on his own rations. What soldier in war is called upon to support himself? If you force him to do it, you make him a robber ; and if ministers be required to support themselves, the danger is that they will be forced to become men of the world. It is not, however, the evil consequences, so much as the injustice of such a course, that the apostle has in view. What is true of the soldier is true of the farmer and of the shepherd, and of every other class of men.

8. Say I these things as a man ? or saith not the law the same also ?

Say I these things as a man ? This phrase (κατὰ ἄνθρωπον λαλεῖν), *to speak as a man,* or after the manner of men, means in general, to speak as men are wont to speak, to utter their thoughts, or principles, or to use illustrations derived from their customs. Rom. 3, 5. Gal. 3, 15. comp. Rom. 6, 19. The apostle means here to ask whether it was necessary to appeal to the usages of men in support of the principle that labour should be rewarded. *Does not the law also say the same ?* i. e. does not the word of God sanction the same principle ? *The law* (ὁ νόμος) means in general that which binds. It is applied to the law of God, however revealed, whether in the heart, the decalogue, the Pentateuch, or in the whole Scriptures. The context must determine the specific reference in each particular case. Here the law of Moses is intended.

9. For it is written in the law of Moses, Thou shalt not muzzle the mouth of the ox that treadeth out the corn. Doth God take care for oxen ?

For refers to the answer implied to the preceding question. 'Does not the law say the same ? It does : *for* it is written,' &c. The passage quoted is found in Deut. 25, 4, where it is forbidden to put a muzzle on the oxen which draw the threshing machine over the corn, or which tread it out with their feet ; as both methods of threshing were common in Palestine as well as the use of the flail or rods. Comp. Is. 28, 28. 41, 15. Hosea 10, 11. *Doth God take care of oxen ?* It is perfectly certain that God does care for oxen ; for he feeds the young ravens when they cry ; Job 38, 41. Ps. 147, 9. Matt. 6, 26. Luke 12, 24. This, therefore, the apostle cannot intend to deny. He only means to say that the law had a higher reference. Although the proximate end of the command was that the labouring brute should be treated justly, yet its ultimate design was to teach men the moral truth involved in the precept. If God requires that even the ox, which spends his strength in our service, should not be defrauded of his reward, how much more strict will he be in enforcing the application of the same principle of justice to his rational creatures.

10. Or saith he (it) altogether for our sakes? For our sakes, no doubt, (this) is written : that he that plougheth should plough in hope; and that he that thresheth in hope should be partaker of his hope.

"He sayeth it *altogether*." This is not the meaning here; for this would make the apostle assert that the command in question had exclusive reference to men. The word (πάντως) should be rendered *assuredly*, as in Luke 4, 43. Acts 18, 21. 21, 22, and frequently elsewhere. 'This command was as-suredly given, says the apostle, for *our sakes*,' i. e. for the sake of man—not, *for us ministers*, or *us apostles*. It was intended to enforce the principle that labour should have its reward, so that men may labour cheerfully. *That* (ὅτι); *because.* 'It is written on our account, *because* he that ploughs should (ὀφείλει, 2 Cor. 12, 11,) plough in hope,' i. e. of being rewarded. "And he that threshes should thresh in hope of partaking of his hope," i. e. of what he hoped for. The text is here doubtful. The reading preferred by most editors gives a simpler form to the passage *—'He that thresheth (should thresh) in hope of partaking,' (ἐπ' ἐλπίδι τοῦ μετέχειν). The sense is the same. Some of the ancient, and not a few of the most distinguished modern commentators assume that Paul gives an allegorical interpretation to the passage in Deuteronomy. They under-stand him to say that the passage is not to be understood of oxen, but of us, ministers. 'This command was given on ac-count of us ministers, that we ploughers might plough in hope, and we threshers might thresh in hope.' But this is entirely foreign from the manner of the New Testament writers. † They never argue except from the true historical sense of Scripture. Gal. 4, 21–31, is no exception to this remark; for that passage is an illustration and not an argument.

---

* The common text is τῆς ἐλπίδος αὐτοῦ μετέχειν ἐπ' ἐλπίδι. Griesbach, Lachmann, Scholz and Tischendorf all read ἐπ' ελιπίδι τοῦ μετέχειν, on the au-thority of the MSS. A. B. C.

† In reference to this mode of expounding the passage, Calvin says : Neque etiam quasi velit allegorice exponere praeceptum illud : quemadmodum non-nulli vertiginosi spiritus occasionem hinc arripiunt omnia ad allegorias trans-ferendi : ita ex canibus faciunt homines, ex arboribus angelos, et totam Scrip-turam ludendo pervertunt.

11. If we have sown unto you spiritual things, (is it) a great thing if we shall reap your carnal things?

That is, if we have bestowed on you one class of benefits, is it unreasonable that we should receive from you another class? And if the benefits which we bestow are *spiritual*, such as knowledge, faith and hope, the fruits of the Spirit, and therefore of infinite value, is it much that we should derive from you *carnal* things, i. e. things necessary for the support of the body? On every principle of commutative justice, the minister's right to a support must be conceded.

12. If others be partakers of (this) power over you, (are) not we rather? Nevertheless we have not used this power; but suffer all things, lest we should hinder the gospel of Christ.

This is an argument directed specially to the Corinthians. They had recognized in other teachers the right to a support; they could not, therefore, with any show of reason, deny it to the apostle. *This power over you* (τῆς ὑμῶν ἐξουσίας), i. e. the right of which you are the objects. For this use of the genitive, (*power of you*, for *power over you*), compare Matt. 10, 1. John 17, 2. Undisputable as this right was in the case of Paul, he did not exercise it, *but suffered all things*, i. e. endured all kinds of privations. The word means *to bear in silence*. *Lest we should hinder* (place any hinderance in the way of,) *the gospel of Christ*. Under the circumstances in which Paul was placed, surrounded by implacable enemies, it would have hindered the gospel had he done any thing which gave the least ground to question the purity of his motives. He was willing to suffer any thing rather than to give his opponents the slightest pretext for their opposition to him.

13. Do ye not know that they which minister about holy things live (of the things) of the temple? and they which wait at the altar are partakers with the altar?

What Paul here says is true of all religions, though his reference is probably only to the Jewish. *Those which minister about holy things* (οἱ τὰ ἱερὰ ἐργαζόμενοι); *those who perform the sacred services*, i. e. those who offer sacrifices. *Eat of the temple*, i. e. they derive their support from the temple. *Those attending the altar share with the altar*, i. e. the priests receive a portion of the sacrifices offered on the altar. If this was an institution ordained by God himself, under the old dispensation, it has the sanction of divine authority. The apostle's concluding and conclusive argument on this subject is contained in the following verse.

14. Even so hath the Lord ordained that they which preach the gospel should live of the gospel.

Even so (οὕτω καί), *so also*, i. e. as God had ordained under the Old Testament, *so also* the Lord (i. e. Christ) had ordained under the New. Christ has made the same ordinance respecting the ministers of the gospel, that God made respecting the priests of the law. *The Lord hath ordained that*, &c., (διέταξε τοῖς), *he commanded those who preach*, &c. It was a command to ministers themselves not to seek their support from secular occupations; but *to live of the gospel*, as the priests lived of the temple. Matt. 10, 10. Luke 10, 8. This is the law of Christ, obligatory on ministers and people; on the latter to give, and on the former to seek a support from the church and not from worldly avocations. There are circumstances under which, as the case of Paul shows, this command ceases to be binding on preachers. These are exceptions, to be justified, each on its own merits; the rule, as a rule, remains in force. If this subject were viewed in this light, both by preachers and people, there would be little difficulty in sustaining the gospel, and few ministers would be distracted by worldly pursuits.

15. But I have used none of these things: neither have I written these things, that it should be so done unto me: for (it were) better for me to die, than that any man should make my glorying void.

None of these things, may refer to the various arguments above mentioned. 'I have availed myself of none of these arguments;' or, it may refer to the right itself, which was manifold, the right of a recompense for labour, v. 7; the right to an equivalent for benefits conferred, v. 11; the right to be treated as other ministers were, v. 12; the right to be dealt with according to the law of God in the Old Testament, and of Christ in the New. 'I have used none of these rights. *Neither have I written these things that it should* (in future) *be so done* (i. e. according to what I have written) *unto me* (ἐν ἐμοί), in my case. Paul had no intention of changing his course in this matter. The reason for this determination he immediately assigns. *For it were better for me to die than that any man should make my glorying void,* that is, deprive me of my ground of glorying. What enabled Paul to face his enemies with joyful confidence, was his disinterested self-denial in preaching the gospel without reward. And this he calls his (καύχημα), or ground of boasting. That this, and not merely preaching the gospel, was the proof of his integrity to which he could confidently refer, he shows in the following verses.

16. For though I preach the gospel, I have nothing to glory of : for necessity is laid upon me ; yea, woe is unto me, if I preach not the gospel !

The reason why it was so important to him to refuse all remuneration as a minister was, that *although he preached the gospel* that was no (καύχημα), ground of boasting to him. That he was bound to do, yea, woe was denounced against him unless he did preach it. Nothing could be a ground of boasting, but something which he was free to do, or not to do. He was free to receive or to refuse a remuneration for preaching ; and therefore his refusing to do so was a ground of glorying, that is, a proof of integrity to which he could with confidence appeal.

17. For if I do this thing willingly, I have a reward : but if against my will, a dispensation (of the gospel) is committed unto me.

This is the proof that preaching was no ground of boasting. If he preached *willingly,* i. e. if it were optional with him to preach or not to preach, then it would be a ground of boasting ; but if he did it *unwillingly,* i. e. if it was not optional with him, (as was in fact the case), he was only discharging an official duty, and had nothing to boast of. That Paul preached the gospel willingly, that he esteemed it his highest

joy and glory, is abundantly evident from his history and
his writings. Rom. 1, 5. 11, 13. 15, 15. 16. 1 Cor. 15, 9.
10. Gal. 1, 15. 16. Eph. 3, 8. The difference, therefore, here
expressed between (ἑκών and ἄκων), *willing* and *unwilling*, is
not the difference between cheerfully and reluctantly, but between optional and obligatory. He says he had a dispensation
or stewardship (οἰκονομία) committed to him. These stewards
(οἰκονόμοι) were commonly slaves. There is a great difference
between what a slave does in obedience to a command, and
what a man volunteers to do of his own accord. And this is
the precise difference to which the apostle here refers. The
slave may feel honoured by the command of his master, and
obey him gladly, still it is but a service. So Paul was commanded to preach the gospel, and he did it with his whole
heart; but he was not commanded to refuse to receive a support from the churches. The former, therefore, was not a
ground of boasting, not a thing for which he could claim the
reward of special confidence; the latter was. He could appeal to it as a proof, not only of his obedience, but of the
purity of the motive which prompted that obedience. A phy-
sician may attend the sick from the highest motives, though
he receives a remuneration for his services. But when he attends the poor gratuitously, though the motives may be no
higher, the evidence of their purity is placed beyond question.
Paul's ground of glorying, therefore, was not preaching, for
that was a matter of obligation; but his preaching gratuitously, which was altogether optional. If, says he, my preaching
is optional, *I have a reward ;* not in the sense of merit in the
sight of God, but in the general sense of recompense. He
gained something by it. He gained the confidence even of
his enemies. But as preaching was not optional but obligatory, he did not gain confidence by it. Mere preaching, therefore, was not a (καύχημα) ground of boasting, but preaching
gratuitously was. *A dispensation of the gospel is committed
to me ;* in the Greek it is simply, ' *I am intrusted with a stewardship* (comp. Gal. 2, 7, i. e. an office), which I am bound to
discharge. I am in this matter a mere servant.' The principle on which the apostle's argument is founded is recognized
by our Lord, when he said, " When ye shall have done all
those things which are commanded you, say, We are unprofitable servants: we have done that which was our duty to do,"
Luke 17, 10.

18. What is my reward then? (Verily) that, when I preach the gospel, I may make the gospel of Christ without charge, that I abuse not my power in the gospel.

To do what he was commanded was no ground of reward; but to preach the gospel without charge was something of which he could boast, i. e. make a ground of confidence. *What then is my reward?* i. e. what constitutes my reward? in the sense explained; what gives me a ground of boasting? The answer follows, (ἵνα being used instead of the exegetical infinitive; comp. John 15, 8. 1 John 4, 17.) *that preaching I should make the gospel free of charge.* In other words, *that I should not use my right in the gospel.* In other words, Paul's reward was to sacrifice himself for others. He speaks of his being permitted to serve others gratuitously as a reward. And so it was, not only because it was an honour and happiness to be allowed to serve Christ in thus serving his people; but also because it secured him the confidence of those among whom he laboured by proving his disinterestedness. The common version, *that I abuse not,* although agreeable to the common meaning of καταχράομαι, is not consistent with the context, and is not demanded by the usage of the word; see 7, 31. It was not the abuse, but the use of his right to be supported, that the apostle had renounced.

19. For though I be free from all (men), yet have I made myself servant unto all, that I might gain the more.

The apostle's self-denial and accommodation of himself to the weakness and prejudices of others, was not confined to the point of which he had been speaking. He constantly acted upon the principle of abstaining in things indifferent, from insisting on his rights. *Though free from all,* i. e. independent of all men, and under no obligation to conform my conduct to their opinions, *I subjected myself to all.* In what way he did this, and to what extent, is explained by what follows. His motive in thus accommodating himself to others, was, *that he might gain the more,* or the greater number, the majority; comp. 10, 5. No one was more yielding in matters of indifference, no one was more unyielding in matters of principle that this apostle. So long as things indifferent were regarded as such, he was ready to accommodate himself to the most unreasonable prejudices; but when they were insisted upon as matters of necessity, he would not give place, no not for an hour, Gal. 2, 5.

20. And unto the Jews I became as a Jew, that I might gain the Jews; to them that are under the law, as under the law, that I might gain them that are under the law;

To the Jews he became as a Jew, i. e. he acted as they acted, he conformed to their usages, observed the law, avowing at the same time that he did it as a matter of accommodation. Wherever the fair inference from his compliance would have been that he regarded these Jewish observances as necessary, he strenuously refused compliance. His conduct in relation to Timothy and Titus, before referred to, shows the principle on which he acted. The former he circumcised, because it was regarded as a concession. The latter he refused to circumcise, because it was demanded as a matter of necessity. There are two things, therefore, to be carefully observed in all cases of concession to the opinions and practices of others: first, that the point conceded be a matter of indifference; for Paul never yielded in the smallest measure to any thing which was in itself wrong. In this his conduct was directly the opposite to that of those who accommodate themselves to the sins of men, or to the superstitious observances of false religions. And secondly, that the concession does not involve any admission that what is in fact indifferent is a matter of moral obligation. The extent to which Paul went to conciliate the Jews may be learnt from what is recorded in Acts 21, 18–27.

To those under the law. These were not converted Jews, because they were already gained to the gospel, and did not need to be won, which is the sense in which the expression *to gain* is used in this verse, as he had just spoken of gaining the Jews. Perhaps *those under the law*, as distinguished from Jews, were proselytes, i. e. Gentiles who had embraced Judaism. But most of these proselytes were not strictly *under the law*. They acknowledged Jehovah to be the only true God, but did not subject themselves to the Mosaic institutions. The common opinion is, that this clause is only explanatory of the

former, 'To the Jews, i. e. to those under the law, I became
as a Jew, i. e. as one under the law.'

"Not being myself under the law," μὴ ὢν αὐτὸς ὑπὸ νόμον.
This clause happened to be omitted from the Elziver edition
of the Greek Testament from which our translation was made,
and therefore fails in the common English version. It is
found, however, in all the more ancient manuscripts, in many
of the fathers and early versions, and is therefore adopted by
most modern editors. The internal evidence is also in its
favour. It was important for Paul to say that although acting
as under the law, he was not under it; because it was a fundamental principle of the gospel which he preached, that believers are freed from the law. "We are not under law, but
under grace," Rom. 6, 14. It was necessary, therefore, that
his compliance with the Jewish law should be recognized as a
matter of voluntary concession.

21. To them that are without law, as without law,
(being not without law to God, but under the law to
Christ,) that I might gain them that are without law.

Those without law were the heathen, who had no written
revelation as the rule of their conduct; comp. Rom. 2, 12.
As, however, the word (ἄνομος), *without law*, means also *reckless*, regardless of moral restraints, Paul is careful to explain
in what sense he acted as without law. When among the
Gentiles he did not conform to the Jewish law; in that sense,
he was without law; but he did not act as *without law to
God*, i. e. without regard to the obligation of the moral law;
but as *under law to Christ*, i. e. as recognizing his obligation
to obey Christ, whose will is the highest rule of duty. In
other words, he was not under the Jewish law; but he was
under the moral law. He disregarded the Jewish law that he
might gain those without law, i. e. the Gentiles. When in
Jerusalem, he conformed to the Jewish law; when in Antioch
he refused to do so, and rebuked Peter for acting as a Jew
among the Gentiles, Gal. 2, 11–21. It would have greatly im-
peded, if not entirely prevented, the progress of the gospel
among the heathen, had it been burdened with the whole
weight of the Jewish ceremonies and restrictions. Peter himself had told even the Jews that the Mosaic law was a yoke
which neither they nor their fathers had been able to bear,
Acts 15, 10. And Paul said to the Galatians, that he had re-

sisted the Judaizers, in order that the truth of the gospel
might remain with them, Gal. 2, 5.

**22. To the weak became I as weak, that I might
gain the weak : I am made all things to all (men), that
I might by all means save some.**

By *the weak* many understand the Jews and Gentiles considered under another aspect, i. e. as destitute of the power to
comprehend and appreciate the gospel. The only reason for
this interpretation is the assumption that *to gain* in this connection must mean to convert, or make Christians of, and
therefore, those to be gained must be those who were not
Christians. But the word means merely *to win over*, to bring
to proper views, and therefore may be used in reference to
weak and superstitious believers as well as of unconverted
Jews and Gentiles. As in the preceding chapter *the weak*
mean weak Christians, men who were not clear and decided
in their views, and as the very design of the whole discussion
was to induce the more enlightened Corinthian Christians to
accommodate themselves to those weaker brethren, it is altogether more natural to understand it in the same way here.
Paul holds himself up as an example. To the weak he became
as weak ; he accommodated himself to their prejudices that
he might win them over to better views. And he wished the
Corinthians to do the same. *I am made all things to all men.*
This generalizes all that had been said. It was not to this or
that class of men, that he was thus conciliatory, but to all
classes, and as to all matters of indifference ; that he might *at
all events* (πάντως) *save some.*

**23. And this I do for the gospel's sake, that I
might be partaker thereof with (you).**

This I do ; or, according to the reading now generally
adopted (πάντα instead of τοῦτο), *I do all things ;* ' my whole
course of action, not merely in thus accommodating myself to
the prejudices of others, but in every thing else, is regulated
for the promotion of the gospel.' This gives a better sense ;
for to say, *This I do*, would be only to repeat what is included
in the preceding verse. Paul lived for the gospel. He did all
things for it. *That I may be a joint-partaker thereof*, i. e. a
partaker with others ; not, *with you*, as there is nothing to

confine the statement to the Corinthians. To be a partaker of the gospel, means, of course, to be a partaker of its benefits; the subject of the redemption which it announces. It is necessary to live for the gospel, in order to be a partaker of the gospel.

24. Know ye not that they which run in a race run all, but one receiveth the prize ? So run, that ye may obtain.

An exhortation to self-denial and exertion, clothed in figurative language. As the exhortation is addressed principally to the Gentile converts, the imagery used is derived from the public games with which they were so familiar. These games, the Olympian and Isthmian, the latter celebrated every third summer in the neighbourhood of Corinth, were the occasions for the concourse of the people from all parts of Greece. The contests in them excited the greatest emulation in all classes of the inhabitants. Even the Roman emperors did not refuse to enter the lists. To be a victor was to be immortalized with such immortality as the breath of man can give. To Greeks, therefore, no allusions could be more intelligible, or more effective, than those to these institutions, which have nothing to answer to them in modern times.

Know ye not. He took for granted they were familiar with the rules of the games to which he referred. *That those running in a race ;* literally in the *stadium* or *circus* in which the games were celebrated, so called because it was a *stadium* (a little more than two hundred yards) in length. *All run, but one obtains the prize.* It was not enough to start in this race; it was not enough to persevere almost to the end; it was necessary to outrun all competitors and be first at the goal. But one took the prize. *So run that ye may obtain.* That is, run as that one runs, *in order that* ye may obtain. The greatest self-denial in preparation, and the greatest effort in the contest, were necessary to success. In the Christian race there are many victors; but the point of the exhortation is, that all should run as the one victor ran in the Grecian games.

25. And every man that striveth for the mastery is temperate in all things. Now they (do it) to obtain a corruptible crown ; but we an incorruptible.

Every one who striveth, &c. (πᾶς ὁ ἀγωνιζόμενος) *every one accustomed to contend,* i. e. every professional athlete. The word includes all kinds of contests, whether in running, wrestling or fighting. *Is temperate in all things,* i. e. controls himself as to all things. He exercises self-denial in diet, in bodily indulgences, and by painful and protracted discipline. The ancient writers abound in rules of abstinence and exercise, to be observed by competitors in preparation for the games. *They indeed for a corruptible crown, we for an incorruptible.* If the heathen submitted to such severe discipline to gain a wreath of olive or garland of pine leaves, shall not Christians do as much for a crown of righteousness which fadeth not away ?

26. I therefore so run, not as uncertainly; so fight I, not as one that beateth the air :

I therefore, i. e. because so much effort is necessary to success. *So run,* i. e. run not in such a manner as one who runs *uncertainly* (ἀδήλως). That may mean *unconspicuously,* not as one unseen, but as one on whom all eyes are fixed. Or more probably the idea is, not as one runs who is uncertain where or for what he is running. A man who runs uncertain as to his course or object, runs without spirit or effort. *So fight I.* The allusion is here to boxing, or fighting with the fist. *Not as one beating the air.* Here again the figure is doubtful. A man who is merely exercising, without an antagonist, may be said to smite the air. A man puts forth little strength in such a sham conflict. Or the man who aims at his antagonist, and fails to hit him, smites the air. This is the better explanation. VIRGIL has the same figure to express the same idea. He says of a boxer who missed his antagonist, " vires in ventum effudit." Æn. v. 446. In either way the meaning is the same. Nothing is accomplished. The effort is in vain. In 14, 9, the apostle says of those who speak in an unknown tongue, that they *speak into the air.* That is, they speak to no effect.

27. But I keep under my body, and bring (it) into subjection: lest that by any means, when I have preached to others, I myself should be a cast-away.

In opposition to the fruitless or objectless fighting just described, Paul says, *I keep under my body;* literally *I bruise my body.* (ὑπωπιάζω, *to smite under the eye, to bruise, to smite,* Luke 18, 5.) His antagonist was his body, which he so smote, i. e. so dealt with, as *to bring it into subjection ;* literally, *to lead about as a slave.* Perhaps in reference to the custom of the victor leading about his conquered antagonist as a servant; though this is doubtful. The body, as in part the seat and organ of sin, is used for our whole sinful nature. Rom. 8, 13. It was not merely his sensual nature that Paul endeavoured to bring into subjection, but all the evil propensities and passions of his heart. *Lest having preached to others* (κηρύξας). Perhaps the apostle means to adhere to the figure and say, ' Lest having acted the part of a herald, (whose office at the Grecian games was to proclaim the rules of the contest and to summon the competitors or combatants to the lists,) he himself should be judged unworthy of the prize.' As, however, the word is so often used for *preaching the gospel,* he may intend to drop the figure and say, ' He made these strenuous exertions, lest, having preached the gospel to others, he himself should become (ἀδόκιμος) a reprobate, one rejected.' What an argument and what a reproof is this ! The reckless and listless Corinthians thought they could safely indulge themselves to the very verge of sin, while this devoted apostle considered himself as engaged in a life-struggle for his salvation. This same apostle, however, who evidently acted on the principle that the righteous scarcely are saved, and that the kingdom of heaven suffereth violence, at other times breaks out in the most joyful assurance of salvation, and says that he was persuaded that nothing in heaven, earth or hell could ever separate him from the love of God. Rom. 8, 38. 39. The one state of mind is the necessary condition of the other. It is only those who are conscious of this constant and deadly struggle with sin, to whom this assurance is given. In the very same breath Paul says, " O wretched man that I am ; " and, " Thanks be to God who giveth us the victory," Rom. 7, 24. 25. It is the indolent and self-indulgent Christian who is always in doubt.

CHAPTER X.

A continuation of the exhortation to self-denial and caution, vs. 1–13. Express prohibition of joining in the sacrificial feasts of the heathen, vs. 14–22. Particular directions as to the use of meat sacrificed to idols, vs. 23–33.

The necessity of self-denial argued from the case of the Israelites. Vs. 1–13.

At the close of the preceding chapter the apostle had exhorted his readers to self-denial and effort, in order to secure the crown of life. He here enforces that exhortation, by showing how disastrous had been the want of such self-control in the case of the Israelites. They had been highly favoured as well as we. They had been miraculously guided by the pillar of cloud; they had been led through the Red Sea; they had been fed with manna from heaven, and with water from the rock; and yet the great majority of them perished, vs. 1–5. This is a solemn warning to Christians not to give way to temptation, as the Israelites did, v. 6. That is, not to be led into idolatry, v. 7, nor into fornication, v. 8, nor into tempting Christ, v. 9, nor into murmuring, v. 10. In all these points the experience of the Israelites was a warning to Christians; and therefore those who thought themselves secure should take heed lest they fall, vs. 11. 12. God is merciful, and would not suffer them to be too severely tempted, v. 13.

1. Moreover, brethren, I would not that ye should be ignorant, how that all our fathers were under the cloud, and all passed through the sea;

Moreover. The true reading is not (δέ) *moreover*, but (γάρ) *for*, which marks the connection with what precedes. 'We must use self-denial and effort; *for*, brethren, our fathers, notwithstanding all they experienced, perished.' *I would not have you ignorant*, Rom. 1, 10. 11, 25, a formula used when something specially important is to be presented. *That* (not *how that*). *All our fathers.* The emphasis is on *all*. 'All our fathers left Egypt; Caleb and Joshua alone entered the promised land.' All run, but one obtains the prize. The history of the church affords no incident better suited to enforce the necessity of guarding against false security, than that selected by the apostle. The Israelites doubtless felt, as they stood on the other side of the Red Sea, that all danger was over, and that their entrance into the land of promise was secured. They had however a journey beset with dangers before them, and perished because they thought there was no need of exertion. So the Corinthians, when brought to the knowledge of the gospel, thought heaven secure. Paul reminds them that they had only entered on the way, and would certainly perish unless they exercised constant self-denial. *Our fathers.* Abraham is our father, though we are not his natural descendants. And the Israelites were the fathers of the Corinthian Christians, although most of them were Gentiles. Although this is true, it is probable that the apostle, although writing to a church, many, if not most, of whose members were of heathen origin, speaks as a Jew to Jews; as he often addresses a congregation as a whole, when what he says has reference only to a part.

Were under the cloud, not underneath it, but under its guidance. Ex. 13, 21. "The Lord went before them by day in a pillar of cloud, to lead them; and by night in a pillar of fire to give them light, to go by day and night." See Num. 9, 15. 23. 14, 14. Deut. 1, 33. Ps. 78, 14. &c. No more decisive evidence could have been given of their election as a people, than this supernatural guidance. The symbol of the divine presence and favour was before their eyes day and night. If any people ever had reason to think their salvation secure, it was those whom God thus wonderfully guided. *They all passed through the sea.* Would God permit those to perish for whom he had wrought so signal a deliverance, and for whose sake he sacrificed the hosts of Egypt? Yet their carcasses were strewed in the wilderness. It is not enough, therefore, to be recipients of extraordinary favours; it is not enough to begin well. It is only by constant self-denial and vigilance, that the promised reward can be obtained. This is the lesson the apostle intends to inculcate.

2. And were all baptized * unto Moses in the cloud and in the sea;

Baptized unto Moses, i. e. in reference to Moses, so as by

* The MSS. A. C. D. E. F. G. all read ἐβαπτίσθησαν, *were baptized*, instead of ἐβαπτίσαντο, *allowed themselves to be baptized;* and yet the majority of editors prefer the latter reading as the more difficult.

baptism to be made his disciples. See 1, 13. Rom. 6, 3. *In the cloud and in the sea.* The cloud and the sea did for them, in reference to Moses, what baptism does for us in reference to Christ. Their passage through the sea, and their guidance by the cloud, was their baptism. It made them the disciples of Moses; placed them under obligation to recognize his divine commission and to submit to his authority. This is the only point of analogy between the cases, and it is all the apostle's argument requires. One class of commentators says that they were immersed in the sea, and therefore it was a baptism; another says, the cloud rained upon them, and on that account they are said to have been baptized. Both suggestions are equally forced. For the people were baptized as much in the cloud as in the sea; but they were not immersed in the cloud nor sprinkled by the sea. There is no allusion to the mode of baptism. Neither is the point of analogy to be sought in the fact, that the cloud was vapour and the sea water. The cloud by night was fire. The point of similarity is to be found, not in any thing external, but in the effect produced. The display of God's power in the cloud and in the sea, brought the people into the relation of disciples to Moses. It inaugurated the congregation, and, as it were, baptized them to him, bound them to serve and follow him.

3. And did all eat the same spiritual meat;

As they had their baptism, so they had their eucharist; and they all had it. They all eat *the same* spiritual meat. They were all alike favoured, and had therefore equal grounds of hope. Yet how few of them reached the promised rest!

The reference is here obviously to the manna, which the apostle calls spiritual meat. Why it is so called is very doubtful. 1. The word *spiritual* may mean, partaking of the nature of spirit, a sense attributed to the word in 15, 44, where, "spiritual body" is assumed to mean a refined, aetherial body. The manna, according to this view, is called spiritual meat, because it was a refined kind of food; much in the way in which we use the word *celestial* as an epithet of excellence. This interpretation derives some support from Ps. 78, 25, where the manna is called "angels' food." By Josephus, *A.* III. 1, 6, it is called, "divine and wonderful food." 2. A second interpretation assumes that *spiritual* means having a spiritual import. "Spiritual meat" would then be equivalent to *typical.* 'They eat of that bread which was the type of the true bread from heaven.' Neither of these views, however, is consistent with the scriptural use of the word. *Spiritual* neither means refined nor typical. In 15, 44, " spiritual body " means a body adapted to the spirit as its organ. 3. Others give the word here its very common sense, *pertaining to the spirit ;* as, in the preceding chapter, " carnal things " are things pertaining to the body, and " spiritual things " are things pertaining to the soul. The manna, according to this interpretation, was designed not only for the body, but for the soul. It was spiritual food; food intended for the spirit, because attended by the Holy Spirit and made the means of spiritual nourishment. This is a very commonly received interpretation. Calvin assumes it to be the only possible meaning of the passage, and founds on it an argument for his favourite doctrine, that the sacraments of the Old Testament had the same efficacy as those of the New. But this exalts the manna into a sacrament, which it was not. It was designed for ordinary food; as Nehemiah (9, 15) says, " Thou gavest them bread from heaven for their hunger, and broughtest forth for them water out of the rock for their thirst." And our Lord represents it in the same light, when he said, " Your fathers did eat manna in the wilderness and are dead." John 6, 49. He contrasts himself, as the true bread from heaven which gives life to the soul, with the manna which had no spiritual efficacy. 4. One of the most common meanings of the word *spiritual* in Scripture is, *derived from the Spirit*. Spiritual gifts and spiritual blessings are gifts and blessings of which the Spirit is the author. Every thing which God does in nature and in grace, he does by the Spirit. He garnished the heavens by the Spirit; and the Spirit renews the face of the earth. When therefore it is said, God gave them bread from heaven to eat, it means that the Spirit gave it; for God gave it through the Spirit. Thus God is said to renew and sanctify men, because the Spirit of God is the author of regeneration and sanctification. The manna therefore was spiritual food, in the same sense in which the special gifts of God are called spiritual gifts. That is, it was given by the Spirit. It was not natural food, but food miraculously provided. In the same sense, in the next verse, the water is called *spiritual drink*, because miraculously produced. In Gal. 4, 29, the natural birth of Isaac is said to have been *after the Spirit*, because due to the special intervention of God. As the miraculous deliverance and miraculous guidance of the Israelites was their baptism, so their being miraculously fed was their Lord's Supper. They were as signal marks of the divine presence and favour as sacraments are to us. If their privileges did not prevent their perishing in the wilderness, ours will not save us. If the want of self-denial and vigilance destroyed them, it will destroy us.

4. And did all drink the same spiritual drink ; for they drank of that spiritual Rock that followed them : and that Rock was Christ.

The water which they drank was *spiritual*, because derived from the Spirit, i. e. by the special intervention of God. They all drank (ἔπιον) of it once when first provided, and they continued to drink (ἔπινον) of it, for it followed them. Whatever difficulties may be connected with the interpretation of this verse, two things are therein plainly taught. First, that the Israelites were constantly supplied in a miraculous manner with water; and secondly, that the source of that supply was Christ. The principal difficulties in the passage are, the declaration that the rock followed the Israelites; and that the rock was Christ. How are these statements to be understood? 1. Some take the passage literally, and assume that the rock smitten by Moses actually rolled after the Israelites during all their journey. Such was the tradition of the Jews, as is abundantly proved by the quotations from their writings, by Wetstein, Schoettgen and Lightfoot.* According to the local tradition, as old at least as the Koran, the rock smitten by Moses was not part of the mountain, but a detached rock, pierced with holes whence the water is said to have flowed. This view of the passage makes the apostle responsible for a Jewish fable, and is inconsistent with his divine authority. Those who adopt this interpretation do not suppose that the rock actually followed the Israelites, but that the apostle was misled by the tradition of his times. 2. Others say that by the rock following them is meant that the water out of the rock followed them. There is nothing unnatural in this. To say that the vines of France follow the people wherever they go, would be no violent figure to express the fact that the wine produced by those vines followed them. No man at least would be disposed to understand the expression literally.

---

* Fuit (ille puteus Num. 21, 16) sicut petra, sicut alveus apum et globosus, et volutavit, &c., et ivit cum ipsis in itineribus ipsorum. *Bammidhbar* R. S. 1.

In Ps. 105, 41, it is said, "He opened the rock, and the waters gushed out ; they ran in dry places like a river," which at least proves that the supply of water was very copious, and flowed to a considerable distance. 3. It is not necessary, however, to assume that either the rock or the water out of the rock followed them. The rock that followed them was Christ. The Logos, the manifested Jehovah, who attended the Israelites in their journey, was the Son of God who assumed our nature, and was the Christ. It was he who supplied their wants. He was to them the fountain of living waters. He was the *spiritual* rock of which they drank. The word *spiritual* may have the same general force here as in the preceding clauses. The bread and water are called spiritual because supernatural. So the rock was a supernatural rock, though in a somewhat different sense. The manna was supernatural as to its origin ; the rock, as to its nature. It is not uncommon for a word to be taken in the same connection in different, though nearly allied senses. Compare the use of this word *spiritual* in 2, 15 and 3, 1 ; and φθείρει and φθερεῖ in 3, 17. But in what sense was the rock Christ? Not that Christ appeared under the form of a rock ; nor that the rock was a type of Christ, for that does not suit the connection. The idea is not that they drank of the typical rock ; it was not the type but the antitype that supplied their wants. The expression is simply figurative. Christ was the rock in the same sense that he is the vine. He was the source of all the support which the Israelites enjoyed during their journey in the wilderness.

This passage distinctly asserts not only the preëxistence of our Lord, but also that he was the Jehovah of the Old Testament. He who appeared to Moses and announced himself as Jehovah, the God of Abraham, who commissioned him to go to Pharaoh, who delivered the people out of Egypt, who appeared on Horeb, who led the people through the wilderness, who dwelt in the temple, who manifested himself to Isaiah, who was to appear personally in the fulness of time, is the person who was born of a virgin, and manifested himself in the flesh. He is called, therefore, in the Old Testament, an angel, the angel of Jehovah, Jehovah, the Supreme Lord, the Mighty God, the Son of God—one whom God sent—one with him, therefore, as to substance, but a distinct person. Our Lord said, Abraham saw his day, for he was before Abraham, John 8, 58 ; John says, 12, 41, Isaiah beheld his glory in the temple ; Paul says, the Israelites tempted him in the wilder-

ness, 1 Cor. 10, 9, and that Moses suffered his reproach, Heb.
11, 26 ; Jude 5. says, the Lord, or (as Lachmann, after the ancient MSS. and versions, reads) Jesus, saved his people out of
Egypt. This truth early impressed itself on the mind of the
Christian church, as appears from the prayer in the ancient
Liturgies, O Adonai (Supreme Lord), et Dux Domûs Israel,
qui Mosi in igne flammeo rubi apparuisti, et ei in Sina aquam
dedisti, veni ad redimendum nos in brachio extracto.

**5. But with many of them God was not well
pleased : for they were overthrown in the wilderness.**

But, i. e. *notwithstanding* they had been thus highly favoured. *With many ;* literally, with the greater number.
God was not well pleased, that is, he was displeased. The
proof of his displeasure was that they *were overthrown* in the
wilderness. Literally, *they were strewed* as corpses *in the wilderness*. Their path through the desert could be traced by
the bones of those who perished through the judgments
of God.

**6. Now these things were our examples, to the in-
tent we should not lust after evil things, as they also
lusted.**

These things were our examples ; literally, *our types*. A
type is an impression; any thing produced by blows; then an
impression which has a resemblance to something else ; then
a model to which some other person or thing should be, or in
point of fact would be, conformed. The Israelites and the
facts of their history were our types, because we shall be conformed to them if we do not exercise caution. Our doom will
correspond to theirs. They therefore stand as warnings to us.
The particular thing against which their fate was designed to
warn us, is lusting after evil. According to Num. 11, 4, the
people lusted after, i. e. they inordinately longed for, the flesh-
pots of Egypt, and said, Who shall give us flesh to eat ? God
gave them their desire—" but while the flesh was yet between
their teeth, he smote them with a great plague, and the place
was called the ' graves of lust,' for there they buried the people that lusted," Num. 11, 34. Comp. Ps. 78, 27–31, and 105,
14. 15. This was a perpetual warning against the indulgence
of inordinate desires for forbidden objects. It was specially

appropriate as a warning to the Corinthians not to desire participation in the sacrificial feasts of the heathen in which they had been accustomed to indulge.

7. Neither be ye idolaters, as (were) some of them; as it is written, The people sat down to eat and drink, and rose up to play.

The Corinthians were as much exposed to temptation on this subject as the Israelites had been, and were quite as liable to fall into idolatrous practices. The Israelites did not consider themselves as idolaters when they made the golden calf; they did not believe that the second commandment forbade the worship of the true God by images, and it was Jehovah whom they designed to worship. The feast was proclaimed as a feast to Jehovah, Ex. 32, 6. They made the same excuse for the use of images as the Romanists now do; and the same in effect as that which the Corinthians made for their compliance with heathen usages. The latter did not consider the participation of the feasts in the idol's temple as an act of idolatry. As the Israelites perished for their sin, their excuse notwithstanding, so those who are in fact idolaters, whether they so regard themselves or not, must expect a like fate. It is not enough to make a thing right, that we think it to be so. Things do not change their nature according to our thoughts about them. Murder is murder, though man in his self-conceit and pride may call it justifiable homicide.

They sat down to eat and to drink, i. e. of the sacrifices offered to Jehovah in the presence of the golden calf, as a symbol of creative power—and rose up *to play*, i. e. to dance, as that amusement was, among the ancients, connected with their religious feasts. Homer, Od. 8, 251.

8. Neither let us commit fornication, as some of them committed, and fell in one day three and twenty thousand.

Idolatry and fornication have always been so intimately connected that the former seldom fails to lead to the latter. This was illustrated in the case of the Israelites. Num. 25, 1–9, " And the people began to commit whoredom with the daughters of Moab; and they called the people unto the sacrifices of their gods. . . . And Israel joined himself unto Baal-peor." This was a god of the Moabites, who was worshipped by the prostitution of virgins. Idolatry and fornication were in that case inseparable. In Corinth the principal temple was dedicated to Venus, and the homage paid to her was almost as corrupt as that rendered to Baal-peor. How could the Corinthians escape this evil if they allowed themselves to attend the sacrificial feasts within her temple—under the pretence that an idol is nothing?

And were slain in one day three and twenty thousand. In the Hebrew Scriptures, the Septuagint, by Philo, Josephus and the Rabbis, the number is given as twenty-four thousand. Both statements are equally correct. Nothing depended on the precise number. Any number between the two amounts may, according to common usage, be stated roundly as either the one or the other. The infallibility of the sacred writers consists in their saying precisely what the Spirit of God designed they should say; and the Spirit designed that they should speak after the manner of men—and call the heavens solid and the earth flat, and use round numbers, without intending to be mathematically exact in common speech. The Bible, although perfectly divine, because the product of the Spirit of God, is perfectly human. The sacred writers spoke and wrote precisely as other men in their circumstances would have spoken and written, and yet under such an influence as to make every thing they said correspond infallibly with the mind of the Spirit. When the hand of a master touches the organ we have one sound, and when he touches the harp we have another. So when the Spirit of God inspired Isaiah we had one strain, and when he inspired Amos, another. Moses and Paul were accustomed, like most other men, to use round numbers; and they used them when under the influence of inspiration just as they used other familiar forms of statement. Neither intended to speak with numerical exactness, which the occasion did not require. What a wonderful book is the Bible, written at intervals during a period of fifteen hundred years, when such apparitions of inaccuracy as this must be seized upon to impeach its infallibility!

9. Neither let us tempt Christ,* as some of them also tempted, and were destroyed of serpents.

---

* Instead of Χριστόν, the MSS. B. C., and the Coptic and Ethiopic versions read κύριον. The MS. A. has θεόν. The common text is sustained by the MSS. D. E. F. G. H. I. K., by the Syriac, Vulgate, the old Latin and Sahidic ver-

To tempt is to try, either in the sense of *attempting*, or of putting to the test, with a good or evil intent. God is said to tempt his people, when he puts their faith and patience to the test for the sake of exercising and strengthening those graces, Heb. 11, 17. Satan and evil men are said to tempt others, when they put their virtue to the test with the design of seducing them into sin, Gal. 6, 1. James 1, 3. Matt. 4, 1, &c. Men are said to tempt God when they put his patience, fidelity or power to the test. Acts 5, 9. Matt. 4, 7. Heb. 3, 9. It was thus the Israelites tempted him in the wilderness. They tried his forbearance, they provoked him. The exhortation is that we should not thus *tempt Christ*. This supposes that Christ has authority over us, that he is our moral governor to whom we are responsible, and who has the power to punish those who incur his displeasure. In other words, the passage assumes that we stand in the relation to Christ which rational creatures can sustain to God alone. Christ, therefore, is God. Whether the Corinthians are warned against tempting Christ by their impatience and discontent, as the Israelites did in the particular case here referred to ; or whether they are cautioned against putting his fidelity to the test by running unnecessarily into danger (see Matt. 4, 7), is uncertain. Probably the former.

As some of them also tempted. As Christ is mentioned in the immediate context, it is most natural to supply the pronoun *him*. 'Let us not tempt Christ, as they tempted *him*.' This is not only the most natural explanation, but it is sustained by a reference to v. 4, and by the analogy of Scripture, as the Bible elsewhere teaches that the leader of the Israelites was the Son of God. It is only on theological grounds, that is, to get rid of the authority of the passage as a proof of our Lord's divinity, that others interpret the passage thus, 'Let us not tempt Christ, as they tempted God.' It is only one form of the argument, however, which is thus met. For according to this view the passage still teaches that we sustain the relation to Christ which the Israelites sustained to God. *And were destroyed of serpents.* Num. 21, 6. The people provoked God by their complaints and by their regretting their deliverance out of Egypt. " And the Lord sent fiery serpents

---

sions, and by Chrysostom and other Fathers. It is retained, therefore, by the majority of editors. As the more difficult reading it is the more likely to be the original one. The temptation was strong to change χριστόν into κύριον, but no one would be disposed to put the former word for the latter.

among the people, and they bit the people; and much people of Israel died." Similar judgments awaited the Corinthians if they exhausted the forbearance of the Lord.

10. Neither murmur ye, as some of them also murmured, and were destroyed of the destroyer.

To murmur is to complain in a rebellious spirit. The reference is to Num. 14, 2, "And all the children of Israel murmured against Moses and against Aaron: and the whole congregation said unto them, Would God we had died in the land of Egypt! or would God we had died in the wilderness." Vs. 11. 12, "And the Lord said unto Moses, How long will this people provoke me? and how long will it be ere they believe me for all the signs which I have shown among them? I will smite them with the pestilence, &c." V. 27, "How long shall I bear with this evil congregation which murmur against me? ... Their carcasses shall fall in the wilderness." Or the reference is to Num. 16, in which the rebellion of Korah is related, and the subsequent murmuring of the people, v. 41, in consequence of which fourteen thousand and seven hundred were destroyed by a plague, v. 49. In both cases the offence and punishment were the same. *Were destroyed of the destroyer*, i. e. by an angel commissioned by God to use the pestilence as an instrument of destruction. Hence sometimes the destruction is referred to the pestilence, as in Num. 14, 14; sometimes to the angel, as here; and sometimes both the agent and the instrument are combined, as in 2 Sam. 24, 16. See Acts 12, 23.

11. Now all these things happened unto them for ensamples: and they are written for our admonition, upon whom the ends of the world are come.

All these happened (i. e. continued to happen) *to them for ensamples*. Literally, they were *types*, see v. 6. They were intended as historical pictures, to represent, as Calvin says, the effects of idolatry, fornication, murmuring, &c. *And they are written*, &c. They were recorded that we might have the benefit of these dispensations, so that we might be admonished to avoid the sins which brought such judgments upon them. *Upon whom the ends of the world* (literally, *of the ages*) *are come*. That is, upon us who live during the last ages. Duration is sometimes conceived of as one, and is therefore expressed by the singular αἰών; sometimes as made up of distinct periods, and is then expressed by the plural αἰῶνες. Hence we have the expressions συντέλεια τοῦ αἰῶνος, and τῶν αἰώνων, Matt. 24, 3. Heb. 9, 26, both signifying the completion of a given portion of duration, considered either as one or as made up of several periods. Sometimes these expressions refer to the close of the Jewish dispensation, and indicate the time of Christ's first coming; sometimes they refer to the close of the present dispensation, and indicate the time of his second advent. Matt. 13, 39, &c. See Eph. 1, 10, and Heb. 1, 1, for equivalent forms of expression. As in Heb. 9, 26, *the completion of the ages* means the end of the Jewish dispensation, so *the ends of the ages* may have the same meaning here. Or what, in this case, may be more natural, the meaning is that we are living during the last of those periods which are allotted to the duration of the world, or of the present order of things. One series of ages terminated with the coming of Christ; another, which is the last, is now passing.

12. Wherefore let him that thinketh he standeth, take heed lest he fall.

This indicates the design of the apostle in referring to the events above indicated in the history of the Israelites. There is perpetual danger of falling. No degree of progress we may have already made, no amount of privileges which we may have enjoyed, can justify the want of caution. *Let him that thinketh he standeth*, that is, let him who thinks himself secure. This may refer either to security of salvation, or against the power of temptation. The two are very different, and rest generally on different grounds. False security of salvation commonly rests on the ground of our belonging to a privileged body (the church), or to a privileged class (the elect). Both are equally fallacious. Neither the members of the church nor the elect can be saved unless they persevere in holiness; and they cannot persevere in holiness without continual watchfulness and effort. False security as to our power to resist temptation rests on an overweening self-confidence in our own strength. None are so liable to fall as they who, thinking themselves strong, heedlessly run into temptation. This probably is the kind of false security against which the apostle warns the Corinthians, as he exhorts them immediately after to avoid temptation.

13. There hath no temptation taken you but such
as is common to man: but God (is) faithful, who will
not suffer you to be tempted above that ye are able;
but will with the temptation also make a way to escape,
that ye may be able to bear (it).

No temptation, i. e. no trial, whether in the form of seductions or of afflictions, *has taken you but such as is common to
man;* literally *human*, accommodated to human strength,
such as men are able to bear. 'You have been subjected to
no superhuman or extraordinary temptations. Your trials
hitherto have been moderate; and God will not suffer you to
be unduly tried.' This is the ordinary interpretation of this
passage, and one which gives a simple and natural sense. It
may, however, mean, 'Take heed lest ye fall. The temptations which you have hitherto experienced are moderate compared to those to which you are hereafter to be subjected.'
In this view, it is not so much an encouragement, as a warning
that all danger was not over. The apostle is supposed to refer to those peculiar trials which were to attend "the last
times." As these times were at hand, the Corinthians were in
circumstances which demanded peculiar care. They should
not run into temptation, for the days were approaching when,
if it were possible, even the elect would be deceived. As,
however, there is no contrast between the present and the future intimated in the passage, the common interpretation is
the more natural one.

But God is faithful. He has promised to preserve his
people, and therefore his fidelity is concerned in not allowing
them to be unduly tempted. Here, as in 1, 9, and every where
else in Scripture, the security of believers is referred neither
to the strength of the principle of grace infused into them by
regeneration, nor to their own firmness, but to the fidelity of
God. He has promised that those given to the Son as his inheritance, should never perish. They are kept, therefore, by
the power of God, through faith, unto salvation, 1 Peter 1, 4.
This promise of security, however, is a promise of security
from sin, and therefore those who fall into wilful and habitual
sin are not the subjects of the promise. Should they fall, it is
after a severe struggle, and they are soon renewed again unto
repentance. The absolute security of believers, and the necessity of constant watchfulness, are perfectly consistent.

Those whom God has promised to save, he has promised to render watchful. *Who will not suffer you to be tempted above that you are able*, i. e. able to bear. This is the proof of his fidelity. *But will with the temptation make a way of escape.* This means either, that when the temptation comes, God will make a way of escape; or, that when God brings the temptation he will also bring the way of escape. In the latter sense God is regarded as the author of the temptation, in the former he is not. The latter is to be preferred on account of the σύν, *with.* 'He will make *with* the temptation a way of escape,' i. e. he makes the one, he will make the other. The apostle James indeed says, "God cannot be tempted with evil, neither tempteth he any man," James 1, 3. *To tempt* there, however, means to solicit, or attempt to seduce into sin. In that sense God tempts no man. But he does often put their virtue to the test, as in the case of Abraham. And in that sense he tempts or tries them. What the apostle here says is, that when God thus tries his people it will not be beyond their strength, and that he will always make a way of escape *that they may be able to bear it.* This expresses the design of God in making a way of escape. (The genitive τοῦ δύνασθαι, &c., is the genitive of design).

Proof that attendance on sacrificial feasts in a heathen temple is idolatry. Vs. 14–22.

This whole discussion arose out of the question whether it was lawful to eat the sacrifices offered to idols. Paul, while admitting that there was nothing wrong in eating of such meat, exhorts the Corinthians to abstain for the sake of their weaker brethren. There was another reason for this abstinence; they might be led into idolatry. By going to the verge of the allowable, they might be drawn into the sinful. There was great danger that the Corinthians, convinced that an idol was nothing, might be induced to join the sacrificial feasts within the precincts of the temples. The danger was the greater, because such feasts, if held in a private house, lost their religious character, and might be attended without scruple. To convince his readers, that if the feast was held in a temple, attendance upon it was an act of idolatry, is the object of this section. The apostle's argument is from analogy. Attendance on the Lord's Supper is an act of communion with Christ, the object of Christian worship, and with all those who unite with us in the service. From its very nature, it brings all who partake of the bread and wine into fellowship with Christ and with one another, vs. 14–17. The same is true of Jewish sacrifices. Whoever eats of those sacrifices, is thereby brought into communion with the object of Jewish worship. The act is in its nature an act of worship, v. 18. The conclusion is too plain to need being stated—those who join in the sacrificial feasts of the heathen, join in the worship of idols. Such is the import of the act, and no denial on the part of those who perform it can alter its nature. It is not to be inferred from this mode of reasoning, that the objects of heathen worship are what the heathen suppose them to be. Because Paul argued that, as partaking of the Lord's Supper is an act of Christian worship, partaking of an idol-feast must be an act of heathen worship, it is not to be inferred that he regarded Jupiter or Juno as much real beings as Christ is. Far from it. What the heathen sacrifice, they sacrifice to demons; and therefore, to partake of their sacrifices under circumstances which gave religious significance to the act, brought them into communion with demons, vs. 19. 20. The two things are incompatible. A man cannot be a worshipper of Christ and a worshipper of demons, or in communion with the one while in communion with the other. Going to the Lord's table is a renunciation of demons; and going to the table of demons is a renunciation of Christ, v. 21. By this conduct the jealousy of the Lord would be excited against them, as of old it was excited against the Jews who turned aside after false gods, v. 22.

14. Wherefore, my dearly beloved, flee from idolatry.

Wherefore, i. e. because such severe judgments came upon the idolatrous Israelites; because you, as well as they, are in danger of being involved in that sin; and because your distinguished privileges can protect you neither from the sin nor from its punishment any more than their privileges protected them. *My dearly beloved.* Paul addresses them in terms of affection, although his epistle is so full of serious admonition and warning. *Flee from idolatry*, i. e. avoid it by fleeing from it. This is the only safe method of avoiding sin. Its presence is malarious. The only safety is keeping at a distance. This includes two things; first, avoiding what is ques-

tionable; that is, every thing which lies upon the border of
what is allowable, or which approaches the confines of sin;
and secondly, avoiding the occasion and temptations to sin;
keeping at a distance from every thing which excites evil passion, or which tends to ensnare the soul.

15. I speak as to wise men; judge ye what I say.

Unto wise men ; i. e. as to men of sense; men capable of
seeing the force of an argument. Paul's appeal is not to
authority, whether his own or that of the Scriptures. The
whole question was, whether a given service came within the
scriptural definition of idolatry. He was willing, as it were,
to leave the decision to themselves; and therefore said, *judge
ye what I say,* i. e. sit in judgment on the argument which I
present. Should they differ from the apostle, that would not
alter the case. The service was idolatrous, whatever they
thought of it. But he takes this way of convincing them.

16. The cup of blessing which we bless, is it not the communion of the blood of Christ? The bread which we break, is it not the communion of the body of Christ?

It is here assumed that partaking of the Lord's Supper
brings us into communion with Christ. If this be so, partaking
of the table of demons must bring us into communion with
demons. This is the apostle's argument. It is founded on
the assumption, that a participation of the cup is a participation of the blood of Christ; and that a participation of the
bread is a participation of the body of Christ. So far Romanists, Lutherans, and Reformed agree in their interpretation of
this important passage. They all agree that a participation
of the cup is a participation of the blood of Christ; and that
a participation of the bread, is a participation of the body of
Christ. But when it is asked, what is the nature of this participation, the answers given are radically different. The Reformed answer, negatively, that it is "not after a corporal or
carnal manner." That is, it is not by the mouth, or as ordinary food is received. Affirmatively, they answer that it is
by faith, and therefore by the soul. This, of course, determines the nature of the thing partaken of, or the sense in
which the body and blood of Christ are received. If the re-

ception is not by the mouth, but by faith, then the thing received is not the material body and blood, but the body and blood as a sacrifice, i. e. their sacrificial virtue. Hence all Reformed churches teach (and even the rubrics of the Church of England), that the body and blood of Christ are received elsewhere than at the Lord's table, and without the reception of the bread and wine, which in the Sacrament are their symbols and the organs of communication, as elsewhere the word is that organ. Another point no less clear as to the Reformed doctrine is, that since the body and blood of Christ are received by faith, they are not received by unbelievers.

Romanists answer the above question by saying, that the mouth is the organ of reception; that the thing received is the real body and blood of Christ, into the substance of which the bread and wine are changed by the act of consecration; and consequently, that believers and unbelievers are alike partakers. Lutherans teach, that although the bread and wine remain unchanged, yet, as the body and blood of Christ are locally present in the sacrament, in, with, and under the bread and wine, the organ of reception is the mouth; the thing received is the real body and blood of Christ; and that they are received alike or equally by believers and unbelievers; by the latter, however, to their detriment and condemnation; by the former, to their spiritual nourishment and growth in grace. Lutherans and Romanists further agree in teaching, that there is a reception of the body and blood of Christ in the Lord's Supper, which is elsewhere impossible.

These are the three great forms of doctrine which have prevailed in the Church on this subject; and this passage is interpreted by each party in accordance with their peculiar views. The passage decides no point of difference. If the Romish doctrine of transubstantiation can be elsewhere proved, then, of course, this passage must be understood in accordance with it. And if the Lutheran doctrine of consubstantiation can be established by other declarations of the Word of God, then this passage must be explained in accordance with that doctrine. But, if it can be clearly demonstrated from Scripture and from those laws of belief which God has impressed upon our nature, that those doctrines are false, then the passage must be understood as teaching a spiritual, and not a corporal participation of Christ's body and blood. All that the passage asserts is the fact of a participation, the nature of that participation must be determined from other sources.

The cup of blessing. The word (εὐλογέω), *to bless*, means, 1. To speak well of. 2. To praise and thank; as when we bless God. 3. To confer blessings, as when God blesses us. In virtue of the second of these meanings, the word is used interchangeably with (εὐχαριστέω), *to give thanks*. That is, the same act is sometimes expressed by the one word and sometimes by the other. In Matt. 26, 26 and Mark 14, 22, what is expressed by saying, *having blessed*, in Luke 22, 17. 19. and 1 Cor. 11, 25, is expressed by saying, *having given thanks*. And in the account of the Lord's Supper in Matthew and Mark, the one word is used in reference to the bread, and the other in reference to the cup. They therefore mean the same thing, or rather express the same act, for that act was both a benediction and thanksgiving; that is, it was an address to God, acknowledging his mercy and imploring his blessing, and therefore may be expressed either by the word benediction or thanksgiving. It is not necessary to infer that in these cases (εὐλογήσας) *having blessed* is used in the restricted sense of (εὐχαριστήσας) *having given thanks*. This cannot be the fact, because the object of (εὐλογήσας), at least in some of these passages, is not God, but the bread or the cup. The meaning is, 'having blessed the bread.' The phrase, therefore, the *cup of blessing*, so far as the signification of the words is concerned, may be rendered either—the cup of thanksgiving (the eucharistical cup), or the cup of benediction, the consecrated cup. The latter is no doubt the true meaning, because the explanation immediately follows, *which we bless*. The cup, and not God, is blessed. To take the phrase actively, *the cup which confers blessing* is not only inconsistent with usage, but incompatible with the explanation which immediately follows. The cup of blessing is the cup which we bless. In the Paschal service the cup was called "the cup of blessing," because a benediction was pronounced over it. The idea of consecration is necessarily included. Wine, as wine, is not the sacramental symbol of Christ's blood, but only when solemnly consecrated for that purpose. Even our ordinary food is said to "be sanctified by the word of God and prayer," 1 Tim. 4, 5, because it is set apart by a religious service to the end for which it was appointed. So the cup of blessing is the cup which, by the benediction pronounced over it, is "set apart from a common to a sacred use."

Which we bless. This is the explanation of the preceding clause. The cup of blessing is the cup which we bless; which can only mean the cup on which we implore a blessing; that is, which we pray may be blessed to the end for which it was appointed, viz. to be to us the communion of the blood of Christ. That is, the means of communicating to us the benefits of Christ's death. Just as we bless our food when we pray that God would make it the means of nourishing our bodies. The other interpretations of this clause are unnatural, because they require something to be supplied which is not in the text. Thus some say the meaning is, "taking which," or "holding which in our hands," or "over which," we give thanks. All this is unnecessary, as the words give a perfectly good sense as they stand (ὃ εὐλογοῦμεν), *which* (cup) *we bless*. This passage, therefore, seems to determine the meaning of such passages as Matt. 26, 26 and Mark 14, 22, "Having blessed (viz. the bread) he brake it." The bread or cup was the thing blessed. Comp. Luke 9, 16, where it is said our Lord, "having taken the five loaves and the two fishes, and having looked up to heaven, he blessed *them*." This also shows that "having given thanks" in such connections means "having with thanksgiving implored the blessing of God." The cup therefore is blessed by the prayer, in which we ask that God would make it answer the end of its appointment.

Is it not the communion of the blood of Christ? That is, is it not the means of participating of the blood of Christ? He who partakes of the cup, partakes of Christ's blood. This, of course, is true only of believers. Paul is writing to believers, and assumes the presence of faith in the receiver. Thus baptism is said to wash away sin, and the word of God is said to sanctify, not from any virtue in them; not as an external rite or as words addressed to the outward ear; not to all indiscriminately who are baptized or who hear the word; but as means of divine appointment, when received by faith and attended by the working of his Spirit. The believing reception of the cup is as certainly connected with a participation of Christ's blood, as the believing reception of the word is connected with an experience of its life-giving power. The whole argument of the apostle is founded on this idea. He wishes to prove that partaking of the sacrificial feasts of the heathen brought men into real communion with demons, because participation of the Lord's supper makes us really partakers of Christ. The word κοινωνία, *communion*, means *participation*, from the verb κοινωνέω, *to partake of;* in Heb. 2, 14, it is said, Christ took part of flesh and blood. Rom. 15, 17, the Gentiles took part in the spiritual blessings of the Jews. Hence we have such expressions as the following : participation of his Son, 1 Cor. 1, 9 ; participation of the Spirit, 2 Cor. 13, 13. Phil. 2, 1 ; participation of the ministry, 2 Cor. 8, 4 ; of the gospel, Phil. 1, 5 ; of sufferings, Phil. 3, 5. Of course the nature of this participation depends on the nature of its object. Participation of Christ is sharing in his Spirit, character, sufferings and glory ; participation of the gospel is participation of its benefits ; and thus participation of the blood of Christ is partaking of its benefits. This passage affords not the slightest ground for the Romish or Lutheran doctrine of a participation of the substance of Christ's body and blood. When in 1, 9 it is said, "We are called into the fellowship or participation of his Son," it is not of the substance of the Godhead that we partake. And when the Apostle John says, "We have fellowship one with another," i. e. we are (κοινωνοί) partners one of another, 1 John 1, 7, he does not mean that we partake of each other's corporeal substance. To share in a sacrifice offered in our behalf is to share in its efficacy ; and as Christ's blood means his sacrificial blood, to partake of his blood no more means to partake of his literal blood, than when it is said his blood cleanses from all sin, it is meant that his literal corporeal blood has this cleansing efficacy. When we are said to receive the sprinkling of his blood, 1 Pet. 1, 1, it does not mean his literal blood.

The bread which we break, is it not the communion of the body of Christ ? That is, by partaking of the bread we partake of the body of Christ. This is but a repetition of the thought contained in the preceding clause. The cup is the means of participation of his blood ; the bread the means of participation of his body. *The body of Christ* cannot here mean the church, because his blood is mentioned in the same connection, and because in the institution of the Lord's supper the bread is the symbol of Christ's literal, and not of his mystical body. To partake of his body, is to partake of the benefits of his body as broken for us. *Which we break.* This is in evident allusion to the original institution of the sacrament. Our Lord "took bread, and having given thanks, he brake it and said, Take, eat ; this is my body which is broken for you." 1 Cor. 11, 24. The whole service, therefore, is often called the "breaking of bread." Acts 2, 42. 20, 7. The custom, therefore, of using a wafer placed unbroken in the mouth of the communicant, leaves out an important significant element in this sacrament.

17. For we (being) many are one bread, (and) one body : for we are all partakers of that one bread.

Literally rendered this verse reads : *Since it is one bread, we the many are one body ; for we are all partakers of one bread.* We are not said to be one bread ; but we are one body because we partake of one bread. The design of the apostle is to show that every one who comes to the Lord's supper enters into communion with all other communicants. They form one body in virtue of their joint participation of Christ. This being the case, those who attend the sacrificial feasts of the heathen form one religious body. They are in religious communion with each other, because in communion with the demons on whom their worship terminates. Many distinguished commentators, however, prefer the following interpretation. "For we, though many, are one bread (and) one body." The participation of the same loaf makes us one bread, and the joint participation of Christ's body makes us one body. This is, to say the least, an unusual and harsh figure. Believers are never said to be one bread ; and to make the ground of comparison the fact that the loaf is the joint product of many grains of wheat is very remote. And to say that we are literally one bread, because by assimilation the bread passes into the composition of the bodies of all the communicants, is to make the apostle teach modern physiology.

In the word κοινωνία, *communion*, as used in the preceding verse, lies the idea of joint participation. 'The bread which we break is a joint participation of the body of Christ ; because (ὅτι) it is one bread, so are we one body.' The thing to be proved is the union of all partakers of that one bread. Instead of connecting this verse with the 16th, as containing a confirmation of what is therein stated, many commentators take it as an independent sentence introducing a passing remark. 'The Lord's supper brings us into communion with Christ. Because this is the case, we are one body *and should act accordingly.*' But this not only breaks the connection, but introduces what is not in the text. The idea is, ' Partaking of the sacrament is a communion, *because* we the many all partake of one bread.'

18. Behold Israel after the flesh: are not they which eat of the sacrifices partakers of the altar?

Israel after the flesh, i. e. the Jews, as a nation, as distinguished from Israel *after the Spirit*, or the spiritual Israel or true people of God. As Israel was a favourite term of honour, Paul rarely uses it for the Jews as a people without some such qualification. Comp. Rom. 2, 28. 9, 8. Gal. 4, 29. 6, 16.

Are not they which eat of the sacrifices. With the Jews, as with other nations, only a portion of most sacrifices was consumed upon the altar; the residue was divided between the priest and the offerer. Lev. 7, 15. 8, 31. Deut. 12, 18. To eat of the sacrifices in the way prescribed in the Law of Moses, was to take part in the whole sacrificial service. "Thou must eat them before the Lord thy God, in the place which the Lord thy God shall choose." Deut. 12, 18. Therefore the apostle says that those who eat of the sacrifices are *partakers of the altar;* that is, they are in communion with it. They become worshippers of the God to whom the altar is dedicated. This is the import and the effect of joining in these sacrificial feasts. The question is not as to the intention of the actors, but as to the import of the act, and as to the interpretation universally put upon it. To partake of a Jewish sacrifice as a sacrifice and in a holy place, was an act of Jewish worship. By parity of reasoning, to partake of a heathen sacrifice as a sacrifice, and in a holy place, was of necessity an act of heathen worship. As all who attended the Jewish sacrifices, to which none but Jews were admitted, professed to be Jews and to be the joint-worshippers of Jehovah, and as they could not be in communion with the altar without being in communion with each other, therefore all who attended the sacrificial feasts of the heathen brought themselves into religious communion with idolaters. It need hardly be remarked that this passage gives no ground for the opinion that the Lord's supper is a sacrifice. This is not the point of comparison. The apostle's argument does not imply that, because the Jewish and heathen feasts were sacrificial feasts, therefore the Christian festival had the same character. The whole stress lies on the word κοινωνία. 'Because participation of Christian ordinances involves communion with Christ, participation of heathen ordinances involves communion with devils.'

19. What say I then ? that the idol is any thing, or that which is offered in sacrifice to idols is any thing ?

This is evidently intended to guard against a false inference from this mode of reasoning. It was not to be inferred from what he had said, that he regarded the professed objects of heathen worship as having the same objective existence as the God whom Jews and Christians worshipped ; or that he considered the heathen sacrifices as having any inherent power. The idol was nothing, and that which was offered to the idol was nothing. This however does not alter the case. For although there are no such beings as those whom the heathen conceive their gods to be, and although their sacrifices are not what they consider them, still their worship is real idolatry, and has a destructive influence on the soul. How this is, is explained in the following verse.

20. But (I say), that the things which the Gentiles sacrifice, they sacrifice to devils, and not to God : and I would not that ye should have fellowship with devils.

That is, ' I do not say the gods of the heathen have a real existence, that there are any such persons as Jupiter or Minerva ; but I do say that the heathen worship is the worship of demons.' This verse presents two questions for consideration. First, in what sense does Paul here use the word δαιμόνια, translated *devils ;* and secondly, in what sense can it be truly said that the heathen worship devils.

The words δαίμων and δαιμόνιον were used by the Greeks for any deity or god, or spirit, and generally for any object of reverence or dread. The only case in the New Testament where they have this sense is Acts 17, 18, (" He seems to be a setter forth of strange gods.") Elsewhere they always mean fallen angels. Our translators have not adhered to the distinction which in the New Testament is constantly made in the use of the words διάβολος and δαιμόνιον. They translate both terms by the word *devil,* and hence, when the latter occurs in the plural form, they render it *devils.* The former, however, is never applied in Scripture (except in its appellative sense of *accuser*) to any other being than Satan. He is the Devil, and the Scriptures never speak of more than one. By

devils, therefore, in this case are to be understood *demons*, or
the fallen angels or evil spirits. That this is the sense in which
the Greek word is to be here taken is plain, 1. Because it is
its only scriptural sense. The passage in Acts 17, 18, being
the language of Athenians, proves nothing as to the usage of
Jews speaking Greek. 2. In the Septuagint we have precisely
the words used by the apostle, and in the same sense. Deut.
32, 17. See also Ps. 95, 5, where the Septuagint version is, ὅτι
πάντες οἱ θεοὶ τῶν ἐθνῶν δαιμόνια, *all the gods of the heathen are
devils*. It can hardly be doubted that the apostle meant to
use the word in its established scriptural sense. Comp. also
Rev. 9, 20. 3. The classical sense of the word does not suit
the context. Paul had just said that the heathen gods were
nothing; to admit now that there were *deities* in the Grecian
sense of the word δαιμόνιον, would be to contradict himself.
We must understand the apostle, therefore, as saying on the
one hand, that the gods of the heathen were imaginary beings;
and on the other, that their sacrifices were really offered to
evil spirits. In what sense, however, is this true? The hea
then certainly did not intend to worship evil spirits. Nevertheless they did it. Men of the world do not intend to serve
Satan, when they break the laws of God in the pursuit of
their objects of desire. Still in so doing they are really obeying the will of the great adversary, yielding to his impulses,
and fulfilling his designs. He is therefore said to be the god
of this world. To him all sin is an offering and an homage.
We are shut up to the necessity of worshipping God or Satan.;
for all refusing or neglecting to worship the true God, or giving to any other the worship which is due to him alone, is the
worshipping of Satan and his angels. It is true therefore, in
the highest sense, that what the heathen offer they offer to
devils. Although their gods have no existence, yet there are
real beings, the rulers of the darkness of this world, wicked
spirits in heavenly places (Eph. 6, 12), on whom their worship
terminates.

And I would not that ye have fellowship with devils. By
fellowship or communion, the apostle means here what he
meant by the same term in the preceding verses. We are
said to have fellowship with those between whom and us there
are congeniality of mind, community of interest, and friendly
intercourse. In this sense we have fellowship with our fellow
Christians, with God and with his Son. And in this sense the
worshippers of idols have fellowship with evil spirits. They

are united to them so as to form one community, with a common character and a common destiny. Into this state of fellowship they are brought by sacrificing to them; that is, by idolatry, which is an act of apostasy from the true God, and of association with the kingdom of darkness. It was of great importance for the Corinthians to know that it did not depend on their intention whether they came into communion with devils. The heathen did not intend to worship devils, and yet they did it; what would it avail, therefore, to the reckless Corinthians, who attended the sacrificial feasts of the heathen, to say that they did not intend to worship idols? The question was not, what they meant to do, but what they did; not, what their intention was, but what was the import and effect of their conduct. A man need not intend to burn himself when he puts his hand into the fire; or to pollute his soul when he frequents the haunts of vice. The effect is altogether independent of his intention. This principle applies with all its force to compliance with the religious services of the heathen at the present day. Those who in pagan countries join in the religious rites of the heathen, are just as much guilty of idolatry, and are just as certainly brought into fellowship with devils, as the nominal Christians of Corinth, who, although they knew that an idol was nothing, and that there is but one God, yet frequented the heathen feasts. The same principle also applies to the compliance of Protestants in the religious observances of Papists. Whatever their intention may be, they worship the host if they bow down to it with the crowd who intend to adore it. By the force of the act we become one with those in whose worship we join. We constitute with them and with the objects of their worship one communion.

21. Ye cannot drink the cup of the Lord, and the cup of devils: ye cannot be partakers of the Lord's table, and of the table of devils.

The cup of the Lord is that cup which brings us into communion with the Lord, v. 16; *the cup of devils* is that cup which brings us into communion with devils. The reference is not exclusively or specially to the cup of libation, or to the wine poured out as an offering to the gods, but to the cup from which the guests drank at these sacrificial feasts. The whole service had a religious character; all the provisions, the wine as well as the meat, were blessed in the name of the idol, and thereby consecrated to him, in a manner analogous to that in which the bread and the wine on the Lord's table were consecrated to him; comp. 1 Sam. 9, 12. 13. *The table of the Lord* is the table at which the Lord presides, and at which his people are his guests. *The table of devils* is the table at which devils preside, and at which all present are their guests. What the apostle means to say is, that there is not merely an incongruity and inconsistency in a man's being the guest and friend of Christ and the guest and friend of evil spirits, but that the thing is impossible. It is as impossible as that the same man should be black and white, wicked and holy at the same time. In neither case is this attendance an empty, ineffective service. A man cannot eat of the table of demons without being brought under their power and influ- ence; nor can we eat of the table of the Lord, without being brought into contact with him, either to our salvation or con- demnation. If we come thoughtlessly, without any desire after communion with Christ, we eat and drink judgment to ourselves. But if we come with a humble desire to obey our divine master and to seek his presence, we cannot fail to be welcomed and blessed. Compare, in reference to this verse, 2 Cor. 6, 14–18.

22. Do we provoke the Lord to jealousy? are we stronger than he?

Jealousy is the feeling which arises from wounded love, and is the fiercest of all human passions. It is therefore em- ployed as an illustration of the hatred of God towards idola- try. It is as when a bride transfers her affections from her lawful husband, in every way worthy of her love, to some de- graded and offensive object. This illustration, feeble as it is, is the most effective that can be borrowed from human rela- tions, and is often employed in Scripture to set forth the hein- ousness of the sin of idolatry. Deut. 32, 21. Ps. 78, 58 and elsewhere. *Or do we provoke*, i. e. is it our object to provoke the Lord to jealousy. The Corinthians ought not to attend these feasts unless they intended to excite against themselves in the highest measure the displeasure of the Lord. And they ought not thus to excite his anger, unless they were *stronger than he.* By *the Lord* is to be understood Christ, as the con- text requires. It was the Lord's table that was forsaken,

and the same Lord that was provoked thereby to jealousy.
Here, again, the relation in which Christians stand to Christ,
is said to be analogous to that in which the Israelites stood to
Jehovah. Christ is therefore our Jehovah. He is our husband, to whom our supreme affection is due, and who loves us
as a husband loves his wife. "Thy maker is thy husband,
Jehovah is his name," Is. 54, 5; see Eph. 5, 25–31.

*Under what circumstances it was lawful to eat meat offered
to idols.* Vs. 23–33.

The apostle having, in the preceding paragraph, proved
that eating of the sacrifices offered to idols under circumstances which gave a religious character to the act, was idolatry, comes to state the circumstances under which those
sacrifices might be eaten without scruple. He begins by re-
verting to the general law of Christian liberty stated with the
same limitations as in ch. 6, 12. The right to use things
offered to idols, as well as other things in themselves indifferent, is limited by expediency. We should be governed in this
matter by a regard to the good of others, and to our own
edification, vs. 23. 24. If the meat of sacrifices be sold in the
market, v. 25, or found at private tables, it may be eaten without any hesitation, v. 27. But if any one at a private table,
from scruples on the subject, should apprise us that a certain
dish contained part of a sacrifice, for his sake, and not for our
own, we ought to abstain, v. 28. We should not make such
a use of our liberty as to cause our good to be evil spoken of,
v. 29. The general rule of action, not only as to meats and
drinks, but as to all other things is, first, to act with a regard
to the glory of God, v. 31; and secondly, so as to avoid giving offence (i. e. occasion for sin) to any class of men, v. 32.
In this matter Paul presents himself as an example to his
fellow-believers, v. 33.

23. All things are lawful for me, but all things are
not expedient: all things are lawful for me, but all
things edify not.

The apostle had already, in ch. 6, 12, and in ch. 8, conceded that eating of the sacrifices offered to idols, was, in
itself, a matter of indifference. But the use of things indifferent is limited by two principles; first, a regard to the welfare

of others; secondly, regard to our own welfare. The word
(συμφέρει) *is expedient* expresses the one of these ideas, and
(οἰκοδομεῖ) *edifieth* the other.   All things are not expedient
or useful to others; and all things are not edifying to ourselves. The latter phrase might indeed have reference to
others as well as to ourselves—but as contrasted with the
former clause, it appears to be used here with this restricted
application. In this view it agrees with the clause, "I will
not be brought under the power of any thing," in 6, 12.

24. Let no man seek his own, but every man another's (wealth).

That is, let every man, in the use of his liberty, have regard to the welfare of others. The maxim is indeed general.
It is not only in the use of things indifferent, but in all other
things we should act, not, in exclusive regard to our own interests, but also with a view to the good of others, Self, in
other words, is not to be the object of our actions. The context, however, shows, that the apostle intended the maxim to
be applied to the subject under discussion. Another's *wealth*,
i. e. another's *weal* or welfare, according to the old meaning
of the word wealth.

25. Whatsoever is sold in the shambles, (that) eat, asking no question for conscience' sake :

The general principle that sacrifices might be eaten under
any circumstances which deprived the act of a religious character, is here, and in what follows, applied to particular cases.
Meat, when exposed for public sale in the market, lost its
character as a sacrifice, and might be eaten with impunity.
The word μάκελλον is a Latin word which passed into the
Greek, and means a *meat market.*

Eat, asking no questions for conscience' sake. This clause
admits of three interpretations. 1. It may mean, 'When you
go to the market, buy what you want, and make no matter
of conscience about the matter. You need have no conscientious scruples, and therefore ask no questions as to whether
the meat had been offered to idols or not.' This is the simplest and most natural interpretation. These verses contain
the conclusion of the whole discussion. An idol is nothing;
the sacrifices are nothing sacred in themselves; but as the

heathen are really worshippers of evil spirits, to join in their
worship by eating their sacrifices as sacrifices, is idolatry; but
to eat them as meat is a matter of indifference; therefore do
not make it a matter of conscience. This interpretation is
confirmed by the following verse, which assigns the reason
why we need have no scruples in the case. 2. Or, the meaning may be, Ask no questions, for fear of awakening scruples
in your own mind. A man might eat with a good conscience
of meat which he knew not was a sacrifice, when he would
have serious scruples if informed that it had been offered to
an idol. Therefore it was wise, for his own sake, to ask no
questions. Paul, however, would not advise men to act blind-
fold. If a man thought it wrong to eat meat offered to idols,
it would be wrong for him to run the risk of doing so by buying meat in the markets where sacrifices were exposed for
sale. 3. Others say the apostle means to caution the strong
against instituting such inquiries, for fear of giving rise to
scruples in others. In favour of this view it is urged, that
throughout the whole discussion the object of the apostle is
to induce the strong to respect the conscientious scruples of
the weak. And in v. 29 he says expressly, that he means the
conscience of others. The former of these considerations has
not much weight, for we have here general directions suited
to all classes. Having shown in the preceding paragraph,
that it was idolatrous to eat of these sacrifices under certain
circumstances, it was perfectly natural that he should tell both
the strong and the weak when they might be eaten without
scruple. As to the second argument, it is rather against than
in favour of this interpretation. For if, when he means the
conscience of another, he expressly says so, the inference is,
that when he makes no such explanation, he means the man's
own conscience. Besides, the following verse gives the reason
why we need not have any scruples in the case, and not why
we should regard the scruples of others.

26. For the earth (is) the Lord's, and the fulness
thereof.

This was the common form of acknowledgment among the
Jews before meals. It was the recognition of God as the pro-
prietor and giver of all things, and specially of the food provided for his children. The words are taken from Ps. 24, 1.
The fulness of the earth is that by which it is filled; all the

fruits and animals with which it is replenished; which were created by God, and therefore good. Nothing, therefore, can in itself be polluting, if used in obedience to the design of its creation. And as the animals offered in sacrifice were intended to be food for man, they cannot defile those who use them for that purpose. This is the reason which the apostle gives to show that, so far as God is concerned, the Corinthians need entertain no scruples in eating meat that had been offered to idols. It was a creature of God, and therefore not to be regarded as unclean. Comp. 1 Tim. 4, 4, where the same doctrine is taught, and for the same purpose.

27. If any of them that believe not bid you (to a feast), and ye be disposed to go; whatsoever is set before you, eat, asking no question for conscience' sake.

As the sacrifices lost their religious character when sold in the market, so also at any private table they were to be regarded not as sacrifices, but as ordinary food, and might be eaten without scruple. The apostle did not prohibit the Christians from social intercourse with the heathen. If invited to their tables, they were at liberty to go.

28. But if any man say unto you, This is offered in sacrifice unto idols, eat not for his sake that shewed it, and for conscience' sake : for the earth (is) the Lord's, and the fulness thereof:

This is an exception. They might without scruple eat any thing set before them. But if any of the guests apprised them that a particular dish contained meat which had been offered to an idol, out of regard to the conscientious scruples of him who made the intimation, they should abstain. *But, on the contrary, if any one.* That is, any of your fellow-guests. The only person likely to make the suggestion was a scrupulous Christian. *For his sake that showed it and for conscience' sake;* the latter clause is explanatory. 'On account of him making the intimation, i. e. on account of his conscience.' Though it is right to eat, and though you know it to be right, yet, to avoid wounding or disturbing the conscience of your weaker brother, it is your duty to abstain. The union of the most enlightened liberality with the humblest concession to the weakness of others, exhibited in this whole connection, may well excite the highest admiration. The most enlightened man of his whole generation, was the most yielding and conciliatory in all matters of indifference.

The clause, "For the earth is the Lord's and the fulness thereof," at the end of this verse, is not found in the best manuscripts, and therefore omitted in all the critical editions of the Greek Testament. They seem to be here entirely out of place. In verse 26 they assign the reason why the Corinthians might eat without scruple whatever was sold in the market. But here they have no connection with what precedes. The fact that the earth is the Lord's, is no reason why we should *not eat* of sacrificial meat out of regard to a brother's conscience. There is little doubt, therefore, that it should be omitted.

29, 30. Conscience, I say, not thine own, but of the other: for why is my liberty judged of another (man's) conscience? For if I by grace be a partaker, why am I evil spoken of for that for which I give thanks?

As in the preceding vs. 25. 27 the word conscience refers to one's own conscience, to prevent its being so understood in v. 28, Paul adds the explanation, 'Conscience, I say, not thine own, but of the other's.' That is, 'I do not mean your conscience, but the conscience of the man who warned you not to eat.' *For why is my liberty judged of another man's conscience?* These and the words following admit of three interpretations. 1. If connected with the preceding clause, they must give the reason why Paul meant "the conscience of the other." 'Conscience I say, not one's own, but of the other; *for* why is my liberty (or conscience) to be judged by another man's conscience? if I eat with thanksgiving (and with a good conscience, why am I blamed?') The obvious objection to this interpretation is, that it exalts a subordinate clause into the principal matter. It was plain enough that Paul did not mean the man's own conscience, and therefore it is unnecessary to take up two verses to prove that he did not. Besides, this interpretation makes the apostle change sides. He has from the beginning been speaking in behalf of the weak. This interpretation makes him here speak almost in terms of indignation in behalf of the strong, who certainly need no advocate. They did not require to be told that their liberty was not to be restricted by the scruples of the weak. 2. A much better sense is obtained by connecting this passage with the 28th verse. 'Do not eat out of regard to the conscience of your brother; for why should my (your) liberty be judged (i. e. condemned) by another conscience; why should I be blamed for what I receive with thanksgiving?' That is, why should I make such a use of my liberty as to give offence? This brings the passage into harmony with the whole context, and connects it with the main idea of the preceding verse, and not with an intermediate and subordinate clause. The very thing the apostle has in view is to induce the strong to respect the scruples of the weak. They might eat of sacrificial meat at private tables with freedom, so far as they themselves were concerned; but why, he asks, should they do it so as to give offence, and cause the weak to condemn and speak evil of them. 3. This passage is by some commentators regarded as the language of an objector, and not as that of the apostle. The strong, when told not to eat on account of the conscience of a weak brother, might ask, 'Why is my liberty judged by another's conscience—why should I be blamed for what I receive with thanksgiving?' (The γάρ, according to this view, is not *for*, but intensive, ἱνατί γάρ, *why then*.) This gives a very good sense, but it is not consistent with the following verse (which is connected with v. 30 by οὖν, and not by δέ). Paul does not go on to answer that objection, but considers the whole matter settled. The second interpretation is the only one consistent alike with what precedes and with what follows. 'Do not eat when cautioned not to do so; for why should you so use your liberty as to incur censure? Whether therefore you eat or drink, do all for the glory of God.' Why is my liberty *judged* (κρίνεται), i. e. judged unfavourably or condemned. *If I by grace am a partaker;* literally, *if I partake with thanksgiving.* The word χάρις, *grace,* is here used in the sense of *gratia, thanks,* as in the common phrase to *say grace.* See Luke 6, 32. 1 Tim. 1, 12, &c.

31. Whether therefore ye eat, or drink, or whatso-ever ye do, do all to the glory of God.

This may mean either, 'Do all things with a view to the glory of God.' Let that be the object constantly aimed at;

or, 'Do all things in such a way that God may be glorified.'
There is little difference between these modes of explanation.
God cannot be glorified by our conduct unless it be our object to act for his glory. The latter interpretation is favoured
by a comparison with 1 Peter 4, 11, "That God in all things
may be glorified." See Col. 3, 17. All the special directions
given in the preceding discussion are here summed up. ' Let
self be forgotten. Let your eye be fixed on God. Let the
promotion of his glory be your object in all you do. Strive
in every thing to act in such a way that men may praise that
God whom you profess to serve.' The sins of the people of
God are always spoken of as bringing reproach on God himself. Rom. 2, 24. Ezek. 36, 20. 23. It is by thus having the
desire to promote the glory of God as the governing motive
of our lives, that order and harmony are introduced into all
our actions. The sun is then the centre of the system. Men
of the world have themselves for the end of their actions.
Philosophers tell us to make the good of others the end; and
thus destroy the sentiment of religion, by merging it into phi-
lanthropy or benevolence. The Bible tells us to make the
glory of God the end. This secures the other ends by making
them subordinate, while at the same time it exalts the soul
by placing before it an infinite personal object. There is al.
the difference between making the glory of God (the personal
Jehovah) the end of our actions, and the good of the universe,
or of being in general, that there is between the love of Christ
and the love of an abstract idea. The one is religion, the
other is morality.

32. Give none offence, neither to the Jews, nor to
the Gentiles, nor to the church of God :

Give none offence, i. e. give no occasion to sin. An offence
is something over which men stumble. The exhortation is to
avoid being the cause of sin to others, 8, 9. Rom. 14, 13. 21.
They were to be thus careful with respect to all classes of
men, Christians and non-Christians. The latter are divided
into the two great classes, the Jews and Gentiles. *The church
of God*, i. e. his people. Those whom God has called out of
the world to be his peculiar possession. They are therefore
distinguished as the κλητοί, *the called*, or, collectively considered, the ἐκκλησία, *the church*. The first great principle of Christian conduct is to promote the glory of God; the second is

to avoid giving offence, or causing men to sin. In other words, love to God and love to men should govern all our conduct.

33. Even as I please all (men) in all (things), not seeking mine own profit, but the (profit) of many, that they may be saved.

What he urged them to do, he himself did. His object was not his own advantage, but the benefit of others. He therefore, in all things allowable, accommodated himself to all men, that they might be saved. " I am made all things to all men, that I might by all means save some." 9, 22.

The principle which the apostle here avows, and which he so strenuously recommends in the preceding chapters, is one which has often been lamentably perverted. On the plea of becoming all things to all men, Christians are tempted into sinful conformity with the habits and amusements of the world. On the same plea the church of Rome adopted heathen festivals, ceremonies and rites, until the distinction be-tween Paganism and Christianity was little more than nominal. Heathen temples were called churches; pagan gods were baptized as saints, and honored as before. Modern Rome, in the apprehension of the people, is almost as polytheistic as ancient Rome. In like manner Romish missionaries accommodate themselves to such a degree to heathen ideas and forms, that the difference between what they call Christianity and the religion of the country is almost lost. Even Protestant missionaries are often perplexed how to decide between what is to be tolerated and what prohibited of the previous usages and ceremonies of their converts. That the principle on which Paul and the other apostles acted in reference to this matter, is radically different from that adopted by the church of Rome, is apparent from their different results. Rome has become paganized. The apostle so acted as to preserve the church from every taint of either Paganism or Judaism. The rules which guided the apostles may be easily deduced from the conduct and epistles of Paul. 1. They accommodated themselves to Jewish or Gentile usages only in matters of indifference. 2. They abstained from all accommodation even in things indifferent, under circumstances which gave to those things a religious import. They allowed sacrifices to be eaten; but eating within a temple was forbidden.

3. They conceded when the concession was not demanded as a matter of necessity; but refused when it was so regarded. Paul said circumcision was nothing and uncircumcision was nothing; yet he resisted the circumcision of Titus when it was demanded by the Judaizers. 4. The object of their concessions was not to gain mere nominal converts, nor to do away with the offence of the cross, Gal. 4, 11, but to save men. No concession therefore, whether to the manners of the world or to the prejudices of the ignorant, can plead the sanction of apostolic example, which has not that object honestly in view. 5. It is included in the above particulars that Paul, in becoming all things to all men, never compromised any truth or sanctioned any error.

XI., 1. Be ye followers of me, even as I also (am) of Christ.

This verse should belong to the tenth chapter, as it is the conclusion of the preceding discussion, and as a new subject is introduced with the following verse. Paul had referred to his own conciliatory conduct as an example to the Corinthians, and he exhorts them to imitate him, as he did Christ, who is the ultimate standard.

CHAPTER XI.

The impropriety of women appearing unveiled in the public assemblies, vs. 2–16. The improper manner of celebrating the Lord's Supper which prevailed in the Corinthian church, vs. 17–34.

On the impropriety of women appearing in public unveiled, vs. 2–16.

HAVING corrected the more private abuses which prevailed among the Corinthians, the apostle begins in this chapter to consider those which relate to the mode of conducting public worship. The first of these is the habit of women appearing in public without a veil. Dress is in a great degree conventional. A costume which is proper in one country, would be

indecorous in another. The principle insisted upon in this
paragraph is, that women should conform in matters of dress
to all those usages which the public sentiment of the community in which they live demands. The veil in all eastern countries was, and to a great extent still is, the symbol of modesty
and subjection. For a woman, therefore, in Corinth to discard the veil was to renounce her claim to modesty, and to
refuse to recognize her subordination to her husband. It is
on the assumption of this significancy in the use of the veil,
that the apostle's whole argument in this paragraph is founded.
He begins by praising the Corinthians for their obedience in
general to his instructions, v. 2. He then reminds them of
the divinely constituted subordination of the woman to the
man, v. 3. Consequently it was disgraceful in the man to assume the symbol of subordination, and disgraceful in the
woman to discard it, vs. 4. 5. If the veil were discarded as
the symbol of subordination, it must also be discarded as the
symbol of modesty. An unveiled woman, therefore, in Corinth
proclaimed herself as not only insubordinate, but as immodest,
v. 6. The man ought not to wear a veil because he represents
the authority of God ; but the woman is the glory of the man,
v. 7. This subordination is proved by the very history of her
creation. Eve was formed out of Adam, and made for him,
vs. 8. 9. and, therefore, women should wear, especially in the
religious assemblies where angels are present, the conventional
symbol of their relation, v. 10. This subordination, however,
of the woman is perfectly consistent with the essential equality
and mutual dependence of the sexes. Neither is, or can be,
without the other, vs. 11. 12. The apostle next appeals to
their instinctive sense of propriety, which taught them that,
as it is disgraceful in a man to appear in the costume of a
woman, so it is disgraceful in a woman to appear in the costume of a man, vs. 13–15. Finally he appeals to authority ;
the custom which he censured was contrary to the universal
practice of Christians, v. 16.

2. Now I praise you, brethren, that ye remember
me in all things, and keep the ordinances, as I delivered (them) to you.

Now I praise you. The particle (δέ) rendered *now*, either
simply indicates the transition to a new subject, or it is ad-
versative. ' Though I exhort you to imitate me as though

you were deficient, *yet* I praise you that you remember me.'
The Corinthians, although backward in following the self-
denial and conciliatory conduct of the apostle, were nevertheless in general mindful of the ordinances or rules which he had
delivered to them. The word (παράδοσις) *tradition*, here rendered *ordinance*, is used not only for instructions orally trans-
mitted from generation to generation, as in Matt. 15, 2. 3. 6,
but for any instruction, whether relating to faith or practice,
and whether delivered orally or in writing. 2 Thess. 2, 15.
3, 6. In reference to the rule of faith it is never used in the
New Testament, except for the immediate instructions of inspired men. When used in the modern sense of the word *tradition*, it is always in reference to what is human and untrustworthy, Gal. 1, 14. Col. 2, 8, and frequently in the gospels of
the traditions of the elders.

3. But I would have you know, that the head of every man is Christ ; and the head of the woman (is) the man ; and the head of Christ (is) God.

Though the apostle praised the Corinthians for their general obedience to his prescriptions, yet there were many things
in which they were deserving of censure. Before mentioning
the thing which he intended first to condemn, he states the
principle on which that condemnation rested ; so that, by as-
senting to the principle, they could not fail to assent to the
conclusion to which it necessarily led. That principle is, that
order and subordination pervade the whole universe, and is
essential to its being. The head of the man is Christ; the
head of the woman is the man ; the head of Christ is God. If
this concatenation be disturbed in any of its parts, ruin must
be the result. The head is that on which the body is dependent, and to which it is subordinate. The obvious meaning of
this passage is, that the woman is subordinate to the man, the
man is subordinate to Christ, and Christ is subordinate to God.
It is further evident, that this subordination is very different
in its nature in the several cases mentioned. The subordination of the woman to the man is something entirely different
from that of the man to Christ ; and that again is at an infinite
degree more complete than the subordination of Christ to God.
And still further, as the subordination of the woman to the
man is perfectly consistent with their identity as to nature, so
is the subordination of Christ to God consistent with his being

of the same nature with the Father. There is nothing, therefore, in this passage, at all inconsistent with the true and proper divinity of our blessed Lord. For a brief statement of the scriptural doctrine of the relation of Christ to God, see the comments on 3, 23. It need here be only further remarked, that the word Christ is the designation, not of the Logos or second person of the Trinity as such, nor of the human nature of Christ as such, but of the Theanthropos, the God-man. It is the incarnate Son of God, who, in the great work of redemption, is said to be subordinate to the Father, whose will he came into the world to do. *When Christ is said to be the head of every man*, the meaning is of every believer; because it is the relation of Christ to the church, and not to the human family, that is characteristically expressed by this term. He is the head of that body which is the church, Col. 1, 18. Eph. 1, 22. 23.

4. Every man praying or prophesying, having (his) head covered, dishonoureth his head.

Such being the order divinely established, (viz., that mentioned in v. 3,) both men and women should act in accordance with it; the man, by having the head uncovered, the woman by being veiled. As the apostle refers to their appearance in public assemblies, he says, *Every man praying or prophesying*, i. e. officiating in public worship. *Prophesying.* In the scriptural sense of the word, a prophet is one who speaks for another, as Aaron is called the prophet or *spokesman* of Moses. "Thou shalt speak unto him, and put words into his mouth, . . . and he shall be thy spokesman," Ex. 4, 15. 16; or, as he is called, 7, 1, *thy prophet*. The prophets of God, therefore, were his spokesmen, into whose mouth the Lord put the words which they were to utter to the people. To *prophesy*, in Scripture, is accordingly, to speak under divine inspiration; not merely to predict future events, but to deliver, as the organ of the Holy Ghost, the messages of God to men, whether in the form of doctrine, exhortation, consolation, or prediction. This public function, the apostle says, should not be exercised by a man with *his head covered;* literally, *having something on his head downward.* Among the Greeks, the priests officiated bareheaded; the Romans with the head veiled; the Jews (at least soon after the apostolic age) also wore the Tallis or covering for the head in their public services. It is not to be inferred from what is here said, that the Christian prophets (or inspired men) had introduced this custom into the church. The thing to be corrected was, women appearing in public assemblies unveiled. The apostle says, the veil is inconsistent with the position of the man, but is required by that of the women. Men are mentioned only for the sake of illustrating the principle.

Dishonoureth his head. It is doubtful whether we should read *his* or *his own* head, (αὐτοῦ or αὑτοῦ). This is a point the ancient ·manuscripts do not decide, as they are not furnished with the diacritical marks. It depends on the connection. It is also doubtful whether the apostle meant to say that he dishonoured Christ who is his head, or that he dishonoured himself. The latter, perhaps, is to be preferred, 1. Because, in the immediately preceding clause the word is used literally, 'If he cover his head, he dishonours his head.' 2. Because, in v. 5, the woman who goes unveiled is said to dishonour *her own* head, i. e. as what follows shows, *herself,* and not her husband. 3. It is more obviously true that a man who acts inconsistently with his station disgraces himself, than that he disgraces him who placed him in that station. A commanding military officer, who appears at the head of his troops in the dress of a common soldier, instead of his official dress, might more properly be said to dishonour himself than his sovereign. For a freeman to appear in the distinguishing dress of a slave, was a disgrace. So the apostle says, for a man to appear with the conventional sign of subjection on his head, disgraced himself. If the man be intended to represent the dominion of God, he must act accordingly, and not appear in the dress of a woman.

5. But every woman that prayeth or prophesieth with (her) head uncovered dishonoureth her head; for that is even all one as if she were shaven.

Praying and prophesying were the two principal exercises in the public worship of the early Christians. The latter term, as above stated, included all forms of address dictated by the Holy Spirit. It was Paul's manner to attend to one thing at a time. He is here speaking of the propriety of women speaking in public unveiled, and therefore he says nothing about the propriety of their speaking in public in itself. When that subject comes up, he expresses his judgment in the clearest terms, 14, 34. In here disapproving of the one, says Calvin, he does not approve of the other.

The veils worn by Grecian women were of different kinds. One, and perhaps the most common, was the *peplum*, or mantle, which in public was thrown over the head, and enveloped the whole person. The other was more in the fashion of the common eastern veil which covered the face, with the exception of the eyes. In one form or other, the custom was universal for all respectable women to appear veiled in public.— The apostle therefore says, that a woman who speaks in public with her *head uncovered, dishonoureth her head.* Here ἑαυτῆς is used, *her own* head; not her husband, but herself. This is plain, not only from the force of the words, but from the next clause, *for that is even all one as if she were shaven.* This is the reason why she disgraces herself. She puts herself in the same class with women whose hair has been cut off. Cutting off the hair, which is the principal natural ornament of women, was either a sign of grief, Deut. 21, 12, or a disgraceful punishment. The literal translation of this clause is *she is one and the same thing with one who is shaven.* She assumes the characteristic mark of a disreputable woman.

6. For if the woman be not covered, let her also be shorn : but if it be a shame for a woman to be shorn or shaven, let her be covered.

That is, let her act consistently. If she wishes to be regarded as a reputable woman, let her conform to the established usage. But if she have no regard to her reputation, let her act as other women of her class. She must conform either to the reputable or disreputable class of her sex, for a departure from the one is conforming to the other. These imperatives are not to be taken as commands, but rather **as** expressing what consistency would require. *Shorn* or *shaven,* the latter is the stronger term; it properly means to cut with a razor.

7. For a man indeed ought not to cover (his) head, forasmuch as he is the image and glory of God : but the woman is the glory of the man.

The woman, and the woman only, ought to be veiled; *for* the man ought not to cover his head. This does not mean, he

is not bound to do it, but should not do it. The negative belongs not to ὀφείλει, but to κατακαλύπτεσθαι. The reason is
that *he is the image and glory of God*. The only sense in
which the man, in distinction from the woman, is the image
of God, is that he represents the authority of God. He is invested with dominion. When, in Genesis 1, 26. 27, it is said
God created man in his own image, the reference is as much
to woman as to man; for it is immediately added, "male and
female created he them." So far, therefore, as the image of
God consists in knowledge, righteousness and holiness, Eve as
truly, and as much as Adam, bore the likeness of her Maker.
But in the dominion with which man was invested over the
earth, Adam was the representative of God. He is the glory
of God, because in him the divine majesty is specially manifested. *But the woman is the glory of the man.* That is, the
woman is in this respect subordinate to the man. She is not
designed to reflect the glory of God as a ruler. She is the
glory of the man. She receives and reveals what there is of
majesty in him. She always assumes his station; becomes a
queen if he is a king, and manifests to others the wealth and
honour which may belong to her husband.

8. 9. For the man is not of the woman; but the woman of the man. Neither was the man created for the woman; but the woman for the man.

The subordination of the woman to the man is here proved
from two facts recorded in the history of their creation. First,
the woman was formed out of the man, and derived her origin
from him. He, and not she, was created first. Secondly, she
was created on his account, and not he on hers. In this way
does the New Testament constantly authenticate, not merely
the moral and religious truths of the Old Testament, but its
historical facts; and makes those facts the grounds or proofs
of great moral principles. It is impossible, therefore, for any
Christian who believes in the inspiration of the apostles to
doubt the divine authority of the Old Testament Scriptures,
or to confine the inspiration of the ancient writers to their
doctrinal and preceptive statements. The whole Bible is the
word of God.

10. For this cause ought the woman to have power on (her) head because of the angels.

There is scarcely a passage in the New Testament which has so much taxed the learning and ingenuity of commentators as this. After all that has been written, it remains just as obscure as ever. The meaning which it naturally suggests to the most superficial reader, is regarded by the most laborious critics as the only true one. By ἐξουσία, *power,* the apostle means the sign or symbol of authority; just as *Diodorus Sic.,* 1. 47, speaks of an image as "having three kingdoms on its head." The apostle had asserted and proved that the woman is subordinate to the man, and he had assumed as granted that the veil was the conventional symbol of the man's authority. The inference is that the woman ought to wear the ordinary symbol of the power of her husband. As it was proper in itself, and demanded by the common sense of propriety, that the woman should be veiled, it was specially proper in the worshipping assemblies, for there they were in the presence not merely of men but of angels. It was, therefore, not only out of deference to public sentiment, but from reverence to those higher intelligences that the woman should conform to all the rules of decorum. This is the common and only satisfactory interpretation of the passage. Of those who dissent from this view, some propose various conjectural emendations of the text; others vainly endeavour to prove that the word ἐξουσία may be made to mean a veil; others take the word literally. And as to the last clause, instead of taking the word *angels* in its ordinary sense, some say it here means the angels, or presiding officers, of the church; others, that it means messengers or spies from the heathen who came to observe the mode in which the Christians worshipped, and would report any thing they observed to their disadvantage. The great majority of commentators acquiesce in the interpretation stated above, which satisfies all the demands of the context.

11. Nevertheless, neither is the man without the woman, neither the woman without the man, in the Lord.

That is, although there is this subordination of the woman to the man, they are mutually dependent. The one cannot exist without the other. *In the Lord.* This does not mean that the one is not in the Lord to the exclusion of the other. The apostle is not here speaking of the spiritual equality of the sexes. In Galatians 3, 28 and elsewhere he abundantly teaches that in Christ Jesus there is neither male nor female; that the one is as fully a partaker of all the benefits of redemption as the other. And it is also true that he teaches that this equality of Jews and Greeks, bond and free, before God is perfectly consistent with the social inequalities existing in this world. But these truths, however important, and however they distinguish the Christian doctrine of the equality and dignity of woman from all other forms of religious doctrine on the subject, are foreign to this connection. The apostle's single object is to show the true nature and limitations of the subordination of the woman to the man. It is a real subordination, but it is consistent with their mutual dependence; the one is not without the other. And this mutual dependence is *ἐν κυρίῳ*, i. e. by divine appointment—according to the will of the Lord. These words are used here, as so frequently elsewhere, as an adverbial qualification, meaning *religiously, after a Christian manner*, or *divinely*, i. e. *by divine appointment*. The same idea is substantially expressed by those who explain the words in *the Lord* as tantamount to "in Christianity;" in the sense that it is a Christian doctrine that the man and the woman are thus mutually dependent.

12. For as the woman (is) of the man, even so (is) the man also by the woman; but all things of God.

The one is not without the other, *for* as the woman was originally formed out of the man, so the man is born of the woman. This is a proof, not of the admitted equality of the sexes in the kingdom of God, but of their mutual dependence in the kingdom of nature. It therefore confirms the interpretation given of the preceding verse. *But all things are of God;* these subordinate relations of one creature to another are merged, as it were, in the supreme causality of God. It matters little whether the man was of the woman or the woman of the man, as both alike are of God; just as he before said, it matters little whether a man were a Jew or Gentile, bond or free, since all are alike before God.

13. Judge in yourselves : is it comely that a woman pray unto God uncovered ?

This is an appeal to their own sense of propriety. The apostle often recognizes the intuitive judgments of the mind

as authoritative. Rom. 1, 32. 3, 8. The constitution of our
nature being derived from God, the laws which he has impressed upon it, are as much a revelation from him as any
other possible communication of his will. And to deny this,
is to deny the possibility of all knowledge. *Is it comely* (πρέ-
πον ἐστί), *is it becoming* or *decorous?*

14. 15. Doth not even nature itself teach you, that,
if a man have long hair, it is a shame unto him? But
if a woman have long hair, it is a glory to her: for
(her) hair is given her for a covering.

Doth not nature itself. The word (φύσις), *nature,* sometimes means *essence* or *substance,* sometimes *the laws of nature*
or *of our natural constitution;* sometimes, the instinctive feelings or judgments which are the effects of those laws. The
form which these feelings assume is necessarily determined in
a great measure by education and habit. The instinctive
sense of propriety in an eastern maiden prompts her, when
surprised by strangers, to cover her face. In an European it
would not produce that effect. In writing, therefore, to eastern females, it would be correct to ask whether their native
sense of propriety did not prompt them to cover their heads
in public. The response would infallibly be in the affirmative.
It is in this sense the word *nature* is commonly taken here.
It may, however, mean the laws or course of nature. Nature
gives the man short hair and the woman long hair; and therefore nature itself teaches that long hair is a disgrace to the
one and an ornament to the other; for it is disgraceful in a
man to be like a woman, and in a woman to be like a man.
Wearing long hair was contrary to the custom both of the
Hebrews and Greeks. The Nazarites, as a distinction, allowed
their hair to grow. Num. 6, 5; see also Ezek. 44, 20. It
was considered so much a mark of effeminacy for men to wear
long hair, that it was not only ridiculed by Juvenal, but in
after times seriously censured by church councils. To a woman, however, in all ages and countries, long hair has been
considered an ornament. It is given to her, Paul says, as a
covering, or as a natural veil; and it is a glory to her *because*
it is a veil. The veil itself, therefore, must be becoming and
decorous in a woman.

16. But if any man seem to be contentious, we
have no such custom, neither the churches of God.

The arguments against the custom of women appearing in
public unveiled having been presented, the apostle says, if any
man, notwithstanding these arguments, is disposed to dispute
the matter, or appears to be contentious, we have only further
to say, *that we* (the apostles) *have no such custom, neither
have the churches of God. To be contentious,* i. e. disposed to
dispute for the sake of disputation.   With such persons all argument is useless.   Authority is the only end of controversy
with such disturbers of the peace.   The authority here adduced is that of the apostles and of the churches.   The former
was decisive, because the apostles were invested with authority not only to teach the gospel, but also to organize the
church, and to decide every thing relating to Christian ordinances and worship.   The authority of the churches, although
not coercive, was yet great.   No man is justified, except on
clearly scriptural grounds, and from the necessity of obeying
God rather than man, to depart from the established usages
of the church in matters of public concern.

Calvin, and many of the best modern commentators, give
a different view of this passage.   They understand the
apostle to say, that if any one seems to be disputatious, neither we nor the churches are accustomed to dispute.   It is not
our wont to waste words with those who wish merely to make
contention.   The only reason assigned for this interpretation,
is Paul's saying *we have* no such custom; which they say cannot mean the custom of women going unveiled.   But why
not ?   The apostles and the churches constituted a whole—
neither the one nor the other, neither the churches nor their
infallible guides, sanctioned the usage in question.   Besides,
no other custom is mentioned in the context than the one
which he has been discussing.   "If any one appear contentious," is not a custom and suggests nothing to which the
words *such a custom* can naturally refer.

Celebration of the Lord's Supper, vs. 17–34.

This section relates to the disorders connected with the
celebration of the Lord's supper.   These disorders were of a
kind which, according to our method of celebrating that
sacrament, seems almost unaccountable.   It was, however,
the early custom to connect the Lord's supper in the strict

sense of the words with an ordinary meal. As this sacrament was instituted by our Lord at the close of the Paschal supper, so it appears to have been customary at the beginning for the Christians to assemble for a common meal and to connect with it the commemoration of the Redeemer's death. Intimations of this usage may be found in such passages as Acts 2, 42. "They continued steadfastly in the apostle's doctrine and fellowship, and in breaking of bread, and in prayer." In v. 46 it is said, this breaking of bread was from house to house. In Acts 20, 7, it is said, "The disciples came together on the first day of the week to break bread," which, from the narrative which follows, appears to have been an ordinary meal. Whatever may be thought of these passages, it is clear from the paragraph before us that at Corinth at least, the sacrament of the Lord's supper was connected with a regular meal. This may have arisen, not so much from the original institution of the Eucharist in connection with the Paschal supper, as from the sacred festivals both of the Jews and Greeks. Both classes had been accustomed to unite with their sacrifices a feast of a more or less public character. It is also evident that, agreeably to a familiar Grecian custom, the persons assembled brought their own provisions, which being placed on the table formed a common stock. The rich brought plentifully, the poor brought little or nothing. It was, however, essential to the very idea of a Christian feast, that it should be a communion; that all the guests at the table of their common Lord should be on the terms of equality. Instead of this fraternal union, there were divisions among the Corinthians even at the Lord's table. The rich eating by themselves the provisions which they had brought, and leaving their poorer brethren mortified and hungry. It is to the correction of these disorders that the concluding portion of this chapter is devoted.

It was no matter of praise that the assemblies of the Corinthians made them worse rather than better, v. 17. The prominent evil was, that there were schisms even in their most sacred meetings; an evil necessary in the state in which they were, and which God permitted in order that the good might be made manifest, vs. 18. 19. The evil to which he referred was not merely that they had degraded the Lord's supper into an ordinary meal, but that in that meal they were divided into parties, some eating and drinking to excess, and others left without any thing, vs. 20. 21. This was not only making the Lord's supper a meal for satisfying hunger—contrary to its original design, but a cruel perversion of a feast of love into a means of humiliating and wounding their poorer brethren, v. 22. In order to show how inconsistent their conduct was with the nature of the service in which they professed to engage, the apostle recounts the original institution of the Lord's supper, vs. 23–25. From this account it follows, first, that the Lord's supper was designed not as an ordinary meal, but as a commemoration of the death of Christ; secondly, that to participate in this ordinance in an unworthy manner, was an offence against his body and blood, the symbols of which were so irreverently treated; thirdly, that no one ought to approach the Lord's table without self-examination, in order that with due preparation and with a proper understanding of the ordinance, he may receive the bread and wine as the symbols of Christ's body and blood, vs. 26–29. In this way they would escape the judgments which the Lord had brought upon them on account of their profanation of his table, vs. 30–32. In conclusion, he exhorts them to use their houses for their ordinary meals, and to make the Lord's supper a real communion, vs. 33. 34.

17. Now in this that I declare (unto you) I praise (you) not, that ye come together not for the better, but for the worse.

In v. 2 he said, *I praise you.* His praise was consistent with grave disapprobation of many things in their condition as a church. He did not praise them for the manner in which they conducted their public worship. Their assemblies were disgraced not only by women appearing unveiled, contrary to the established rules of decorum, but also by the unfraternal and irreverent manner of celebrating the Lord's supper—and also by the disorderly manner in which they used their spiritual gifts. These evils he takes up in their order. Having dispatched the first, he comes now to the second.

*Now in this that I declare unto you.** The Greek is not *in this,* but *this.* The passage may be rendered, *Declaring this I do not applaud.* To this, however, it is objected that

---

* The common Text here reads παραγγέλλων οὐκ ἐπαινῶ. Lachmann and Tischendorf read παραγγέλλω οὐκ ἐπαινῶν on the authority of the Mss. A. C. F. G. and others of later date, and the Syriac, Vulgate, and Ethiopic versions. The common reading is preferred by the majority of editors.

παραγγέλλειν in the New Testament never means *to declare*, but always *to command*. Hence, the better translation is, *Commanding* or *enjoining this I do not applaud*. It is doubtful whether *this* refers to what precedes or to what follows. If the former, then the sense is, 'While I command what precedes respecting women appearing veiled, I do not praise you, that,' &c. If the latter, the meaning is, 'Commanding what follows, I do not praise,' &c. *That ye come together not for the better, but for the worse.* That is, your public assemblies are so conducted that evil rather than good results. The censure is general, embracing all the grounds of complaint which are specified in this and the following chapters.

18. For first of all, when ye come together in the church, I hear that there be divisions among you; and I partly believe it.

For first of all, or, *For in the first place.* Paul often begins an enumeration which he does not follow out. There is nothing to answer to these words in what follows. According to one view the first censure is directed against the divisions, and the second against their mode of celebrating the Lord's supper. But the only divisions which he here refers to are those connected with their public worship, and especially with the celebration of the sacrament. Besides, the subject of divisions was treated in the beginning of the epistle. He is here speaking of their assemblies. The second ground of censure is to be found in the following chapter. *When ye come together in the church.* The word (ἐκκλησία) *church* never means in the New Testament, a building. The meaning is, when ye come together in convocation, or assemble as a church. *I hear that there be divisions among you.* Literally, *schisms.* For the meaning of that word, see 1, 10. The nature of these schisms is described in what follows. They were *cliques*, not sects, but parties, separated from each other by alienation of feeling. It is evident that the rich formed one of these parties, as distinguished from the poor. And probably there were many other grounds of division. The Jewish converts separated from the Gentiles; those having one gift exalted themselves over those having another. It is not outward separation, but inward alienation, which is here complained of. *And I partly believe it.* Paul intimates that he was loath to believe all he had heard to their disadvantage in this matter; but he was forced to believe enough to excite his serious disapprobation.

19. For there must be also heresies among you, that they which are approved may be made manifest among you.

This is the reason why he believed what he had heard. He knew that such things must happen, and that God had a wise purpose in permitting them; comp. Matt. 18, 7, "It must needs be that offences come." Evil as well as good is included in the divine purpose. It is purposed not as evil, but for the sake of the good which infinite wisdom evolves from it. *Also heresies.* This does not mean heresies in addition to schisms, as something different from them. But heresies as well as other evils. 'I hear there are divisions (σχίσματα) among you, and I believe it, for such divisions (αἱρέσεις) must occur.' What in the one verse are called *schisms*, in the next are called *heresies ;* both words having the general sense of divisions. The nature of these divisions is to be determined by the context. The word (αἵρεσις) *heresy* means literally *an act of choice*, then a chosen way of life, a sect or party; not always in a bad sense, but in the sense of schools; as, "the heresies of philosophers" means "the schools or different classes of philosophers." So in the New Testament it is repeatedly used of "the *sect* of the Pharisees," or "of the Sadducees," Acts 15, 5. 5, 17. Here and in Gal. 5, 20 it means *dissension.* The ecclesiastical sense of the word *heresy*, is, the choice of an opinion different from that of the church, or a doctrine contrary to Scripture. There is nothing to favour the assumption that such is its meaning here

That they which are approved may be made manifest. This is the end which God has in view in permitting the occurrence of such divisions. It is, *that they which are approved* (οἱ δόκιμοι), *the tried*, those who have stood the test, and are worthy of approbation. The opposite class are called (ἀδόκιμοι) *reprobate.* By the prevalence of disorders and other evils in the church, God puts his people to the test. They are tried as gold in the furnace, and their genuineness is made to appear. It is a great consolation to know that dissensions, whether in the church or in the state, are not fortuitous, but are ordered by the providence of God, and are designed, as storms, for the purpose of purification.

20. When ye come together therefore into one place, (this) is not to eat the Lord's supper.

Ye coming together then into one place. Verse 19 is an interruption. The connection with v. 18 is resumed by the particle (οὖν) *then.* When you assemble *it is not to eat the Lord's supper.* This is not the real, though it is your professed purpose. 'You come together for a common, and that too, a disorderly, unbrotherly meal.' The words, however, admit of two other interpretations. We may supply, as our translators have done, the word *this.* 'This is not to eat the Lord's supper; your meal does not deserve that sacred character.' Or, 'Ye cannot eat the Lord's supper.' The substantive verb (ἔστι) followed by an infinitive often means *can ;* οὐκ ἔστιν εἰπεῖν, *one cannot say ;* οὐκ ἔστι φαγεῖν, *one cannot eat.* 'Coming together as you do it is impossible to celebrate the Lord's supper.' This gives a very pertinent sense. *The Lord's supper* is the supper instituted by the Lord, one to which he invites the guests, and which is celebrated in commemoration of his death. That was a very different service from the Agapae, or love feasts, as they were afterwards called, and which, on account of the disorders attending them, were subsequently prohibited by the Council of Carthage. These Agapae were feasts to which each one brought his contributions, during and after which (the bread *during,* and the cup *after*) the consecrated elements were distributed. See *Augusti's* Antiquities of the Christian Church, I. p. 299; and *Pool's* Synopsis on Matt. 26, 26. *Coleman's* Ancient Christianity, p. 443.

21. For in eating every one taketh before (other) his own supper: and one is hungry, and another is drunken.

For, i. e. the reason why the Corinthian suppers were not the Lord's supper, is (so far as here stated) that there was no communion, or eating together. They were not all partakers of one bread, 10, 17. They did not wait for each other. Comp. v. 33. On the contrary, each one took beforehand, i. e. before others could join with him, *his own supper,* i. e. that which he had brought. The consequence was, that *one was hungry ;* the poor had nothing; while another *was drunk.* Such is the meaning of the word. Whether the apostle intended to say that any of the Corinthians actually became intoxicated at the table which they called the table of the Lord, or whether he meant simply to say, that while one had more, another had less, than enough, it is not easy to decide. As they seem to have accommodated their service to the sacrificial feasts to which they had, while yet heathens, been accustomed, it is the less improbable that in some cases they were guilty of actual excess. "It is wonderful, and well nigh portentous," says Calvin, "that Satan could have accomplished so much in so short a time. We may learn from this example, what is the worth of mere antiquity; that is, what authority is due to custom unsustained by the word of God. ... Yet this is the firmest foundation of Popery: it is ancient; it was done of old, therefore it has divine authority!" If, within twenty years of its institution, the Corinthians turned the Lord's supper into a disorderly feast, although the apostles were then alive, we need not wonder at the speedy corruption of the church after their death.

22. What! have ye not houses to eat and to drink in? or despise ye the church of God, and shame them which have not? What shall I say to you? shall I praise you in this? I praise (you) not.

The two grounds on which the apostle condemned this conduct of the Corinthians were, first, that it was a perversion of the Lord's supper; and secondly, that it was disrespectful and mortifying to their poorer brethren. It was a perversion of the Lord's supper, because it made it an ordinary meal designed to satisfy hunger. For that purpose they had their own houses. The church comes together to worship God and to celebrate his ordinances, not for the purpose of eating and drinking. It is important that the church, as the church, should confine itself to its own appropriate work, and not as such undertake to do what its members, as citizens or members of families, may appropriately do. The church does not come together to do what can better be done at home. *Or despise ye the church of God?* This was the second ground of condemnation. Their conduct evinced contempt of their brethren. They treated them as unfit to eat with them. Yet the poor were constituent members of the church of God. They were his people; those whom he had chosen, whom he had made kings and priests unto himself. These persons, thus highly honoured of God, the richer Corinthians treated with contempt; and that too at the Lord's table, where all external distinctions are done away, and the master is not a hair's breadth above his slave. *And shame those who have not. To shame*, i. e. to mortify and humble, by rendering conscious of inferiority. *Those who have not* may mean, either those who have not houses to eat or drink in, or simply *the poor.* Those who have, are the rich; those who have not, are the poor. The latter interpretation is not only consistent with the Greek idiom, but gives a better sense. Even the poorer members of the church did not, and ought not, come to the Lord's table for the sake of food. Much as Paul was disposed to praise the Corinthians, in this matter he could not praise them.

23. For I have received of the Lord that which also I delivered unto you, That the Lord Jesus, the (same) night in which he was betrayed, took bread:

'I cannot praise you, *for* your manner of celebrating the Lord's supper is utterly inconsistent with its original institution.' They were the more inexcusable in departing from the original mode of celebrating this ordinance, first, because the account of its original institution had been received by Paul from the Lord himself; and secondly, because he had delivered it to them. Their sin was therefore one of irreverent disobedience, without the excuse of ignorance. *For I have received of the Lord.* Paul asserts that he received from the Lord the account here given. The whole context shows that he intends to claim for this narrative the direct authority of th Lord himself. As with regard to his doctrines generally, so with regard to the institution and design of this ordinance, he disclaims all indebtedness to tradition or to the instructions of men, and asserts the fact of a direct revelation to himself. Of the gospel he says, "I neither received it of man, neither was I taught it, but by the revelation of Jesus Christ," Gal. 1, 12. To this interpretation, however, it is objected, 1. That he uses the preposition ἀπό, which properly expresses a mediate derivation (i. e. through the instrumentality of others), and not παρά, which would imply a direct communication. This objection supposes a refinement in the use of the Greek particles, which is not consistent with the character of the Greek of the New Testament. The Apostle John says: "This is the message which we have heard of him (ἀπ᾽ αὐτοῦ)," 1 John 1, 5, which certainly does not refer to an indirect communication received through others. In this place ἀπὸ τοῦ κυρίου, *from the Lord*, is evidently opposed to ἀπ᾽ ἀνθρώπων, *from men*. He received his knowledge from the Lord, and not from men. Comp. Gal. 1, 12. So in Gal. 1, 1, he says he was an apostle *not by men* (οὐκ ἀπ᾽ ἀνθρώπων), but *by Jesus Christ* (διὰ Ἰησοῦ Χριστοῦ). Must it be inferred from this latter expression that Christ was only the medium of Paul's call to the apostleship, because διά expresses the instrumental cause? This would be as reasonable as to infer from the use of ἀπό in the text, that the knowledge of Paul was derived indirectly from the Lord. The apostle however says in Gal. 1, 1, that he received his apostleship, not only *through Jesus Christ*, but also *through God the Father ;* must this also mean *through the instrumentality* of God? is God the Father a mere instrument? No writer uses language with such strict grammatical accuracy as this objection supposes; much less did Jews writing Greek. It is of course important to adhere as far as possible to the exact meaning of the words; but to sacrifice the sense and obvious intent of the writer to such niceties is unreasonable. The use of ἀπό, in this case, probably arose from the desire to avoid the triple repetition of παρά; παρέλαβον, παρά, παρέδωκα. 2. It is objected that, as the Lord's supper had been celebrated without interruption from the time of its institution, the facts concerning it must have been universally known, and therefore needed no direct revelation. The same objection might be made to a special revelation of the gospel to Paul. Why might he not have been allowed to learn it from the other apostles? Besides, Paul, as he shows in the first and second chapters of his epistle to the Galatians, had no communication with the other apostles for three years after his conversion. 3. It is objected that ideas and truths may be communicated by visions and inward influences, but not historical facts. Then a large part of the prophecies of the Old Testament must be fabulous. The evidence is so strong from the context, that Paul claims independent authority for what he here says, that many who bow to the force of the Greek preposition, say that the account received by Paul from Christ through others, was authenticated to him by an inward revelation. But this is not what he says. He says he received it from Christ, which, in the connection, can only mean that he received it directly from Christ; for his object is to give authority to his account of the ordinance. It was not only of importance for the Corinthians, but for the whole church, to be assured that this account of the Lord's supper, was communicated immediately by Christ to the apostle. It shows the importance which our Lord attributes to this ordinance.

The account which Paul received was, *That the same night in which he was betrayed,* i. e. while he was being betrayed—while the traitorous scheme was in progress. Under these affecting circumstances the ordinance was instituted. This fact, which Christ saw fit to reveal to Paul, must be of permanent interest to his people. It is not a matter of indifference, that this sacred rite was instituted on the last night of our Redeemer's life, and when he knew what the morrow was to bring forth. This fact gives a peculiar solemnity and interest to the institution. Romanists, in answer to the objections made by Protestants to the mass, that it is a departure from the original mode of celebrating the Lord's supper, say that if the example of Christ be obligatory, we should celebrate the ordinance at night, after a meal, and at a table covered with provisions, &c. Protestants, however, do not hold that the church in all ages is bound to do whatever Christ and the apostles did, but only what they designed should be afterwards done. It is not apostolic example which is obligatory, but apostolic precept, whether expressed in words or in examples declared or evinced to be preceptive. The example of Christ in celebrating the Lord's supper is binding as to every thing which enters into the nature and significancy of the institution; for those are the very things which we are commanded to do. They constitute the ordinance.

Took bread. Matt. 26, 26, it is said, "as they were eating," i. e. during the repast, "Jesus took bread," that is, he took of the bread lying on the table; and as it was at the time of the Passover, there is no doubt that the bread used was unleavened. It was the thin Passover bread of the Jews. But as no part of the significancy of the rite depends on the kind of bread used, as there is no precept on the subject, and as the apostles subsequently in the celebration of the ordinance used ordinary bread, it is evidently a matter of indifference what kind of bread is used. It was however for a long time a subject of bitter controversy. At first the Latins and Greeks used leavened bread; when the Latins introduced the unleavened wafer from superstitious fear of any of the fragments being dropped, the Greeks retained the use of fermented bread, and accused the Latins of Judaizing. Romanists and Lutherans use unleavened wafers; Protestants generally ordinary bread.

24. And when he had given thanks, he brake (it), and said, Take, eat; this is my body, which is broken for you : this do in remembrance of me.

Having given thanks. In Matt. 26, 26, and Mark 14, 22, it is, " Having blessed *it*." In Luke 22, 19, it is as here. The two expressions mean the same thing. Both express the act of consecration, by a grateful acknowledgment of God's mercy and invocation of his blessing. See the remarks on 10, 16. *He brake* it. This circumstance is included in all the accounts; in those of Matthew, Mark, and Luke, as well as in Paul's. This is one of the significant parts of the service, and ought not to be omitted as is done by Romanists, by the Greek church and by Lutherans. *And said.* The words uttered by our blessed Lord at this moment are differently reported by the different evangelists. In Matt. 26, 26, it is, "Take, eat." In Mark 14, 22, the latter word (according to the best authorities) is omitted. In Luke 22, 19, both are omitted. Here, although both are found in the common text, yet, as they are wanting in the oldest MSS., they should probably be omitted; so that Paul's account agrees as to this point with that of Luke. The proper inference from this diversity is, that the words were uttered by our Lord; but as the ideas which they express were sufficiently indicated by the gesture of reaching the bread to his disciples, they were omitted by some of the narrators as unnecessary. The idea, whether expressed by words or gesture, is however of importance. The bread was to be taken and eaten.—There must be a distribution of the elements to those participating in the service. Otherwise it is not a communion. This distribution is omitted by Romanists in the ordinary celebration of the Mass. The priest alone eats the consecrated wafer. The next words, *this is my body*, are found in all the accounts. Probably the history of the world does not furnish a parallel to the controversies occasioned by these simple words. The ordinary and natural interpretation of them is, that the pronoun *this* refers to the bread. 'This bread which I hold in my hand, and

which I give to you, is my body.' That is, is the symbol of
my body; precisely as we say of a statue, it is the person
which it represents; or as the Scriptures say that the sign is
the thing of which it is the symbol, Ez. 5, 4. 5. Gal. 4, 24; or as
our Saviour says, I am the vine, ye are the branches. I am
the door; or as in the preceding chapter it was said, "that
rock was Christ;" or as in John 1, 32, the dove is said to be
the Holy Ghost; or as baptism is said to be regeneration.
This is a usage so familiar to all languages that no one disputes that the words in question will bear this interpretation.
That they must have this meaning, would seem to be plain,
1. From the impossibility of the bread in Christ's hand being
his literal body then seated at the table; and the wine the
blood then flowing in his veins. 2. From the still more obvious impossibility of taking the words "this cup is the New
Testament" in a literal sense. In Matt. 26, 28 it is said, "this
(cup) is my blood." But Romanists do not hold to a transubstantiation of the *cup*, but only of the wine. But if the words
are to be taken literally, they necessitated the belief of the one
as well as of the other. 3. From the utter subversion of all
the rules of evidence and laws of belief necessarily involved in
the assumption that the bread in the Lord's supper is literally
the crucified body of Christ. 4. From the infidelity on the one
hand, and the superstitious idolatry on the other, which are
the unavoidable consequences of calling upon men to believe
so glaring a contradiction. It is only by denying all distinction between matter and spirit, and confounding all our ideas
of substance and qualities, that we can believe that wine is
blood, or bread flesh.

The Romish interpretation of these words is, that the
bread is the body of Christ, because its whole substance is
changed into the substance of his body. The Lutherans say,
It is his body, because his body is locally present in and with
the bread. Calvin says, It is his body in the same sense that
the dove (John 1, 32) was the Holy Ghost. The Holy Ghost
appeared under the form of a dove, which was the pledge of
his presence. So the bread is the symbol of Christ's body,
because with the one we receive the other. What is received,
however, and what Calvin calls Christ's body, and sometimes
the substance of his body, is not the body itself, which, he admits, is in heaven only, but a life-giving power (vim vivificam)
which flows to us from the glorified body of our Lord. The
only presence of Christ's body in the sacrament admitted by

Calvin was this presence of power.* The Reformed churches teach that the bread is called the body of Christ in the same sense that the cup is called the new covenant. He who in faith receives the cup, receives the covenant of which it was the pledge; and he who receives in faith the bread receives the benefits of Christ's body as broken for sin. The one is the symbol and pledge of the other.

Broken for you. In Luke it is, *given for you.* In Matthew and Mark these words are omitted. In some manuscripts † the word (κλώμενον), *broken*, is wanting in this passage; so that it would read simply *for you*, leaving the participle to be supplied from the context. *Broken* or *given* for you means slain, or given unto death for you. The sacrificial character of the death of Christ enters essentially into the nature of this ordinance. It is the commemoration of his death, not as a teacher, or a benefactor, but as a sacrifice; so that if this idea be kept out of view the sacrament loses all its significance and power.

This do in remembrance of me. These words are not found in Matthew or Mark. They occur in Luke 22, 19, as they do here. *This* do, i. e. 'Do what I have just done; take bread, consecrate it, break it, distribute and eat it. *In remembrance of me*, i. e. that I may be remembered as he who died for your sins. This is the specific, definite object of the Lord's Supper, to which all other ends must be subordinate, because this alone is stated in the words of institution. It is of course involved in this, that we profess faith in him as the sacrifice for our sins; that we receive him as such; that we acknowledge the obligations which rest upon us as those who have been redeemed by his blood; and that we recognize ourselves as constituent members of his church and all believers as our brethren. We are thus, as taught in the preceding chapter, brought into a real communion with Christ and with all his people by the believing participation of this ordinance.

25. After the same manner also (he took) the cup, when he had supped, saying, This cup is the new testa-

* Hæc communicatio corporis Christi, quam nobis in coena exhiberi dico, nec localem praesentiam, nec Christi descensum, nec infinitam extensionem, nec aliud quicquam tale flagitat. . . . Locum non mutat, ut nobis adsit, sed e coelo praesentem in nos carnis suae virtutem transmittat.

† The MSS. A. B. C. omit κλώμενον, Griesbach questioned its genuineness, Lachmann and Tischendorf reject it.

ment in my blood : this do ye, as oft as ye drink (it), in remembrance of me.

This second part of the service is introduced by Luke with the same words which are here used, though our translators there render them *Likewise also the cup, after supper.* This latter version is the literal and simple rendering of the original. In Matthew and Mark it is said, "Having taken the cup, and having given thanks." This explains what Paul and Luke mean by *likewise,* or *after the same manner.* They intend to say that Christ did with the cup what he had done with the bread, i. e. he took it, and pronounced over it the eucharistical benediction, i. e. a blessing connected with thanksgiving. In this particular there is a slight departure in our mode of administering this ordinance, from the example of Christ. With us there is generally but one eucharistical blessing at the introduction of the service, having reference both to the bread and to the cup. Whereas it seems that our Lord blessed the bread, and having broken, distributed it to his disciples ; and then took the cup, and having blessed it, gave it to them to drink. *After supper*, i. e. after the conclusion of the paschal supper.

Saying, This cup is the New Testament in my blood. The same words occur in Luke 22, 20. In Matthew and Mark the corresponding expression is, "This is my blood of the New Testament." The sense must be the same. "The blood of the covenant" means here, as in Ex. 24, 8, the blood by which the covenant was ratified and its blessings secured. The passage referred to in Exodus shows the manner in which covenants were anciently ratified in the East. A victim was slain and the blood sprinkled upon the contracting parties, by which they were solemnly bound to their mutual engagements. The word διαϑήκη so constantly, after the Vulgate, rendered Testament by our translators, always in the New Testament means a covenant, unless Heb. 9, 16 be an exception. Here that sense is required by the context, as a covenant and not a testament was ratified by blood. This covenant is called *new* in reference to the Mosaic covenant. The latter was ratified by the blood of animals; the new, by the blood of the eternal Son of God; the one in itself could secure only temporal benefits and the remission of ceremonial offences ; the other secures eternal redemption, and the remission of sin in the sight of God. As the Hebrews entered into covenant with God when the blood of the heifer was sprinkled upon them, and thereby bound themselves to be obedient to the Mosaic institutions, and as God thereby graciously bound himself to confer upon them all its promised blessings on condition of that obedience; so, in the Lord's supper, those who receive the cup profess to embrace the covenant of grace, and bind themselves to obedience to the gospel; and God binds himself to confer on them all the benefits of redemption. In receiving the cup, therefore, they receive the pledge of their salvation. The death of Christ, which is so often compared to a sin-offering, is here, as well as in the Epistle to the Hebrews, compared to a federal sacrifice. The two, however, do not differ. The death of Christ is the latter only in virtue of its being the former. It ratifies the covenant of grace and secures its benefits, only because it was a propitiation, i. e. because it was a satisfaction to divine justice, as is so clearly taught in Rom. 3, 25. 26. Every time, therefore, the consecrated wine touches the believer's lips, he receives anew the application of the blood of Christ for the remission of his sins and his reconciliation with God. If the Bible says we are sprinkled with the blood of Jesus, 1 Peter 1, 2, why may we not be said to receive his blood? If the former expression means the application of the benefits of his sacrificial death, why may not the latter mean the reception of those benefits? Here, as elsewhere, the difficulty is the want of faith. He who by faith appropriates a divine promise recorded in the word, receives the blessing promised; and he who in the exercise of faith receives the sacramental cup receives the benefits of the covenant of which that cup is the symbol and the pledge. But what is faith? or rather, what is it that we are required to believe, in order to experience all this? 1. We must believe that Jesus is the Son of God, and that he loved us and gave himself for us. 2. That his blood cleanses from all sin. 3. That in the sacrament he offers us, with the symbols of his broken body and his shed blood, the benefits of his death; and that he will certainly convey those benefits to all those who hold out even a trembling hand to receive them.

In Luke, after the words *in my blood*, it is added, *which is shed for you.* In Mark the explanation is, *which is shed for many;* and in Matthew, still more fully, *which is shed for many for the remission of sins.* These are different forms of expressing the sacrificial character of the death of Christ. Though it was the blood of the covenant, yet it was at the same time *shed for many*, not merely for their benefit in the general, but for the specific object of securing *the remission of sins*. It was, therefore, truly a sin-offering. Thus does Scripture explain Scripture. What is said concisely in one place is more fully and clearly stated in another.

This do, as oft as ye drink it, in remembrance of me. These words do not occur in Luke. In Matthew the words are, *Drink ye all of it.* Mark says, *They all drank of it.* In each account the fact is made plain that the cup was distributed to all at the table and that all drank of it. The words *This do* are to be understood here as in v. 24, 'Do what I have done, i. e. bless the cup and distribute it among yourselves.' *As oft as ye drink of it.* This does not mean that every time Christians drank wine together they should do it in commemoration of Christ's death; but, 'as often as this ordinance is celebrated, do what I have done, to commemorate my death.' The Lord's Supper is a commemoration of Christ's death, not only because it was designed for that purpose, but also because the bread and wine are the significant symbols of his broken body and shed blood. In this ordinance therefore Christ is set forth as a sacrifice which at once makes expiation for sin and ratifies the covenant of grace.

26. For as often as ye eat this bread, and drink this cup, ye do shew the Lord's death till he come.

What Paul had received of the Lord is recorded in the preceding verses. Here and in what follows we have his own inferences from the account which the Lord had given him. The first of those inferences is, that the Lord's supper is, and was designed to be, a proclamation of the death of Christ to continue until his second advent. Those who come to it, therefore, should come, not to satisfy hunger, nor for the gratification of social feelings, but for the definite purpose of bearing their testimony to the great fact of redemption, and to contribute their portion of influence to the preservation and propagation of the knowledge of that fact. *For* indicates the connection with what precedes. 'It is a commemoration of his death, *for* it is in its very nature a proclamation of that great fact.' And it was not a temporary institution, but one designed to continue until the consummation. As the Passover was a perpetual commemoration of the deliverance out of Egypt, and a prediction of the coming and death of the

Lamb of God, who was to bear the sins of the world; so the Lord's supper is at once the commemoration of the death of Christ and a pledge of his coming the second time without sin unto salvation.

27. Wherefore whosoever shall eat this bread, and drink (this) cup of the Lord, unworthily, shall be guilty of the body and blood of the Lord.

This is the second inference. *Wherefore*, i. e. so that, hence it follows. If the Lord's Supper be in its very nature a proclamation of the death of Christ, it follows that those who attend upon it as an ordinary meal, or in an irreverent manner, or for any other purpose than that for which it was appointed, are guilty of the body and blood of the Lord. That is, they contract guilt in reference to the body and blood of Christ. See James 2, 10. The man who tramples on the flag of his country, insults his country; and he who treats with indignity the representative of a sovereign, thereby offends the sovereign himself. In like manner, he who treats the symbols of Christ's body and blood irreverently is guilty of irreverence towards Christ. The idea that he is so evil that he would have joined in the crucifixion of the Lord; or that he makes himself a partaker of the guilt of his death, does not lie in the words. It is also obvious that this passage affords no ground for either the Romish or Lutheran view of the local presence of Christ's body in the sacrament, since an insult to the appointed symbol of his body, is an insult to his body itself. Neither does the passage countenance the doctrine held by both Romanists and Lutherans, that unbelievers receive the body and blood of Christ. If they do not receive them, it is asked, how can they be guilty in respect to them? By treating them, in their appointed symbols, irreverently. It is not necessary, therefore, in order to the guilt here spoken of, either that the body of Christ should be locally present, or that the unworthy receiver be a partaker of that body, which is received by faith alone. In our version it is, " whosoever shall eat this bread *and* drink this cup;" in the Greek it is (ἤ) *or*, not *and*. And this the sense requires. The irreverent use of either the bread or the cup in this ordinance involves the guilt of which the apostle here speaks; because the indignity extends to the whole service.

But what is it to eat and drink *unworthily?* It is not to

eat and drink with a consciousness of unworthiness, for such a sense of ill-desert is one of the conditions of acceptable communion. It is not the whole, but the consciously sick whom Christ came to heal. Nor is it to eat with doubt and misgiving of our being duly prepared to come to the Lord's table; for such doubts, although an evidence of a weak faith, indicate a better state of mind than indifference or false security. In the Larger Catechism of our Church, in answer to the question, whether one who doubts of his being in Christ, may come to the Lord's supper, it is said, "One who doubteth of his being in Christ, or of his due preparation to the sacrament of the Lord's supper, may have true interest in Christ, though he be not yet assured thereof; and in God's account hath it, if he be duly affected with the apprehension of the want of it, and unfeignedly desires to be found in Christ, and to depart from iniquity; in which case (because promises are made, and this sacrament is appointed, for the relief even of weak and doubting Christians) he is to bewail his unbelief, and labour to have his doubts resolved; and so doing, he may and ought to come to the Lord's supper, that he may be further strengthened." To eat or drink *unworthily* is in general to come to the Lord's table in a careless, irreverent spirit, without the intention or desire to commemorate the death of Christ as the sacrifice for our sins, and without the purpose of complying with the engagements which we thereby assume. The way in which the Corinthians ate unworthily was, that they treated the Lord's table as though it were their own; making no distinction between the Lord's supper and an ordinary meal; coming together to satisfy their hunger, and not to feed on the body and blood of Christ; and refusing to commune with their poorer brethren. This, though one, is not the only way in which men may eat and drink unworthily. All that is necessary to observe is, that the warning is directly against the careless and profane, and not against the timid and the doubting.

28. But let a man examine himself, and so let him eat of (that) bread, and drink of (that) cup.

This is the third inference from the account of the Lord's supper which Paul had received. It requires self-examination and preparation in order to being worthily received. If it be a commemoration of Christ's death; if we are therein "made

partakers of his body and blood;" if we contract such guilt
by eating and drinking unworthily; in other words, if such
blessings attend the worthy receiving, and such guilt the
unworthy receiving of this ordinance, it is evident that we
should not approach it without due self-inspection and preparation. *Let a man examine himself.* In other words, let him
ascertain whether he has correct views of the nature and design of the ordinance, and whether he has the proper state of
mind. That is, whether he desires thankfully to commemorate the Lord's death, renewedly to partake of the benefits of
that death as a sacrifice for his sins, publicly to accept the covenant of grace with all its promises and obligations, and to
signify his fellowship with his brethren as joint members with
himself of the body of Christ. *And so let him eat.* That is,
after this self-examination, and, as is evidently implied, after
having ascertained that he possesses the due preparation. It
is not essential, however, to this preparation, as before remarked, that we should be assured of our good estate, but
simply that we have the intelligent desire to do what Christ
requires of us when we come to his table. If we come humbly
seeking him, he will bid us welcome, and feed us with that
bread whereof if a man eat, he shall never die.

29. For he that eateth and drinketh unworthily,*
eateth and drinketh damnation to himself, not discerning the Lord's body.

This verse assigns the reason why self-examination in preparation for the Lord's supper is necessary. It is because he
that eateth and drinketh unworthily (in the sense before explained), *eateth and drinketh judgment to himself.* That is,
he incurs the manifestation of God's displeasure by the act of
eating. The word *damnation*, used in our version, originally
and properly means simply condemnation, and not hopeless
and final perdition, which is its modern and popular sense. In
the original the word is κρίμα without the article, and there-

---

* The word ἀναξίως, *unworthily*, is omitted by the MSS. A. C., and is rejected by Lachmann and Tischendorf. If discarded, the sense of the passage
is either, 'The eater and drinker, i. e. he who eats and drinks at the Lord's
table as at an ordinary meal, eats judgment to himself;' or, 'He that eats,
not discerning the Lord's body, eats judgment to himself.' The common text
has in its support the majority of ancient MSS., and is followed by most
editors.

fore simply *judgment*, not *the* judgment. The meaning obviously is, that the unworthy eater contracts guilt; he exposes himself to the judgments of God. What kind of judgments the apostle had in his mind is plain from the next verse, where he refers to sickness and death.* This verse is only a repetition of the sentiment expressed in v. 27, where he who eats unworthily is said to contract guilt in reference to the body of the Lord. *Not discerning*, i. e. because he does not discern *the Lord's* body. The word διακρίνω, translated *to discern*, means *to separate*, then to cause to differ, as 4, 7; and also, judge of, either in the sense of discriminating one thing from another, or in the sense of estimating aright. This passa‚ e may therefore mean, not discriminating the Lord's body, i. e. making no difference between the bread in the sacrament and ordinary food; or, it may mean, not estimating it aright, not reverencing it as the appointed symbol of the body of the Lord. In either case the offence is the same. The ground of the condemnation incurred is, regarding and treating the elements in the Lord's supper as though there was nothing to distinguish them from ordinary bread and wine. Here, as before, it is the careless and profane who are warned. There is, therefore, nothing in these passages which should surround the Lord's table with gloom. We are not called unto the mount covered with clouds and darkness, from which issue the signs of wrath, but unto Mount Zion, to the abode of mercy and grace, where all is love—the dying love of him who never breaks the bruised reed.

30. For this cause many (are) weak and sickly among you, and many sleep.

For this cause, that is, because those who partake of the Lord's supper unworthily incur the judgment of God; *many are weak and sickly*. The distinction between these words made by commentators, is, that the former designates those whose strength decays as it were of itself, and the latter, those rendered *infirm* by sickness. The latter term is the stronger of the two. *And many sleep*, i. e. have already died. As there is nothing in the context to intimate that these terms

---

* BENGEL's remark on this clause is: κρίμα sine articulo judicium aliquod, morbum, mortemve corporis, ut qui Domini corpus non discernunt, corpore suo luant. Non dicit τὸ κατάκριμα, condemnationem.

are used figuratively of moral infirmities and spiritual declension, they should be taken in their literal sense. Paul knew that the prevailing sickness and frequent deaths among the Christians of Corinth were a judgment from God on account of the irreverent manner in which they had celebrated the Lord's supper.

31. For if we would judge ourselves, we should not be judged.

For, i. e. these afflictions are judgments from God, because of your sin in this matter; for, if *we judge ourselves*, that is, if we examine ourselves (see v. 28) and prepare ourselves for the Lord's table, *we should not be judged*, i. e. thus afflicted. It is because we do not sit in judgment on ourselves, that God judges us.

32. But when we are judged, we are chastened of the Lord, that we should not be condemned with the world.

These judgments were chastisements designed for the benefit of those who suffered, to bring them to repentance, that they might not be finally condemned with the world; that is, with unbelievers. The world often means mankind as distinguished from the church, or those chosen out of the world. "They are not of the world, even as I am not of the world," John 17, 16. What Paul says of the design of these judgments, proves that even the extreme irreverence with which he charges the Corinthians in reference to the Lord's supper, was not an unpardonable sin.

33. 34. Wherefore, my brethren, when ye come together to eat, tarry one for another. And if any man hunger, let him eat at home; that ye come not together unto condemnation. And the rest will I set in order when I come.

The two great evils connected with the observance of the Lord's supper at Corinth were, first, that it was not a communion, one took his supper before another, v. 21; and secondly, that they came to the Lord's table to satisfy their hunger. That is, they made it an ordinary meal. They thus sinned against their brethren, v. 22, and they sinned against Christ, v. 27. In the conclusion, therefore, of the whole discussion, he exhorts them to correct these evils; to wait for each other, and make it a joint service; and to satisfy their hunger at home, and come together only to commemorate the Lord's death. Mildly as this exhortation is expressed, it is enforced by the solemn warning already given, *that ye come not together to condemnation*, that is, so as to incur the displeasure of God. *The rest will I set in order when (whenever* ὡς ἄν) *I may come.* There were, it seems, other irregularities of less importance than those above mentioned, which the apostle leaves to be corrected until he should again visit Corinth. The epistles of Paul abound in evidence of the plenary authority exercised by the apostles over the churches. The word διατάσσω, *to set in order*, implies authoritative direction; see 7, 17. 16, 1. Matt. 11, 1. The apostles were rendered infallible, as the representatives of Christ, to teach his doctrines, to organize the church and determine its form of government, and to regulate its worship. And what they ordained has binding force on the church to this day. What Paul teaches in this chapter concerning the nature and mode of celebrating the Lord's supper, has determined the views and practice of evangelical Christians in every part of the world. It is not at all wonderful, considering that the festivals of the Jews, and especially the Passover, as well as the sacrificial feasts of the Gentiles, were social repasts, and especially considering that our Lord instituted this ordinance in connection with the Paschal supper, that the early Christians should have so generally combined it with a social meal; or that this custom should have continued so long in the church. Nor is it a matter of surprise, that the social element in this combined service should so often have prevailed over the religious one. That this was to a lamentable degree the case in Corinth, is evident from this chapter; and it is probable from Jude 12, that the evil was by no means confined to Corinth. That apostle, speaking of certain sensual persons, says, " These are spots in your feasts of charity, when they feast with you without fear." Hence the unspeakable importance of the instructions and directions given by St. Paul, which are specially designed to separate the Lord's supper as a religious rite from the social element with which it was combined. The apostle urges that neither the sacrament itself, nor any feast with which it might be connected, should be regarded as the occasion of satisfying hunger. The communion of saints and the commemoration of the death of Christ as a sacrifice for our sins, are the only legitimate objects which could be contemplated in the service. And by exhibiting the intimate fellowship with the Lord involved in the right use of this ordinance, and the dreadful consequences of unworthily participating, he has raised it to a purely religious service, and made it the highest act of worship. From one extreme the church gradually passed over to the opposite. From regarding it as it had been in Corinth, little more than an ordinary meal, it came to be regarded as an awful mystery, a sacrifice which the people were to witness, and in which they were to adore the Redeemer as locally present in his corporeal nature under the form of a wafer! So strong a hold had this unscriptural view taken of the mind of the church, that Luther found it impossible to emancipate himself from the belief of the local presence of Christ's real body in this sacrament. And even Calvin could not divest himself of the conviction, not only of its supernatural character, which all admit who regard it as a means of grace, but also of its being truly miraculous. It was only after a severe struggle that the Reformed church got back to the simple, yet sublime view of the ordinance presented by the apostle Paul. The danger has often since been that the church should go back to the Corinthian extreme, and look upon the Lord's supper as a simple commemoration, involving nothing supernatural either in its nature or effects. Our only safety is in adhering strictly to the teachings of the Scriptures. The apostle tells us, on the authority of a direct revelation from the Lord himself, that while the ordinance is designed as a memorial of Christ's death, it involves a participation of his body and blood, not of their material substance, but of their sacrificial efficacy, so that, "although the body and blood of Christ are not corporally or carnally present in, with, or under the bread and wine in the Lord's supper; and yet are spiritually present to the faith of the receiver, no less truly and really than the elements themselves are to their outward senses; so they that worthily communicate in the sacrament of the Lord's supper, do therein feed upon the body and blood of Christ, not after a corporal or carnal, but in a spiritual manner; yet truly and really, while by faith they receive and apply unto themselves Christ crucified and all the benefits of his death." *Larger Catechism.*

CHAPTER XII.

Of Spiritual Gifts, vs. 1–31.

THE ancient prophets had clearly predicted that the Messianic period should be attended by a remarkable effusion of the Holy Spirit. "And it shall come to pass in those days," it is said in the prophecies of Joel, "saith God, I will pour out of my Spirit upon all flesh; and your sons and your daughters shall prophesy, and your young men shall see visions, and your old men shall dream dreams." Our Lord, before his crucifixion, promised to send the Comforter, who is the Holy Ghost, to instruct and guide his church, John 14, &c. And after his resurrection he said to his disciples, "These signs shall follow them that believe. In my name shall they cast out devils; they shall speak with new tongues; they shall take up serpents; and if they drink any deadly thing it shall not hurt them; they shall lay hands on the sick and they shall recover," Mark 16, 17. 18. And immediately before his as. cension he said to the disciples, "Ye shall be baptized with the Holy Ghost not many days hence," Acts 1, 5. Accordingly, on the day of Pentecost, these promises and prophecies were literally fulfilled. The peculiarity of the new dispensation consisted, in the first place, in the general diffusion of these gifts. They were not confined to any one class of the people, but extended to all classes; male and female, young and old; and secondly, in the wonderful diversity of these supernatural endowments. Under circumstances so extraordinary it was unavoidable that many disorders should arise. Some men would claim to be the organs of the Spirit, who were deluded or impostors; some would be dissatisfied with the gifts which they had received, and envy those whom they regarded as more highly favoured; others would be inflated, and make an ostentatious display of their extraordinary powers; and in the public assemblies it might be expected that the greatest confusion would arise from so many persons being desirous to exercise their gifts at the same time. To the correction of these evils, all of which had manifested themselves in the church of Corinth, the apostle devotes this and the two following chapters. It is impossible to read these chapters without being deeply impressed by the divine wisdom with which they are pervaded. After contrasting the condition of the Corinthians, as members of that body which was instinct with the life-giving Spirit of God, with their former condition as the senseless worshippers of dumb idols, he, First, lays down the criterion by which they might decide whether those who pretended to be the organs of the Spirit were really under his influence. How do they speak of Christ? Do they blaspheme, or do they worship him? If they openly and sincerely recognize Jesus as the Supreme Lord, then they are under the influence of the Holy Ghost, vs. 1–3. Secondly, these gifts, whether viewed as graces of the Spirit, or as forms of ministering to Christ, or the effects of God's power, that is, whether viewed in relation to the Spirit, to the Son, or to the Father, are but different manifestations of the Holy Ghost dwelling in his people, and are all intended for the edification of the church, vs. 4–7. Thirdly, he arranges them under three heads, 1. The word of wisdom and the word of knowledge. 2. Faith, the gift of healing, the power of working miracles, prophesying, and the discerning of spirits. 3. The gift of tongues and the interpretation of tongues, vs. 8–10. Fourthly, these gifts are not only all the fruits of the Spirit, but they are distributed according to his sovereign will, v. 11. Fifthly, there is therefore in this matter a striking analogy between the church and the human body. For, 1. As the body is one organic whole, because animated by one spirit, so the church is one because of the indwelling of the Holy Ghost as the principle of its life. 2. As the unity of life in the body is manifested in a diversity of organs and members; so the indwelling of the Spirit in the church is manifested by a diversity of gifts and offices. 3. As the very idea of the body as an organization supposes this diversity in unity, the same is true in regard to the church. 4. As in the human body the members are mutually dependent, and no one exists for itself alone but for the body as a whole, so also in the church there is the same dependence of its members on each other, and their various gifts are not designed for the exclusive benefit of those who exercise them, but for the edification of the whole church. 5. As in the body the position and function of each member are determined not by itself, but by God, so also these spiritual gifts are distributed according to the good pleasure of their author. 6. In the body the least attractive parts are those which are indispensable to its existence, and so in the church it is not the most attractive gifts which are the most useful. Sixthly, the apostle draws from this analogy the following inferences. 1. Every one should be contented with the gift which he has received of the Lord, just as the hand and foot are contented with their position and office in the body. 2. There should be no exaltation of one member of the church over others, on the ground of the supposed superiority of his gifts. 3. There should, and must be mutual sympathy between the members of the church, as there is between the members of the body. One cannot suffer without all the others suffering with it. No one lives, or acts, or feels for itself alone, but each in all the rest, vs. 12–27. In conclusion the apostle shows that what he had said with regard to these spiritual gifts, applies in all its force to the various offices of the church, which are the organs through which the gifts of the Spirit are exercised, vs. 28–31.

1. Now concerning spiritual (gifts), brethren, I would not have you ignorant.

Instead of beginning with, *in the second place*, in continuance of the enumeration begun in 11, 17, he passes to the second ground of censure, by the simple *now* (δέ) as the particle of transition. The misuse of the spiritual gifts, especially of the gift of tongues, was the next topic of rebuke. *Concerning spiritual*, whether *men* or *gifts*, depends on the context, as the word may be either masculine or neuter. The latter is the more natural and common explanation, because the gifts rather than the persons are the subject of discussion ; and because in v. 31, and 14, 1, the neuter form is used. *I would not have you ignorant*, i. e. I wish you to understand the origin and intent of these extraordinary manifestations of divine power, and to be able to discriminate between the true and false claimants to the possession of them.

2. Ye know that ye were Gentiles, carried away unto these dumb idols, even as ye were led.

Here, as in Ephesians 2, 11, the apostle contrasts the former with the present condition of his readers. Formerly, they were Gentiles, now they were Christians. Formerly, they were the worshippers and consulters of dumb idols, now they worshipped the living and true God. Formerly, they were swayed by a blind, unintelligent impulse, which carried them away, they knew not why nor whither ; now they were under the influence of the Spirit of God. Their former condition is here adverted to as affording a reason why they needed instruction on this subject. It was one on which their previous experience gave them no information.

*Ye know that** ye were Gentiles.* This is the comprehensive statement of their former condition. Under it are included the two particulars which follow. First, they were addicted to the worship of *dumb* idols, i. e. voiceless, comp. Hab. 2, 18. 19, "Woe unto him that saith unto the wood, Awake; unto the dumb stone, Arise, it shall teach," and Ps. 115, 5. 135, 16. To worship dumb idols, gods who could neither hear nor save, expresses in the strongest terms at once their folly and their misery. Secondly, they were *carried away* to this worship *just as they were led*, i. e. they were controlled by an influence which they could not understand or resist. Compare, as to the force of the word here used, Gal. 2, 13. 2 Pet. 3, 17. It is often spoken of those who are led away to judgment, to prison, or to execution. Mark 14, 53. John 18, 13. Matt. 27, 21. Paul means to contrast this (ἀπάγεσθαι) *being carried away*, as it were, by force, with the (ἄγεσθαι πνεύματι), *being led by the Spirit.* The one was an irrational influence controlling the understanding and will; the other is an influence from God, congruous to our nature, and leading to good.

3. Wherefore I give you to understand, that no man speaking by the Spirit of God calleth Jesus accursed: and (that) no man can say that Jesus is the Lord, but by the Holy Ghost.

Wherefore, i. e. because I would not have you ignorant on this subject. The first thing which he teaches is the criterion or test of true divine influence. This criterion he states first negatively and then positively. The negative statement is, that *no man speaking by the Spirit of God calleth Jesus accursed.* To speak by (or *in*) the Spirit, is to speak under the influence of the Spirit, as the ancient prophets did. Matt. 22, 43. Mark 12, 36. *No one speaking* (λαλῶν, *using his voice*), *calleth* (λέγει *pronounces*) *Jesus to be accursed.* Or, according to another reading, utters the words, "Jesus is accursed."

---

* The common text is ὅτι, the MSS. A. C. D. E. F. I., and many of the versions and Fathers have ὅτι ὅτε (*that when*), which reading is adopted by Lachmann, Scholz, and Tischendorf. The construction is then irregular.

By *Jesus*, the historical person known among men by that name is indicated. And, therefore, Paul uses that word and not *Christ*, which is a term of office. *Accursed*, i. e. anathema. This word properly means something consecrated to God; and as among the Jews what was thus consecrated could not be redeemed, but, if a living thing, must be put to death, Lev. 27, 28. 29, hence the word was used to designate any person or thing devoted to destruction; and then with the accessory idea of the divine displeasure, something devoted to destruction as accursed. This last is its uniform meaning in the New Testament. Rom. 9, 3. Gal. 1, 8. 9. 1 Cor. 16, 22. Hence to say that Jesus is anathema, is to say he was a malefactor, one justly condemned to death. This the Jews said who invoked his blood upon their heads. The affirmative statement is, *no man can say Jesus is the Lord, but by the Holy Ghost.* The word κύριος, LORD, is that by which the word Jehovah is commonly rendered in the Greek version of the Old Testament. To say Jesus is the Lord, therefore, in the sense of the apostle, is to acknowledge him to be truly God. And as the word *Jesus* here as before designates the historical person known by that name, who was born of the Virgin Mary, to say that Jesus is Lord, is to acknowledge that that person is God manifest in the flesh. In other words, the confession includes the acknowledgment that he is truly God and truly man. What the apostle says, is that no man can make this acknowledgment but by the Holy Ghost. This of course does not mean that no one can utter these words unless under special divine influence; but it means that no one can truly believe and openly confess that Jesus is God manifest in the flesh unless he is enlightened by the Spirit of God. This is precisely what our Lord himself said, when Peter confessed him to be the Son of God. "Blessed art thou, Simon Bar-jona; for flesh and blood hath not revealed it unto thee, but my Father who is in heaven." Matt. 16, 17. The same thing is also said by the apostle John. "Hereby know ye the Spirit of God; every spirit that confesseth that Jesus Christ is come in the flesh is of God: and every spirit that confesseth not that Jesus Christ is come in the flesh is not of God," 1 John 4, 2. 3; and in v. 15, "Whosoever shall confess that Jesus is the Son of God, God dwelleth in him, and he in God." To blaspheme Christ, *maledicere Christo*, Plin. Epist. X. 97, was the form for renouncing Christianity before the Roman tribunals; and saying, "I believe that Jesus is the Son of God," Acts 8, 37, was the form of professing allegiance to Christ. Men acknowledged themselves to be Christians, by acknowledging the divinity of Christ. These passages, therefore, teach us first, whom we are to regard as Christians, viz., those who acknowledge and worship Jesus of Nazareth as the true God; secondly, that the test of the divine commission of those who assume to be teachers of the gospel, is not external descent, or apostolic succession, but soundness in the faith. If even an apostle or angel teach any other gospel, we are to regard him as accursed, Gal. 1, 8. And Paul tells the Corinthians that they were to discriminate between those who were really the organs of the Holy Ghost, and those who falsely pretended to that office, by the same criterion. As it is unscriptural to recognize as Christians those who deny the divinity of our Lord; so it is unscriptural for any man to doubt his own regeneration, if he is conscious that he sincerely worships the Lord Jesus.

4–6. Now there are diversities of gifts, but the same Spirit. And there are differences of administrations, but the same Lord. And there are diversities of operations, but it is the same God which worketh all in all.

The second thing which the apostle teaches concerning these gifts is, their diversity of character in connection with the unity of their source and design. He is not, however, to be understood as here dividing these gifts into three classes, under the heads of *gifts, ministrations,* and *operations;* but as presenting them each and all under three different aspects. Viewed in relation to the Spirit, they are gifts; in relation to the Lord, they are ministrations; and in relation to God, they are operations, i. e. effects wrought by his power. And it is the same Spirit, the same· Lord, and the same God who are concerned in them all. That is, the same Spirit is the giver; it is he who is the immediate and proximate author of all these various endowments. It is the same Lord in whose service and by whose authority these various gifts are exercised. They are all different forms in which he is served, or ministered to. And it is the same God the Father, who having exalted the Lord Jesus to the supreme headship of the church, and having sent the Holy Ghost, works all these effects in the

minds of men. There is no inconsistency between this statement and v. 11, where the Spirit is said to work all these
gifts; because God works by his Spirit. So in one place we
are said to be born of God, and in another to be born of the
Spirit. Thus, the doctrine of the Trinity underlies the whole
scheme of redemption in its execution and application as well
as in its conception.

Those who understand this passage as describing three distinct classes of gifts, one as derived from the Spirit, the other
from the Son, and the other from the Father, suppose that to
the first class belong wisdom, knowledge, and faith; to the
second, church-offices; and to the third, gift of miracles. But
this view of the passage is inconsistent with the constant and
equal reference of these gifts to the Holy Spirit; they all come
under the head of " spiritual gifts; " and with what follows in
vs. 8–10, where a different classification is given. That is, the
nine gifts there mentioned are not classified in reference to
their relation to the Father, Son, and Spirit; and therefore it
is unnatural to assume such a classification here. They are all
and equally gifts of the Spirit, modes of serving the Son, and
effects due to the efficiency of the Father.

7. But the manifestation of the Spirit is given to
every man to profit withal.

But, i. e. notwithstanding these gifts have the same source,
they are diverse in their manifestations. *To each one*, i. e. to
every believer, or every recipient of the Holy Ghost, *is given
a manifestation of the Spirit.* That is, the Spirit who dwells
in all believers as the body of Christ, manifests himself in one
way in one person, and in another way in another person.
The illustration which the apostle subsequently introduces is
derived from the human body. As the principle of life manifests itself in one organ as the faculty of vision, and in another
as the faculty of hearing, so the Holy Ghost manifests himself
variously in the different members of the church; in one as
the gift of teaching, in another as the gift of healing. This is
one of those pregnant truths, compressed in a single sentence,
which are developed in manifold forms in different parts of
the word of God. It is the truth of which this whole chapter
is the exposition and the application. *To profit withal* ($\pi\rho\grave{o}s$
$\tau\grave{o}$ $\sigma\upsilon\mu\phi\acute{e}\rho\omicron\nu$), i. e. for edification. This is the common object
of all these gifts. They are not designed exclusively or mainly

for the benefit, much less for the gratification of their recipients; but for the good of the church. Just as the power of vision is not for the benefit of the eye, but for the man. When, therefore, the gifts of God, natural or supernatural, are perverted as means of self-exaltation or aggrandizement, it is a sin against their giver, as well as against those for whose benefit they were intended.

With regard to the gifts mentioned in the following verses, it is to be remarked, first, that the enumeration is not intended to include all the forms in which the Spirit manifested his presence in the people of God. Gifts are elsewhere mentioned which are not found in this catalogue; comp. Rom. 12, 4–8, and v. 28 of this chapter. Secondly, that although the apostle appears to divide these gifts into three classes, the principle of classification is not discernible. That is, we can discover no reason why one gift is in one class rather than in another; why, for example, prophecy, instead of being associated with other gifts of teaching, is connected with those of healing and working miracles. The different modes of classification which have been proposed, even when founded on a real difference, cannot be applied to the arrangement given by the apostle. Some would divide them into natural and supernatural. But they are all supernatural, although not to the same degree or in the same form. There are gifts of the Spirit which are ordinary and permanent, such as those of teaching and ruling, but they are not included in this enumeration, which embraces nothing which was not miraculous, or at least supernatural. Others, as Neander, divide them into those exercised by word, and those exercised by deeds. To the former class belong those of wisdom, knowledge, prophecy, and speaking with tongues; and to the latter the gifts of healing and miracles. Others, again, propose a psychological division, i. e. one founded on the different faculties involved in their exercise. Hence they are distinguished as those which concern the feelings, those which pertain to the intelligence, and those which relate to the will. But this is altogether arbitrary, as all these faculties are concerned in the exercise of every gift. It is better to take the classification as we find it, without attempting to determine the principle of arrangement, which may have been in a measure, so to speak, fortuitous, or determined by the mere association of ideas, rather than by any characteristic difference in the gifts themselves. The Scriptures are much more like a work of nature than a work of art; much more like a landscape than a building. Things spring up where we cannot see the reason why they are there, rather than elsewhere, while every thing is in its right place.

8. For to one is given by the Spirit the word of wisdom; to another the word of knowledge by the same Spirit;

In v. 7, he had said, " To each one is given a manifestation of the Spirit," *for* to one is given one gift, and to another, another. What follows, therefore, is the illustration and confirmation of what precedes. The point to be illustrated is the diversity of forms in which the same Spirit manifests himself in different individuals. " To one is given the word of wisdom, to another the word of knowledge." The *word* of wisdom, is the gift of speaking or communicating wisdom; and the *word* of knowledge is the gift of communicating knowledge. As to the difference, however, between wisdom and knowledge, as here used, it is not easy to decide. Some say the former is practical, and the latter speculative. Others, just the reverse; and passages may be cited in favour of either view. Others say that wisdom refers to what is perceived by intuition, i. e. what is apprehended (as they say) by the reason; and knowledge what is perceived by the understanding. The effect of the one is spiritual discernment; of the other, scientific knowledge; i. e. the logical nature and relations of the truths discerned. Others say that wisdom is the gospel, the whole system of revealed truth, and the *word* of wisdom is the gift of revealing that system as the object of faith. In favour of this view are these obvious considerations, 1. That Paul frequently uses the word in this sense. In ch. 2 he says, we speak wisdom, the wisdom of God, the hidden wisdom which the great of this world never could discover, but which God has revealed by his Spirit. 2. That gift stands first as the most important, and as the characteristic gift of the apostles, as may be inferred from v. 28, where the arrangement of offices to a certain extent corresponds with the arrangement of the gifts here presented. Among the gifts, the first is the word of wisdom; and among the offices, the first is that of the apostles. It is perfectly natural that this correspondence should be observed at the beginning, even if it be not carried out. This gift in its full measure belonged to the apostles alone; partially, however, also, to the prophets of the New Testament. Hence apostles and prophets are often associated as possessing the same gift, although in different degrees. "Built on the foundation of the apostles and prophets," Eph. 2, 20. "As now revealed unto the holy apostles and prophets by the Spirit," Eph. 3, 5 ; see also 4, 11. The characteristic difference between these classes of officers was, that the former were endowed with permanent and plenary, the latter with occasional and partial, inspiration. By the *word of knowledge*, as distinguished from *the word of wisdom*, is probably to be understood the gift which belonged to teachers. Accordingly, they follow the apostles and prophets in the enumeration given in v. 28. *The word of knowledge* was the gift correctly to understand and properly to exhibit the truths revealed by the apostles and prophets. This agrees with 13, 8, where the gift of knowledge is represented as pertaining to the present state of existence. *By the same Spirit*, literally, *according to* the same Spirit, i. e. according to his will, or as he sees fit ; see v. 11. The Spirit is not only the author, but the distributor of these gifts. And therefore sometimes they are said to be given (διά) *by*, and sometimes (κατά) *according to*, the Spirit.

9. To another faith by the same Spirit; to another the gifts of healing by the same Spirit ;

There is a distinction indicated in the Greek which is not expressed in our version. The main divisions in this enumeration seem to be indicated by ἕτερος, and the subordinate ones by ἄλλος, though both words are translated by *another ;* the former, however, is a stronger expression of difference. Here, therefore, where ἑτέρῳ is used, a new class seems to be introduced. To the first class belong the word of wisdom and the word of knowledge ; to the second, all that follow except the last two. *To another faith.* As faith is here mentioned as a gift peculiar to some Christians, it cannot mean saving faith, which is common to all. It is generally supposed to mean the faith of miracles to which our Lord refers, Matt. 17, 19. 20, and also the apostle in the following chapter, "Though I have all faith, so that I could remove mountains," 13, 2. But to this it is objected, that the gift of miracles is mentioned immediately afterwards as something different from the gift of faith. Others say it is that faith which manifests itself in all the forms enumerated under this class, that is, in miracles, in healing, in prophecy, and in discerning of spirits. But then it is nothing peculiar; it is a gift common to all under this head, whereas it is as much distinguished from them, as they are from each other. Besides, no degree of faith involves inspiration which is supposed in prophecy. In the absence of distinct data for determining the nature of the faith here intended, it is safest, perhaps, to adhere to the simple meaning of the word, and assume that the gift meant is a higher measure of the ordinary grace of faith. Such a faith as enabled men to become confessors and martyrs, and which is so fully illustrated in Heb. 11, 33–40. This is something as truly wonderful as the gift of miracles. *To another the gifts of healing,* i. e. gifts by which healing of the sick was effected, Acts 4, 30. This evidently refers to the miraculous healing of diseases.

10. To another the working of miracles ; to another prophecy ; to another discerning of spirits ; to another (divers) kinds of tongues ; to another the interpretation of tongues :

Working of miracles, literally, *effects which are miraculous,* or which consist in miracles. This is more comprehensive than the preceding gift. Some had merely the gift of healing the sick, while others had the general power of working miracles. This was exemplified in the death of Ananias, in raising Dorcas, in smiting Elymas with blindness, and in many other cases.

To another prophecy. The nature of this gift is clearly exhibited in the 14th ch. It consisted in occasional inspiration and revelations, not merely or generally relating to the future, as in the case of Agabus, Acts 11, 28, but either in some new communications relating to faith or duty, or simply an immediate impulse and aid from the Holy Spirit, in presenting truth already known, so that conviction and repentance were the effects aimed at and produced ; comp. 14, 25. The difference, as before stated, between the apostles and prophets, was, that the former were permanently inspired, so that their teaching was at all times infallible, whereas the prophets were infallible only occasionally. The ordinary teachers were uninspired, speaking from the resources of their own knowledge and experience.

To another discerning of spirits. It appears, especially from the epistles of the apostle John, that pretenders to inspiration were numerous in the apostolic age. He therefore exhorts his readers, " to try the spirits, whether they be of God; for many false prophets are gone out into the world," 1 John 4, 1. It was therefore of importance to have a class of men with the gift of discernment, who could determine whether a man was really inspired, or spoke only from the impulse of his own mind, or from the dictation of some evil spirit. In 14, 29, reference is made to the exercise of this gift. Compare also 1 Thess. 5, 20. 21.

To another divers *kinds of tongues.* That is, the ability to speak in languages previously unknown to the speakers. The nature of this gift is determined by the account given in Acts 2, 4–11, where it is said, the apostles spoke " with *other* tongues as the Spirit gave them utterance;" and people of all the neighbouring nations asked with astonishment, " Are not all these that speak Galileans? And how hear we every man in our own tongue wherein we were born?" It is impossible to deny that the miracle recorded in Acts consisted in enabling the apostles to speak in languages which they had never learnt. Unless, therefore, it be assumed that the gift of which Paul here speaks was something of an entirely different nature, its character is put beyond dispute. The identity of the two, however, is proved from the sameness of the terms by which they are described. In Mark 16, 17, it was promised that the disciples should speak " with *new* tongues." In Acts 2, 4, it is said they spoke " with *other* tongues." In Acts 10, 46, and 19, 6, it is said of those on whom the Holy Ghost came, that " they spake with tongues." It can hardly be doubted that all these forms of expression are to be understood in the same sense; that to speak " with tongues" in Acts 10, 46, means the same thing as speaking " with other tongues," in Acts 2, 4, and that this again means the same as speaking " with new tongues," as promised in Mark 16, 17. If the meaning of the phrase is thus historically and philologically determined for Acts and Mark, it must also be determined for the Epistle to the Corinthians. If *tongues* means languages in the former, it must have the same meaning in the latter. We have thus two arguments in favour of the old interpretation of this passage. First, that the facts narrated in Acts necessitate the interpretation of the phrase " to speak with other tongues " to mean to speak with foreign languages.

Second, that the interchange of the expressions, *new* tongues, *other* tongues, and *tongues*, in reference to the same event, shows that the last mentioned (to speak with tongues) must have the same sense with the two former expressions, which can only mean to speak in new languages. A third argument is, that the common interpretation satisfies all the facts of the case. Those facts are, 1. That what was spoken with tongues was intelligible to those who understood foreign languages, as appears from Acts 2, 11. Therefore the speaking was not an incoherent, unintelligible rhapsody. 2. What was uttered were articulate sounds, the vehicle of prayer, praise, and thanksgiving, 1 Cor. 14, 14–17. 3. They were edifying, and therefore intelligible to him who uttered them, 1 Cor. 14, 4. 16. 4. They admitted of being interpreted, which supposes them to be intelligible. 5. Though intelligible in themselves, and to the speaker, they were unintelligible to others, that is, to those not acquainted with the language used; and consequently unsuited for an ordinary Christian assembly. The folly which Paul rebuked was, speaking in Arabic to men who understood only Greek. The speaker might understand what he said, but others were not profited, 1 Cor. 14, 2. 19. 6. The illustration employed in 1 Cor. 14, 7. 11, from musical instruments, and from the case of foreigners, requires the common interpretation. Paul admits that the sounds uttered were "not without signification," v. 10. His complaint is, that a man who speaks in an unknown tongue is to him a foreigner, v. 11. This illustration supposes the sounds uttered to be intelligible in themselves, but not understood by those to whom they were addressed. 7. The common interpretation is suited even to those passages which present the only real difficulty in the case; viz., those in which the apostle speaks of the understanding as being unfruitful in the exercise of the gift of tongues, and those in which he contrasts praying with the spirit and praying with the understanding, 14, 14. 15. Although these passages, taken by themselves, might seem to indicate that the speaker himself did not understand what he said, and even that his intellect was in abeyance, yet they may naturally mean only that the understanding of the speaker was unprofitable to others; and speaking with the understanding may mean speaking intelligibly. It is not necessary, therefore, to infer from these passages, that to speak with tongues was to speak in a state of ecstasy, in a manner unintelligible to any human being 8. The common interpretation is also consistent with the fact that the gift of interpretation was distinct from that of speaking with tongues. If a man could speak a foreign language, why could he not interpret it? Simply, because it was not his gift. What he said in that foreign language, he said under the guidance of the Spirit; had he attempted to interpret it without the gift of interpretation, he would be speaking of himself, and not " as the Spirit gave him utterance." In the one case he was the organ of the Holy Ghost, in the other he was not.

Fourth argument. Those who depart from the common interpretation of the gift of tongues, differ indefinitely among themselves as to its true nature. Some assume that the word *tongues* (γλῶσσαι) does not here mean languages, but *idioms* or peculiar and unusual forms of expression. To speak with tongues, according to this view, is to speak in an exalted poetic strain, beyond the comprehension of common people. But it has been proved from the expressions *new* and *other* tongues, and from the facts recorded in Acts, that the word γλῶσσαι (*tongues*) must here mean languages. Besides, to speak in exalted language is not to speak unintelligibly. The Grecian people understood the loftiest strains of their orators and poets. This interpretation also gives to the word γλῶσσαι a technical sense foreign to all scriptural usage, and one which is entirely inadmissible, at least in those cases where the singular is used. A man might be said to speak in "phrases," but not in " a phrase." Others say that the word means the tongue as the physical organ of utterance ; and to speak *with the tongue* is to speak in a state of excitement in which the understanding and will do not control the tongue, which is moved by the Spirit to utter sounds which are as unintelligible to the speaker as to others. But this interpretation does not suit the expressions *other tongues* and *new tongues*, and is irreconcilable with the account in Acts. Besides it degrades the gift into a mere frenzy. It is out of analogy with all Scriptural facts. The spirits of the prophets are subject to the prophets. The Old Testament seers were not beside themselves, and the apostles in the use of the gift of tongues were calm and rational, speaking the wonderful works of God in a way which the foreigners gathered in Jerusalem easily understood. Others, again, admit that the word *tongues* means languages, but deny that they were languages foreign to the speaker. To speak with tongues, they say, was to speak in an incoherent, unintelligible manner, in a state of ecstasy, when the mind is entirely abstracted from the external world, and unconscious of things about it, as in a dream or trance. This, however, is liable to the objections already adduced against the other theories. Besides, it is evident from the whole discussion, that those who spake with tongues were self-controlled. They could speak or not as they pleased. Paul censures them for speaking when there was no occasion for it, and in such a manner as to produce confusion and disorder. They were, therefore, not in a state of uncontrollable excitement, unconscious of what they said or did. It is unnecessary to continue this enumeration of conjectures; what has already been said would be out of place if the opinions referred to had not found favour in England and in our own country.

The arguments against the common view of the nature of the gift of tongues, (apart from the exegetical difficulties with which it is thought to be encumbered,) are not such as to make much impression upon minds accustomed to reverence the Scriptures. 1. It is said the miracle was unnecessary, as Greek was understood wherever the apostles preached. This, no doubt, is in a great degree true. Greek was the language of educated persons throughout the Roman empire, but it had not superseded the national languages in common life; neither was the preaching of the apostles confined to the limits of the Roman empire. Besides, this supposes that the only design of the gift was to facilitate the propagation of the gospel. This was doubtless one of the purposes which it was intended to answer; but it had other important uses. It served to prove the presence of the Spirit of God; and it symbolized the calling of the Gentiles and the common interest of all nations in the gospel. See the remarks on Acts 2, 4. 2. It is said God is not wont by miracles to remove difficulties out of the way of his people, which they can surmount by labour. 3. Others pronounce it impossible that a man should speak in a language which he had never learnt. But does it thence follow that God cannot give him the ability? 4. It appears that Paul and Barnabas did not understand the speech of Lycaonia, Acts 14, 11–14. The gift of tongues, however, was not the ability to speak all languages. Probably most of those who received the gift, could speak only in one or two. Paul thanked God that he had the gift in richer measure than any of the Corinthians. 5. The gift does not appear to have been made subservient to the missionary work. It certainly

was in the first instance, as recorded in Acts, and may have
been afterwards. 6. Paul, in 1 Cor. 14, 14–19, does not place
speaking with tongues and speaking in one's own language in
opposition; but speaking with the understanding and speaking with the spirit; and therefore to speak with tongues, is to
speak without understanding, or in a state of ecstasy. This
is a possible interpretation of this one passage considered in
itself, but it is in direct contradiction to all those passages
which prove that speaking with tongues was not an involuntary, incoherent, ecstatic mode of speaking. The passage referred to, therefore, must be understood in consistency with
the other passages referring to the same subject. Though
there are difficulties attending any view of the gift in question,
arising from our ignorance, those connected with the common
interpretation are incomparably less than those which beset
any of the modern conjectures.

To another, the interpretation of tongues. The nature of
this gift depends on the view taken of the preceding. Commonly, at least, the man using a foreign language was able to
understand it, see 14, 2. 4. 16, and may have had the gift of
interpretation in connection with the gift of tongues. It is
possible, however, that in some cases he did not himself understand the language which he spoke, and then of course he
would need an interpreter. But even when he did understand
the language which he used, he needed a distinct gift to make
him the organ of the Spirit in its interpretation. If speaking
with tongues was speaking incoherently in ecstasy, it is hard
to see how what was said could admit of interpretation. Unless coherent it was irrational, and if irrational, it could not be
translated.

**11. But all these worketh that one and the self-
same Spirit, dividing to every man severally as he will.**

But all these, &c., i. e. notwithstanding the diversity of
these gifts they have a common origin. They are wrought by
the same Spirit. What therefore in v. 6 is referred to the
efficiency of God, is here referred to the efficiency of the
Spirit. This is in accordance with constant scriptural usage.
The same effect is sometimes attributed to one, and sometimes
to another of the persons of the Holy Trinity. This supposes
that, being the same in substance (or essence) in which divine
power inheres, they coöperate in the production of these ef-

fects. Whatever the Father does, he does through the Spirit. The Holy Ghost not only produces these gifts in the minds of men, but he distributes them *severally* (ἰδίᾳ) *to every man as he will*, i. e. not according to the merits or wishes of men, but according to his own will. This passage clearly proves that the Holy Spirit is a person. *Will* is here attributed to him, which is one of the distinctive attributes of a person. Both the divinity and personality of the Holy Ghost are therefore involved in the nature of the work here ascribed to him.

12. For as the body is one, and hath many members, and all the members of that one body, being many, are one body : so also (is) Christ.

For introduces an illustration of the truth taught in the preceding verses. Every organism, or organic whole, supposes diversity and unity. That is, different parts united so as to constitute one whole. The apostle had taught that in the unity of the church there is a diversity of gifts. This is illustrated by a reference to the human body. It is one, yet it consists of many members. And this diversity is essential to unity ; for unless the body consisted of many members, it would not be a (σῶμα) *body*, i. e. an organic whole. *So also is Christ*, i. e. the body of Christ, or the Church. As the body consists of many members and is yet one ; so it is with the church, it is one and yet consists of many members, each having its own gift and office. See Rom. 12, 4. 5. Eph. 1, 23, and 4, 4. 16.

13. For by one Spirit are we all baptized into one body, whether (we be) Jews or Gentiles, whether (we be) bond or free ; and have been all made to drink into one Spirit.

This is the proof of what immediately precedes. The church is one, *for* by one Spirit we were all baptized into one body. The word is not in the present tense, but in the aorist. 'We *were*, by the baptism of the Spirit, constituted one body.' This is commonly, and even by the modern commentators, understood of the sacrament of baptism ; and the apostle is made to say that by the Holy Ghost received in baptism we were made one body. But the Bible clearly distinguishes between baptism with water and baptism with the Holy Ghost. "I indeed baptize you with water . . . but he shall baptize you with the Holy Ghost," Matt. 3, 11. "He that sent me to baptize with water, the same said unto me, Upon whom thou shalt see the Spirit descending, and remaining on him, the same is he which baptizeth with the Holy Ghost," John 1, 33. "John truly baptized with water, but ye shall be baptized with the Holy Ghost, not many days hence," Acts 1, 5. These passages not only distinguish between the baptism of water and the baptism of the Spirit, but they disconnect them. The baptism to which Acts 1, 5 refers took place on the day of Pentecost, and had nothing to do with the baptism of water. It is not denied that the one is sacramentally connected with the other; or that the baptism of the Spirit often attends the baptism of water; but they are not inseparably connected. The one may be without the other. And in the present passage there does not seem to be even an allusion to water baptism, any more than in Acts 1, 5. Paul does not say that we are made one body by baptism, but by the baptism of the Holy Ghost; that is, by spiritual regeneration. Any communication of the Holy Spirit is called a baptism, because the Spirit is said to be poured out, and those upon whom he is poured out, whether in his regenerating, sanctifying, or inspiring influences, are said to be baptized. In all the passages above quoted the expression is ἐν πνεύματι, *by the Spirit*, as it is here.* It is not therefore by baptism as an external rite, but by the communication of the Holy Spirit that we are made members of the body of Christ. *Unto one body* means *so as to constitute one body* (εἰς, *unto*, expressing the result). No matter how great may have been the previous difference, whether they were Jews or Gentiles, bond or free, by this baptism of the Spirit, all who experience it are merged into one body; they are all intimately and organically united as partaking of the same life. Comp. Gal. 3, 28. And this is the essential point of the analogy between the human body and the church. As the body is one because pervaded and animated by one soul or principle of life, so the church is one because pervaded by one Spirit. And as all parts of the body which partake of the common life belong to the body, so all

---

* It may be remarked in passing that βαπτίζεσθαι ἐν πνεύματι cannot mean *to be immersed in the* Spirit, any more than βαπτίζεσθαι ὕδατι, Luke 3, 16, Acts 1, 5, can by possibility mean *to be immersed in water*.

those in whom the Spirit of God dwells are members of the church which is the body of Christ. And by parity of reasoning, those in whom the Spirit does not dwell are not members of Christ's body. They may be members of the visible or nominal church, but they are not members of the church in that sense in which it is the body of Christ. This passage, therefore, not only teaches us the nature of the church, but also the principle of its unity. It is one, not as united under one external visible head, or under one governing tribunal, nor in virtue of any external visible bond, but in virtue of the indwelling of the Holy Spirit in all its members. And this internal spiritual union manifests itself in the profession of the same faith, and in all acts of Christian fellowship.

And have all been made to drink into one Spirit. This is a difficult clause. *To drink into* is an unexampled phrase, whether in English or Greek. The text varies. In some MSS. it is εἰς ἓν πνεῦμα, *into one Spirit*, in others, ἓν πνεῦμα, *one Spirit*. The latter is adopted by Lachmann and Tischendorf. If this be preferred, the sense is, 'We have all drank one Spirit.' That is, we have all been made partakers of one Spirit. Compare John 7, 37, and other passages, in which the Spirit is compared to water of which men are said to drink. The meaning of the passage according to this reading is simple and pertinent. 'By the baptism of the Holy Ghost we have all been united in one body and made partakers of one Spirit.' If the common text be preferred, the most natural interpretation would seem to be, 'We have all been made to drink so as to become one Spirit.' The words (εἰς ἓν πνεῦμα) *unto one Spirit*, would then correspond to (εἰς ἓν σῶμα) *unto one body*. The allusion is supposed by Luther, Calvin and Beza to be to the Lord's Supper. 'By baptism we become one body, and by drinking (of the cup, i. e. by the Lord's Supper) we become one body.' But this allusion is not only foreign to the context, but is not indicated by the words. How can the simple word ἐποτίσθημεν, *made to drink*, in such a connection, mean to partake of the Lord's Supper? Besides, as the modern commentators all remark, the tense of the verb forbids this interpretation. It must express the same time with the preceding verb. 'We were all baptized (ἐβαπτίσθημεν), and we were all made to drink (ἐποτίσθημεν).' It is something done in the past, not something continued in the present that the word expresses. If any thing is to be supplied it is not the word *cup*, but *the Spirit*, i. e. the water of life. 'We have been made to drink (i. e. of the Spirit) so as to become one spirit.' Another interpretation of the common text supposes that the preposition (εἰς) *into* belongs to the construction of the verb—*to drink into* being equivalent to *drink of*. The sense is then the same as in the reading without the εἰς, 'We have all drank of one Spirit.' The doctrine taught is clear, viz., that by receiving the Spirit we are all made members of the body of Christ, and that it is in virtue of the indwelling of the Spirit that the church is one.

14. For the body is not one member, but many.

This is a proof that diversity of gifts and members is necessary to the unity of the church. The church no more consists of persons all having the same gifts, than the body is all eye or all ear. As the body is not one member, but many, so the church is not one member, but many. The word *member* means a constituent part having a function of its own. It is not merely a multiplicity of parts that is necessary to the body; nor a multiplicity of persons that is necessary to the church; but in both cases what is required is a multiplicity of members in the sense just stated. To a certain extent what Paul says of the diversity of gifts in individual members of the church, may, in the existing state of things, be applied to different denominations of Christians. No one is perfect or complete in itself; and no one can say to the others, I have no need of you. Each represents something that is not so well represented in the others. Each has its own function to exercise and work to perform, which could not so well be accomplished without it. As, therefore, harmony and coöperation, sympathy and mutual affection, are required between individual Christians as constituent members of Christ's body, so also should they prevail between different denominations. It is only when the hand undertakes to turn the foot out of the body, that the foot is bound in self-defence and for the good of the whole, to defend its rights.

15. 16. If the foot shall say, Because I am not the hand, I am not of the body; is it therefore not of the body? And if the ear shall say, Because I am not the eye, I am not of the body; is it therefore not of the body?

The first and most obvious conclusion from the view which
Paul had given of the nature of the church is the duty of contentment.   It is just as unreasonable and absurd for the foot
to complain that it is not the hand, as for one member of the
church to complain that he is not another; that is, for a
teacher to complain that he is not an apostle; or for a dea-
coness to complain that she is not a presbyter; or for one who
had the gift of healing to complain that he had not the gift of
tongues.   This, as the apostle shows, would destroy the very
idea of the church.

17. If the whole body (were) an eye, where (were)
the hearing?   If the whole (were) hearing, where
(were) the smelling?

The obvious meaning of this verse is, that the very existence of the body as an organization depends on the union of
members endowed with different functions.   And the application of this idea to the church is equally plain.   It also requires to its existence a diversity of gifts and offices.   If all
were apostles where would be the church?

18. But now hath God set the members every one
of them in the body, as it hath pleased him.

But now, i. e. as the matter actually is.   Instead of the
body being all one member, God has arranged and disposed
the parts each in its place so as to constitute one living organic whole.   The eye did not give itself the power of vision,
nor the ear its ability to discriminate sounds.   Each member
occupies in the body the position which God has seen fit to
assign it, and which is most conducive to the good of the
whole.   It is so also in the church; the position and the gifts
of every member are determined by the Lord.   One has one
gift and another another; one is a pastor and another is
a missionary; one labours in a city, another in the wilderness, not according to their relative merits, nor in virtue of
their own selection, but as God wills and orders.   It is therefore as inconsistent with the idea of the church that each
member should decide on his own position and functions, as
that the members of the body should arrange themselves according to their own notions.   The nature of the church sup-

poses, that as in the body the principle of life manifests itself under one form in the eye, and in another form in the ear, so the Spirit of God dwelling in the church manifests himself under one form in one member and under a different form in another; and that the selection of his organs and distribution of his gifts are according to his sovereign pleasure. We are contending against him, therefore, when we contend against the position and the office which he has assigned us in the church. It is easy to give this principle a wider application. One is born in Europe, another in Asia; one in America, another in Africa; one is rich, another poor; one has ten talents, another one; not because one is better than the other, but simply because God has so ordained. His will, as thus manifested, is not only sovereign but infinitely wise and benevolent. It is on this diversity, whether in the world, in the church, or in the human body, that the life and the good of the whole depend. This verse thus contains the second practical inference from the nature of the church as the body of Christ. The place and gifts of each member are determined by the Lord.

19. 20. And if they were all one member, where (were) the body? But now (are they) many members, yet but one body.

These verses are a repetition of the idea that diversity of organs in the body is essential to its nature as a body, i. e. as an organization; and that this diversity is perfectly consistent with unity.

21. And the eye cannot say unto the hand, I have no need of thee: nor again the head to the feet, I have no need of you.

The third inference from the doctrine taught above, is the mutual dependence of the members of the church. As in the body the eye cannot dispense with the hand, nor the head with the feet, so in the church the most highly gifted are as much dependent on those less favoured as the latter are on the former. Every thing like pride, therefore, is as much out of place in the church as discontent.

22. 23. Nay, much more those members of the body, which seem to be more feeble, are necessary : and those (members) of the body, which we think to be less honourable, upon these we bestow more abundant honour ; and our uncomely (parts) have more abundant comeliness.

The fourth inference from the apostle's doctrine is, that the least attractive gifts are the most important. As in the human frame the heart is more important than the tongue, so in the church the gift of prayer is more important than eloquence. Those who in the closet, however obscure, wrestle with God, often do more for his glory and for the advancement of his kingdom than those who fill the largest space in the public eye. What would the tongue do without the lungs, which are neither seen nor heard ? God's thoughts are not as our thoughts. The childish Corinthians prized the gift of tongues, which, as they used it, could edify no one, to the gift of prophecy by which the whole body of Christ could be instructed and comforted. And those persons and offices in the church which are most admired or coveted, are often of little account in the sight of God. There is another idea presented in these verses. It is an instinct of nature to adorn most the least comely portions of the body ; and it is an instinct of grace to honour most those members of the church who least attract admiration. *Those members of the body which we think to be less honourable,* i. e. less likely to be honoured ; *on those we bestow the more abundant honour,* i. e. we on that account honour them the more. It is thus with a mother. The child which is the least admired, she cherishes with special affection. And it is thus with the church. The true people of God are only the more disposed to honour those of their number who are undervalued or despised. In the body, as the apostle says, *our uncomely parts* have (i. e. they receive) *more abundant comeliness,* i. e. are specially adorned.

24. For our comely (parts) have no need : but God hath tempered the body together, having given more abundant honour to that (part) which lacked :

Our comely parts have no need, i. e. of being thus adorned. The face is uncovered ; the feet are clothed and decked. The former needs no adorning, the latter does. *God hath tempered the body together*, i. e. he has so adjusted it and combined its several members, as to secure the result that more abundant honour should be given to those which lacked. By making the uncomely parts essential to the well-being of the rest, and by diffusing a common life through all the members, he has made the body a harmonious whole.

25. 26. That there should be no schism in the body; but (that) the members should have the same care one for another. And whether one member suffer, all the members suffer with it; or one member be honoured, all the members rejoice with it.

God has so constituted the body *that there should be no schism in it*, i. e. no diversity of feeling or interest. *Schism* means simply *division*, but when spoken of an organized body, or of a society, it commonly includes the idea of alienation of feeling. Such was the schism which existed among the Corinthians, see 1, 10. 11, 18. *But that the members should have the same care one for another.* That is, that one member should have the same care for another member that it has for itself. The body is so constituted that the eye is as solicitous for the welfare of the foot as it is for its own well-being. The consequence is that if one member suffers all the members suffer with it; and if one member be honoured, all the members rejoice with it. This is the law of our physical nature. The body is really one. It has a common life and consciousness. The pain or pleasure of one part is common to the whole.

27. Now ye are the body of Christ, and members in particular.

That is, collectively ye are the body of Christ; individually or severally, ye are members. This is the application of the preceding analogy to the case of the Corinthians. What had been said of the body, of its unity; of the diversity of its members; of their mutual dependence; of the greater importance of the weaker than of the stronger members; of the community of feeling and interest that pervades the whole; is all true in its application to the church. The body of Christ is really one, pervaded by one and the same spirit; it consists of many members of different gifts and functions, each according to the will of the Spirit; these members are mutually dependent; the humble and obscure are more necessary to the being and welfare of the church than those distinguished by attractive gifts; and the law of sympathy pervades the whole, so that if one Christian suffers all his fellow Christians suffer with him, and if one believer is honoured, all believers rejoice with him. It is to be observed that Paul is not speaking of what ought to be, but of what is. He does not say that it is the duty of one member of the human body to care for another member, but that it does thus care. Such is the law of our nature. The want of this sympathy in any part with all the rest, would prove that it was a mere excrescence which did not partake of the common life. The same is true with regard to the body of Christ. It is not merely the duty of one Christian to have sympathy with another, to suffer when he suffers, and to rejoice when he is honoured; but such is the nature of their relation that it must be so. The want of this sympathy with our fellow Christians, no matter by what name they may be called, is proof that we do not belong to the body of Christ. In this, as in all other respects, Christians are imperfect. The time has not yet come when every believer shall have the same care for another that he has for himself, and rejoice in his joy and grieve in his sorrow as though they were his own. The ideal is here set before us, and blessed are those who approach nearest to the standard.

28. And God hath set some in the church, first apostles, secondarily prophets, thirdly teachers, after that miracles, then gifts of healings, helps, governments, diversities of tongues.

In Eph. 4, 11, Paul says, "God gave *some* apostles, *some* prophets," &c. He began here to use the same form, 'God hath set *some* in the church,' but varies the construction, and says, First, apostles. This verse is an amplification of the preceding one. In v. 27 he said the church is analogous to the human body. He here shows that the analogy consists in the common life of the church, or the indwelling Spirit of God, manifesting itself in a diversity of gifts and offices, just as the common life of the body manifests itself in different organs and members. In the church some were apostles, i. e. immediate messengers of Christ, rendered infallible as teachers and rulers by the gift of plenary inspiration. Secondly, prophets, i. e. men who spoke for God as the occasional organs of the Spirit. Thirdly, *teachers*, i. e. uninspired men who had received the gift of teaching. Fourthly, *miracles ;* here and in what follows abstract terms are used for concrete—*miracles* mean men endowed with the power of working miracles. Fifthly, *gifts of healing*, i. e. persons endowed with the power of healing diseases. Sixthly, *helps*, i. e. persons qualified and appointed to help the other officers of the church, probably in the care of the poor and the sick. These, according to the common understanding from Chrysostom to the present day, were deacons and deaconesses. Seventhly, *governments*, i. e. men who had the gift and authority to rule. As this gift and office are distinguished from those of teachers, it cannot be understood of the presbyters or bishops who were required "to be apt to teach." It seems to refer clearly to a class of officers distinct from teachers, i. e. rulers, or as they are called in the Reformed churches, "ruling elders," and in the ancient church, *seniores plebis*. Finally, *diversities of tongues*, i. e. persons having the gift of speaking in foreign lauguages. This is put last probably· because it was so unduly valued and so ostentatiously displayed by the Corinthians.

On this enumeration it may be remarked, first, that it was not intended to be exhaustive. Gifts are mentioned in vs. 8–10, and elsewhere, which have nothing to correspond to them here. Secondly, every office necessarily supposes the corresponding gift. No man could be an apostle without the gift of infallibility; nor a prophet without the gift of inspiration; nor a healer of diseases without the gift of healing. Man may appoint men to offices for which they have not the necessary gifts, but God never does, any more than he ordains the foot to see or the hand to hear. If any man, therefore, claims to be an apostle, or prophet, or worker of miracles, without the corresponding gift, he is a false pretender. In the early church, as now, there were many false apostles, i. e. those who claimed the honour and authority of the office without its gifts. Thirdly, the fact that any office existed in the apostolic church is no evidence that it was intended to be permanent. In that age there was a plenitude of spiritual manifestations and endowments demanded for the organization and propagation of the church, which is no longer required. We have no longer prophets, nor workers of miracles, nor gifts of tongues. The only evidence that an office was intended to be permanent is the continuance of the gift of which it was the organ, and the command to appoint to the office those who are found to possess the gift. The only evidence that God intended the eye to be a permanent organ of the body, is, that he has perpetuated the faculty of vision. Had the gift of sight been discontinued, it would avail little that men should call the mouth and nose eyes, and demand that they should be recognized as such. This is precisely what Romanists and others do, when they call their bishops apostles, and require men to honour and obey them as though they were. Fourthly, the only evidence of a call to an office, is the possession of the requisite gifts. If a man received the gift of prophecy, he was thereby called to be a prophet; or if he received the gift of healing, he was thereby called to exercise that gift. So if any man has received ministerial gifts, he has received a call to the ministry. What those gifts are the Bible has taught us. They are such as these: soundness in the faith, competent knowledge, ability to teach, the love of Christ and zeal for his glory, an intelligent conviction of an obligation to preach the gospel, and in short the qualifications which are necessary in one who is to be an example and guide of the flock of Jesus Christ. The office of the church in the matter is, first to examine whether the candidate for the ministry really possesses ministerial gifts; and then, if satisfied on that point, authoritatively to declare its judgment in the appointed way. The same remarks may be made in reference to a call to the missionary work or to any other department of labour in the church of Christ. The fundamental idea is that the church is the body of Christ, filled by his Spirit, and that the Spirit distributes to every one severally as he wills, the gifts which he designs him to exercise for the edification of the whole.

29. 30. (Are) all apostles? (are) all prophets? (are) all teachers? (are) all workers of miracles? Have all the gifts of healing? do all speak with tongues? do all interpret?

As in the body all is not eye, or all ear, so in the church all have not the same gifts and offices. And as it would be preposterous in all the members of the body to aspire to the same office, so it is no less preposterous in the members of the church that all should covet the same gifts. It is the design of the apostle to suppress, on the one hand, all discontent and envy, and on the other, all pride and arrogance. God distributes his gifts as he pleases; all are necessary, and the recipients of them are mutually dependent.

31. But covet earnestly the best gifts : and yet shew I unto you a more excellent way.

All cannot have every gift, *but* covet earnestly the better ones. *To covet* (ζηλόω) is *earnestly to desire*, with the implication of corresponding effort to obtain. The extraordinary gifts of the Spirit were bestowed according to his own good pleasure. But so also are his saving benefits. Yet both may be, and should be sought in the use of the appointed means. *The best gifts;* literally, *the better gifts*, by which is meant, as appears from 14, 5, those which were the more useful. The Corinthians had a very different standard of excellence; and coveted most the gifts which were the most attractive, although the least useful. *And yet* (or, *moreover*) *I shew you an excellent way.* The expression is not in itself comparative, *more* excellent; but simply *a way according to excellence*, i. e. an excellent way. Whether it is excellent compared to something else, or most excellent, depends on the context. Here no comparison is implied. The idea is not that he intends to show them a way that is better than seeking gifts, but a way *par excellence* to obtain those gifts. The other view is indeed adopted by Calvin and others, but it supposes the preceding imperative (*covet ye*) to be merely concessive, and is contrary to 14, 1, where the command to seek the more useful gifts is repeated. The sense is, 'Seek the better gifts, and *moreover* I show you an excellent way to do it.'

CHAPTER XIII.

Christian Love. Vs. 1–13.

Love is superior to all extraordinary gifts. It is better than the gift of tongues, v. 1 ; than the gifts of prophecy and knowledge, v. 2 ; and than the gift of miracles, v. 2. All outward

works of charity without it are worthless, v. 3. Love has this
superiority, first, because of its inherent excellence; and secondly, because of its perpetuity. As to its superior excellence,
it implies or secures all other excellence. 1. It includes all
the forms of kindness. 2. It is humble and modest. 3. It is
unselfish. 4. It sympathizes with all good, vs. 4–7. It is perpetual—all the extraordinary gifts mentioned in the preceding
chapter were designed for the present state of existence, or
were temporary. Love is never to cease, v. 8. Knowledge,
as a special gift, and perhaps also in the form in which it exists in this world, is to pass away. It is now the apprehension
of truth as through a mirror—hereafter it will be lost in immediate vision, vs. 9–12. The permanent graces are faith,
hope, and love, and the greatest of these is Love, v. 13.

This chapter, although devoted to a single Christian grace,
and therefore not to be compared with the eighth chapter of
Romans, or with some chapters in the epistle to the Ephesians,
as an unfolding of the mysteries of redemption, still has ever
been considered as one of the jewels of Scripture. For moral
elevation, for richness and comprehensiveness, for beauty and
felicity of expression, it has been the admiration of the church
in all ages.—With regard to the word *charity*, as the translation of the Greek ἀγάπη, it has already been remarked in the
comment on 8, 1, that it is peculiarly unhappy. Neither in
its primary signification, nor in the sense which usage has attached to it, does it properly answer to the Greek term. The
latter occurs about one hundred and sixteen times in the New
Testament, and is translated *love* in all places except twenty-
three; and in those the departure from the common usage is
altogether arbitrary. The word charity is just as inappropri-
ate in this chapter as it would be in such phrases as, "the Son
of his charity," or, "the charity of God is shed abroad in our
hearts," or, "the charity of Christ." The Greek word ἀγάπη
is not of heathen origin. The heathen had no conception of
the grace which in the Scriptures is expressed by that term;
neither ἔρως nor φιλία answers to the Scriptural sense of ἀγάπη;
nor do the Latin words *amor* or *caritas*. It was the unsuita-
bleness of the former that induced Jerome to adopt the latter
as the more elevated of the two. The one properly expresses
love founded on sympathy; the latter came to mean love
founded on respect. Its English derivative (*charity*) retains
more of the original force of the Latin word. Caritas (from
carus, *a carendo, dear,* i. e. costly) is properly dearness or

costliness; and then it came to express the feeling arising
from the sight of want and suffering. And this is the common meaning still attached to the English word, which renders it unsuitable as the substitute of the comprehensive word
love. Many have been led to think that almsgiving covers a
multitude of sins, because charity is said to have that effect;
and that kindness to the poor and the sick is the sum of all
religion, because Paul exalts charity above faith and hope. It
is not of charity, but of love, of which the Bible thus speaks.

Superiority of Love to all other gifts.

1. Though I speak with the tongues of men and of
angels, and have not charity, I am become (as) sounding brass, or a tinkling cymbal.

The gift of tongues, on which the Corinthians so much
valued themselves, is mentioned first, because it was the prominent subject in this whole discussion. *The tongues of men*
are the languages which men speak. As this is the obvious
meaning of the expression, it serves to prove that the gift
of tongues was the gift of speaking foreign languages. *The
tongues of angels* are the languages which angels use. A
mode of expression equivalent to 'all languages human or
divine.' Paul means to say, that the gift of tongues in its
highest conceivable extent without love is nothing. *Without
love I am become*, i. e. the mere want of love has reduced me,
notwithstanding the gift in question, to a level with *sounding
brass;* not a musical instrument made of brass, which has
some dignity about it, but to a piece of clattering brass which
makes a senseless noise; or, at least, to a *tinkling cymbal,* the
lowest and least expressive of all musical instruments. *Tinkling* (ἀλαλάζον), properly *clanging,* expressive of the loud
shrill noise made by the cymbal. These instruments were of
two kinds, one small, worn on the thumb and middle finger,
answering, it is thought, to the modern *castanets;* the other
large, broad plates, like our common cymbals. Joseph. Ant.
7. 12. 3. Both kinds are perhaps referred to in Ps. 150, 5,
where the Septuagint distinguishes them as the *sweet-toned*
and the *loud.* The latter is the kind here specified. The
illustration was probably adopted from the shrill, discordant
noise made by the speakers with their tongues, each endeavouring to drown the voice of all the others, as seems from

what follows to have been the case with the Corinthians. Paul says, 14, 23, the meetings for worship in Corinth, if all spoke with tongues, would be so confused as to make strangers think they were mad.

2. And though I have (the gift of) prophecy, and understand all mysteries, and all knowledge; and though I have all faith, so that I could remove mountains, and have not charity, I am nothing.

There are three gifts here referred to, prophecy, "the word of knowledge," and miracles. 'Though I have the gift of prophecy, so as to understand all mysteries, and (though I have) all knowledge, and all faith,' &c. As the particle ἐάν, *though*, by which the distinction of gifts is indicated in the context, is here omitted, the first two clauses are commonly combined. 'Though I have the gift of prophecy, so as to understand all mysteries, and *so as to possess* all knowledge.' There are two objections to this. The passage literally reads, that I may know all mysteries and all knowledge;' so that the words *mysteries* and *knowledge* grammatically depend on (εἰδῶ), *I may know*. But this would make Paul use an unexampled phrase, 'to know knowledge.' Something, therefore, must be supplied, and it is as natural to borrow from the context the words, *though I have*, as simply, *that I may have*. And secondly, Paul distinguishes between prophecy and knowledge as distinct gifts, v. 8 and 12, 8–10. The understanding or apprehension of mysteries, and not the possession of knowledge, in its distinctive sense, was the result of the gift of prophecy. *Mysteries* are secrets, things undiscoverable by human reason, which divine revelation alone can make known. And the gift of prophecy was the gift of revelation by which such mysteries were communicated; see 14, 30. *All mysteries*, therefore, here means, *all the secret purposes of God* relating to redemption. This limitation is required by the context. Paul intends to say, that though he was the recipient of all the revelations which God ever designed to make concerning the plan of salvation and the kingdom of Christ, without love he would be nothing.

And all knowledge, i. e. and though I have all knowledge. By knowledge is meant the intellectual apprehension or cognition of revealed truth. It was the prerogative of the prophet to reveal, of the teacher to know and to instruct. Compare 14, 6, where Paul connects revelation with prophecy, and knowledge with doctrine or teaching. *And all faith*, i. e. all degrees of the faith of miracles, so that the greatest wonders, such as removing mountains, could be thereby accomplished. Compare our Lord's language in Matt. 21, 21. *I am nothing*, i. e. worthless. Neither intellectual gifts nor attainments, nor power, without love, are of any real value. They do not elevate the character or render it worthy of respect or confidence. Satan may have, and doubtless has, more of intelligence and power than any man ever possessed, and yet he is Satan still. Those, therefore, who seek to exalt men by the mere cultivation of the intellect, are striving to make satans of them.

3. And though I bestow all my goods to feed (the poor), and though I give my body to be burned, and have not charity, it profiteth me nothing.

Paul here advances one step further. All outward acts of beneficence are of no avail without love. A man may give away his whole estate, or sacrifice himself, and be in no sense the gainer. He may do all this from vanity, or from the fear of perdition, or to purchase heaven, and only increase his condemnation. Religion is no such easy thing. Men would gladly compound by external acts of beneficence, or by penances, for a change of heart; but the thing is impossible. Thousands indeed are deluded on this point, and think that they can substitute what is outward for what is inward, but God requires the heart, and without holiness the most liberal giver or the most suffering ascetic can never see God. The original word (ψωμίζω) here used, literally means, *to feed by morsels*. It is generally followed by two accusatives, *to feed a person with something*. Here the accusative of the person is omitted, so that the passage stands, 'Though I feed out my property,' i. e. distribute it in food. *And though I give my body to be burned*, i. e. though I make the most painful sacrifice of myself. A man may not only give his property but his life, and be nothing the better. It is not probable that the apostle refers to martyrdom, or that the idea is, that a man may, from wrong motives, submit to be a martyr. The context requires that the reference should be to a sacrifice made for the good of others. Some suppose that the reference is to the branding of slaves to indicate their ownership. The

meaning would then be, 'Though I not only give away all my
goods, but should sell myself as a slave for the sake of the
poor, it would profit me nothing.' Had Paul intended to say
this, he would probably have used the appropriate term for
branding. We do not express the idea that an animal was
branded, by saying it was burnt. There is no necessity for
departing from the simple sense of the words. 'Though I
give my body to be burnt for others, i. e. though I should die
for them, without love it profiteth me nothing.'

4. Charity suffereth long, (and) is kind; charity envieth not; charity vaunteth not itself, is not puffed up,

Almost all the instructions of the New Testament are suggested by some occasion, and are adapted to it. We have
not in this chapter a methodical dissertation on Christian love,
but an exhibition of that grace as contrasted with extraordinary gifts which the Corinthians inordinately valued. Those
traits of love are therefore adduced which stood opposed to
the temper which they exhibited in the use of their gifts.
They were impatient, discontented, envious, inflated, selfish,
indecorous, unmindful of the feelings or interests of others,
suspicious, resentful, censorious. The apostle personifies love,
and places her before them and enumerates her graces, not in
logical order, but as they occurred to him in contrast to the
deformities of character which they exhibited.
Love suffereth long, i. e. is long-minded, or slow to be
roused to resentment. It patiently bears with provocation,
and is not quick to assert its rights or resent an injury. *It is
kind*, i. e. is inclined to perform good offices; is good-natured.
The root of the verb (χρηστός, from χράομαι) means *useful*, and
hence its primary sense is, *disposed to be useful*. The excellence here indicated is the positive side of that already mentioned. Love is not quick to resent evil, but is disposed to do
good. *It envieth not*. The word (ζηλόω) here used may express any wrong feeling excited in view of the good of others;
not only envy, but hatred, emulation, and the like. *It vaunteth not itself* (περπερεύεται), this includes all forms of the desire
to gain the applause of others. Love does not seek to win
admiration and applause. *Is not puffed up*, i. e. conceited.
This is the root of the preceding. The man who has a high
conceit of himself is apt to be boastful and desirous of praise.
Love, on the other hand, is modest and humble; modest because humble.

5. Doth not behave itself unseemly, seeketh not her own, is not easily provoked, thinketh no evil;

Doth not behave itself unseemly, i. e. does nothing of which one ought to be ashamed. Its whole deportment is decorous and becoming. *Seeketh not her own*; is disinterested, 10, 33. *Is not easily provoked*, i. e. is not quick tempered; or, does not suffer itself to be roused to resentment. And, therefore, *it thinketh no evil*, or rather, *it does not think evil*. This may mean, 1. It does not plan or devise evil. But the expression is (τὸ κακόν) *the* evil, and not (κακά) *evil*. Comp. Matt. 9, 4.   2. It does not impute evil, i. e. attribute evil motives to others, or is not suspicious. The sense is good in itself, but not so suitable to the connection as, 3. It does not lay the evil which it suffers to the charge of the wrong-doer. Instead of being resentful, it is forgiving.

6. Rejoiceth not in iniquity, but rejoiceth in the truth;

The general sentiment of this verse is, that love does not sympathize with evil, but with good. *It rejoiceth not in iniquity*, i. e. in any thing which is not conformed to the standard of right. The word is usually translated unrighteousness; but this is not to be limited to injustice, but includes all forms of moral evil. *Truth* is often used antithetically in Scripture to *unrighteousness*, as it is here. Rom. 1, 8. comp. John 3, 21. 1 John 1, 6, and other passages, in which men are said to do the truth. Hence it is commonly interpreted in such cases as meaning *righteousness*. 'Love does not rejoice in unrighteousness, but it rejoices together with (συγχαίρει) righteousness,' i. e. sympathizes with it, and has a common joy with it. As, however, the word so commonly in Paul's epistles stands for religious truth as revealed in the gospel, perhaps the majority of commentators so understand it here. 'Love rejoices together with the truth.' This, however, not only destroys the antithesis, but introduces a disturbing element into the description; for it is of love as a virtue of which Paul is speaking. Its sympathy with the gospel, therefore, does not seem to be appropriate in this connection.

7. Beareth all things, believeth all things, hopeth all things, endureth all things.

Beareth all things. This may either mean, bears in silence all annoyances and troubles, or *covers up all things* (as στέγω may have either meaning), in the sense of concealing or excusing the faults of others, instead of gladly disclosing them. The latter interpretation harmonizes better with what follows, but it is contrary to Paul's usage as to this word. See 9, 12. 1 Thess. 3, 1. 5. With him the word always means *to bear patiently.* Further, love *believes all things,* is not suspicious, but readily credits what men say in their own defence. *Hopeth all things,* i. e. hopes for the best with regard to all men. It would be contrary to the context to understand the faith and hope here spoken of as referring to the truths and promises of the gospel. *Endureth all things.* The word (ὑπομένω) is properly a military word, and means to sustain the assault of an enemy. Hence it is used in the New Testament to express the idea of sustaining the assaults of suffering or persecution, in the sense of bearing up under them, and enduring them patiently. 2 Tim. 2, 10. Heb. 10, 32. 12, 2. This clause, therefore, differs from that at the beginning of the verse; as that had reference to annoyances and troubles, this to suffering and persecutions.

8. Charity never faileth: but whether (there be) prophecies, they shall fail; whether (there be) tongues, they shall cease; whether (there be) knowledge, it shall vanish away.

Love never fails, i. e. it endures for ever. It is not designed and adapted, as are the gifts under consideration, merely to the present state of existence, but to our future and immortal state of being. *Whether* there be *prophecies,* or *be it prophecies, they shall fail,* i. e. be done away with. The gift shall cease to be necessary, and therefore shall not be continued. *Be it tongues,* &c., i. e. the gift of tongues shall cease. *Be it knowledge, it shall vanish away,* i. e. cease to exist. It is the same word as that used above in reference to prophecies. It is not knowledge in the comprehensive sense of the term that is to cease, but knowledge as a gift; as one of the list of extraordinary endowments mentioned above, 12, 8–11. Knowledge, considered as the intellectual apprehension of truth, is, as the apostle immediately states, hereafter to be rendered perfect. But the λόγος γνώσεως, *the word of knowledge,* 12, 8,

i. e. knowledge in that form in which it was the foundation of the office of teacher, is to be done away with. Whether this means that hereafter there will be no need of the office of teacher, and therefore that the gift which qualified for that office shall cease; or whether Paul means to say that the immediate vision of truth is to be hereafter so different from our present discursive, obscure, and imperfect mode of cognition, that it deserves to be called by a different name, may be matter of doubt. Both are probably true. There will be no ignorance in heaven to be removed through the intervention of human instructors; and there will probably be as great a difference between knowledge hereafter and what we call knowledge here, as there is between hearing of an object and seeing it. We may hear a description of a person or place and have thereby a certain form of knowledge of him or it; but that form passes away, or is merged in a higher, as soon as we see what we had before only heard about.

9. 10. For we know in part, and we prophesy in part. But when that which is perfect is come, then that which is in part shall be done away.

This is the reason why knowledge and prophecy are to cease. They are partial or imperfect, and therefore suited only to an imperfect state of existence. The revelations granted to the prophets imparted mere glimpses of the mysteries of God; when those mysteries stand disclosed in the full light of heaven, what need then of those glimpses? A skilful teacher may by diagrams and models give us some knowledge of the mechanism of the universe; but if the eye be strengthened to take in the whole at a glance, what need then of a planetarium or of a teacher? The apostle employs two illustrations to teach us the difference between the present and the future. The one is derived from the difference between childhood and maturity; the other from the difference between seeing a thing by imperfect reflection, or through an obscure medium, and seeing it directly.

11. When I was a child, I spake as a child, I understood as a child, I thought as a child: but when I became a man, I put away childish things.

When I was a child; not an infant, but as opposed to one

of mature age, *a child. I spake as a child.* This does not
refer to the gift of tongues as something childish, but simply
to the mode of speaking characteristic of children. *I understood as a child*, rather, *I felt and acted* as a child; otherwise
too little distinction is made between this and the next clause.
I thought as a child. My language, feelings and thoughts
were all childish. The words (φρονέω and λογίζομαι), however,
are so comprehensive that the two clauses may be rendered,
'I had the opinions of a child and I reasoned as a child.' The
former word, however, is so often used to express feeling,
Matt. 16, 23. Rom. 8, 5. Phil. 3, 19. Col. 3, 2, that the first
mentioned interpretation is to be preferred. *When I became
a man*, or having become a man, I have put away *childish
things*, i. e. my former childish mode of speaking, feeling and
thinking. The feelings and thoughts of a child are true and
just, in so far as they are the natural impression of the objects
to which they relate. They are neither irrational nor false, but
inadequate. The impression which the sight of the heavens
makes on the mind of the child, is for the child a just and true
impression. The conception which it forms of what it sees is
correct in one aspect of the great object contemplated. Yet
that impression is very different from that which is made on
the mind of the astronomer. In like manner our views of
divine things will hereafter be very different from those which
we now have. But it does not thence follow that our present
views are false. They are just as far as they go, they are only
inadequate. It is no part of the apostle's object to unsettle
our confidence in what God now communicates by his word
and Spirit to his children, but simply to prevent our being
satisfied with the partial and imperfect.

12. For now we see through a glass, darkly ; but
then face to face : now I know in part; but then shall
I know even as also I am known.

This is a confirmation of what precedes. Our present
knowledge is imperfect, *for* we now see *through a glass.*
These words admit of three interpretations. 1. The preposition (διά) may have its ordinary instrumental sense, we see *by
means* of a glass; or, 2. It may have its local sense, *through.*
Then, assuming *glass* (ἐσόπτρον) to mean a window, the meaning is, we see as through a window; and as the windows
were commonly made of mica, and therefore imperfectly

transparent, to see through a window was to see dimly. As the word, however, properly means a mirror, James 1, 23, the best interpretation probably is, 3. We see as through a mirror; the optical impression is that the object is behind the mirror, and the spectator seems to look through it. The ancient mirrors were of imperfectly polished metal, and the reflection which they gave was very obscure. *Darkly*, literally, *in an enigma.* This may be taken adverbially, as by our translators, *we see enigmatically*, i. e. obscurely ; or the idea may be that we see divine things as it were wrapped up in enigmas. We do not see the things themselves, but those things as set forth in symbols and words which imperfectly express them. The reference seems to be to Num. 12, 8. Of an ordinary prophet God said, " I will make myself known unto him in a vision, and speak to him in a dream ; " but of Moses he says, " With him will I speak mouth to mouth, even apparently, and not in dark sayings," i. e. in enigmas. (The Septuagint version is δι' αἰνιγμάτων). The clearest revelation of the things of God in words is as an enigma, when compared to sight. Every thing is comparative. The revelations made to Moses were clear in comparison to the communications made to others by visions and dreams. Paul says the writings of Moses were enigmas compared to the revelations contained in the gospel, 2 Cor. 3, 12. 13. And the gospel itself is obscure compared to the lucid medium through which we shall see hereafter. *But then face to face*, i. e. no longer through a mirror, but immediately. Comp. Gen. 32, 31. Num. 12, 8. The word of God is a mirror wherein even now we behold the glory of the Lord (2 Cor. 3, 18), but what is that to seeing him face to face !

Now I know in part (imperfectly), *but then shall I know even as I am known*, i. e. perfectly. As we are required to be perfect as our Father in heaven is perfect, Matt. 5, 48, so we may be said to know even as we are known. We may be perfect in our narrow sphere, as God is perfect in his; and yet the distance between him and us remain infinite. What Paul wishes to impress upon the Corinthians is, that the gifts in which they so much prided themselves, were small matters compared to what is in reserve for the people of God.

13. And now abideth faith, hope, charity, these three ; but the greatest of these (is) charity.

The words *and now* may either indicate time, *now*, during
the present state; or they may be inferential, *now*, i. e. *since
things are so, rebus sic stantibus*. In the latter case, the
sense is, 'Since these extraordinary gifts are to pass away,
faith, hope, and love abide.' The former are temporary, the
latter are permanent. The only objection to this interpretation arises from the apostle's speaking of faith and hope abiding in a future state, whereas elsewhere, Rom. 8, 24. 2 Cor. 5,
7, and Heb. 11, 1, faith and hope seem to be represented as
pertaining only to our present state of existence, and as being
hereafter merged, the one in sight, and the other in fruition.
This apparent inconsistency arises from the comprehensiveness
of the terms. The state of mind indicated by faith and hope
as now exercised, will not continue in the future life; but the
state of mind, so to speak, of the saints in heaven, may be designated by these same terms, because confidence and expectation will continue for ever. Faith in one form, ceases when
merged in sight; but in another form it continues; and the
same is true of hope. Or perhaps the same idea may be more
correctly expressed by saying that some exercises of faith and
hope are peculiar to the present state, while others will never
cease. Certain it is that there will always be room even in
heaven for confidence in God, and for hope of the ever ad-
vancing and enlarging blessedness of the redeemed.

If, however, (νυνὶ δέ), *but now*, be taken, as is commonly
done, as relating to time, the meaning is, 'Now, i. e. so long
as we continue in this world, there remain faith, hope and
love.' These are the three great permanent Christian graces,
as opposed to the mere temporary gifts of prophecy, miracles,
and tongues. But this does not seem to be consistent with
what precedes. The contrast is not between the more or less
permanent gifts pertaining to our present state; but between
what belongs exclusively to the present, and what is to continue for ever. In v. 8 it is said of love, as a ground or reason
of its pre-eminence, that *it never fails;* and here the same
idea is expressed by saying, *it abides*. 'To abide,' therefore,
must mean, that it continues for ever. The same permanence
is attributed to faith, hope, and love. They are all contrasted
with the temporary gifts, and they are all said to abide. The
one is to continue as long as the others. The former interpretation is, therefore, to be preferred.

The greatest of these is love. In what sense is love greater
than faith? Some say, because it includes, or is the root of

faith and hope. It is said that we believe those whom we love, and hope for what we delight in. According to Scripture, however, the reverse is true. Faith is the root of love. It is the believing apprehension of the glory of God in the face of Jesus Christ, that calls forth love to him. Others say, the ground of superiority is in their effects. But we are said to be sanctified, to be made the children of God, to overcome the world, to be saved, by faith. Christ dwells in our hearts by faith; he that believes hath eternal life, i. e. faith as including knowledge, is eternal life. There are no higher effects than these so far as we are concerned. Others say that love is superior to faith and hope, because the latter belong to the present state only, and love is to continue for ever. But, according to the true interpretation of the verse, all these graces are declared to abide. The true explanation is to be found in the use which Paul makes of this word *greater*, or the equivalent term *better*. In 12, 31, he exhorts his readers to seek *the better* gifts, i. e. the more useful ones. And in 14, 5, he says, 'Greater is he that prophesies, than he that speaks with tongues;' i. e. he is more useful. Throughout that chapter the ground of preference of one gift to others is made to consist in its superior usefulness. This is Paul's standard; and judged by this rule, love is greater than either faith or hope. Faith saves ourselves, but love benefits others.

———•••———

CHAPTER XIV.

Superiority of the gift of prophecy to that of tongues, vs. 1–25. Special directions for the conduct of public worship, vs. 26–40.

Superiority of the gift of prophecy to that of tongues. Vs. 1–25.

THE superiority of the gift of prophecy to that of tongues is founded, 1. On the consideration that he who speaks with tongues speaks to God, whereas, he who prophesies, speaks to men, vs. 2. 3. 2. That he who speaks with tongues edifies only himself, whereas, he who prophesies edifies the church, vs. 4. 5. That this must be so, is proved, 1. By an appeal to their own judgment and experience. If Paul came to them speaking in a way which they could not understand, what good could it do them? But if, as a prophet, he brought them a revelation from God, or as a teacher, set before them a doctrine, they would be edified, v. 6. 2. From the analogy of musical instruments. It is only when the sounds are understood, that they produce the desired effect. If a man does not know that a given note of the trumpet is a signal for battle, he will not prepare himself for the conflict, vs. 7–9. 3. From their experience in intercourse with strangers. If a man comes to me speaking a language which I cannot understand, no matter how polished or significant that language may be, he is a barbarian to me, and I to him, vs. 10. 11. In their zeal, therefore, for spiritual gifts, they should have regard to the edification of the church, v. 12. Hence, he who had the gift of tongues should pray for the gift of interpretation; as without the latter gift, however devotional he might be, his prayers could not profit others, vs. 13. 14. It was not enough that the prayers and praises should be spiritual, they must be intelligible; otherwise those who were unlearned could not join in them, vs. 15–17. For himself, the apostle says, although more richly endowed with the gift of tongues than any of his readers, he would rather speak five words so as to be understood, than ten thousand words in an unknown tongue, vs. 18. 19. It was mere childishness in the Corinthians to be so delighted with a gift which they could not turn to any practical account, v. 20. They should learn wisdom from the experience of the Hebrews. It was as a judgment that God sent among them teachers whom they could not understand. So long as they were obedient, or there was hope of bringing them to repentance, he sent them prophets speaking their own language, vs. 21. 22. Their experience would not be dissimilar. If they came together, each speaking in an unknown tongue, the effect would be only evil. But if, when they assembled, all the speakers spoke so as to be understood, and under the influence of the Spirit, then men would be convinced and converted, and God glorified, vs. 23–25.

In the comment on 12, 10, reasons have already been presented for adhering to the common view, that the gift of tongues, of which the apostle here speaks, was the gift miraculously conferred, of speaking in foreign languages. Every one must feel, however, the truth of the remark of Chrysostom in his commentary on this chapter: "This whole pas-

sage is very obscure; but the obscurity arises from our ignorance of the facts described, which, though familiar to those
to whom the apostle wrote, have ceased to occur." That this
gift should be specially connected with prophesying, as in
Acts 19, 6, "they spake with tongues and prophesied," and
elsewhere, is to be explained from the fact that all speaking
under divine, supernatural influence, was included under the
head of prophesying; and as all who spake with tongues
"spake as the Spirit gave them utterance," in the wide sense
of the word they all prophesied. But it is not so easy to
understand why this gift should have been so common, nor
why it should so often attend on conversion; see Acts 10, 46.
19, 6. There are many things also in this chapter which it is
not easy to understand on any theory of the nature of the
gift. Under these circumstances it is necessary to hold fast
what is clear, and to make the certain our guide in explaining
what is obscure. It is clear, 1. That the word *tongues* in this
connection, as already proved, means languages. 2. That the
speaker with tongues was in a state of calm self-control. He
could speak, or be silent, 14, 28. 3. That what he said was
intelligible to himself, and could be interpreted to others.
4. That the unintelligibleness of what was said, arose not from
the sounds uttered being inarticulate, but from the ignorance
of the hearer. The interpretation of particular passages must,
therefore, be controlled by these facts.

1. Follow after charity, and desire spiritual (gifts), but rather that ye may prophesy.

In the preceding chapters Paul had taught, 1. That all the
extraordinary gifts of the Spirit were proper objects of desire.
2. That they were of different relative importance. 3. That
love was of greater value than any gift. In accordance with
these principles, the apostle exhorts his readers to *follow after
love ;* i. e. to press forward towards it, as men do towards the
goal in a race, Phil. 3, 12. 14. Pursue it earnestly as the greatest good. But at the same time, *desire spiritual* gifts. Because love is more important than miraculous gifts, it does not
follow that the latter were not to be sought. The same word
is used here as in 12, 31. *But rather that ye may prophesy.*
The two gifts specially in the apostle's mind were the gift of
speaking with tongues, and that of prophecy, i. e. the gift of
speaking as the organ of the Spirit in a manner adapted to in-

struct and edify the hearer. Of these two gifts, he says, the latter is to be preferred. The reason for this preference is given in what follows.

2. For he that speaketh in an (unknown) tongue speaketh not unto men, but unto God: for no man understandeth (him); howbeit in the spirit he speaketh mysteries.

What is here taught is, First, that he who speaks with tongues speaks not to men, but to God. Second, that this means that men do not understand *him*. Thirdly, that the reason of his not being understood is in the medium of communication, not in the things communicated. *Speaketh not unto men, but unto God;* or, speaks not *for* men, but *for* God. Sibi canit et musis, according to the Latin proverb. CALVIN. His communion is with God, and not with man. *For no man understandeth* him. Literally, *no man hears*, i. e. hears any articulate sounds. He hears the sound, but does not distinguish the words. This, however, does not imply that the sounds uttered were in themselves unintelligible, so that no man living (unless inspired) could understand them. When the apostles spake with tongues on the day of Pentecost, what they said was understood. The meaning is, not that no man *living*, but that no man *present*, could understand. It is not the use of the gift of tongues that he censures, but the use of that gift when no one was present who understood the language employed. *Howbeit in the spirit he speaketh mysteries.* *Spirit* does not mean the man's own spirit as distinguished from his understanding. The Scriptures do not distinguish between the νοῦς and πνεῦμα as distinct faculties of the human intelligence. The latter is not the higher spiritual powers of our nature, but the Holy Spirit; comp. 2, 14. In favour of this interpretation is, 1. The prevailing use of the word *spirit* in reference to the Holy Ghost in all Paul's epistles, and especially in this whole connection. 2. That the expression to speak *in* or *by* the Spirit, is an established Scriptural phrase, meaning to speak under the guidance of the Holy Spirit. 3. When *spirit* is to be distinguished from the *understanding*, it designates the affections; a sense which would not at all suit this passage. 4. The meaning arrived at by this interpretation is natural, and suitable to the connection. 'Although he who speaks with tongues is not understood, yet, guided by the Spirit, he speaks mysteries. *Mysteries* mean divine truths; things which God has revealed. In Acts 2, 11, they are called "the wonderful things (τὰ μεγαλεῖα) of God." To make the word mean, things not understood by the hearer, is contrary to the usage of the word. A secret disclosed, is no longer a secret; and a mystery revealed ceases to be a mystery, for a mystery is something hidden. Besides, Paul would then say, 'No man understands him, yet he speaks what is not understood.'* The meaning obviously is, that although not understood, yet what he utters contains divine truth. The difficulty was in the language used, not in the absence of meaning, or in the fact that inarticulate sounds were employed. This verse, therefore, contains nothing inconsistent with the commonly received view of the nature of the gift in question. 'He who speaks with tongues, speaks to God and not to men, for no one (in the case supposed) understands him, although what he says is replete with the highest meaning.' The implication is that these *tongues* were foreign to the hearers; and therefore it is said, 'no man understands him.'

3. But he that prophesieth speaketh unto men (to) edification, and exhortation, and comfort.

The prophet spoke in the native language of his hearers; the speaker with tongues in a foreign language. This made the difference between the cases. The one was understood and the other was not. The prophet spoke with a view to *edification.* This is a general term including the sense of the two following. He edified the church either by exhortation or comfort; either by arousing believers to do or suffer, or by pouring into their hearts the consolations of the Spirit.

4. He that speaketh in an (unknown) tongue edifieth himself; but he that prophesieth edifieth the church.

* CALVIN says, *Mysteria* et res occultas, ideoque nullius utilitatis. Mysteria hic Chrysostomus accepit honorifice, pro eximiis Dei revelationibus: ego vero in malam partem pro aenigmatibus obscuris et involutis, quasi diceret, loquitur quod nemo percipiat. Calvin's view of the gift of tongues seems to have been very little higher than that of some of the moderns.

This follows from what had been said. The speaker with tongues did not edify the church, because he was not understood; he did edify himself, because he understood himself. This verse, therefore, proves that the understanding was not in abeyance, and that the speaker was not in an ecstatic state.

5. I would that ye all spake with tongues, but rather that ye prophesied : for greater (is) he that prophesieth than he that speaketh with tongues, except he interpret, that the church may receive edifying.

I would that ye all spake with tongues. It was not to be inferred from what he had said, that the apostle undervalued this gift. He admitted its importance as one of the manifestations of the Spirit, and he subsequently, v. 18, gives thanks that he himself possessed it in rich measure. From this it is evident that it was something of a higher nature than modern theories would represent it. *But rather that ye prophesied,* (θέλω ἵνα). *I would that.* The same particle often follows verbs of wishing, praying, exhorting, &c. *For greater is he that prophesieth,* &c., i. e. he is more useful than the speaker with tongues, unless the latter interpret. " Nam si accedat interpretatio, jam erit prophetia." CALVIN. Speaking under the supernatural influence of the Spirit was common to both gifts ; the only difference was in the language used. If the speaker interpreted, then he prophesied. *That the church may receive edification.* This proves that the contents of these discourses, delivered in an unknown tongue, were edifying; and therefore did not consist in mysteries in the bad sense of that term; i. e. in enigmas and dark sayings. This passage also proves that the gift of interpretation, although distinct from that of tongues, might be, and doubtless often was, possessed by the same person, and consequently, that he understood what he said. The absence of the gift of interpretation does not prove that the speaker himself in such cases was ignorant of what he uttered. It only proves that he was not inspired to communicate in another language what he had delivered. Had he done so, it would have been on his own authority, and not as an organ of the Spirit. It is conceivable that a man might speak connectedly in a foreign language under the inspiration of the Spirit, so as to be perfectly understood by those acquainted with the language, though he himself did not understand a word of what he uttered. But this hypothesis, though it would suit some passages in this chapter, is inconsistent with others, and therefore cannot be adopted.

6. Now, brethren, if I come unto you speaking with tongues, what shall I profit you, except I shall speak to you either by revelation, or by knowledge, or by prophesying, or by doctrine?

Now (νυνὶ δέ), *since things are so*, i. e. since speaking with tongues without interpreting is unedifying, what shall I profit you, asks the apostle, if I should come to you speaking in a language which you do not understand? He then varies the question, 'What shall I profit you unless I speak to you as a prophet, by (or rather *with*, ἐν) a revelation, or as a teacher with a doctrine.' There are not four, but only two modes of address contemplated in this verse. Revelation and prophecy belong to one; and knowledge and doctrine to the other. He who received revelations was a prophet, he who had "the word of knowledge" was a teacher.

7. And even things without life giving sound, whether pipe or harp, except they give a distinction in the sounds, how shall it be known what is piped or harped?

This verse in Greek begins with the word ὅμως, *yet*, which is variously explained. The most natural interpretation is to assume that the word here, as in Gal. 3, 15, is out of its logical place, and that the sentence should read thus: 'Things without life giving sound, *yet*, unless they give a distinction of sound, how shall it be known," &c. The obvious design of the illustration is to show the uselessness of making sounds which are not understood. But what is the point of the analogy? According to some it is this, as musical instruments emit a mere jargon of sounds, unless the regular intervals be observed, so the speakers with tongues utter a mere jargon. The sounds which they utter are not articulate words, but a

confused noise.* From this it is inferred that the speaking
with tongues was not the gift of speaking foreign languages.
This would make Paul wish (v. 5) that all the Corinthians
would utter unmeaning sounds, and give thanks that he produced more such jargon than any of them! It is plain from
what follows, as well as from the drift of the whole discourse,
that the simple point of the analogy is, that as we cannot
know what is piped or harped, or be benefited by it, unless
we can discriminate the sounds emitted; so we cannot be
benefited by listening to one who speaks a language which
we do not understand. It is not the nature of the gift, but
the folly of the use made of it, which is the point which the
apostle has in view.

8. For if the trumpet give an uncertain sound, who shall prepare himself to the battle?

This is a confirmation of the last clause of the preceding
verse. The sound emitted does not produce its proper effect
if it be unintelligible or uncertain. This teaches us the point
of the whole illustration. The trumpet may sound the battle
call, but if that call is not understood, who will heed it? So
the speaker with tongues may announce the most important
truths, he may unfold mysteries, or pour forth praises as from
a harp of gold, what can it profit those who do not understand him?

9. So likewise ye, except ye utter by the tongue words easy to be understood, how shall it be known what is spoken? for ye shall speak into the air.

This is the application of the preceding illustration, and
affords another proof of what the apostle intended to illustrate.
It was not the nature of the sounds uttered, but their unintelligibleness to the hearer, which was to be considered. *By
the tongue,* i. e. by means of the tongue as the organ of speech.
Words easy to be understood, or rather, *an intelligible dis-*

---

* Acsi diceret: Non potest homo dare citharae aut tibiae animam : vocem
tamen affingit ita temperatam, ut discerni queat; quam igitur absurdum est,
homines ipsos intelligentiae praeditos confusum nescio quid sonare ?—Calvin.
This would seem to mean that the speaker with tongues uttered a confused
noise, with ro more meaning in it than thrumming on a harp.

course. This does not imply, as is contended by tl e advocates
of the modern theories, that those who spoke with tongues
uttered inarticulate sounds. The opposite of εὔσημος, is not
inarticulate, but unintelligible, i. e. what is not in fact understood. *Ye shall speak into the air,* i. e. in vain. Your words
are lost in the air, no ear receives them. In 9, 26, the man
who struck in vain is said to smite the air.

10. There are, it may be, so many kinds of voices
in the world, and none of them (is) without signification.

There are, it may be, so many kinds of voices. The words
(εἰ τύχοι), properly rendered, *it may be,* are often used to render a statement indefinite, where precision is impossible or
unimportant. It was no matter, so far as the apostle's object
was concerned, whether the "kinds of sound" in the world
were more or less. *There are so many,* or, as we should say,
'There are *ever so many,* it may be, languages in the world.'
Kinds of voices. Calvin understands this of the voices or
natural cries of animals. All animated nature is vocal; no
living creature is mute or utters unintelligible sounds: tota
igitur naturæ series quæ est a Deo ordinata, nos ad distinctio-
nem invitat. The context, however, shows that the reference
is to human speech, therefore the words (γένη φωνῶν) should
be translated *kinds of languages,* Gen. 1, 11. And no one of
them *is without signification,* i. e. inarticulate. The phrase
is (φωνὴ ἄφωνος), *a language which is no language,* that is,
without significancy, which is the essence of a language. The
illustration contained in this verse goes to prove that speaking
with tongues was to speak in foreign languages. The very
point is that as all languages are significant, so the languages
used by those who spoke with tongues were significant. The
difficulty was not in the language used, but in the ignorance
of the hearer. This is still plainer from what follows.

11. Therefore if I know not the meaning of the
voice, I shall be unto him that speaketh a barbarian,
and he that speaketh (shall be) a barbarian unto me.

Therefore, i. e. because the sounds uttered are significant;
because the man does not make a mere senseless noise, but

speaks a real language, therefore, if I know not the meaning of the voice (i. e. the language), I shall stand in the relation of a foreigner to him and he to me. Otherwise it would not be so. If a man utters incoherent, inarticulate sounds, which no man living could understand, that would not make him a foreigner. It might prove him to be deranged, but not a stranger. The word *barbarian* means simply one of another country. All other people, whether civilized or not, were barbarians to the Greeks, or to the Romans. As ancient civilization came to be confined to those nations, not to be a Greek or Roman, was to be uncivilized, and hence barbarian or foreigner came to mean without civilization. Just as the true religion being confined to the Jews, *Gentile* (one not a Jew) came to be synonomous with *heathen*. In this passage, however, barbarian means simply foreigner. Comp. Rom. 1, 14. Acts 28, 24. Col. 3, 11.

12. Even so ye, forasmuch as ye are zealous of spiritual (gifts), seek that ye may excel to the edifying of the church.

Even so ye. That is, as the man who speaks a language which I do not understand, is a foreigner to me and I to him, so are ye. You too are foreigners to those who do not understand the language which you use. As all such unintelligible speaking is worthless, the apostle exhorts them to seek to edify the church. *As ye are zealous of spiritual* gifts; literally, *of spirits.* The most probable explanation of this expression is to be sought from 12, 7, where it is said that "to every one is given a manifestation of the Spirit." One and the same Spirit manifests himself in different ways in different persons; and these different manifestations are called spirits. Somewhat analogous are the expressions, "spirits of the prophets," v. 32; "discernment of spirits," 12, 11; "try the spirits," 1 John 4, 1; and "the seven Spirits of God," spoken of in the Apocalypse. In all these cases *spirits* mean manifestations of the Spirit, or forms under which the Spirit manifests himself. It is not an unusual metonomy when the effect receives the name of its cause. Comp. Gal. 5, 17, "The spirit lusteth against the flesh," where *spirit* may mean the renewed principle produced by the Spirit.

Seek that ye may excel (or *abound*) *to the edifying of the church.* This is the common explanation of this clause. But taking the words in their order the passage reads, 'Seek (these gifts) with a view to the edification of the church, in order that ye may excel.' The former explanation is the more natural. The end or object to be sought is not *that they might excel;* that is not the ultimate object, but the edification of the church. The words ζητεῖτε ἵνα, κτλ., therefore, naturally go together. 'Seek that ye may abound unto the edification of the church,' i. e. that ye may possess in rich abundance those gifts which are useful.

13. Wherefore let him that speaketh in an (unknown) tongue pray that he may interpret.

This is an inference not only from the preceding verse but from the whole preceding argument, which was designed to show how useless it is to speak in a language which no one present understands. The verse admits of two interpretations. It may mean that the speaker with tongues should pray for the gift of interpretation; or, that he should pray with the purpose (ἵνα) of interpreting what he said. The principal reason for this latter interpretation is the assumption that the gift of tongues was exercised only in prayer and praise; in other words, that it consisted in an ecstatic but unintelligible and unintelligent pouring out of the heart to God. It is therefore inferred that "to speak with a tongue," v. 13, and "to pray with a tongue," v. 14, mean exactly the same thing; the former being no more comprehensive than the latter. But this whole assumption is not only gratuitous but contrary to Scripture. The gift of tongues was, according to Acts 2, 5–11, exercised in declaring the "wonderful works of God." It is also apparent from what is said in this chapter, vs. 22–25, and v. 27, that the gift in question was not confined to acts of devotion. The former interpretation is therefore to be preferred. 'Let him pray that (ἵνα) he may interpret.' For this use of ἵνα after verbs of *entreating*, &c., see Robinson's Greek Lex. p. 352.

14. For if I pray in an (unknown) tongue, my spirit prayeth, but my understanding is unfruitful.

This is the reason why the speaker with tongues should pray for the gift of interpretation. Unless he interprets his prayer can do no good; or, as the same idea is expressed in vs. 16, 17, those who are unlearned cannot join in it. Praying with a tongue is specified, by way of example, as one mode of speaking with tongues. Though the general meaning of this verse is thus plain, it is the most difficult verse in the whole chapter. What does Paul mean by saying, His spirit prays? There are three answers given to this question. 1. That *spirit* (my spirit) here means the higher intellectual powers of the soul, as distinguished from the understanding. This verse and those which immediately follow, are the principal foundation of the theory that the speaker with tongues was in a state of ecstatic excitement in which his understanding was not exercised, so that he knew not what he said or did. How inconsistent this theory is with the facts of the case has already been shown. This view of the passage, therefore, cannot be admitted. Besides, it has already been remarked, that the Scriptures know nothing of this distinction between the *reason* and the *understanding*. 2. Others say that *spirit* here means the affections. 'My feelings find utterance in prayer, but my understanding is unfruitful.' This would give a good sense; but this meaning of the word spirit is of rare occurrence. In most of the passages quoted by lexicographers as examples of this use of the term, it really means the Holy Spirit. And in this whole discussion, *spirit* is not once used for the feelings. 3. *My spirit* may mean the Holy Spirit in me; that is, my spiritual gift; or, my spirit as the organ of the Spirit of God. Each man has his own spirit, (comp. v. 12) i. e. his own spiritual gift. And Paul means to say, that when a man prays in an unknown tongue, his spiritual gift is indeed exercised; in other words, the Holy Spirit is active in him, but others are not profited. The speaker with tongues is not to be set down as an enthusiast, or as a man in a frenzy, or, as the mockers said, as a man full of new wine. He is really the organ of the Holy Ghost. But as the influence of the Spirit under which he acts, is not irresistible, he should not exercise his gift where it can do no good to others. He may pray in silence, v. 28. This interpretation seems much more in accordance with the use of the word and with the whole drift of the chapter.

What is meant by saying, *my understanding is unfruit-ful?* It may mean, My understanding is not profited, gains no fruit; that is, I do not understand what I say. Though the words in themselves may have this meaning, this interpretation contradicts all those passages which teach that the speaker with tongues did understand himself. The words, therefore, must be understood to mean, 'my understanding produces no fruit,' i. e. it does not benefit others. This is in accordance with all that precedes, and with the uniform use of the word, Eph. 5, 11. Tit. 3, 14. 2 Pet. 1, 8. Matt. 13, 22. Paul had, from the beginning, been urging his readers to have regard to the edification of the church, and he here says, that if he prayed in an unknown tongue, though he acted under the guidance of the Spirit, his prayer could not profit others.* This interpretation is confirmed by vs. 16. 17, as remarked above, where the same idea is expressed by saying, the unlearned could not say Amen to such a prayer. By his understanding being unfruitful is therefore meant, that others did not understand what he said.

The great objection to the preceding interpretation is, that *my* spirit and *my* understanding must be explained in the same way. If the latter means *my own* understanding, the former must mean *my own* spirit. The Holy Ghost, it is said, never is, and cannot be called *my* spirit, for the very reason that it is distinct from the spirit of man. The interpretation given above, however, does not suppose that *my spirit* means the Holy Spirit as a person, but the Holy Spirit as a manifestation; it is the way in which the Spirit manifests himself in me. In other words, it is my spiritual gift. The objection, if it have any force, bears as much against the conceded meaning of the phrase, " the spirits of the prophets," as it does against the explanation just given of the expression, " my

* CALVIN says, Sensus planus est. Si ergo idiomate mihi ignoto preces concipiam, ac spiritus mihi verba suppeditet : ipse quidem spiritus qui linguam meam gubernat, orabit ; sed mens mea vel alibi vagabitur, vel saltem non erit orationis particeps. This implies, that the gift of tongues, at least when disjoined from the gift of interpretation, was the power to speak in a language which the speaker himself did not at the time understand. Accordingly, just before he had asked, Si donum linguae ab intelligentia separetur, ita ut qui pronuntiat, sit ipse sibi barbarus, quid proficiet sic balbutiendo ? Yet Calvin himself regarded this as ridiculous. Quam ridiculum fuisset, linguam hominis Romani formari Dei Spiritu ad pronuntiandas voces Graecas, quae loquenti essent prorsus ignotae : qualiter psittaci, et picae, et corvi humanas voces fingere docentur ? It is very certain, however, that the gift of tongues was possessed by those who had not the gift of interpretation, and yet, even in those cases, it was edifying to the speaker. It therefore follows, that this view of the nature of the gift must be erroneous. Those speaking with tongues were not parrots or ravens. The expression in the text, *my understanding is unfruitful*, consequently cannot mean, "I do not myself understand what I say."

spirit." The spirits of the prophets means the Holy Ghost as manifested in the prophets, or the spiritual influence of which they were the subjects. And that is just the meaning of *my spirit* in this passage.

15. What is it then? I will pray with the spirit, and I will pray with the understanding also: I will sing with the spirit, and I will sing with the understanding also.

What is it then? i. e. what is the practical conclusion from what has been said? That conclusion is expressed by Paul's avowal of his own purpose. The interpretation of this verse of course depends on that of the preceding. Accordingly, some say, the meaning is, I will pray not only with the reason, but with the understanding also, i. e. not only with the higher powers of my nature in exercise, but also with such a command of the understanding as to be able to comprehend and to interpret what I say.* 2. Others say the passage means, 'I will pray with the heart and with the understanding; my mind and feelings shall unite in the exercise.' A very good sense, but entirely foreign to the context. The sentiment is correct in itself, but it is not what Paul here says. 3. According to the third interpretation the sense is, 'I will not only pray in the exercise of my spiritual gift, but so as to be understood by others;' i. e. not only spiritually but intelligibly. If τῷ νοΐ, *with the understanding*, may mean, as the moderns say it does, 'with a view to interpret' (MEYER); it certainly may mean, 'with a view to be understood.' That is, this is what is implied and intended in what the apostle says. When a man spoke τῷ πνεύματι, *with the Spirit*, the Spirit was the *principium movens*, the moving principle, determining him to speak, and what to say. When he spake with τῷ νοΐ, *with the understanding*, the understanding was that controlling principle. These two could be combined. The man could so speak under the guidance of the Spirit as to be intelligible to others.

---

* This view of the subject supposes the speakers with tongues to have been in a state somewhat analogous to that of somnambulists; whose spiritual nature is in activity, but their ordinary intellectual consciousness is suspended, so that when they are recovered, they do not remember any thing they said or did when in their somnambulistic condition.

I will sing. The word (ψάλλειν) means *to touch ;* then *to touch the cords* of a stringed instrument, i. e. to play upon it ; then to sing or chant in harmony with such instrument ; and then to sing or chant. This last is its New Testament meaning. It appears from this as well as from other passages, that singing was from the beginning a part of Christian worship. Pliny, about forty years later, says, Christianos solitos fuisse canere antelucanos hymnos Christo.

16. 17. Else, when thou shalt bless with the spirit, how shall he that occupieth the room of the unlearned say Amen at thy giving of thanks, seeing he understandeth not what thou sayest ? For thou verily givest thanks well, but the other is not edified.

Else, i. e. since in that case. That is, in case you do not speak intelligibly (τῷ νοΐ as well as τῷ πνεύματι). *If thou shalt bless with the spirit.* That is, bless God, including praise and thanksgiving. The word translated *to give thanks,* in the last clause of the verse expresses the same idea. *By the Spirit,* i. e. under the influence of the Spirit, or in the exercise of your spiritual gift, as in the preceding verse. *How shall he that occupieth the place of the unlearned,* i. e. (ἰδιώτου) *of a private person.* The word is used to designate one out of office in opposition to officers ; and in general, one who does not possess the distinguishing characteristic of the class to which it is opposed. It here designates the ungifted in opposition to those who had the gift of tongues ; or rather, it is applicable to any one who was ignorant of the language used by the speaker. Comp. vs. 23. 24. Acts 4, 13. 2 Cor. 11, 6. The context shows that Paul does not refer to laymen in opposition to church officers ; for the officers were just as likely to be (ἰδιῶται) *unlearned* as to the language used as others. *To fill the place* means to occupy the position ; not a particular part of the place of assembly assigned to laymen, but to sustain the relation to the speaker of one unacquainted with the tongue which he uses. *Say Amen at thy giving of thanks,* i. e. assent or respond to it. *Amen* is a Hebrew adjective signifying *true* or *faithful,* often used adverbially at the end of a sentence to express assent to what is said, in the sense of *so let it be.* In the Jewish synagogue it was the custom for the people to respond to the prayers by audibly saying Amen, by which they signified their assent and participation in the petitions which had been offered. *Buxtorf's* Talm. Lexicon, *Vitringa* de Synag. Great importance was attached by the Jews to saying Amen. Schoettgen quotes numerous passages to show to what a superstitious extreme this was carried. "He who says Amen is greater than he that blesses." "Whoever says Amen, to him the gates of Paradise are opened." "Whoever says Amen shortly, his days shall be shortened; whoever answers Amen distinctly and at length, his days shall be lengthened." According to Justin Martyr, Apolog. ii. 97, the custom passed over to the Christian church. This seems also intimated in this passage; the expression is, "Say *the* Amen," i. e. utter the familiar formula of assent. The unlearned cannot thus assent, *since he knows not what thou sayest*. Men cannot assent to what they do not understand, because assent implies the affirmation of the truth of that to which we assent. It is impossible, therefore, to join in prayers uttered in an unknown tongue. The Romish church persists in the use of the Latin language in her public services not only in opposition to the very idea and intent of worship, but also to the express prohibition of the Scriptures. For the very thing here prohibited is praying in public in a language which the people do not understand. It is indeed said that words may touch the feelings which do not convey any distinct notions to the mind. But we cannot say Amen to such words, any more than we can to a flute. Such blind, emotional worship, if such it can be called, stands at a great remove from the intelligent service demanded by the apostle. *Thou verily givest thanks well*, i. e. in a way acceptable to God and profitable to yourself. This proves that the speaker must have understood what he said. For if the unintelligible is useless, it must be so to the speaker as well as to the hearer. If it was necessary that they should understand in order to be edified, it was no less necessary that he should understand what he said in order to be benefited. This verse is therefore decisive against all theories of the gift of tongues which assume that those who used them did not understand their own words. The Scriptures recognize no unintelligent worship of God, or any spiritual edification (in the case of adults) disconnected from the truth; whether that edification be sought by sounds or signs, whether by prayers or sacraments.

18. 19. I thank my God, I speak with tongues

more than ye all : yet in the church I had rather speak five words with my understanding, that (by my voice) I might teach others also, than ten thousand words in an (unknown) tongue.

That Paul should give thanks to God that he was more abundantly endowed with the gift of tongues, if that gift consisted in the ability to speak in languages which he himself did not understand, and the use of which, on that assumption, could according to his principle benefit neither himself nor others, is not to be believed. Equally clear is it from this verse that to speak with tongues was not to speak in a state of mental unconsciousness. The common doctrine as to the nature of the gift, is the only one consistent with this passage. Paul says that although he could speak in foreign languages more than the Corinthians, he would rather speak five words *with his understanding*, i. e. so as to be intelligible, than ten thousand words in an unknown tongue. *In the church*, i. e. in the assembly. *That I might teach others also*, (κατηχέω) to instruct orally, Gal. 6, 6. This shows what is meant by speaking *with the understanding*. It is speaking in such a way as to convey instruction.

20. Brethren, be not children in understanding : howbeit in malice be ye children, but in understanding be men.

There are two characteristics of children ; the one a disposition to be pleased with trifles, or to put a false estimate on things; the other, comparative innocence. There is a great difference as to every thing evil between a little child and a full-grown man. The former of these characteristics the apostle wished the Corinthians to lay aside. The latter he wished them to cultivate. They had displayed a childish disposition in estimating the gift of tongues above more useful gifts, and in using it when it could answer no good purpose. A little child, however, is some thing so lovely, and is so often held up in Scripture for imitation, that he could not say, without qualification, *Be not children*. He therefore says, Be not children *as to understanding ;* but as *to malice*, a comprehensive word for evil dispositions, *be ye children*. So our Lord said, Except ye be converted, and become as little children, ye shall not enter into the kingdom of heaven, Matt. 18, 3.

21. In the law it is written, With (men of) other tongues and other lips will I speak unto this people ; and yet for all that will they not hear me, saith the Lord.

In the law. The word *law* signifies that which binds; especially that which binds the conscience as a rule of faith and practice. That rule may be revealed in our hearts, in the whole Scriptures, in the Pentateuch, or in the moral law ; and hence the word as used in Scripture may refer to any one of these forms in which the will of God is made known; or it may include them all. The context must decide its meaning in each particular case. Here, as in John 10, 34. Rom. 3, 20, and elsewhere, the reference is not to the Pentateuch, but to the Old Testament. The passage quoted is Is. 28, 11. 12, which in our version stands thus, "For with stammering lips, and another tongue, will he speak to this people. To whom he said, This is the rest wherewith ye may cause the weary to rest; and this is the refreshing : yet they would not hear." The apostle gives the 11th verse in a free translation, and the concluding words of the 12th. He does not quote the passage as having any prophetic reference to the events in Corinth ; much less does he give an allegorical interpretation of it in order to make it a condemnation of speaking with tongues. It is a simple reference to a signal event in the Jewish history from which the Corinthians might derive a useful lesson. The Jews had refused to hear the prophets speaking their own language, and God threatened to bring upon them a people whose language they could not understand. This was a judgment; a mark of displeasure designed as a punishment and not for their conversion. From this the Corinthians might learn that it was no mark of the divine favour to have teachers whose language they could not understand. They were turning a blessing into a curse. The gift of tongues was designed, among other things, to facilitate the propagation of the gospel, by enabling Christians to address people of various nations each in his own language. Used for this purpose it was a blessing ; but to employ it for the sake of display, in addressing those who could not understand the language employed, was to make it a curse. The Spirit of God often confers gifts on men, and then holds them responsible for the way in which they exercise them.

22. Wherefore tongues are for a sign, not to them that believe, but to them that believe not : but prophesying (serveth) not for them that believe not, but for them which believe.

There are two inaccuracies in this version which obscure the sense. The first is the introduction of the word *serveth* after prophesying. The clauses are parallel. Tongues are for a sign to one class, and prophesying to another. Nothing need be supplied; what is implied is, that prophesying *is for a sign*. The introduction of the word *serveth* is not only unnecessary, but contrary to the context. The second inaccuracy is expressing the force of the datives (πιστεύουσι and ἀπίστοις) by *to* in the first member of the verse, and by *for* in the second member. There is no reason for this change. The relation expressed is the same in both cases. 'Tongues are *for* the one, prophesying are *for* the other;' or, 'Tongues are for a sign *to* the one, and prophesying *to* the other.' The connection between this verse and what precedes is indicated by the word *wherefore*, or *so that*. The inference may be drawn either from the immediately preceding clause, viz., "For all that they will not hear me, saith the Lord;" or from the historical fact referred to in the whole verse. If the former, then the design of the apostle is to show that as teaching the Hebrews by men of other tongues did not render them obedient; so speaking in other tongues would not profit the Corinthians. If the latter, then the design is to show, that as sending foreigners among the Hebrews was a mark of God's displeasure, so speaking in the Christian assemblies in foreign languages would be a curse and not a blessing. The latter view is demanded by the whole context.

The inference from the preceding verse is that tongues are a sign not to the believing but to the unbelieving, and prophesying just the reverse. This difficult verse is variously explained. 1. The word *sign* is taken in the sense of *mark* or *proof*, as when it is said, "the signs of an apostle," 2 Cor. 12, 12, that is, the tokens by which an apostle may be known. Comp. Luke 2, 12. 2 Thess. 3, 17. The meaning of the passage would then be, 'Tongues are a proof that those among whom they are used are not believers, but unbelievers; and prophesying is a proof that they are believers, and not unbelievers.' But when the word is used in this sense, the thing of which it is a sign is put in the genitive. It is a sign *of*, not *to* or *for*. 2. It may mean a *prodigy* or *wonder*. This is a very common sense of the word, as in the familiar phrase, " signs and wonders." The meaning is then commonly made to be, 'Tongues are a wonder designed not for the benefit of believers, but for unbelievers; and on the other hand, prophesy is a wonder designed not for the benefit of unbelievers, but for the benefit of believers.' But this is neither true nor in accordance with v. 24. It is not true that the gift of tongues was designed exclusively for the conversion of unbelievers. Why should not that gift be exercised for the edification, as well as for the conversion of men? Their conversion would not enable them to understand the native language of the apostles. Much less is it true that prophecy was designed exclusively for the edification of believers. The prophets and apostles were sent forth for the conversion of the world. And in v. 24 the conversion of unbelievers is specified as the very effect to be anticipated from the use of this gift. A still more decisive objection to this interpretation is, that it does not give the true conclusion from the preceding verse. The nature of the premises must decide the nature of the inference. It is not a fair inference from the fact that although God sent foreigners to teach the Hebrews they still continued disobedient, that foreign tongues were designed for the conversion of unbelievers. The very opposite conclusion would naturally follow from that fact. 3. *Sign* may here mean *a warning* or sign of punishment. 'Tongues are a warning, designed not for believers, but for unbelievers,' who are understood to be, not those merely without faith, but positive infidels, or obstinate rejectors of the truth. To this, however, it may be objected, that the word unbeliever (ἄπιστος) is used in v. 24 for those without faith, and that to assume a change of meaning in the same context is most unnatural. A still more serious objection is, that this interpretation cannot be carried out. It cannot be said that prophecy is a warning designed for believers. The two members of the sentence are so related that whatever is said of the gift of tongues, must be true, *mutandis mutatis*, of prophecy. If the one be a punishment designed for unbelievers, the other must be a punishment designed for believers. 4. The most satisfactory explanation is to take *sign* in the general sense of any indication of the divine presence. 'Tongues are a manifestation of God, having reference, not to believers, but to unbelievers; and prophecy is a similar manifestation, having reference, not to unbelievers, but to believers.' By *tongues*, however, is not to be understood the gift of tongues, but, as v. 21 requires, foreign languages, i. e. languages unknown to the hearers. The meaning is, that when a people are disobedient, God sends them teachers whom they cannot understand; when they are obedient, he sends them prophets speaking their own language. This is the natural conclusion from the premises contained in v. 21. When the Hebrews were disobedient God sent foreigners among them; when obedient, he sent them prophets. *Wherefore*, i. e. hence it follows, that unintelligible teachers are for the unbelieving; those who can be understood are for the believing. This view is also consistent with what follows, which is designed to show that speaking in a language which those who hear cannot understand is the cause of evil; whereas speaking intelligibly is the source of good. It must be remembered that it is not the gift of tongues of which the apostle speaks, but speaking to people in a language which they do not understand. And therefore this interpretation does not imply any disparagement of the gift in question. When used aright, that is, when employed in addressing those to whom the language used was intelligible, it was prophecy. The obscurity of the passage arises in a great measure from the ambiguity of the expression *to speak with tongues*. It means to speak in foreign or unknown languages. But a language may be said to be unknown either in reference to the speaker or to the hearer. It is said to be unknown to the speaker, if not previously acquired; and it is said to be unknown to the hearers if they do not understand it. The apostle uses the expression sometimes in one sense and sometimes in the other. When it is said that the apostles, on the day of Pentecost, spake with tongues, it means that they used languages which they had never learned; but when Paul says he would rather speak five words intelligibly than ten thousand words with a tongue, he means in a language unknown to the hearers. Speaking with tongues in the one sense, was a grace and a blessing; in the other sense, it was a folly and a curse. It was of speaking with tongues in the latter sense the apostle treats in these verses.

23. If therefore the whole church be come together into one place, and all speak with tongues, and there come in (those that are) unlearned, or unbelievers, will they not say that ye are mad?

If *therefore*. The inference from the preceding representation is, that speaking in languages not understood by the people is undesirable and useless. To show the justness of this conclusion the apostle supposes the case which follows. *If the whole church be come together in one place.* That is, if all the Christians of the place, or the whole congregation, be assembled. This is one of the conditions of the hypothesis. Another is, that *all should speak with tongues.* This does not necessarily imply either that all present had the gift of tongues, or that all who possessed the gift spoke at one and the same time, although from vs. 27 and 30 it may be inferred that this was sometimes done. All that the words here require is that all who spoke used foreign languages. *To speak with tongues* must mean to speak in languages unknown to the hearers. The third condition of the case supposed is, that unlearned and unbelievers should come into the meeting. Who are the (ἰδιῶται), *the unlearned* here intended? 1. Some say they were Christians ignorant of the gift of tongues, because they are distinguished from *unbelievers*, or those not Christians. 2. Others say that the *unlearned* are those who were ignorant of Christianity, and the (ἄπιστοι) *unbelieving*, are those who knew and rejected it, i. e. infidels. This is giving to the word a force which it has not in itself, and which the context does not give it. 3. The simplest explanation is that the *unlearned* were those ignorant of the language spoken, and the *unbelieving* those not Christians, whether Jews or Gentiles. Such persons were doubtless often led, from curiosity or other motives, to attend the Christian assemblies. The two classes (the unlearned and the unbelieving) are not so distinguished that the same person might not belong to both classes. The same persons were either ἰδιῶται or ἄπιστοι, according to the aspect under which they were viewed. Viewed in relation to the languages spoken, they were *unlearned ;* viewed in relation to Christianity, they were *unbelievers.* The apostle asks what impression such persons, in the case supposed, would receive? Would they not say *ye are mad ?* John 12, 20. Acts 12, 15. 26, 24.

24. 25. But if all prophesy, and there come in one that believeth not, or (one) unlearned, he is convinced of all, he is judged of all : and thus are the secrets of his heart made manifest ; and so falling down on (his)

face he will worship God, and report that God is in
you of a truth.

This is another part of the inference from what was said in
vs. 21. 22. Speaking in languages unknown to the hearers is
not adapted to do good; speaking intelligibly is suited to
produce the happiest effects. *If all prophesy,* i. e. if all the
speakers speak under the guidance of the Spirit in a language
which the hearers can understand. *If one that believeth not,
or one unlearned.* From these words it is manifest that the
unlearned were not Christians as distinguished from Jews or
Gentiles here called unbelievers, for the same effect is said to
be produced on both. The unlearned were therefore as much
the subjects of conversion as the unbelieving. The meaning
is, if any person, either ignorant or destitute of faith, should
come in, he would be *convinced by all.* That is, what he
heard from all would carry conviction to his mind. He would
be convinced of the truth of what he heard; convinced of sin,
of righteousness and of judgment, John 16, 8; convinced that
Jesus is the Christ, the Son of the living God, Acts 9, 20. 22;
and that it is a faithful saying, and worthy of all acceptation,
that Jesus Christ is come into the world to save sinners, 1
Tim. 1, 15. *He is judged of all,* i. e. examined, searched into
(ἀνακρίνεται); for the word of God is a discerner (κριτικός) of
the thoughts and intents of the heart, Heb. 4, 12. The result
of this searching examination is, *that the secrets of his heart
are made manifest;* that is, they are revealed to himself.
His real character and moral state, with regard to which he
was before ignorant, are made known to him. The effect of
this is humility, contrition, self-condemnation, and turning
unto God. This is expressed by saying, *so* i. e. in this condition of a convinced sinner who has been brought to the
knowledge of himself, *falling down on his face, he will worship God.* The first step in religion is entire self-abasement;
such a conviction of sin, i. e. of guilt and pollution, as shall
lead to self-condemnation and self-abhorrence, and to a complete renunciation of all dependence on our own righteousness
and strength. When the soul is thus humbled God reveals
himself sooner or later, in mercy, manifesting himself as reconciled in Jesus Christ; and then we *worship him.* This expresses reverence, love and confidence. It is the return of the
soul to the favour and fellowship of God. One who has had
such an experience cannot keep it to himself. The apostle

therefore describes the convert as *declaring*, i. e. *proclaiming aloud that God is in you of a truth.* "With the heart man believeth unto righteousness, and with the mouth confession is made unto salvation," Rom. 10, 10. It is not enough to believe the truth, it must be publicly professed; because confession is the natural fruit of faith. When there is a proper apprehension of the value of the truth, and a sincere appropriation of the promises of God to ourselves, there will be the desire to acknowledge his goodness and to proclaim the truth to others. The thing acknowledged is, *that God is in you,* i. e. that Christianity is divine; that Christians are not deluded fanatics, but the true children of God, in whom he dwells by his Spirit. The convert therefore joins himself to them to share their fate, to take part in whatever of reproach or persecution falls to their lot. This confession is made with confidence. *Declaring that God is in you of a truth.* It is not a mere conjecture, but a firm conviction, founded on experience, i. e. on the demonstration of the Spirit, 2, 4.

Special directions as to the mode of conducting their public assemblies, vs. 26–40.

The apostle concludes this chapter with certain practical directions derived from the principles which he had laid down. He neither denied the reality of the extraordinary gifts with which the Corinthians were so richly endowed, nor forbade their exercise. He only enjoined that mutual edification should be the end aimed at, v. 26. With regard to those having the gift of tongues, he directed that not more than two, or at most three, should speak, and that in succession, while one interpreted. But in case no interpreter was present, there was to be no speaking with tongues, vs. 27. 28. Of the prophets also only two or three were to speak, and the rest were to sit in judgment on what was said. In case a new revelation was made to one of the prophets, he was not to interrupt the speaker, but wait until he had concluded; or the one was to give way to the other. Both were not to speak at the same time, for God did not approve of confusion. As the influence of which the prophets were the subjects did not destroy their self-control, there could be no difficulty in obeying this injunction, vs. 29–33. Women were not to speak in public; but to seek instruction at home. This prohibition rests on the divinely established subordination of the women, and on the instinct of propriety, vs. 34. 35. The Corinthians were not to act in this matter as though they were the oldest or the only church, v. 36. The apostle requires all classes, no matter how highly gifted, to regard his directions as the commands of Christ, vs. 37. 38. He sums up the chapter in two sentences. 1. Earnestly to seek the gift of prophecy, and not to prohibit the exercise of the gift of tongues. 2. To do all things with decency and order.

26. How is it then, brethren? when ye come together, every one of you hath a Psalm, hath a doctrine, hath a tongue, hath a revelation, hath an interpretation. Let all things be done unto edifying.

How is it then? i. e. as in v. 15, What is the conclusion from what has been said? What is the condition of things among you? How, in point of fact, do you conduct your public worship? *When ye come together.* That is, as often as ye come together. *Every one of you hath,* &c. *Every one* is used distributively; one has this and another that. *A psalm,* a song of praise to God. This can hardly mean one of the Psalms of the Old Testament; but something prepared or suggested for the occasion. One was impelled by the Spirit to pour forth his heart in a song of praise. Comp. v. 15. *Hath a doctrine,* i. e. comes prepared to expound some doctrine. *Hath a tongue,* i. e. is able and impelled to deliver an address or to pray in an unknown tongue. *Hath a revelation,* i. e. as a prophet he has received a revelation from God which he desires to communicate. *Hath an interpretation,* i. e. is prepared to give the interpretation of some discourse previously delivered in an unknown tongue. This passage, and indeed the whole chapter, presents a lively image of an early Christian assembly. Although there were officers in every church, appointed to conduct the services and especially to teach, yet as the extraordinary gifts of the Spirit were not confined to them or to any particular class, any member present who experienced the working of the Spirit in any of its extraordinary manifestations, was authorized to use and exercise his gift. Under such circumstances confusion could hardly fail to ensue. That such disorder did prevail in the public assemblies in Corinth is clear enough from this chapter. To correct this evil is the apostle's design in this whole passage. It was only so long as the gifts of tongues, of prophecy, of miracles, and others of a like kind continued in the church that the state of things here described prevailed. Since those gifts have ceased, no one has the right to rise in the church under the impulse of his own mind to take part in its services. The general rule which the apostle lays down, applicable to all gifts alike, is that every thing *should be done unto edifying.* That is, that the edification of the church should be the object aimed at in the exercise of these gifts. It was not enough that a man felt himself the subject of a divine influence; or that acting under it would be agreeable or even profitable to himself, he must sit in silence unless the exercise of his gift would benefit the brethren as a worshipping assembly.

27. If any man speak in an (unknown) tongue, (let it be) by two, or at the most (by) three, and (that) by course; and let one interpret.

As to the use of the gift of tongues, the directions were that only two or three having that gift should speak; that they were not to speak together, but in succession; and that one should interpret what the others said.

28. But if there be no interpreter, let him keep silence in the church ; and let him speak to himself, and to God.

If neither the speaker himself, nor any other person present, have the gift of interpretation, the former was to keep *silence in the church*, i. e. in the public assembly. *And let him speak to himself, and to God*, or, *for* himself, and *for* God. That is, let him commune silently with God in the exercise of his gift. As, according to Paul, all true worship is intelligent, it is evident that if in the exercise of the gift of tongues, there was communion with God, the understanding could not have been in abeyance. In that gift, not only the words, but also the thoughts and the accompanying emotion were communicated or excited by the Spirit. Those having that gift spake as the Spirit gave them utterance, Acts 2, 4.

29. 30. Let the prophets speak two or three, and let the others judge. If (any thing) be revealed to another that sitteth by, let the first hold his peace.

The number of prophets who were to speak at any one

meeting was also limited to two or three. The others were *to judge*, i. e. exercise the gift of "the discerning of spirits," 12, 10. From this passage it may be inferred that this latter gift was a concomitant of the gift of prophecy; for the other prophets, i. e. those who did not speak were to sit in judgment on what was said, in order to decide whether those claiming to be prophets were really inspired. The case, however, might occur that a communication from the Spirit might be made to one prophet while another was speaking. What was to be done then? As it was contrary to order for two to speak at the same time, the one speaking must either at once stop, or the receiver of the new revelation must wait until his predecessor had concluded his discourse. The imperative form of the expression (ὁ πρῶτος σιγάτω), *let the first be silent*, is in favour of the former view. This would suppose that the fact of a new communication being made, indicated that it was entitled to be heard at once. There are two reasons, however, which may be urged for the second view. The interruption of a speaker was itself disorderly, and therefore contrary to the whole drift of the apostle's directions; and secondly, what follows is most naturally understood as assigning the reason why the receiver of the new revelation should wait. The meaning may be, 'Let the first be silent *before the other begins.'*

31. For ye may all prophesy one by one, that all may learn, and all may be comforted.

This verse assigns the reason why two prophets should not speak at the same time. They could all have the opportunity of speaking one by one. Not indeed at the same meeting, for he had before limited the number of speakers to two or three for any one occasion. *That all may learn, and all may be comforted.* This is the end to be attained by their all speaking. The discourse of one might suit the wants of some hearers; and that of another might be adapted to the case of others. Thus all hearers would receive instruction and consolation. The latter word (*consolation*), however, is not so comprehensive as the original, which means not only to comfort, but also to exhort and to admonish.

32. And the spirits of the prophets are subject to the prophets.

This verse is connected by *and* to the preceding as containing an additional reason for the injunction in v. 31. 'You need not speak together, because you can all have the opportunity of speaking successively, *and* you are not compelled to speak by any irresistible impulse.' *The spirits of the prophets.* The word *spirit* is used here (comp. vs. 12. 14. 15) for the divine influence under which the prophets spoke. That influence was not of such a nature as to destroy the self-control of those who were its subjects. It did not throw them into a state of frenzy analogous to that of a heathen pythoness. The prophets of God were calm and self-possessed. This being the case, there was no necessity why one should interrupt another, or why more than one should speak at the same time. The one speaking could stop when he pleased; and the one who received a revelation could wait as long as he pleased. The spirits of the prophets are subject to the prophets, i. e. under their control. According to another interpretation the *spirits of the prophets* means their own *spirits* (or minds), considered as the organs of the Holy Spirit. But this is contrary to the use of the word in the context; and moreover it is inconsistent with the sense assigned to the word by the advocates of this interpretation. They say that *spirit* means the higher powers of the mind in distinction from the understanding. In this sense every man, whether the subject of divine influence or not, has a spirit. In other words, according to their theory it is not because the higher powers of the mind are the organs of the Spirit of God that they are called *spirits*. It is therefore inconsistent to assign that reason for the use of the word here. The interpretation above given of this verse is the one commonly adopted. Many commentators, however, understand the apostle to say, that the spirits of the prophets are subject to one another, i. e. to other prophets; and therefore if one is speaking he should yield to another who wishes to speak. This idea is not suited to the context. It would suggest merely a reason why one *ought* to yield to the other. What the apostle says and wishes to prove is, that one *can* yield to the other. A prophet was not forced to speak by the spirit which he had received.

33. For God is not (the author) of confusion, but of peace, as in all churches of the saints.

This is the reason why the spirits of the prophets must be

assumed to be subject to the prophets. They are from God; but God is not a God of disorder or of commotion, but of peace. Therefore every spirit which is from him, must be capable of control. He never impels men to act contrary to the principles which he has ordained. If he wills order to prevail in the church, he never impels men to be disorderly. This is a truth of wide application. When men pretend to be influenced by the Spirit of God in doing what God forbids, whether in disturbing the peace and order of the church, by insubordination, violence or abuse, or in any other way, we may be sure that they are either deluded or impostors.

34. Let your women keep silence in the churches: for it is not permitted unto them to speak; but (they are commanded) to be under obedience, as also saith the law.

The words *as in all the churches of the saints*, if connected with verse 33, contain a proof of what had just been said. 'I may appeal to all the churches of the saints in proof that God is the God not of commotion, but of peace.' Most commentators, however, connect them with v. 34. 'As in all the churches of the saints, let your women keep silence in the churches; for it is not permitted to them to speak; but *they are commanded* to be under obedience, as also saith the law.' The reasons for preferring this connection are, 1. That verse 33 has an appropriate conclusion in the words "God is not a God of confusion but of peace." 2. The words *as in all the churches of the saints*, if connected with v. 33, do not give a pertinent sense. The apostle would be made to prove a conceded and undeniable truth by an appeal to the authority or experience of the church. 3. If connected with v. 34, this passage is parallel to 11, 16, where the custom of the churches in reference to the deportment of women in public is appealed to as authoritative. The sense is thus pertinent and good. 'As is the case in all other Christian churches, let your women keep silence in the public assemblies.' The fact that in no Christian church was public speaking permitted to women was itself a strong proof that it was unchristian, i. e. contrary to the spirit of Christianity. Paul, however, adds to the prohibition the weight of apostolic authority, and not of that only but also the authority of reason and of Scripture. *It is not permitted to them to speak.* The speaking intended is public speaking, and especially in the church. In the Old Testament it had been predicted that "Your sons and your daughters shall prophesy;" a prediction which the apostle Peter quotes as verified on the day of Pentecost, Acts 2, 17; and in Acts 21, 9 mention is made of four daughters of Philip who prophesied. The apostle himself seems to take for granted, in 11, 5, that women might receive and exercise the gift of prophecy. It is therefore only the public exercise of the gift that is prohibited. The *rational* ground for this prohibition is that it is contrary to the relation of subordination in which the woman stands to the man that she appear as a public teacher. Both the Jews and Greeks adopted the same rule; and therefore the custom, which the Corinthians seemed disposed to introduce, was contrary to established usage. The *scriptural* ground is expressed in the words *as also saith the law*, i. e. the will of God as made known in the Old Testament. There, as well as in the New Testament, the doctrine that women should be in subjection is clearly revealed.

35. And if they will learn any thing, let them ask their husbands at home: for it is a shame for women to speak in the church.

The desire for knowledge in women is not to be repressed, and the facilities for its acquisition are not to be denied them. The refinement and delicacy of their sex, however, should be carefully preserved. They may learn all they wish to know without appearing before the public. *For it is a shame for women to speak in the church.* The word used is αἰσχρός, which properly means *ugly, deformed.* It is spoken of any thing which excites disgust. As the peculiar power and usefulness of women depend on their being the objects of admiration and affection, any thing which tends to excite the opposite sentiments should for that reason be avoided.

36. What! came the word of God out from you? or came it unto you only?

That is, Are you the mother church? or are you the only church? *The word of God* here means the gospel. Paul means to ask, whether the gospel took its rise in Corinth?

U

The disregard which the people of that church manifested for the customs of their sister churches seemed to evince an assuming and arrogant temper. They acted as though they were entitled to be independent, if not to prescribe the law to others. Paul takes the authority of the church for granted. He assumes that any thing contrary to the general sentiment and practice of the people of God is wrong. This he does because he understands by the church the body of Christ, those in whom the Holy Spirit dwells, and whose character and conduct are controlled and governed by his influence.

37. If any man think himself to be a prophet, or spiritual, let him acknowledge that the things that I write unto you are the commandments of the Lord.

If any man think, &c. That is, If any man, with or without just reason, assumes to be *a prophet*, i. e. inspired; or *spiritual*, i. e. the possessor of any gift of the Spirit, let him prove himself what he claims to be by submitting to my authority. Here, as in 1 John 4, 6, ("He that knoweth God, heareth us; he that is not of God, heareth not us,") submission to the infallible authority of the apostles is made the test of a divine mission and even of conversion. This must be so. If the apostles were the infallible organs of the Holy Ghost, to disobey them in any matter of faith or practice is to refuse to obey God. The inference which Romanists draw from this fact is, that as the apostleship is a permanent office in the church, and as the prelates are the bearers of that office, therefore to refuse submission in matters of faith or practice to the bishops is a clear proof that we are not of God. This is the chain with which Rome binds the nations to her car which she drives whithersoever she wills. The inference which Protestants draw from the fact in question is, that as we have the infallible teaching of the prophets and apostles in the Bible, therefore any man who does not conform in faith and practice to the Scriptures cannot be of God. This is the rule by which Protestants try all who claim to have a divine commission. It is nothing to them what their ecclesiastical descent may be. He that heareth not the Scriptures, is not of God. *The things which I write.* There is not only no reason for confining these words, as some do, to the preceding verse, but every reason against it. It is not merely for the prohibition against women speaking in the church for which the apostle claims divine authority. The specification of prophets and spiritual persons shows that the reference is primarily to the whole contents of this chapter. All the directions which he had given with respect to the exercise of spiritual gifts were of divine authority. What is true, however, of this chapter, is no less true of all apostolical instructions; because they all rest on the same foundation. *Are the commandments of the Lord*, i. e. of Christ, because he is the person known in the Christian church as Lord. The continued influence of Christ by the Spirit over the minds of his apostles, which is a divine prerogative, is here assumed or asserted.

38. But if any man be ignorant, let him be ignorant.

That is, if any man be ignorant or refuses to acknowledge the divine authority of my instructions, let him be ignorant. Paul would neither attempt to convince him, nor waste time in disputing the point. Where the evidence of any truth is abundant and has been clearly presented, those who reject it should be left to act on their own responsibility. Further disputation can do no good.

39. Wherefore, brethren, covet to prophesy, and forbid not to speak with tongues.

Prophecy and the gift of tongues are the two gifts of which this chapter treats. The former is to be preferred to the latter. The one is to be coveted, i. e. earnestly desired and sought after; the exercise of the other, even in Christian assemblies, was not to be prohibited; provided, as stated above, any one be present who possessed the gift of interpretation.

40. Let all things be done decently and in order.

Decently, i. e. in such a way as not to offend against propriety. The adjective, the adverbial form of which is here used, means *well-formed, comely;* that which excites the pleasing emotion of beauty. The exhortation therefore is, so to conduct their worship that it may be beautiful; in other words, so as to make a pleasing impression on all who are right-minded. *And in order* (κατὰ τάξιν), not tumultuously as in a mob, but as in a well-ordered army, where every one keeps his place, and acts at the proper time and in the proper way. So far as external matters are concerned, these are the two principles which should regulate the conduct of public worship. The apostle not only condemns any church acting independently of other churches, but also any member of a particular church acting from his own impulses, without regard to others. The church as a whole, and in every separate congregation, should be a harmonious, well-organized body.

CHAPTER XV.

The Resurrection of the Dead.

In treating this subject the apostle first proves the fact of Christ's resurrection, vs. 1–11. He thence deduces, first, the possibility, and then the certainty of the resurrection of his people, vs. 12–34. He afterwards teaches the nature of the resurrection, so far as to show that the doctrine is not liable to the objections which had been brought against it, vs. 35–58.

The Resurrection of Christ as securing the Resurrection of his People, vs. 1–34.

THAT certain false teachers in Corinth denied the resurrection of the dead is plain, not only from the course of argument here adopted but from the explicit statement in v. 12. Who these persons were, and what were the grounds of their objections, can only be conjectured from the nature of the apostolic argument. The most common opinion is that the objectors were converted Sadducees. The only reason for this opinion is that the Sadducees denied the doctrine of the resurrection, and that Paul, as appears from Acts 24, 6–9 and 26, 6–8, had been before brought into collision with them on this subject. The objections to this view are of no great weight. It is said that such was the hostility of the Sadducees to the gospel that it is not probable any of their number were among the converts to Christianity. The case of Paul himself proves that the bitterest enemies could, by the grace of God, be converted into friends. It is further objected that Paul could not, in argument with Sadducees, make the resurrection of Christ the basis of his proof. But he does not assume that fact as conceded, but proves it by an array of the testimony by which it was supported. Others suppose that the opponents of the doctrine were Epicureans. There is, however, no indication of their peculiar opinions in the chapter. In v. 32 Epicurean carelessness and indulgence are represented as the consequence, not the cause, of the denial of the resurrection. Nothing more definite can be arrived at on this point than the conjecture that the false teachers in question were men of Grecian culture. In Acts 17, 32 it is said of the Athenians that "some mocked" when they heard Paul preach the doctrine of the resurrection. From the character of the objections answered in the latter part of the chapter, vs. 35–58, it is probable that the objections urged against the doctrine were founded on the assumption that a material organization was unsuited to the future state. It is not unlikely that oriental philosophy, which assumed that matter was the source and seat of evil, had produced an effect on the minds of these Corinthian sceptics as well as on the Christians of Colosse. The decision of the question as to what particular class of persons the opponents of the doctrine of the resurrection belonged, happily is of no importance in the interpretation of the apostle's argument. As in 2 Tim. 2, 17. 18 he speaks of Hymeneus and Philetus as teaching that the resurrection was passed already, it is probable that these errorists in Corinth also refused to acknowledge any other than a spiritual resurrection.

After reminding the Corinthians that the doctrine of the resurrection was a primary principle of the gospel, which he had preached to them, and on which their salvation depended, vs. 1–3, he proceeds to assert and prove the fact that Christ rose from the dead on the third day. This event had been predicted in the Old Testament. Its actual occurrence is proved, 1. By Christ appearing after his resurrection, first to Peter and then to the twelve.   2. By his appearing to upward of five hundred brethren at one time, most of whom were still alive.   3. By a separate appearance to James.   4. And then again to all the apostles.   5. Finally by his appearance to Paul himself. There never was a historical event established on surer evidence than that of the resurrection of Christ, vs. 4–8. This fact, therefore, was included in the preaching of all the apostles, and in the faith of all Christians, v. 11. But if this be so, how can the doctrine of the resurrection be

denied by any who pretend to be Christians? To deny the
resurrection of the dead is to deny the resurrection of Christ;
and to deny the resurrection of Christ, is to subvert the gospel, vs. 12–14; and also to make the apostles false witnesses,
v. 15. If Christ be not risen, our faith is vain, we are yet in
our sins, those dead in Christ are perished, and all the hopes
of Christians are destroyed, vs. 16–19. But if Christ be risen,
then his people will also rise, because he rose as a pledge of
their resurrection. As Adam was the cause of death, so Christ
is the cause of life; Adam secured the death of all who are *in*
him, and Christ secures the life of all who are *in* him, vs. 20–22.
Although the resurrection of Christ secures the resurrection
of his people, the two events are not contemporaneous. Christ
rose first, his people are to rise when he comes the second
time. Then is to be the final consummation, when Christ
shall deliver up his providential kingdom as mediator to the
Father, after all his enemies are subdued, vs. 23. 24. It is
necessary that Christ's dominion over the universe, to which
he was exalted after his resurrection, should continue until his
great work of subduing or restraining evil was accomplished.
When that is done, then the Son (the Theanthropos, the Incarnate Logos), will be subject to the Father, and God as
God, and not as Mediator, reign supreme, 25–28.

Besides the arguments already urged, there are two other
considerations which prove the truth or importance of the
doctrine of the resurrection. The first is, "the baptism for
the dead" (whatever that means) prevailing in Corinth, assumes the truth of the doctrine, v. 29. The other is, the intimate connection between this doctrine and that of a future
state is such, that if the one be denied, the other cannot, in a
Christian sense, be maintained. If there be no resurrection,
there is for Christians no hereafter, and they may act on the
principle, "Let us eat and drink for to-morrow we die," vs.
30–32. The apostle concludes this part of the subject by
warning his readers against the corrupting influence of evil associations. Whence it is probable that the denial of the doctrine had already produced the evil effects referred to among
those who rejected it, vs. 33. 34.

1. 2. Moreover, brethren, I declare unto you the
gospel which I preached unto you, which also ye have
received, and wherein ye stand; by which also ye are

saved, if ye keep in memory what I have preached unto
you, unless ye have believed in vain.

There is no connection between this and the preceding
chapter. The particle δέ, rendered *moreover*, indicates the introduction of a new subject. *I declare unto* (γνωρίζω), literally, *I make known* to you, as though they had never heard it
before. 'Moreover, brethren, I proclaim to you the gospel.'
This interpretation is more consistent with the signification
of the word, and more impressive than the rendering adopted
by many, 'I remind you.' Comp. however, 12, 3. 2 Cor. 8, 1.
Of this gospel Paul says, 1. That he had preached it. 2. They
had received it, i. e. embraced it as true. 3. That they then
professed it. They still stood firm in their adherence to the
truth. It was not the Corinthians as a body, but only "some
among them," v. 12, who denied the doctrine of the resurrection. 4. That by it they *are saved*. The present tense is
used to express either the certainty of the event, or the idea
that believers are in this life partakers of salvation. They are
already saved. There is to them no condemnation. They are
renewed and made partakers of spiritual life. Their salvation,
however, is conditioned on their perseverance. If they do not
persevere, they will not only fail of the consummation of the
work of salvation, but it becomes manifest that they never
were justified or renewed. 'Ye are saved (εἰ κατέχετε) *if ye
hold fast*.' The word does not mean, *if ye keep in memory*.
It simply means, *if ye hold fast ;* whether that be by a physical holding fast with the hand, or a retaining in the memory,
or a retaining in faith, depends on the connection. Here it is
evident that the condition of salvation is not retaining in the
memory, but persevering in the faith. 'The gospel saves
you,' says the apostle, 'if you hold fast the gospel which I
preached unto you.'

The only difficulty in the passage relates to the words τίνι
λόγῳ, literally, *with what discourse ;* which in our version is
expressed by the word *what*. This may express the true
sense. The idea is, 'If you hold fast to the gospel *as* I
preached it to you.' The principal objection to this interpretation is the position of the words. The order in which they
stand is, ' With what discourse I preached unto you if ye hold
fast.' The interpretation just mentioned reverses this order.
This clause is therefore by many connected with the first
words of the chapter. 'I bring to your knowledge, brethren,

the gospel which I preached unto you, which ye received, wherein ye stand, by which ye are saved, (I bring to your knowledge, I say,) how, *qua ratione*, I preached, if ye hold fast.' This, however, breaks the connection. It is, therefore, better to consider the words τίνι λόγῳ as placed first for the sake of emphasis. ' You are saved if ye hold fast (the gospel) as I preached it to you.' *Unless ye have believed in vain.* The word εἰκῆ, *in vain*, may mean either *without cause*, Gal. 2, 18, or *without effect*, i. e. to no purpose, Gal. 3, 4. 4, 11. If the former, then Paul means to say, ' Unless ye believed without evidence, i. e. had no ground for your faith.' If the latter, the meaning is, ' Unless your faith is worthless.' The clause may be connected with the preceding words, ' If ye hold fast, which ye do, or will do, unless ye believed without cause.' The better connection is with the words *ye are saved*, &c. ' Ye are saved, if ye persevere, unless indeed faith is worthless.' If, as the errorists in Corinth taught, there is no resurrection, Paul says, v. 14, our faith is vain; it is an empty, worthless thing. So here he says, the gospel secures salvation, unless faith be of no account.

3. For I delivered unto you first of all that which I also received, how that Christ died for our sins according to the Scriptures :

For introduces the explanation of ' *what* he had preached.' *I delivered unto you first of all ; first*, not in reference to time; nor *first* to the Corinthians, which would not be historically true, as Paul did not preach first at Corinth ; but ἐν πρώτοις means, among the first, or principal things. The death of Christ for our sins and his resurrection were therefore the great facts on which Paul insisted as the foundation of the gospel. *Which also I received*, i. e. by direct revelation from Christ himself. Comp. 11, 23. Gal. 1, 12. " I did not receive it (the gospel) from man, neither was I taught it; but by revelation of Jesus Christ." The apostle, therefore, could speak with infallible confidence, both as to what the gospel is and as to its truth. *That Christ died for our sins*, i. e. as a sacrifice or propitiation for our sins. Comp. Rom. 3, 23–26. Some commentators remark that as ὑπὲρ ἁμαρτιῶν, *for sin*, cannot mean in *the place of* sin, therefore ὑπὲρ ἡμῶν, *for us*, cannot mean *in our place*. This remark, however, has no more force in reference to the Greek preposition, ὑπέρ, than it has in relation to the English preposition, *for*. Whether the phrase, *to die for any one*, means to die for his benefit, or in his place, is determined by the connection. It may mean either or both; and the same is true of the corresponding scriptural phrase.

According to the Scriptures, i. e. the fact that the Messiah was to die as a propitiation for sin had been revealed in the Old Testament. That the death of Christ as an atoning sacrifice was predicted by the law and the prophets is the constant doctrine of the New Testament. Our Lord reproved his disciples for not believing what the prophets had spoken on this subject, Luke 24, 25. 26. Paul protested before Festus, that in preaching the gospel he had said "none other things than those which Moses and the prophets say should come; that Christ should suffer, and that he should be the first that should rise from the dead, and should show light unto the people, and to the Gentiles," Acts 26, 22. 23. He assured the Romans that his gospel was "witnessed (to) by the law and the prophets," Rom. 3. 21. The epistle to the Hebrews is an exposition of the whole Mosaic service as a prefiguration of the office and work of Christ. And the fifty-third chapter of Isaiah is the foundation of all the New Testament exhibitions of a suffering and atoning Messiah. Paul and all other faithful ministers of the gospel, therefore, teach that atonement for sin, by the death of Christ, is the great doctrine of the whole word of God.

4. And that he was buried, and that he rose again the third day according to the Scriptures :

There are two things taught in this, as in the preceding verse. First, the truth of the facts referred to; and secondly, that those facts had been predicted. It is true that Christ was buried, and that he rose again on the third day. These facts were included in the revelation made to Paul, and the truth of which he proceeds to confirm by abundant additional testimony. That these facts were predicted in the Old Testament, is taught in John 20, 9. Acts 26, 23. The passage especially urged by the apostles as foretelling the resurrection of Christ, is Ps. 16, 10. Peter proves that that Psalm cannot be understood of David, because his body was allowed to see corruption. It must, he says, be understood of Christ, who was raised from the dead, and "saw no corruption," Acts 13, 34–37. The prophetic Scriptures, however, are full of this doctrine; for on the one hand they predict the sufferings and death of the Messiah, and on the other his universal and perpetual dominion. It is only on the assumption that he was to rise from the dead that these two classes of prediction can be reconciled.

5. And that he was seen of Cephas, then of the twelve :

As the resurrection of Christ is an historical fact, it is to be proved by historical evidence. The apostle therefore appeals to the testimony of competent witnesses. All human laws assume that the testimony of two witnesses, when uncontradicted, and especially when confirmed by collateral evidence, produces such conviction of the truth of the fact asserted as to justify even taking the life of a fellow-creature. Confidence in such testimony is not founded on experience, but on the constitution of our nature. We are so constituted that we cannot refuse assent to the testimony of good men to a fact fairly within their knowledge. To render such testimony irresistible it is necessary, 1. That the fact to be proved should be of a nature to admit of being certainly known. 2. That adequate opportunity be afforded to the witnesses to ascertain its nature, and to be satisfied of its verity. 3. That the witnesses be of sound mind and discretion. 4. That they be men of integrity. If these conditions be fulfilled, human testimony establishes the truth of a fact beyond reasonable doubt. If, however, in addition to these grounds of confidence, the witnesses give their testimony at the expense of great personal sacrifice, or confirm it with their blood; if, moreover, the occurrence of the fact in question had been predicted centuries before it came to pass; if it had produced effects not otherwise to be accounted for, effects extending to all ages and nations; if the system of doctrine with which that fact is connected so as to be implied in it, commends itself as true to the reason and conscience of men ; and if God confirms not only the testimony of the original witnesses to the fact, but also the truth of the doctrines of which that fact is the necessary basis, by the demonstration of his Spirit, then it is insanity and wickedness to doubt it. All these considerations concur in proof of the resurrection of Christ, and render it the best authenticated event in the history of the world.

The apostle does not refer to all the manifestations of our

Lord after his resurrection, but selects a few which he details in the order of their occurrence. The first appearance mentioned is that to Cephas; see Luke 24, 34. The second occurred on the same day " to the eleven and those who were with them," Luke 24, 33–36. To this Paul refers by saying, " then to the twelve ; " comp. also John 20, 19. On this occasion, when the disciples were terrified by his sudden appearance in the midst of them, he said, " Why are ye troubled ? and why do thoughts arise in your hearts ? Behold my hands and my feet, that it is I myself: handle me, and see; for a spirit hath not flesh and bones, as ye see me have. And when he had thus spoken, he showed them his hands and his feet." Luke 24, 38–40. The apostles collectively, after the apostasy of Judas, are spoken of as the twelve according to a common usage, although at the time there were only eleven.

6. After that, he was seen of above five hundred brethren at once ; of whom the greater part remain unto this present, but some are fallen asleep.

There is no distinct record of this event in the evangelical history. It may have taken place on the occasion when Christ met his disciples in Galilee. Before his death he told them, " After I am risen again, I will go before you into Galilee," Matt. 26, 32. Early in the morning of his resurrection he met the women who had been at his tomb, and said to them, " Be not afraid ; go tell my brethren, that they go into Galilee, and there shall they see me," Matt. 28, 10 ; and accordingly in v. 16, it is said, " Then the eleven went away into Galilee, into a mountain where Jesus had appointed them." This, therefore, was a formally appointed meeting, and doubtless made known as extensively as possible to his followers, and it is probable, therefore, that there was a concourse of all who could come, not only from Jerusalem, but from the surrounding country, and from Galilee. Though intended specially for the eleven, it is probable that all attended who knew of the meeting, and could possibly reach the appointed place. Who would willingly be absent on such an occasion ? Others think that this appearance took place at Jerusalem, where, in addition to the one hundred and twenty who constituted the nucleus of the church in the holy city, there were probably many disciples gathered from all parts of Judea in attendance on the passover. The special value of this testimony to the fact of

Christ's resurrection, arises not only from the number of the witnesses, but from Paul's appeal to their testimony while the majority of them were still alive. *Some have fallen asleep.* This is the Christian expression for dying, v. 18, and 11, 30. Death to the believer is a sleep for his body; a period of rest to be followed by a glorious day.

7. After that, he was seen of James; then of all the apostles.

Which James is here intended cannot be determined, as the event is not elsewhere recorded. The chronological order indicated in this citation of witnesses, renders it improbable that the reference is to our Lord's interview with the two disciples on their way to Emmaus, and is inconsistent with the tradition preserved by Jerome, that Christ appeared to James immediately after his resurrection. It has been inferred that the James intended was James the brother of our Lord, who presided over the church in Jerusalem, because he was so conspicuous and universally known. *Then to all the apostles.* This, for the reason given above, probably does not refer to the appearance of Christ to the eleven on the day in which he rose from the dead. It may refer to what is recorded in John 20, 26; or to the interview mentioned in Acts 1, 4. Whether James was one of the apostles is not determined by any thing in the verse. The word πᾶσιν may be used to indicate that the appearance was to the apostles collectively; and this, from its position, is the most natural explanation. Or the meaning may be, he appeared to James separately, and then to all the apostles including James. If the James intended was James of Jerusalem; and if that James were a different person from James the son of Alpheus (a disputed point), then the former interpretation should be preferred. For "the apostle" answers to "the twelve," and if James of Jerusalem was not the son of Alpheus, he was not one of the twelve.

8. And last of all he was seen of me also, as of one born out of due time.

Last of all may mean last of all the apostles; or, as is more probable, *last of all* means *the very last. As to an abortion, he appeared to me.* Such is Paul's language concerning himself. Thus true is it, that unmerited favours produce self-abasement.   Paul could never think of the distinction conferred on him by Christ, without adverting to his own unworthiness.

9.   For I am the least of the apostles, that am not meet to be called an apostle, because I persecuted the Church of God.

The least, not because the last in the order of appointment, but in rank and dignity.   *Who am not worthy to be called an apostle.*   See Matt. 3, 11. Luke 3, 16.   This deep humility of the apostle, which led him to regard himself as the least of the apostles, was perfectly consistent with the strenuous assertion of his official authority, and of his claim to respect and obedience.   In 2 Cor. 11, 5 and 12, 11, he says, he was "not behind the very chiefest apostles;" and in Gal. 2, 6–9, he claims full equality with James, Cephas and John. Those of his children whom God intends to exalt to posts of honour and power, he commonly prepares for their elevation by leading them to such a knowledge of their sinfulness as to keep them constantly abased.   *Because I persecuted the church of God.*   This is the sin which Paul never forgave himself. He often refers to it with the deepest contrition, 1 Tim. 1, 13–15.   The forgiveness of sin does not obliterate the remembrance of it; neither does it remove the sense of unworthiness and ill-desert.

10.   But by the grace of God I am what I am : and his grace which (was bestowed) upon me was not in vain; but I laboured more abundantly than they all : yet not I, but the grace of God which was with me.

Christian humility does not consist in denying what there is of good in us; but in an abiding sense of ill-desert, and in the consciousness that what we have of good is due to the grace of God.   *The grace of God*, in this connection, is not the love of God, but the influence of the Holy Spirit considered as an unmerited favour.   This is not only the theological and popular, but also the scriptural sense of the word *grace* in many passages.   *By the grace of God I am what I am.* That is, divine grace has made me what I am.   'Had I been left to myself, I should have continued a blasphemer, a perse-cutor, and injurious. It is owing to his grace that I am now an apostle, preaching the faith which I once destroyed.' The grace of which he was made the subject, he says, *was not in vain*, i. e. without effect. *But*, on the contrary, *I laboured more abundantly than they all.* This may mean either, more than any one of the apostles, or more than all of them to-gether. The latter is more in keeping with the tone of the passage. It serves more to exalt the grace of God, to which Paul attributes every thing good; and it is historically true, if the New Testament record is to be our guide. *Yet not I,* i. e. the fact that I laboured so abundantly is not to be refer-red to me; I was not the labourer—*but the grace which was with me.* By some editors the article is omitted in the last clause, ἡ σὺν ἐμοί. The sense would then be *with me*, instead of, *which was* with me. In the one case grace is represented as co-operating with the apostle; in the other, the apostle loses sight of himself entirely, and ascribes every thing to grace. ' It was not I, but the grace of God.' Theologically, there is no difference in these different modes of statement. The common text is preferred by most editors on critical grounds; and the sense, according to the common reading, is more in accordance with the spirit of the passage, and with Paul's manner; comp. Rom. 7, 17. True, he did co-operate with the grace of God, but this co-operation was due to grace —so that with the strictest propriety he could say, ' Not I, but the grace of God.'

11. Therefore whether (it were) I or they, so we preach, and so ye believed.

This verse resumes the subject from which vs. 9. 10 are a digression. ' Christ appeared to the apostles and to me; whether therefore I or they preached, we all proclaimed that fact, and ye all believed it.' The resurrection of Christ was included in the preaching of all ministers, and in the faith of all Christians.

12. 13. Now if Christ be preached that he rose from the dead, how say some among you that there is no resurrection of the dead? But if there be no resur-rection of the dead, then is Christ not risen :

The admission of the resurrection of Christ is inconsistent with the denial of the resurrection of the dead. What has happened, may happen. The actual is surely possible. This mode of arguing shows that the objections urged in Corinth bore equally against the resurrection of Christ, and against the general doctrine of the resurrection. They, therefore, could not have been founded on the peculiar difficulties attending the latter doctrine. They must have been derived from the assumption that the restoration to life of a body once dead, is either an impossibility, or an absurdity. Most probably, these objectors thought, that to reunite the soul with the body was to shut it up again in prison; and that it was as much a degradation and retrocession, as if a man should again become an unborn infant. ' No,' these philosophers said, ' the hope of the resurrection " is the hope of swine." The soul having once been emancipated from the defiling encumbrance of the body, it is never to be re-imprisoned.'

The argument of the apostle does not imply that the objectors admitted the resurrection of Christ. He is not arguing with them, but against them. His design is to show that their objections to the resurrection proved too much. If they proved any thing, they proved what no Christian could admit, viz., that Christ did not rise from the dead. The denial of the resurrection of the dead involves the denial of the resurrection of Christ. The question discussed throughout this chapter is not the continued existence of the soul after death, but the restoration of the body to life. This is the constant meaning of the expression "resurrection of the dead," for which the more definite expression "resurrection of the body" is often substituted. Whether the false teachers in Corinth, who denied the doctrine of the resurrection, also denied the immortality of the soul, is uncertain. The probability is that they did not. For how could any one pretend to be a Christian, and yet not believe in an hereafter? All that is certain is, that they objected to the doctrine of the resurrection on grounds which logically involved the denial of the resurrection of Christ.

14. And if Christ be not risen, then (is) our preaching vain, and your faith (is) also vain.

This is the first consequence of denying the resurrection of Christ. The whole gospel is subverted. The reason why this fact is so essential, is, that Christ rested the validity of all his claims upon his resurrection. If he did rise, then he is truly the Son of God and Saviour of the world. His sacrifice has been accepted, and God is propitious. If he did not rise, then none of these things is true. He was not what he claimed to be, and his blood is not a ransom for sinners. In Rom. 1, 3, the apostle expresses this truth in another form, by saying that Christ was by his resurrection demonstrated to be the Son of God. It was on account of the fundamental importance of this fact that the apostles were appointed to be the witnesses of Christ's resurrection, Acts 1, 22. *Then*, i. e. in case Christ be not risen, *our preaching is vain*, i. e. empty, void of all truth, reality, and power. *And your faith is also vain*, i. e. empty, groundless. These consequences are inevitable. For, if the apostles preached a risen and living Saviour, and made his power to save depend on the fact of his resurrection, of course, their whole preaching was false and worthless, if Christ were still in the grave. The dead cannot save the living. And if the object of the Christian's faith be the Son of God as risen from the dead and seated at the right hand of God in heaven, they believed a falsehood if Christ be not risen.

15. Yea, and we are found false witnesses of God; because we have testified of God that he raised up Christ: whom he raised not up, if so be that the dead rise not.

This is the second consequence. The apostles were false witnesses. They were guilty of deliberate falsehood. They testified that they had seen Christ after his resurrection; that they had handled him, felt that he had flesh and bones; that they had put their hands into his wounds, and knew assuredly that it was their Lord. *We are found*, i. e. we are detected or manifested as being *false witnesses;* not such as falsely claim to be witnesses; but those who bear witness to what is false, Matt. 26, 60. *Because we testified of God;* literally, *against* God. We said he did, what in fact he did not do, *if so be the dead rise not.* Here again it is assumed that to deny that the dead rise is to deny that Christ has risen. But why is this? Why may not a man admit that Christ, the incarnate Son of God, arose from the dead, and yet consistently deny that there is to be a general resurrection of the dead?

Because the thing denied was that the dead could rise. The denial was placed on grounds which embraced the case of Christ. The argument is, If the dead cannot rise, then Christ did not rise; for Christ was dead.

16. For if the dead rise not, then is not Christ raised :

This is a reassertion of the inseparable connection between these two events. If there be no resurrection, Christ is not risen. If the thing be impossible, it has never happened. The sense in which Christ rose, determines the sense in which the dead are said to rise. As it is the resurrection of Christ's body that is affirmed, so it is the resurrection of the bodies of the dead, and not merely the continued existence of their souls which is affirmed. The repetition in this verse of what had been said in v. 13, seems to be with the design of preparing the way for v. 17.

17. And if Christ be not raised, your faith (is) vain ; ye are yet in your sins.

This is the third consequence of the denial of Christ's resurrection. In v. 14 it was said, your faith is κενή, *empty ;* here it is said to be ματαία, *fruitless.* In what sense the following clause explains; *ye are yet in your sins,* i. e. under the condemnation of sin. Comp. John 8, 21, "Ye shall die in your sins." As Christ's resurrection is necessary to our justification, Rom. 4, 25, if he did not rise, we are not justified. To teach, therefore, that there is no resurrection, is to teach that there is no atonement and no pardon. Errorists seldom see the consequences of the false doctrines which they embrace. Many allow themselves to entertain doubts as to this very doctrine of the resurrection of the body, who would be shocked at the thought of rejecting the doctrine of atonement. Yet Paul teaches that the denial of the one involves the denial of the other.

18. Then they also which are fallen asleep in Christ are perished.

This is the fourth disastrous consequence of the denial of the doctrine in question. All the dead in Christ are lost. *To*

fall asleep in Christ is to die in faith, or in communion with
Christ for salvation. See 1 Thess. 4, 14. Rev. 14, 13. *Are
perished ;* rather, *they perished.* 'They perished when they
died.' Perdition, according to Scripture, is not annihilation,
but everlasting misery and sin. It is the loss of holiness and
happiness for ever. If Christ did not rise for the justification
of those who died in him, they found no advocate at the bar
of God; and have incurred the fate of those who perish in
their sins. Rather than admit such conclusions as these, the
Corinthians might well allow philosophers to say what they
pleased about the impossibility of a resurrection. It was
enough for them that Christ had risen, whether they could
understand how it can be that the dead should rise, or not.

19. If in this life only we have hope in Christ, we are of all men most miserable.

Not only the future, but even the present is lost, if Christ
be not risen. Not only did the departed sink into perdition
when they died, but we, who are alive, are more miserable
than other men. This is the last conclusion which the apostle
draws from the denial of the resurrection. *If in this life only*,
the word μόνον, *only*, admits of a threefold connection. Although it stands at the end of the clause it may be connected,
as in our translation, with the words "in this life." 'If in this
life only.' That is, if all the good we expect from Christ is to
be enjoyed in this life, we are more miserable than other men.
We are constantly exposed to all manner of persecutions and
sufferings, while they are at their ease. 2. It may be connected with the word *Christ.* This is a very natural construction,
according to the position of the words in the common text,
for (ἐν Χριστῷ μόνον), *in Christ only*, stand together. The
sense would then be, 'If we have set all our hopes on Christ,
and he fails us, we are of all men most miserable.' This,
however, supposes the important clause, on which every thing
depends (*if he fails us*), to be omitted. It also leaves the
words *in this life* without importance. 3. Recent editors,
following the older manuscripts, place ἐν Χριστῷ before the
verb, and make μόνον qualify the whole clause. 'If we have
only hoped in Christ, and there is to be no fulfilling of our
hopes, we are more miserable than others.' Or, 'If we are
only such (nothing more than such) who in life, and not in
death, have hope in Christ,' &c. The apposition between the

dead in v. 18, and the living in this verse, is in favour of the
first-mentioned explanation. 'Those who died in Christ, perished when they died. And we, if all our hopes in Christ are
confined to this life, are the most miserable of men.' *We have
hoped.* The Greek is ἠλπικότες ἐσμέν, which, as the commentators remark, expresses not what we do, but what we are.
We are hopers. This passage does not teach that Christians
are in this life more miserable than other men. This is contrary to experience. Christians are unspeakably happier than
other men. All that Paul means to say is, that if you take
Christ from Christians, you take their all. He is the source
not only of their future, but of their present happiness.
Without him they are yet in their sins, under the curse of the
law, unreconciled to God, having no hope, and without God
in the world; and yet subject to all the peculiar trials incident
to a Christian profession, which in the apostolic age often included the loss of all things.

20. But now is Christ risen from the dead, (and) become the first-fruits of them that slept.

But now, νυνὶ δέ, i. e. as the matter actually stands. All
the gloomy consequences presented in the preceding verses
follow from the assumption that Christ did not rise from the
dead. But as in point of fact he did rise, these things have no
place. Our preaching is not vain, your faith is not vain, ye
are not in your sins, the dead in Christ have not perished, we
are not more miserable than other men. The reverse of all
this is true. Christ has not only risen, but he has risen in a
representative character. His resurrection is the pledge of
the resurrection of his people. He rose as *the first-fruits of
them that slept,* and not of them only, but as the first-fruits of
all who are ever to sleep in Jesus. The apostle does not mean
merely that the resurrection of Christ was to precede that of
his people; but as the first sheaf of the harvest presented to
God as a thank-offering, was the pledge and assurance of the
ingathering of the whole harvest, so the resurrection of Christ
is a pledge and proof of the resurrection of his people. In
Rom. 8, 23 and 11, 16, the word ἀπαρχή, *first-fruits,* has the
same force. Comp. also Col. 1, 18, where Christ is called
"the first begotten from the dead," and Rev. 1, 5. Of the
great harvest of glorified bodies which our earth is to yield
Christ is the first-fruits. *As* he rose, *so* all his people must; as

certainly and as gloriously, Phil. 3, 21. The nature of this causal connection between the resurrection of Christ and that of his people, is explained in the following verses.

21. For since by man (came) death, by man (came) also the resurrection of the dead.

The connection between this verse and the preceding is obvious. The resurrection of Christ secures the resurrection of his people, *for* as there was a causal relation between the death of Adam and the death of his descendants, so there is a causal relation between the resurrection of Christ and that of his people. What that causal relation is, is not here expressed. It is simply asserted that as death is δι᾽ ἀνϑρώπου, *by means of a man ;* so the resurrection is δι᾽ ἀνϑρώπου, *by means of a man.* Why Adam was the cause of death, and why Christ is the cause of life, is explained in the following verse, and abundantly elsewhere in Scripture, but not here. By *death*, in this verse, is meant the death of the body; and by *the resurrection* is meant the restoration of the body to life. This, however, only proves that the death of which Adam was the cause includes physical death, and that the life of which Christ is the cause includes the future life of the body. But as the life which we derive from Christ includes far more than the life of the body, so the death which flows from Adam includes far more than physical death.

22. For as in Adam all die, even so in Christ shall all be made alive.

This is the reason why Adam was the cause of death, and why Christ is the cause of life. We die *by means of* Adam, because we were *in* Adam; and we live *by means of* Christ, because we are *in* Christ. Union with Adam is the cause of death; union with Christ is the cause of life. The nature of this union and its consequences are more fully explained in Rom. 5, 12–21. In both cases it is a representative and vital union. We are in Adam because he was our head and representative, and because we partake of his nature. And we are in Christ because he is our head and representative, and because we partake of his nature through the indwelling of his Spirit. Adam, therefore, is the cause of death, because his sin is the judicial ground of our condemnation; and because we derive from him a corrupt and enfeebled nature. Christ is the cause of life, because his righteousness is the judicial ground of our justification ; and because we derive from him the Holy Ghost, which is the source of life both to the soul and body. Comp. Rom. 8, 9–11.

That the word *all* in the latter part of this verse is to be restricted to all believers (or rather, to all the people of Christ, as infants are included) is plain, 1. Because the word in both clauses is limited. It is the all who are in Adam that die; and the all who are in Christ who are made alive. As union with Christ is made the ground of the communication of life here spoken of, it can be extended only to those who are in him. But according to the constant representation of the Scriptures, none are in him but his own people. "If any man be in Christ, he is a new creature," 2 Cor. 5, 17. 2. Because the verb (ζωοποιέω) here found is never used of the wicked. Whenever employed in reference to the work of Christ it always means to communicate to them that life of which he is the source, John 5, 21. 6, 63. Rom. 8. 11. 1 Cor. 15, 45. Gal. 3, 21. The real meaning of the verse therefore, is, 'As in Adam all die, so in Christ shall all be made partakers of a glorious and everlasting life.' Unless, therefore, the Bible teaches that all men are in Christ, and that all through him partake of eternal life, the passage must be restricted to his own people. 3. Because, although Paul elsewhere speaks of a general resurrection both of the just and of the unjust, Acts 24, 15, yet, throughout this chapter he speaks only of the resurrection of the righteous. 4. Because, in the parallel passage in Rom. 5, 12–21, the same limitation must be made. In v. 18 of that chapter it is said, "As by the offence of one judgment came upon all men to condemnation; even so by the righteousness of one the free gift came upon all men to justification of life." That is, as for the offence of Adam all men were condemned, so for the righteousness of Christ all men are justified. The context and the analogy of Scripture require us to understand this to mean, as all who are in Adam are condemned, so all who are in Christ are justified. No historical Christian church has ever held that all men indiscriminately are justified. For whom God justifies them he also glorifies, Rom. 8, 30.

There are two other interpretations of this verse. According to one, the verb, *shall be made alive,* is taken to mean no more than *shall be* raised from the dead. But this, as already remarked, is not only inconsistent with the prevailing use of the word, but with the whole context. Others, admitting that the passage necessarily treats of a resurrection to glory and blessedness, insist that the word *all* must be taken to include all men. But this contradicts the constant doctrine of the Bible, and has no support in the context. It is not absolutely all who die through Adam, but those only who were in him; so it is not absolutely all who live through Christ, but those only who are in him.

23. But every man in his own order: Christ the first-fruits; afterward they that are Christ's at his coming.

In his own *order*. The word τάγμα is properly a concrete term, meaning *a band*, as of soldiers. If this be insisted upon here, then Paul considers the hosts of those that rise as divided into different cohorts or companies; first Christ, then his people, then the rest of mankind. But the word is used by later writers, as Clemens in his Epistle to the Corinthians I. 37, and 41, in the sense of τάξις, *order of succession*. And this best suits the context, for Christ is not a band. All that Paul teaches is, that, although the resurrection of Christ secures that of his people, the two events are not contemporaneous. First Christ, then those who are Christ's. There is no intimation of any further division or separation in time in the process of the resurrection. The resurrection of the people of Christ is to take place *at his coming*, 1 Thess. 3, 13. 4, 14–19.

24. Then (cometh) the end, when he shall have delivered up the kingdom to God, even the Father; when he shall have put down all rule, and all authority and power.

This is a very difficult passage, and the interpretations given of it are too numerous to be recited. The first question is, What is the end here spoken of? The common answer is, That it is the end of the world. That is, the close of the present order of things; the consummation of the work of redemption. In favour of this view, it may be urged, 1. That where there is nothing in the context to determine otherwise, *The end* naturally means the end of all things. There is nothing here to limit the application, but the nature of the subject spoken of. 2. The analogy of Scripture is in favour of this explanation. In 1 Pet. 4, 7 we find the expression "the end of all things is at hand." Matt. 24, 6, "The end is not yet;" v. 14, "Then shall the end come." So in Mark 13, 7. Luke 21, 9. In all these passages *the end* means the end of the world. 3. The equivalent expressions serve to explain the meaning of this phrase. The disciples asked our Lord, "What shall be the sign of thy coming, and of the end of the world?" (i. e. the consummation of the present dispensation.) In answer to this question, our Lord said certain things were to happen, but "the end is not yet;" and afterwards, "then shall the end come." See Matt. 24, 3. 6. 14. The same expression occurs in the same sense, Matt. 13, 39. 28, 20, and elsewhere. "The end," therefore, means the end of the world. In the same sense the phrase "until the restoration of all things" is probably used in Acts 3, 21. 4. What immediately follows seems decisive in favour of this interpretation. The end is, when Christ shall deliver up his kingdom, after having subdued all his enemies; i. e. after having accomplished the work of redemption.

Many commentators understand by *the end*, the end of the resurrection. That work, they say, is to be accomplished by distinct stages. First the resurrection of Christ, then that of his people, then that of the wicked. This last, they say, is expressed by *then cometh the end*, viz., the end of the resurrection. Against this view, however, are all the arguments above stated in favour of the opinion that *the end* means the end of the world. Besides, the doctrine that there are to be two resurrections, one of the righteous and another of the wicked, the latter separated from the former by an unknown period of time, is entirely foreign to the New Testament, unless what is said in the 20th chapter of Revelation teaches that doctrine. Admitting that a twofold resurrection is there spoken of, it would not be proper to transfer from that passage an idea foreign to all Paul's representations of the subject. If that fact was revealed to John, it does not prove that it was revealed to Paul. All that the most stringent doctrine of inspiration requires is, that the passages should not contradict each other. The passage in Revelation, however, is altogether too uncertain to be made the rule of interpretation for the plainer declarations of the epistolary portions of the New Testament. On the contrary, what is doubtful in the former should be explained by what is clearly taught in the latter. Secondly, it is clearly taught in the gospels and epistles that the resurrection of the righteous and of the wicked is to be contemporaneous. At least, that is the mode in which the subject is always presented. The element of time (i. e. the chronological succession of the events) may indeed in these representations be omitted, as is so often the case in the prophecies of the Old Testament. But unless it can be proved from other sources, that events which are foretold as contemporaneous, or as following the one the other in immediate succession, are in fact separated by indefinite periods of time, no such separation can properly be assumed. In the evangelists and epistles the resurrection of the righteous and that of the wicked are spoken of as contemporaneous, and since their separation in time is nowhere else revealed, the only proper inference is that they are to occur together. In Matt. 24, 3, the coming of Christ and the end of the world are coupled together as contemporaneous. And throughout that chapter our Lord foretells what is to happen before that event, and adds, "Then shall appear the sign of the Son of Man in heaven . . . and he shall send his angels with the sound of a great trumpet, and they shall gather together the elect from the four winds, from one end of heaven to the other," vs. 30. 31. In John 5, 28. 29 it is said, "The hour is coming when all (good and bad) who are in their graves shall hear the voice of the Son of Man, and shall come forth, they that have done good unto the resurrection of life, and they that have done evil unto the resurrection of damnation." In 2 Thess. 1, 7–10, Christ is said to come to take vengeance on those who obey not the gospel, and to be glorified in the saints. These events go together. Besides, our Lord repeatedly says that he will raise up his people " at the last day," John 6, 39. 40. 11, 24, and therefore not an indefinitely long period before the last day. According to the uniform representations of the Scriptures, when Christ comes he is to raise all the dead and separate the wicked from among the just as a shepherd divides his sheep from the goats. Or, according to another figure, he is to send forth his angels and separate the tares from the wheat. It has therefore been the constant faith of the church that the second advent of Christ, the resurrection of the just and of the unjust, the final judgment and end of the world—are parts of one great transaction, and not events which are to succeed each other at long intervals of time. All this, however, is said with diffidence and submission. It may prove to be otherwise. The predictions of the Old Testament produced the universal impression that the first coming of Christ was to be attended at once by events which we learn from the New Testament require ages to bring about. Still, we are bound to take the Scriptures as they stand, and events which are described as contemporaneous are to be assumed to be so, until the event proves the contrary. We may be perfectly sure that the Scriptures will prove infallibly true. The predictions of the Old Testament, although in some points misinterpreted, or rather interpreted too far, by the ancient church, were fully vindicated and explained by the event.

The second question to be considered is, When is the end of the world to take place? According to some, at Christ's coming; according to others, at an indefinite period after his second coming. It may be admitted that this verse is not decisive on this point. It marks the succession of certain events, but determines nothing as to the interval between them. First, Christ's resurrection; then the resurrection of his people; then the end of the world. But as it is said that those who are Christ's shall rise at his coming, and then cometh the end; the natural impression is that nothing remains to be done after the resurrection before the end comes. This view is confirmed by the numerous passages of the New Testament, several of which have already been quoted, which connect the general judgment and end of the world as intimately with the coming of Christ as the resurrection of his people. Some of those who assume that an indefinite period is to elapse between the coming of Christ and the end of the world, suppose that the intervening period is to be occupied not in the work of conversion, but in the subjugation of the enemies of Christ spoken of in the following verses. The common opinion among those who adopt this interpretation is, that the interval in question is to be occupied by the personal reign of Christ on earth. This is the doctrine of the ancient Chiliasts, and of modern Millenarians. The form which this doctrine has commonly assumed in ancient and modern times is only a modified Judaism, entirely at variance with the spirituality of the gospel and with the teachings of the apostle in this chapter. He tells us that flesh and blood, i. e. bodies organized as our present bodies are, i. e. natural bodies, cannot inherit the kingdom of God. The whole design of the latter portion of this chapter is to show that after the resurrection, the bodies of believers will be like the glorious body of the Son of God, adapted to a heavenly, and not to an earthly condition.

A third question which this verse presents is, In what sense is Christ to deliver up the kingdom to the Father? In the common text the words are ὅταν παραδῷ, *when he shall have delivered up;* most of the modern editors read παραδιδῷ, *when he delivers up.* That is, when the end comes, Christ is to deliver up the kingdom to his Father. What does this mean? The Scriptures constantly teach that Christ's kingdom is an everlasting kingdom, and of his dominion there is no end. In what sense, then, can he be said to deliver up his kingdom? It must be remembered, that the Scriptures speak of a threefold kingdom as belonging to Christ. 1. That which necessarily belongs to him as a divine person, extending over all creatures, and of which he can never divest himself. 2. That which belongs to him as the incarnate Son of God, extending over his own people. This also is everlasting. He will for ever remain the head and sovereign of the redeemed. 3. That dominion to which he was exalted after his resurrection, when all power in heaven and earth was committed to his hands. This kingdom, which he exercises as the Theanthropos, and which extends over all principalities and powers, he is to deliver up when the work of redemption is accomplished. He was invested with this dominion in his mediatorial character for the purpose of carrying on his work to its consummation. When that is done, i. e. when he has subdued all his enemies, then he will no longer reign over the universe as Mediator, but only as God; while his headship over his people is to continue for ever. *To God even the Father,* i. e. to him who is at once his God and Father. This is the Scriptural designation of the first person of the Trinity. He is the God of the Lord Jesus Christ, inasmuch as he is the God whom Christ came to reveal, and whose work he performs. He is his Father in virtue of the eternal relation subsisting between the first and second persons in the Godhead.

The fourth question which this pregnant verse suggests is presented in the last clause. *When he shall have put down all rule, and authority and power.* Calvin and others understand this to mean, ' When he shall have abrogated all other dominion than his own.' Whatever authority is now exercised by one man over others is at last to be abolished, and merged in the all-pervading authority of God. Most commentators, in obedience to the context, understand the passage to refer to all hostile powers, whether demoniacal or human. These are *to be put down*, i. e. effectually subdued; not annihilated, and not converted; but simply deprived of all power to disturb the harmony of his kingdom.

25. For he must reign, till he hath put all enemies under his feet.

This verse assigns the reason why Christ cannot relinquish his dominion over the universe as mediator until the end comes, and why he will then deliver it up. He must reign until the purpose for which he was invested with this universal dominion is accomplished. As in Ps. 110 it is said to the Messiah, "Sit thou on my right hand until I make thy enemies thy footstool," many assume that *God* is the subject of the verb *has put*. The meaning would then be, 'He must reign until *God* has put all his enemies under his feet.' But this is inconsistent with the context. Christ is to put down all rule, authority and power, v. 24, and he reigns until he has accomplished that work. The two modes of representation are perfectly consistent. The Father created the world, though he did it through the Son, Heb. 1, 3. The work, therefore, is sometimes ascribed to the one and sometimes to the other. In like manner the Father subdues the powers of darkness, but it is through Christ to whom all power in heaven and earth has been committed. It is therefore equally proper to say that God makes the enemies of Christ his footstool, and that Christ himself puts his enemies under his feet. The enemies who are to be thus subdued are not only intelligent beings hostile to Christ, but all the forms of evil, physical and moral, because death is specially included. By subduing, however, is not meant destroying or banishing out of existence. The passage does not teach that Christ is to reign until all evil is banished from the universe. Satan is said to be subdued, when deprived of his power to injure the people of God. And evil in like manner is subdued when it is restrained within the limits of the kingdom of darkness.

26. The last enemy (that) shall be destroyed (is) death.

Death shall reign until the resurrection. Then men shall never more be subject to his power. Then death shall be swallowed up in victory, Luke 20, 36. "Neither shall they die any more," 2 Tim. 1, 10. Rev. 20, 14.

27. For he hath put all things under his feet. But
when he saith, All things are put under (him, it is)
manifest that he is excepted, which did put all things
under him.

The proof that death is finally to be destroyed is derived
from the 8th Psalm, where the subjection of *all things* to the
Messiah is predicted. There are two passages of the Old
Testament frequently quoted in the New Testament as foretelling the absolutely universal dominion of the Messiah, Ps.
110 and Ps. 8. The former is quoted, or its language appropriated, in v. 25. Matt. 22, 44. Acts 2, 34. Eph. 1, 22. Heb. 1,
13. 10, 12. 13. 1 Pet. 3, 22. In this there is no difficulty, as
that Psalm clearly refers to the Messiah and to none else.
The 8th Psalm is quoted and applied to Christ in this passage,
and in Eph. 1, 22. Heb. 2, 8, and 1 Pet. 3, 22. As this Psalm
has no apparent reference to the Messiah, but is a thanksgiving to God for his goodness to man, the use made of it in the
New Testament is to be understood as an inspired exposition
of its hidden meaning. That is, when the Psalmist said,
"Thou madest him to have dominion over the works of thy
hands, thou hast put all things under his feet," we learn from
the New Testament that the Spirit of God intended by these
words far more than that man was invested with dominion
over the beasts of the field. There is no limit to the *all things*
here intended. Heb. 2, 8. Man is clothed with dominion
over the whole universe, over all principalities and powers,
and every name that is named, not only in this world but also
in that which is to come. This is fulfilled in the man Christ
Jesus, into whose hands all power in heaven and earth has
been committed. This may be called the hidden meaning of
the Psalm, because it never would have been discovered without a further revelation such as we find in the exposition given
by the inspired apostles. *When he saith,* ὅταν εἴπῃ. This may
mean either, when the Scripture saith, or *when God saith.*
The latter is better on account of what follows. The verb is
not to be translated as in the present tense, but, as the better
commentators agree, in the past future, see v. 24. Heb. 1, 6.
'When God shall have said.' That is, when God shall have
declared his purpose to subject all things to Christ accomplished, it will then be manifest that all things are subject to
him, God only excepted.

28. And when all things shall be subdued unto him, then shall the Son also himself be subject unto him that put all things under him, that God may be all in all.

When the work of redemption has been accomplished, the dead raised, the judgment held, the enemies of Christ all subdued, then, and not till then, will the Son also himself be subject to him who put all things under him. This passage is evidently parallel with that in v. 24. The subjection of the Son to the Father here means precisely what is there meant by his delivering up the kingdom to God even the Father. The thing done, and the person who does it, are the same. The subjection here spoken of is not predicated of the eternal Logos, the second person of the Trinity, any more than the kingdom spoken of in v. 24 is the dominion which belongs essentially to Christ as God. As there the word *Christ* designates the Theanthropos, so does the word *Son* here designate, not the Logos as such, but the Logos as incarnate. And as the delivery of the kingdom or royal authority over the universe committed to Christ after his resurrection, is consistent at once with his continued dominion as God over all creatures, and with his continued headship over his people; so is the subjection here spoken of consistent with his eternal equality with the Father. It is not the subjection of the Son as Son, but of the Son as Theanthropos of which the apostle here speaks. The doctrine of the true and proper divinity of our Lord is so clearly revealed in Scripture, and is so inwrought into the faith of his people, that such passages as these, though adduced with so much confidence by the impugners of that doctrine, give believers no more trouble than the ascription of the limitations of our nature to God. When the Bible says that God repents, we know that it is consistent with his immutability; and when it says the Son is subject or inferior to the Father, we know that it is consistent with their equality, as certainly as we know that saying that man is immortal is consistent with saying he is mortal. We know that both of the last-mentioned propositions are true; because mortality is predicated of man in one aspect, and immortality in another aspect. In one sense he is mortal, in another sense he is immortal. In like manner we know that the verbally inconsistent propositions, the Son is subject to the Father, and, the Son is equal with the Father, are both true. In one sense he is subject, in another sense he is equal. The son of a king may be the equal of his father in every attribute of his nature, though officially inferior. So the eternal Son of God may be coëqual with the Father, though officially subordinate. What difficulty is there in this? What shade does it cast over the full Godhead of our adorable Redeemer? The subordination, however, here spoken of, is not that of the human nature of Christ separately considered, as when he is said to suffer, or to die, or to be ignorant; but it is the official subordination of the incarnate Son to God as God. The words αὐτὸς ὁ υἱός, *the Son himself*, here designate, as in so many other places, not the second person of the Trinity as such, but that person as clothed in our nature. And the subjection spoken of, is not of the former, but of the latter, i. e. not of the Son as Son, but of the Son as incarnate; and the subjection itself is official and therefore perfectly consistent with equality of nature.

There is another difficulty connected with this verse which it may be well to notice. According to the Scriptures and the creeds of all the great historical churches (Greek, Latin, Lutheran and Reformed), the term Son, as applied to Christ, designates his divine nature. It is a term of nature and not of office. He was from eternity the Son of God. Yet it is of the Son that subjection is here predicated. This is urged as an argument against his eternal sonship. The fact, however, is, that the person of Christ may be designated from one nature, when the predicate belongs either to the opposite nature or to the whole person. That is, he may be called God when what is said of him is true only of his human nature or of his complex person as God and man; and he may be called man, when what is said is true only of his divine nature. Thus he is called the Son of Man when omnipresence and omniscience are ascribed to him; and he is called God, the Son of God, the Lord of glory when he is said to die. These passages do not prove that the human nature of Christ is every where present; or that his divine nature suffered and died. Neither do such expressions as that in the text prove that the Son as such is inferior to the Father, nor that the term Son is not a scriptural designation of his divine nature. The principle here adverted to is so important, and serves to explain so many passages of Scripture, that it will bear to be often repeated.

That God may be all in all. Before the ascension of Christ, God reigned as God; after that event he reigned and still reigns through the Theanthropos; when the end comes, the Theanthropos will deliver up this administrative kingdom, and God again be all in all. Such is the representation of Scripture, and such seems to be the simple meaning of this passage. When our Lord ascended up on high all power in heaven and earth was given to him. It was given to him then, and therefore not possessed before. He is to retain this delegated power in his character of Mediator, God-man, until his enemies are put under his feet. Then he, the God-man, is to deliver it up. And God as God will reign supreme. The phrase here used, τὰ πάντα (or πάντα) ἐν πᾶσιν, *all in all*, depends (as is the case with all similar formulas), for its precise meaning on the connection. If words be taken by themselves, and made to mean any thing which their signification will admit, without regard to the context or to the analogy of Scripture, then the authority of the word of God is effectually subverted. No book, human or divine, can be interpreted on a principle so unreasonable. Some, however, regardless of this universally admitted rule of interpretation, say that these words teach that the whole universe is to be merged in God—he is to become all in all—he will be all, and all will be God. Others limit the last *all* to intelligent creatures, and the sense in which God is *all* is restricted to his gracious influence; so that while the continued personal existence of rational creatures is provided for, it is assumed that God is to reign supreme in all intelligent beings. All sin and evil will thus be banished from the whole universe. This interpretation is, in the first place, perfectly arbitrary. If the meaning of the words is to be pressed beyond the limits assigned by the context and the analogy of Scripture, why limit ἐν πᾶσι to intelligent creatures, and τὰ πάντα to mere gracious control? The passage teaches pantheism, if it teaches universalism. Secondly, this interpretation is contrary to the context. Paul is speaking simply of the continuance of the mediatorial dominion of Christ over the universe. That dominion was given to him for a specific purpose; when that purpose is accomplished, he will give it up, and God, instead of reigning through Christ, will be recognized as the immediate sovereign of the universe; his co-equal, co-eternal Son, clothed in our nature, being, as the everlasting head of the redeemed, officially subordinate to him. In other words, the whole question, so to speak, is whose hands are to hold the reins of universal dominion. They are now in the hands of Christ; hereafter they are to be in the hands of God as such. The passage does not teach us the design of redemption, but what is to happen when the redemption of God's people is accomplished. Then the Messianic reign is to cease, and God is to rule supreme over a universe reduced to order, the people of God being saved, and the finally impenitent shut up with Satan and his angels in the prison of despair. Thirdly, the interpretation which makes this passage teach the restoration of all intelligent creatures to holiness, is contrary to the express declarations of Scriptures and to the faith of the church universal. This the most accomplished of its advocates virtually admit. See for example Olshausen's commentary on this epistle. If the evidence in support of the doctrine of the everlasting perdition of the wicked were not overwhelming, it never could have become a part of the faith of the universal church. And that doctrine being once established on its own grounds, doubtful passages must be interpreted in accordance with it.

There is another orthodox interpretation of this passage. It is assumed to treat of the final result of the work of redemption. God will reign supreme in all. But the *all* is restricted to the subjects of redemption. The whole chapter treats of those who are in Christ. It is of their resurrection, and of the effect of redemption in their case, the apostle is assumed to speak. 'All who are in Christ shall be made alive, v. 22, and God shall reign in them all.' The sense is good, but this interpretation overlooks what intervenes between vs. 22 and 28 concerning the kingdom of Christ and its being given up.

29. Else what shall they do which are baptized for the dead, if the dead rise not at all ? why are they then baptized for the dead?

The apostle, after the preceding digression, returns to his argument for the resurrection. 'The dead are certainly to be raised, *otherwise* (ἐπεί) what shall they do who are baptized for the dead?' This practice (whatever it was) of baptizing for the dead, takes for granted that the dead are to rise. *What shall they do*, i. e. What account will they give of themselves? what explanation of their conduct can they make? The most important of the numerous interpretations of this verse admit of being reduced to the following classes : 1. Those which turn on the sense given to the word *baptize*. 2. Those which depend on the explanation of the preposition ὑπέρ, *for*.

3. Those which assume an ellipsis in the verse.   **4.** Those which turn on the explanation of τῶν νεκρῶν, *the dead.*   **1.** The simplest and most natural interpretation takes the word baptize in its ordinary sense. 'What do they do who allow themselves to be baptized in the place of the dead?' This supposes that the custom of vicarious baptism, as afterwards practised by the Cerinthians and Marcionites, had already been introduced into Corinth. Among those heretical sects, if a catechumen died before baptism, some one was baptized in his name, in order that he might be enrolled among Christians and receive the benefit of the ordinance. The objections to this interpretation are, that the practice was superstitious, founded on wrong views of the nature and efficacy of baptism.   **2.** That there are no traces elsewhere of the prevalence of vicarious baptism before the second century.   **3.** That it was universally condemned by the churches as heretical.   **4.** That it cannot be supposed that the apostle would refer to such a superstitious custom without condemning it.   These objections are in a measure met by the following considerations: **1.** Paul, so far from intimating any approbation of the custom, distinctly separates himself from its abettors. He does not say, 'What shall we do'—'What shall *they* do.' It was something with which he had no fellowship.   **2.** That this method of arguing against others from their own concessions, is one which the apostle frequently employs.   **3.** That when his mind is full of a particular subject he does not leave it, to pronounce judgment on things incidentally introduced. Thus, in chap. 11, 5, when treating of women speaking in the church unveiled, he expresses no disapprobation of their speaking in public, although he afterwards condemned it. A still more striking example of the same thing is to be found 10, 8, where he speaks of the Corinthians " sitting at meat in an idol's temple," without any disapprobation of the thing itself, but only of its influence on the weaker brethren. Yet, in 10, 14–22, he proves that the thing itself was an act of idolatry.   **4.** That the entire disappearance of this custom in the orthodox church, although other superstitious observances not less objectionable soon prevailed, is probably to be referred to the practice having been forbidden by the apostle as soon as he reached Corinth. This may have been one of the things which he left " to be set in order when he came," 11, 34.   **5.** The state of the church in Corinth, as disclosed by this epistle, was not such as to render the adoption of such a custom by a portion of the people, incredible. Baptizing for the dead was not so bad as sitting at the table of devils, 10, 21. A second interpretation under this head gives the word *baptize* the figurative sense which it has in Matt. 20, 22. Luke 12, 50, " I have a baptism to be baptized with; and how am I straitened until it be accomplished!" According to this view, Paul here refers to the baptism of afflictions. 'Why do men suffer so for the hopelessly dead? if the dead are not to rise, what is the use of suffering so much for them? i. e. of labouring so much, and enduring so much for men who, when dead, are never to live again.' This, however, evidently puts a sense on the word *dead*, which it will not bear. It is assumed to designate not those actually dead, but men who when dead are not to rise again.

Of the second class of interpretations some propose to render ὑπέρ by *over*. 'Why do they baptize over the dead? i. e. over their graves.' Sometimes, for the sake of expressing their faith in the resurrection, Christians are said to have been baptized over the graves of the martyrs. Others say that ὑπέρ means in *the place of*. 'Why should men be baptized in place of the dead? i. e. to supply their places in the church, and thus keep up the ranks of believers.' A third class propose to take νεκρῶν for the singular, and to read, 'Why are they baptized for one dead?' Others say the meaning is, *for the dead*, i e. for bodies. What is the use of being baptized for a dead body? a body which is never to live again. He that is baptized receives the ordinance believing that his body is not to remain dead. Calvin and others understand the *dead* to mean here, those about to die. 'Why should baptism be administered for those on the verge of the grave—if there be no resurrection?' Finally, some suppose the passage is elliptical. Fully expressed it would be, 'What do they do who are baptized for the resurrection of the dead?' i. e. in hope of the resurrection which was professed by all who receive baptism. The darkness which rests on this passage can never be entirely cleared away, because the reference is to a custom of which no account is extant. *If the dead rise not at all* belongs to the latter member of the verse. 'If the dead rise not at all, why are they baptized for them?' Instead of τῶν νεκρῶν, *the dead*, modern editors read αὐτῶν, *them*.

30. And why stand we in jeopardy every hour?

Here Paul speaks for himself. With baptizing for the

dead, he had nothing to do. ' Why do *they* allow themselves,'
he asks, ' to be baptized for the dead ? ' That, as would appear, is what his opponents did. As an additional argument for
the doctrine which he is defending, he urges, that its denial
destroys at least one of the great motives to self-denial. ' If
there be no resurrection, on which all our hopes as Christians
depend, why should we voluntarily encounter perpetual danger ? ' It is to be remembered that, according to Paul's doctrine
and previous argument, if there be no resurrection, then Christ
is not risen, and if Christ be not risen, there is no atonement,
no reconciliation with God. We are in a state of final and
hopeless condemnation. What is the use of labouring to save
men, if there be no salvation ?

**31. I protest by your rejoicing which I have in
Christ Jesus our Lord, I die daily.**

Paul solemnly assures his readers that he was constantly
in jeopardy, for, says he, *I die daily*, i. e. I am constantly ex-
posed to death, 2 Cor. 4, 10. *By your boasting which I have.*
This is not the meaning, but, '*By my boasting concerning you.*'
That is, ' as surely as I boast of you, and rejoice over you.'
The pronoun ὑμετέραν, *your*, is to be taken objectively (as in
Rom. 11, 31 ; comp. also 1 Cor. 9, 12) the boasting of which
you are the object. *Which I have in Christ Jesus*, i. e. which
I have in communion with Christ. It was a rejoicing which
he, as a Christian minister, had over them as the seals of his
ministry.

**32. If after the manner of men I have fought with
beasts at Ephesus, what advantageth it me, if the dead
rise not ? let us eat and drink ; for to-morrow we die.**

The apostle refers to one, and probably a recent instance
of his exposure to death. *If after the manner of men*, i. e.
with those views and interests which determine the conduct
of ordinary men, i. e. without hope in the resurrection. *I have
fought with beasts at Ephesus.* This may be understood
either literally or figuratively. Against the literal interpretation is urged, 1. The improbability that, as a Roman citizen,
he should have been subjected to that punishment. But his
being a Roman citizen did not prevent his being thrice beaten
with rods, by Roman magistrates, or at least, by others than

Jews, and contrary to law, 2 Cor. 11, 25. 2. The silence of The Acts on the subject. But we learn from 2 Cor. 11, 23–29, that scarcely a tithe of what Paul did and suffered is recorded in The Acts. 3. The omission of any reference to his exposure to wild beasts in the long enumeration of his sufferings in 2 Cor. 11, 23–29. This is a more serious objection. Considering, moreover, that Paul was at Ephesus exposed to the violent tumult of the people, and that this expression is often used by the ancients figuratively for contests with enraged men, the probability is, that it is to be so understood here. *What to me is the advantage?* 'If I have no other views or hopes than ordinary men, whose expectations are confined to this world, what is the use of incurring so many dangers?' *If the dead rise not.* This clause does not belong to the one preceding, as it is pointed in our version, but to what follows. 'If the dead rise not, let us eat and drink, for to-morrow we die.' The natural consequence of denying the doctrine of the resurrection, involving as it does the denial of the gospel, and the consequent rejection of all hope of salvation, is to make men reckless, and to lead them to abandon themselves to mere sensual enjoyments. If man has no glorious hereafter, he naturally sinks towards the level of the brutes, whose destiny he is to share.

33. Be not deceived : evil communications corrupt good manners.

This warning flows naturally from what had been said. If the tendency of the denial of the resurrection be to render men reckless and sensual, then the Corinthians should not be deceived by the plausible arguments or specious conduct of the errorists among them. They should avoid them, under the conviction that all evil is contagious. Evil *communications.* The word properly means *a being together, companionship.* It is contact, association with evil, that is declared to be corrupting. This is a fact of common experience, and therefore the apostle expresses it in a verse borrowed from the Greek poet, Menander, which had probably become a proverb. It is only when men associate with the wicked with the desire and purpose to do them good, that they can rely on the protection of God to preserve them from contamination.

34. Awake to righteousness, and sin not; for some have not the knowledge of God : I speak (this) to your shame.

Surrounded by evil teachers, the Corinthians had need not only of being on their guard against deception, but also of vigilance. *Awake.* The word properly means, *to become sober*, to arouse from a state of drunkenness or torpor. The call is to prompt exertion to shake off the delusion under which they were lying as to their security. *To righteousness*, literally, *righteously*, i. e. in a proper manner. ' Awake rightly,' or, as Luther renders it, *Wake right up. And sin not*, i. e. do not allow yourselves to be carried away into sin. This was the end to be answered by their vigilance. There was need of this exhortation, *for some have not the knowledge of God ;* literally, *have ignorance of God.* They are ignorant of God, and therefore they deny the resurrection. Comp. Matt. 22, 29, where our Lord says to the Sadducees who denied the resurrection, " Ye do err, not knowing the Scriptures, nor the power of God." *I speak this to your shame.* It should make you ashamed that there are men among you capable of calling in question one of the great essential facts of the gospel—the resurrection of the dead.

Nature of the resurrection body, vs. 35–58.

Having proved the fact of the resurrection, the apostle comes to illustrate its nature, or to teach with what kind of bodies the dead are to rise. It seems that the great objection against the doctrine in the minds of his readers rested on the assumption that our future bodies are to be of the same nature with those which we now have; that is, natural bodies consisting of flesh and blood, and sustained by air, food and sleep. Paul says this is a foolish assumption. Our future bodies may be material and identical with our present bodies, and yet organized in a very different way. You plant a seed; it does not come up a seed, but a flower. Why then may not the future be to the present body what the flower is to the seed ? vs. 35–37. Matter admits of indefinite varieties in organization. There is not only immense diversity in the vegetable productions of the earth, but even flesh is variously modified in the different orders of animals, vs. 38. 39. This is true not only as to the earth, for there are heavenly as well as earthly bodies. And even the sun, moon and stars differ from each other in glory; why then may not our future differ from our present bodies in glory? vs. 40. 41. Such not only may be, but will be the case. The body deposited in the grave is corruptible, mean, weak, and, in a word, natural; as raised from the grave, it will be incorruptible, glorious, powerful, and spiritual, vs. 42–44. This is according to Scripture. Adam was created with a natural body, adapted to an earthly state of existence; Christ, as a life-giving spirit, has a spiritual body. As Adam was before Christ, so our earthly tabernacles are before our heavenly ones. As we have borne the image of the earthly, we shall bear the image of the heavenly, vs. 45–49. It is freely admitted that flesh and blood, i. e. bodies organized as ours now are, are unfit for heaven. Corruption cannot inherit incorruption, v. 50. But our bodies are to be changed. This change shall be instantaneous and at the last day. It shall embrace both the living and the dead. Corruption shall put on incorruption, mortality shall put on immortality, vs. 51–53. When this is done, the original promise that death shall be swallowed up in victory, will be fully accomplished, v. 54. Death, therefore, to the believer, has lost its sting, and the grave is conquered. Death has no sting but sin; sin has no strength but from the law; the law has no power over those who are in Christ Jesus, therefore thanks be to God, who giveth us the victory through Christ Jesus our Lord! vs. 55–57. Seeing then that we have such a glorious hereafter, we should be steadfast, unmoveable, always abounding in the work of the Lord, v. 58.

35. But some (man) will say, How are the dead raised up? and with what body do they come?

The discussion of the fact of the resurrection being ended, the apostle comes to consider the manner of it. He supposes some objector to ask, *How are the dead raised up?* This may mean, How can a corrupted and disorganized body be restored to life? And the next question, *With what body do they come?* may refer to the result of the process. What is to be the nature of our future bodies? Or the latter question may be merely explanatory of the former, so that only one point is presented. *How,* i. e. with what kind of body are the dead raised? There are, however, two distinct questions, for although the two are not connected by καί, *and,* but by the particle δέ, which might be merely explanatory, yet the apostle really answers, in what follows, both questions, viz., How it is possible for life to come out of death, and, What is to be the nature of the body after the resurrection. The latter difficulty was the main one, and therefore to that the most of what follows refers. The great objection in the minds of the Corinthians to the doctrine of the resurrection was evidently the same as that of the Sadducees. Both supposed our future bodies are to be like our present ones. Our Lord's answer to the Sadducees, therefore, is the same as that which Paul gives to the Corinthian objectors. The future body is not to be like the present. To reject a plainly-revealed and most important doctrine on such grounds as these is wicked as well as foolish, and therefore the apostle says in the next verse—

36. (Thou) fool, that which thou sowest is not quickened, except it die.

It is not, *Thou* fool, but simply, Fool! an exclamation both of disapprobation and contempt. Luke 12, 20. Rom. 1, 22. Eph. 5, 15. It does not, however, necessarily express any bitterness of feeling; for our blessed Lord said to his doubting disciples, " O fools, and slow of heart to believe all that the prophets have spoken! " Luke 24, 25. It was the senselessness of the objection that roused the apostle's indignation. The body cannot live again because it dies. Fool! says Paul, a seed cannot live unless it does die. Disorganization is the necessary condition of reorganization. If the seed remain a seed there is an end of it. But if it die, it bringeth forth much fruit, John 12, 24. The seed is as much disorganized, it as really ceases to be a seed when sown in the ground, as the body when laid in the grave. If the one dies, the other dies. Death is not annihilation, but disorganization; the passing from one form or mode of existence to another. How then can the disorganization of the body in the grave be an objection to the doctrine of a resurrection ? It may be said that the apostle does not pursue the objection; that the body is not only disorganized but dispersed; its elements scattered over the earth, and embraced in new combinations; whereas in the seed the germ remains, so that there is no interruption of the organic life of the plant. To those who make this objection our Saviour's answer is, that they err, " not knowing the power of God." Who knows where the principle of the organic life of the body is? It may be in the soul, which when the time comes may unfold itself into a new body, gathering or regathering its materials according to its own law; just as the principle of vegetable life in the seed unfolds itself into some gorgeous flower, gathering from surrounding nature the materials for its new organization. The identity between the present and future body is implied in the apostle's illustration. But it is his object neither to assert that identity, nor to explain its nature. The latter is a very subordinate point. The Bible clearly teaches that our bodies hereafter are to be the same as those which we now have; but it nowhere teaches us wherein that sameness consists. In what sense is a sprouting acorn the same with the full-grown oak? Not in substance, not in form, not in appearance. It is, however, the same individual organism. The same is true of the human body. It is the same in old age that it was in infancy. But in what sense? The materials of which the body is composed change many times in the course of an ordinary life, yet the body remains the same. We may rest assured that our future bodies will be the same with those which we now have in a high and satisfying sense, though until the time comes we may be as little able to explain the nature of that identity as we are to tell what constitutes the identity of the body in this life. The same body which is sown in tears, shall be reaped in joy. To doubt the fact of the resurrection, because we cannot understand the process, is, as the apostle says, a proof of folly.

37. And that which thou sowest, thou sowest not that body that shall be, but bare grain, it may chance of wheat, or of some other (grain):

The first clause of this verse stands, as it were, absolutely. And *as to* that which thou sowest—*thou sowest not the body that shall be.* That is, you do not sow the plant, but the *bare grain,* i. e. the simple, naked grain—*it may be of wheat, or of some other grain.* The point of the illustration is, that what comes up is very different from that which is deposited in the ground. You sow a seed, a plant appears. You sow a natural, corruptible body; a spiritual, incorruptible body appears. Nature itself therefore teaches that the objection that the future body must be like the present, is of no force.

38. But God giveth it a body as it hath pleased him, and to every seed his own body.

What is deposited in the earth is very different from that which springs from it. Every seed produces its own plant. The product depends on the will of God. It was determined at the creation, and therefore the apostle says that God, in the continual agency of his providence, gives to each seed its own appropriate product, *as he willed*, i. e. he originally purposed. The point of this is, if God thus gives to all the products of the earth each its own form, why may he not determine the form in which the body is to appear at the resurrection? You cannot infer from looking at a seed what the plant is to be; it is very foolish, therefore, to attempt to determine from our present bodies what is to be the nature of our bodies hereafter.

39. All flesh (is) not the same flesh : but (there is) one (kind of) flesh of men, another flesh of beasts, another of fishes, (and) another of birds.

If even here, where the general conditions of life are the same, we see such diversity in animal organizations, flesh and blood appearing in so many forms, why should it be assumed that the body hereafter must be the same cumbrous vehicle of the soul that it is now?

40. (There are) also celestial bodies, and bodies terrestrial : but the glory of the celestial (is) one, and the (glory) of the terrestrial (is) another.

There is no limit to be set to the possible or actual modifications of matter. We not only see it in all the diversified forms of animal and vegetable life, but in the still greater diversities of heavenly and earthly bodies. What Paul here means by *bodies celestial*, is doubtful. 1. Many suppose the reference is to angels, either on the assumption that they too have bodies, or that the apostle refers to the forms in which they appear to men. When they become visible they must assume some material vehicle, which was always luminous or glorious. Of the angel who appeared at the sepulchre of Christ it is said, "His countenance was like lightning, and his raiment white as snow," Matt. 28, 3. There is a great contrast between the bodies of these celestial beings and those of men. 2. Others suppose that the reference is to the bodies of the saints in heaven. There are many kinds of bodies here on earth, and there are also celestial as well as terrestrial bodies. The one differing from the other in glory. 3. The common opinion is that the apostle means what is now generally meant by "the heavenly bodies," viz., the sun, moon and stars. To this it is objected that it is to make the apostle use the language of modern astronomy. This, however, has little force; for whatever the ancients conceived the sun, moon and stars to be, they regarded them as bodies, and used the word σῶμα in reference to them or to the universe. Galen, who was born not more than sixty or seventy years after the date of this epistle, uses nearly the same language as the apostle does. He too contrasts τὰ ἄνω σώματα (meaning the sun, moon and stars,) with τὰ γήϊνα σώματα. See Wetstein. The common interpretation is also sustained by the context, for the sun, moon and stars mentioned in the next verse are evidently included in the heavenly bodies here intended.

41. (There is) one glory of the sun, and another glory of the moon, and another glory of the stars; for (one) star differeth from (another) star in glory.

Not only do the heavenly bodies differ from the earthly bodies in glory, but there is great diversity among the heavenly bodies themselves. How different is the sun from the moon, the moon from the stars, and even one star from another. Standing, therefore, as we do in the midst of this wonderful universe, in which we see matter in every conceivable modification, from a clod of earth to a sunbeam, from dust to the lustre of the human eye, how unutterably absurd is it to say that if we are to have bodies hereafter, they must be as gross, and heavy, and as corruptible as those which we have now.

42. So also (is) the resurrection of the dead. It is sown in corruption, it is raised in incorruption:

So also is the resurrection of the dead. That is, as the heavenly bodies differ from the earthly bodies, and as one star differs from another star, so the resurrection body will differ from our present body. The apostle does not mean that as one star differs from another star in glory, so one risen believer will differ from another. This, no doubt, is true; but it is not what Paul here says or intimates. His object is simply to show the absurdity of the objection founded on the assumption that the body hereafter must be what it is here. He shows that it may be a body and yet differ as much from what it is now as the light of the sun differs from a piece of clay. He therefore proceeds to show wherein this difference consists. The body *is sown in corruption; it is raised in incorruption.* The figure of the seed is again introduced. The bodies of the saints are as seed sown in the ground, not there to be lost or to remain; but at the appointed time, to rise in a state the very reverse of that in which they were committed to the dust. *It is sown in corruption,* i. e. it is now a corruptible body, constantly tending to decay, subject to disease and death, and destined to entire dissolution. *It is raised in incorruption.* Hereafter it will be imperishable; free from all impurity, and incapable of decay.

43. 44. It is sown in dishonour, it is raised in glory : it is sown in weakness, it is raised in power : it is sown a natural body, it is raised a spiritual body. There is a natural body, and there is a spiritual body.

The apostle contemplates the body as at the moment of interment, and therefore these predicates are to be understood with special reference to its condition at that time. It is the dead body that is sown in dishonour, despoiled of the short-lived attractiveness which it had while living. It is raised *in glory,* i. e. in that resplendent brightness which diffuses light and awakens admiration. It is to be fashioned like unto the glorious body of the Son of God, Phil. 3, 21. *It is sown in weakness.* Nothing is more absolutely powerless than a corpse —it can do nothing and it can resist nothing. The weakness which belonged to it in life, is perfected in death. *It is raised in power.* The future body will be instinct with energy, endowed, it may be, with faculties of which we have now no conception. *It is sown a natural body, it is raised a spiritual body.* This comprehends all that has been said. A natural body, σῶμα ψυχικόν, is a body of which the ψυχή, or animal life, is the animating principle; and a spiritual body, σῶμα πνευματικόν, is a body adapted to the πνεῦμα, the rational, immortal principle of our nature. We know from experience what a natural body is. It is a body which has essentially the same properties as those of brutes. A natural body consists of flesh and blood; is susceptible of pain and decay; and needs air, food, and rest. It is a mere animal body, adapted to the conditions of an earthly existence. What a spiritual body is, we know only from Paul's description, and from the manifestation of Christ in his glorified body. We know that it is incorruptible, glorious, and powerful, adapted to the higher state of existence in heaven, and therefore not adapted to an earthly condition. *Spiritual*, in this connection, does not mean ethereal, refined, much less *made of spirit*, which would be a contradiction. Nor does it mean animated by the Holy Spirit. But as σῶμα ψυχικόν is a body adapted to the ψυχή or principle of animal life, the σῶμα πνευματικόν is a body adapted to the πνεῦμα or principle of rational life. The Bible uses these terms just as we do, without intending to teach that the ψυχή or *life*, is a distinct substance or subject from the πνεῦμα or *rational spirit*, but only that as we have certain attributes, considered as living creatures, in common with irrational animals, so we have now a body suited to those attributes; and, on the other hand, as we have attributes unspeakably higher than those which belong to brutes, we shall hereafter possess bodies adapted to those higher attributes. The Bible recognizes in man only two subjects or distinct separable substances, the soul and body. And this has ever been a fundamental principle of Christian anthropology.

There is a natural body, and there is a spiritual body. This is a vindication of the apparently contradictory expression, *spiritual body*, which, according to the letter, is tantamount to *immaterial matter*. If, however, it is proper to speak of σῶμα ψυχικόν, *a natural body*, i. e. a body adapted to the principle of animal life; it is right to speak of a σῶμα πνευματικόν, *a spiritual body*, i. e. a body adapted to the spirit. Lachmann, Rückert, and Tischendorf, after the ancient MSS. and versions, adopt the reading εἰ ἔστι, κ.τ.λ. *If* there is a natural body, there is a spiritual body. Just as certainly as we have a body adapted to our lower nature, we shall have one adapted to our higher nature. If the one exists, so does the other.

45. And so it is written, The first man Adam was made a living soul; the last Adam (was made) a quickening spirit.

So it is written, i. e. the Scriptures are in accordance with the preceding representation. They represent Adam as having been created with an animal nature, and therefore as having an animal body. Whereas, the second Adam is a person of a far higher order. The proof with regard to the nature of Adam does not rest exclusively on the words quoted, but on the whole account of his creation, of which those words form a part. It is evident from the entire history, that Adam was formed for an existence on this earth, and therefore with a body adapted to the present state of being; in its essential attributes not differing from those which we have inherited from him. He was indeed created immortal. Had he not sinned, he would not have been subject to death. For death is the wages of sin. And as Paul elsewhere teaches, death is by sin. From what the apostle, however, here says of the contrast between Adam and Christ; of the earthly and perishable nature of the former as opposed to the immortal, spiritual nature of the latter, it is plain that Adam as originally created was not, as to his body, in that state which would fit him for his immortal existence. After his period of probation was passed, it is to be inferred, that a change in him would have taken place, analogous to that which is to take place in those believers who shall be alive when Christ comes. They shall not die, but they shall be changed. Of this change in the constitution of his body, the tree of life was probably constituted the sacrament. For when he sinned, he was excluded from the garden of Eden, "lest he put forth his hand and take of the tree of life, and eat, and live for ever," Gen. 3, 22. Some change, therefore, was to take place in his body, to adapt it to live for ever. *He was made a living soul,* ψυχὴν ζῶσαν. He had a ψυχή, and therefore a body adapted to it. Both the Greek word ψυχή and the corresponding Hebrew term are frequently used for the immortal principle of our nature—the rational soul—but they also, and perhaps most frequently, mean life in that form which we have in common with other animals. This idea is included in the passage quoted from Genesis. It is to be remembered that the quotations given in the New Testament from the Old Testament are not mere quotations, but authoritative expositions. Paul tells us what the Spirit of God meant, when he called Adam a *living soul.*

The last Adam, i. e. Christ. This was not an unusual designation for the Messiah among the Jews, though not found in Scripture elsewhere than here. The appropriateness of the designation is evident. Christ is the second great head and representative man, of whom Adam is declared to have been the type, Rom. 5, 14. Was made *a quickening spirit.* Adam was in his distinctive character, that is, as distinguished from Christ, an animal—a creature endowed with animal life, whereas Christ has life in himself, and can give life to as many as he will, John 5, 21. 26. This does not of course mean that Adam had nothing more than animal life. It does not deny that he had a rational and immortal soul. Neither does it imply that our Lord had not, while on earth, a ψυχή or principle of life in common with us. The apostle simply contrasts the first and second Adam as to their distinguishing characteristics. The one was a man; the other infinitely more.

There are two questions suggested by this passage. The first is, on what ground does the apostle assert that Christ was made a quickening spirit? When he says, at the beginning of the verse, "So it is written," does he intend to appeal to the support of Scripture not only for what he says of the nature of Adam, but also for what he says of the person of Christ? If so, the proof cannot rest on the passage quoted, for that relates exclusively to Adam. If the apostle intended to cite the Scriptures for both parts of the declaration in the preceding verse, "there is a natural body, and there is a spiritual body," he must mean the Scriptures in express terms declare Adam to have had a living soul, and they set forth Christ as a life-giving Spirit. It is more commonly assumed, however, that the quotation is limited to the first clause. 'The Scriptures say that the first Adam "was made a living soul;" the last Adam (we know) was made a life-giving Spirit.'

The second question is, When was Christ made a quickening spirit? The apostle does not refer to what Christ was before his incarnation, but to what he became. The subject of discourse is, *the last Adam.* When did he become a quickening spirit? Some say at his incarnation. This is undoubtedly true. As the incarnate Son of God he was life-giving. "It pleased the Father that he should have life in himself," John 5, 26. That is, that the divine and human nature should be united in his person. And in this constitution of his person it was already determined that, although while on earth he should have a body like our own, yet his whole person, including 'his true body and reasonable soul,' should be adapted to sit at the right hand of God. Adam was first formed for this earth, and had an earthly body; the person of Christ was constituted in reference to his reigning in heaven, and therefore he has a spiritual body. The apostle argues from the nature of Adam to the nature of his body; and from the nature of Christ to the nature of his body. This argument does not involve the assumption that the body of Christ was here a spiritual one—for we know that it was flesh and blood; but that such was the state to which, from the very constitution of his person, he was destined, a spiritual body alone could be suited to him. The last Adam, therefore, was made a quickening spirit, by the union of the divine with the human in the constitution of his person. Others say that it was at his resurrection; and others, at his ascension. As to the former opinion, it is enough to say, that no change took place at his resurrection in the nature of Christ's body. It was necessary in order to its satisfactory identification that it should remain the same that it was before. He therefore not only called upon his disciples to handle his risen body and to satisfy themselves of its identity by probing the wounds in his hands and feet, but he also repeatedly ate before them. He did not assume his permanent pneumatic state until his ascension. But this did not make him a quickening spirit. It only affected his body, which then assumed the state adapted to its condition in heaven.

46. Howbeit that (was) not first which is spiritual, but that which is natural; and afterward that which is spiritual.

This does not mean simply that the natural *body* precedes the spiritual *body*. But it announces, as it were, a general law. The lower precedes the higher; the imperfect the perfect. This is true in all the works of God, in which there is a development. Adam's earthly state was to be preparatory to a heavenly one. The present life is like a seed time, the harvest is hereafter. The natural comes before the spiritual; as Calvin says, we are born before we are regenerated, we live before we rise.

47. The first man (is) of the earth, earthy: the second man (is) the Lord from heaven.

The general principle stated in the preceding verse, that

the natural precedes the spiritual, is here illustrated by the fact that Adam came before Christ. *The first man was of the earth,* i. e. formed out of the earth, and therefore *earthy. The second man is the Lord from heaven.* Here the text is doubtful. The authorities are about equally divided for and against the reading ὁ κύριος, *the Lord.* The sentence is more simple if that word be omitted. 'The first man was from the earth; the second man was from heaven.' If the common text be retained, the word *Lord* is in apposition with the words *the second man.* 'The second man, the Lord, was from heaven.' This passage was used by the early heretics of the Gnostic school to sustain their doctrine that our Lord was not really born of the Virgin Mary, but was clothed in a body derived from heaven, in opposition to whom the early creeds declare that he was as to his human nature consubstantial with man, and as to his divine nature consubstantial with God. The text, however, simply asserts the heavenly origin of Christ. Adam was of the earth; Christ was from heaven; comp. John 3, 13. Adam, therefore, had a body suited to the earth; Christ has a body suited to heaven.

48. As (is) the earthy, such (are) they also that are earthy; and as (is) the heavenly, such (are) they also that are heavenly.

The earthy is of course Adam; *they that are earthy* are his descendants. *The heavenly* is Christ; *they that are heavenly* are his risen people. The descendants of Adam derive from him an earthly body like his. Those who are Christ's are to have a body fashioned like unto his glorious body, Phil. 3, 21.

49. And as we have borne the image of the earthy, we shall also bear the image of the heavenly.

In this passage, instead of the future φορέσομεν, *we shall bear,* the great majority of the oldest MSS. read the conjunctive φορέσωμεν, *let us bear.* The context, however, so evidently demands the future, that the common reading is preferred by almost all editors. An exhortation here would be entirely out of place. The apostle is evidently proceeding with his discussion. He is obviating the objection to the doctrine of the resurrection founded on the assumption that our bodies hereafter are to be of the same kind as those which we have here. This is not so. They are to be like the body of Christ. As we have borne the image of Adam as to his body, we shall bear the image of Christ as to his body. The idea that as we have derived a corrupt nature from Adam, we derive a holy nature from Christ, though true in itself, is altogether foreign to the connection.

50. Now this I say, brethren, that flesh and blood cannot inherit the kingdom of God; neither doth corruption inherit incorruption.

This I say. These words admit of three interpretations. 1. They may be understood concessively. 'This I concede, brethren. I admit that flesh and blood, our bodies as now organized, cannot inherit the kingdom of God. But that is not what I teach when I preach the doctrine of the resurrection. Our bodies are to be changed.' 2. The sense may be, 'This is what I say, the sum of what I have said is that flesh and blood,' &c. 3. The words may mean, 'This I assert, brethren. I assure you of this fact, that flesh and blood,' &c. In 7, 29 the expression is used in this sense. Comp. also Rom. 3, 8 and 1 Cor. 10, 19.

Flesh and blood means our body as now constituted, not sinful human nature. The phrase never has this latter sense. In Heb. 2, 14, it is said, "Inasmuch as the children are partakers of flesh and blood, he (Christ) also himself likewise took part of the same," Matt. 16, 17. Gal. 1, 16. Eph. 6, 12. It is indeed true, that our unsanctified nature, or unrenewed man, cannot inherit the kingdom of God. But that is not what the apostle is speaking about. He is speaking of the body and of its state after the resurrection. It is of the body as now constituted that he says, *it cannot inherit the kingdom of heaven,* i. e. the kingdom of Christ as it is to exist after the resurrection, Matt, 8, 11. Luke 13, 28. 1 Cor. 6, 9. Gal. 5, 21. 2 Tim. 4, 18. The same idea is repeated in abstract terms and as a general proposition in the next clause, *neither can corruption inherit incorruption.* The mortal cannot be immortal; the perishable imperishable. Incorruption cannot be an attribute of corruption. Our bodies, therefore, if they are to be immortal and imperishable must be changed. And this the apostle in the next verse announces on the authority of a direct revelation, is actually to occur.

51. Behold, I shew you a mystery; We shall not all sleep, but we shall all be changed,

A mystery ; something revealed, and which could not otherwise be known, Matt. 13, 11. 1 Cor. 4, 1, and often elsewhere. What is here expressed by saying, *I show you a mystery,* is in 1 Thess. 4, 15 expressed by saying, 'This I say unto you *by the word of the Lord,*' i. e. by divine revelation. The revelation which Paul now declares, and to which he calls special attention by the word, Behold ! is, that all are not to die, but all are to be changed, i. e. so changed that their corruptible body shall be rendered incorruptible. The common text is, πάντες μὲν οὐ κοιμηθησόμεθα, the negative being connected with the verb, so that the literal sense would be, *all are not to die.* This is said of *all* whom Paul addressed. The apostle tells them all that they are not to die. To avoid this impossible sense, for Paul certainly did not mean to assure the Corinthians that it had been revealed to him that none of them should die, most of the older commentators assume in common with our translators a not unusual trajection of the negative particle, πάντες οὐ standing for οὐ πάντες. Others explain the verse thus : 'We all — shall indeed not die (before the resurrection) — but we shall all be changed.' It is said this is contrary to the context, inasmuch as *being changed* is something peculiar to those who should be alive at the coming of Christ, and is not affirmed of the dead. This, however, is contrary to the fact. Paul had said, v. 50, that flesh and blood could not inherit the kingdom of God. All, therefore, who enter that kingdom, whether they die before the second advent or survive the coming of Christ, must be changed. And that is the fact which Paul says had been revealed to him. Those who died before the advent would not fail of the blessings of Christ's kingdom, and those who should be alive when he came, would not be left in their corruptible bodies. Both should be changed, and thus prepared for the heavenly state.*

* The difficulty, however, attending the common text, has given rise to a great variety of readings in the MSS. and versions. A. C. F. G. have πάντες μὲν κοιμηθησόμεθα, οὐ πάντες δὲ ἀλλαγησόμεθα, *we shall indeed all die, but we shall not all be changed.* D. and the Vulgate have : πάντες μὲν ἀναστησόμεθα, οὐ πάντες δὲ ἀλλαγησόμεθα, *we shall all rise, but we shall not all be changed.* There are several less important variations. These are all explained as attempts on the part of transcribers to escape making the apostle say that the Christians of that generation were not to die. But as the common text does not make him say that, there is no necessity for departing from it.

Comp. 1 Thess. 4, 15–17. The modern commentators, both German and English, understand the apostle as expressing the confident expectation that he and others of that generation should survive the coming of Christ. 'Though we (who are now alive) shall not all die, we shall all be changed.' But 1. This is altogether unnecessary. The *we all* includes all believers who had lived, were living, or ever should live. There is nothing either in the form of expression or in the context to limit it to the men of that generation. In the same way Paul says in 1 Thess. 4, 15, "We that are alive at the coming of the Lord shall not prevent them that are asleep." This does not imply that he expected to be alive when Christ came. In his second Epistle to the Thessalonians he warns them against the expectation of the speedy advent of Christ, telling them that a great apostasy and the revelation of the Man of Sin were to occur before that event. 2. The plenary inspiration of the sacred writers rendered them infallible in all they taught ; but it did not render them omniscient. They could not err in what they communicated, but they might err, and doubtless did err, as to things not included in the communications of the Spirit. The time of the second advent was not revealed to them. They profess their ignorance on that point. They were, therefore, as to that matter, on a level with other men, and may have differed in regard to their private conjectures on the subject just as others differ. It would not, in the least, therefore, encroach on their authority as infallible teachers, if it should be apparent that they cherished erroneous expectations with regard to that about which they professed to know nothing. Knowing that Christ was to come, and not knowing when he was to come, it was perfectly natural that they should look on his advent as constantly imminent, until it was revealed that certain events not yet accomplished, were to occur before Christ came. But all this is very different from any didactic statement that he was to come within a certain period. Paul might exhort Christians to wait and long for the coming of the Lord ; but he could not tell them *by the word of the Lord* that he and others then living would be alive when he came. This would not only be teaching error, but it would be claiming divine authority, or a special revelation, for that error. It is, therefore, only at the expense of all confidence in the inspiration of the apostle that the exposition above mentioned can be adopted.

52. In a moment, in the twinkling of an eye, at the last trump: for the trumpet shall sound, and the dead shall be raised incorruptible, and we shall be changed.

The change in question is to be instantaneous; *in a moment*, literally, *an atom*, i. e. in a portion of time so short as to be incapable of further division. It is to take place *at the last trump*, i. e. on the last day. As the trumpet was used for assembling the people or marshalling a host, it became the symbol for expressing the idea of the gathering of a multitude. So, in Matt. 24, 31, Christ says, "He will send his angels with a great sound of a trumpet; and they shall gather his elect from the four winds, from one end of heaven to another." Comp. Is. 27, 13. 1 Thess. 4, 16. This trumpet is called the *last*, not because several trumpets (the Jews say seven) are to sound in succession, but because it is the last that ever is to sound. In other words, the resurrection is to take place on the last day. *For the trumpet shall sound.* This is a confirmation of the preceding. That day shall surely come—the voice of the archangel, the trump of God, shall certainly resound as it did from Sinai, Ex. 19, 16. *And*, i. e. and then, in consequence of the summons of God, *the dead shall be raised* in the manner described in vs. 42. 43, incorruptible, glorious and powerful. *And we shall be changed.* This is in exact accordance with 1 Thess. 4, 15. Those who are alive when Christ comes "shall not prevent them which are asleep." The dead in Christ shall rise first, and then the living shall undergo their instantaneous change. As remarked on the preceding verse, it is not necessary to understand the apostle as including himself and fellow believers in Corinth, when he says *We* shall be changed. The connection indeed is different here from what it is there. There he says, "*We* shall not all die." If that means that the men of that generation should not all die, it is a positive assertion of what the event has proved to be false. But here he simply says, all who are alive when Christ comes shall be changed. If he hoped that he might be of the number there would be nothing in that expectation inconsistent with his inspiration. Calvin, therefore, so understands the passage.* Considering, however, his ex-

---

* Quum autem dicit, *Nos immutabimur* in eorum numero se comprehendit qui victuri sunt ad Christi adventum; quoniam jam erant postrema tempora, expectandus fuit dies ille in singulas horas.

press teaching in 2 Thess. 2, 2–12 on the subject, it is far more natural to understand him as contemplating the vast company of believers as a whole, and saying 'Those of us who are dead shall rise, and all who are alive shall be changed.'

53. For this corruptible must put on incorruption, and this mortal (must) put on immortality.

This is the reason why we must be changed. 'We must all be changed, for this corruptible must put on incorruption.' It is impossible that corruption should inherit incorruption. This reason applies equally to the quick and to the dead. With regard to both classes it is true that these vile bodies must be fashioned like unto Christ's glorious body.

54. So when this corruptible shall have put on incorruption, and this mortal shall have put on immortality, then shall be brought to pass the saying that is written, Death is swallowed up in victory.

When the change above described has been accomplished, when once the resurrection has taken place, then, according to the language of Scripture, death shall be completely conquered. Not only shall those over whom he had triumphed, and whom he had so long detained in the prison of the grave, be delivered from his power, but there shall be no more death. The passage quoted is Isaiah 25, 8, "He will swallow up death in victory." In Hebrew the last words mean literally *for ever*. They are, however, frequently translated by the LXX. as they are here rendered by the apostle. The sense is the same. The victory over death is to be complete and final.

55. O death, where (is) thy sting?   O grave, where (is) thy victory?

The apostle places himself and his readers in presence of the Saviour and of the risen dead arrayed in immortality; and in view of that majestic scene he breaks out in these words of triumph: 'Christ has conquered. His people are redeemed. Death is disarmed. Hades is no more.' Death is addressed under the figure of an animal armed with a poisonous sting which pierces even to the soul; for that sting is sin. *The grave*, or the Greek word Hades, means, *what is un-*

seen, the invisible world, the abode of the dead in the widest
sense. It depends on the context whether the immediate
reference be to the grave, the place of departed spirits, or
hell, in the modern sense of that word. Here where the special reference is to the bodies of men and to the delivery of
them from the power of death, it is properly rendered the
grave. The only sense in which the body can be in Hades is
that it is in the grave. The apostle is not speaking of the delivery of the souls of men from any intermediate state, but of
the redemption of the body. In Hosea 13, 14 God says, "O
death, I will be thy plagues; O grave, I will be thy destruction." This is a literal version of the Hebrew. The Vulgate
comes near to it, Ero mors tua, O mors! Morsus tuus ero,
inferne! The LXX. depart from the figure, "Where is thy
judgment (or vengeance), O death? where is thy sting, O
grave?" These are all different forms of expressing the idea
that death and the grave are completely conquered. The
apostle does not quote the prophet. He expresses an analogous idea in analogous terms. In speaking of death as furnished with a sting, the most natural figure is that of a scorpion. Others say that κέντρον here means *a goad,* and that
death is compared to a man driving animals before him with
such an instrument. The power of a goad is as nothing to
that of the sting of a scorpion, Rev. 9, 5. 6. 10, and the figure
is therefore far more forcible as commonly understood.*

56. The sting of death (is) sin; and the strength of sin (is) the law.

The sting of death is sin; that is, death would have no
power to injure us if it were not for sin. This is true for two
reasons. 1. Because if there were no sin there would be no
death. Death is by sin, Rom. 5, 12. 2. Because sin gives
death, when it has been introduced, all its terrors. If sin be
pardoned, death is harmless. It can inflict no evil. It becomes a mere transition from a lower to a higher state. *The
strength of sin is the law.* This must be the law of God in its
widest sense; not the Mosaic law, which would make the
declaration amount to nothing. The law is the strength of

* The MSS. B. D. E. F. G., and most of the versions, read, ποῦ σοῦ, θάνατε, τὸ κέντρον; ποῦ σοῦ, θάνατε, τὸ νῖκος; *where, O death, is thy sting? where,
O death, thy victory?* A reading which Tischendorf and other modern editors
have adopted.

sin for two reasons. 1. Because without law there would be no sin, Rom. 4, 15. The very idea of sin is want of conformity on the part of moral creatures to the law of God. If there be no standard to which we are bound to be conformed, there can be no such thing as want of conformity. Sin is the correlative, not of reason, nor of expediency, but of law. If you take away law, men may act unreasonably, or in a way injurious to themselves or others, but they cannot sin. 2. Because if there be no law there can be no condemnation. Sin is not imputed where there is no law, Rom. 5, 13. There is still another reason, which, though presented elsewhere by the apostle, is foreign to this connection, and that is, that the law not only reveals and condemns sin, but it exasperates and excites it, and thus gives it strength, Rom. 7, 8–12.

57. But thanks (be) to God, which giveth us the victory through our Lord Jesus Christ.

The victory here meant is, of course, the victory over death and the grave. Thanks be to God, who delivers us from the power of death, redeeming even our bodies from the grave, and making us partakers of everlasting life. This is done through Jesus Christ our Lord, i. e. our divine possessor and absolute ruler. It is through him, and through him alone. 1. Because he has satisfied the demands of the law. It has no power to condemn those who are clothed in his righteousness. There is no condemnation to those who are in Christ Jesus, Rom. 8, 1. Who shall lay any thing to the charge of God's elect? It is God that justifieth, who is he that condemneth? Rom. 8, 33. 34. Christ by his death hath destroyed him that had the power of death, that is, the devil, and delivered them who through fear of death were all their lifetime subject to bondage, Heb. 2, 14. 15. That is, in virtue of the death of Christ, by which the demands of justice are satisfied, Satan, the great executioner of divine justice, has no longer the right or power to detain the people of Christ under the power of death. If, therefore, it be the law which gives sin its reality and strength, and if sin gives death its sting, he who satisfies the law destroys the strength of sin, and consequently the sting of death. It is thus that Christ deprives death of all power to injure his people. It is for them disarmed and rendered as harmless as an infant. 2. But Christ not only gives us this victory through his justifying righteousness, but by his almighty power, he new creates the soul after the image of God, and, what is here principally intended, he repairs all the evils which death had inflicted. He restores us to that state, and even to more than that state, from which sin had cast us down. He rescues our bodies from the grave, and fashions them like unto his glorious body, even by that power whereby he is able to subdue all things unto himself, Phil. 3, 21. Had it not been for Christ, death would have reigned for ever over our fallen race; but thanks be to God, Christ hath given us the victory; so that the believer may even now say, O death, where is thy sting? O grave, where is thy victory?

58. Therefore, my beloved brethren, be ye steadfast, unmoveable, always abounding in the work of the Lord, forasmuch as ye know that your labour is not in vain in the Lord.

Such being the truth and importance of the doctrine of the resurrection, Christians should be firm in their adherence to it, not suffering themselves to be moved by the specious objections of philosophy falsely so called. They should remember that if the dead rise not, then is Christ not risen; and if Christ be not risen, their faith is vain, and they are yet in the power of sin. But as Christ has risen, and as his resurrection illustrates and renders certain that of his people, what more natural and proper than that they should abound in the work of the Lord. *The work of the Lord* is either that work in which the Lord is engaged, the destruction of death by destroying sin; or, it is the work which the Lord has given us to do, as parents and children, as husbands and wives, as ministers and Christians. In this work we should abound, i. e. be abundant. As Paul says, 2 Cor. 11, 23, "In labours more abundant." *Forasmuch as ye know that your labour is not in vain in the Lord.* This with Paul was more than faith; it was knowledge. He knew that labour in the work of the Lord would not be in vain. The reward secured for it by the grace of God and merit of Christ is participation of the glories of a blessed resurrection.

CHAPTER XVI.

Treats, 1. Of the collection to be made for the saints in Jerusalem, vs. 1–9.
2. Of Timothy and Apollos, whom the apostle commends to the confidence
of the Corinthians, vs. 10–14.   3. The third paragraph contains exhortations and greetings, vs. 15–20.   4. The last paragraph is the salutation
written with Paul's own hand, vs. 21–24.

Concerning the Collection for the Saints at Jerusalem.

FOR some reason not now to be certainly ascertained, poverty
prevailed in Jerusalem among the believers more than in any
other part of the church.   Almost all the special exhortations
to provide for the poor, in Paul's epistles, have primary reference to the poor in Jerusalem.   He had exhorted the churches
of Galatia to make a collection for their relief; and then those
of Macedonia, and he now addresses the Corinthians on the
subject.   It is a very common opinion that the poverty of the
Christians in Jerusalem arose from the community of goods
introduced among them at the beginning; an error which
arose from an excess of love over knowledge.   In thirty years
that mistake may have produced its legitimate effects.   Perfection in one thing requires perfection in all.   Perfect equality
in goods requires perfect freedom from selfishness and indo-
lence.   The collection made by the Syrian churches, as recorded in Acts 11, 29, was in consequence of the dearth the Christian prophet Agabus warned his brethren was to come on all
the world.   Whatever may have been the cause, the fact is
certain that the saints in Jerusalem stood in special need of
the assistance of their richer brethren.   Paul, therefore, undervalued and suspected as he was by the Jewish Christians,
laboured assiduously in their behalf.   He exhorts the Corinthians to adopt the same arrangements in reference to this matter,
which he had established in the churches of Galatia.   A contribution was to be made on the Lord's day every week, proportioned to their resources, so that the collection might be
ready when he came, vs. 1. 2.   He would either send it by
persons whom they might approve to Jerusalem, or if the sum
were of sufficient magnitude to make it worth while, he would
himself accompany their messengers, vs. 3. 4.   He announces
his purpose to visit the Corinthians after having passed over
Macedonia, and perhaps to pass the winter with them.   His

prospects of usefulness in Ephesus would detain him in that city until Pentecost, vs. 5–9.

As *to Timothy and Apollos* he exhorts them to treat the former in such a manner that he might be free from fear among them, for he was worthy of their confidence, vs. 10. 11. Of the latter he says he had urged him to go to Corinth with the other brethren, but that he was unwilling to do so then, but would go when a suitable occasion offered, vs. 12–14. He exhorts them to submission to the household of Stephanas, and to every one who was labouring in the good cause, vs. 15. 16. He expresses his gratification in seeing the brethren from Corinth, and sends salutations from those around him to the Christians in Achaia, vs. 17–20. The conclusion of the epistle was written with his own hand as an authentification of the whole, vs. 21–24.

1. Now concerning the collection for the saints, as I have given order to the churches of Galatia, even so do ye.

But concerning the collection which is for the saints. What saints were intended was already known to the Corinthians. Instead of *for the saints*, in Rom. 15, 26 we have the more definite expression, "for the poor of the saints who are in Jerusalem," in whose behalf, he tells the Romans, Macedonia and Achaia had made a contribution. The Greek word λογία, in the sense of συλλογή, *collection*, is only found in this passage. *As I have given orders*, i. e. as I arranged or ordered. This is the language of authority. For although these contributions were voluntary, and were required to be made cheerfully, 2 Cor. 9, 7, yet they were a duty, and therefore both the collection itself, and the mode in which it should be accomplished, were proper subjects for apostolic direction. In the epistle to the Galatians there is no mention of this collection. It was probably ordered when Paul visited those churches. *So do ye*, i. e. adopt the same plan as to the mode of making the collection. What that was, is stated in the following verse.

2. Upon the first (day) of the week let every one of you lay by him in store, as (God) hath prospered him, that there be no gatherings when I come.

The collection was to be made every Lord's day; every one was to contribute; and the contributions were to be in proportion to the means of the giver. These are the three principles which the apostle had established among the churches of Galatia, and which he urged the Corinthians to adopt. *Upon the first day of the week*, literally, *upon one of the Sabbath*, according to the Jewish method of designating the days of the week. The Hebrew word, sabbath (*rest*), is used not only in the singular, but also in the plural form, both for the seventh day, and for the whole week, Luke 18, 12. That the first day of the week was, by divine appointment, made the sacred day for Christians, may be inferred, 1. From the distinction put upon that day by our Lord himself, John 20, 19. 26. 2. From the greatness of the event which its observance was intended to commemorate. The sanctification of the seventh day of the week was intended to keep in mind the great truth of the creation of the world, on which the whole system of revealed religion was founded; and as Christianity is founded on the resurrection of Christ, the day on which Christ rose became for that reason the Christian Sabbath. 3. From its being called by the apostle John the Lord's day, i. e. the day set apart for the service of the Lord, Rev. 1, 10. 4. From the evidence that it was from the beginning the day on which Christians assembled for worship, Acts 20, 7. 5. From the uniform practice of the whole church, which practice, having the clear evidence of apostolic sanction, is authoritative.

Let every one of you. It was an important feature of these apostolic arrangements, that the contributions were not to be confined to any one class of the people. The same amount might perhaps have been raised from the rich few. But this would not have answered one important end which the apostle had in view. It was the religious effect which these gifts were to produce in promoting Christian fellowship, in evincing the truth and power of the gospel, and in calling forth gratitude and praise to God, even more than the relief of the temporal necessities of the poor, that Paul desired to see accomplished, 2 Cor. 9, 12–14. Every one was to *lay by himself*, i. e. most modern commentators say, *at home*, παρ' ἑαυτῷ. Compare πρὸς ἑαυτόν, in Luke 24, 12 ; see also John 20, 10. The direction then is that every one should, on the first day of the week, lay aside at home whatever he was able to give, thus *treasuring up* his contribution. To this interpretation it may

be objected that the whole expression is thus obscure and
awkward. 'Let every one at home place, treasuring up what
he has to give.' The words do not mean *to lay by at home*,
but *to lay by himself*. The direction is nothing more definite
than, *let him place by himself*, i. e. let him take to himself
what he means to give. What he was to do with it, or where
he was to deposit it, is not expressed. The word θησαυρίζων
means *putting into the treasury*, or *hoarding up*, and is perfectly consistent with the assumption that the place of deposit
was some common treasury, and not every man's own house.
2. If Paul directed this money to be laid up *at home*, why
was the first day of the week selected? It is evident that the
first day must have offered some special facility for doing
what is here enjoined. The only reason that can be assigned
for requiring the thing to be done on the first day of the week,
is, that on that day the Christians were accustomed to meet,
and what each one had laid aside from his weekly gains could
be treasured up, i. e. put into the common treasury of the
church. 3. The end which the apostle desired to accomplish
could not otherwise have been effected. He wished that *there
might be no collections when he came*. But if every man had
his money laid by at home, the collection would be still to be
made. The probability is, therefore, Paul intended to direct
the Corinthians to make a collection every Lord's day for the
poor, when they met for worship. *As God hath prospered
him ;* literally, *whatever has gone well with him*. He was to
lay aside what by his success in business he was able to give.
This is another principle which the apostle would have Christians to act upon. Their contribution should be in proportion
to their means.

3. And when I come, whomsoever ye shall approve
by (your) letters, them will I send to bring your liberality unto Jerusalem.

Paul was not to receive the money himself. It was to be
given to men selected and approved by the Corinthians, whom
Paul promised to send, furnished with letters from himself, to
Jerusalem. The words δι' ἐπιστολῶν, *with letters*, are not to be
connected with what precedes, "approved by *your* letters,"
but with what follows, "I will send with letters." Otherwise
there would have been no need of Paul's sending them, i. e.
the persons approved by the Corinthians. The people were

to collect the money; it was to be committed to men of their own selection; but Paul, as the author of the collection, was to send it to Jerusalem. If the apostle deemed it wise to place himself above suspicion, and to avoid giving even the most malicious the opportunity of calling his integrity in question, as is intimated here, and expressly stated in 2 Cor. 8, 19. 20, it must be wise for other men and ministers to act with equal caution. If called to disburse the money of others or of the church, let that money, if possible, be in some other custody than their own, that others may know what is done with it. Thus at least Paul acted.

4. And if it be meet that I go also, they shall go with me.

And if it is deserving of my going; that is, if the collection be of an amount to make it proper for me also to go with it to Jerusalem, your messengers shall go with me. According to Acts 19, 21, Paul purposed, after visiting Macedonia and Achaia, to go to Jerusalem. But whether he would go at the time the contribution of the Corinthians was sent, depended on its amount. He would not modify his plans for the sake of having charge of the distribution of an inconsiderable sum.

5. Now I will come unto you, when I shall pass through Macedonia: for I do pass through Macedonia.

It appears from 2 Cor. 1, 15. 16, that Paul's original plan was to go directly from Ephesus to Corinth, and from there into Macedonia, and then back again to Corinth, and thence to Jerusalem. He now informs them that he would go to Macedonia before going to Corinth. So eager were the false teachers in Corinth to find grounds of complaint against him, that they made this change of plan a grievous offence, and a proof that he was not to be depended upon either as to his purposes or his doctrine. This is apparent from the vindication of himself in the second Epistle. *For I do pass through Macedonia;* not, *I am passing;* the present tense expresses the purpose of the apostle as settled. The mistake as to the force of the tense here, probably led transcribers to date this epistle from Philippi; whereas, it is clear from v. 8, that it was written from Ephesus.

6. And it may be that I will abide, yea, and winter with you, that ye may bring me on my journey whithersoever I go.

'I pass through Macedonia, but I will abide with you.' His visit to the former was to be transient, to the latter prolonged. In the second Epistle he speaks of himself as in Macedonia, and in Acts 20, 2. 3, we find that he left Ephesus after the uproar in that city and went to Macedonia, and thence to Greece, where he abode three months. The plan here sketched was therefore executed. He would remain with them for the winter, he says, *in order that* they might help him forward on his journey, i. e. attend him on his way, which was the customary mark of respect. Paul wished to receive this courtesy from the Corinthians rather than from others, as his affection for them, notwithstanding the trouble and anxiety they occasioned him was, as is evident from his second Epistle, peculiarly strong.

7. For I will not see you now by the way; but I trust to tarry a while with you, if the Lord permit.

By some ἄρτι, *now*, is connected with θέλω, *I will.* 'I do not now wish, as I formerly intended.' Its natural connection is with ἰδεῖν, *to see.* 'I do not wish to see you now in passing.' "*But* I hope;" instead of δέ, *but*, the older MSS. read γάρ; "*for* I hope to tarry with you." It seems that the intelligence which Paul received in Ephesus concerning the disorders in Corinth, determined him to write them this letter, instead of making them a passing visit, and to defer his visit for some months in order that his letter might have time to produce its effect. The same reason determined him, when he did go to Corinth, to remain there some time, that he might correct the abuses which had sprung up in his absence. The second Epistle shows how anxious he was about the effect of this letter, and how overjoyed he was when Titus brought him the intelligence that it had brought the people to repentance. *If the Lord permit*, (ἐπιτρέπῃ), or, 'If the Lord shall have permitted' (ἐπιτρέψῃ). The latter reading is adopted by the later editors. *The Lord* is Christ, whom Paul recognized as ordering all events, and whose guidance he sought and always submitted to.

8. 9. But I will tarry at Ephesus until Pentecost. For a great door and effectual is opened unto me, and (there are) many adversaries.

There were two reasons, therefore, for his remaining at Ephesus, his abundant opportunities of usefulness, and the necessity of withstanding the adversaries of the gospel. Paul's plan was to spend the spring at Ephesus, the summer in Macedonia, and the winter in Corinth. The Pentecost of the following year he spent in Jerusalem. He could not leave Ephesus soon, *for*, he says, *a great and effectual door is opened to me.* *A door* is a way of entrance, and figuratively an opportunity of entering into the possession of the convictions and hearts of men. A great door was opened to the apostle, he had a wide field of usefulness. The epithet *effectual* does not agree with the figure, but the meaning is plain—the opportunities were such as could be turned to good effect. *And there are many adversaries.* The opponents of the gospel varied very much in character in different places. Those in Ephesus were principally men interested in the worship of Diana. The pressure of the heathen seems to have driven the Jews and Christians to make common cause, Acts 19, 22. Whereas, in Corinth, Paul's most bitter opponents were Judaizers. The presence of such violent adversaries rendered the personal support of the apostle more necessary to the church.

10. Now if Timotheus come, see that he may be with you without fear : for he worketh the work of the Lord, as I also (do.)

In Acts 19, 22, we read that Paul "sent into Macedonia two of those who ministered to him, Timotheus and Erastus; but he himself stayed in Asia for a season." Timothy, therefore, at this time, was travelling through Macedonia, and expected to reach Corinth, whither the apostle had sent him ; see 4, 17. Besides this mission of Timothy, there was another some time later, consisting of Titus and other brethren, who were sent to learn the effect produced by this letter ; and whose return the apostle so anxiously awaited, 2 Cor. 2, 12. 13. Paul requests the Corinthians so to receive Timothy that he might be there *without fear.* It was not fear of personal violence, but the fear of not being regarded with respect and confidence. The reason by which he enforces his request shows the nature of the evil which he apprehended, *for he worketh the work of the Lord.* If they would recognize this, Timothy would be satisfied. *The work of the Lord,* as in 15, 58, may mean either that work in which the Lord himself is engaged; or that which he has prescribed. *As I also do.* A comprehensive commendation. Timothy preached the same gospel that Paul preached; and with like assiduity and fidelity.

11. Let no man therefore despise him : but conduct him forth in peace, that he may come unto me : for I look for him with the brethren.

Therefore, i. e. because he works the work of the Lord, he is entitled to respect, and ought not to be despised. Perhaps it was Timothy's youth that made the apostle specially solicitous on this account, 1 Tim. 4, 12. *But conduct him forth in peace;* i. e. attend him on his journey in a friendly manner. *That he may come to me.* It was not Paul's wish that Timothy should remain in Corinth ; but after having executed his commission, 4, 17, he was to return to the apostle. He did thus return, and was with Paul when he wrote the second Epistle, 2 Cor. 1, 1. *I expect him with the brethren,* i. e. the brethren whom Paul had appointed as Timothy's travelling companions. It is rare in the New Testament that we read of any one going on a missionary tour alone.

12. As touching (our) brother Apollos, I greatly desired him to come unto you with the brethren : but his will was not at all to come at this time ; but he will come when he shall have convenient time.

Either the Corinthians, among whom Apollos had already laboured, had requested Paul to send him to them again; or for some other reason, the apostle earnestly wished that he would accompany the brethren from Corinth, who were to carry this epistle back with them ; see v. 17. It appears from this verse that Apollos was not under Paul's authority. No reason is given for his declining to go to Corinth but that he was not willing. Why he was not willing is matter of conjecture. Many suppose it was because his name had been mixed up with the party strifes which disturbed the church there.

1, 12. *I greatly desired him ;* or, *I often exhorted him, that he would come,* &c. ἵνα does not here mean, *in order that,* but indicates the purport of the request.

13. 14. Watch ye, stand fast in the faith, quit you like men, be strong. Let all your things be done with charity.

These concise exhortations form a fitting close to the epistle ; each being adapted to the peculiar circumstances of the Corinthians, though of course applicable to all Christians in their conflicts with the world.   1. He exhorts *them to watch,* i. e. to be wakeful, constantly on the alert, that their spiritual enemies might not gain advantage over them before they were aware of their danger.   2. Beset as they were with false teachers, who handled deceitfully the word of God, 2 Cor. 4, 2, he exhorts them to *stand fast in the faith.* Do not consider every point of doctrine an open question.   Matters of faith, doctrines for which you have a clear revelation of God, such for example as the doctrine of the resurrection, are to be considered settled, and, as among Christians, no longer matters of dispute.   There are doctrines embraced in the creeds of all orthodox churches, so clearly taught in Scripture, that it is not only useless, but hurtful, to be always calling them into question.   3. *Quit you like men.* The circumstances of the Corinthians called for great courage.   They had to withstand the contempt of the learned, and the persecutions of the powerful.   4. *Be strong.* Not only courage, but strength, was needed to withstand their enemies, and to bear up under the trials which were to come upon them.   5. *Let all your affairs be conducted in love,* i. e. let love prevail, in your hearts, in your families, in your assemblies.   The preceding parts of the epistle show how much need there was for this exhortation ; as the church was rent with factions, and even the Lord's supper, every where else a feast of love, had become in Corinth a fountain of bitterness.

15. 16. I beseech you, brethren, [ye know the house of Stephanas, that it is the first-fruits of Achaia, and (that) they have addicted themselves to the ministry of the saints,] that ye submit yourselves unto such, and to every one that helpeth with (us,) and laboureth.

The family of Stephanas was the first family in Achaia that embraced the gospel. In Rom. 16, 5, Epenetus, according to the common text, is said to have been the first fruits of *Achaia ;* but there the true reading is *Asia ;* so that there is no conflict between the two passages. Of the family of Stephanas it is said, that *they addicted themselves to the ministering of the saints*, i. e. devoted themselves to the service of believers. The expression does not necessarily involve the idea of any official service. The exhortation is, *that ye also submit yourselves to such.* ' As they serve you, do you serve them.' Nothing is more natural than submission to the good. *And to every one that helpeth with* (such), *and laboureth.* This may mean, submit yourselves to every one who co-operates with such persons ; i. e. to all who in like manner are addicted to the service of believers. Those who serve, should be served.

17. I am glad of the coming of Stephanas and Fortunatus and Achaicus : for that which was lacking on your part they have supplied.

These were members of the church in Corinth, who visited Ephesus probably for the express purpose of seeing the apostle, and of consulting him on the condition of the church. They were probably the bearers of the letter from the Corinthians to Paul, to which he alludes in 7, 1. The reason why he rejoiced in their presence was, that they *supplied what was lacking on the part of the Corinthians ;* or rather, *the want of you* (τὸ ὑμέτερον ὑστέρημα; ὑμέτερον being objective, as in 15, 31.) The presence of these brethren made up to the apostle, in a measure, the absence of the Corinthians. Another explanation is, 'they have done what you failed to do,' i. e. informed me of the true state of things in Corinth. The former view of the meaning is the common one, and is more in keeping with the tone of the passage, which is affectionate and conciliatory. This too is confirmed by what follows.

18. For they have refreshed my spirit and yours : therefore acknowledge ye them that are such.

For, i. e. They have supplied your place, for their presence has had the same effect as would have followed from our being together. It has refreshed me, and it has had a corresponding effect on you. 'To them,' as Meyer and others explain it, 'you owe whatever in my letter serves to refresh you.' Others think that the apostle refers to the effect of the return of these brethren to Corinth, and the assurances they would carry with them of the apostle's love. Or, Paul may mean, that what refreshed him, must also gratify them. They would rejoice in his joy. However understood, it is one of the examples of urbanity with which this apostle's writings abound. *Therefore acknowledge them that are such*, i. e. recognize and appreciate them properly.

19. The churches of Asia salute you. Aquila and Priscilla salute you much in the Lord, with the church that is in their house.

Asia here means proconsular Asia, of which Ephesus was the capital, and which included the seven apocalyptic churches. *To salute*, in a general sense, is to wish safety to; in a Christian sense, it is to wish salvation to any one. This was included in the Hebrew formula of salutation, "Peace be with you," which passed into the service of Christians. To salute any one *in the Lord*, is to salute him as a Christian and in a Christian manner. It is to salute him because he is in the Lord, and in a way acceptable to the Lord. Aquila and Priscilla, when driven from Rome, as mentioned in Acts 18, 2, settled in Corinth. They accompanied the apostle to Ephesus, and remained there, Acts 18, 18. *The church which is in their house*, i. e. the company of Christians which meet in their house. As the same expression is used Rom. 16, 5, in connection with their names, it is probable that both at Rome and Ephesus, they opened their house as a regular place of meeting for Christians. Their occupation as tent-makers probably required spacious apartments, suited for the purpose of such assemblies.

20. All the brethren greet you. Greet ye one another with a holy kiss.

As *all the brethren* in this verse are distinguished from the church in the house of Aquila and Priscilla, mentioned in v. 19, it may be inferred that only a portion, and probably a small portion of the Christians of Ephesus were accustomed to meet in that place. The apostle exhorts them to *greet one another with a holy kiss*, Rom. 16, 16. 2 Cor. 13, 12. 1 Thess. 5, 26.

This was the conventional token of Christian affection. In the East the kiss was a sign either of friendship among equals, or of reverence and submission on the part of an inferior. The people kissed the images of their gods, and the hands of princes. In the early church, the custom was for Christians when they met to kiss; and in their assemblies, especially after the Lord's supper, this token of Christian brotherhood was interchanged. Paul seems here to request, that when his letter was publicly read, the members of the church would give to each other this pledge of mutual forgiveness and love.

21. The salutation of (me) Paul with mine own hand.

As Paul commonly wrote by an amanuensis, he was accustomed to write with his own hand the concluding sentences of his epistle as an authentication of them, Col. 4, 18. 2 Thess. 3, 17. He remarks in Gal. 6, 11, on his having written that epistle with his own hand as something unusual, and as indicating a peculiar stress of feeling.

22. If any man love not the Lord Jesus Christ, let him be Anathema. Maran atha.

This and what follows is what Paul himself wrote. They are words which need no explanation. They carry with them their awful import to every heart. *If any man love not our Lord Jesus Christ.* If our Lord be "God over all and blessed for ever," want of love to him is the violation of our whole duty. If he be not only truly God, but God manifested in the flesh for our salvation; if he unites in himself all divine and all human excellence; if he has so loved us as to unite our nature to his own, and to humble himself and become obedient unto death, even the death of the cross, that we might not perish, but have everlasting life; then our own hearts must assent to the justness of the malediction pronounced even against ourselves, if we do not love him. We must feel that in that case we deserve to be *anathema*. Nay, we thereby are a thing accursed; we are an object of execration and loathing to all holy beings by the same necessity that holiness is opposed to sin. *Maran atha* are two Aramæan words signifying "The Lord," or "our Lord comes." It is a solemn warning. The Lord, whom men refuse to recognize and love, is about to come in the glory of his Father and with all his holy angels, to take vengeance on those who know not God, and who obey not the gospel.   So deeply were the apostles impressed with the divinity of Christ, so fully were they convinced that Jesus was God manifest in the flesh, that the refusal or inability to recognize him as such, seemed to them a mark of reprobation. If this truth be hid, they say, it is hid to them that are lost, 2 Cor. 4, 3–6.

23.   The grace of our Lord Jesus Christ (be) with you.

As to be anathema from Christ, to be the subject of his curse, is everlasting perdition ; so his favour is eternal life. " May his love be with you," is a prayer for all good.

24.   My love (be) with you all in Christ Jesus. Amen.

" My love in Christ " is my Christian love.   Paul in conclusion assures them all, all the believers in Corinth, even those whom he had been called upon to reprove, of his sincere love.

2 CORINTHIANS

II. CORINTHIANS.

———•••———

CHAPTER I.

Paul's gratitude for the deliverance and consolation which he had experienced. Vs. 1–11.

AFTER the apostle had written his former letter to the Corinthians, and had sent Titus, either as the bearer of the letter or immediately after its having been sent by other hands, to ascertain the effect which it produced, he seems to have been in a state of unusual depression and anxiety. The persecutions to which he had been exposed in Asia placed him in continued danger of death, 1, 8; and his solicitude about the church in Corinth allowed him no inward peace, 7, 5. After leaving Ephesus he went to Troas; but although the most promising prospects of usefulness there presented themselves, he could not rest, but passed over into Macedonia in hopes of meeting Titus and obtaining from him intelligence from Corinth, 2, 12. 23. This letter is the outpouring of his heart occasioned by the information which he received. More than any other of Paul's epistles, it bears the impress of the strong feelings under the influence of which it was written. That the Corinthians had received his former letter with a proper spirit, that it brought them to repentance, led them to excommunicate the incestuous person, and called forth, on the part of the larger portion of the congregation, the manifestation of the warmest affection for the apostle, relieved his mind from a load of anxiety, and filled his heart with gratitude to God. On the other hand, the increased boldness and influence of the false teachers, the perverting errors which they inculcated, and the frivolous and calumnious charges which they brought against himself, filled him with indignation. This accounts for the abrupt transitions from one subject to another, the sudden changes of tone and manner which characterize this epistle. When writing to the Corinthians as a church obedient, affectionate, and penitent, there is no limit to his tenderness and love. His great desire seems to be to heal the temporary breach which had occurred between them, and to assure his readers that all was forgiven and forgotten, and that his heart was entirely theirs. But when he turns to the wicked, designing corrupters of the truth among them, there is a tone of severity to be found in no other of his writings, not even in his epistle to the Galatians. Erasmus compares this epistle to a river which sometimes flows in a gentle stream, sometimes rushes down as a torrent bearing all before it; sometimes spreading out like a placid lake; sometimes losing itself, as it were, in the sand, and breaking out in its fulness in some unexpected place. Though perhaps the least methodical of Paul's writings, it is among the most interesting of his letters as bringing out the man before the reader and revealing his intimate relations to the people for whom he laboured. The remark must be borne in mind (often made before), that the full play allowed to the peculiarities of mind and feeling of the sacred writers, is in no way inconsistent with their plenary inspiration. The grace of God in conversion does not change the natural character of its subjects, but accommodates itself to all their peculiarities of disposition and temperament. And the same is true with regard to the influence of the Spirit in inspiration.

The salutation in this epistle is nearly in the same words as in the former letter, vs. 1. 2. Here also as there, the introduction is a thanksgiving. As these expressions of gratitude are not mere forms, but genuine effusions of the heart, they vary according to the circumstances under which each epistle was written. Here the thanksgiving was for consolation. Paul blesses God as the God of all mercy for the consolation which he had experienced. He associates, or rather identifies himself with the Corinthians; representing his afflictions as theirs and his consolation also as belonging to them, vs. 3–7. He refers to the afflictions which came upon him in Asia, so that he despaired of life, but through their prayers God who had delivered, still delivered, and he was assured, would continue to deliver him, vs. 8–11.

1. 2. Paul, an apostle of Jesus Christ by the will of God, and Timothy (our) brother, unto the church of God which is at Corinth, with all the saints which are in all Achaia : Grace (be) to you, and peace, from God our Father, and (from) our Lord Jesus Christ.

The sense in which the word *apostle* is to be here taken, the force of the expression *by the will of God*, the scriptural meaning of the words *church* and *saints*, are all stated in the remarks on the first verse of the former epistle. In the first epistle Paul associates Sosthenes with himself in the salutation ; here it is Timothy who is mentioned. In neither case is there any community of office or authority implied. On the contrary, a marked distinction is made between Paul the apostle and Sosthenes or Timothy the brother, i. e. the Christian companion of the apostle. From 1 Cor. 4, 17 it appears that Timothy was in Macedonia, on his way to Corinth, when the first epistle was written. From the form of expression (if Timothy come) in 1 Cor. 16, 10, and from the absence of any intimation in this epistle that Paul had received from him the information from Corinth which he was so desirous to obtain, it is doubtful whether Timothy had been able to reach that city. At any rate he was now with the apostle at Nicopolis or some other city in Macedonia. *With all the saints which are in all Achaia.* This epistle was not intended exclusively for the Christians in Corinth, but also for all the believers scattered through the province who were connected with the church in Corinth. These believers were probably not collected into separate congregations, otherwise the apostle would have used the plural form, as when writing to the *churches* of Galatia, Gal. 1, 3. Achaia was originally the name of the northern part of the Peloponnesus including Corinth and its isthmus. Augustus divided the whole country into the two provinces, Macedonia and Achaia; the former included Macedonia proper, Illyricum, Epirus and Thessaly ;

and the latter all the southern part of Greece. It is in this wide sense *Achaia* is always used in the New Testament. From this it appears that the converts to Christianity in Greece were at this time very few out of Corinth, as they were all members of the church in that city. *Grace* and *peace*, the favour of God and its fruits, comprehend all the benefits of redemption. The apostle's prayer is not only that believers may be the objects of the love of God our Father and of Jesus Christ our Lord, but that they may have the assurance of that love. He knew that the sense of the love of God would keep their hearts in perfect peace. God is our Father, Jesus Christ is our Lord. Every one feels the distinction in this relationship, whether he reduces it to clear conceptions in his own mind or not. God, as God, is our father because he is the father of all spirits, and because, if believers, we are born again by his Spirit, and adopted as his children, made the objects of his love and the heirs of his kingdom. Jesus Christ, the eternal Son of God clothed in our nature, is our Lord, for two reasons: first, because as God he is our absolute sovereign; and secondly, because as Redeemer he has purchased us by his own most precious blood. To him, therefore, as God and Redeemer, our allegiance as Christians is specially due.

3. Blessed (be) God, even the Father of our Lord Jesus Christ, the Father of mercies, and God of all comfort.

This richness and variety of designations for the object of his reverence and gratitude, shows how full was the apostle's heart, and how it yearned after fellowship with God, to whom he places himself in every possible connection by thus multiplying the terms expressive of the relations which God bears to his redeemed people. *Blessed.* The word εὐλογητός (*blessed*) is used in the New Testament only of God. (In Luke 1, 28, where the Virgin Mary is spoken of, εὐλογημένη is used.) It expresses at once gratitude and adoration. Adored be God! is the expression of the highest veneration and thankfulness. It is not God merely as God, but as *the Father of our Lord Jesus Christ* who is the object of the apostle's adoration and gratitude. The expression does not refer to the miraculous conception of our Lord, but the person addressed is he whose eternal Son assumed our nature, who, as invested with that nature, is our Lord Jesus Christ. It is he who so loved the world that he gave his only-begotten Son, that whoso believeth in him might not perish but have everlasting life. It is therefore the peculiar, characteristic Christian designation of God, as it presents him as the God of redemption. Rom. 15, 6. 2 Cor. 11, 31. Col. 1, 3. 1 Pet. 1, 3. This God who has revealed himself as the God of love in sending his Son for our redemption, the apostle still further designates as *the Father of mercies*, i. e. the most merciful Father; he whose characteristic is mercy. Comp. Ps. 86, 5. 15. Dan. 9, 9. Micah 7, 18.   The explanation which makes the expression mean *the author of mercies* is inconsistent with the signification of the word οἰκτιρμός, which always means *mercy* as a feeling. *The God of all comfort.* This most merciful Father is the God, i. e. the author of all, i. e. of all possible, consolation. God is the author of consolation not only by delivering us from evil, or by ordering our external circumstances, but also, and chiefly, by his inward influence on the mind itself, assuaging its tumults and filling it with joy and peace in believing. Rom. 15, 13.

4. Who comforteth us in all our tribulation, that we may be able to comfort them which are in any trouble, by the comfort wherewith we ourselves are comforted of God.

Us here refers to the apostle himself. Throughout this chapter he is speaking of his own personal trials and consolations. He blessed God as the author of comfort, because he had experienced his consolations. And the design, he adds, of God in afflicting and in consoling was to qualify him for the office of a consoler of the afflicted. In this design Paul acquiesced; he was willing to be thus afflicted in order to be the bearer of consolation to others. A life of ease is commonly stagnant. It is those who suffer much and who experience much of the comfort of the Holy Ghost, who live much. Their life is rich in experience and in resources. *In all our tribulation*, i. e. on account of (ἐπί). His tribulation was the ground or reason why God comforted him. The apostle was one of the most afflicted of men. He suffered from hunger, cold, nakedness, stripes, imprisonment, from perils by sea and land, from robbers, from the Jews, from the heathen, so that his life was a continued death, or, as he expressed it, he died daily. Besides these external afflictions he was overwhelmed with cares and anxiety for the churches. And as though all this were not enough, he had "a thorn in the flesh, a messenger of Satan," to buffet him. See 11, 24–30, and 12, 7. In the midst of all these trials God not only sustained him, but filled him with such a heroic spirit that he actually rejoiced in being thus afflicted. "I take pleasure," he says, "in infirmities, in reproaches, in necessities, in persecutions, in distresses for Christ's sake; for when I am weak, then am I strong," 12, 10. This state of mind can be experienced only by those who are so filled with the love of Christ, that they rejoice in every thing, however painful to themselves, whereby his glory is promoted. And where this state of mind exists, no afflictions can equal the consolations by which they are attended, and therefore the apostle adds, that he was enabled to comfort those who were in any kind of affliction by the comfort wherewith he was comforted of God.

5. For as the sufferings of Christ abound in us, so our consolation aboundeth by Christ.

This is a confirmation of what precedes. 'We are able to comfort others, *for* our consolations are equal to our sufferings.' *The sufferings of Christ*, do not mean 'sufferings on account of Christ,' which the force of the genitive case does not admit; nor sufferings which Christ endures in his own members; but such sufferings as Christ suffered, and which his people are called upon to endure in virtue of their union with him and in order to be like him. Our Lord said to his disciples, "Ye shall indeed drink of my cup, and be baptized with the baptism wherewith I am baptized with," Matt. 20, 23. Paul speaks of his *fellowship*, or participation in the sufferings of Christ, Phil. 3, 10; and the apostle Peter calls upon believers to rejoice, inasmuch as they are "partakers of Christ's sufferings," 1 Peter 4, 24. Comp. Rom. 8, 17. Col. 1, 24. Gal. 6, 17. In many other passages it is taught that believers must share in the sufferings, if they are to be partakers of the glory of Christ. *So*, i. e. in equal measure, *our consolation aboundeth through Christ*. As union with Christ was the source of the afflictions which Paul endured, so it was the source of the abundant consolation which he enjoyed. This makes the great difference between the sorrows of believers and those of unbelievers. Alienation from Christ does not secure freedom from suffering, but it cuts us off from the only source of consolation. Therefore the sorrow of the world worketh death.

6, 7. And whether we be afflicted, (it is) for your consolation and salvation, which is effectual to the enduring of the same sufferings which we also suffer : or whether we be comforted, (it is) for your consolation and salvation. And our hope of you (is) stedfast, knowing that as ye are partakers of the sufferings, so (shall ye be) also of the consolation.

Although the ancient manuscripts differ very much in the order in which the several clauses of these verses are arranged, yet the sense expressed in all is substantially the same. The text adopted by Beza, Griesbach, Knapp, Meyer, &c., on the authority of the manuscripts A, C, and several of the ancient versions, reads thus, "Whether we be afflicted, (it is) for your consolation and salvation; whether we are comforted, (it is) for your consolation, which is effectual in enduring the same sufferings which we also suffer; and our hope of you is stedfast, knowing that as ye are partakers of the suffering, so also (shall ye be) of the consolation." The reading adopted by Lachmann, Tischendorf, Rückert and others, differs from the common text in placing the clause *our hope of you is stedfast*, immediately after the first member of the sentence, and before the words, *whether we are comforted*. For this arrangement are the MSS. B, D, E, F, G, I. The reading of Beza gives the text in its simplest and most perspicuous form. In either way the main idea is, ' Whether we be afflicted, it is for your good; or whether we be comforted, it is for your good.' All the rest is subordinate. The relation in which the apostle stood to the Corinthians was such that he felt assured that they would share both in his sufferings and in his consolation, and therefore experience the benefit of both. It was not that Paul's constancy in suffering set them a good example; nor simply that Paul suffered in behalf of the Gospel, and therefore for the benefit of others; nor does he mean merely that the experience of the Corinthians would correspond to his, if they were similarly afflicted, they would be similarly comforted; but the main idea is that such was the intimate bond between them and him that he had a firm hope they would be partakers both of his affliction and of his consolation. Though this appears to be the primary idea of the passage, the others are not to be excluded. Paul no doubt felt, and intended to intimate, that his diversified experience would redound to their advantage by qualifying him more abundantly for his work, and especially for the office of consoling them in the afflictions which they, as well as he, would be called to endure. *Whether we be afflicted* (it is) *for your consolation and salvation;* i. e. my afflictions will contribute to your consolation and salvation. To the former, because those whom God afflicts, or, who suffer for Christ's sake and with Christ's people, God never fails to console; to the latter, because suffering and salvation are so intimately connected. "If we suffer with him we shall also be glorified together," Rom. 8, 17. It is not of suffering as suffering that the apostle here speaks. There is no tendency in pain to produce holiness. It is only of Christian suffering and of the sufferings of Christians, that is, of suffering endured for Christ and in a Christian manner, that the apostle says it is connected with salvation, or that it tends to work out for those who suffer an eternal weight of glory. *Or whether we be comforted it is for your consolation.* That is, our consolation is also yours. If we are consoled, so are you. If we suffer together, we rejoice together. Or, if you suffer as I do, you will enjoy similar consolation. My being consoled enables me to console you. According to the common text the reading here is, "your consolation *and salvation.*" But the repetition of the words *and salvation* is not sustained by some of the oldest manuscripts, and they do not cohere so well with the following clause; as it can hardly be said that "salvation is effectual in enduring affliction." On these grounds, as before remarked, Beza and many other editors omit the words in question. *Which is effectual;* that is, which consolation is operative or efficacious, not *to* the enduring, as in our version, but *in* the enduring (ἐν ὑπομονῇ). This consolation shows its efficacy in the patient endurance of suffering. According to another interpretation ἐνεργουμένης is taken passively, *which is wrought out.* The sense would then be good. 'This consolation is wrought out or experienced in patient endurance.' But as Paul always uses this word actively, the rendering adopted in our version is generally and properly preferred. *The same sufferings which I also suffer.* The sufferings of the Corinthians were the same with those of the apostle, because they sympathized in his afflictions, because they in a measure suffered as he did, and because their sufferings were "the sufferings of Christ," in the same sense that his were. They were not only such sufferings as Christ endured, but they were incurred because those who suffered were Christians. *And our hope of you is stedfast.* That is, 'we have a stedfast hope that you will be partakers of our consolation.' *Knowing*, i. e. because we know, *that as ye are partakers of the sufferings, so also of the consolation.* The two go together. Those who share in our sorrows, share in our joys. There are two ideas apparently united here as in the preceding context. The one is that the sufferings of the apostle were also the sufferings of the Corinthians because of the union between them. The other is, that his readers were in their measure exposed to the same kind of sufferings. In this twofold sense they were the κοινωνοί, the communicants or joint-partakers of his joys and sorrows.

8. For we would not, brethren, have you ignorant of our trouble, which came to us in Asia, that we were pressed out of measure, above strength, insomuch that we despaired even of life.

The apostle confirms from the facts of his recent history, what he had said of his afflictions. *Asia* is probably to be understood here in reference to proconsular Asia, which comprehended the western provinces of Asia Minor, viz., Mysia, Lydia, Caria, and part of Phrygia. What afflictions and dangers the apostle here refers to is uncertain. It is generally assumed that he alludes to the uproar in Ephesus, of which mention is made in Acts 19, 23–41. But to this it is objected that Paul does not appear to have been in personal danger during that tumult; that instead of saying *in Asia* he would probably have said *in Ephesus*, had he referred to that special event; and that the language used seems obviously to imply a succession and continuance of severe trials. Others think that the reference is to some severe illness. But there is nothing in the context to indicate that particular form of affliction. Neither could *illness* naturally be included under the "afflictions of Christ," under which head the apostle com-

prehends all the afflictions to which in this connection he refers. The probability is that he alludes to trials of different
kinds, and especially to plots and attempts against his life.
He was surrounded by enemies, Jews and heathen, who thirst-
ed for his blood. And we know, as remarked above, that the
Acts of the Apostles contains the record of only a small portion of his afflictions. *That we were pressed,* ἐβαρήθημεν, *we
were burdened.* The allusion is to a wearied animal that sinks
in despair under a burden beyond its strength. *Out of measure, above strength ;* if thus separated, the former of these
phrases refers to the character of his afflictions in themselves,
' they were excessive ; ' and the latter, expresses their relation
to his ability to bear them. Absolutely, they were too great,
relatively, they were above his strength. Many commentators make the former qualify the latter, " We were burdened
far beyond our strength " (καθ᾽ ὑπερβολὴν ὑπὲρ δύναμιν). *Insomuch that we despaired even of life.* The expression is intensive, ἐξαπορηθῆναι, *to be utterly at a loss,* or, absolutely
without a way (πόρος) of escape. It seemed impossible to the
apostle that he could escape from the enemies who beset him
on every side. These enemies were not only men, but perils
and trials of all kinds.

9. But we had the sentence of death in ourselves, that we should not trust in ourselves, but in God who raiseth the dead.

So far from expecting to live, the apostle says, *on the contrary* (ἀλλά) he had in himself *the sentence of death.* This
may mean that he was as one who was actually condemned to
die. God appeared to have passed upon him the sentence of
death, from which there could be no reprieve. This supposes
ἀπόκριμα to have the sense of κατάκριμα. This meaning of the
word is very doubtful. It properly signifies *response, answer.*
' We had in ourselves the answer of death.' That is, when he
put to himself the question, whether life or death was to be
the issue of his conflicts, the answer was, Death! In other
words, he did not expect to escape with his life. God brought
him into these straits *in order that* he might not trust in himself, but in God who raiseth the dead. These two things are
so connected that the former is the necessary condition of the
latter. There is no such thing as implicit confidence or reli-

ance on God, until we renounce all confidence in ourself. When Paul was convinced that no wisdom nor efforts of his own could deliver him from death, then he was forced to rely on the power of God. God is here described as he *who raiseth the dead*, because the apostle's deliverance was a deliverance from death. It was only that Being who could call the dead to life who could rescue him from the imminent peril in which he was placed. So when Abraham's faith was put to the severe trial of believing what was apparently impossible, it is said, "He believed God who quickeneth the dead, and calleth those things which be not as though they were," Rom. 4, 17. Comp. Heb. 11, 19. No man until he is tried knows how essential the omnipotence of God is as a ground of confidence to his people. They are often placed in circumstances where nothing short of an almighty helper can give them peace.

10. Who delivered us from so great a death, and doth deliver : in whom we trust that he will yet deliver (us).

Paul's trust in God was not disappointed. He did deliver him from *such a death*, i. e. one so fearful and apparently so inevitable. It is evident from the whole context that the apostle had not only been in imminent peril, but exposed to a more than ordinarily painful death. Whether this was from disease or from enemies is a matter of conjecture. The latter is the more probable. Though he had been delivered from the instant and fearful death with which he was threatened, the danger was not over. The machinations of his enemies followed him wherever he went. He therefore says that God had not only delivered, but that he continued to deliver him. He was still beset with danger. He was however confident for the future. For he adds, *in whom we trust*, εἰς ὃν ἠλπίκαμεν, *on whom we have placed our hope that he will also henceforth deliver*. He did, he does, he will, deliver, ἐρρύσατο, ῥύεται, ῥύσεται. The experience of past deliverances and mercies is the ground of present peace and of confidence for the future. These words of Paul sound continually in the ears of the people of God in all times of emergency.

11. Ye also helping together by prayer for us, that

for the gift (bestowed) upon us by the means of many persons, thanks may be given by many on our behalf.

Intercessory prayer has great power, otherwise Paul would not so often solicit it on his own behalf, and enjoin the duty on his readers. His confidence in his safety for the future was not founded simply on the experience of God's past mercy, but also on the prayers of Christians in his behalf. God will yet deliver me, he says, *you also helping together by prayer*. That is, provided you join your prayers with those of others for my safety. *Helping together* probably refers to their co-operation in the work of intercession with other churches, rather than with the apostle himself. The design of God in thus uniting his people in praying for each other when in affliction or danger, is that the deliverance may be matter of common gratulation and praise. Thus all hearts are drawn out to God and Christian fellowship is promoted. This is expressed in the latter part of this verse; *that*, i. e. in order that *the gift being bestowed on us by means of many* (διὰ πολλῶν) *thanks may be rendered by many* (ἐκ πολλῶν). In the Greek it is ἐκ πολλῶν προσώπων, which most commentators render as our translators do, *by many persons*. The word πρόσωπον, however, always elsewhere in the New Testament means *face* or *presence*, which sense many retain here. 'That thanks may be rendered from many (upturned) faces.' According to the interpretation given above, the words διὰ πολλῶν are connected with τὸ χάρισμα, "the favour to us by means of many;" and ἐκ πολλῶν προσώπων with εὐχαρεσθῇ, 'thanks may be rendered by many persons (or faces).' This gives a good sense, and is perhaps better suited to the force of the prepositions ἐκ and διά. It is more correct to say that the 'favour was (διά) by means of many,' i. e. by means of their prayer, than that it 'was (ἐκ) *out of*, or *by*,' as expressing the efficient cause. The order of the clauses, however, favours the connection adopted by our translators. 'The favour was by many persons, and the thanks to be rendered by means of many.' This construction of the sentence is also sanctioned by the majority of commentators.

The apostle's defence against the charge of inconstancy.
Vs. 12–24.

Paul had informed the Corinthians that it was his purpose

to go direct from Ephesus to Corinth, thence into Macedonia, and back again to Corinth, v. 16. This plan he had been induced to modify before the former epistle was sent, as in 1 Cor. 16, 5 he tells them he would not visit them until he had passed through Macedonia. On this slight ground his enemies in Corinth represented him as saying one thing and meaning another. They seem also to have made this an occasion for charging him with like inconsistency in doctrine. If his word could not be depended on in small matters, what dependence could be placed on his preaching? Paul shows there was no levity or insincerity involved in this change of his plans, and no inconsistency in his preaching; but that to spare them he had deferred his visit to Corinth, vs. 12–24.

12. For our rejoicing is this, the testimony of our conscience, that in simplicity and godly sincerity, not in fleshly wisdom, but by the grace of God, we have had our conversation in the world, and more abundantly to you-ward.

The connection between this verse and what precedes, as indicated by the particle *for*, is, 'I look for your sympathy in my afflictions, and for your prayers in my behalf, *for* my conscience bears testimony to the simplicity and sincerity of my conversation among you.' Unless we are conscious of integrity towards others, we cannot be assured of their confidence in us. *Our rejoicing*, says Paul, *is this, the testimony of our conscience.* This may mean that the testimony of conscience was the *ground* of his rejoicing. This assumes a metonymical sense of the καύχησις, a meaning which is often attributed to the word. But as the word may express the inward feeling of exultation as well as the outward expression of it, which latter is its proper sense, the meaning may be (without assuming any metonomy), 'My joyful confidence consists in the consciousness of sincerity.' The testimony of the conscience is consciousness; and that of which Paul was conscious was integrity. And that consciousness sustained and elevated him. It was in its nature a joy. What follows is explanatory. His conscience testified that *in simplicity and godly sincerity*, &c. The word ἁπλότης means *singleness of mind*, the opposite of duplicity. The ancient manuscripts Α, B, C, read ἁγιότης, *purity* or *sanctity*, which the recent editors generally adopt. The former word is much more common in Paul's writings, and is better suited to the following term, εἰλικρίνεια, which means *translucence*, clearness, sincerity of mind. It is called the *sincerity of God*, which our translators explain as meaning *godly sincerity*, either in the sense of religious, as distinguished from mere natural sincerity as a moral virtue; or in the sense of *divine*, what comes from God. The latter is the true explanation. It is the sincerity which God gives. The Bible often uses such expressions as "the peace of God," "joy of the Spirit," &c., meaning the peace or joy of which God or the Spirit is the author. There is a specific difference between moral virtues and spiritual graces, although they are called by the same names. Simplicity, sincerity, meekness, long-suffering, when the fruits of the Spirit differ from the moral virtues designated by those terms, as many external things, though similar in appearance, often differ in their inward nature. A religious man and a moral man may be very much alike in the eyes of men, though the inward life of the latter is human, and that of the former is divine. What Paul means here to say is, that the virtues which distinguished his deportment in Corinth were not merely forms of his own excellence, but forms of the divine life; modes in which the Spirit of God which dwelt in him manifested itself. This is expressed more clearly in what follows. *Not in fleshly wisdom*, that is, not in that wisdom which has its origin in our own nature. The familiar meaning of the word *flesh* in the New Testament, especially in the writings of St. Paul, is human nature as it now is, as distinguished from the Spirit of God. " Ye are not in the flesh," says this apostle, " but in the Spirit, if so be that the Spirit of God dwell in you," Rom. 8, 9. As our nature is corrupt, natural or fleshly necessarily involves more or less the idea of corruption. The natural man, carnal mind, fleshly wisdom, all imply that idea more or less, according to the context. *Fleshly wisdom*, therefore, is that kind of wisdom which unrenewed men are wont to exhibit, wisdom guided by principles of self-interest or expediency. It stands opposed to *the grace of God*. Paul was not guided by the former, but by the latter. The grace of God controlled his conduct; and by grace is here meant, as so often elsewhere, the gracious influences of the Spirit. *We have had our conversation ;* ἀνεστράφημεν, *we moved about*, we conducted ourselves. The expression includes all the mani-

festations of his inward life. *In the world*, i. e. among men
generally; *and more especially to you-ward.* That is, the
evidence of my sincerity is much more abundant to you than
to others. The Corinthians had enjoyed more opportunities
of learning the character of the apostle, and of seeing his simplicity and integrity, than the world, or men outside of the
church, had possessed. He could therefore the more confidently assume that they confided in him.

13. 14. For we write none other things unto you,
than what ye read or acknowledge, and I trust ye shall
acknowledge even to the end; as also ye have acknowledged us in part, that we are your rejoicing,
even as ye also (are) ours in the day of the Lord
Jesus.

The same sincerity and honesty marked his correspondence that characterized his life. He never wrote one thing
and meant another. The connection with the preceding verse
is, ‘We are perfectly honest, *for* we write none other things
than what ye read.’ The simple, obvious meaning of my letter, is the true meaning. *I write*, i. e. I mean none other
things than what you-understand me to intend when you
read my letters, *or know* from other sources. The word
ἐπιγινώσκετε may be rendered as in our version, *ye acknowledge.* The sense would then be, ‘I mean nothing else but
what you read or acknowledge to be my meaning.’ But this
is not so clear. The design of the apostle is to show that his
purposes really were what his letters indicated, or what the
Corinthians, by other means, had been led to understand them
to be. The words are, “Ye read, *or also* (ἢ καί) know,” *and
I trust ye shall acknowledge to the end.* This clause may be
connected with what precedes. ‘I mean what you know, and
I trust shall continue to acknowledge, to be my meaning.’
That is, ‘I have confidence that you will not misunderstand
or misinterpret my intentions until we all come to the end;’
ἕως τέλους, *to the end*, either of life, or of the world. A much
better sense is obtained by connecting this clause with what
follows, so that the clause (ὅτι καύχημα ὑμῶν ἐσμεν), *that we are
your rejoicing*, is the object of the verb (ἐπιγνώσεσθε) *ye shall*

acknowledge. 'I trust ye shall acknowledge unto the end (as ye have acknowledged us in part), that we are your rejoicing.' The verb ἐπιγινώσκειν combines the ideas of recognition and of complete knowledge. The words *in part* are most naturally referred to the Corinthians, *ye in part*, i. e. a part of you. Paul knew that there were some in Corinth who did not rejoice in him. Others understand them to qualify the verb. It was only a partial recognition of him that the Corinthians had as yet manifested. Compare 1 Cor. 13, 12, "I know in part." This, however, would give a tone of reproach to the language which is foreign to the character of the passage. *We are your rejoicing*, i. e. the ground of your exultation and delight. *As ye also ours, in the day of the Lord Jesus.* Paul believed that in the day of the Lord Jesus the Corinthians would rejoice over him as he would rejoice over them. In that day they would appreciate the blessedness of having had him for their teacher, as he would rejoice in having had them for his converts. The joy, however, which he anticipated in its fulness when Christ should come, was in a measure already theirs. 'We are, and shall be, your rejoicing, as ye are and shall be ours, in the day of the Lord Jesus.' Instead of rendering ὅτι in the above clause *that* many commentators render it *because*. This gives a different sense to the whole passage. 'We hope you will acknowledge—*because* we are your rejoicing, as ye are ours.' This, however, leaves the verb *acknowledge* without an object. What were they to acknowledge? We may indeed supply from the context the words *our sincerity*, but it is more natural so to construe the passage as to avoid the necessity of supplying any thing. The sense also is better according to the common interpretation. Paul does not design to prove that the Corinthians confided in him because he was their rejoicing, which would be to prove a thing by itself.

15. 16. And in this confidence I was minded to come to you before that ye might have a second benefit; to pass by you into Macedonia, and to come again out of Macedonia unto you, and of you to be brought on my way to Judea.

And in this confidence, that is, in the confidence that we are your rejoicing, Paul was not afraid to go to Corinth. He did not doubt that the great majority of the church would receive him with confidence and affection. The change in the plan of his journey arose, as he afterwards states, from very different motives. Paul says *he was minded,* i. e. intended to come to them *before,* i. e. before going to Macedonia; *that ye might have a second benefit,* i. e. the benefit of seeing me twice, once before going to Macedonia, and again after my return. The other explanation of this passage is, that *second* here refers to his first visit to Corinth. The first benefit was their conversion, the second would be the good effects to be anticipated from another visit. But it appears from 12, 14 and other passages that Paul had already been twice in Corinth, and therefore he could not speak of his intended visit as the second; and the word *second* here evidently refers to the word *before.* He was to see them *before* and *after* going to Macedonia. *Benefit,* χαρίν, *grace,* a term generally in the New Testament used of religious blessings. The word sometimes signifies *joy,* so the sense here may be, 'That ye might have the pleasure of seeing me twice.' The former explanation is not only better suited to the common use of the word, but also gives a higher sense. *And of you to be brought on my way to Judea.* Προπεμφθῆναι, *to be brought on my way,* i. e. to be aided in my journey. The word often, and perhaps most frequently, means *to escort* on a journey, or to furnish with the means of travelling. Acts 15, 3. 20, 38. &c. In ancient times when there were no established modes of travelling, it was customary for the friends of the traveller in one city to send him forward to the next, or at least to escort him on his way. This office of friendship Paul was willing and desirous to receive at the hands of the Corinthians. He was not alienated from them. And his purpose to seek this kindness from them was a proof of his confidence in their affection for him.

17. When therefore I was thus minded did I use lightness? or the things that I purpose, do I purpose according to the flesh, that with me there should be yea, yea, and nay, nay?

Paul did not execute the plan of his journey above indicated. His having changed his purpose was made the ground of a twofold charge against him; first, of levity, and secondly, of inconsistency; saying one thing, and doing another; or saying one thing at one time, and the opposite at another, so that he was utterly untrustworthy either as a man or as a teacher. This was indeed a slight foundation on which to rest such a charge. It is no wonder therefore that it excited the apostle's indignation. The first charge is that he *used lightness*, i. e. that in purposing to visit Corinth and in announcing his purpose he had no serious intention of doing what he promised. It was a careless, inconsiderate avowal such as none but a man of levity would make. In the Greek the article is used (τῇ ἐλαφρίᾳ) *the* lightness, which may mean, *the* lightness with which they charged him; or that which belongs to our nature; or it may have no more force than when used in other cases before abstract nouns. *Or the things that I purpose, do I purpose according to the flesh?* The first charge related to the past, *did* I use lightness? This relates to his general character. 'Am I habitually governed in my plans by the flesh,' i. e. am I influenced and controlled by those considerations which govern ordinary men, who have nothing to guide them but their own corrupt nature? The word *flesh* here, as in v. 12, stands for our whole nature, considered as distinguished from the Spirit of God. All who are not *spiritual* (governed by the Spirit) are, according to the Scripture, *carnal* (governed by the flesh). What Paul therefore intends to deny in these two questions, is that his original purpose of visiting Corinth was formed in levity, and secondly, that his plans in general were controlled by worldly or selfish considerations. *That with me there should be yea, yea, and nay, nay. That* (ἵνα) here expresses the result, not the design. 'Do I so act after the flesh that the consequence is,' &c. The repetition of the particles *yea, yea,* and *nay, nay,* is simply intensive, as in Matthew 5, 37, "Let your communication be yea, yea, and nay, nay." The meaning, therefore, is, 'Do I affirm and deny the same thing? Do I say both yes and no at the same time and in reference to the same subject? Is no dependence to be placed on my word?' This is the common interpretation and the one demanded by the context. Many commentators from Chrysostom downwards give a very different view of the passage. They understand the apostle to defend himself for his change of plan by saying that he was not like men of the world who obstinately adhered to their purposes, without regard to the manifested will of God, so that with him a yea should be yea, and a nay, nay, let what would be the consequence. But in the 18th v. this interpretation is impossible, because it is there simply " yea and nay." That verse therefore determines the meaning of this. Besides, what he goes on to defend himself against is not a charge of obstinacy, but of saying first one thing and then another. Luther's translation assumes still another interpretation. "Are my purposes carnal? *Not so,* but my yea is yea, and my nay is nay." But this arbitrarily introduces into the text what is not expressed, and thus changes the whole sense.

18. But as God is true, our word towards you was not yea and nay.

That is, ' My preaching, or the doctrine which I preached, was not inconsistent and contradictory. I did not preach first one thing and then another.' This sudden transition from the question as to his veracity as a man to his consistency as a preacher, shows two things; first, that his enemies had brought both charges against him, founding the latter on the former; and secondly, that Paul was much more concerned for the gospel than for his own reputation. They might accuse him, if they pleased, of breaking his word; but when they charged him with denying Christ, that was a very different affair. He therefore drops the first charge and turns abruptly to the second. 'Whatever you may think of my veracity as a man, as God is true, my preaching was not yea and nay,' i. e. unworthy of confidence. *As God is true.* The words are, *God is faithful, that,* &c. Comp. 1 Cor. 1, 9. 10, 13. 1 Thess. 5, 24. They may be understood as an appeal to the fidelity of God as the ground and evidence of the truth and reliableness of his preaching. 'God is faithful, *that* our preaching is not yea and nay.' That is, his fidelity secures the trustworthiness of the gospel. It is his word and therefore is unchangeably true. It abideth forever. 'If,' says the apostle, ' there is no dependence to be placed on my word, God is trustworthy. My preaching, which is his word, is to be relied upon. That is not yea and nay, but firm and true.' It must be admitted, however, that this interpretation is constrained; it is not the simple meaning of the words. The passage must be paraphrased to get this sense out of it. It is perhaps better with our translators, after Calvin, Beza, and many other commentators, ancient and modern, to take the words as an asseveration. *So true as God is faithful*, so true is it, *that*, &c. Comp. 11, 10, ἔστιν ἡ ἀλήθεια Χριστοῦ ἐν ἐμοί, ὅτι. Rom. 14, 11, ζῶ ἐγώ—ὅτι, *as I live—every knee shall bow to me*. Judith 12, 4, ζῇ ἡ ψυχή σου—ὅτι. It is therefore according to the usage of the language to understand πιστὸς ὁ θεός—ὅτι as an oath, and the sense given is much more natural. An oath is an act of worship. To predict that men shall everywhere swear by the name of Jehovah, Is. 65, 16, is to predict that Jehovah shall everywhere be worshipped. Men may, therefore, appeal to God for the truth of what they say on any solemn occasion, if they do it devoutly as an act of worship. It is a formal recognition of his being, of his omniscience, of his holiness and power, and of his moral government. Our Lord himself did not refuse to answer when put upon his oath, Matt. 27, 63; and the apostles often call on God to witness the truth of their declarations. When, therefore, our Saviour commands us, " Swear not at all," he must be understood to forbid profane swearing, that is, calling on God in an irreverent manner and on trivial occasions. *That our word towards you was not yea and nay;* ὁ λόγος ἡμῶν. This may mean *our preaching*, 1 Cor. 1, 17. 2, 1. 4, and often; or, *our word* generally, i. e. what I said. The apostle may be understood to assert the truth and consistency of his instructions as a teacher, or the trustworthiness of his declarations and promises as a man. The decision depends on the context. In favour of the latter it is urged that the charge against him, as intimated in v. 17, was that of breaking his promise, and therefore to make this verse refer to his preaching is to make him evade the point entirely. But the following verses, which are intimately connected with the one before us, clearly refer to matters of doctrine, and therefore this verse must have the same reference. The sudden transition from the charge of levity in v. 17, to that of false doctrine in v. 18, as before remarked, is sufficiently accounted for from the association of the two charges in the minds of his enemies. They said he was not to be depended upon as a preacher, because he had shown himself to be untrustworthy as a man. " As God is true, my preaching is true." The one is as true as the other. Hence in Gal. 1, 8 he pronounces an angel accursed should he preach another gospel. Paul's confidence in the truth of the gospel as he preached it was one and the same with his confi-

dence in God. To tell him that his preaching was not to be
depended upon, was in his mind the same as to say that God
was not to be believed; for he knew that he was the infallible
organ of God in all his teaching. 1 John 5, 10.

19. For the Son of God, Jesus Christ, who was
preached among you by us, (even) by me and Silvanus
and Timotheus, was not yea and nay, but in him was yea.

My preaching is true, for Christ is true. There is no contradiction, no yea and nay, in him, therefore there is no contradiction in my doctrine. There was no room in Paul's mind
for doubt as to his preaching being a trustworthy exhibition
of the person and work of Christ, and therefore if Christ be
one and the same, i. e. self-consistent truth, so was his doctrine or teaching. With such self-evidencing light and irresistible conviction does the Spirit attend his communications
to the human mind. Even in ordinary religious experience,
the testimony of the Spirit becomes the testimony of consciousness. Much more was this the case when plenary inspiration
was combined with the sanctifying power of the truth. *The
Son of God, Jesus Christ;* that is, Christ, who is the Son of
God, the same in nature with the eternal Father, and because
he is the Son, and, therefore, eternally and immutably true,
was not yea and nay. There was nothing in him contradictory or untrustworthy. This Christ *was* preached in Corinth
by Paul, Silvanus and Timotheus. These persons are mentioned because the apostle probably refers to his first visit to
Corinth when they were his companions. Acts 18, 5. His
appeal is to the experience of his readers. They had found
Christ to be the way, the truth and the life. He had been
made unto them wisdom, righteousness, sanctification and redemption. 1 Cor. 1, 32. By *Christ* here the apostle does
not mean the doctrine of Christ. He does not intend to assert simply that there was perfect consistency in his own
preaching, and that it agreed with the preaching of his associates. The truth asserted is that Christ, the Son of God, had
not been manifested among them, or experienced by them to
be unsatisfying or uncertain, but *in him was yea.* That is,
he was simple truth. *In him,* i. e. in Christ, was truth. He
proved himself to be all that was affirmed of him. He was
and continued to be (γέγονεν) all that they had been led to

expect. Let, therefore, what will become of me and of my
reputation for veracity, Christ is the same yesterday, to-day,
and forever.

20. For all the promises of God in him are yea,
and in him amen, unto the glory of God by us.

This verse is the confirmation of what precedes. Christ
was, and is, not yea and nay, not uncertain and inconsistent,
for in him all the promises of God were fulfilled. All that
God had promised relative to the salvation of man met its full
accomplishment in him. Instead of, *all the promises*, the
Greek is, *as many promises*. That is, as many promises as
had from the beginning been made as to what the Messiah
was to be and to do. *In him were the yea.* That is, in him
they found their affirmation or accomplishment. The article
(τὸ ναί), *the* yea, has reference to the promises. Christ, as regards the promises of God, was *the* yea, i. e. their affirmation
and accomplishment. *And in him the Amen.* This is saying in Hebrew what had just been said in Greek; *Amen* being equivalent to *yea*. It is not unusual with the sacred
writers to give solemn or impressive formulas in both languages. The promises of God are amen in Christ, because he
is the sum and substance of them. He says in a sense which
includes the idea here expressed, "I am the truth," John 14,
6; and in Rev. 3, 7 he is designated as "He that is true;"
and in Rev. 3, 14 he is called, "The Amen, the faithful and
true witness." The common text, which is expressed in our
version, has the support of the manuscripts D, E, I, K, which
read καὶ ἐν αὐτῷ, *and in him*. A, B, C, F, G have διὸ καὶ δὶ
αὐτοῦ, *wherefore also through him* the Amen. This reading,
which most recent editions adopt, was preferred by Calvin,
who renders the passage, *quare et per ipsum sit Amen.* The
Vulgate has the same reading, *ideo et per ipsum Amen.* The
sense thus expressed is certainly better and fuller. The verse
then teaches not only that the promises of God receive their
confirmation in Christ, but also that we experience and assent
to their truth. We say Amen, it is even so, to all God had
promised, when we come to know Christ. *To the glory of
God by us.* As these words are commonly pointed the natural interpretation is, that by us, i. e. by the preaching of the
apostles, men are brought thus to say Amen to the divine
promises, to the glory of God. God is glorified by the faith

in his promises thus expressed. The words, however, admit of a different construction. *By us* may be connected with the first part of the clause. 'The Amen is said by us to the glory of God.' This may mean, 'We Christians render a glad assent to the promises thus ratified in Christ.' But *us* in the immediate context refers to the apostles, and therefore cannot be naturally here made to refer to Christians generally. Or, the meaning may be, 'By us apostles testimony is given to the truth of the promises, to the glory of God.' This last-mentioned interpretation, however, is inconsistent with the scriptural use of the expression "to say Amen," which means simply to assent to, or to sanction. 1 Cor. 14, 16. The apostles did not say Amen to the promises by preaching the gospel; but through their preaching men were brought to say Amen; that is, they were led to the joyful experience and avowal of faith in what God had promised. In Christ, therefore, the promises were fulfilled; and in him also men were brought, through the apostles, joyfully to assent to them. Bengel's pithy comment on this verse is: *Nae* respectu Dei promittentis, *amen* respectu credentium. "He that hath received his testimony, hath set to his seal that God is true." John 3, 33. 1 John 5, 9. 10. To receive God's testimony concerning his Son, to say Amen, and to believe, all mean the same thing.

21. 22. Now he which stablisheth us with you in Christ, and hath anointed us, (is) God; who hath also sealed us, and given the earnest of the Spirit in our hearts.

In the preceding verse the apostle had spoken of Christ as the truth and substance of all the divine promises, and of the cordial assent which believers gave to those promises; he here brings into view God as the author and preserver of their faith, who would assuredly grant them the salvation of which he had already given them the foretaste and the pledge. *Now* he; or, *but he who stablisheth us with you in Christ.* The word is ὁ βεβαιῶν, *who renders firm* or *stedfast;* i. e. who causes us with you to stand firm, εἰς Χριστόν, in reference to Christ, so that we adhere to him with unshaken constancy. As by the pronouns *we* and *us*, in what precedes, the apostle had meant himself and Silas and Timothy, here where he has reference to all believers he unites them with himself, *us with you*. The constancy in faith which God gave was not a gift peculiar to teachers, but common to all true Christians. *And hath anointed us*. Kings, prophets, and priests were anointed when inaugurated in their several offices; *to anoint* may therefore mean to qualify by divine influence, and thereby to authorize any one to discharge the duties of any office. In Luke 4, 18 our Lord applies to himself the language of Isaiah 61, 1, "The Spirit of the Lord is upon me, because he hath anointed me to preach the gospel to the poor." Acts 4, 27. 10, 38. "God anointed Jesus of Nazareth with the Holy Ghost." In like manner Christians are spoken of as anointed, because by the Spirit they are consecrated to God and qualified for his service. 1 John 2, 20. 27. When Paul says here, *hath anointed us*, he means by *us* all Christians, and of course the anointing to which he refers is that which is common to all believers. This is plain, 1. Because the object of the two participles, βεβαιῶν and χρίσας, here used, must be the same; 'who establisheth *us*, and hath anointed *us*.' But with the former Paul expressly associates the Corinthians. He says, *us with you*. They as well as he were the subjects of the confirmation, and therefore also of the anointing. 2. What follows of sealing and receiving the earnest of the Spirit, cannot with any propriety be restricted to ministers. 3. In the New Testament *official* anointing is spoken of only in relation to Christ, never of apostles or preachers; whereas believers are said to receive the unction of the Holy Spirit. The design of the apostle is not, as some of the later commentators say, to assert that God had given to him the assurance of the Spirit as to his fidelity in preaching the gospel; but to show that believers were indebted to God for their faith, and that he would certainly cause them to persevere. *Is God;* God it is who confirms and anoints his people. Comp. 5, 5 for a similarly constructed passage. This is the common and natural explanation. Billroth and Olshausen render it thus: 'God, who establishes and anointed us, also sealed us.' But this makes the first part of the verse too subordinate; the *sealing* is not the dominant idea. It is only one of the several benefits specified. It is God who establishes, anoints, seals and gives the earnest of the Spirit. *Who also hath sealed us.* A seal is used, 1. To indicate proprietorship. 2. To authenticate or prove to be genuine. 3. To preserve safe or inviolate.

The Holy Spirit, which in one view is an unction, in another view is a seal. He marks those in whom he dwells as belonging to God. They bear the seal of God upon them. Rev. 7, 2. 2 Tim. 2, 19. *Act. Thom.* § 26, ὁ θεὸς διὰ τῆς αὑτοῦ σφραγῖδος ἐπιγινώσκει τὰ ἴδια πρόβατα, *God knows by his seal his own sheep.* He also bears witness in the hearts of believers that they are the children of God. He authenticates them to themselves and others as genuine believers. And he effectually secures them from apostasy and perdition. Eph. 1, 3. 4, 30. This last idea is amplified in the next clause; and hath *given the earnest of the Spirit in our hearts.* The Holy Spirit is itself *the earnest,* i. e. at once the foretaste and pledge of redemption. The word ἀῤῥαβών, *pledge,* is a Hebrew word, which passed as a mercantile term, probably from the Phenician, into the Greek and Latin. It is properly that part of the purchase money paid in advance, as a security for the remainder. The indwelling of the Holy Spirit in the hearts of his people, is that part of the blessings of redemption, which God gives them as a pledge of their full and final salvation. So certain, therefore, as the Spirit dwells in us, so certain is our final salvation. " If any man have not the Spirit of Christ, he is none of his. . . But if the Spirit of him that raised up Jesus from the dead dwell in you, he that raised up Christ from the dead shall also quicken your mortal bodies by his Spirit that dwelleth in you," Rom. 8, 9–11. The indwelling of the Spirit is therefore called the first-fruits of redemption. Rom. 8, 23. Comp. Eph. 1, 14. 2 Cor. 5, 5. There is but one thing stated in these verses, and that is that God establishes or renders his people firm and secure in their union with Christ, and in their participation of the benefits of redemption. How he does this, and the evidence that he does it, is expressed or presented by saying he hath anointed, sealed, and given us the earnest of the Spirit. The indwelling of the Spirit, therefore, renders the believer secure and steadfast; it is his anointing; it is the seal of God impressed upon the soul, and therefore the pledge of redemption. The fruits of the Spirit are the only evidence of his presence; so that while those who experience and manifest those fruits may rejoice in the certainty of salvation, those who are destitute of them have no right to appropriate to themselves the consolation of this and similar declarations of the word of God. The perseverance of the saints is a perseverance in holiness.

23. Moreover, I call God for a record upon my soul, that to spare you I came not as yet unto Corinth.

Paul here returns to the original charge. The complaint against him for not having executed his purpose of going at once from Ephesus to Corinth, he had left on one side to meet the more serious charge of inconsistency in his teaching. Having answered that accusation, he here says, *But I sparing you*, i. e. for the sake of avoiding giving you pain, *came not again to Corinth*. The obvious implication is, that such was the state of things in Corinth that had he gone there immediately on leaving Ephesus, as he had originally intended, he would have been obliged to appear among them with a rod. 1 Cor. 4, 21. It was to avoid that necessity, and to give them the opportunity to correct abuses before he came, that he had deferred his visit. As there was no available testimony by which the apostle could prove that such was his motive, he confirms it by an oath. *I invoke God as a witness*, i. e. I call upon the omniscient God, who is the avenger of all perjury, to bear testimony to the truth of what I say. "An oath for confirmation is the end of all strife," Heb. 6, 16. All the bonds of society are loosened, and all security of life and property is lost, if men are not to be believed upon their oaths. This shows that human society depends on the sanctity of an oath; and as the oath derives all its sacredness from faith in God, as the providential and moral governor of the world, it is obvious that society cannot exist without religion. Superstition and false religion, although great evils, are far better than atheism. The words ἐπὶ τὴν ἐμὴν ψυχήν, rendered *on my soul*, may mean *against* my soul; or, I summon God *to* me as a witness. The latter idea includes the former, for, as Calvin says, "He who uses God as a witness, cites the punisher of falsehood."

24. Not for that we have dominion over your faith, but are helpers of your joy : for by faith ye stand.

This is intended to moderate and explain what precedes. 'When I speak of sparing you, I do not wish to intimate that I consider myself the lord over your faith.' *Not for that*, οὐχ ὅτι, equivalent to, *I do not say that* we have dominion over your faith. Some say *faith* is here used for believers, (the abstract for the concrete,) we have not dominion over believers; or, as

St. Peter says, are not lords over God's heritage. 1 Pet. 5, 3. Others say *faith* here means faith-life; we have not dominion over your Christian life. Both of these interpretations are unnatural and unnecessary. The word is to be taken in its ordinary sense. Paul disclaims all authority over their faith, either as a man or as an apostle. It was not for him, and if not for him, surely for no other man or set of men, to determine what they should believe. He called upon the Galatians to denounce him, or even an angel from heaven, as accursed, if he preached another gospel. Gal. 1, 8. Faith rests not on the testimony of man, but on the testimony of God. When we believe the Scriptures, it is not man, but God whom we believe. Therefore faith is subject not to man but to God alone. This is perfectly consistent with the plenary inspiration of the apostles, and with our confidence in them as the infallible witnesses of the truth. When a man speaks through a trumpet, it is the man and not the trumpet that we believe. Or when we read a printed page, we have confidence in the trustworthiness of the words as symbols of thought, but it is the mind expressed by those symbols with which we are in communion. So the apostles were but the organs of the Holy Ghost; what they spoke as such, they could not recall or modify. What they should communicate was not under their control; they were not the lords, so to speak, of the gospel, so that they could make it what they pleased. Not at all; they were as much subject to the communication which they received, and as much bound to believe what they were made the instruments of teaching, as other men. Paul therefore places himself alongside of his brethren, not over them as a lord, but as a joint-believer with them in the gospel which he preached, and *a helper of their joy*. That is, his office was to co-operate with them in the promotion of their spiritual welfare. It was not the end of the apostleship to give pain or to inflict punishment, but to promote the real happiness of the people. *For by faith ye stand.* The meaning of this clause is doubtful. Taken by themselves the words may mean, 'Ye stand firm or independently as to faith.' This would suit the connection as indicated by *for*. 'We are not lords over your faith, but merely helpers, for you stand independently as to faith.' Or the meaning may be what is expressed in our version, 'Ye stand *by* faith.' Then the connection, as explained by Calvin, is, 'Since it is the effect and nature of faith to sustain or cause you to stand, it is absurd that it should be subject to man, or that we should have dominion over your faith.' This, however, is rather an obscure argument. According to Meyer the connection is with the immediately preceding words, 'We are helpers of your joy, because ye are steadfast as to faith.' That is, steadfastness in faith is necessary to joy. The most natural interpretation probably is that given by Erasmus: fidei nomine nullum habemus in vos dominium, in qua perseveratis; sed est in vita quod in vobis correctum volebam. 'Over your faith I have no dominion, for in that ye stand; but, when I speak of not sparing, I had reference to your conduct.' He had authority in matters of discipline, but not in matters of faith. As to the latter, he and they were equally under subjection to the revelation of God. He indeed, as the organ of the Spirit, could declare infallibly what that revelation was, but he could not go counter to it, and was to be judged by it. If the inspired apostles recognised not only their subjection to the word of God, but also the right of the people to judge whether their teachings were in accordance with the supreme standard, it is most evident that no church authority can make any thing contrary to Scripture obligatory on believers, and that the ultimate right to decide whether ecclesiastical decisions are in accordance with the word of God, rests with the people. In other words, Paul recognises, even in reference to himself, the right of private judgment. He allowed any man to pronounce him anathema, if he did not preach the gospel as it had been revealed and authenticated to the church. Quum eorum fidei dominari se negat, significat injustam hanc esse et minime tolerandam potestatem, imo tyrannidem in ecclesia. Fides enim prorsus ab hominum jugo soluta, liberrimaque esse debet. Notandum autem, quis loquatur: nam siquis omnino sit mortalium qui jus habeat tale dominium sibi vindicandi, Paulus certe dignus hac prærogativa fuit, fatetur autem sibi non competere. Itaque colligimus, fidem non aliam subjectionem agnoscere, quam verbi Dei: hominum imperio minime esse obnoxiam. Calvin.

CHAPTER II.

The first paragraph, vs. 1–4, relates to the change of his plan of going immediately to Corinth. In vs. 5–11 he refers to the case of discipline mentioned in his former letter. In vs. 12–14 he states why he did not remain in Troas. And in vs. 14–17 he pours out his heart in gratitude to God for the continued triumph of the gospel.

The true reason why the apostle did not go immediately to Corinth, and his views in reference to the offender whose excommunication he had insisted upon in his former letter.

THERE is no change of subject in this chapter. The apostle after defending himself from the charge of levity in conduct and inconsistency in doctrine, had said, in v. 23 of the preceding chapter, that he did not go to Corinth before giving the church time to comply with the injunctions contained in his former letter, because he did not wish to appear among them as a judge. He here says, in amplification, that he had determined not again to visit Corinth under circumstances which could only give pain to the Corinthians and to himself. He knew that he could not give them sorrow without being himself grieved, and he was assured that if he was happy they would share in his joy, vs. 1–4. The sorrow occasioned by the incestuous person was not confined to the apostle, but shared by the church. He was satisfied with the course which the church had pursued in reference to that case, and was willing the offender should be restored to their fellowship if they were, vs. 5–11. His anxiety about them was so great that not finding Titus, from whom he expected to receive intelligence, he was unable to remain at Troas, but passed over into Macedonia to meet him on his way, vs. 12. 13. The intelligence which he received from Titus being favourable, the apostle expresses in strong terms his gratitude to God who always caused him to triumph, vs. 15–17.

1. But I determined this with myself, that I would not come again to you in heaviness.

The connection is with what immediately precedes. 'I deferred my visit in order to spare you, not that I assume to be a lord over your faith, but a helper of your joy. *But* the true reason for my not coming was that I did not wish to come with heaviness.' The words ἔκρινα ἐμαυτῷ, rendered *I determined with myself*, may mean simply *I determine as to myself*. I had made up my mind; or, 'I determined *for myself*,' i. e. for my own sake. This perhaps is to be preferred. The apostle thus delicately intimates that it was not merely to spare them, but also himself, that he put off his visit. The word *this* refers to the purpose which the apostle had formed, and which is explained by the following infinitive, μὴ ἐλθεῖν, *not to come*. Two explanations are given of the following clause. According to the one, the meaning is, 'I determined that my second visit should not be with sorrow;' according to the other, 'I determined not a second time to visit you in sorrow.' In the one case the implication is that Paul had, at this time, been only once in Corinth; in the other, the passage implies that he had already (i. e. after his first visit) been to Corinth under circumstances painful to himself and to the church. There are two reasons for preferring this latter view. The first is, that according to the position of the words, as given in all the older manuscripts, (μὴ πάλιν ἐν λύπῃ πρὸς ὑμᾶς ἐλθεῖν,) the πάλιν, *again*, belongs to the whole clause and not exclusively to ἐλθεῖν. The sense, therefore, is that he determined not a second time to come with sorrow, (he had done that once.) The other reason is, that there is evidence from other passages that Paul had been twice to Corinth before this letter was written. See 12, 14. 21. 13, 1. That there is no mention in the Acts of this intermediate journey, is no sufficient reason for denying it, as the passages referred to are so explicit. To make the second visit one by letter, as Calvin (venerat enim semel per epistolam) and others have done, is evidently unnatural. Having gone once to correct abuses and to exercise severity, he was anxious not to have a second painful interview of the same kind, and therefore, instead of going to them, as he had intended, directly from Corinth, he waited to learn through Titus what had been the effect of his letter. *With heaviness*, ἐν λύπῃ, *with sorrow*, i. e. causing sorrow to you. This explanation is required by the following verse, otherwise the meaning would more naturally be *in sorrow*, i. e. in a sorrowful state of mind, as the word λύπη everywhere else with Paul means a state of grief.

2. For if I make you sorry, who is he that maketh me glad, but the same that is made sorry by me?

This is the reason why he did not wish to come bringing sorrow with him; 'For if,' says he, 'I make you sorry, who is there to make me glad? How can I be happy, if you are afflicted? Unless my visit cause you joy, it can bring no joy to me.' As inspiration leaves full play to all the characteristic peculiarities of its subject, in reading the writings of inspired men we learn not only the mind of the Spirit, but also the personal character of the writers. The urbanity of the apostle Paul, his refinement and courtesy, are just as plainly revealed in his epistles as his intellectual power and moral courage. The passage before us is one of many illustrations of the truth of this remark, furnished by this epistle. *Who is he that maketh me glad, but the same that is made sorry by me.* The singular is used, not because a particular individual, much less because the incestuous person, is specially referred to, but because the case is stated in the form of a general proposition. 'I cannot expect joy from one to whom I bring sorrow.' Such was the apostle's love for the Corinthians that unless they were happy he could not be happy. This is the natural and commonly received interpretation of the passage. Chrysostom, and many of the ancient commentators, and some also of the moderns, give a different view of its meaning. 'Who gives me joy, but he who allows himself (λυπούμενος as middle and not passive) to be grieved by me.' That is, no one causes me so much joy as he who is brought to repentance by me. But this is obviously inconsistent with the context. The verse, as thus explained, gives no reason why Paul did not wish to go to Corinth bringing sorrow. On the contrary, the more of that kind of sorrow he brought with him, or was occasioned by his visit, the better. This interpretation would make the apostle say, 'I will not come with sorrow, for nothing gives me so much pleasure as to cause (godly) sorrow.' To avoid this incongruity Olshausen says the connection is to be thus understood: Paul determined that he would not come with sorrow, because he feared that few of the Corinthians would give him the happiness of seeing that they had been made sorry by his former reproofs. But this makes the passage itself a reproof, an insinuation that they had not profited by his first letter. This is contrary to the whole spirit of the passage, which is overflowing with confidence and affection.

3. And I wrote this same unto you, lest, when I
2*

came, I should have sorrow from them of whom I
ought to rejoice; having confidence in you all that my
joy is (the joy) of you all.

Having said that his motive for not coming at once to Corinth was to avoid giving them sorrow, he here adds, 'And I
wrote what I did in my former letter that, when I came, I
might not have sorrow.' Instead of going in person to correct the evils which existed in the church of Corinth, he wrote
to them that those evils might be corrected before he came,
and thus his coming would be a source of joy to both parties.
It is evident from the preceding context, and from vs. 4 and
9, that ἔγραψα here refers not to this epistle, but to the former
one. *This same*, τοῦτο αὐτό, *that very thing*, that is, the very
thing which I did write respecting the incestuous person.
The expression seems to have special reference to that case,
because that is evidently the case to which the following
verses relate. It appears that the point about which the
apostle was most anxious was, how the Corinthians would act
in regard to his command, 1 Cor. 5, 13, to put away from
among them "that wicked person." He seems to have feared
that his enemies might have had influence enough with the
church, to prevent their executing his command. He therefore waited in painful suspense to learn the issue. And when
Titus, on his return from Corinth, informed him that they had
not only promptly obeyed his directions, but that the offender
himself and the whole church had been brought to deep and
genuine repentance, his heart was filled with gratitude to God,
and with love to the people who had manifested such a Christian spirit. All this is plain from what is said in ch. 7. Erasmus and several other commentators render τοῦτο αὐτό *hac
eadem de causa*, for this very reason. The sense would then
be, 'I determined I would not come to you with sorrow, *and
for that very reason* I wrote to you that I might not.'
This, although it suits the preceding context, is not so consistent with what follows as the common interpretation; for
in the following verses the apostle states the reasons for his
writing as he had done in his former letter.

*Lest when I came I should have sorrow from them of
whom I ought to rejoice.* That is, 'I wrote what I did that I
might not have sorrow from those, who should be to me a
source of joy.' He wished all painful questions settled before
he came. *Having confidence in you all that my joy is the joy*

of you all. Paul in saying that he wished all causes of painful collision might be removed out of the way before he went to Corinth, did not isolate himself from the people, as though concerned only for his own peace of mind, but was satisfied that what made him happy would make them happy. My joy will be the joy of you all. This does not mean merely that it would give them pleasure to see him happy, but also that obedience on their part, and the consequent purity and prosperity of the church, were as necessary to their happiness as to his. Paul says he had this confidence in them *all*, although it is abundantly evident that there were men among them who were his bitter opponents. These latter he here leaves out of view, and speaks of the majority, probably the great body, of the church as though it were the whole.

4. For out of much affliction and anguish of heart I wrote unto you with many tears; not that ye should be grieved, but that ye may know the love which I have the more abundantly towards you.

The connection is either with the immediately preceding clause, 'I have confidence in you, for otherwise it would not have given me so much pain to write as I did;' or, what is more natural because more direct, the reference is to the motives which dictated his letter. 'I was influenced by the desire of promoting your happiness, for to me it was a most painful duty.' *Out of* (ἐκ) indicates the source. His letter flowed from a broken heart. *Affliction and anguish* refer to his inward feelings, not to his outward circumstances, for both are qualified by the word *heart.* It was out of an afflicted, an oppressed heart, that he wrote. *With many tears,* (διά,) *through* many tears. The union of fidelity and love which renders parental discipline peculiarly effective, gives also peculiar power to ecclesiastical censures. When the offender is made to feel that, while his sin is punished, he himself is loved; and that the end aimed at is not his suffering but his good, he is the more likely to be brought to repentance. Every pastor must see in the apostle's love for the Corinthians, and in the extreme sorrow with which he exercised discipline in the case of offenders, an instructive example for his imitation. *Not that ye should be grieved,* my object in writing was not to cause you sorrow, *but that ye may know the love that I have the more abundantly towards you.* The ends which the apostle desired to accomplish by his former letter were numerous, and he therefore sometimes specifies one, and sometimes another. Here, he says, it was to manifest his love; in v. 9 he says it was to test their obedience; in ch. 7 he says it was to bring them to repentance. These are not incompatible ends, and therefore there is no inconsistency between these several statements. *The love which I have the more abundantly towards you.* This naturally means *the special* love which I have for you. His love for them was more abundant, or greater, than that which he had for any other church. This view is borne out by numerous other passages in these two epistles, which go to show that Paul's love for the Corinthian church was, for some reason, peculiarly strong. As vs. 5–11 have direct reference to the case of the incestuous person, it is the more probable that all that he says in the preceding verses as to his reasons for not coming sooner to Corinth, and as to the sorrow and anxiety which he felt about the state of the church there, had special reference to that case.

5. But if any have caused grief, he hath not grieved me, but in part, that I may not overcharge you all.

The connection between this paragraph, vs. 5–11, and what precedes is natural and obvious. Paul had been speaking of his motives for writing his former letter. It was not intended to give them sorrow. If sorrow had been occasioned, it had not come from him. This led him to speak more particularly of the case which had occasioned so much distress. The proper interpretation of this particular verse is, however, a matter of great doubt. The translation is of necessity, in this case, an exposition, and therefore the grounds of doubt do not appear to the English reader. Our translators, after Luther, assume that ἀπὸ μέρους, *in part*, are to be connected with the preceding clause, and πάντας ὑμᾶς, *you all*, with ἐπιβαρῶ, *overcharge*. Thus construed the sense can only be, 'If any one has caused grief, he has not grieved me, but in part, that is, I am not the only person aggrieved. I say this, lest I should bear hard upon you all. It would be a severe reflection on you to say that you did not feel any sorrow for the offence in question.' According to this view, the design of the passage is to guard against the impression that he

meant to charge them with indifference. But to this it is objected that to express this sense εἰ μή, and not ἀλλά, would be
required. "He hath not grieved me *except* in part." And
secondly, that the idea thus expressed is not suited to the
context. The main idea evidently is, 'He hath not grieved
me but you.' The subordinate words and clauses therefore
must be accommodated to that idea. Hence ἀλλ' ἀπὸ μέρους
must be connected with what follows, and πάντας ὑμᾶς with
λελύπηκεν. Then the sense will be, 'He hath not grieved me,
but in part, or, to a certain extent, (lest I should bear too
hard *on him*,) you all.' The design of the passage, according
to this view, is to soften the charge against the penitent offender of having been the cause of sorrow. This the apostle
does, first, by saying, "he did not grieve me," i. e. it was no
personal offence against me that he committed ; and second,
that all the Corinthians were not afflicted, it was not a universal sorrow that he caused. This substantially is the interpretation given by Calvin after Chrysostom, and is the one
adopted by the great majority of modern commentators. It
has the advantage of being not only suited to the meaning of
the words, but to the whole tone of the following context,
which is eminently mild and conciliatory. The apostle's heart
was overflowing with the tenderest feelings towards his Corinthian brethren, and he was evidently solicitous to heal the
salutary wounds inflicted by his former letter. There is still
another view of the passage which should be mentioned. It
may be pointed so as to read thus : 'He hath not grieved me,
but in part (that I may not overcharge all) you.' This, however, unnaturally separates the words πάντας ὑμᾶς, *you all*.

6. Sufficient to such a man is this punishment,
which (was inflicted) of many.

I do not wish to be severe towards him, for the punishment which he has received is sufficient. The word ἡ ἐπιτιμία,
rendered *punishment*, occurs only in *Wisdom* 3, 10 in this
sense, and therefore many assume that it here does not mean
punishment, but *reproof*. The word rendered *sufficient*, ἱκανόν,
is used substantively. "This punishment is a sufficiency, or a
satisfaction." Comp. Matt. 6, 34 for a similar construction.
Paul says the punishment or reproof was administered ὑπὸ τῶν
πλειόνων, *by the majority*, intimating that all did not concur in

it. This, however, is not a necessary inference, because οἱ πλείονες may mean *the many*, the whole body considered as many, because composed of many members. There are three views taken of this verse in connection with what follows. In his former letter the apostle had not only commanded the church to excommunicate the person here referred to, but declared his own determination to deliver him to Satan for the destruction of the flesh. 1 Cor. 5, 5. Grotius supposes that in consequence of that judgment he was seized with some bodily malady, for delivery from which Paul, in this connection, declares his willingness that the Corinthians should pray. Of this, however, the passage gives no intimation. A second view is that the sentence of excommunication had not been carried into effect, but as the reproof administered by many had had the effect of leading the offender to repentance, the apostle here intimates his satisfaction with what the church had done, although his injunctions had not been fully complied with. This is the view of Calvin, Beza, and of many others. In favour of this explanation it is urged that the expression "*this* punishment" naturally refers to that punishment or reproof which the Corinthians had administered as distinguished from that which he had enjoined; and his saying "*this* punishment," of which he had heard, was enough, implies that he did not wish them to proceed any further, but rather that they should console the penitent by the assurance of their love. On the other hand, however, v. 9 (as well as ch. 7) clearly intimates that the church had rendered a prompt obedience to the apostle's directions. The great majority of commentators, therefore, understand the passage to mean that Paul did not wish the excommunication to be continued any longer. As it had produced its desired effect, he was willing that the offender should be restored to the communion of the church. The whole passage indicates that Paul was more lenient than the church, for he exhorts his readers not to be too severe in their treatment of their offending brother. A passage, says Calvin, himself a severe disciplinarian, well to be observed, as it teaches with what equity and clemency the discipline of the church is to be attempered; *qua æquitate et clementia temperanda sit disciplina ecclesiæ.* Paul, he adds, was satisfied with the repentance of the offender; whereas the ancient bishops gave forth their canons requiring a penance of three, or seven years, or even for a life-time, without regard to the contrition of the unhappy victims of their severity.

7. So that contrariwise ye (ought) rather to forgive (him) and comfort (him), lest perhaps such a one should be swallowed up with overmuch sorrow.

The consequence of what is expressed in v. 8 is indicated by the words *so that*. 'The punishment being sufficient, the consequence is that, instead of its being increased or continued, you should forgive and comfort the offender.' As the apostle seems to indicate what *ought* to be done, most commentators supply before the infinitives χαρίσασθαι καὶ παρακαλέσαι the word δεῖ or δεῖν, '*it is necessary* to forgive and comfort.' The infinitive itself, however, often expresses, after verbs of saying, and the like, not what is, but what should be, e. g. λέγοντες περιτέμνεσθαι, *saying you ought to be circumcised.* Acts 15, 24. 21, 4. 21. *Winer*, p. 371, says that neither of these modes of explanation is necessary, as the infinitives may be connected immediately with ἱκανόν, 'The reproof is sufficient —in order to your pardoning and comforting him.' The delicacy of the apostle towards this offender is indicated by his abstaining either from naming him, or designating him as he had before done, 1 Cor. 5, 13, as *that wicked person.* He refers to him simply *as such an one*, without any appellation which could wound his feelings. The apostle combined, therefore, the strictest fidelity with the greatest tenderness. As long as the offender was impenitent and persisted in his offence, Paul insisted upon the severest punishment. As soon as he acknowledged and forsook his sin, he became his earnest advocate. *Lest he should be swallowed up with overmuch sorrow*, that is, lest he should be driven to despair and thus destroyed. Undue severity is as much to be avoided as undue leniency. The character which Paul here exhibits reflects the image of our heavenly Father. His word is filled with denunciations against impenitent sinners, and at the same time with assurances of unbounded pity and tenderness towards the penitent. He never breaks the bruised reed or quenches the smoking flax.

8. Wherefore I beseech you that ye would confirm (your) love towards him.

The connection is either with v. 6, 'His punishment is sufficient—*wherefore* confirm your love towards him;' or with what immediately precedes. 'There is danger of his being swallowed up with overmuch sorrow unless you forgive him, wherefore confirm your love to him.' The latter method is to be preferred, though the sense is substantially the same. *I beseech you*, παρακαλῶ, the same word which in the preceding verse is used in the sense of consoling. Paul not unfrequently uses the same word in the immediate connection in different senses. 1 Cor. 3, 17. 11, 23. *That ye would confirm*, literally, *to confirm*, κυρῶσαι. The word properly means *to ratify* with authority by some public or formal act. Gal. 3, 15. And this sense is generally adopted here. The apostle is understood to call upon them by a formal act to reinstate the offender in the communion of the church, to assure him of their love, so that he might not have to infer it merely from their treatment of him. The word, however, may mean nothing more than is expressed in our version. 'I exhort you to make your love towards him a matter of certainty.' But as the implication is that they had already begun to manifest their brotherly affection for him, the probability is that the apostle wished them to give their love a formal ratification.

9. For to this end also did I write, that I might know the proof of you, whether ye be obedient in all things.

Verses 9 and 10 are sometimes regarded as a parenthesis, so as to connect the 11th verse with the 8th. 'Confirm your love towards him, lest Satan get an advantage over us.' But a parenthesis is never to be assumed where the grammatical construction continues unbroken, and the logical connection is uninterrupted. The 11th verse is naturally connected with the 10th, and the 9th with the 8th. 'Confirm your love to him, for the object of my writing to you to exclude him from your fellowship, has been accomplished.' *To this end* means the end specified in the latter part of the verse. *I wrote*, ἔγραψα, a form of the verb which is often in the epistolary style used of the letter in the process of being written. Rom. 15, 15. 1 Cor. 9, 15. 1 Pet. 5, 12, &c. The whole context, however, shows that Paul refers to his former letter. See vs. 3. 4. He did not write this letter to test their obedience, though that was one of the objects of his former epistle. Paul says, 'I *also* wrote.' This *also* may indicate that it was the object of his former letter as well as of the exhortation which he had just given them, to test their obedience. But such was not

the object of that exhortation. It is better therefore to understand the (καί) *also*, as simply intended to give prominence
to the words *I wrote*, as something additional to other things
which he had done with the same general object. 'To this
end I also wrote, as well as did many other things,' &c. The
end (although not the only one), which the apostle had in view
in enjoining on the church the excommunication of the person
here referred to, was, as he says, *that I might know the proof
of you.* The word used is δοκιμή, which means *trial*, 8, 2,
" trial of affliction ; " or, *proof, test*, 13, 3, " As ye seek a proof
of Christ speaking in me ; " or, the result of trial, what is approved, *integrity that has been tested.*   Phil. 2, 22, " Ye know
his tried integrity." The last meaning is the best suited to
this place. 'That I might know your integrity, i. e. your true
Christian temper.' This is explained by saying he wished to
see whether they would be *obedient in all things*, εἰς πάντα,
in reference to all things. These latter words stand first,
'Whether as to all things ye are obedient,' which is more emphatic. Obedience to legitimate authority is one of the fruits
and evidences of Christian sincerity. A rebellious, self-willed,
disobedient spirit is a strong indication of an unsanctified
heart. As the Corinthians had proved themselves obedient
to the apostle's directions, and as the offender was truly penitent, the object of his letter, both as it related to them and to
him, had been attained, and therefore there was no reason for
the continuance of the punishment.

10. To whom ye forgive any thing, I (forgive) also :
for if I forgave any thing, to whom I forgave (it),* for
your sakes (forgave I it) in the person of Christ.

The apostle having exhorted the Corinthians to forgive
their repentant brother, says he was ready to join in that forgiveness. *To whom ye forgive any thing, I also.* Although
this is stated generally, as though he meant to say that he
would forgive any one whom they were ready to forgive, yet
it is obvious from the context that he intended to be under-

* The received text here reads καὶ γὰρ ἐγὼ εἴ τι κεχάρισμαι, ᾧ κεχάρισμαι,
for also I if I have forgiven any thing, to whom I forgave. Griesbach, Lachmann, Tischendorf, Rückert, Meyer, and others, after the majority of ancient
MSS. read, καὶ γὰρ ἐγὼ ὅ κεχάρισμαι, εἴ τι κεχάρισμαι, *for also I what I have
forgiven, if I have forgiven any thing.*

stood as referring to that particular case. He was satisfied with their course, and also with the evidence of the repentance of the offender, and therefore he was ready to sanction his restoration to their communion. His reason for this is stated in what follows, he did it for their sake. His forgiving, however, was suspended upon theirs. He would not interfere to restore the person in question unless they were satisfied to receive him. He therefore says, *If I have forgiven any thing*, that is, if the forgiveness expressed in the foregoing clause is to take effect and to be considered as already done, I have done it for your sake. He was influenced by no personal consideration either in the censure originally pronounced, or in his present course, but solely by a desire to promote their best interests. *In the person of Christ*, or, *in the presence* of Christ. This latter interpretation is the more consistent with usage, and is generally adopted. The meaning is that he acted in this matter as in the presence of Christ, i. e. as though Christ were looking on. The other explanation, which is preferred by Luther and many others, is consistent with the meaning of the words, and gives a good sense. He acted in the person of Christ, i. e. as his representative and by his authority. This idea, however, is commonly expressed by the phrase *in the name* of Christ. 1 Cor. 5, 4. Calvin prefers the former view, and adds, Christ is to be placed before us, or we " are to act as in his presence, for nothing is better adapted to incline us to mercy." No man can be severe in his judgment who feels that the mild eyes of Christ are fixed upon him.

The word χαρίζομαι, rendered *to forgive* in this verse, is a deponent verb, but is, in several of its forms, used in a passive sense. It is so taken here by Rückert and Meyer, who give an entirely different explanation of the passage. They adopt the reading of Griesbach, given in the margin, and render it thus: 'I forgive—for what I have been forgiven, if I have been forgiven anything, it is for your sake.' That is, if God has really pardoned my great sin in persecuting Christ, it was for your sake. Comp. 1 Tim. 1, 16. But this interpretation is inconsistent with the common use of the word, with the whole context, and with Paul's manner of speaking. His humility manifested itself in deep remorse and repentance for his past conduct, but not in doubting whether he had been forgiven. Besides, this interpretation would require a very unnatural explanation of the following clause. 'If I have been forgiven for your sake *in the presence of Christ,*' that is, Christ is the witness of my being forgiven. This is contrary to all scriptural representations. God is said to forgive for Christ's sake; and Christ is said to forgive, but he is never represented as the mere witness or spectator of our forgiveness.

11. Lest Satan should get an advantage of us : for we are not ignorant of his devices.

This verse, as above remarked, is by some made to depend on v. 8, the vs. 9 and 10 being parenthetical. 'Confirm your love towards him—lest Satan should get an advantage of us.' Others make it depend on the preceding words, 'We should act (or, I was pardoned) in the presence of Christ, lest,' &c. The most natural connection is with the first clause of v. 10, which contains the main idea of the context. 'I will join you in pardoning the offender lest Satan get an advantage of us,' i. e. make a gain of us. The expression is μὴ πλεονεκτηθῶμεν ὑπὸ τοῦ σατανᾶ, *lest we should be made gain of, or defrauded, by Satan.* It was a gain to Satan if either an individual soul could be driven to despair, or the peace of the church could be disturbed. Both of these evils were to be apprehended if discipline were carried too far. This dread of Satan was not chimerical or unreasonable, for he really does seek to turn every thing to the disadvantage of Christ and his kingdom. *We are not ignorant,* says the apostle, *of his devices.* This and similar passages of the Word of God teach that Satan is a personal being; that he exerts great influence over the minds of men ; that although finite, and, therefore, not ubiquitous, he is nevertheless represented as operating on the minds of men generally, and not merely on those in any one place. His powers of intelligence and agency therefore must be great beyond our conceptions. No individual and no community can ever be sure that he is not plotting their destruction. Paul might have said to the Romans or the Ephesians, as he did to the Corinthians, that they must take heed lest Satan make a gain of them, and in some way secure them as his own.

12. 13. Furthermore, when I came to Troas to (preach) Christ's gospel, and a door was opened to me of the Lord, I had no rest in my spirit because I found

not Titus my brother; but taking my leave of them, I went from thence into Macedonia.

Furthermore, when I came; literally, *But having come.* The particle δέ (*but*) serves to resume the connection broken by the digression, vs. 5–11. In v. 4 he said he had written his former letter in great anguish and distress of heart, to manifest his love for them. And as a still further proof of the deep interest which he took in their welfare, he refers to the incident mentioned in these verses. In execution of his plan of going from Ephesus through Macedonia to Corinth, 1 Cor. 16, 5, Paul came *to Troas,* literally, *to the Troad* (εἰς τὴν Τρωάδα), a name given to the whole district around the site of ancient Troy. The city itself was on the coast of Mysia opposite to the island of Tenedos. It had been made a Roman colony by Augustus, and was a place of considerable importance, in constant commercial intercourse with the cities of Macedonia and Greece. Paul did not intend to make a rapid journey to Corinth, but a regular missionary tour; he therefore says he came to Troas to preach *Christ's gospel,* i. e. the gospel of which Christ is the author. It is also called the gospel of God, and Paul speaks of it as his gospel, i. e. the gospel which he preached. When spoken of as the gospel *of the kingdom of God,* Matt. 4, 23, the gospel *of salvation,* Eph. 1, 13, *of peace,* Eph. 6, 15, the genitive expresses either the subject of which the gospel treats or the effects which it produces. *And a door was opened to me,* i. e. a way of access, an opening to labour with effect. *Of the Lord,* according to this interpretation the words, ἐν κυρίῳ, are to be connected with the immediately preceding participle, " door opened by the Lord." See 1 Cor. 15, 58. Gal. 5, 10. Eph. 2, 21. It is, however, more in accordance with Paul's style, who so frequently uses, these words in such expressions as ' work in the Lord,' ' temple in the Lord,' ' fellow-labourer in the Lord,' to refer them to the whole clause. " There was an open door in the Lord." The kind of door is thus indicated, or the sphere of labour pointed out. It was an opportunity for labouring successfully in the Lord's service. Though the prospects were so favourable, Paul says, *I had no rest in my spirit;* τῷ πνεύματι μοῦ, *for my spirit.* The word *spirit* is here used because it is the highest term to designate the soul, Rom. 8, 16, and the anxiety or distress which the apostle experienced concerned the highest feelings of his nature. *Be-*

cause I found not Titus my brother. He calls Titus his brother, both because of his relation to him as a fellow-Christian,
and because he was a joint labourer with him in the gospel.
He expected to meet Titus at Troas, and to learn from him the
state of things in Corinth, and especially the effect produced
by his former letter. It seems that he regarded this as a
turning point in the history of that church. If they submitted
to his authority and corrected the abuses which he had pointed out, and especially if they excommunicated the member
guilty of the unheard-of offence so often referred to in this
chapter, then he had hopes of their stability in faith and progress in holiness. But if they refused to regard his injunctions,
and persisted in the course on which they had entered, then he
foresaw their speedy destruction. So much was at stake that
he could not endure the state of suspense which he was in;
and therefore, *taking leave of them,* that is, of the brethren in
Troas, he passed over into Macedonia. On his first visit to this
city, Paul was prevented from remaining by a vision, from which
he gathered that the Lord called him to preach the gospel in
Macedonia. Acts 16, 8. And on his return from his present
journey, it is said, he sailed from Philippi and came in five days
to Troas, and abode there seven days. Acts 20, 6. From the
circumstances connected with this last visit it is evident that
there was an established church at that time in Troas. The
word ἀποτάσσομαι, *to take leave of,* means *to separate oneself
from,* to bid farewell to. Luke 16, 61. Acts 18, 18. 21. *I
went from thence into Macedonia ;* ἐξῆλθον, *I went forth.*
He crossed over the northeastern corner of the Mediterranean
sea to one of the ports of Macedonia; the same voyage which
he made on his return, which then required five days. As
Titus was to return from Corinth through Macedonia to Troas,
Paul thus went to meet him on his journey.

14. Now thanks (be) unto God, which always causeth us to triumph in Christ, and maketh manifest the
savour of his knowledge by us in every place.

Agreeably to the impulsive character of this epistle, instead of stating what was the intelligence which he received
from Titus, the apostle breaks out into a thanksgiving to God,
which assumes a form which might be taken for self-commendation, which he, however, disclaims, and humbly acknowl-
edges that all his qualifications for his work, and all his success

in it, are to be attributed to God. This leads him to speak of the ministry of the gospel, which he contrasts with that of the law, and himself with Moses, so that it is not until the seventh chapter that he pauses, as it were, to take breath, and resumes the narrative here broken off. The thing for which the apostle gives thanks is his success; which includes both his triumph over obstacles and enemies, and his efficiency in spreading abroad the knowledge of the truth. The word θριαμβεύειν, rendered here to *cause to triumph*, means *to triumph over*, *to lead in triumph*. This is its uniform sense in the classics, and it is so used by Paul in Col. 2, 5. Meyer and others so render the word here. 'Thanks be to God who triumphs over us,' i. e. who disappoints our fears and puts our anxieties to shame. But this is evidently incongruous. Paul does not represent himself as humbled and conquered, but just the reverse. Calvin and others retain the literal meaning of the word, and say the sense is, 'Thanks be to God who leads us in triumph, not as captives, but as sharers of his victory.' This gives a suitable meaning, but is not so consistent with the use of the word, which means *to triumph over*, not, to make one a sharer in our triumph. The great majority of commentators therefore modify the sense of the word as is done by our translators. This they justify by referring to the fact that many verbs which in ordinary Greek are neuter, in the Hellenistic dialect are used in a causative sense (*Winer*, p. 304), as μαθητεύειν, *to be a disciple*, in Matt. 28, 19 and elsewhere, means *to make disciples;* βασιλεύειν, *to reign*, in 1 Sam. 8, 22, and often in the Septuagint, means *to cause to reign;* and thus θριαμβεύειν, *to triumph*, may in obedience to the context be fairly rendered, *to cause to triumph*. *In Christ*, in virtue of union with Christ, or, as united to him. These words determine the nature of the triumph of which the apostle speaks. It was the triumph of a Christian minister in the service of Christ.

And maketh manifest the savour of his knowledge, i. e. diffuses or spreads abroad his knowledge, which is compared to the savour of a sacrifice (Gen. 8, 21. Eph. 5, 2. Phil. 4, 18), or to incense. *His* knowledge; the pronoun *his* is commonly referred to God, but as this clause is explanatory of the former, or an amplification of the idea therein expressed, it is perhaps better to refer it to Christ. ' He causes us to triumph in Christ, and to spread abroad the savour of his knowledge,' i. e. the knowledge of Christ. That Christ should be known was the great end of Paul's mission, and is of all things the most acceptable to God. Knowledge here, as so often elsewhere in Scripture, means not merely intellectual cognition, but spiritual apprehension and recognition. That men should know the Lord Jesus Christ in the sense of recognizing, loving and worshipping him as God manifest in the flesh, is the consummation of redemption; the sum of all blessedness and excellence. *In every place.* Wherever Paul went, there the knowledge of Christ was spread abroad. Comp. Rom. 15, 19. Can this be said of us?

15. For we are unto God a sweet savour of Christ, in them that are saved, and in them that perish.

We as ministers, and our work of preaching Christ, are acceptable to God, whatever may be the result of our labours. This idea is connected with the preceding as an amplification and confirmation. 'God by us diffuses the knowledge of Christ everywhere as a savour; *for* (ὅτι, *because*) it is well pleasing to God whatever be the effect which it produces.' There is, as is so common in Paul's epistles, a slight change in the figure. In v. 14 the knowledge of Christ is declared to be a savour as of incense, here the apostle is the sweet savour. But it is the apostle not as a man, not the purity or devotion of his life; but the apostle as a preacher of the gospel, and therefore the gospel which he preached; so that the thought remains the same. In both verses the diffusion of the knowledge of Christ is said to be well pleasing to God. *Savour of Christ*, does not mean a savour of which Christ is the author. The idea is not that Christ rendered Paul or his life acceptable to God. That indeed is true, but it is not what is intended. When we speak of the perfume of the rose, or of the violet, we mean that perfume which the rose or the violet emits and which is characteristic of it. When Paul says, "We are a sweet smelling savour of Christ," he means we are the means of diffusing the knowledge of Christ. When a man's garments are perfumed with myrrh or frankincense, he fills with the fragrance every place he enters. So Paul, wherever he went, diffused abroad the fragrance of the name of Christ, and that was acceptable to God. *In them*, i. e. among them, that are saved; *and in* (among) *them that perish*. This does not mean among them predestined to be saved, and those predestined to perish. The idea of predestination is not included. The

two classes are designated *ab eventu*. The gospel and those
who preach it are well pleasing to God, whether men receive
it and are saved, or reject it and are lost. The light is inesti-
mably precious, whether the eye rejoices in it, or through disease is destroyed by it. Comp. 1 Cor. 1, 18. 2 Thess. 2, 10.

16. To the one (we are) the savour of death unto
death; to the other the savour of life unto life. And
who is sufficient for these things?

The words *we are* are not in the text, but are necessarily
implied. The apostle and all faithful ministers are to God an
εὐωδία, *a sweet savour*, to men an ὀσμή, *a savour*, salutary or
destructive according to circumstances. *We are*, i. e. we as
preachers. The idea is the same whether we say that preachers of the gospel, or the gospel itself, or Christ, are the cause
of life to some, and of death to others. As Christ is to some
a tried corner stone, elect and precious, the rock of their salvation, to others he is a stone of offence. 1 Pet. 2, 7. 8. So
the gospel and its ministers are the cause of life to some, and
of death to others, and to all they are either the one or the
other. The word of God is quick and powerful either to save
or to destroy. It cannot be neutral. If it does not save, it
destroys. "This is the condemnation, that light is come into
the world, and men loved darkness rather than light," John
3, 19. "If I had not come and spoken unto them they had
not had sin," John 15, 22. If a man rejects the gospel, it had
been far better for him never to have heard it. It will be
more tolerable for Sodom and Gomorrah in the day of judgment than for him. This, which is the doctrine of the Bible,
is plainly the doctrine of this passage. The gospel and those
who preach it, are either a savour of life or a savour of death.
If not the one, they must be the other. In the phrase "a
savour of death unto death," *of death* expresses the quality,
unto death, the effect. It is a deadly savour, and it produces
death. And so of the corresponding clause, "a savour of life
unto life," is a salutary savour producing life. The Rabbins
often use a similar expression in reference to the Law, which
they say is either an odour of life or of death.

On the authority of two of the older MSS. (A and C), and
several of the more modern ones, Lachmann, Tischendorf and
Meyer read ἐκ θανάτου and ἐκ ζωῆς instead of the simple geni-

tive. It is then not a savour *of death* or *of life*, but a savour
arising from death, and a savour arising from life. To the
one class Christ is dead and yields only a savour of death; to
the other, he is alive, and yields a savour of life. According
to either reading the main idea is the same. Christ and his
gospel, and therefore his ministers, are to believers the source
of life, and to unbelievers the source of death. See Matt. 21,
44. Luke 2, 34. John 9, 39. The common text has more external authority, and certainly gives a simpler sense, and is
therefore preferred by the majority of editors.

And who is sufficient for these things? Καί (*and*) before
a question often indicates a consequence of what precedes.
It is frequently in our version in such cases rendered *then*.
"Who then can be saved?" Mark 10, 26. "How is he then
David's son?" Luke 20, 44. So here, Who then is sufficient
for these things? If the work is so great, if eternal life or
eternal death must follow the preaching of the gospel, who
then is sufficient (ἱκανός) for so responsible a calling? The
most natural answer to this question would seem to be, 'No
one in himself.' The following verse, however, which begins
with (γάρ) *for*, and is designed to confirm the implied answer,
requires that answer to be, "I am." 'I am sufficient for this
work, *for* I do not handle the word of God deceitfully.'
"My sufficiency," however, the apostle immediately adds, 3,
5, "is of God." Of himself he was not fit or able to do any
thing. There is, as Calvin remarks, an implied antithesis.
'The object of preaching is the diffusion of the knowledge of
Christ; the effect of that diffusion is life to some and death to
others. Who then is competent to this work? Not your
false teachers who corrupt the word of God, but I and others
who preach the pure gospel from pure motives.' This view is
sustained by what follows, for the apostle immediately proceeds to vindicate his claim to this sufficiency or fitness, which
he denies to the false teachers.

17. For we are not as many, which corrupt the
word of God; but as of sincerity, but as of God, as in
the sight of God, speak we in Christ.

The connection indicated by *for* is obvious. 'We are
competent to this work, for we are not like the false teachers,
but are sincere.' We are not *as many*, οἱ πολλοί, *the* many.

This some understand to mean the mass or majority of those who preach the gospel. The apostle would thus be made to condemn, as corrupters of the faith, the great body of the ministers of the apostolic church. This, however, is unnecessary. *The* many, means the definite many known to the Corinthians as false teachers, to whom in the course of this epistle the apostle so often refers. *Which corrupt the word of God.* The word used is καπηλεύω, *to be a huckster*, and then *to act as one*. Paul says, We do not act as hucksters in reference to the word of God. The word is frequently used in the Greek writers in a figurative sense, to express the ideas of adulterating, and of making merchandise of any thing for the sake of gain. Both ideas may be united, for both are included in the disclaimer of the apostle. He neither adulterated the word of God, by mixing it with Judaism or false philosophy (i. e. with his own speculations), nor did he use it for any selfish or mercenary purpose. *But as of sincerity.* The (ὡς) *as*, is not redundant. The meaning is, 'We speak as those who are sincere,' i. e. those whose characteristic is εἱλικρίνεια, *transparent purity*, or integrity; who can bear being looked through and through; all whose motives will sustain inspection. *As of God*, not merely sent of God, but godly, influenced by God, and belonging to God, and therefore like him. Our Lord said to the Jews, "He which is of God, heareth God's words: ye therefore hear them not because ye are not of God," John 8, 47. *As in the sight of God*, i. e. as in his presence and conscious of his inspection. We speak *in Christ;* not of Christ, nor, according to Christ, but in communion with him, as a member of his body and actuated by his Spirit. We have here then Paul's description of a faithful minister, of one who is (ἱκανός) *sufficient*, or qualified for the fearful responsibility of being a savour of life or of death. He does not corrupt the word of God by any foreign admixtures, nor use it as a means of his own advancement by dispensing it so as to please men; but he is governed by pure motives, is of God, and speaks as in the presence of God, and as a true Christian man.

CHAPTER III.

The apostle shows that he does not need to commend himself or to be commended by the Corinthians; that God had qualified him for the work of a minister of the new, and not of the old covenant, vs. 1–11. He exercised his ministry in accordance with the peculiar character of the new dispensation, vs. 12–18.

Proof of the Apostle's fitness for his work, and its nature.
Vs. 1–11.

ALTHOUGH the concluding paragraph of the preceding chapter contained a strong assertion of the integrity and fidelity of the apostle, he says, it was not written for the purpose of self-commendation. He needed no commendation from any source, v. 1. The Corinthians themselves were his commendation. Their conversion was an epistle of Christ authenticating his mission and his fidelity, which all men could read, vs. 2. 3. His fitness or sufficiency for his work was due in no measure to himself, but to God, who had endowed him with the qualifications of a minister of the new covenant, vs. 4–6. This covenant and its ministry are far superior to the old covenant and the ministry of Moses, because the one was a ministry of death, the other of life; the one was of condemnation, the other of righteousness; the glory of the one was transient, the glory of the other is abiding, vs. 7–11.

1. Do we begin again to commend ourselves? or need we, as some (others), epistles of commendation to you, or (letters) of commendation from you?

Many of the peculiarities of this epistle are due to the fact that at the time of writing it the apostle's mind was filled with conflicting feelings. On the one hand, he was filled with gratitude to God and love to the Corinthians on account of their repentance and ready obedience; and on the other, with feelings of indignation at the perverse and wicked course adopted by the false teachers in Corinth. Hence even in the expression of the former class of feelings, he is interrupted or turned aside by the thought that his opponents were on the watch to turn every thing to his disadvantage. Thus although there was nothing of a spirit of self-commendation in his thanking God for causing him to triumph, or in the assertion of his sincerity, in 1, 15–17, yet he knew that his enemies would put that construction on what he had said. He seems to hear them say, 'He is commending himself again.' It is plain from the use of the word *again* in this connection, that the charge of praising himself had before been made against the apostle, whether founded on his former epistle or what he said on other occasions, is uncertain and unimportant.

The authorities are divided as to whether ἡ μη or εἰ μη is the true reading in the following clause. If the former, the sense is, "Or do we need," &c.; if the latter, "Unless we need," &c. The latter gives an ironical turn to the passage. The apostle sets it forth as certain that his apostolic mission and authority were so authenticated, that he did not need, as certain people did, letters of commendation either to them or from them. These false teachers had no doubt gained access to Corinth on the strength of certain letters of recommendation. They were so little known and had so little character, that when they went elsewhere, they would need to be commended by the Corinthians. With Paul the case was different.

2. Ye are our epistle written in our hearts, known and read of all men.

Ye are our epistle, &c., or, *The epistle which we have ye are.* You as Christians, your conversion is, as it were, a letter from Christ himself authenticating our mission and fidelity. *Written in our hearts.* The plural form, *our hearts,* may be explained either on the assumption that the apostle is speaking of Timothy as well as of himself; or on the ground that he says *hearts* instead of *heart* for the same reason that he says *We* instead of *I;* or that the word is used figuratively for the affections. It is not Paul's manner to make his associates the joint authors of his letters, and in no one of his epistles does he speak more out of the fulness of his personal feelings than he does in this. It was not Timothy who was accused of self-commendation, who needed no letters of commendation, and it was not of Timothy's mission that the conversion of the Corinthians was the authentication, and therefore it was not in Timothy's heart that the epistle referred to was written. Paul is speaking of himself. A thing is said to be written in the heart when it is a matter of consciousness;

when it is a matter of subjective, as distinguished from objective knowledge. Thus the law of God is said to be written on the heart when the knowledge of it is inward and not merely outward. Jer. 31, 33. Heb. 8, 10. Rom. 2, 15. Any thing of which a man is certain, or of which he has a conviction founded upon his inward experience, may be said to be written on his heart. That the Corinthians were his epistle was to the apostle a matter of consciousness. It was a letter written on his heart which he could neither misunderstand nor be ignorant of. Comp. Rom. 10, 8. Any thing also that is very dear to us is said to be written on the heart, or to be in the heart. So Paul says to the Corinthians, " Ye are in our hearts," 7, 3. The apostle therefore may be understood to mean either that he was perfectly certain that the conversion of the Corinthians was for him a letter of commendation; or that it was most dear to him. A letter cherished in his heart. The context is in favour of making the former idea the prominent one. This letter, however, was not only well known to the apostle, it was *known and read of all men.* It was a palpable evidence of his divine mission, which no one could be ignorant of, and which no one could gainsay. Men could not doubt its genuineness, nor could they question its import. He expresses the same idea when he says, " The seal of my apostleship are ye in the Lord," 1 Cor. 9, 2.

3. (Forasmuch as ye are) manifestly declared to be the epistle of Christ ministered by us, written not with ink, but with the Spirit of the living God; not in tables of stone, but in fleshly tables of the heart.

The fact that the Corinthians were to Paul an epistle of commendation, is here confirmed; ὑμεῖς—φανερούμενοι ὅτι ἐστέ, *ye are conspicuous or publicly known as the epistle of Christ.* That is, an epistle of which Christ is the author. *Ministered by us.* The conversion of the Corinthians was the work of Christ, effected by the ministry of Paul. Considered as a letter, they were a letter of Christ written by the hand of Paul as Christ's instrument. The importance or superior worth of this epistle is set forth in what follows by a twofold contrast or comparison. First, it was not a letter written with ink, but by the Spirit of the living God. Any man could write with ink; Christ alone can write with the Spirit of God.

This is a figurative way of expressing the idea that the conversion of the Corinthians was a divine, supernatural work, and therefore an irrefragable proof that Paul, by whose instrumentality the work was effected, was the minister of Christ. This was a letter, therefore, infinitely above any ordinary letter written with ink. Secondly, it was not an outward, but an inward, spiritual work. The decalogue, written on tables of stone by the finger of God, was indeed a divine work, and proved the divine mission of Moses; but what was that to writing the law upon the fleshly tables of the heart! The work of regeneration and sanctification is always represented in the Scripture as a much higher manifestation of divine power and grace than any mere external miracle. In predicting the new dispensation in contrast with the old, God says, "Behold the days come when I will make a new covenant with the house of Israel—not according to the covenant that I made with their fathers,—but I will put my law in their inward parts, and write it in their hearts," Jeremiah 31, 31–33. To this the apostle evidently refers to show that the evidence of his mission was of a higher character than that of Moses, and that his ministry was far more exalted and glorious.

Instead of the genitive, καρδίας, the great body of ancient MSS. have the dative, καρδίαις; *on tables which are hearts of flesh*, instead of fleshly tables *of the heart*. The majority of editors adhere to the common text on the authority of the Greek fathers. The sense is the same.

4. And such trust have we through Christ to God-ward.

This confidence in the divinity and glory of his mission, and in his sufficiency for the apostleship he had from Christ and in the presence of God. It was a confidence so strong (and yet so humble) that it did not quail even under the eye of God; much less therefore under the scrutiny of the bleared eyes of his opponents. *Such confidence*, not merely confidence in the fact that the Corinthians were to him a letter of commendation, but the confidence expressed in the whole context, and especially in 2, 15–17. This confidence he had *through Christ*. It was not self-confidence. It was not the consciousness of superior excellence; but a conviction of the truth of the gospel and of the reality of that vocation which he had received from Christ. This confidence of the apostle that he was what God had called him to be, an able or fit minister of the gospel, was not a trait of natural character; it was not a conclusion from his inward and outward experience; it was one of the forms in which the Spirit of God which was in him manifested itself; just as that Spirit manifested itself in his humility, faith, courage, or constancy. It is easy to determine whether such confidence is self-inflation, or the strength of God in the soul. If the former, it has its natural concomitants of pride, arrogance, indifference, contempt of others. If the latter, it is attended by self-abhorrence, meekness, long-suffering, a willingness to be the least and lowest, and by all other graces of the Spirit. *To God-ward*, πρὸς τὸν Θεόν. This may mean in reference to God, i. e. a confidence exercised toward God as its object. Or, πρός may be used here as in Rom. 4, 2. Abraham, it is there said, had no καύχημα, *ground of boasting*, πρὸς Θεόν, *before God;* that is, none that could stand his inspection. Paul says he had a confidence before God; that is, one which could endure in his sight.

5. Not that we are sufficient of ourselves to think any thing as of ourselves; but our sufficiency (is) of God.

The apostle had strongly asserted his sufficiency or fitness for his work. He here tells us what was not, and then what was, the source of his sufficiency. *Not that*, i. e. I do not say, or, I do not mean, that we are sufficient of ourselves. In most of the older MSS. the words ἀφ' ἑαυτῶν, *of ourselves*, stand after λογίζασθαί τι, "sufficient to think any thing of ourselves," instead of, as in the common text, 'sufficient of ourselves to think any thing.' The former order of the words has greater authority, and gives perhaps the better sense. There is a difference in the prepositions in Greek which is not expressed in the English. Paul says his sufficiency or ability to think any thing was not ἀφ' ἑαυτῶν ὡς ἐξ ἑαυτῶν, not *from* himself as *out of* himself. He was not the source of this sufficiency either remotely or immediately. We should express much the same idea by saying, 'Our sufficiency is not in or of ourselves.' Comp. Gal. 1, 1. What he disclaims is sufficiency or ability *to think any thing ;* the implication is any thing right or good. He had no power of himself to accomplish any thing. His fitness for his work, whether consisting in knowledge, or grace, or fidelity, or efficiency, did not arise out of any thing he was in or of himself. The word λογίζασθαι does not here mean *to judge*, or *to think out* or *determine*. The idea is not that Paul was of himself unable to judge what was best and right, i. e. to think out the means of rendering his ministry successful. The word is to be taken in its simplest sense, *to think.* Thought is the lowest form of our efficiency, in so far as it is much easier to think good, than either to will or to do it. Paul means to say that so far as the subject in hand is concerned, he could do nothing, not even think. He was in himself absolutely empty and powerless. *Our sufficiency is of God.* All our fitness for our work—all our knowledge, holiness and power are of God. They are neither self-acquired nor self-sustained. I am nothing, the apostle would say; God in me is every thing. The same truth and feeling are expressed in 1 Cor. 15, 10.

6. Who also hath made us able ministers of the new testament; not of the letter, but of the spirit: for the letter killeth, but the spirit giveth life.

This verse is a confirmation of the preceding. The relative ὅς is here used as in Luke 8, 13, and elsewhere, as implying the cause or reason. Our sufficiency is of God, *who ;* equivalent to *for he* hath made us able ministers. The same radical word is retained, ἱκάνωσε, hath rendered us ἱκανούς, *sufficient,* able, well qualified, *ministers of the new testament,* καινῆς διαθήκης, *of the new covenant,* as the word διαθήκη always means in the New Testament, unless Heb 9, 16 be an exception. The covenant formed between God and the Hebrews at Mount Sinai is called the Old Covenant; the gospel dispensation as distinguished from the Mosaic is called the New Covenant. Matt. 26, 28. 1 Cor. 11, 25. Heb. 8, 8. 9, 15. &c. As, however, the promises of the gospel, and especially the great promise of redemption by the blood of Christ, underlay both the patriarchal and Mosaic dispensations, the plan of salvation or the covenant of grace, is also called the New Covenant, although older than the Mosaic covenant, to distinguish it from the covenant of works formed with Adam. This gives rise to no little obscurity. It is not always easy to determine whether the words "new covenant" refer to the gospel dispensation introduced by Christ, or to the covenant of grace inaugurated in the first promise made to our fallen parents. And in like manner it is not easy always to decide whether the words the "old covenant" designate the Mosaic covenant or the covenant of works. The context must in every case be our guide in deciding these questions. In the present case it is plain that by the New Covenant the apostle means the gospel as distinguished from the Law,—the Christian as distinguished from the Mosaic dispensation. It was of that he was made a minister, and it is that which he contrasts with the Old Testament economy. *Not of the letter, but of the spirit.* These words admit of two constructions. They may depend on the word covenant. 'Covenant not of the letter, but of the spirit.' They thus determine the nature of the New Covenant as being not of the letter but of the spirit. This is the construction adopted by perhaps the majority of modern commentators. The older interpreters, followed by our translators, make the words in question depend on *ministers.* "Ministers not of the letter, but of the spirit." This latter is not only more familiar to the readers of the English version, but is favoured by the whole context. Paul contrasts two dispensations; one he calls the letter, the other the spirit. He says he is minister of the one, not of the other, and afterwards, vs. 7. 8, he speaks of the ministry of death and ministry of the spirit; the ministry of condemnation and the ministry of righteousness. That the words *letter* and *spirit* as here used mean the law and the gospel is plain, first, because it is the law and the gospel which he proceeds to compare in the following verses; and secondly, because these are terms which he elsewhere uses in the same sense. Thus in Rom. 7, 6 he speaks of the oldness of the letter and newness of the spirit. In Rom. 2, 27 he characterizes the Jew as being of the letter, i. e. as having the law. Comp. also Gal. 3, 3. If it be asked what is the ground of these designations, why the law is called *letter*, and the gospel *spirit*, it may be answered in the first place, that the law is called γράμμα, *letter*, for the same reason that it is called γράφη, *scripture*. It was something written. Not only was the decalogue, the kernel of the Mosaic economy, originally written on stones, but the whole law was a volume known as *the writings*. And in the second place, the law as written was something external and objective. It was addressed to the eye, to the ear, to the understanding. It was not an inward principle or power. It held up the rule of duty to which men were to be conformed, but it could not impart the disposition or ability to obey. It was, as it were, a mere writing or book. On the other hand, the gospel is spiritual, as distinguished from what was external and ritual. It is the power of God, Rom. 1, 6; the organ through which the Spirit works in giving life to the soul. These words therefore express concisely the characteristic difference between the law and the gospel. The one was external, the other spiritual; the one was an outward precept, the other an inward power. In the one case the law was written on stone, in the other on the heart. The one therefore was *letter*, the other *spirit*.

For the letter (i. e. the law) *killeth*, but the spirit (i. e. the gospel) *giveth life*. This is the reason why God hath made Paul the minister of the spirit. 'God had made us able ministers not of the law but of the gospel, *for* the law kills, but the gospel gives life.' This passage and the following context present two important questions. First, in what sense does the law kill? And second, How is it that the apostle attributes to the Mosaic system this purely legal character, when he elsewhere so plainly teaches that the gospel was witnessed or taught both in the law and the prophets? As to the former of these questions, the answer furnished by the Scriptures is plain. The law demands perfect obedience. It says, "Do this and live," Rom. 10, 5. Gal. 3, 12, and "Cursed is every one who continueth not in all things written in the book of the law to do them," Gal. 3, 10. As no man renders this perfect obedience, the law condemns him. It pronounces on him the sentence of death. This is one way in which it kills. In the second place, it produces the knowledge or consciousness of sin, and of course of guilt, that is, of just exposure to the wrath of God. Thus again it slays. And thirdly, by presenting the perfect standard of duty, which cannot be seen without awakening the sense of obligation to be conformed to it, while it imparts no disposition or power to obey, it exasperates the soul and thus again it brings forth fruit unto death. All these effects of the law are systematically presented by the apostle in the 6th and 7th chapters of his epistle to the Romans, and in the 3d chapter of the epistle to the Galatians.

The second question is more difficult. Every reader of the New Testament must be struck with the fact that the apostle often speaks of the Mosaic law as he does of the moral law considered as a covenant of works; that is, presenting the promise of life on the condition of perfect obedience. He represents it as saying, Do this and live; as requiring works, and not faith, as the condition of acceptance. Rom. 10, 5–10. Gal. 3, 10–12. He calls it a ministration of death and condemnation. He denies that it can give life. Gal. 3, 21. He tells those who are of the law (that is, Judaizers) that they had fallen from grace; that is, had renounced the gratuitous method of salvation, and that Christ should profit them nothing. Gal. 5, 2. 4. In short, when he uses the word law, and says that by the law is the knowledge of sin, that it can only condemn, that by its works no flesh can be justified, he includes the Mosaic law; and in the epistle to the Galatians all these things are said with special reference to the law of Moses. On the other hand, however, he teaches that the plan of salvation has been the same from the beginning; that Christ was the propitiation for the sins committed under the old covenant; that men were saved then as now by faith in Christ; that this mode of salvation was revealed to Abraham and understood by him, and taught by Moses and the prophets. This view is presented repeatedly in Paul's epistles, and is argued out in due form in Rom. 3, 21–31. Rom. 4, and Gal. 3. To reconcile these apparently conflicting representations it must be remembered that the Mosaic economy was designed to accomplish different objects, and is therefore presented in Scripture under different aspects. What, therefore, is true of it under one aspect, is not true under another. 1. The law of Moses was, in the first place, a re-enactment of the covenant of works. A covenant is simply a promise suspended upon a condition. The covenant of works, therefore, is nothing more than the promise of life suspended on the condition of perfect obedience. The phrase is used as a concise and convenient expression of the eternal principles of justice on which God deals with rational creatures, and which underlie all dispensations, the Adamic, Abrahamic, Mosaic and Christian. Our Lord said to the lawyer who asked what he should do to inherit eternal life, "What is written in the law? How readest thou? And he answering said, Thou shalt love the Lord thy God with all thy heart, and with all thy soul, and with all thy strength, and with all thy mind; and thy neighbour as thyself. And he said unto him, Thou hast answered right, this do and thou shalt live," Luke 10, 26–28. This is the covenant of works. It is an immutable principle that where there is no sin there is no condemnation, and where there is sin there is death. This is all that those who reject the gospel have to fall back upon. It is this principle which is rendered so prominent in the Mosaic economy as to give it its character of law. Viewed under this aspect it is the ministration of condemnation and death. 2. The Mosaic economy was also a national covenant; that is, it presented national promises on the condition of national obedience. Under this aspect also it was purely legal. But 3, as the gospel contains a renewed revelation of the law, so the law of Moses contained a revelation of the gospel. It presented in its priesthood and sacrifices, as types of the office and work of Christ, the gratuitous method of salvation through a Redeemer. This necessarily supposes that faith and not works was the condition of salvation. It was those who trusted, not those free from sin, who were saved. Thus Moses wrote of Christ, John 5, 46; and thus the law and the prophets witnessed of a righteousness of faith, Rom. 3, 21. When therefore the apostle spoke of the old covenant under its legal aspect, and especially when speaking to those who rejected the gospel and clung to the law of Moses as law, then he says, it kills, or is the ministration of condemnation. But when viewing it, and especially when speaking of those who viewed it as setting forth the great doctrine of redemption through the blood of Christ, he represented it as teaching his own doctrine. The law, in every form, moral or Mosaic, natural or revealed, kills. In demanding works as the condition of salvation, it must condemn all sinners. But the gospel, whether as revealed in the promise to Adam after his fall, or in the promise to Abraham, or in the writings of Moses, or in its full clearness in the New Testament, gives life. As the old covenant revealed both the law and the gospel, it either killed or gave life, according to the light in which it was viewed. And therefore Paul sometimes says it does the one, and sometimes the other. *But the spirit giveth life.* The spirit, or the gospel, gives life in a sense correlative to that in which *the letter* (i. e. the law) kills. 1. By revealing a righteousness adequate to our justification, and thus delivering us from the sentence of death. 2. By producing the assurance of God's love and the hope of his glory in the place of a dread of his wrath. 3. By becoming, through the agency of the Holy Spirit, an inward principle or power transforming us into the image of God; instead of a mere outward command.

7. 8. But if the ministration of death, written (and) engraven in stones, was glorious, so that the children of Israel could not steadfastly behold the face of Moses for the glory of his countenance ; which (glory) was to be done away : how shall not the ministration of the Spirit be rather glorious ?

It was the design and effect of the law to kill. This is true, so far as the work of salvation is concerned, of the law in all its forms, whether the moral law as revealed in the Scriptures, or as written in the heart, or as the Mosaic law. In all these forms it was designed to bring men to the knowledge of sin and helplessness ; to produce a sense of guilt and misery, and a longing for redemption, and thus be a schoolmaster to bring men to Christ. Gal. 3, 24. This was a necessary office, and therefore glorious. But how can it compare with the gospel? How can that which only makes us know that we are sinful and condemned, be compared with that which delivers us from sin and condemnation? This is the idea which the apostle expands, and, as it were with exultation, turns over as though he could not let it go, in vs. 7–11. *But if the ministration of death, written* (and) *graven in stones.* The Greek is, εἰ δὲ ἡ διακονία τοῦ θανάτου ἐν γράμμασιν ἐντετυπωμένη ἐν λίθοις, *but if the ministration of death in letters engraven in stones.* The simplest interpretation of these words is that the ministration of death was in letters, i. e. by means of letters, engraven on stone ; which is the sense expressed by the free translation given in our common version. According to this view ἐν γράμμασιν are connected with what follows. But more commonly they are connected with what precedes ; *the ministration of death in letters,* which Luther makes to mean, "the ministration which by means of letters (i. e. the written law) produces death." This certainly gives a good sense and consistent with the context ; but it is not so simple or natural as the one first mentioned. It will be observed that Paul says that the *ministration* was engraven on stone. It was, however, of course not the ministration (the office of a minister) but the law itself that was thus engraven. There are two things here stated. First, that Moses was the minister of a covenant that produced death ; and secondly, that that covenant was an external economy or system. These two ideas are combined at the expense of mere verbal accuracy in a single clause. The word διακονία, *ministration*, means either *the service*, i. e. the act of ministering, or the office of a διάκονος or minister. Commonly the former. In what sense the ministry of the law was a ministry of death, and the reason why the law is described as engraven on stone, have already been stated. The law is thus exhibited as external, as opposed to what is spiritual.

Was glorious, ἐγενήθη ἐν δόξᾳ, *existed in glory ;* was surrounded, as it were, by a halo. The reference here is only indirectly to the brightness of Moses's face, which was but a symbol of the glory of his ministration. The glory which pertained to the old dispensation was not the illumination of the countenance of Moses, which was merely an incident. It was of the same kind, though less in degree, as the glory of the gospel. The one dispensation was indeed glorious, but the other was more so. *So that the children of Israel could not steadfastly behold the face of Moses.* The whole service was so glorious that even the face of Moses was so bright that the people could not look upon it. This brightness of the face of Moses was in two respects a symbol of the glory of the old dispensation. In the first place, it was an outward brightness. So too the glory of the Mosaic dispensation was derived in large measure from its pompous ritual, its temple, its priesthood, its sacrifice, and, above all, its Shekinah, or visible symbol of the divine presence. But what was all this to the glory of the gospel ? What was a bright cloud overhanging the cherubim, to the light of God's presence filling the soul ? And secondly, the brightness of the face of Moses was transient. The participle καταργουμένην may be taken as imperfect —They could not behold it as *it was vanishing away ;* or as present, *which is evanescent*, or *perishable*. It was in its own nature a mere transient brightness, analogous to the temporary splendour of the service committed to him. *How shall not the ministration of the Spirit be rather glorious ?* If the one was glorious, how much more the other ! The future *shall* is not to be understood in reference to the future world. The idea is not that hereafter, when Christ's kingdom is consummated, the ministration of the gospel shall be found more glorious than that of the law. The future expresses the certain sequence. If the ministration of death was glorious, the ministration of the Spirit shall assuredly, if rightly considered, be regarded as glorious. This is plain from the fact that the things compared are the ministration committed to Moses and the ministration committed to Paul; and also from the reason assigned for the superiority of the latter, which is not what is to be realized in the future, but what is experienced in the present. It was because it is *the ministration of the spirit* that it is more glorious than the ministration of death. The ideas of life and life-giving are inseparable from that of spirit. Hence the Holy Ghost in the ancient creeds of the church is designated as τὸ πνεῦμα τὸ ἅγιον, τὸ κύριον, τὸ ζωοποιόν. And hence the gospel as the source of life is called spirit. It is doubtful, however, whether the word *spirit* here refers to the Holy Spirit, or to the gospel. Luther renders the phrase ἡ διακονία τοῦ πνεύματος, *das Amt, das den Geist giebt*, i. e. the office which gives the Spirit; because it is by the ministration of the gospel the Holy Spirit is imparted to men. This view is perhaps commonly adopted. But as in v. 6, *spirit*, as opposed to *letter*, evidently means the gospel as opposed to the law, and as the things compared are the law and gospel, or the ministry of the one and the ministry of the other, the probability is that Paul intended the word to be so understood here. The gospel is *spirit* because it is the source of life. Instead of being something external and powerless, it is inward and saving; and this is the ground of its superiority to the law.

9. For if the ministration of condemnation (be) glory, much more doth the ministration of righteousness exceed in glory.

This verse is a confirmation of the preceding. The gospel is more glorious than the law, for the ministration of righteousness is more glorious than the ministration of condemnation. *The ministration of condemnation* is that ministration which brings men into a state of conscious condemnation; that is, which makes them know and feel that they are condemned. *The ministration of righteousness* is that ministration which reveals a righteousness by which men are justified, and thus freed from the condemnation pronounced upon them by the law. As much better therefore as justification is than condemnation to eternal death, so much better is the gospel than the law. Although the words κατάκρισις, *condemnation*, and δικαιοσύνη, *righteousness*, are here in antithesis, it does not follow that the latter means *justification*, which is a sense it

never has in the New Testament. It retains its proper meaning, *righteousness*, i. e. that which the law demands. It is
not justification, but the ground of it; that on account of
which a man is justified or pronounced righteous. The gospel, being the ministration of the spirit, is the ministration of
righteousness, because as what is spirit is life-giving, the gospel must reveal a righteousness which satisfies the demands
of the law, and thus free us from judicial death, or it could
not be the source of life. It is true that the life of which the
gospel is the source is more than mere justification; but as
justification is the necessary condition of spiritual life, Paul
here exalts the gospel by making it the means of securing
that righteousness which is necessary to sanctification and inseparable from it. The use of the present tense, περισσεύει,
doth abound, in this verse, serves to confirm the explanation
given of v. 8. Paul in both instances is speaking of the glory
which now belongs to the ministry of the gospel, not of what
is to be hereafter.

10. For even that which was made glorious hath
no glory in this respect, by reason of the glory that
excelleth.

For even, καὶ γάρ, *for moreover*. Too little was said in
simply asserting that the gospel excelled the law. The law,
though glorious in itself, ceased to be glorious in the presence
of the gospel, as the moon loses its brightness in the presence
of the sun. *That which was made glorious*, τὸ δεδοξασμένον,
that which was and is glorious, viz. the ministry of Moses, and,
by implication, the law or dispensation of which he was the
minister. *Hath no glory*, οὐ δεδόξασται, *is not glorious*, ἐν
τούτῳ τῷ μέρει, *in this particular*. This is explained by what
follows. *Because of the glory that excelleth*. The ministry
of the gospel so much excels the ministry of the law, that the
latter ceases in the comparison to be glorious at all. This is
the common and natural interpretation of the text. Two other
explanations have been proposed. First, the words ἐν τούτῳ
τῷ μέρει are connected with δεδοξασμένον, *that which was glorious* (viz. the ministry of Moses), in this particular, viz. that the
face of Moses was rendered luminous. This gives a very insignificant sense. The shining of the face of Moses was not
the glory of his ministry or of the old economy. It was but

a symbol of it. Second, Meyer and others, retaining the ordinary construction of the passage, make the apostle say, that the general truth that the lesser glory is eclipsed by the greater, was illustrated *in this case*, i. e. in the case of Moses and his ministry. This brings out the same sense as that given by the ordinary interpretation, but in a less natural way. *That which was made glorious*, τὸ δεδοξασμένον, naturally refers to the definite subject of which the context treats, which is the ministry of Moses.

11. For if that which was done away (was) glorious, much more that which remaineth (is) glorious.

A new ground of superiority. The old dispensation and its ministry were temporary, the new is permanent. There is nothing to intervene, no new revelation, no new economy, between the gospel and its ministry, and the final consummation. Whoever are to be converted, whatever nations are to be brought in, it must be by the preaching of the gospel, *which remaineth*, or is to continue, according to Christ's promise, until the end of the world. In the former clause the apostle says the law was διὰ δόξης, *with glory*, in the latter, that the gospel was ἐν δόξῃ, *in glory*. This is a mere variation of expression without any difference of meaning. Comp. Rom. 3, 30. 5, 10. That the binding authority of the law ceased on the introduction of the gospel, is a doctrine which the apostle had to sustain against the Judaizing tendency of the early Christians, on many occasions. To this point the epistles to the Galatians and to the Hebrews are principally directed. As Paul's opponents in Corinth were of this class, there is little doubt that what he here says of the inferiority and temporary character of the old economy had a special reference to them; while his strong assertion of his divine mission, of the dignity and superiority of the ministry which he had received, was intended to counteract the influence of their invidious attacks upon his authority. No less clear is the inculcation of the other great truth here presented. The gospel did away the law, but is itself never to be superseded. These are "the last times," the last dispensation, which is to continue until the consummation of all things.

*The clearness and freedom of the Gospel as contrasted with
the obscurity of the Law.* Vs. 12–18.

The apostle having referred to the transient brightness of
Moses's face, as a symbol of the passing glory of his ministry,
here employs the fact that Moses veiled his face as a twofold
illustration. In the first place, it is symbolical of the obscurity of the revelation made under the old dispensation. As the
brightness of Moses's face was covered, so spiritual or evangelical truth was of old covered under the types and shadows
of the Mosaic economy. In the second place, it is symbolical
of the blindness which rested on the minds of the Jews, which
prevented their seeing the true import of their own institutions, vs. 12–15. Nevertheless, as Moses removed the veil
from his face when he turned to the Lord, so both the obscurity which rests on the law, and the blindness which rests
upon the mind of the Jew, are dispelled when he turns
towards Christ. The vision of his glory transforms the soul
into his likeness, vs. 16–18.

**12. Seeing then that we have such hope, we use
great plainness of speech.**

Seeing then that we have such hope, literally, *Having then
such hope,* i. e. because we have it. The hope to which he refers
must be that mentioned in the context, v. 14, that the gospel
and its ministry were, and would prove themselves to be, far
superior to the law and to the ministry of Moses. What in
v. 4 he calls πεποίθησις, *confidence,* he here calls ἐλπίς, *hope,*
because the confidence which he felt had reference not only to
the present, but also to the future. *We use great plainness
of speech,* i. e. παρρησία, *outspokenness.* This stands opposed
to all concealment, whether from timidity or from a desire to
deceive; and also to all fear of consequences. It is a frank,
open, courageous manner of speech. Paul therefore says that
in his case it was the result of his firm conviction of his divine
mission and of the truth and glory of the gospel which he
preached, that he proclaimed it fully, intelligibly, and without regard to consequences. Its being to the Greeks foolishness, and to the Jews a stumblingblock, did not prevent his
declaring the whole counsel of God. The same cause will
ever produce the same effect. If Paul's experience of the
truth and excellence of the gospel led him to declare it with-

out reserve, a similar experience will produce a similar openness and boldness in other ministers of the gospel. This indeed is one of the glories of Christianity. It is characteristic
of error to practise reserve and to seek concealment. In all
the religions of antiquity there was an esoteric and exoteric
doctrine; one for the people and the other of the initiated.
They all had mysteries carefully concealed from the public
eye. So in the Romish church, just in proportion as it is in-
fected with the spirit of heathenism the doctrine of reserve is
avowed and practised. The gospel is not preached with
openness, so that all may understand it. The people are kept
in ignorance. They are told they need not know; that faith
without knowledge, a blind confidence in rites which they do
not understand, is all-sufficient. But if a man in a church has
the conviction that the gospel is of God, that it is unspeakably
glorious, adapted to all and needed by all in order to salvation, then the word will be preached openly and without
reserve.

13. And not as Moses, (which) put a veil over his
face, that the children of Israel could not steadfastly
look to the end of that which is abolished.

And not as Moses, that is, we do not do what Moses did.
Paul had just said that he used great plainness of speech, that
he practised no concealment or reserve. Of course he means
that Moses did the reverse. He did use concealment and
practise reserve. This is no impeachment of the character
of Moses. Paul is not speaking of his personal character, but
of the nature of his office. The truth concerning man's redemption was not "in other ages made known unto the sons
of men as it is now revealed unto the holy apostles and
prophets by the Spirit," Eph. 3, 5. It was not consistent
with the nature of the ministry of Moses to use the παῤῥησία,
the openness, in communicating the doctrines of redemption,
which it is the glory of the Christian ministry to be permitted
to employ. He was sent to speak in parables and in types, to
set forth truth in the form of significant rites and ceremonies.
He put a veil over the glory, not to hide it entirely from
view, but to obscure its brightness. The people saw the
light, but only occasionally and imperfectly. Paul had already spoken of the brightness of Moses's face as a symbol of his

ministry, and therefore he represents him as veiling himself, to express the idea that he communicated the truth obscurely. Paul was sent to let the truth shine forth clearly; he did not put a veil over it as Moses did, and was commanded to do. *That the children of Israel could not steadfastly look to the end of that which is abolished.* That is, to prevent their seeing the end or fading away of the brightness of his face. The word καταργούμενος (*that which is abolished*) is used, v. 7, in reference to the glory of the face of Moses, and v. 11 in reference to his ministry and the dispensation to which it belonged. Here the reference is to the former, because his face is spoken of, and its brightness was veiled, and therefore, it was the brightness the end of which the Israelites were prevented from seeing. If this be so, then τέλος, *the end*, must mean the termination, and not the design or scope. In Rom. 10, 4, Christ is said to be the end of the law, not only as abrogating it, but as being the object towards which it tended. He was that which it was intended to reveal. Those commentators who make καταργούμενον (*that which is abolished*) refer to the old law and its ministry, give τέλος the sense of end or object. They understand the apostle to say that Moses put a veil over his face to prevent the children of Israel seeing Christ, who was the end of the law. But this gives a most incongruous meaning. How could Moses's veiling his face prevent the Israelites seeing Christ? The first part of the verse cannot be taken literally, and the latter part figuratively. If the veiling was a literal covering of the face, that which the veil hid must be something which a literal veil could cover. The majority of commentators, therefore, understand the words, *that which is abolished,* to refer to the visible brightness of the face of Moses, and *the end* to mean the termination of that brightness. The whole clause therefore means that Moses veiled his face in order to prevent the Israelites seeing how soon its brightness faded. But what has this to do with the point in hand? In answering this question it must be remembered that the apostle had referred to the brightness of the face of Moses as a fit symbol of his ministry, inasmuch as it was external and transient. To say, therefore, that Moses veiled his face that the people might not see the end of its brightness, is a figurative way of saying that Moses hid the light, or taught obscurely, that the people might not understand the true nature and intent of his ministry. But how is it consistent with the character of God that he should commission Moses to teach

obscurely in order that he might not be understood? Some
endeavour to obviate this difficulty by saying that πρὸς τὸ μὴ
ἀτενίσαι expresses the result and not the design. 'He put a
veil over his face, *so that* (not, *in order that*) the children of
Israel did not see the end of that which is abolished.' Or, to
drop the figure, 'He taught obscurely, *so that* the people did
not understand him.' This explanation, however, is forbidden
by the force of the preposition πρός, which in such connections
properly expresses the design or intention. There is no special difficulty in the matter. Whatever is, God intended
should be. If Moses taught obscurely or in types, God intended that he should do so. If, in point of fact, the Jews
misunderstood the nature of their own economy, regarding as
ultimate and permanent what was in fact preparatory and
temporary, this was included in the divine purpose. It was
evidently the plan of God to make the revelation of the
scheme of redemption gradually. The whole was by slow
degrees evolved from the original promise made to our first
parents. Perhaps the object of their faith was the simple
promise of redemption. To Abraham it was revealed that
the Redeemer was to be one of his descendants. To Moses it
was made known that he was to be a prophet like himself, and
the nature of his work was obscurely set forth in the priesthood and sacrifices which he ordained. This was enough for
salvation, so long as nothing more had been revealed. It was
in accordance with this plan that Moses spoke in such a way
that the people did not understand the full import of his
teaching, God having purposed "that they without us should
not be made perfect," Heb. 11, 40. The passage before us is
parallel, in a measure, to Mark 4, 11, where our Lord says,
"Unto you it is given to know the mysteries of the kingdom
of God; but unto them that are without all these things are
done in parables; that seeing they may see, and not perceive." There is, therefore, as just remarked, no special difficulty in this passage, even if it is understood to teach that
Moses was commissioned so to veil his teachings that they
should not be clearly understood. There is another difficulty
connected with this verse. It does not seem to agree with
Exodus 34, 30. There it is said that the people were afraid
to approach Moses on account of the brightness of his face,
and the implication (according to the English version, at least)
is, that it was to calm their fears he put on a veil. Whereas
here it is said that he put a veil over his face that the people

might not see the transient nature of that brightness. There is no inconsistency between the two accounts. The veiling had both effects; it calmed the fears of the people, and it prevented their seeing how fleeting the brightness was. As both effects followed, both were intended. Paul in this epistle assigns in different places three or four reasons why he commanded the Corinthians to excommunicate the incestuous member of their church. That it was meant as a test of their obedience, 2, 9, is not incompatible with its being a proof of his care for them, 7, 12. There is, however, not even the appearance of discrepancy between what the apostle here says and Exodus 34, 30–33, as it is rendered both in the Septuagint and Vulgate. The English version of that passage is, "And when Aaron and all the children of Israel saw Moses, behold, the skin of his face shone; and they were afraid to come nigh him. And Moses called unto them; and Aaron and all the rulers of the congregation returned unto him: and Moses talked with them. . . . And *till* Moses had done speaking with them, he put a veil on his face." According to this Moses put a veil over his face when he spoke to the people, and the implication is that he did it because they were afraid on account of the brightness of his countenance. But the Hebrew, in v. 33, is simply, "Moses ceased to speak with them, and put a veil over his face." The natural meaning of which is that he did not veil his face until he had ceased speaking. The Septuagint therefore renders the passage, "And when he ceased speaking with them, he put a veil over his face." And the Vulgate, *impletisque sermonibus, posuit velamen super faciem suam.* It appears from the following verses that when Moses went in before the Lord, he removed the veil; and when he came out his face shone, and he spake to the people, and again resumed the veil. According to this interpretation of the original, the object of putting on the veil was not to calm the fear of the people, but, as Paul says, to prevent their seeing how the brightness of his face vanished.

14. But their minds were blinded; for until this day remaineth the same veil untaken away in the reading of the Old Testament; which (veil) is done away in Christ.

In the preceding verse Paul was speaking of his ministry;

the same subject is resumed in the following chapter. Verses 14–18 are therefore a digression, although intimately connected with what precedes and follows. The particle ἀλλά either introduces something just the reverse of what precedes, and means *on the contrary*, or simply something different, and is to be rendered *but*. This verse admits of two modes of connection with what precedes. 'The Jews did not understand the ministry of Moses, *on the contrary*, their minds were blinded.' Or, the connection may be with the main idea of the preceding context. 'We use great plainness of speech, *but* their minds are blinded.' That is, notwithstanding the clearness with which the gospel is presented as the substance and true meaning of the old economy, still the Jews were so blinded they did not perceive it. In either way the sense is good. But as it is so much the habit of the apostle to connect what follows with what immediately precedes, and as the figure of the veil, which is not mentioned in v. 12, is continued in v. 14, it is most natural to make the connection with v. 13, where that figure is introduced, especially as Paul's immediate object in v. 12 is not to exhibit his plainness of speech in opposition to the hebetude of the Jews. It is the general fact that under the new dispensation the truth is exhibited plainly which he asserts. The blindness of the Jews is only incidentally introduced. *Their minds*, νοήματα, *thoughts, affections*. It means the whole inner man. *Were blinded*, ἐπωρώθη, properly *were rendered hard* or *callous*. The word is used both of the understanding and of the feelings. It expresses an inaptitude both of seeing and feeling. They neither understood nor felt the power of the truth. *For until this day remaineth untaken away the same veil.* This is a confirmation derived from experience of the fact previously stated. That the minds of the Israelites were thus blinded and hardened, is proved from the fact that until this day they do not understand the law. *The same veil*, i. e. the same obscurity. A veil was thrown over the truth as first revealed by Moses, and that same veil is there still. The Israelites of Paul's day understood their Scriptures as little as their fathers did. They remained satisfied with the external, ritual and ceremonial, without penetrating to what was beneath, or asking the real import of the types and shadows of the old economy. *In the reading of the Old Testament*, that is, when the Old Testament (covenant) is read. This metonymical use of the word *covenant* for the books in which that covenant is contained, is perfectly familiar to our ears, as we are accustomed to call the two great divisions of the Scriptures the Old and New Testaments or covenants; but this is the only instance of this use of the word in the New Testament. The English version does not in this passage follow the order of the Greek, which reads, "For until this day the same veil in the reading of the old covenant remains." Here the sense is complete. The following clause, μὴ ἀνακαλυπτόμενον ὅτι ἐν Χριστῷ καταργεῖται, admits of three interpretations. 1. The first is that adopted by our translators; μὴ ἀνακαλυπτόμενον is referred to the preceding clause (*remains untaken away*), and ὅτι (*because,* or *that*) is read as two words, ὅ τι, *which,* i. e. which veil is done away in Christ. So Luther, in his free translation: Denn bis auf den heutigen Tag bleibet dieselbige Decke unaufgedeckt über das Alten Testament wenn sie es lesen, welche in Christo aufhöret. The great majority of editors, however, read ὅτι. 2. The word ἀνακαλυπτόμενον, *untaken away,* is, as before, referred to κάλυμμα, *veil,* and ὅτι is rendered *because.* 'The veil remains untaken away, *because* it is removed (only) in Christ.' 3. ἀνακαλυπτόμενον is taken absolutely, and ὅτι is rendered *that.* 'The veil remains, it being unrevealed *that* it (viz. the old covenant) is done away in Christ.' In favour of this last-mentioned interpretation it is urged, that the old covenant was in fact done away in Christ, and that ignorance of that fact prevented the Jews understanding their own Scriptures. The sense therefore is good. Besides, the word καταργεῖται, *is done away,* is the proper term to express the abrogation of the law, but not so suitable to express the idea of the removal of a veil, for which, in v. 16, Paul uses the word περιαιρεῖται, *is removed.* The word καταργέω is used in verses 7. 11 and 13, to express the passing away of the brightness of the face of Moses, and of his ministry and dispensation, of which that brightness was the symbol, and therefore it is the more probable that it has the same reference here. On the other hand, however, it must be admitted that ἀνακαλυπτόμενον naturally agrees with κάλυμμα, *the veil remains untaken away,* and that ἀνακαλύπτω, to *uncover* or *unveil,* is not the common word to express the idea of making known or revealing. See v. 18, ἀνακαλυπτομένῳ προσώπῳ, *with unveiled face.* The second interpretation, therefore, above mentioned, is on the whole to be preferred. 'The veil which hid the meaning of the Old Testament remained unremoved, *because* it is done away in Christ, whom the Jews rejected.'

The Old Testament Scriptures are intelligible only when understood as predicting and prefiguring Christ. The present
καταργεῖται (*is done away*) is used as expressing the certain
consequence. The knowledge of Christ, as a matter of fact
and as a matter of course, removes the veil from the Old
Testament.

15. But even unto this day, when Moses is read, the veil is upon their heart.

But, ἀλλά, *on the contrary*, i. e. so far from being taken
away, the veil remains until this day. *When Moses is read.*
The word ἡνίκα, *when*, is used in the New Testament only
here and in v. 16. As it occurs often in the Septuagint, and
is used in Exodus 34, 34, it is the more probable that the language of that version was before the apostle's mind, and determined the mode in which he presents the incident of Moses
veiling his face, which, as shown above, accords better with
the view which the Septuagint gives of the original than with
that presented in the English version. In Acts 15, 21, Moses,
it is said, was read every sabbath day in the synagogues.
The veil, or, as the article is wanting, *a veil*, was, however,
over his face. The apostle presents the idea that the Jews
did not understand their Scriptures in two forms. He says,
in v. 14, that a veil rests on the Old Testament, and here that
a veil was over the hearts of the Jews. The true source of
the want of knowledge was subjective. The revelation of
Christ, even in the writings of the Old Testament, though obscure when compared with that contained in the writings of
the apostles, was sufficiently clear to be understood if the
Jews had only been in a right state of mind. Hence our Lord
upbraided his disciples, saying, " O fools and slow of heart to
believe all that the prophets have spoken," Luke 24, 25. Compare Acts 13, 27–29. The darkness was not so much in the
Scriptures, as in their minds.

16. Nevertheless, when it shall turn to the Lord, the veil shall be taken away.

According to the narrative in Ex. 34, 29–35, as understood
by the Septuagint, and as expounded by the apostle, the face
of Moses was made to shine by speaking with the Lord; when
among the people (except when delivering his message) he

wore a veil; when he turned to the Lord he removed the veil. To this allusion seems to be here made. So long as the people were turned from the Lord, the veil was on their heart; they could not understand the Scriptures; as soon as they turn to the Lord, the veil is removed, and all is bright and intelligible. *When it shall turn to the Lord;* ἡνίκα δ᾽ ἂν ἐπιστρέψῃ, *when it has turned,* i. e. when that conversion is accomplished, and as often as it occurs. The most natural subject of the verb ἐπιστρέψῃ (*turned*) is καρδία (*heart*). A veil is on the heart, but when it turns to the Lord, the veil is removed. As, however, the apostle is speaking of the heart of the Jews, and as the turning of their heart is their turning, so the sense is the same if the word Israel be supplied. The veil is on the heart of the people, but when the people turn to the Lord the veil is taken away. Calvin and others supply *Moses* as the nominative. By Moses, however, Calvin understands the Law. ‘When Moses is read, a veil is on the heart of the Jews; but when he, i. e. the law, is directed to Christ, who is the end of the law, then the veil is removed.’ That is, as soon as the Jews see that their law relates to Christ, then they understand it. This, however, is obviously an unnatural interpretation, as ἐπιστρέψῃ expresses the turning of the heart or of the people to God, and not giving the law a particular interpretation. Stanley, who also says that *Moses* must be the nominative of the verb, makes him, however, the representative, not of the law, but of the people. ‘When Moses turns to the Lord he strips off the veil.’ The word περιαιρεῖται he gives an active sense, according to its common use in the Septuagint. This too is less simple and natural than the common interpretation given above. The veil was on the heart of the people, and when *it,* i. e. their heart, turns to the Lord, *it is stripped off;* περιαιρεῖται is the word used in Ex. 34, 34. By *Lord* here, as the context shows, we are to understand Christ. He is the Lord whom Moses saw face to face on Mount Sinai, and to whom the Jews and all others must turn if they would enjoy the light of salvation.

17. Now the Lord is that Spirit: and where the Spirit of the Lord (is), there (is) liberty.

The first point to be determined with regard to this difficult passage, is the relation in which it stands to what precedes. It may be either an explanation or an inference. If

the former, then it is designed to show why turning to the
Lord secures the removal of the veil from the heart. It is
because the Lord is the Spirit, and where the Spirit is, there
is liberty, freedom from the law, from its bondage and ob-
scurities. If the latter, then the idea is, that since the veil is
removed by turning to the Lord, it follows as a further consequence that by thus turning we have liberty. The force of
the particle δέ, which so often introduces an explanation, and
the whole structure of the passage is in favour of the first interpretation. 2. It is plain that *the Lord* here means Christ.
This is clear not only because the word *Lord*, as a general
rule, in the New Testament, refers to Christ, but also because
the context in this case demands that reference. In v. 14 it
is said that the veil is done away in Christ, and in v. 16 that it
is removed when the heart turns to the Lord, and here that
the Lord is the Spirit. The main idea of the whole context
is, that the recognition of Jesus Christ as Lord, or Jehovah, is
the key to the Old Testament. It opens all its mysteries, or,
to use the figure of the apostle, it removes the veil which hid
from the Jews the true meaning of their own Scriptures. As
soon as they turn to the Lord, i. e. as soon as they recognize Jesus Christ as their Jehovah, then every thing becomes
bright and clear. It is plain, therefore, that the Lord spoken
of is Christ. This also determines another point, viz. that
Lord is here the subject, and *Spirit* the predicate. Paul says
that "The Lord is the Spirit," and not "The Spirit is the
Lord." The latter view of the passage is taken by many of
the Fathers, who regard it as a direct assertion of the divinity
of the Holy Ghost. Although the words would admit of this
interpretation, it is evidently inconsistent with the context.
It also follows from the fact that "Lord" here means Christ,
that it must designate his person and not his doctrine. The
apostle does not mean to say that the doctrine of Christ, or
the gospel, or new covenant, is the Spirit. It is true that in
v. 6, when contrasting the law and the gospel, he calls the one
the letter and the other the spirit; but this does not authorize
us to make *Lord* mean the gospel because the Lord is said to
be the Spirit. As in the preceding verses Christ and Lord
refer to Christ as a person; the word Lord must have the
same reference here. 3. When Paul says "The Lord is *the*
Spirit," he does not mean to say that 'the Lord is *a* spirit,'
agreeably to the analogy of John 4, 24, where it is said "God
is a spirit." This is not only opposed to the force of the arti-

cle τὸ before πνεῦμα, *the* Spirit, but also to the connection, as
Paul is speaking of Christ's office rather than of his nature. It is not his object to say that Christ is a spiritual being. Neither is the idea that he is replenished with the Holy
Spirit, so as to be in that sense and on that account called the
Spirit. This is not the meaning of the words, nor is the idea
demanded by the context. The two interpretations which
the words admit are either, first, that which our translators
probably intended to indicate when they rendered τὸ πνεῦμα
that Spirit. "The Lord is that Spirit," that is, the spirit
spoken of in v. 6; the spirit which stands opposed to the letter, that which gives life and righteousness; the inner sense
of the law, the saving truth and power hidden under the types
and forms of the Mosaic economy. Christ, says Calvin, is the
life of the law. Accedat anima ad corpus: et fit vivus homo,
præditus intelligentia et sensu, ad vitales actiones idoneus:
tollatur anima a corpore, et restabit inutile cadaver, omnique
sensu vacuum. Thus if Christ is present in the Mosaic law,
it is living and life-giving; if he is absent from it, it is dead and
death-dispensing. Christ is therefore *that* spirit which animates the law or institutions of Moses, and when this is recognized, the veil which hides their meaning is removed. True
as all this is, it can hardly be expressed by the simple words
ὁ κύριος τὸ πνεῦμά ἐστι, *the Lord is the Spirit.* The words τὸ
πνεῦμα, "the Spirit," have in the New Testament a fixed and
definite meaning, which is not to be departed from unless the
context renders such departure necessary. Besides, this interpretation requires that "the Spirit" should mean one thing,
and "the Spirit of the Lord" another, in the same verse.
This, however, can hardly be admitted. If "the Spirit of the
Lord," in the last clause, means the Holy Spirit, which will
not be questioned, "the Spirit," in the first clause, must have
the same meaning. The other interpretation, therefore, must
be adopted. "The Lord is the Spirit," that is, Christ is the
Holy Spirit; they are one and the same. Not one and the
same person, but one and the same Being, in the same sense
in which our Lord says, "I and the Father are one." It is an
identity of essence and of power. Christ is the Holy Spirit,
because, being the same in substance, where Christ is, there
the Spirit is, and where the Spirit is, there is Christ. Therefore this same apostle interchanges the three forms of expression as synonymous, "the Spirit of Christ," "Christ," and
"the Spirit." Rom. 8, 9. 10. The Holy Ghost is everywhere

in the Bible recognized as the source of all life, truth, power, holiness, blessedness and glory. The apostle, however, had in the context spoken of Christ as the source of life, as delivering from the death and bondage of the law. He is and does this because he and the Spirit are one; and therefore wherever Christ is, or in other words, wherever the Spirit of Christ is, or in other words still, wherever the Spirit is, *there is liberty*. By turning unto Christ we become partakers of the Holy Spirit, the living and life-giving, because he and the Spirit are one, and Christ dwells in his people, redeeming them from the law and making them the children of God, by his Spirit. *The Spirit of the Lord*, as a designation of the Holy Ghost, shows that the Spirit stands in the same relation to the Son that he does to the Father. Therefore he is called the "Spirit of Christ," Rom. 8, 10, and "Spirit of His Son," Gal. 4, 6. And, therefore, also the Son is said to send and give the Spirit. John 16, 7. All this of course supposes the supreme divinity of our Lord. *The liberty* of which the apostle here speaks, must be that liberty which is consequent on the indwelling of the Holy Spirit, that is, which flows from the application to us of the redemption purchased by Christ. We have not received, says the apostle, the Spirit of bondage again to fear, but the Spirit of adoption. Rom. 8, 15. The liberty here intended is the glorious liberty of the children of God. Rom. 8, 21. It is the liberty wherewith Christ has made us free. Gal. 5, 1. This includes, 1. Freedom from the law in all its forms, Mosaic and moral, Rom. 6, 14. 7, 4, i. e. freedom from the obligation to fulfil the law as the condition of our justification before God; which involves freedom from condemnation and from a legal, slavish spirit. 2. Freedom from the dominion of sin, Rom. 7, 6, and from the power of Satan. Heb. 2, 14. 15. 3. Freedom from the bondage of corruption, not only as to the soul, but as to the body. Rom. 8, 21–23. This liberty, therefore, includes all that is involved in being the sons of God. Incidental to this liberty is freedom from all ignorance and error, and all subjection to the authority of men, except so far as it represents the authority of Christ, and therefore liberty of conscience or freedom from all authority in matters of religion other than that of the Spirit of God. There is not only no reason for restricting the idea of the liberty of which the apostle speaks to any one of these forms, but the context requires that it should include all that liberty of which the presence of the Spirit is the source and the assurance. As no man in this life is perfectly and at all times filled with the Spirit of Christ, he is never in this life a partaker of the full liberty of which Christ is the author.

18. But we all, with open face beholding as in a glass the glory of the Lord, are changed into the same image from glory to glory, (even) as by the Spirit of the Lord.

This verse is connected with the preceding by the simple particle of transition δέ, *but*. The natural consequence of the liberty mentioned in v. 17 is what is here stated. *We all*, i. e. all whom the indwelling of the Spirit of the Lord has made free. They are delivered from the bondage of the law, the veil has been removed from their face, and being turned to the Lord, they behold his glory *with open face*, ἀνακεκαλυμμένῳ προσώπῳ, i. e. with a face which has been, and which remains unveiled. The darkness arising from alienation, ignorance, misconception and prejudice has been dissipated, so that we can see clearly. *Beholding as in a glass or mirror*. This is probably the proper interpretation of the word here used. Κατοπτρίζω, in the active voice, means *to show in a mirror*, and in the middle, (the form here used,) it generally means, *to see one's self in a mirror*. This is its constant use in the classics. But in Philo it is used to express the idea of seeing by means of a mirror. As this sense is perfectly suited to this passage it is generally adopted by commentators, because the other explanations given to the word are either contrary to usage or to the context. Some render it simply *beholding*. But to this it is objected that it overlooks the special etymological signification of the word, and that ἀτενίζω, which occurs twice in this chapter, vs. 7 and 13, is the proper term for that idea. Besides, this interpretation loses sight of the figure involved in the passage. It is an *image* we see, and therefore we see, as it were, by reflection, or as in a glass. Luther, after Chrysostom, renders the word, *reflecting as in a mirror*. This explanation is adopted by Bengel, Billroth, Olshausen and others. They understand the apostle to say that Christians reflect, with an unveiled face, the glory of the Lord. They suppose that allusion is had to the glory of God as reflected from the face of Moses, which was transient and veiled; whereas, in the case of Christians, the glory of the Lord is constantly and clearly manifested in them and by them. They reflect his image wherever they go. But, in the first place, this explanation is inconsistent with the signification of the word, which never means to reflect; secondly, it is contrary to the context. The contrast is not between Moses and Christians, but between the Jews, or the unconverted, and Christians. The former were blinded by a veil, the latter see with an unveiled face. The one see and the others do not. This is obviously the antithesis implied, and not that the one class do, and the other do not reflect the glory of the Lord. In the third place, the relation in which this verse stands to the preceding forbids this interpretation. We have here the effect of turning to the Lord. We are delivered from the law, we are made free, we are introduced into the presence of the Lord, and enabled to behold his glory. And, finally, this interpretation overlooks the causal relation between the two clauses of this verse. We are transformed into the image of the Lord by beholding it, not by reflecting it. The common interpretation is therefore to be preferred; *beholding as in a mirror*. Though in comparison with the unconverted those who are turned to the Lord see clearly, or with an unveiled face, still it is only as in a mirror. 1 Cor. 13, 12. It is not the immediate, beatific vision of the glory of the Lord, which is only enjoyed in heaven, but it is that manifestation of his glory which is made in his word and by his Spirit, whose office it is to glorify Christ by revealing him to us. John 16, 14.

The object which we behold is *the glory of the Lord*, i. e. as the context evidently demands, of Christ. The glory of Christ is his divine excellence. The believer is enabled to see that Jesus is the Son of God, or God manifested in the flesh. This is conversion. Whoever shall confess that Jesus is the Son of God, God dwelleth in him, and he in God. 1 John 4, 15. The turning unto the Lord mentioned in the preceding verse is recognizing Christ as Jehovah. This is not only conversion, it is religion. It is the highest state of the human soul. It is eternal life. John 17, 3. Hence our Lord prays that his disciples may behold his glory, as the consummation of their blessedness. John 17, 24. And the apostle John says of all who received Christ, that they beheld "his glory as of the only begotten of the Father," John 1, 14. The idea here presented is more fully unfolded in the beginning of the following chapter.

Beholding his glory *we are changed into the same image;*

τὴν αὐτὴν εἰκόνα μεταμορφούμεθα, *we are transformed into the same image.* The verb is commonly construed with εἰς, *into*, or κατά, *after*, but sometimes, as here, with the simple accusative. *The same image*, that is, the same which we are by the Spirit enabled to behold. 'Beholding we are transformed;' there is a causal relation between the one and the other. This is a truth everywhere recognized in the word of God. While, on the one hand, it is taught that the natural man cannot see the things of the Spirit, because they are spiritually discerned, 1 Cor. 2, 14, and that this blindness is the cause of alienation and pollution, Eph. 4, 18; on the other hand, it is no less clearly taught that knowledge is the source of holiness, Eph. 5, 9; that spiritual discernment implies and produces congeniality. We shall be like Christ, because we shall see him as he is. 1 John 3, 2. The conformity to the image of Christ, as it arises from beholding his glory, must of course begin here. It is the vision of that glory, although only as in a glass, which has this transforming power. As the vision is imperfect, so the transformation is imperfect; when the vision is perfect, the conformity will be perfect. Rom. 8, 29. 1 John 3, 2. Only they are Christians, who are like Christ. The conformity of which the apostle speaks, although it is spiritual, as here presented, is not confined to the soul. Of the body it is said, since we have borne the image of the earthy, we shall bear the image of the heavenly. 1 Cor. 15, 49. Phil. 3, 21. *From glory to glory.* This may mean that the transformation proceeds *from glory* (i. e. from the glory of Christ as apprehended by us), and results in glory. This explanation is adopted by the Greek fathers. Or the expression indicates progression from one stage of glory to another. Comp. Ps. 84, 7, "They go from strength to strength." This is the common and most natural interpretation. The transformation is carried forward without intermission, from the first scarce discernible resemblance, to full conformity to the image of Christ, both as to soul and body. *As by the Spirit of the Lord.* As, i. e. as might be expected from such an agent. It is a work which corresponds to the nature of its author. *By;* the preposition is ἀπό, *from*, as indicating the source whence this glorious effect flows. *The Spirit of the Lord.* The Greek is κυρίου πνεύματος, which the Vulgate renders *Domini Spiritu*, an explanation which is adopted by Augustin, Calvin and many others, as well as by our translators. But this inverts the order of the words, and

is the more unnatural here because in the immediately preceding verse the apostle had said τὸ πνεῦμα κυρίου, *Spirit of the
Lord;* he would therefore hardly express the same idea in the
same connection by κυρίου πνεύματος. Others render the words
the Lord Spirit, i. e. the Spirit who is Lord. We have in the
Old Testament and in the apocalypse the familiar phrase, "the
Lord God;" but this is only the translation of יְהֹוָה אֱלֹהִים Je-
hovah Elohim, Jehovah who is God, which the Septuagint ren-
der κύριος ὁ θεός, the Vulgate Dominus Deus, and the English,
"Lord God." More analogous to the passage in the text is the
Hebrew אֲדֹנָי יְהֹוָה, which the Septuagint render κύριος κύριος,
the Vulgate Dominus Deus, and the English Lord God. In
Joshua 22, 22, we have the unusual combination, אֵל אֱלֹהִים יְהֹוָה;
Septuagint, ὁ θεὸς θεὸς κύριός ἐστι; and immediately after ὁ
θεὸς θεός; Vulgate, Fortissimus Deus Dominus; the English,
"The LORD God of gods." As then in Hebrew אֲדֹנָי יְהֹוָה, in
Greek κύριος κύριος (or κύριος ὁ θεός), in Latin, Dominus Deus,
and in English, Lord God, all meaning *God who is Lord,* so
κύριος πνεῦμα may mean *the Spirit who is Lord,* i. e. the divine
Spirit. This is the explanation adopted by Chrysostom, Theodoret and some of the moderns, in accordance with the interpretation which they give of the first clause of v. 17, which,
as stated above, they understand to mean, *the Spirit is Lord,*
πρὸς τὸ Πνεῦμα ἐπιστρέφων, πρὸς Κύριον ἐπιστρέφεις κύριος γὰρ τὸ
Πνεῦμα, καὶ ὁμόθρονον, ὁμοπροσκύνητον καὶ ὁμοούσιον Πατρὶ καὶ υἱῷ.
But as in v. 17 Paul does not say the Spirit is the Lord, but
on the contrary that the Lord is the Spirit, so it would be
unnatural to make him here say we are transformed by *the
Spirit who is the Lord.* If *Lord* is the subject in the one
case, it must be in the other. According to others, the phrase
in question should be rendered *Lord of the Spirit,* i. e. Christ,
who may be said to be Lord of the Spirit, in a sense analogous
to that in which God is said to be the God of Christ. That
is, as God sent Christ, and was revealed by him, so Christ
sends the Spirit and is revealed by him. This is the interpretation of Billroth, Olshausen, Meyer and others. But the
"Lord of the Spirit" is an expression without any scriptural
authority or analogy. It is only of the incarnate Son of God
that the Father is said to be his God. There is no grammatical necessity for this interpretation, and it does not accord
with v. 17. Luther, Beza and others render the phrase ἀπὸ
κυρίου πνεύματος, *the Lord who is the Spirit.* In favour of this
interpretation is, first, the analogy of such expressions as ἀπὸ

Θεοῦ πατρός, *from God who is Father*, Gal. 1, 3 ; and secondly, the authority of v. 17. There the apostle had said, 'The Lord is the Spirit,' and here he says, the transforming power by which we are made like Christ flows from 'the Lord who is the Spirit.' The former passage determines the meaning of the latter. The Lord who is the Spirit means, the Lord who is one with the Spirit, the same in substance, equal in power and glory; who is where the Spirit is, and does what the Spirit does.

-----••----

CHAPTER IV.

In vs. 1–6 the apostle resumes the theme of 3, 12, viz. the open and faithful manner in which he preached the gospel. In vs. 7–15 he shows that his own personal insufficiency and suffering served to manifest more clearly the power of God, who rendered such a feeble instrument the means of producing so great effects. Therefore, vs. 16–18, he was not discouraged or faint-hearted, but exultingly looked above the things seen to those unseen.

As Paul had been made a minister of the new covenant, intrusted with the ministration of righteousness and life, he acted as became his high commission. He was neither timid nor deceitful. He doubted not the truth, the power, or the success of the gospel which he preached; nor did he in any way corrupt or conceal the truth, but by its open proclamation commended himself to every man's conscience, vs. 1. 2. If, notwithstanding this clear exhibition of the truth, the gospel still remained hid, that could only be accounted for by the god of this world blinding the eyes of men. Nothing short of this can account for the fact; for, says the apostle, we preach Christ and not ourselves, and Christ is the image of God. In him there is a revelation of the glory of God to which there is nothing analogous but the original creation of light out of darkness, vs. 3–6. This treasure, however, is in earthen vessels. The gospel is the revelation of God. It is to do for the world what the creation of light did for the chaotic earth. But we ministers are to have none of the glory of the work. We are nothing. The whole power is of God;

who so orders events as to make his power apparent. I am
so perplexed, persecuted, down-trodden and exposed to death,
as to render it evident that a divine power is exercised in my
preservation and continued efficiency. My continuing to live
and labour with success is a proof that Jesus lives. This he
tells the Corinthians is for their benefit. vs. 7–12. Having the
same faith that David had, he spoke with equal confidence,
assured that God, who raised up Christ, would not only preserve him while in this world, but also raise him hereafter
from the dead. As all Paul endured and did was for the
benefit of the Church, thanks would be rendered by the people of God for his preservation and success, vs. 13–15. Therefore, adds this great apostle, I do not faint; although my outward man perishes, my inward man is renewed day by day;
for I know that my present afflictions are not only temporary,
but that they are to be succeeded by an eternal weight of
glory, vs. 16–18.

1. Therefore, seeing we have this ministry, as we
have received mercy, we faint not.

Therefore, i. e. on this account. This is explained by what
follows; *seeing we have this ministry,* that is, because we
have it. In the former chapter he had proclaimed himself a
minister of the new covenant, not of the letter, but of the
spirit, 3, 6; a ministry far more glorious than that of the law,
inasmuch as the law could only condemn, whereas the gospel
conveys righteousness and life. The possession of such an office he assigns as the reason why he does not *faint;* οὐκ ἐκκα-
κοῦμεν, *we do not turn out bad,* or prove recreant. That is,
we do not fail in the discharge of duty, either through weariness or cowardice. *As we have received mercy.* The position
of these words in the text admits of their being connected
either with what precedes or with what follows. In the former case, the sense is, having through the mercy of God obtained this ministry; in the latter, the meaning would be, as
we have obtained mercy we faint not. The former is almost
universally preferred, both because his not fainting is referred
to his having so glorious an office, and because he so often refers to his call to the apostleship as a signal manifestation of
the mercy and grace of God. Rom. 15, 15. 16. 1 Cor. 15,
9. 10. Eph. 3, 8. 'Having through the mercy of God obtained such a ministry, we faint not.'

2. But have renounced the hidden things of dis-
honesty, not walking in craftiness, nor handling the
word of God deceitfully; but by manifestation of the
truth commending ourselves to every man's conscience
in the sight of God.

But, ἀλλά, *on the contrary,* i. e. so far from proving recreant to his duty as a minister of the new covenant he acted in
the manner set forth in this verse. The apostle in the description which he here gives of his official conduct, evidently
intends to describe the false teachers in Corinth. What he denies of himself he impliedly affirms of them. First, Paul says,
we have renounced, declared off from, *the hidden things of dis-
honesty,* τὰ κρυπτὰ τῆς αἰσχύνης. The word αἰσχύνη (from αἰσχρός,
ugly), means either *shame* as a feeling, or the cause of shame,
any thing disgraceful or scandalous. The above phrase therefore may mean either those things which men conceal, or do in
secret, because they are ashamed of them, or, secret scandals or
crimes. It may be taken in a general sense, as including any
course of conduct which men conceal from fear of being disgraced; or in a specific sense for secret immoralities, or for
secret machinations and manœuvres. The last is probably the
true view, because the emphasis is rather on *secret* than *shame.*
It was secrecy or concealment, the opposite of openness and
honest frankness, that the apostle charges on his opponents.
In the preceding context he had spoken of his openness of
speech and conduct, and in the latter part of this verse he
speaks of the manifestation of the truth, i. e. of its open proclamation. What therefore he says he renounced, that which
he represents as characteristic of false teachers, is the want of
openness, adopting secret methods of accomplishing their
ends, which they would be ashamed to avow openly; *puden-
das latebras,* as Beza says, *minime convenientes iis, qui tantœ
dignitatis ministerium tractant. Not walking in craftiness,*
this is an amplification of what precedes. A πανοῦργος is a
man who can do every thing, and is willing to do any thing to
accomplish his ends; and hence πανουργία includes the ideas
of shrewdness or acuteness in seeing how things can be done,
and unscrupulousness as to the character of the means to be
employed. It is the quality manifested by Satan when he beguiled Eve, 2 Cor. 11, 3; which the Jews exhibited when
they endeavoured to entrap our Lord, Luke 20, 23; and

which false teachers are wont to exercise when they would seduce the unwary into heresy. Eph. 4, 14. All such cunning, all such sly and secret ways of accomplishing his purposes Paul renounced. *Nor handling the word of God deceitfully.* The word δολόω means not only *to deceive,* but also *to falsify.* The latter is its meaning here. Not falsifying or corrupting the word of God, i. e. not adulterating it with the doctrines or traditions of men. Comp. 2, 17. The gospel which Paul preached was the word of God; something divinely revealed, having therefore a divine, and not merely human authority. The apostles always thus speak with the consciousness of being the mouth of God or organs of the Spirit, so that we cannot deny their inspiration without denying not only their authority but their integrity. *But by the manifestation of the truth.* This stands opposed to the preceding clauses. Instead of availing ourselves of secret and cunning arts, and corrupting the word of God, we declared it openly and purely. *The truth,* therefore, here is not moral truth or integrity, nor truth in general, but revealed truth, i. e. the word of God. *Commending ourselves to every man's conscience.* Paul's opponents endeavoured to recommend themselves and to secure the confidence of others by cunning, and by corrupting the gospel; but he relied simply on the manifestation of the truth. He knew that the truth had such a self-evidencing power that even where it was rejected and hated it commended itself to the conscience as true. And those ministers who are humble and sincere, who are not wise in their own conceit, but simply declare the truth as God has revealed it, commend themselves to the consciences of men. That is, they secure the testimony of the conscience even of wicked men in their favour. *In the sight of God,* that is, he acted thus in the sight of God. This is an assertion of the purity of the motives which governed his official conduct. He acted as in the sight of that God before whose eye nothing unholy or selfish could stand. The assertion of conscious integrity is not self-praise.

3. But if our gospel be hid, it is hid to them that are lost.

Although the gospel is thus glorious in itself, and although it was clearly set forth, yet to some it remained hid. That is, its true character and excellence as a revelation from God and of God was not apprehended or recognized. The reason or

cause of this fact was not to be sought either in the nature of
the gospel, or in the mode of its exhibition, but in the state
and character of those who rejected it. The sun does not
cease to be the sun although the blind do not see it. And if
any man cannot see the sun on a clear day at noon, he must
be blind. So Paul does not hesitate to say that if any man
does not receive the gospel when clearly presented, he is lost.
If our gospel be hid, it is hid to them that are lost, ἐν τοῖς
ἀπολλυμένοις, *among*, or *before* them who are lost. See 1 Cor.
1, 18, where it is said that the gospel is foolishness to them
that perish. *The lost* are those who are in a state of perdition
and who are certain (if they continue to reject the gospel) to
perish forever. Nothing can be plainer than the doctrine of
this passage. A man's faith is not a matter of indifference.
He cannot be an atheist and yet be saved. He cannot reject
the gospel and yet go to heaven when he dies. This is not an
arbitrary decision. There is and must be an adequate ground
for it. Atheism implies spiritual death, the absence of all that
constitutes the true life of the soul, of all its highest and best
aspirations, instincts and feelings. The rejection of the gospel
is as clear a proof of moral depravity, as inability to see the
light of the sun at noon is a proof of blindness. Such is the
teaching of the Bible, and such has ever been the faith of the
church. Men of the world cry out against this doctrine.
They insist that a man is not accountable for his opinions.
He is, however, accountable for the character by which those
opinions are determined. If he has such a character, such an
inward moral state, as permits and decides him to believe that
there is no God, that murder, adultery, theft and violence are
right and good, then that inward state which constitutes his
character, and for which he is responsible, (according to the
intuitive perception and universal judgment of men,) is reprobate. A good infidel is, according to the Bible, as much a
contradiction as good wickedness or sweet bitterness. It is
not for nothing that infinite truth and love, in the person of
our Lord, said, "He that believeth not shall be damned."

4. In whom the god of this world hath blinded the
minds of them which believe not, lest the light of the
glorious gospel of Christ, who is the image of God,
should shine unto them.

In this verse the apostle assigns the reason why those who are lost do not see the truth and excellence of the gospel. It is that the god of this world hath blinded their minds. *In whom* (ἐν οἷς). The relative is used here as implying a cause or reason. 'Our gospel is hid to them who are lost, *because* in them,' &c. See 3, 6. *The god of this world*, i. e. Satan, who is called the god of this world because of the power which he exercises over the men of the world, and because of the servile obedience which they render to him. They are taken captive by him at his will. 2 Tim. 2, 26. It is not necessary in order that men should serve Satan, and even worship him, that they should intend to do so, or even that they should know that such a being exists. 1 Cor. 10, 20. It is enough that he actually controls them, and that they fulfil his purposes as implicitly as the good fulfil the will of God. Not to serve God, is to serve Satan. There is no help for it. If Jehovah be not our God, Satan is. He is therefore called the prince of this world. John 12, 31. 14, 30. Comp. Matt. 4, 8. 9. Eph. 2, 2. 6, 12. This was one of the designations which the Rabbins applied to Satan. The true God, they said, is Deus primus, Satan, Deus secundus. Or as old Calovius said, *Diabolus est simia Dei.* As the Arians argued from the fact that Satan is called god of this world, that Christ's being called God is no proof of his true divinity; and as the Manicheans quoted the passage in favour of their doctrine of two eternal principles, the one good and the other evil, many of the fathers, including even Chrysostom and Augustine, in violation of its obvious construction, make it to mean, "God hath blinded the minds of this world, i. e. of unbelievers." On which Calvin remarks, We see how far the spirit of controversy can lead men in perverting Scripture. The word *god* may be used figuratively as well as literally. That we say mammon is the god of the world, or that Paul said of certain men, "their belly is their god," does not prove that calling Jehovah God is no assertion of his divinity. And as to the Manichean argument, unless it can be shown that when Baal is called god of the Syrians, eternity and self-existence are ascribed to him, it cannot be inferred that these attributes belong to Satan because he is called the god of this world. Satan is said to *blind the minds of those that believe not;* that is, he exerts such an influence over them as prevents their apprehending the glory of the gospel. This control of Satan over the human mind, although so effectual, is analogous to

the influence of one created intellect over another in other
cases, and therefore is perfectly consistent with free agency
and responsibility. It should, however, make us feel our danger and need of divine assistance, seeing that we have to contend not only against the influence of evil men, but against
the far more powerful influence of the rulers of darkness; the
pantocrators of this world. Eph. 6, 12. The grammatical
construction of this clause is somewhat doubtful. The words
are ἐν οἷς ἐτύφλωσε τὰ νοήματα τῶν ἀπίστων. The common explanation makes the genitive, τῶν ἀπίστων, virtually in apposition with ἐν οἷς. 'In whom, i. e. in unbelievers, he had blinded the minds.' The simple meaning then is, 'The gospel is
hid to them who are lost, because Satan hath blinded their
eyes.' The *lost* and the *unbelieving* are identical. According
to this view unbelief is the effect of the blinding. The same
idea is expressed if, according to Fritzsche and Billroth, τῶν
ἀπίστων be taken proleptically. 'Whose minds Satan hath
blinded so that they believe not.' Comp. 1 Thess. 3, 13, "To
establish your hearts unblamable," i. e. so that they may be
unblamable; and Phil. 3, 21, (according to the corrected
text,) "changed like," i. e. changed so as to be like. According to Meyer this would require the accusative, τὰ νοήματα
ἄπιστα, as the genitive of adjectives taken substantively is
never thus proleptically used. His explanation is, 'Blinding
the eyes of unbelievers is the business of Satan, and this he
has done in them who are lost.' According to this view,
blindness does not precede, but follows unbelief. Those who
will not believe, Satan blinds so that they cannot see. Comp.
Rom. 1, 21, "Their foolish heart was darkened." Their inexcusable folly was the ground of their judicial blindness. The
doctrine thus taught is one clearly recognized in Scripture.
Those who resist the truth, God gives up to a reprobate mind.
Rom. 1, 24. 28. The logical connection, however, is here opposed to this interpretation. Paul had said that the gospel
was hid to the lost. This he accounts for by saying that Satan had blinded their minds. The blindness therefore precedes the unbelief and is the cause of it.

*Lest the light of the glorious gospel of Christ, who is the
image of God, should shine unto them.* This is both the design and effect of the blindness spoken of. Satan intends by
the darkness which he spreads over the minds of men, to prevent their seeing the glory of Christ. *Lest the light,* φωτισμός,
a word which does not occur in common Greek, but is used

in the Septuagint, Ps. 44, 3, in the phrase rendered, "in the light of thy countenance," and Ps. 78, 14, "He led them all night with a light of fire." The word therefore signifies the brightness emitted by a radiant body. *Of the glorious gospel of Christ*, literally, *the gospel of the glory of Christ*, i. e. that gospel which reveals the glory of Christ. The word δόξης, *glory*, is not to be taken as a merely qualifying genitive of εὐαγγελίον, *gospel*. It is the genitive of the object. The glory of Christ is the sum of all the divine and human excellence which is centred in his person, and makes him the radiant point in the universe, the clearest manifestation of God to his creatures, the object of supreme admiration, adoration and love, to all intelligent beings, and especially to his saints. To see this glory is to be saved; for we are thereby transformed into his likeness from glory to glory, 3, 18. Therefore it is that Satan, the great adversary, directs all his energy to prevent men becoming the subjects of that illumination of which the gospel, as the revelation of the glory of Christ, is the source. *Who is the image of God*, i. e. who being God represents God, so that he who hath seen the Son hath seen the Father also. John 14, 9. 12, 45. Christ, as to his divine nature, or as the Logos, is declared to be the brightness of the Father's glory, Heb. 1, 3, to be in the form of God and equal with God, Phil. 2, 6, and perhaps also Col. 1, 15; but here it is the incarnate Logos, the exalted Son of God clothed in our nature, who is declared to be the image of God, because in him dwells the fulness of the Godhead bodily. Col. 2, 9.

5. For we preach not ourselves, but Christ Jesus the Lord; and ourselves your servants for Jesus' sake.

The connection indicated by the particle *for* is with the main idea of the preceding verse. 'Our gospel,' says Paul, 'is the gospel of the glory of Christ, *for* we do not preach ourselves, but him.' To preach one's self is to make self the end of preaching; that is, preaching with the design to attract to ourselves the admiration, the confidence or homage of men. This Paul declares he did not do, but he preached *Christ Jesus the Lord*. His object in preaching was to bring men to recognize Jesus the son of Mary as Christ, i. e. as him whom Moses and the prophets designated as the Messiah, and consequently that this Jesus was, had done, is doing, and would hereafter do, all that had been asserted or predicted of the Messiah; and further that he is LORD in that sense in which every tongue in heaven, and on earth, and under the earth shall confess that he is Lord. The great end of Paul's preaching, therefore, was to bring men to receive and acknowledge Jesus of Nazareth as the Messiah and as the supreme Lord, the maker of heaven and earth. This is the only proper end of preaching. It is the only way by which men can be made either virtuous or religious. It is the only way in which either the true interests of society or the salvation of souls can be secured. To make the end of preaching the inculcation of virtue, to render men honest, sober, benevolent and faithful, is part and parcel of that wisdom of the world that is foolishness with God. It is attempting to raise fruit without trees. When a man is brought to recognize Jesus Christ as Lord, and to love and worship him as such, then he becomes like Christ. What more can the moralist want? Paul cared little for the clamour of the Greeks that he should preach wisdom and virtue. He knew that by preaching Christ he was adopting the only means by which men can be made wise and virtuous here and blessed hereafter.

And ourselves your servants (slaves) *for Jesus' sake.* Paul presented Christ as Lord; himself as a servant. A servant is one who labours, not for himself, but for another. Paul did not labour for himself, but for the Corinthians. *For Jesus' sake.* The motive which influenced him to devote himself to the service of the Corinthians was the love of Christ. Here again the wisdom of the world would say the proper motive would be a desire for their good. Paul always puts God before man. A regard for the glory of Christ is a far higher motive than regard for the good of men; and the former is the only true source of the latter. The ideal of a Christian minister, as presented in this pregnant passage, is, that he is a preacher of Christ, and a servant of the church, governed and animated by the love of Jesus.

6. For God, who commanded the light to shine out of darkness, hath shined in our hearts, to (give) the light of the knowledge of the glory of God in the face of Jesus Christ.

There are two different views taken of the meaning of this verse. First, it may be understood to assign the reason why

Paul was the servant of the Corinthians. He devoted himself to their service, because God had revealed to him the knowledge of Christ, in order that he might communicate that knowledge to others. According to this view the connection is with the last clause of v. 5. "I am your servant, ὅτι, *because*," &c.; "in our hearts," means in Paul's heart; and πρὸς φωτισμόν (for the light) is equivalent to πρὸς τὸ φωτίζειν, *to diffuse the light*. Second, it may be understood to state the reason why Paul preached Christ. 'We preach not ourselves, but Christ Jesus the Lord, ὅτι, *because* in him is revealed the glory of God.' In this case the connection is with the first clause of v. 5, and not with the last; "in our hearts" means in the hearts of believers; and πρὸς φωτισμόν (for light) means, as our version expresses it, *to give us the light*. The end or design of God's shining into our hearts is that we should apprehend the glory of God in the face of Jesus Christ. The latter of these interpretations is adopted by Calvin, the former by Luther and by almost all the modern commentators. With regard to the former it must be admitted that the sense is good and consistent with the meaning of the words. It accords also with Gal. 1, 16, where the apostle says that God had revealed his Son in him that he might preach him among the Gentiles. The following considerations, however, are in favour of the other view of the passage. 1. The connection is better. The main idea of the context is that Paul preached Christ, and therefore it is more natural to understand him to give the reason for so doing, than why he served the Corinthians, which is a subordinate matter. 2. The phrase "in our *hearts*" is much more naturally understood to mean "in the hearts of believers" than in Paul's own heart. It is indeed possible that here, as in 3, 2, the plural (hearts) may be used in reference to the apostle himself. Still this is admissible only when the context requires it. Had Paul meant himself he would probably have said "in our heart," as in the parallel passage in Galatians 1, 16 he says, ἐν ἐμοί, *in me*. To explain the plural form here by assuming that Paul means himself and Timothy is contrary to his uniform habit of speaking for himself. His epistles are his and not Timothy's. 3. The former interpretation supposes φωτισμός to have a different meaning here from what it has in v. 4. There it means *light*, here it is made to mean *the act of communicating light*. But if φωτισμὸς τοῦ εὐαγγελίου means the light which flows from the gospel (or the gospel itself as lumi-

nous), then φωτισμός τῆς γνώσεως means the light of which the
knowledge of Christ is the source, (or that knowledge as
light.) In v. 4, it is said that Satan hath blinded the eyes of
unbelievers so that they cannot see the light of the gospel of
the glory of Christ. Here it is said that God has enlightened
us so that we do see it. In Test. XII. Patr. p. 578, it is said,
τὸ φῶς τοῦ κόσμου, τὸ δοθὲν ἐν ὑμῖν πρὸς φωτισμὸν πάντος ἀνθρώπου,
*the light of the world deposited in you, for the (subjective) il-
lumination of every man.* 4. It is an additional reason in favour of this interpretation that it suits the antithesis between
vs. 4 and 6. The gospel is hid to one class of men, but God
has opened the eyes of another class to see its glory. Here,
as elsewhere, particularly in 1 Cor. 2, 14, the apostle recognizes a twofold illumination, the one external by the word, to
which Satan renders unbelievers blind; and the other internal
by the Spirit, whereby we are enabled to see the glory which
is objectively revealed.

The literal translation of this passage is, ' God who commanded the light to shine out of darkness, who shined into
our hearts.' Something must be supplied to complete the
sense. We may read either ' *It is* God who commanded, &c.,
who shined into our hearts;' or, 'God who commanded the
light to shine out of darkness, *is he* who shined,' &c.   There
is an obvious reference to the work of creation as recorded in
Genesis. Darkness originally brooded over chaos, until God
said, Let there be light. So spiritual darkness broods over
the minds of men, until God shines into their hearts. *Shined
into our hearts.* The word λάμπω, means either, *to be luminous ;* or as here, to *illuminate,* or *cause light,* as the analogy
with the physical creation, just referred to, requires. The
idea is not that God becomes luminous in us, but that he produces light in our hearts. The design of this inward illumination is expressed by the words πρὸς φωτισμὸν τῆς γνώσεως, which,
according to the former of the two interpretations mentioned
above, means, *to the shining abroad of the knowledge,* &c.
He illuminates us that we may diffuse light, and thus illuminate others. According to the second interpretation, the
meaning is, *to give us the light of the knowledge.* God illuminates our minds so that we apprehend that light which
flows from the knowledge of *the glory of God,* or which consists in that knowledge. By *the glory of God* is of course
meant the divine majesty or excellence, which is the proper
object of admiration and adoration. *In the face of Jesus*

Christ; the position of these words and the sense require that they should be connected with the word *glory*, notwithstanding the omission in the Greek of the connecting article (τῆς). It is the glory of God as revealed in Christ that men are by the illumination of the Holy Ghost enabled to see. There are two important truths involved in this statement. First, that God becomes in Christ the object of knowledge. The clearest revelation of the fact that God is, and what he is, is made in the person of Christ, so that those who refuse to see God in Christ lose all true knowledge of him. "No man hath seen God at any time; the only begotten Son, who is in the bosom of the Father, he hath declared him," John 1, 18. "Neither knoweth any man the Father, save the Son, and he to whomsoever the Son will reveal him," Matt. 11, 27. "Whosoever denieth the Son, the same hath not the Father," 1 John 2, 23. 2 John 9. John 15, 23. Insignis locus, says Calvin, unde discimus Deum in sua altitudine non esse investigandum (habitat enim lucem inaccessibilem), sed cognoscendum quatenus se in Christo patefacit. Proinde quicquid extra Christum de Deo cognoscere appetunt homines, evanidum est, vagantur enim extra viam. . . . Nobis utilius est Deum conspicere, qualis apparet in Filio unigenito, quam arcanam ejus essentiam investigare. The other truth here taught is, that this knowledge of God in Christ is not a mere matter of intellectual apprehension, which one man may communicate to another. It is a spiritual discernment, to be derived only from the Spirit of God. God must shine into our hearts to give us this knowledge. Matt. 16, 17. Gal. 1, 16. 1 Cor. 2, 10. 14. As the glory of God is spiritual, it must be spiritually discerned. It is therefore easy to see why the Scriptures make true religion to consist in the knowledge of Christ, and why they make the denial of Christ, or want of faith in him as God manifest in the flesh, a soul-destroying sin. If Christ is God, to know him, is to know God; and to deny him, is to deny God.

7. But we have this treasure in earthen vessels, that the excellency of the power may be of God, and not of us.

This treasure is not the light or inward illumination spoken of in v. 6, but the ministry of the gospel which Paul had received, and of which he had spoken in such exalted terms. It was a ministration of life, of power, and of glory. It revealed the grandest truths. It produced the most astonishing effects. It freed men from the condemnation and power of sin; it transformed them into the image of Christ; it delivered them from the power of the god of this world, and made them partakers of eternal life. These are effects which infinitely transcend all human power; and to render this fact conspicuous God had committed this treasure *to earthen vessels.* By earthen vessels is not meant frail bodies, but weak, suffering, perishing men, because it is not on account of the frailty of the body merely that ministers are so incompetent to produce the effects which flow from their ministrations. The apostle means to present the utter disproportion between the visible means and the effects produced, as proof that the real efficiency is not in man, but in God. *The excellency of the power,* i. e. the exceedingly great power, the wonderful efficiency of the gospel. *May be,* i. e. may be known and acknowledged to be, *of God,* i. e. to flow from him as its source, and not from us. Although what the apostle here says is true of all ministers, yet he had, no doubt, special reference to himself and to his own peculiar circumstances. He had magnified in the highest degree his office, but he himself was a poor, weak, persecuted, down-trodden man. This, he says, only renders the power of God the more conspicuous, not only in the success of my ministry, but in my preservation in the midst of dangers and sufferings which it seems impossible any man could either escape or bear. It is to show, on the one hand, how weak he is, how truly a mere earthen vessel, and, on the other, how great and manifest God's power is, that in the following verses he contrasts his trials and his deliverances.

8. 9. (We are) troubled on every side, yet not distressed; (we are) perplexed, but not in despair; persecuted, but not forsaken; cast down, but not destroyed.

Our version supplies the words *we are,* turning the participles into verbs, which, in the Greek, are all connected with the verb ἔχομεν (*we have*) in the preceding verse. 'We, troubled, perplexed, persecuted and cast down, have, &c.' *On every side,* ἐν παντί, in every way and on every occasion.

These words belong to all the clauses, and not merely to the
first. He was not only troubled, but perplexed and persecuted, ἐν παντί, *in every way.* *Troubled, but not distressed,* ϑλι-
βόμενοι, ἀλλ᾽ οὐ στενοχωρούμενοι, "pressed for room, but still
having room." The figure is that of a combatant sore pressed
by his antagonist, but still finding room to turn himself. *Perplexed, but not in despair,* constantly doubtful what way to
take, and yet always finding some way open. The word ἀπο-
ρέω (ἄπορός εἰμι) means to be at a loss what to say or do; ἐξα-
πορέω is intensive, to be absolutely shut up so as to have no
way or means available. *Persecuted, but not forsaken;* that
is, although God allowed men to persecute him, and seek to
destroy his life and usefulness, yet he never deserted him or
gave him up to the power of those who thus followed him.
Cast down, but not destroyed. The allusion is still to a com-
bat. Paul was not only persecuted or pursued by his enemies,
but actually overtaken by them and cast to the ground, but
not killed. When they seemed to have him in their power,
God delivered him. This occurred so often, and in cases so
extreme, as to make it manifest that the power of God was
exerted on his behalf. No man from his own resources could
have endured or escaped so much. There is in these verses
an evident climax, which reaches its culmination in the next
succeeding sentence. He compares himself to a combatant,
first hardly pressed, then hemmed in, then pursued, then actually cast down. This was not an occasional experience, but
his life was like that of Christ, an uninterrupted succession of
indignities and suffering.

10. Always bearing about in the body the dying
of the Lord Jesus, that the life also of Jesus might be
made manifest in our body.

We constantly illustrate in our person the sufferings of
Christ. We are treated as he was treated; neglected, defamed, despised, maltreated; oppressed with hunger and
thirst, and constantly exposed to death. *Always bearing
about.* Wherever he went, among Jews or Gentiles, in Jerusalem and Ephesus; in all his journeyings, he met everywhere, from all classes of persons, the same kind of treatment
which Christ himself had received. *In his body.* This is
said because the reference is to his external trials and suffer-

ings, and not to his internal anxieties and sorrows. *The dying of* [the Lord] *Jesus.* The word κυρίου, *of the Lord,* is not found in the majority of the ancient manuscripts, and is therefore omitted in the later editions of the Greek Testament. If this word be left out, the two clauses more nearly correspond. *The dying of Jesus* then answers to *the life of Jesus* in the following clause. The word νέκρωσις is used figuratively in Rom. 4, 19, "the deadness of Sarah's womb." Here it is to be taken literally. It means properly *a slaying* or *putting to death,* and then violent death, or simply death. *The death of Jesus* does not mean death on his account; but such death as he suffered. Comp. 1, 5. Though the reference is principally to the dying of Christ, and the climax begun in the preceding verse is here reached, yet his other sufferings are not to be excluded. "The mortification of Jesus," says Calvin, "includes every thing which rendered him (i. e. Paul) despicable before men." Paul elsewhere refers to his constant exposure to death in terms as strong as those which he here uses. In Rom. 8, 36 he says, "We are killed all the day long," and 1 Cor. 15, 31, "I die daily." Compare also 1 Cor. 4, 9. 2 Cor. 11, 23. The death or sufferings of Christ were constantly, as it were, reproduced in the experience of the apostle. In the use of another figure he expresses the same idea in Gal. 6, 17. "I bear in my body the marks of the Lord Jesus." The scars which I bear in my body mark me as the soldier of Christ, and as belonging to him as my divine Master, and as suffering in his cause.

That the life also of Jesus might be made manifest in our body. This expresses the design of God in allowing Paul to be thus persecuted and involved in the constant danger of death. The treasure of the gospel was committed not to an angel, but to Paul, an earthen vessel, and he was pressed, persecuted, cast down, and beset with deadly perils, in order that his preservation, his wonderful efficiency and astonishing success, should be a constant proof that Jesus lives, and not only exercises a providential care over his servants, delivering them out of all their perils, but also attends their labours with his own divine efficiency. Paul's deliverances, and the effects of his preaching, made it manifest that Jesus lives. In Rom. 15, 18 the apostle says, "I will not dare to speak of those things which Christ hath not wrought by me, to make the Gentiles obedient, by word and deed;" and in Gal. 2, 8, "He that wrought effectually in Peter to the apostleship of the cir-

·cumcision, the same was mighty in me towards the Gentiles." As the life of every believer is a manifestation of the life of Christ, (for it is not we that live, but Christ liveth in us, Gal. 2, 20,) so also was the apostolic life of Paul. As the life of Christ, however, is not only manifested in the spiritual life of his followers, and in the deliverance and success of his ministers, as it is not only made known in rescuing them from deadly perils, but is hereafter to be more conspicuously revealed in delivering them from death itself, it seems from v. 14 that Paul includes the resurrection in the manifestation of the life of Jesus of which he here speaks. We die (daily, and at last, literally) in order that the life of Christ may be revealed. This passage is thus brought into unison with Rom. 8, 17, "If so be that we suffer with him, that we may be also glorified together;" and with 2 Tim. 2, 11, "If we be dead with him, we shall live with him." See 1 Peter 4, 13. 14. Rom. 6, 8. 9. John 14, 19, "Because I live, ye shall live also." The association is natural between deliverance from the danger of death, and the ultimate deliverance from death itself. The following verses show that this association actually existed in the apostle's mind, and that both were regarded as manifestations of the life of Christ, and therefore proofs that he still lives. *In our body ;* this does not mean simply *in me.* A special reference is made to the body, because Paul was speaking of bodily sufferings and death.

11. For we which live are always delivered unto death for Jesus' sake, that the life also of Jesus might be made manifest in our mortal flesh.

This is a confirmation and explanation of what precedes. Paul constantly bore about the dying of Jesus, *for* he was always delivered to death for Jesus' sake. He was, as he says 1 Cor. 4, 9, ὡς ἐπιθανάτιος, *as one condemned,* and constantly expecting death. *We which are alive ;* ἡμεῖς οἱ ζῶντες, *we the living,* i. e. although living, and therefore, it might seem, not the subjects of death. Death and life are opposed to each other, and yet in our case they are united. Though living we die daily. The words in this connection do not mean 'as long as we live,' or, 'we who are alive,' as in 1 Thess. 4, 17, where they designate the living as a class distinguished from the dead. They mark the peculiarity of Paul's condition as living although constantly delivered to death.

That the life also of Jesus might be made manifest in our mortal flesh. The only variation between this and the corresponding clause of the preceding verse is, that here the phrase *in our mortal flesh* is substituted for *in our body.* The word *body* does not of itself involve the idea of weakness and mortality, but the word *flesh* does. Hereafter we are to be clothed with bodies, but not with flesh and blood. The contrast, therefore, between the power of the life of Christ, and the feebleness of the instrument or organ through which that life is revealed, is enhanced by saying it was manifested in our mortal flesh. In himself Paul was utter weakness; in Christ he could do and suffer all things.

12. So then death worketh in us, but life in you.

This verse expresses the conclusion or the result of the preceding exhibitions. *So then* I have the suffering and you the benefit. I am constantly dying, but the life of Jesus manifested in me is operative for your good. The death and life here spoken of must be the same as in vs. 10. 11. The death is Paul's sufferings and dying; the life is not his physical life and activity by which the life of Christ is represented, but the divine life and efficiency of Jesus. Death and life are personified. The one is represented as operative in Paul; the other in the Corinthians. The divine power manifested in the support of the apostle, and in rendering his labours so successful, was not primarily and principally for his benefit, but for the benefit of those to whom he preached. It was, however, to him and to them a consolation that his labours were not in vain. There is no analogy between this passage and 1 Cor. 4, 8–10, where the apostle in a tone of irony contrasts his own condition with that of the Corinthians, "Now ye are full, now ye are rich, ye have reigned as kings without us," &c., and therefore there is no propriety in understanding the apostle here to represent the Corinthians as living at their ease while he was persecuted and afflicted. According to this view, *life* here signifies a state of enjoyment and prosperity, and *death* the opposite. But it is plain from the connection that the life spoken of is "the life of Jesus" which was manifested in the apostle, the fruits of which the Corinthians enjoyed.

13. We having the same spirit of faith, according

as it is written, I believed, and therefore have I spoken; we also believe, and therefore speak.

The afflictions and dangers to which the apostle was exposed, were adapted to discourage and even to drive him to despair. He, however, was not discouraged; but having the same faith which of old animated the Psalmist, he also, as David did, proclaimed his confidence in God. Our version omits the connecting particle, δέ, which expresses the contrast between what follows and what precedes. 'We are delivered unto death, *but* having,' &c. *The same spirit of faith.* "The spirit of faith" may be a periphrase for faith itself; or the word spirit may refer to the human spirit, and the whole mean 'having the same believing spirit.' It is more in accordance with scriptural usage, and especially with Paul's manner, to make spirit refer to the Holy Spirit, who is so often designated from the effects which he produces. He is called the Spirit of adoption, Rom. 8, 15; the Spirit of wisdom, Eph. 1, 17; Spirit of grace, Heb. 10, 29; Spirit of glory, 1 Pet. 4, 14. The apostle means to say that the same blessed Spirit which was the author of faith in David he also possessed. *According as it is written,* i. e. the same faith that is expressed in the passage where it is written, 'I believed, therefore have I spoken.' This is the language of David in Ps. 116, 10. The Psalmist was greatly afflicted; the sorrows of death compassed him, the pains of hell gat hold of him, but he did not despair. He called on the Lord, and he helped him. He delivered his soul from death, his eyes from tears, and his feet from falling. David's faith did not fail. He believed, and therefore, in the midst of his afflictions, he proclaimed his confidence and recounted the goodness of the Lord. Paul's experience was the same. He also was sorely tried. He also retained his confidence, and continued to rely on the promises of God. The apostle follows the Septuagint in the passage quoted. The Hebrew expresses the same idea in a rather different form. "I believed *for* I speak." In either way, *speaking* is represented as the effect and proof of faith. See ALEXANDER on the Psalms.

We also believe, therefore we also speak. As Paul's faith was the same, its effect was the same. The faith of David made him proclaim the fidelity and goodness of God. The faith of Paul made him, despite all the suffering it brought upon him, proclaim the gospel with full assurance of its truth and of his own participation of its benefits. This clause, "we also believe," depends on the participle at the beginning of the verse. 'Having the Holy Spirit, the author of faith, we speak.' The interpretation here given of this passage is the common one. Calvin and many other commentators take a very different view. They say that by the *same* faith is to be understood, not the same the Psalmist had, but the same that the Corinthians had. Paul, says Calvin, is to be understood as saying, 'Although there is a great difference between my circumstances and yours; although God deals gently with you and severely with me, yet, notwithstanding this difference, we have the same faith; and where the faith is the same, the inheritance is the same.' But this supposes that the design of the preceding part of the chapter is to contrast the external condition of Paul with that of the Corinthians; and it supposes that by *we* is meant *we* Christians, whereas the apostle evidently means himself. 'We are persecuted, cast down, and delivered to death, but we, having the same faith with David, do as he did. We retain our confidence and continue to confess and to proclaim the gospel.' It is his own experience and conduct, and not those of the Corinthians, that Paul is exhibiting.

14. Knowing, that he which raised up the Lord Jesus, shall raise up us also by Jesus, and shall present (us) with you.

That this is to be understood of the literal resurrection, and not of a mere deliverance from dangers, is evident, 1. Because wherever a figurative sense is preferred to the literal meaning of a word or proposition, the context or nature of the passage must justify or demand it. Such is not the case here. There is nothing to forbid, but every thing to favour the literal interpretation. 2. Because the figurative interpretation cannot be carried through without doing violence to the passage and to the analogy of Scripture. "To present us with you" cannot be made to mean, 'to exhibit us with you as rescued from danger.' 3. The figurative interpretation rests on false assumptions. It assumes that Paul confidently expected to survive the second coming of Christ, and therefore could not say he expected to be raised from the dead. In this very connection, however, he says he longs to be ab-

sent from the body and to be present with the Lord; as he
said to the Philippians, at a later period of his career, that he
had a desire to depart and to be with Christ. Again, it is
said that according to the true reading of the passage, Paul
says he knows we shall be raised up *with* (not *by*) Christ, and
therefore he cannot refer to the literal resurrection. But admitting the reading to be as assumed, to be raised up *with*
Christ does not mean to be raised contemporaneously with
him, but in fellowship with him, and in virtue of union with
him. This figurative interpretation, therefore, although at
first adopted by Beza and advocated by many of the most distinguished modern commentators, is generally and properly
rejected.

The apostle here indicates the ground of the confidence
expressed in the preceding verse. He continued to speak,
i. e. to preach the gospel, notwithstanding his persecutions,
knowing, i. e. because he was sure that he and his fellow-
believers should share in its glorious consummation. The
word *to know* is often used in the sense of being convinced or
sure of. Rom. 5, 3. 1 Cor. 15, 58. It is assumed as a fact
which no Christian did or could doubt, that God had raised
up Jesus from the dead. What Paul was fully persuaded of
is, that God would raise us (i. e. him, for he is speaking of himself) *with* or *by Jesus*. The majority of the ancient manuscripts and versions here read σύν, *with*, instead of διά, *by*, and
that reading is adopted in most critical editions. Both forms
of representation occur in Scripture. Believers are said to be
raised up *by* Christ and *with* Christ. Our Lord often says,
"I will raise him up at the last day;" and in 1 Cor. 15, 21,
the resurrection is said to be (διά) *by* man, i. e. *by* Christ.
On the other hand, believers are said to be raised up *with* or
in him. 1 Cor. 15, 22. Eph. 2, 6. Col. 3, 3. 4. 1 Thess. 5, 10.
The two modes of statement are nearly coincident in meaning.
The believer is united to Christ, as a member of his body, and
therefore a partaker of his life. It is in virtue of this union,
or of this participation of life, which the apostle expressly
teaches, extends to the body as well as to the soul, Rom. 8,
8–11. 1 Cor. 6, 13–20. 15, 21. 22, that our bodies are raised
from the dead. It is therefore immaterial whether we say we
are raised by him, i. e. by the power of his life, or, we are
raised with, i. e. in union with him, and in virtue of that
union. As our resurrection is due to this community of life,
our bodies shall be like his glorious body. Phil. 3, 21. And

this congeniality and conformity are included in the idea which is expressed by saying, we shall be raised up with him, i. e. in his fellowship and likeness. The resurrection, therefore, was the one great, all-absorbing object of anticipation and desire to the early Christians, and should be to us. It is then that we shall be introduced into the glorious liberty of the sons of God; it is then that the work of redemption shall be consummated, and Christ be admired in his saints. *And present us together with you.* To present, παρίστημι, is to cause to stand near or by, to offer to. We are required to present our members (Rom. 6, 13,) or our bodies (Rom. 12, 1,) unto God; Paul says he desired to present the Corinthians as a chaste virgin unto Christ, 11, 2; God is said to have reconciled us to present us holy in his sight, Col. 1, 22; and Jude (v. 24) gives thanks to him who is able to present us faultless before the presence of his glory with exceeding joy. This is the idea here. It is true that in the following chapter it is said that we must all appear before the judgment seat of Christ, whence many suppose that the apostle means here that having been raised from the dead, believers shall be presented before the tribunal of the final judge. But the idea of judgment is foreign from the connection. It is a fearful thing to stand before the judgment seat of Christ, even with the certainty of acquittal. The apostle is here exulting in the assurance that, however persecuted and down-trodden here, God, who had raised up Jesus, would raise him up and present him with all other believers before the presence of his glory with exceeding joy. This it was that sustained him, and has sustained so many others of the afflicted of God's people, and given them a peace which passes all understanding.

The resurrection of Christ here, as in other passages, is represented as the pledge of the resurrection of his people. "He that raised Christ from the dead shall also quicken your mortal bodies," Rom. 8, 11. "God hath both raised up the Lord, and will also raise us up by his own power," 1 Cor. 6, 14. "Christ is risen from the dead and become the first fruits of them that slept; for . . . in Christ shall all be made alive," 15, 19–22. "For if we believe that Jesus died and rose again, even so them also which sleep in Jesus will God bring with him," 1 Thess. 4, 14. See also John 11, 25. Eph. 2, 6. Col. 2, 12. In the view of the sacred writers, therefore, the glorious resurrection of believers is as certain as the resurrection of Christ, and that not simply because God who has raised up

Jesus has promised to raise his followers, but because of the union between him and them. They are in him in such a sense as to be partakers of his life, so that his life of necessity secures theirs. If he lives, they shall live also. Now as the fact of Christ's resurrection was no more doubted by the apostles, who had seen and heard and even handled him after he rose from the dead, than their own existence, we may see how assured was their confidence of their own resurrection to eternal life. And as to us no event in the history of the world is better authenticated than the fact that Christ rose from the dead, we too have the same ground of assurance of the resurrection of those who are Christ's at his coming. Had we only the faith of the apostle, we should have his constancy and his joy even in the midst of the greatest afflictions.

15. For all things (are) for your sakes, that the abundant grace might through the thanksgiving of many redound to the glory of God.

In the preceding verse Paul had expressed his confident hope of being delivered even from the grave and presented before God in glory with his Corinthian brethren, *for* all things are for your sakes. They were to be partakers of the salvation which he proclaimed and for which he suffered. All he did and all he suffered was for them. According to this interpretation the *all things* are limited to all things of which he had been speaking, viz. his sufferings, his constancy, and his deliverance. In 1 Cor. 3, 21, however, he says in a much more comprehensive sense, 'All things are yours, whether things present or things to come.' Hence some understand the expression with the same latitude in this passage: 'I expect to be presented *with you*, for all things are for your sakes.' But this does not agree with the latter part of the verse. He evidently means all that he did, and suffered, and experienced. 'They are for your sake, *that* (ἵνα, in order that) the abundant grace or favour manifested to me, might, through the thanksgiving of many, i. e. through your gratitude, called forth by your experience of the blessings flowing from my labour and sufferings, as well as from my deliverance, redound to the glory of God.' This is the sense of the passage, according to the construction of the original, adopted by our translators. Paul says that the favour shown him redounds the more to the glory of God, because others besides himself are led to give thanks for it.   This supposes that in the Greek, διὰ τῶν πλειόνων, κ.τ.λ. are to be connected with περισσεύσῃ, *might abound through.*   Those words, however, may be connected with πλεονάσασα, *the grace rendered abundant by many.*   This may mean either that the favour shown the apostle was the more abundant because so many interceded in his behalf.   Comp. 1, 11, and Phil. 1, 19.   "I know that this shall turn to my salvation through your prayer."   Or the meaning may be, 'The favour shown me, rendered abundant, or greatly multiplied, through the participation of many.'   In the one case, Paul says the grace was the greater because so many prayed for him; in the other, it was the greater because so many enjoyed the fruits of it.   The passage admits of either of these constructions and explanations; and whichever is preferred the general idea is the same.   The church is one.   If one member be honoured, all the members rejoice with it.   If Paul was redeemed from his enemies, all the church gave thanks to God.   A favour shown to him was a favour shown to all, and was thereby multiplied a thousand-fold and rendered a thousand-fold more prolific of thanksgiving unto God.   Whichever construction be adopted, περισσεύσῃ is to be taken transitively, as in Eph. 1, 8. 1 Thess. 3, 12.   'Grace causes thanksgiving to abound.'

16. For which cause we faint not; but though our outward man perish, yet the inward (man) is renewed day by day.

For which cause, that is, because we are sure of a glorious resurrection, and are satisfied that our present sufferings and labours will advance the glory of God.   *We faint not*, we do not become discouraged and give up the conflict.   On the contrary, though his outward man, his whole physical constitution, *perish*, διαφθείρεται, be utterly worn out and wasted away by constant suffering and labour, yet *the inward man*, the spiritual nature, is renewed, i. e. receives new life and vigour, day by day.   By 'inward man' is not meant simply the soul as distinguished from the body, but his higher nature —his soul as the subject of the divine life.   Rom. 7, 22. Eph. 3, 16.   Of no unholy man could it be said in the sense of the apostle that his inward man was daily renewed.   It is not of renewed supplies of animal spirits or of intellectual vigour that the apostle speaks, but of the renewal of spiritual strength to do and suffer. This constant renewal of strength is opposed to fainting. 'We faint not, but are renewed *day by day*,' ἡμέρᾳ καὶ ἡμέρᾳ. This is a Hebraism, Gen. 39, 10. Ps. 68, 19. familiar to our ears but foreign to Greek usage. The supplies of strength came without fail and as they were needed.

17. For our light affliction, which is but for a moment, worketh for us a far more exceeding (and) eternal weight of glory.

This is the reason why we faint not. Our afflictions are light, they are momentary, and they secure eternal glory. Every thing depends upon the standard of judgment. Viewed absolutely, or in comparison with the sufferings of other men, Paul's afflictions were exceedingly great. He was poor, often without food or clothing; his body was weak and sickly; he was homeless; he was beset by cruel enemies; he was repeatedly scourged, he was stoned, he was imprisoned, he was shipwrecked, robbed, and counted as the off-scouring of the earth; he was beyond measure harassed by anxieties and cares, and by the opposition of false teachers, and the corruption of the churches which he had planted at such expense of time and labour. See 1 Cor. 4, 9–13, and 2 Cor. 11, 23–29. These afflictions in themselves, and as they affected Paul's consciousness, were exceedingly great; for he says himself he was pressed out of measure, above strength, so that he despaired even of life. 1, 8. He did not regard these afflictions as trifles, nor did he bear them with stoical indifference. He felt their full force and pressure. When five times scourged by the Jews and thrice beaten with rods, his physical torture was as keen as that which any other man would have suffered under similar inflictions. He was not insensible to hunger, and thirst, and cold, and contempt, and ingratitude. His afflictions were not light in the sense of giving little pain. The Bible does not teach, either by precept or example, that Christians are to bear pain as though it were not pain, or bereavements as though they caused no sorrow. Unless afflictions prove real sorrows, they will not produce the fruits of sorrow. It was only by bringing these sufferings into comparison with eternal glory that they dwindled into insignificance. So also when the apostle says that his afflictions were for a moment, it is only when compared with eternity. They were not momentary so far as the present life was concerned. They lasted from his conversion to his martyrdom. His Christian life was a protracted dying. But what is the longest life to everlasting ages? Less than a single second to threescore years. The third source of consolation to the apostle was that his afflictions would secure for him eternal glory, i. e. the eternal and inconceivable excellence and blessedness of heaven. This is all the words κατερ-γάζεται ἡμῖν express. Afflictions are the cause of eternal glory. Not the meritorious cause, but still the procuring cause. God has seen fit to reveal his purpose not only to reward with exceeding joy the afflictions of his people, but to make those afflictions the means of working out that joy. This doctrine is taught in many passages of Scripture. Matt. 19, 29. Rom. 8, 17. 2 Tim. 2, 12. 13. 1 Pet. 1, 6. 4, 13. Rev. 7, 14. It is not, however, suffering in itself considered which has this effect; and therefore not all suffering; not self-inflicted suffering, not punishment, but only such sufferings which are either endured for Christ's sake, or which when imposed for the trial of our faith are sustained with a Christian spirit. We are, therefore, not to seek afflictions, but when God sends them we should rejoice in them as the divinely appointed means of securing for us an eternal weight of glory. Our Lord calls on those who were persecuted to rejoice and be exceeding glad, Matt. 5, 12; so does the apostle Peter, 4, 13; and Paul often asserts that he gloried or rejoiced in his afflictions. Phil. 2, 17. Col. 1, 24.

The expression τὸ παραυτίκα ἐλαφρὸν τῆς θλίψεως, *the momentary lightness of affliction*, exhibits the adverb (παραυτίκα) used as an adjective, and the adjective (ἐλαφρόν) used as a substantive. Comp. 8, 8. 1 Cor. 1, 25. Wetstein and other collectors furnish abundant illustrations of this usage from the Greek writers. In this carefully balanced sentence, ἐλαφρόν, *light*, stands opposed to βάρος, *weight*, and παραυτίκα, *momentary*, to αἰώνιον, *eternal*. In Hebrew the same word signifies *to be heavy*, and *to be glorious*, and the literal meaning of the Hebrew word for glory is *weight*, which may have suggested the peculiar expression "weight of glory." The words καθ' ὑπερβολὴν εἰς ὑπερβολήν, *according to excess unto excess*, in the sense of *exceeding exceedingly*, (one of Paul's struggles with the impotency of language to express his conceptions,) may be taken as an adjective qualification of βάρος δόξης, *weight of glory*. This is the explanation adopted by our translators, who render the phrase, "far more exceeding, *and* eternal weight of glory." There is, however, no καί (*and*) in the text. If this view be adopted, it would be better therefore to take "eternal weight of glory" as one idea. The eternal glory exceeds all limits. The words in question, however, may be connected adverbially with κατεργάζεται, as proposed by Meyer and De Wette. 'Our light afflictions work exceedingly, i. e. are beyond measure efficacious in securing or producing an eternal weight of glory.'

18. While we look not at the things which are seen, but at the things which are not seen: for the things which are seen (are) temporal; but the things which are not seen (are) eternal.

The participial clause with which this verse begins (μὴ σκοπούντων ἡμῶν) may have a causal force. 'Our light afflictions are thus efficacious *because* we look not at the things which are temporal.' This, however, is hardly true. The afflictions of Christians do not work out for them eternal glory, *because* their hearts are turned heavenward. It is therefore better to understand the apostle as simply expressing the condition under which the effect spoken of in v. 17 is produced. This is the idea expressed in our version by the word *while*. Afflictions have this salutary operation while (i. e. provided that) we look at the things which are eternal. This clause thus serves to designate the class of persons to whom even the severest afflictions are light, and for whom they secure eternal glory. It is not for the worldly, but for those whose hearts are set on things above. The word translated *look*, σκοπέω, is derived from σκοπός (*scopus, scope*), meaning the mark or goal on which the eye is fixed, as in Phil. 3, 14, κατὰ σκοπὸν διώκω, *I press toward the mark*. Therefore *looking* here means making things unseen the goal on which our eyes are fixed, the end toward which the attention, desires and efforts are directed. As is usual with the apostle, he states both what is not, and what is, the absorbing object of the believer's attention. Not *the visible*, but *the invisible;* i. e. not the world and the things of the world, but the things which pertain to that state which is to us now invisible. The reason why the latter, and not the former class of objects do thus engross the believer, is that the things seen are *temporal*, or rather, *temporary*, lasting only for a time; whereas the things unseen are eternal. Few passages in Paul's writings exhibit so clearly his inward exercises in the midst of sufferings and under the near prospect of death. He was, when he wrote what is here written, in great affliction. He felt that his life was in constant and imminent danger, and that even if delivered from the violence of his enemies, his strength was gradually wearing away under the uninterrupted trials to which he was subjected. Under these circumstances we see him exhibiting great sensibility to suffering and sorrow; a keen susceptibility in reference to the conduct and feelings of others towards him; a just appreciation of his danger, and yet unshaken confidence in his ultimate triumph; a firm determination not to yield either to opposition or to suffering, but to persevere in the faithful and energetic discharge of the duty which had brought on him all his trials, and a heroic exultation in those very afflictions by which he was so sorely tried. He was sustained by the assurance that the life of Christ secured his life; that if Jesus rose, he should rise also; and by the firm conviction that the more he suffered for the sake of Christ, or in such a way as to honour his divine master, the more glorious he would be through all eternity. Suffering, therefore, became to him not merely endurable, but a ground of exceeding joy.

CHAPTER V.

The confidence expressed in the preceding chapter is justified by showing that the apostle was assured of a habitation in heaven, even if his earthly tabernacle should be destroyed, vs. 1–10. His object in what he had said of himself was not self-commendation. He laboured only for the good of the church, impelled by the love of Christ, whose ambassador he was, in exhorting men to be reconciled to God, vs. 11–21.

The state of believers after death. Vs. 1–10.

PAUL did not faint in the midst of his sufferings, because he knew that even if his earthly house should be destroyed, he

had a house in heaven—not like the present perishable tabernacle, but one not made with hands, and eternal, v. 1.   He
looked forward to the things unseen, because in his present
tabernacle he groaned, desiring to enter his heavenly habitation.   He longed to be unclothed that he might be clothed
upon with his house which is from heaven, vs. 2–4.   This confidence he owed to God, who had given him the Holy Spirit
as a pledge of his salvation, v. 5.   Having this indwelling of
the Spirit he was always in good courage, knowing that as
soon as he should be absent from the body, he would be present with the Lord, vs. 6–8.   Therefore his great desire was to
please him, before whose tribunal he and all other men were
to appear to receive according to their works, vs. 9. 10.

1. For we know that if our earthly house of (this)
tabernacle were dissolved, we have a building of God,
a house not made with hands, eternal in the heavens.

The connection between this passage and the preceding
chapter is plain.   Our light afflictions, Paul had said, work
out for us an eternal weight of glory, *for* we know that even
if our earthly house perishes, we have an everlasting habitation in heaven.   The general sense also of the whole of the
following paragraph is clear.   The apostle expresses the assurance that a blessed state of existence awaited him after
death.   There is, however, no little difficulty in determining
the precise meaning of the figurative language here employed.
Few passages in Paul's writings have awakened a deeper or
more general interest, because it treats of the state of the soul
after death; a subject about which every man feels the liveli-
est concern, not only for himself, but in behalf of those dear
to him.   Where are those who sleep in Jesus before the resurrection ?   What is the condition of a redeemed soul when it
leaves the body ?   These are questions about which no Christian can be indifferent.   If Paul here answers those inquiries,
the passage must have peculiar value to all the people of God.
This, however, is the very point about which the greatest difficulty exists.   There are three views taken of the passage;
that is, three different answers are given to the question,
What is that building into which the soul enters when the
present body is dissolved ?   1. The first answer is, that the
house not made with hands is heaven itself.   2. That it is the

resurrection body. If this be the correct view, then the passage throws no light on the state of the soul between death and the resurrection. It treats solely of what is to happen after Christ's second coming. 3. The third opinion is, that the house into which the soul enters at death is, so to speak, an intermediate body; that is, a body prepared for it and adapted to its condition during the state intermediate between death and the resurrection. This, however, is not a scriptural doctrine. Many philosophers indeed teach that the soul can neither perceive nor act unless in connection with a body; nay, that an individual man is nothing but a revelation of the general principle of humanity in connection with a given corporeal organism, as a tree is the manifestation of the principle of vegetable life through a specific material organization. As therefore vegetable life is, or exists, only in connection with vegetable forms, so the soul exists only in connection with a body. Thus Olshausen in his Commentary, 1 Cor. 15, 42–44, says, Wie ohne Leib keine Seele, so ohne Leiblichkeit keine Seligkeit; Leiblichkeit und die dadurch bedingte Persönlichkeit ist das Ende der Werke Gottes. "As without body there is no soul, so without a corporeal organization there can be no salvation; a corporeal organization, as the necessary condition of personality, is the end of God's work." Still more explicitly, when commenting on verses 19 and 20 of the same chapter, he says, Ein Fortleben als reiner Geist ohne körperliches Organ erkennt der Apostle gar nicht als Möglichkeit an; die Lehre von der Unsterblichkeit der Seele ist der ganzen Bibel, ebenso wie der Name, fremd—und zwar mit vollem Recht, indem ein persönliches Bewusstseyn im geschaffenen Wesen die Schranken des Leibes nothwendig voraussetzt. "The continued existence of the soul as a pure spirit without a body is to the apostle an impossibility. The Bible knows nothing of the doctrine of the immortality of the soul; the very expression is strange to it. And no wonder, for self-consciousness in a created being necessarily supposes the limitation of a bodily organization." Of course all angels must have bodies, and of course also if the soul exists between death and the resurrection it must have a body. Strange to say, however, Olshausen, despite his maxim, "no body no soul," admits the existence of the soul during the interval between death and the resurrection, and yet denies that it has a body. His utterly unsatisfactory attempt to reconcile this contradiction in his theory is, first, that self-consciousness in departed spirits is very obscure—a mere dreamy state of existence; and secondly, that it must be assumed that a relation continues between the soul and the elements of its decaying body in the grave. This is a perfect collapse of the theory. If it involves either of these consequences, that the soul is unconscious after death, or that its life is in connection with its disorganized body, and conditioned by that connection, then it comes in direct conflict with the Scripture, and is exploded as a mere product of the imagination. If the Bible teaches or assumes that a body is necessary to the self-consciousness of the soul, or even to its power to perceive and to express, to act and to be acted upon, then it would be not only natural but necessary to understand the apostle to teach in this passage that the moment the soul leaves its present body it enters into another. Then it would follow either that the only resurrection of which the Scriptures speak takes place at the moment of death, or that there is a body specially fitted for the intermediate state, differing both from the one which we now have, and from that which we are to have at the resurrection. The former of these suppositions contradicts the plain doctrine of the Bible that the resurrection is a future event, to take place at the second advent of Christ; and the latter contradicts this very passage, for Paul says that the house on which we enter at death is eternal. Besides, the Bible knows nothing of any body except the σῶμα ψυχικόν, *the natural body*, which we have now, and the σῶμα πνευματικόν, *the spiritual body*, which we are to receive at the resurrection. We are therefore reduced to the choice between the first and second of the three interpretations mentioned above. The building of which the apostle here speaks must be either a house in heaven, or the resurrection body. If the latter, then Paul teaches, not what is to happen immediately after death, but what is to take place at the second coming of Christ. In opposition to this view, and in favour of the opinion that the house here mentioned is heaven itself, it may be argued, 1. Heaven is often in Scripture compared to a house in which there are many mansions, John 14, 2; or to a city in which there are many houses, Heb. 11, 10. 14. 13, 14. Rev. 21, 10; or more generally to a habitation, Luke 16, 9. 2. The figure in this case is peculiarly appropriate. The body is compared to a house in which the soul now dwells, heaven is the house into which it enters when this earthly house is dissolved. Our Lord told his sorrowing disciples that they should soon be

with him, that in his Father's house, whither he went, there
were many mansions, and that he would receive them unto
himself. 3. The description here given of the house of which
the apostle speaks agrees with the descriptions elsewhere
given of heaven. It is a building of God; compare Heb. 11,
10, where heaven is said to be a city whose builder and maker
is God. It is not made with hands, i. e. not of human workmanship or belonging to the present order of things. In the
same sense the true tabernacle in heaven is said to be "not
made with hands," Heb. 9, 11. It is eternal, because the state
on which the soul enters at death is unchanging. And finally,
this house is said to be "in heaven," or, we are said to have
it "in heaven." This last clause is not consistent with the
assumption that the house spoken of is the resurrection body.
That body is not now in heaven awaiting our arrival there,
nor is it to be brought down to us *from* heaven. But the
mansion which Christ has gone to prepare for his people is in
heaven; and therefore the apostle in raising his eyes heavenward could appropriately say, 'If this tabernacle be dissolved
I have a house in heaven.' 4. The principal argument in favour of this interpretation is that the house spoken of is one
on which the soul enters immediately after death. This is
plain because Paul says, that if our earthly house be dissolved
we have, i. e. we have at once, a house in heaven. The whole
context requires this explanation to be given to ἔχομεν, *we
have*. The apostle is speaking of the grounds of consolation
in the immediate prospect of death. He says in effect that
the dissolution of the body does not destroy the soul or deprive it of a home. His consolation was that if unclothed
he would not be found naked. While at home in the body
he was absent from the Lord, but as soon as he was absent
from the body he would be present with the Lord. It is so
obvious that the apostle is here speaking of what takes
place at death, that those who maintain that the building referred to is the resurrection body, propose various methods
of getting over the difficulty. Some, as Usteri, assume that
Paul, when he wrote the first epistle to the Corinthians, believed that the resurrection was not to take place until the
second advent of Christ, but changed his view and here teaches
that it takes place at death. That is, that the soul when it
leaves the present body is furnished with that spiritual body
which in the former epistle he taught was not to be received
until Christ comes the second time. To those who proceed

on the assumption of the inspiration of Scripture, this unnatural explanation needs no refutation. In his epistle to the Philippians, written still later, he teaches the same doctrine that we find in First Corinthians. He must, therefore, have reverted to his former view. Paul was not thus driven about by every wind of doctrine. Even those who deny his inspiration must admit his consistency. Others say that as the apostle confidently expected to survive the second advent, he here speaks of what he anticipated in his own case. He believed he would not die, but be changed at once as described in 1 Cor. 15, 51. 52. But even admitting that Paul at this time did expect to survive the coming of the Lord, that is not the expectation here expressed. On the contrary, he is speaking of what would take place (ἐάν) even in case he should die. If, worn out by his sufferings, his earthly house should be dissolved before Christ came, still he knew he should have a house in heaven. Others again say that the interval between death and the resurrection is not taken into account, but that the apostle, after the manner of the prophets, speaks of events as chronologically coincident which in fact are separated by a long period of time. But this does not meet the difficulty. As the apostle is speaking of the ground of consolation in the prospect of death, he must be understood to refer, not to what might be expected at an indefinite period after that event, but to its immediate consequence. He did not glory in his afflictions because when his earthly house should be dissolved he would sink into a state of unconsciousness until the resurrection; but because he would have another and unspeakably better habitation. This is evident, because he speaks of his being absent from the body as the immediate antecedent of his being present with the Lord; which is only another form of saying he would be clothed upon with his house which is from heaven. 5. A fifth consideration in favour of the interpretation in question, is derived from the analogy of Scripture. The Bible in other places teaches that the souls of believers do at their death immediately pass into glory. Our Lord in refuting the Sadducees, who denied the existence of spirits, said, "Have ye not read that which was spoken unto you by God, saying, I am the God of Abraham, the God of Isaac, and the God of Jacob? God is not the God of the dead, but of the living," Matt. 22, 32. Abraham, Isaac and Jacob therefore are living, and not in a dreamy state of semi-conscious existence. In the parable of the rich man and Lazarus, we are told that when Lazarus died he was carried by angels into Abraham's bosom, i. e. to heaven. On the mount of transfiguration, Moses and Elias appeared talking with Christ. Our Lord said to the dying thief, "This day shalt thou be with me in paradise," and paradise, as we learn from 2 Cor. 12, 2 and 4, is the third heaven. In Phil. 1, 22–24, Paul says that although he had a desire to depart and be with Christ, yet his abiding in the flesh was more needful for them. This clearly implies that as soon as he departed from the flesh he expected to be present with the Lord. This flows from the perfection of Christ's work. As his blood cleanses from all sin, there is no process of expiation or purification to be endured or experienced by believers after death. And as we know, as our Lord says, that they still live, they must enter on the blessedness secured by his merits. Accordingly the apostle says that the saints on earth and the saints in heaven form one communion. "We are come unto Mount Zion—and unto the spirits of just men made perfect," Heb. 12, 23.

The considerations above presented appear decisive in favour of understanding the apostle to mean by the house not made with hands, a mansion in heaven into which believers enter as soon as their earthly tabernacle is dissolved. It is, however, objected to this view of the passage, that as the earthly house is the present body, the heavenly house must also be a body. This, however, does not follow. The comparison is not of one body with another; but of one house with another. We dwell now in an earthly tabernacle; after death, we shall dwell in a heavenly house. This is all that the figure demands. In the second place, it is urged that in v. 2 it is said our house is "from heaven," and if from heaven it is not heaven itself. But our resurrection body is not *from* heaven in the local sense. It is from heaven only in the general sense of being heavenly, and in this sense our house is of heaven. It is not of the earth, does not belong to the present state of existence, but to that on which we enter in heaven. Besides, it is not heaven considered as a state, nor even as a place, (in the wide sense of the word heaven,) that is our house, but the mansion which the Lord has gone to prepare for his people in heaven. The simple idea is that the soul, when it leaves its earthly tabernacle, will not be lost in immensity, nor driven away houseless and homeless, but will find a house and home in heaven. This is the consoling doctrine here taught. The soul of the believer does not cease to exist at death. It does not sink into a state of unconsciousness. It does not go into purgatory; but, being made perfect in holiness, it does immediately pass into glory. As soon as it is absent from the body, it is present with the Lord. This is all that is revealed, and this is enough. What Paul learnt more than this when he was caught up into the third heaven, he was not permitted to make known.

As Paul is speaking of himself in this whole connection, when he says *we know,* he does not refer to a knowledge common to all men, nor to other Christians, but he expresses his personal conviction—*I know. That if,* ἐάν, *if as it may;* (not *although*). The apostle is speaking of his afflictions, which were wearing away his strength; and says, 'Even if my sufferings should prove fatal, and my earthly house be dissolved, I have another habitation.' *Our earthly house of this tabernacle,* i. e. our earthly house which is a tabernacle, ὁ σκῆνος, a frail, temporary abode, as opposed to a stable, permanent building. See 2 Peter 1, 13. 14. *Is dissolved,* i. e. its component parts separated either by violence or decay, so that it falls in pieces. *We have,* i. e. I have, as he is speaking of himself. The present tense, ἔχομεν, is used because the one event immediately follows the other; there is no perceptible interval between the dissolution of the earthly tabernacle and entering on the heavenly house. As soon as the soul leaves the body it *is* in heaven. *A building of God,* οἰκοδομὴν ἐκ θεοῦ, a building from God, one provided by him, and of which he is the builder and maker, Heb. 11, 10, and therefore is said to be *not made with hands,* i. e. not like the buildings erected by man. Comp. Heb. 9, 11 and Col. 2, 11. The latter passage refers to the circumcision of the heart as the immediate work of God; it is therefore said to be ἀχειροποίητος. The soul therefore at death enters a house whose builder is God. This is said to exalt to the utmost our conceptions of its glory and excellence. Being made by God it is *eternal.* It is to last forever; and we are never to leave it. We dwell in our present bodies only for a little while, as in a tent; but heaven is an abode which, once entered, is retained forever. The words *in the heavens* may be connected with *house,* in the sense of heavenly, i. e. a celestial house. This construction is assumed in our version where the words "eternal in the heavens" are made to qualify or describe the house spoken of. The natural connection of the words, however, is with (ἔχομεν) *we have.* 'If our earthly house be dissolved, we have in heaven a house of God, not made with hands, and eternal.'

2. For in this we groan, earnestly desiring to be clothed upon with our house which is from heaven.

This verse must, from the force of the connecting particle (γάρ) *for*, be a confirmation of what precedes, but whether of what is said in v. 1, or at close of preceding chapter, is doubtful. The words καὶ γάρ may mean either *for also*, or *for even*. If the former, this verse is condinate with v. 1, and assigns an additional reason why the apostle looked at the things unseen and eternal. He thus looked *for* he knew he had in heaven a house not made with hands, and *because* he earnestly desired to enter that house. If the latter explanation of the particles be preferred, the sense is, 'I know I have a house in heaven, *for even* in this I groan, desiring to be clothed with my house which is from heaven.' In this case the argument would be, 'There is such a house, for I long for it.' This, however, is hardly a scriptural argument. Paul's confidence in a state of blessedness beyond the grave was not founded on the obscure aspirations of his nature, but on express revelation from God. Rom. 8, 22 is not parallel, for there the groaning of the creation is presented, not as a proof of future blessedness, but to show that the creature is subject to vanity, *not willingly* nor finally. *In this*, i. e. in this tabernacle, as the word σκῆνος is used in v. 1, and also v. 4. *We groan earnestly desiring*, i. e. we groan because we desire. The groaning is the expression of this longing after his heavenly home; and not, as in v. 4, of suffering caused by afflictions. The ἐπί in ἐπιποθοῦντες is either intensive, *earnestly* desiring, or it expresses the tendency of the desire. The word and its cognates are always used in the New Testament to express strong desire or longing. What the apostle thus longed for was, ἐπενδύσασθαι, *to be clothed upon*, i. e. to put on over, as an outer garment. *With our house which is from heaven.* As the body is familiarly compared sometimes to a house in which the soul dwells, and sometimes to a garment with which it is clothed, the two figures are here combined, and the apostle speaks of putting on a house as though it were a garment. Both are a covering and a protection. *Our house*, οἰκητήριον, i. e. *dwelling*, more specific than the general term οἰκία, *a building*. *Which is from heaven*, ἐξ οὐρανοῦ, i. e. heavenly, as distinguished from a

dwelling which is ἐκ γῆς, *of the earth.* 1 Cor. 15, 47. It is not
"of this building," ταύτης τῆς κτίσεως, Heb. 9, 11. Those who
understand this whole passage to treat of the change which is
to take place in those believers who shall be alive when the
Lord comes, and which is described in 1 Cor. 15, 51–54, lay
special stress on this verse. They urge that this house being
from heaven cannot be heaven; and that the verb ἐπενδύω,
meaning *to put on over,* evidently refers to the putting on of
the new body, as it were, over the old one; and therefore can
be understood only of those who, being in the body when
Christ comes, are thus clothed *upon* without being unclothed.
It has already been remarked that there is no force in the former of these arguments, because the new body is not *from*
heaven. It is ἐξ οὐρανοῦ only in the sense of being heavenly,
and in that sense the expression suits the idea of a building as
well as that of a body. As to the second argument, it may be
admitted, that if the context demanded, or even naturally admitted of our understanding "the house not made with
hands" to be the resurrection body, there would be a peculiar propriety in the use of the word ἐπενδύσασθαι, (to be
clothed *upon,*) instead of the simple verb ἐνδύσασθαι, *to be
clothed.* But the use of this word is not sufficient to determine the interpretation of the whole passage. 1. Because
nothing is more common than the use of compound verbs in
the same sense as the corresponding simple ones. 2. Because
in 1 Cor. 15, 53. 54, Paul uses the simple verb (ἐνδύσασθαι) four
times to express the very thing which it is here urged he must
refer to because he uses the compound ἐπενδύσασθαι. That is,
he uses the two words in the same sense. He makes no difference between "putting on" and being "clothed *upon.*"
We are not required, therefore, by the use of the latter expression, to infer that the apostle speaks of the change which
those who are in the body should experience at the coming of
Christ. This view, as remarked above, is out of keeping with
the whole context. Paul was daily exposed to death, his outward man was perishing. His consolation was that if his
earthly tabernacle were dissolved, he had a better house in
heaven. He earnestly longed for that house; to be absent
from the body and to be present with the Lord. All he says
is said on the hypothesis of his dying, and therefore he cannot
say he earnestly desired to escape death. What he longed
for was, not that he might be alive when Christ came, and
thus escape the pains of dissolution, but that he might quit

his mud hovel and enter in that house not made with hands, eternal in the heavens.

3. If so be that being clothed we shall not be found naked.

Few verses in this epistle have been more variously explained than this. In the first place the reading is doubtful. The received text has εἴγε, which the great majority of the critical editions also adopt; Lachmann, on the authority of the manuscripts, B, D, E, F, G, reads εἴπερ. The latter (*if so be, provided*) expresses doubt; the former (*since*) expresses certainty. This distinction, however, is not strictly observed in Paul's writings. See 1 Cor. 8, 5. Gal. 3, 4. Col. 1, 23. 2 Thess. 1, 6. A more important diversity is that several ancient manuscripts and most of the Fathers read ἐκδυσάμενοι (*un*clothed) instead of ἐνδυσάμενοι (*clothed*). The former renders the passage much plainer. 'We earnestly desire to be clothed with our house from heaven, since (or, even if) being unclothed we shall not be found naked.' That is, 'Although despoiled of our earthly tabernacle we shall not be found houseless.' Mill, Semler and Rückert prefer this reading, but the weight of authority is in favour of the received text. There are three general modes of explaining this passage which have been adopted. 1. Calvin among the older commentators, and Usteri and Olshausen among the moderns, say that the words *clothed* and *naked* must be understood to refer to the moral or spiritual state of the soul; to its being clothed with righteousness or being destitute of that robe. Calvin says the apostle's design is to limit the blessedness spoken of in the preceding verses to the righteous. The wicked are to be despoiled of their bodies and will appear naked before God; but believers, being clothed in the righteousness of Christ, will stand before him in the glorious vesture of immortality. There are two garments, therefore, he says, referred to ; the one, the righteousness of Christ, received in this life; the other, immortal glory, received at death. The former is the cause and necessary condition of the latter. Calvin lays special stress on the καί, *also*, which is inserted for the sake of amplification, as though Paul had said, 'A new garment shall be prepared for believers at death if also (or already) in this life they were clothed.' This interpretation, however, is evidently out of keeping with the context. It is very unnatural to make the same words have such different meanings in the same connection. In v. 2 we are said to be clothed with our house from heaven; in v. 3 we are so clothed as not to be found naked, and in v. 4 Paul speaks of being unclothed. If in vs. 2 and 4 the word refers to a body or house, in v. 3 it cannot refer to the robe of righteousness. Being unclothed is evidently the opposite of being clothed. As the former refers to laying aside the earthly tabernacle, the latter must refer to our being invested with the house from heaven. Besides, any such distinction between the righteous and the wicked, or any caution that the unrighteous are not to be received into heaven, as this interpretation supposes, is foreign to the design of the passage. Paul is not speaking of the general destiny of men after death, but of his own personal experience and conviction. 'I know,' he says, 'that if I die I have a house in heaven, and being clothed with that house I shall not be found naked.' There is no room here for a warning to the unrighteous. They are not at all brought into view.

2. The second general view of this passage is founded on the assumption that v. 2 speaks of the change to be effected in those who shall be alive when Christ comes. According to Grotius the meaning is, 'We shall be clothed upon (i. e. invested with a new body over the present one), if so be that day shall find us clothed (i. e. in the body) and not *naked* (i. e. bodiless spirits).' That is, we shall experience the change mentioned in v. 2, provided we are alive when Christ comes. To this, however, it is objected, first, that as the event of Paul's being alive at that time was entirely uncertain, and is here so presented, the appropriate particle would be εἴπερ (*if so be*) and not εἴγε (*if*, as is sure to be the case); and second, that this interpretation is inconsistent with the force of the aorist participle ἐνδυσάμενοι. The sense given to the passage would require the perfect ἐνδεδυμένοι, *being then clothed*. According to Meyer the meaning is, 'If, as is certain to be the case, we in fact (καί) shall be found clothed, and not naked.' That is, 'If clothed upon with our house from heaven (i. e. the new body) we shall not be found bodiless when Christ comes.' This interpretation suits the words, but not the connection. As before remarked, the whole passage proceeds on the hypothesis of death. 'If I die,' says the apostle, 'so and so will happen.' This being the case, he cannot be understood to state what would happen if he did not die, but

survived the coming of the Lord. Besides, the whole basis of
this interpretation is unsound. Paul did not expect to survive
the second advent, as is plain from 2 Thess. 2, 1–6. See the
comment on 1 Cor. 15, 51.

3. The third interpretation assumes that the apostle refers
not to the spiritual body but to a mansion in heaven. In the
preceding verse he said that he earnestly desired to be clothed
upon with his house from heaven, "since," he adds, "being
clothed, we shall not be found (i. e. shall not be) naked." As
the house from heaven is spoken of as a garment, being houseless is expressed by the word *naked*. This interpretation
gives the same translation of the words as the preceding, but
a different exposition of their meaning; and it has the advantage of agreeing logically with the context and with the elevated tone of the whole passage. 'If I die,' says Paul, 'I
know I have a home in heaven, and I earnestly desire to enter
on that heavenly house, since when driven from this earthly
tabernacle I shall not be houseless and homeless.' According
to this view the object of his desire was the glory and blessedness of heaven; according to the other, it was that he might
live until Christ came, and thus escape the pain of dying.
This was an object comparatively insignificant, and utterly
out of keeping with the heroic spirit which pervades the
whole context.

4. For we that are in (this) tabernacle do groan,
being burdened : not for that we would be unclothed,
but clothed upon, that mortality might be swallowed
up of life.

This verse gives the reason of the desire expressed in v. 2.
'We desire our house which is from heaven, *for* in this we
groan, &c.' The words οἱ ὄντες mean *we who are*, not 'whilst
we are,' which would require the simple ὄντες without the article. *In this tabernacle*, ἐν τῷ σκήνει, literally, in *the* tabernacle, i. e. the tabernacle mentioned in v. 1, and implied in v. 2.
Do groan being burdened, i. e. because burdened. The burden meant may be the affliction by which Paul was overwhelmed; or the body itself; or the longing after a better
world. As this passage is intimately connected with the preceding chapter, in which the apostle had spoken so freely of
his sufferings, and as his experience in view of death was de-

termined by those sufferings, it is perfectly natural to understand him to refer to the burden of sorrow. It was because
he suffered so much that he groaned to be delivered, i. e. to
be absent from the body and present with the Lord. *Not
that we would be unclothed.* The words are ἐφ' ᾧ, which in
Rom. 5, 12 mean *propterea quod*, 'because that;' but here
they more naturally mean *quare*, 'wherefore.' They introduce the reason of what follows, not of what precedes. 'On
which account,' i. e. because we are thus burdened we desire,
&c. If ἐφ' ᾧ be taken in the sense of *because that* the sense is
just the opposite. Then this clause states the nature of the
burden under which the apostle groaned. 'We groan *because that* we do not wish to be unclothed.' It was then the
dread of death, or the desire to be glorified without the necessity of dying, that was the object of the apostle's intense
desire. This is altogether unworthy of the man and inconsistent with the context. Paul says, 'We groan being burdened, *wherefore*, i. e. because thus burdened, we do not wish
to die; death is not that for which we long, but that which
comes after death. It is not mere exemption from the burden of life, from its duties, its labours or its sufferings, which
is the object of desire, but to be in heaven.' The passage is
in its spirit and meaning altogether parallel with v. 8. "Willing rather to be absent from the body and present with the
Lord." *To be unclothed* means to lay aside our earthly tabernacle. *To be clothed upon* means to enter the house not made
with hands. As the earthly house is compared to a garment,
so is the heavenly house. *That mortality* (τὸ θνητόν, *that
which is mortal*) *may be swallowed up of life*, i. e. absorbed
by it so that the one ceases to appear and the other becomes
dominant. Comp. 1 Cor. 15, 53. 54. This is the elevated object of the apostle's longing desire. It was not death, not
annihilation, nor mere exemption from suffering; but to be
raised to that higher state of existence in which all that was
mortal, earthly and corrupt about him should be absorbed in
the life of God, that divine and eternal life arising from the
beatific vision of God, and consisting in perfect knowledge,
holiness and blessedness.

5. Now, he that hath wrought us for the selfsame
thing (is) God, who also hath given unto us the earnest
of the Spirit.

It was something very heroic and grand for a poor, persecuted man to stand thus erect in the presence of his enemies and in the immediate prospect of death, and avow such superiority to all suffering, and such confidence of a glorious immortality. The apostle, therefore, adds that neither the elevated feelings which he expressed, nor his preparation for the exalted state of existence which he so confidently expected, was due to himself. *He who hath wrought us for the selfsame thing is God.* The words εἰς αὐτὸ τοῦτο, *to this very thing*, naturally refers to what immediately precedes, the being clothed upon so that mortality should be swallowed up of life. For this elevated destiny God had prepared him; not created him, but (ὁ κατεργασάμενος) made him fit by giving the requisite qualifications. He was, as a believer, looking forward with joyful expectation to his home in heaven, the workmanship of God. *Who also hath given unto us the earnest of the Spirit.* God had not only prepared him for future glory, but had given him the assurance of a blessed immortality, of which the indwelling of the Holy Ghost was the earnest, i. e. a foretaste and pledge. 1, 22. Eph. 1, 13. 14. Rom. 5, 5. 8, 16. According to the view given above of the context, the object of the apostle's desire was not the resurrection, nor the change which the living believer is to experience at Christ's coming, but the state of glory immediately subsequent to death. It is therefore of that the Holy Spirit is here declared to be the earnest. Elsewhere, as in Rom. 8, 11, the indwelling of the Spirit is represented as the pledge of the future life of the body, because he is the source of that life which the believer derives from Christ, and which pertains to the body as well as to the soul. Comp. 1 Cor. 6, 19. All therefore in whom the Spirit dwells, i. e. manifests his permanent presence by producing within them the Christian graces, have the pledge of immediate admission into heaven when they die, and of a glorious resurrection when the Lord comes.

6. Therefore (we are) always confident, knowing that, whilst we are at home in the body, we are absent from the Lord.

The grammatical construction in this and the following verse, 8, is interrupted and irregular, which our translators

have helped out by inserting the words *we are*, thus turning
the participle θαρροῦντες into a verb. The unfinished sentence
in v. 6 is resumed and completed in v. 8. Omitting the words
of resumption in v. 8, the whole sentence stands thus: "Being
confident and knowing that whilst at home in the body, we
are absent from the Lord, we are desirous (εὐδοκοῦμεν) rather
to be absent from the body and present with the Lord." This
verse is introduced as a consequence of what precedes. 'Having the earnest of the Spirit, *therefore* we are confident.'
This confidence is not a mere temporary feeling due to some
transient excitement; but a permanent state of mind. Being
always, πάντοτε, on all occasions and under all circumstances,
even in the midst of dangers and discouragements which, were
it not for divine support, would produce despair. The ground
of the boldness and confidence expressed by the word θαρροῦντες is not any thing in the believer; it is not his natural
courage, not the strength of his convictions; but it is a state
of mind produced by the indwelling of the Spirit, and the
natural consequence of his presence. *Being confident and
knowing;* both these particles are grammatically constructed
with the verb *we are willing*, εὐδοκοῦμεν, in v. 8, and together
express the ground of the apostle's desire to be absent from
the body. *Knowing that, whilst we are at home in the body,
we are absent from the Lord.* The words ἐνδημέω, to be at
home (literally, among one's people), and ἐκδημέω are opposed
to each other. The figure is slightly changed from that used
in the preceding verses. There it was a house, here a city, at
least δῆμος, *people*, naturally suggests that idea. Comp. Phil.
3, 20. Heb. 11, 13. 13, 14.

7. (For we walk by faith, not by sight.)

This is a passing, parenthetical remark, intended as a confirmation of the preceding declaration. 'We are absent from
the Lord, *for* we now, in this life, walk by faith.' The passage
is parallel to Rom. 8, 24, "We are saved by hope (or in hope,
i. e. in prospect)." Salvation is not a present, but a future
good. So here, presence with the Lord is now a matter of
faith, not of fruition. The condition of our present state of
being is that of believing. The faith which is the evidence of
things not seen and the substance (or assurance) of things
hoped for, is the element in which we live, so long as we are
not present with those things. Being the objects of faith they

are of course absent. The preposition, διά, may have its ordinary force, " We walk *by means of* faith ; " it is by faith we regulate our walk through life. Or it may be used here as in Rom. 8, 25. Heb. 12, 1, and elsewhere, to mark the attending circumstances, " we wait *with* patience," " let us run *with* patience," " we walk *with* faith." *And not by sight.* The word εἶδος does not mean the sense of sight, but the thing seen, form, appearance, that which is the object of sight. In Luke 3, 22, the Spirit is said to have descended σωματικῷ εἴδει, *in a bodily shape;* in 9, 29 it is said of our Lord that the εἶδος τοῦ προσώπου αὐτοῦ, *the fashion of his face was changed;* and in John 5, 37 our Lord tells the Jews, speaking of the Father, " Ye have never heard his voice or seen his (εἶδος) shape." If this, the proper signification of the word, be retained, then εἶδος is the object of faith, the form and fashion of the things believed. *Loco rei verbo acquiescimus,* as Calvin expresses it. We are conversant with the report of heavenly things, not with the things themselves. We are absent, not present with them. In this case διά means *with.* ' We are not surrounded with the forms of things in heaven.' It is no objection to this interpretation that the preposition διά has a different force given to it in the second clause, from that commonly given to it in the first clause of the verse. ' We walk *by* faith, and not *with*, or *in presence of* the objects of our faith.' This change in the force of the same preposition in the same sentence is not unusual. See Heb. 9, 11. 12. 10, 20. The majority of commentators, however, depart from the proper signification of the word εἶδος and take it in the sense of ὄψις, because this agrees best with the antithesis to πίστις (*faith*) and with the force of the preposition. " We walk by faith, not by sight; " we believe, but do not see things which govern our life. This, no doubt, is the idea which the apostle intended, although not precisely the form in which he has expressed it.

8. We are confident, (I say,) and willing rather to be absent from the body, and to be present with the Lord.

The sentence begun and left incomplete in v. 6 is here resumed and carried out. Θαῤῥοῦμεν δέ, *we are of good courage.* The particle δέ may either serve to indicate the resumption of what he had begun to say in v. 6, or be taken adversatively in reference to v. 7. 'We walk by faith, not by sight, *nevertheless* we are not discouraged.' We are not only not desponding, but are so confident as to prefer to be absent from the body. Death is not an object of dread, but of desire. That the phrase "to be absent from the body" means *to die* is evident, not only from the import of the expression and from the parallel passage in Phil. 1, 23, but also from the whole context, which treats of the apostle's experience in view of death. He was surrounded by dangers; he could scarcely bear up under the load of his sufferings; he was every day exposed to a violent death, which he had escaped hitherto only, as it were, by miracle; still he was not cast down. He sustained his courage, and even desired to die. There can be no doubt that this verse is parallel with v. 4, where the apostle says he desired to be clothed upon, i. e. with his house which is from heaven. The object of desire is the same in both. It is also plain that in this verse it is absence from the body and presence with the Lord, not the being changed from corruptible to incorruptible without dying, that he earnestly longed for; and therefore this verse shows that the subject treated of in the context is the change which the believer experiences at death, and not that which those who are alive shall experience at Christ's second coming. The words ἐκδημέω and ἐνδημέω, here used as in v. 6, are best rendered 'from home' and 'at home.' 'We would be from home as to the body, and at home with the Lord.' THE LORD is of course Christ, the supreme Lord, who in virtue of the fulness of the Godhead is the rightful sovereign and possessor of the universe, and in virtue of his dying for the redemption of his people, in a peculiar sense the sovereign and possessor of believers. The Christian's heaven is to be with Christ, for we shall be like him when we see him as he is. Into his presence the believer passes as soon as he is absent from the body, and into his likeness the soul is at death immediately transformed; and when at the resurrection, the body is made like unto his glorious body, the work of redemption is consummated. Awaiting this consummation, it is an inestimable blessing to be assured that believers, as soon as they are absent from the body, are present with THE LORD.

9. Wherefore we labour, that, whether present or absent, we may be accepted of him.

Wherefore, διὸ καί, *wherefore also,* i. e. because we desire to be with the Lord. Longing after communion with him produces the desire and secures the effort to be found acceptable to him. Those who have this hope purify themselves as he is pure. 1 John 3, 3. It is impossible that those who regard the presence of Christ, or being with him, as heaven, should not desire and labour to be pleasing to him, by living in obedience to his commandments. *We labour.* The word φιλοτιμεῖσθαι means more than to labour. It signifies literally, to love honour, to be ambitious; and then to make any thing a point of honour, or to set one's honour in doing or attaining something. So Paul says, he made it a point of honour not to build on another man's foundation. Rom. 15, 20. And here he intends to say that as ambitious men desire and strive after fame, so Christians long and labour to be acceptable to Christ. Love to him, the desire to please him, and to be pleasing to him, animates their hearts and governs their lives, and makes them do and suffer what heroes do for glory. *Whether present or absent.* These words may be variously explained. 1. The sense may be, 'Whether present *in the body,* or absent *from the body,*' i. e. whether living or dying. Comp. Rom. 14, 8, "Whether we live, we live unto the Lord; or whether we die, we die unto the Lord." 1 Thess. 5, 10, "Whether we wake or sleep, we live together with him." The connection is then either with φιλοτιμούμεθα, 'we strive whether in the body or out of the body; i. e. the desire in question is active as well in the living as the dead;' or, as is better, with εὐάρεστοι εἶναι, 'we strive to be acceptable whether in the body or absent from it.' 2. The sense may be, 'Whether present *with the Lord,* or absent *from the Lord.*' This is only expressing the same idea in a different form. Whether living or dead, as in Rom. 14, 8. 3. Meyer takes the words literally, 'Whether at home or abroad.' But this is utterly inconsistent with the context. The objection to the first interpretation, that the desire to be acceptable to the Lord when actually saved, must cease, inasmuch as the object is attained, is of no force. The thing desired, τὸ ζητούμενον, as Chrysostom says, is that we may be pleasing to Christ whether here or there, whether in this world or the next.

10. For we must all appear before the judgment-seat of Christ; that every one may receive the things

(done) in (his) body, according to that he hath done, whether (it be) good or bad.

In what precedes Paul had been speaking of himself. It was his own sufferings, hopes, and efforts which the occasion called upon him to exhibit. In all this, however, he spoke as a Christian, and therefore in the name of other Christians. In this verse he expressly comprehends others, and all others. 'I strive to be acceptable to the Lord, *for* we must all (I as well as all believers, and even all men) must, &c.' As Christ is to decide upon our eternal destiny, it is of infinite moment that we should be acceptable, or well-pleasing, in his sight. *We must all appear*, φανερωθῆναι. This means either nothing more than a judicial appearance, as when any one is said to appear in court before a judge; or, as Bengel explains it, *manifestos fieri cum occultis nostris*, 'we must all stand revealed in our true character before the judgment-seat of Christ.' 1 Cor. 4, 5. Col. 3, 4. As there can be no disguise, no deception before an omniscient judge, Paul was assiduous in his efforts to be prepared to stand the scrutiny of an all-seeing eye. *The judgment-seat of Christ;* βῆμα, literally, *step*, then a raised platform, or seat; most frequently used of the elevated seat on which the Roman magistrates sat to administer justice, an object of reverence and fear to all the people. As Christ is to be the judge, as all men are to appear before him, as the secrets of the heart are to be the grounds of judgment, it is obvious that the sacred writers believed Christ to be a divine person, for nothing less than omniscience could qualify any one for the office here ascribed to our Lord. *That every one may receive*, κομίζω, which in the active form means *to take up*, in the middle, as here, *to take for one's self*, properly to take or receive what is one's due, or what on some ground one is entitled to. Matt. 25, 27. Col. 3, 25. 2 Pet. 2, 13. The punishment which men are to receive will be what they have earned, and therefore what is in justice due to them. The reward of the righteous, although a matter of grace and not of justice, yet being, agreeably to the tenor of the covenant of grace, according to their works, it is of the nature of a reward. The pay of a faithful soldier is a matter of debt, titles and estates are matters of favour. There is no inconsistency, therefore, in the Scriptures denying all merit to believers, and yet teaching that they shall be rewarded according to their works. We are said to receive *the things done in the body*, because the matter is conceived of, or is here represented as an investment. Our acts are treasures laid up for the future, whether treasures of wrath, or treasures in heaven; and these (κομιζόμεθα) *we receive back.* The words τὰ διὰ τοῦ σώματος may mean *things (done) through or by the body.* Then bodily acts are taken for acts of all kinds. Compare Rom. 8, 13. Or the διά may be taken as in v. 7, (according to one interpretation of that verse,) as indicating the attending circumstance—*with the body,* i. e. while clothed with the body. This is the sense expressed in our version, which renders the clause "things (done) *in* the body," although διά of course does not mean *in. According to that he hath done,* πρὸς ἃ ἔπραξεν, indicating the rule according to which the retributions of the final judgments are to be administered. Both with regard to the wicked and the righteous, there is to be a great distinction in the recompense, which different members of each class are to receive. Some will be beaten with few stripes, and some with many. It will be more tolerable in that day for Tyre and Sidon than for those who reject the gospel; and on the other hand, those believers who suffer most, will love most and be most blessed. *Whether good or evil,* i. e. whether he did good or evil. Each shall receive according to his deeds whether good or bad. It is from such passages as this that some American theologians have inferred that the only benefit which the believer receives from Christ is the forgiveness of sin, and that being pardoned he is dealt with according to the principles of justice. Others, especially in Germany, have drawn from the same source the conclusion that the doctrine of Paul is that the merit of Christ cleanses only from the sins committed before conversion. If a Jew or Gentile became a Christian his sins were blotted out, and then he was rewarded or punished, saved or lost, according to his works. The merit of Christ availed nothing for the pardon of sin after conversion. And this again is very much the ancient doctrine that there is no forgiveness for post-baptismal sins. The benefits of Christ's work, according to many of the ancients, are conveyed to the soul in baptism, but if once forfeited by sin can never be reapplied. This gloomy doctrine, which belonged to the transition period which preceded the full development of the theology of the Papal church, has been revived by the inchoate Romanists of the present day. But according to the Scriptures and the doctrine of all Protestant churches, the blood of Jesus Christ cleanses from all sin, whether committed before or after baptism or conversion. It is a fountain to which we may daily come for cleansing. He is a priest who ever lives to make intercession for us, and who ever presents before God the merit of his sacrifice as a perpetual offering, typified by the morning and evening sacrifice under the law. According to the anti-scriptural views mentioned above, when a man first comes to Christ his sins are forgiven, and he then commences anew under the covenant of works, and stands in the same relation to God that Adam did before the fall. The condition of salvation is to him as it was to our first parent, "Do this and live." Christ henceforth profits him nothing. But according to the apostle we are not under the law, but under grace. Rom. 6, 14. On the ground of the one offering of Christ, by which those who believe are forever sanctified, (i. e. atoned for,) God does not impute to the penitent believer his sins unto condemnation. He is not judged by the law or treated according to its principles, for then no man could be saved. But he is treated as one for all whose sins, past, present, and future, an infinite satisfaction has been made, and who has a perpetual claim to that satisfaction so long as he is united to Christ by faith and the indwelling of his Spirit. Hence the Scriptures are filled with exhortations not merely to the unconverted, to Jews and Pagans, but to baptized Christians, to repent of sin and to believe in the Lord Jesus Christ; that is, to exercise trust in the merit of his sacrifice and the prevalence of his intercession for the pardon of their daily and manifold transgressions and shortcomings. The sacrifice of Christ avails for the sins committed from the foundation of the world to the final consummation. It affords a permanent and all-sufficient reason why God can be just and yet justify the ungodly.

Paul's defence of himself against the charge of self-commendation. Vs. 11–21.

He declares that he acted under a solemn sense of his responsibility to God, v. 11. This was not said with the view of commending himself; but rather to afford them the means of vindicating his character, v. 12. Whether his way of speaking of himself was extravagant or moderate, sane or insane, his motive in doing as he did was a sincere regard to the glory of God and the good of his church, v. 13. For the love of Christ constrained him to live, not for himself, but for him who died for him and rose again, vs. 14. 15. Acting under the control of this elevated principle, he was raised above the influence of external things. He did not judge of men by their external condition. He was a new creature in virtue of his union with Christ, vs. 16. 17. This great change which he had experienced was not self-wrought; it was of God, who is the author of the whole scheme of redemption. He is reconciled unto the world through Jesus Christ, and he has commissioned his ministers to proclaim this great truth to all men, vs. 18. 19. Therefore, the apostle, as an ambassador of God, exhorted men to accept of this offer of reconciliation, for which the most abundant provision had been made, in that God had made Christ to be sin for us, in order that we might be made the righteousness of God in him, vs. 20. 21.

11. Knowing therefore the terror of the Lord, we persuade men; but we are made manifest unto God; and I trust also are made manifest in your consciences.

This verse is an inference from what precedes, as is indicated by the particle (οὖν) *therefore*. Paul had asserted his earnest desire to be acceptable to the Lord, and, therefore, *knowing the terror of the Lord*, &c. In this version of the clause, τὸν φόβον τοῦ κυρίου, the genitive is taken as the genitive of the subject. It is the terror which belongs to the Lord. 'Knowing how terrible the Lord is.' But this is contrary to the constant use of the phrase. The fear of the Lord is that fear or reverence which the Lord excites, or of which he is the object. Hence it so often stands in Scripture for true religion. "The fear of the Lord is the beginning of wisdom." So in Acts 9, 31, "Walking in the fear of the Lord." Rom. 3, 18, "The fear of God is not before their eyes;" and in 7, 1 of this epistle, "perfecting holiness in the fear of God." See also Eph. 5, 21, "Submitting yourselves one to another in the fear of Christ." In all these cases (φόβος) *fear* means pious reverence. There is no reason for departing from that sense in this place. Knowing, i. e. feeling or experiencing, the pious reverence for Christ, the earnest desire to meet his approbation, asserted in the context, the apostle acted under the influence of that sentiment, and not from selfish or unworthy motives, in all his conduct as a man and as a minister. As the expression " fear of the Lord "

is so uniformly used to express that reverence and submission
which are due only to God, it is clear from this and analogous
passages that Christ was to the apostles the object of the
religious affections; and that they felt themselves to be responsible to him for their moral character and conduct. The
evidence of the divinity of the Lord is thus seen to pervade
the New Testament, and is not confined to a few isolated
passages. Influenced, says the apostle, by the fear of the
Lord, *I persuade men.* What this means is somewhat doubtful. The word πείθειν expresses the endeavour to convince,
as in Acts 18, 4, "He persuaded the Jews," i. e. endeavoured
to convince them of the truth, and in Acts 28, 23, "Persuad-
ing them concerning Jesus." The apostle therefore may here
mean that he endeavoured to convince men of the truth of
the gospel, i. e. to convert them, or bring them to the obedience of faith. Or, he may mean that he endeavoured to convince them of his integrity, or that he was really governed by
the fear of Christ, and was therefore sincere and honest, which
in Corinth had been so unjustly called in question. This latter
explanation is generally preferred, both because it suits the
context, and because the following clause seems to require
this idea. 'We seek to convince men of our integrity, but
God we need not convince, to him our inmost soul is manifest.'
The word (πείθειν), however, also signifies *to conciliate*, to seek
to please, as in Gal. 1, 10, "Do we persuade (i. e. seek to
please) men, or God." Matt. 28, 14. Acts 12, 20. 1 John 3,
19. Many prefer that sense here. Luther, in his idiomatic
style, renders the clause, *fahren wir schön mit den Leuten.*
The apostle is supposed to refer to the fact that he accommodated himself to all classes, and became all things to all men,
that he might save some. 1 Cor. 9, 22. Though he thus acted
still he was manifest unto God; i. e. God knew the purity of
his motives. This, however, is an idea foreign to the connection. His accommodating himself to others was not the specific objection made against him by his enemies in Corinth,
but, as appears from the previous chapters, his "lightness"
or instability of purpose, and his consequent untrustworthiness
as a man and as a teacher. Others again, take πείθειν in a bad
sense. 'We deceive men, (as our enemies say,) but are manifest to God.' But this is utterly incongruous. How could
Paul say in such a solemn connection, 'I deceive men,' and
leave the saving clause, *as my enemies say*, to be supplied by
the reader. The most natural interpretation is that given

above. 'Under the influence of the fear of the Lord, we endeavour to convince men, i. e. as he had said in 4, 2, to commend himself to every man's conscience, and whether successful in this or not he was at least known to God.' *Made
manifest unto God*, i. e. to God I am (φανερός) *apparent*, my
true character is known. *And I trust also are made manifest
in your conscience.* Although misunderstood and defamed
by others, he trusted that the Corinthian Christians as a body
had an inward conviction of his integrity. The evidence of
his sincerity was his moral excellence, and therefore it addressed itself to their consciences. There may be many re-
.ports against a good man which we cannot contradict; many
charges which we cannot refute; and yet the self-evidencing
light of goodness will produce the conviction of his integrity
in the consciences even of wicked men, and much more in the
hearts of the good.

12. For we commend not ourselves again unto
you, but give you occasion to glory on our behalf, that
ye may have somewhat to (answer) them which glory
in appearance, and not in heart.

His object in thus speaking of himself was not self-praise,
nor to secure the confidence of the Corinthians, which he already possessed; but to give them materials for a vindication
of his character against the aspersions of his enemies. The
connection, as indicated by *for*, is with the preceding verse,
of which this is a confirmation. 'I am assured of your confidence, *for* the object of my self-commendation is not to recommend myself to you, but, &c.' In chapter 3, 1, Paul had
had occasion to repel the charge of self-laudation, and hence
he says, he was not about to commend himself *again*, as some
said he had before done. *But give you*, literally, *giving*
(διδόντες), and therefore a verb must be supplied, 'Giving you
occasion *we say these things.'* *An occasion of glorying in
our behalf*, ἀφορμὴν καυχήματος; καύχημα being taken in the
sense of καύχησις. *On our behalf*, ὑπὲρ ἡμῶν, not simply *over*
us, or *about* us, but for our benefit. That is, for our vindication. Some commentators suppose that there is something
ironical in this whole passage. As though the apostle designed to taunt the Corinthians with their readiness to listen
to the false representations of his opponents, and with the

plea that they needed not the disposition, but the ability to defend him. This view, however, is inconsistent with the connection and with the whole drift of the epistle. In the immediately preceding verse he had expressed his assurance of their confidence in his integrity, and throughout the epistle his overflowing love for the faithful in Corinth is mingled with his severe denunciations of the false teachers and their followers. *That ye may have.* There is no object expressed to the verb (ἔχητε), *ye may have.* We may supply (τί) *something,* and insert the words *to answer,* as is done by our translators; or we may borrow from the context the word καύχημα; " That ye may have *some ground of boasting.*" *Against those who glory in appearance and not in heart.* This is evidently descriptive of the false teachers. The words ἐν προσώπῳ, *in face,* may, from the antithesis to ἐν καρδίᾳ, *in heart,* be taken, as in our version, for what is external as opposed to what is inward. Then the expression refers to the fact that those teachers gloried in their Hebrew descent, in their circumcision, their external religious privileges, their churchmanship, &c. It was in these things they placed their confidence, and of them they made their boast. Or the words may be taken literally, and according to their uniform use in other passages. Then the expression describes the sanctimoniousness and hypocrisy of the false teachers. They gloried, says Meyer, in the holiness, the zeal, and devotion which expressed themselves in the face. They wished to appear unto men to fast, to wear the look of sanctity, while their hearts, as our Lord describes the same class of men, were full of all uncleanness. The former explanation is commonly adopted, and is probably the true one, because regard for externals is elsewhere in this epistle represented as the prominent characteristic of Paul's opponents in Corinth. Their great boast was that they belonged to the true church or theocracy, and that Paul and his followers were dissenters and schismatics.

13. For whether we be beside ourselves, (it is) to God: or whether we be sober, (it is) for your cause.

This verse again is a confirmation of the preceding. ' You have good reason to glory on my behalf, *for,* &c.' *Whether we be beside ourselves.* The word ἐξίστημι, *to be out of one's mind,* and other words of like signification, are used either in their strict sense to express insanity or madness, or in a wider sense, to express undue excitement or extravagance. When Festus, Acts 26, 24, said to the apostle, "Paul, thou art beside thyself; much learning doth make thee mad," he did not mean that he was really insane. And when our Lord's zeal provoked his friends to say of him, "He is beside himself," Mark 3, 21, they certainly did not intend to charge him with insanity. There is therefore no necessity for taking the word here in its strict sense, and assuming that Paul's enemies had accused him of being out of his mind. It is the more natural to take the word in a wider sense here, because the opposite term, σωφρονέω, (to be sober, or sane,) and its cognates, are much more frequently used to express moderation and discretion than sanity in the strict sense of that word. The apostle means to say that whether he was extravagant or moderate, whether he exceeded the bounds of discretion, as his enemies asserted, or whether he was sober and discreet, it was not for himself; he had in view only the glory of God and the good of his church, and therefore the Corinthians might safely boast of him, i. e. vindicate him from the aspersions of the false teachers. Whether the extravagance or insanity here referred to, consisted in his self-commendation, or in his zeal and devotion, is matter of dispute. The former is the more probable, both because in the immediate context he had been speaking of that subject, and because in chapters 11 and 12 he speaks so much at large of his commending himself, although forced upon him, as a kind of folly or insanity. In those chapters the ἀφροσύνη, (the want of mind,) of which he accuses himself, was self-praise; and the σωφροσύνη (soberness or sanity) which he desired to exhibit was moderation in speaking of himself and of his labours. Paul, therefore, in this passage, is most naturally understood to mean, that whether he praised himself or whether he did not, whether the manner in which he had spoken of himself be considered as ἀφροσύνη or σωφροσύνη, as insanity or sobriety, he spoke not for himself, but for God and his people.

14. For the love of Christ constraineth us; because we thus judge, that if one died for all, then were all dead.

'In whatever I do,' says the apostle, 'I act for God and his church, *for* the love of Christ constraineth me.' The connection is thus plain. *The love of Christ* here means Christ's love for us, not the love of which he is the object. This is obvious, because the apostle goes on to illustrate the greatness of Christ's love to us, and not of our love to him. Comp. Gal. 2, 20, where the same idea is expressed by the words "who loved me." See Rom. 8, 35. Eph. 3, 19. *Constraineth us*, i. e. controls and governs us. The word συνέχω means also to *restrain*, a sense which many adopt here. 'The love of Christ restrains me from acting for myself.' This is a more limited sense, and is not required by the usage of the word, which is often used to express the idea of being pressed as by a crowd, or figuratively, by calamity or sorrow. There is no better version for it in this passage than that adopted by our translators. 'The love of Christ *constraineth* us.' It coerces, or presses, and therefore impels. It is the governing influence which controls the life. This is a trait of Paul's experience as a Christian, and is therefore common to all Christians. It is not benevolence which makes a man a Christian, for then all philanthropists would be Christians. Nor is it mere piety, in the sense of reverence for God, which makes a man a Christian, for then all devout Mussulmans and Jews would be Christians. Morality does not make us religious, but religion makes us moral. In like manner benevolence and piety (in the wide sense) do not make men Christians, but Christianity makes them benevolent and devout. A Christian is one who recognizes Jesus as the Christ, the Son of the living God, as God manifested in the flesh, loving us and dying for our redemption; and who is so affected by a sense of the love of this incarnate God as to be constrained to make the will of Christ the rule of his obedience, and the glory of Christ the great end for which he lives. The man who does this perfectly, is a perfect Christian. The man who does it imperfectly, yet with the sincere desire to be entirely devoted to Christ, is a sincere Christian. On the other hand, the man who lives supremely for himself, for his family, for science, for the world, for mankind, whatever else he may be, is not a Christian. Whosoever loveth father or mother, son or daughter, more than me, saith our Lord, is not worthy of me, Matt. 10, 37. He that hateth not his own life, cannot be my disciple, Luke 14, 26. The great question is, What constitutes a Christian? It is being so constrained by a sense of the love of our divine Lord to us, that we consecrate our lives to him. Hence faith in his divinity, faith in his love, faith in his having died for us, is the principle or source of the Christian life. And this is the only form in which true religion can now exist. That is, the only true religion now possible is the worship, love, and service of the Lord Jesus Christ. It is impossible for a man to turn his back on Christ and worship the God of nature or the God of the Jews. Should a man reveal himself to us first as an acquaintance, then as a friend, and then as a father, filial reverence and devotion would be the only form in which sincere and true regard for him could exist. To deny him as father, would be to reject him as a friend and acquaintance. Since, therefore, the same God who revealed himself first in nature, and then as the Jehovah of the Hebrews, has revealed himself in the flesh, loving us and dying for our redemption, to deny him in this the clearest revelation of his being and perfection, is to deny him altogether. "Whoso denieth the Son, the same hath not the Father," 1 John 2, 23. It is the practical or experimental form of this great truth, which is presented in this passage.

Because we thus judge. This clause assigns the reason why the love of Christ exerted the constraining power referred to. It was because the apostle judged that the death of Christ for his people not only placed them under the strongest obligation to devote themselves to his service, but it secured this devotion. They died in him. Rom. 6, 4. 5. As the participle (κρίναντας) is in the aorist, it would be more strictly rendered, *because we judged.* That is, 'I live for Christ, because when I became a Christian I regarded his dying for me as involving the obligation and necessity of my living for him.' This was the aspect under which he embraced Christianity; the judgment which he formed of it from the beginning. *That if one died for all.* The contrast presented, especially in the epistle to the Hebrews, between the priest and sacrifices of the old economy on the one hand, and the high priest and sacrifice of the gospel on the other, is that those were many, these are one. The ancient priests could not continue by reason of death. Our high priest, being a divine person, and therefore possessed of an endless life, ever lives to save. The sacrifices of the law were daily repeated, because it was impossible that they should take away sin; Christ by the offering up of himself hath forever perfected them that are sanctified. His blood cleanses from all sin. The apostle here presents him as the one priest and the one sacrifice. *Died for all.* The words are ὑπὲρ πάντων. The preposition ὑπέρ, may have the general sense, *for the benefit of*, *in behalf of*, or the stricter sense, *in the place of*, as in v. 20 of this chapter. Philem. 13. Eph. 6, 20. In many places the choice between these senses depends on the context. In all those passages in which one person is said to die for another, as Rom. 5, 6. 7. 8. 14, 15. 1 Thess. 5, 10. Heb. 2, 9. Comp. Luke 22, 19. 1 Tim. 2, 6. Titus 2, 14. &c., &c., or in which the reference is to a sacrifice, the idea of substitution is clearly expressed. The argument does not rest on the force of the preposition, but on the nature of the case. The only way in which the death of the victim benefited the offerer, was by substitution. When, therefore, Christ is said to die as a sacrifice for us, the meaning is, he died in our stead. His death is taken in the place of ours so as to save us from death. That the preposition ὑπέρ, in this and similar passages, does mean *instead of*, is admitted by the great body of even Rationalistic commentators. See De Wette, Rückert, &c. Christ, it is said, died for *all*, i. e. for all the subjects of redemption. This limitation is not an arbitrary one, but arises of necessity out of the nature of the case, and is admitted almost universally. He did not die for all creatures; nor for all rational creatures; nor for all apostate rational creatures. The *all* is of necessity limited by what the Scriptures teach of the design of his death. If his death was merely didactic, intended to reveal and confirm some truth, then he may be said to have died for all benefited by that revelation, and therefore for angels as well as men. If designed to make it consistent with the interests of God's moral government for him to pardon the sins of men, then he may be said to have died equally for all men. But if his death was intended to save his people, then it had a reference to them which it had not to others. The true design of the death of Christ is to be learned from express assertions of Scripture, and from its effects. It is so obvious that the death of Christ was designed to save those for whom it was offered, that many of the recent as well as ancient commentators justify their explaining ὑπὲρ πάντων as meaning all men, by attributing to Paul the belief that all men are to be saved. This is an admission that the *all* for whom he died, are the all who are saved by his death. One of its effects is stated in the following clause; *Then were all dead*, or, *Then all died*. The word is ἀπέθανον. It is the same verb, and in the same tense. 'If one died, (ἀπέθανεν,)

then all died, (ἀπέθανον).' The word must have the same
sense in both clauses. It cannot mean *were* dead, because
that is inconsistent with the force of the aorist. *All*, (literally, *the* all, οἱ πάντες,) i. e. *the* all for whom the one died. His
death involved, or secured their death. This was its design
and effect, and, therefore, this clause limits the extent of the
word *all* in the preceding clause. Christ died for the all who
died when he died. The meaning of this expression has, however, been variously explained. 1. It is made to mean, 'Then
all died to themselves and sin.' His dying literally, secured
their dying figuratively. 2. Others say the true meaning is,
'Then all *ought* to die.' But this is not included in the words.
The aorist does not express obligation. 3. Chrysostom, Theodoret, Beza and others, give the same explanation which is
implied in our version, 'If one died for all, then were all subject to death.' That is, the vicarious death of Christ proves
that those for whom he died were in a state of condemnation.
But this suits neither the meaning of the word nor the context.
It was not to Paul's purpose to prove that men were in a state
of death. It was not what they *were*, but what the death of
Christ caused them to become, that he evidently intended to
express. 4. The simple meaning of the passage is, that the
death of one was the death of all. If one died for all, the all
died. The Scriptures teach that the relation between Christ
and his people is analogous to that between Adam and his
posterity. Rom. 5, 12–21. 1 Cor. 15, 21. 22. The apostasy
of Adam was the apostasy of all united to him; the work of
Christ was the work of all united to him. In the one, all
died; in the other, all are made alive. As the sin of Adam
was legally and effectively the sin of his race; so the death
of Christ was legally and effectively the death of his people.
This doctrine underlies the whole scheme of redemption. It
is, so to speak, the generic idea of the Epistle to the Romans.
The apostle shows that man, ruined by the sin of Adam, is
restored by the work of Christ. His people are so united to
him that his death is their death, and his life is their life.
"If we be dead with him, we shall also live with him," Rom.
6, 8. Hence believers are said to be crucified with Christ, to
rise with him, to reign with him. Gal. 2, 20. Eph. 2, 5. 6.
The simple meaning of the words, "If one died for all, then all
died," therefore is, that Christ's death was the death of his
people. This as we have seen is according to the analogy
of Scripture; and is also entirely pertinent to the design of

this passage. The apostle denied that he lived for himself.
He asserts that he lived for God and his people. For, he
adds, I died in Christ. This is precisely the argument which
he uses in Rom. 6. Shall we continue in sin that grace may
abound? Far from it, he says, How shall they who have
died on account of sin live any longer therein? If united to
Christ in his death, we must be united to him in his life.
Another consideration in favour of this interpretation is that
it comprehends the others. They are objectionable, not because they are erroneous, but because they are defective.
Death on account of sin, is death to sin. Dying with Christ,
involves death to self and sin ; and of course includes the obligation so to die. The death of Christ reconciles us to God ;
and reconciliation to God secures a life of devotion to his service. This is the doctrine set forth in the Epistle to the
Romans, ch. 7.

15. And (that) he died for all, that they which live
should not henceforth live unto themselves, but unto
him which died for them, and rose again.

This is a continuation of the preceding sentence, and is
designed to express more fully the judgment or conviction
(κρίναντας) which the apostle had formed of his relation to
Christ. He judged that the death of Christ was the death of
his people, and that the design with which he died for them
was that they might live for him. This idea is expressed in
various forms in the word of God. Sometimes our Lord is
said to have died, the just for the unjust, to bring us near to
God, 1 Pet. 3, 18 ; or, that we, being dead to sins, should live
unto righteousness, 1 Pet. 2, 24 ; or, to purify to himself a peculiar people, zealous of good works, Titus 2, 14. In Rom.
14, 9, the mode of statement is exactly parallel to the passage
before us. "To this end Christ both died and rose that he
might be the Lord both of the dead and living." To say
that Christ died that he might be the Lord of his people, is to
say that he died that they might be his servants, i. e. belong
to him and be devoted to him. The proximate design and
effect of the death of Christ is the expiation of sin and reconciliation with God, and the design and effect of reconciliation
with God are devotion to his service. Hence the death of
Christ is sometimes presented in reference to its proximate,

sometimes in reference to its ultimate design; i. e. sometimes he is said to have died to make a propitiation for sin, and sometimes, to bring us near to God. Here it is the latter. He died *that they which live should not henceforth live unto themselves*. "Those who live," οἱ ζῶντες, not, *those who survive his death*; nor, *those who are spiritually living*; nor, *the happy or blessed*, but, those who, although they died in Christ, are still living. Their death in him is not inconsistent with their being alive, for they died in one sense and they live in another. Those for whom Christ died, and on whom his death takes effect, thenceforth, i. e. from the time they apprehend their relation to him, and feel the power of his vicarious death, *do not live unto themselves*, i. e. self is not the object for which they live. This is the negative description of the Christian. He is a man who does not live unto himself. This is what he is not. The positive description is given in the next clause. He lives *for him who died for him and rose again*. This presents both the object and the ground of the Christian's devotion. He lives for him who died for him, and because he died for him. He is not a Christian who is simply unselfish, i. e. who lives for some object out of himself. He only is a Christian who lives for Christ. Many persons think they can be Christians on easier terms than these. They think it is enough to trust in Christ while they do not live for him. But the Bible teaches us that if we are partakers of Christ's death, we are also partakers of his life; if we have any such appreciation of his love in dying for us as to lead us to confide in the merit of his death, we shall be constrained to consecrate our lives to his service. And this is the only evidence of the genuineness of our faith. *And rose again.* We do not serve a dead Saviour. The resurrection of Christ is as essential to redemption as his death. He died for our sins and rose again for our justification. And it is to this risen Saviour, seated at the right hand of God, to whom all power in heaven and earth has been committed, and who ever lives to make intercession for us, who is the object of the supreme love of the believer, to whose service and glory the Christian consecrates his life.

16. Wherefore henceforth know we no man after the flesh: yea, though we have known Christ after the flesh, yet now henceforth know we (him) no more.

This is an inference, (ὥστε, *so that*). 'Such is the nature
of the change which I have experienced through the apprehension of the love of Christ, as just described, that I no
longer see or judge of things according to the flesh.' The *we*
refers primarily to the apostle himself, as he is still engaged
in self-vindication. He was acting from pure motives, he says,
for a sense of the love of Christ constrained him not to live for
himself but for Christ, and therefore he no longer judged of
persons or things as he had been accustomed to do. Paul's experience, however, was his experience as a Christian, and therefore not peculiar to himself. It is true of all Christians that
they do not know (i. e. estimate, judge, feel in reference to)
any man according to the flesh. This may mean, that the
judgment is not regulated or determined by a regard to
what is external. It is not a man's outward circumstances,
his birth, his station, his being rich or poor, Jew or Gentile,
that determines our estimate of him. Or the meaning may
be, that the judgment was not determined by carnal or selfish
considerations. Paul was not led to approve or disapprove,
love or hate any man from selfish or corrupt motives. This
latter view would suit the context, for the apostle had just
said that he lived not for himself but for Christ, and therefore
his judgments of men were not determined by a regard to
himself. It is also consistent with the usage of the word; for
σάρξ means *corrupt nature*, as well as what is outward. The
following part of the verse, however, is decisively in favour of
the former interpretation. Comp. 11, 18. John 8, 15. Phil.
3, 4. Paul evidently contrasts himself as he now was (ἀπὸ τοῦ
νῦν) with what he was before his conversion; and also himself
with his Judaizing opponents in Corinth. *Yea, though we
have known Christ after the flesh.* The words εἰ δὲ καί, *but
even if,* are concessive. Paul admits that he had once done
what he here condemns. *He had known or estimated Christ
after the flesh.* Of course this does not mean that he had
known Christ while in the flesh, as Olshausen supposes, because that would be saying nothing to the purpose, and because there is no evidence of Paul's ever having seen our
Lord before his resurrection. Olshausen's idea is, that as he
formerly regarded men as men, but now only as Christians,
i. e. had reference only to what was spiritual, so also he no
longer thinks of Christ as he once knew him on earth, but as
he is glorified in heaven. But this does not suit the connection nor the facts of the case. The words κατὰ σάρκα must

have the same sense in both parts of the verse; and in the former they do not designate the life before conversion, and therefore when spoken in reference to Christ are not to be understood of his earthly as opposed to his heavenly life. Paul had known Christ after the flesh in the sense of estimating him entirely according to the outward appearance of things. *Christ* does not here mean the Messiah, but is the historical designation of our Lord as an individual. Paul had despised and hated him because he judged him only according to his outward appearance as a poor suffering man, yet claiming to be the Christ the Son of the living God. His Jewish notions of what the Messiah was to be led him to regard with indignation the claims of Jesus to be the Christ. *Yet now henceforth know we* (*him*) *no more.* The order of the words in the original shows that the words κατὰ σάρκα are to be connected with the verb and not with its object; εἰ δὲ καὶ ἐγνώκαμεν κατὰ σάρκα Χριστόν. That is, we no longer judge *after the flesh* concerning Christ; we no longer estimate him according to appearance, but know him to be the Son of God, who loved us and gave himself for us. Gal. 2, 20.

17. Therefore, if any man (be) in Christ, (he is) a new creature : old things are passed away ; behold, all things are become new.

A further inference from what precedes. What was true in Paul's case, must be true in all analogous cases. If the revelation of Christ, the apprehension of his glory and love, had wrought such a change in him, the same illumination must produce a like change in others. He therefore says, *If any man be in Christ he is a new creature.* The proposition is general; it applies to every man. To be in Christ is the common scriptural phrase to express the saving connection or union between him and his people. They are in him by covenant, as all men were in Adam; they are in him as members of his body, through the indwelling of his Spirit; and they are in him by faith, which lays hold of and appropriates him as the life and portion of the soul. Rom. 8, 1. 9. Gal. 5, 6, &c. This union is transforming. It imparts a new life. It effects a new creation. This expression indicates not only the greatness and radical nature of the change effected, but also its divine origin. It is a divine work, i. e. one due to the mighty power of God. It is therefore called a creation, the com-

mencement of a new state of being. Eph. 1, 19. In Gal. 6, 15.
Rom. 8, 9, and elsewhere, the same effects are ascribed to
union with Christ. If we are united to him so as to be interested in the merits of his death, we must also be partakers of
his life. This is the foundation on which the apostle builds
his whole doctrine of sanctification as developed in the sixth
and seventh chapter of his epistle to the Romans. The word
καινός, *new, unimpaired, uncontaminated*, is an epithet of excellence; a new song, a new name, new heavens, new earth,
the new Jerusalem, the new man, a new creature, are scriptural expressions which will occur to every reader. In the
margin of the English Bible this clause is rendered, *Let him
be a new creature*. This is in accordance with Calvin's view
of the passage. "If any man would be in Christ, i. e. if he
would be of consequence in Christ's kingdom, let him become
a new creature." He supposes that the apostle refers to the
ambition of the false teachers, whom he tells that if they wish
to attain the influence to which they aspire, they must like
him be entirely changed from selfishness to devotion to Christ.
There is nothing in the words to require this, and every thing
in the context is opposed to it. The apostle is detailing his
own experience, unfolding the principles on which he acted,
and showing the effect which the apprehension of the love of
Christ had on him and must have on others. If any man is in
Christ he is thereby made a new creature. In the Old Testament, Is. 43, 18. 19. 65, 17, the effects to be produced by the
coming of the Messiah are described as a making all things
new. The final consummation of the Redeemer's kingdom in
heaven is described, Rev. 21, 5, in the same terms. "He that
sat upon the throne said, Behold, I make all things new."
The inward spiritual change in every believer is set forth in
the same words, because it is the type and necessary condition
of this great cosmical change. What would avail any conceivable change in things external, if the heart remained a
cage of unclean birds? The apostle therefore says that if any
man is in Christ he experiences a change analogous to that
predicted by the prophets, and like to that which we still anticipate when earth shall become heaven. "Old things are
passed away; behold, all things have become new." Old
opinions, views, plans, desires, principles and affections are
passed away; new views of truth, new principles, new apprehensions of the destiny of man, and new feelings and purposes
fill and govern the soul.

18. And all things (are) of God, who hath reconciled us to himself by Jesus Christ, and hath given to us the ministry of reconciliation.

All things are of God; this is not spoken of the universe as proceeding from God as its author ; nor does it refer to the providential agency of God, by which all events are controlled. The meaning of τὰ δὲ πάντα here is, *but all is of God,* i. e. the entire change of which he had been speaking. The new creation experienced by those who are in Christ is ἐκ τοῦ Θεοῦ, *is out of God,* proceeds from him as its efficient cause. It is his work. God effects this great moral and spiritual revolution *by reconciling us unto himself.* The word *us* is not to be limited to the apostle, first, because the reconciliation spoken of is not peculiar to him ; and secondly, because the change or new creation effected by this reconciliation belongs to all who are in Christ. *Us,* therefore, must include all who are in Christ. The objection to this interpretation that *to us* in the next clause of the verse must refer to the apostle, is not a serious one, because the passage is perfectly perspicuous even supposing ἡμᾶς, *us,* to refer to all believers, and ἡμῖν, *to us,* to the apostle himself. *To reconcile* is to remove enmity between parties at variance with each other. In this case God is the reconciler. Man never makes reconciliation. It is what he experiences or embraces, not what he does. The enmity between God and man, the barrier which separated them, is removed by the act of God. This is plain, 1. Because it is said to be effected *by Jesus Christ,* that is, by his death. The death of Christ, however, is always represented as reconciling us to God as a sacrifice ; the design and nature of a sacrifice are to propitiate and not to reform. 2. In the parallel passage, Rom. 5, 9. 10, being "reconciled by the death of the Son," is interchanged as equivalent with "being justified by his blood," which proves that the reconciliation intended consists in the satisfaction of the divine justice by the sacrifice of Christ. 3. In this case our reconciliation to God is made the source and cause of our new creation, i. e. of our regeneration and holiness. God's reconciliation to us must precede our reconciliation to him. This, as remarked above, is the great doctrine of the Bible. So long as we are under the wrath and curse of God, due to us for sin, we are aliens and enemies, cut off from his favour and fellowship, which are the life of the soul. Therefore until God's wrath and curse are

removed, there is no possibility of holiness and love. It is
vain to attempt to secure the favour of God by being holy;
we must enjoy his favour before we can be holy. See Rom.
7, 56. As the apostle here ascribes our holiness to our being
reconciled to God, he must of necessity refer to the reconciliation of God to us; i. e. to his being propitious, ready to receive us into his favour and to manifest to us his love. *And
hath given to us*, i. e. to the apostle and to other preachers of
the gospel, for the thing given was not something peculiar to
the apostles but common to all preachers, viz., *the ministry
of reconciliation*, i. e. the office and duty of announcing this
reconciliation. It is therefore the peculiar duty or special
design of the ministry to proclaim to men that God, justly
offended by their sins, can be just and yet justify those who
come to him by Jesus Christ. This is the εὐαγγέλιον, or glad
tidings, which our blessed Lord has commissioned his disciples
to announce to every creature under heaven.

19. To wit, that God was in Christ, reconciling the
world unto himself, not imputing their trespasses unto
them; and hath committed unto us the word of reconciliation.

This verse is an explanation and confirmation of what precedes. According to our version, and to the common interpretation, it is an explanation of the last clause of v. 18, i. e.
of the "reconciliation" there spoken of. 'He hath given to
us the ministry of reconciliation—because God was reconciling
the world unto himself, &c.' To this it is objected by Meyer
and others, that the position of the word θεός (*God*) requires
the emphasis to be thrown on that word; and secondly, that
the two following clauses must, in that case, explain the mode
of that reconciliation. Paul would then say, 'God was reconciling the world unto himself, having committed to us the
word of reconciliation.' But our reconciliation to God is not
the ministry of reconciliation. The former does not consist
in the latter; nor is the first the consequence of the second.
This verse therefore is referred to the first clause of v. 18.
'All things are of God, &c., because God was reconciling, &c.'
The words ὡς ὅτι, rendered *to wit*, mean here *seeing that*, or
because. They are equivalent to the simple ὅτι. The expres
sion is explained either as a pleonasm, or as the mixture of
two constructions, ὡς θεοῦ ὄντος and ὅτι θεός ἐστι.

The principal difference among interpreters in the explanation of this verse relates to the question whether (ἦν) *was* is to be referred to (ἐν Χριστῷ) *in Christ*, or to (καταλλάσσων) *reconciling*. Our version favours the former mode of construction, which is adopted both by Luther and Calvin. The sense then is, 'God was in Christ, when he reconciled the world unto himself;' or, as Luther renders it, "God was in Christ, and reconciled the world with himself, and imputed not to them their sins, &c." This breaks up the verse into distinct propositions, turning all the participles into verbs. Calvin says that by *God* we are not to understand the divine nature, or "the fulness of the Godhead," but God the Father; and refers to John 10, 38, "The father is in me," as a parallel expression. He thinks the design of the apostle is to assure believers that in having Christ, they have the Father also; that Christ is the true Immanuel, whose advent is the approximation of God to man. But all this is foreign to the context. What follows is no proof that "God was in Christ," but it is a proof of his being engaged, so to speak, in the great work of reconciling the world unto himself. Most interpreters, therefore, adopt the other construction, 'God was reconciling the world unto himself in Christ.' As in v. 18 it is said that God reconciled us to himself διὰ Χριστοῦ (*through Christ*), here it is said to be ἐν Χριστῷ (*in Christ*). The imperfect ἦν καταλλάσσων, *was reconciling*, expresses either contemporary or continuous action. The sense may be, 'God was, when Christ died, reconciling the world unto himself;' that was what he was doing and designed to do when he gave his Son up for us all. So Meyer and others. Or, the reference is to what follows; 'He reconciled the world, not imputing unto men their sins, &c.' That is, 'While not imputing, &c.' But this is impossible, because the next clause, 'and given to us the word of reconciliation,' cannot express what was contemporaneous with the reconciling. Others say that the imperfect is used for the aorist. The first explanation is to be preferred. *God was reconciling the world unto himself*, means God was making atonement for the sins of the world. He set Christ forth as a propitiation. Theodoret explains ἦν καταλλάσσων by καταλλαγὰς ἐποιήσατο. By *the world* (κόσμος, without the article) is meant *man, mankind*. The reference or statement is perfectly indefinite; it merely indicates the class of beings towards whom God was manifesting himself as propitious. In the same sense our Lord is called the Saviour of the world, or, the Saviour of men, Jesus Salvator Hominum. *To reconcile unto himself*, does not mean to convert, or to render friendly to himself. This is plain first, because this reconciliation is said to be effected by the death of Christ as a sacrifice; and secondly, because what follows is not a proof of God's converting the world, but it is a proof of his being propitious. The proof that God was reconciling the world to himself in Christ (i. e. in his death) is that he does not impute to men their trespasses, and that he has established the ministry of reconciliation. The forgiveness of sin and the institution of the ministry are clear evidence that God is propitious. Not to impute sin, is to forgive it. Rom. 4, 5. 2 Tim. 4, 16. In Col. 2, 13, the same idea is expressed by saying, "hath forgiven you all trespasses." The participle μὴ λογιζόμενος, *not imputing*, is in the present because continuous action is intended; whereas in the next clause, θέμενος, *having committed*, is a past participle, because the institution of the ministry was done once for all. *To them*, i. e. to men, as included in the κόσμος, *world*. When God is said to forgive men it of course does not mean that all men, penitent and impenitent, believing and unbelieving, are forgiven; but here, as before, the class of beings is indicated towards whom forgiveness is exercised. God is propitious to men, as is manifest by his forgiving their trespasses. *And hath committed unto us*, καὶ θέμενος ἐν ἡμῖν, i. e. *having deposited in us*. This may mean, 'having put within us,' i. e. in our souls. Or the idea may be, 'having placed upon us.' If the former, then the following words, τὸν λόγον τῆς καταλλαγῆς, must mean 'the doctrine of reconciliation.' That is, God hath instructed us apostles in the doctrine of reconciliation. If the latter, then the clause just quoted means, 'the word of reconciliation,' i. e. the preaching of reconciliation, as in 1 Cor. 1, 18, ὁ λόγος τοῦ σταυροῦ means 'the preaching of the cross.' This latter view is to be preferred. The evidence that the death of Christ has been accepted as an expiation for sin, of infinite value and efficiency, is the fact that God hath commissioned his ministers to announce to all men that God is reconciled and ready to forgive, so that whosoever will may turn unto him and live.

20. Now then we are ambassadors for Christ, as though God did beseech (you) by us: we pray (you) in Christ's stead, be ye reconciled to God.

This is an inference from what precedes. *Now then* (οὖν, *therefore*). 'Seeing that God in Christ is reconciled, and that he has commissioned us to make known this great truth, it follows that we, as preachers of the gospel, are ambassadors of Christ.' An ambassador is at once a messenger and a representative. He does not speak in his own name. He does not act on his own authority. What he communicates is not his own opinions or demands, but simply what he has been told or commissioned to say. His message derives no part of its importance or trustworthiness from him. At the same time he is more than a mere messenger. He represents his sovereign. He speaks with authority, as accredited to act in the name of his master. Any neglect, contempt or injury done to him in his official character, is not a personal offence, but an offence to the sovereign or state by whom he is commissioned. All this is true of ministers. They are messengers. They communicate what they have received, not their own speculations or doctrines. What they announce derives its importance not from them, but from him who sends them. Nevertheless, as they speak in Christ's name and by his authority, as he hath ordained the ministry and calls men by his Spirit into the sacred office, the rejection of their message is the rejection of Christ, and any injury done unto them as ministers is done unto him.

For Christ, ὑπὲρ Χριστοῦ, this may mean either 'in Christ's stead,' as his substitute and representative; or, 'in Christ's behalf,' for his sake, to promote his interests by furthering the accomplishment of the object for which he died ; as in Eph. 6, 20, the apostle, speaking of the gospel, says, ὑπὲρ οὗ πρεσβεύω, *for which I act as an ambassador.* The latter sense is good, and is in accordance with the common force of the preposition. The former, however, is better suited to the context. To act as an ambassador for any one, is to act in his name or as his representative. And in the following explanatory clause it is said, 'God beseeches you by us,' where the idea of substitution is clearly expressed. The clause, *as though God did beseech you by us,* is commonly connected with what precedes. 'We are ambassadors for Christ, as though God did beseech you by us.' That is, 'We are the ambassadors of Christ, because it is God that speaks through us; or, we speak in his name.' Beza and others connect the words with the following clause. 'We are the ambassadors of Christ,' here is the pause, and then follows as one clause, 'As though God did beseech you by us we pray, &c.' This is the more natural, because the latter words express the prayer, so to speak, which God through the ministry addresses to sinners. It will be noticed that to be an ambassador for Christ, and that God speaks through us, mean the same thing. Redemption is as much the work of the Father as of the Son. God reconciles the world unto himself in Christ. God gives us the word of reconciliation. We are acting for God, or in his name, when we appear as the ambassadors of Christ. *We pray you in Christ's stead.* Here again ὑπὲρ Χριστοῦ may be either *in Christ's stead*, or, *for Christ's sake.* The former is to be preferred as better suited to the uniformity of the passage. *Be ye reconciled unto God ;* this does not mean, 'Reconcile yourselves unto God.' The word, καταλλάγητε, is passive. *Be reconciled*, that is, embrace the offer of reconciliation. The reconciliation is effected by the death of Christ. God is now propitious. He can now be just, and yet justify the ungodly. All we have to do is not to refuse the offered love of God. Calvin remarks that this exhortation is not directed exclusively to the unconverted. The believer needs daily, and is allowed whenever he needs, to avail himself of the offer of peace with God through Jesus Christ. It is not the doctrine of the Scriptures that the merits of Christ avail only for the forgiveness of sins committed before conversion, while for post-baptismal sins, as they were called, there is no satisfaction but in the penances of the offender. Christ ever lives to make intercession for us, and for every short-coming and renewed offence there is offered to the penitent believer, renewed application of that blood which cleanses from all sin.

21. For he hath made him (to be) sin for us, who knew no sin ; that we might be made the righteousness of God in him.

This verse is designed to enforce the preceding. 'Be reconciled to God, *for* an abundant and trustworthy provision has been made for your reconciliation and acceptance.' It is indeed doubtful whether γάρ, *for*, belongs to the text, as it is omitted in many of the oldest manuscripts. Its omission only renders the transition more abrupt, the relation of the passage remains the same. The apostle states in this verse what God has done for the justification of men. The passage, therefore,

is of special interest, as presenting in a concise form the testimony of the Spirit on that all important subject. *He made
him who knew no sin to be sin for us.* The Greek here is,
τὸν μὴ γνόντα ἁμαρτίαν ὑπὲρ ἡμῶν ἁμαρτίαν ἐποίησεν. Our Lord
is presented as one whom God contemplated as free from sin
and yet he made him sin. Others understand the μή γνόντα as
referring to Christ himself, as one having no consciousness of
sin. Others again, to the necessary judgment of believers, he
whom we know was free from sin. One or the other of these
modes of interpretation is supposed to be necessary, as the
apostle uses μή and not οὐ; the one being, as the grammarians
say, the subjective, the other the objective particle of nega-
tion; the one denying a thing as it appears to the mind, the
other denying it simply as a fact. In either case the thing
here asserted is that Christ was without sin. This was one of
the indispensable conditions of his being made sin for us.
Had he not been free from sin, he could not have taken the
place of sinners. Under the old dispensation the sacrifices
were required to be without blemish, in order to teach the
necessity of freedom from all sin in him who was to bear the
sins of the world. See Heb. 4, 15. 1 Pet. 2, 22. 1 John 3, 5.
He was made sin, may mean either, he was made a sin-offering,
or, the abstract being used for the concrete, he was made a
sinner. Many of the older commentators prefer the former
explanation; Calvin, and almost all the moderns adopt the
latter. The meaning in either case is the same; for the only
sense in which Christ was made sin, is that he bore the guilt
of sin; and in this sense every sin offering was made sin.
Hence in the Hebrew Scriptures the same word is used both
for sin and a sin-offering. This is the principal ground on
which the explanation of ἁμαρτία here in the sense of a sacrifice for sin is defended. The reasons, however, against this
explanation are decisive. 1. In the Septuagint the Hebrew
word for sin, when it means a sin-offering, is always rendered
by ἁμαρτία in the genitive. It is always " of sin," or " for sin,"
(περὶ ἁμαρτίας), Lev. 5, 9. 14, 19. Num. 8, 8, and never simply
" sin," as here. 2. The use of the word in the ordinary sense
in this same clause, ' He made him to be sin who knew no sin.'
It must have the same meaning in both cases. 3. The antithesis between " sin " and " righteousness." He was made sin,
we are made " righteousness." The only sense in which we
are made the righteousness of God is that we are in Christ regarded and treated as righteous, and therefore the sense in

which he was made sin, is that he was regarded and treated as a sinner. His being made sin is consistent with his being in himself free from sin; and our being made righteous is consistent with our being in ourselves ungodly. In other words, our sins were imputed to Christ, and his righteousness is imputed to us. Justitia hic non pro qualitate aut habitu, says Calvin, sed pro imputatione accipitur, eo quod accepta nobis fertur Christi justitia. Quod e converso peccatum? reatus quo in Dei judicio obstringimur. . . . . Personam enim nostram quodammodo suscepit, ut reus nostro nomine fieret, et tanquam peccator judicaretur, non propriis, sed alienis delictis, quum purus foret ipse et immunis ab omni culpa, pœnamque subiret nobis, non sibi debitam. Ita scilicet nunc justi sumus in ipso: non quia operibus propriis satisfaciamus judicio Dei, sed quoniam censimur Christi justitia, quam fide induimus, ut nostra fiat. In Gal. 3, 13, the apostle says that "Christ was made a curse for us," which is equivalent to saying that he was made sin for us. In both cases the idea is that he bore the punishment of our sins. God laid on him the iniquities of us all. His sufferings and death were penal, because inflicted and endured in satisfaction of justice. And in virtue of the infinite dignity of his person they were a perfect satisfaction; that is, a full equivalent for all the law's demands. In Rom. 8, 3, it is said, "What the law could not do, in that it was weak through the flesh, God, sending his own Son in the likeness of sinful flesh, and for sin, condemned sin in the flesh." Here again we have precisely the same doctrine. What in one passage is expressed by saying that Christ was made sin, in the other is expressed by saying, he was sent "for sin," i. e. as a sin-offering (περὶ ἁμαρτίας).

The apostle says Christ was made sin *for us*, ὑπὲρ ἡμῶν, i. e. *in our stead*, because the idea of substitution is involved in the very nature of the transaction. The victim was the substitute for the offender. It was put in his place. So Christ was our substitute, or, was put in our place. This is the more apparent from the following clause, which teaches the design of this substitution. He was made sin, that we might be made righteous. He was condemned, that we might be justified. The very idea of substitution is that what is done by one in the place of another, avails as though that other had done it himself. The victim was the substitute of the offerer, because its death took the place of his death. If both died there was no substitution. So if Christ's being made sin does not secure our being made righteousness, he was not our substitute. Righteousness does not here mean inward rectitude, or moral excellence. It is true that the word often has this sense; and it is true that the work of Christ does secure the holiness of his people, and was designed to produce that effect, as is often asserted in Scripture. But this was neither its only, nor its proximate design. Its immediate end was to reconcile us to God; to propitiate him, by the satisfaction of justice, so that he can be just and yet justify the ungodly. As the apostle is here speaking of the sacrificial effect of Christ's death, that is, of the proximate effect of his being made sin for us, the word righteousness must be understood in its forensic sense. It expresses our relation to the law, not our inward moral state. It is that which justifies, or satisfies the demands of the law. Those who have this δεκαιοσύνη are δίκαιοι, just in the sight of the law, in the sense that the law or justice is satisfied as concerns them. It is called *the righteousness of God*, either because it is from him as its author; or, because it renders us righteous in his sight. Those who possess this righteousness are δίκαιοι παρὰ τῷ θεῷ, i. e. righteous before God. The former is the more common representation in Paul's writings. Rom. 1, 17. 3, 22. 10, 3. Phil. 3, 9, where "the righteousness of God," is explained by "the righteousness which is of God." In this view of the meaning of the phrase, the sense of the clause "we become the righteousness of God," is that we become divinely righteous. We are righteous with the righteousness of God, not with our own which is but as a filthy rag, but with that which he has provided and which consists in the infinitely meritorious righteousness of his own dear Son. All this is true; but the context here favours the other mode of representation. Christ was treated as a sinner, i. e. condemned, that we might be justified, i. e. regarded as just before God. The apostle uses the present tense, γινώμεθα, *we become* righteous, because this justification is continuous. We are introduced into a justified state. *In him*, that is, in Christ. It is by virtue of our union with Christ, and only as we are in him by faith, that we are righteous before God.

There is probably no passage in the Scriptures in which the doctrine of justification is more concisely or clearly stated than in this. Our sins were imputed to Christ, and his righteousness is imputed to us. He bore our sins; we are clothed in his righteousness. Imputation conveys neither pollution

nor holiness. Christ's bearing our sins did not make him
morally a sinner, any more than the victim was morally defiled
which bore the sins of the people; nor does Christ's righteousness become subjectively ours, it is not the moral quality of
our souls. This is what is not meant. What is meant is
equally plain. Our sins were the judicial ground of the sufferings of Christ, so that they were a satisfaction of justice;
and his righteousness is the judicial ground of our acceptance
with God, so that our pardon is an act of justice. It is a
justification; or, a declaration that justice is satisfied. We
are set free by no mere act of sovereignty, but by the judicial
decision of the infinitely just. As we, considered in ourselves,
are just as undeserving and hell-deserving as ever, this justification is to us an act of infinite grace. The special consideration, therefore, by which the apostle enforces the exhortation,
'Be ye reconciled to God,' is that God can be just in the justification of sinners. There is nothing in the perfection of his
character, nothing in the immutability of his law, nothing in
the interests of his moral government, that stands in the way
of our pardon. A full, complete, infinitely meritorious satisfaction has been made for our sins, and therefore we may
come to God with the assurance of being accepted. This is a
ground of confidence which an enlightened conscience, burdened with a sense of sin, absolutely needs. It is not mere
pardon, but justification alone, that gives us peace with God.

CHAPTER VI.

The apostle continues the vindication of himself, vs. 1–10. Asserts his
strong love for the Corinthians, and exhorts them to keep themselves
free from all contaminating alliances, vs. 11–18.

The apostle's fidelity and love. Vs. 1–18.

As the occasion of writing this epistle was the false accusa-
tions of his opponents, a strain of self-vindication runs through
the whole. In 5, 12 he said he spoke of himself to enable his
friends in Corinth to defend him against his enemies. He was

governed by the love of Christ, and acted as his ambassador ; as such he was a fellow-worker with God, and exhorted men not to fail of the grace of God, vs. 1. 2. In the exercise of this office he avoided all offence, v. 3, proving his sincerity and fidelity as a minister of God, by the patient endurance of all kinds of trials, vs. 4. 5 ; by the exercise of all the graces and gifts of the Spirit, vs. 6. 7 ; and under all circumstances, whether of honour or dishonour, prosperity or adversity, whether understood or misunderstood by his fellow men, vs. 8–10. He thus unbosomed himself to the Corinthians, because his heart was enlarged. It was wide enough to take them all in. Whatever there was of the want of love or of due appreciation between them and him, the fault was on their side, not on his, vs. 11. 12. He begs them to be as large-hearted towards him as he was towards them, v. 13, and not to allow themselves to be involved in any intimate alliances with the wicked, vs. 13–18.

1. We then, (as) workers together (with him), beseech (you) also that ye receive not the grace of God in vain.

This verse is intimately connected with the preceding chapter by the particles δὲ καί, *but also.* He is still describing his manner of discharging his apostolic duties. He not only announced that God had made Christ sin for us, that we might become the righteousness of God in him, but also, as a co-worker with God, he exhorted men not to receive the grace of God in vain. In our version the apostle is made to say, " I beseech you also." This is wrong ; the *also* belongs to the verb—" I also beseech you." That the word συνερ-γοῦντες, *co-operating,* refers to the apostle's co-operating with God, is plain from the connection, and from the nature of the work. He had just before, 5, 20, spoken of God's beseeching them ; and now he says, we as co-workers beseech you. So in 1 Cor. 3, 9, he says, " We are co-workers with God." In the Vulgate the word is rendered *adjuvantes,* which favours the idea that he was co-operating with them, assisting them (i. e. the Corinthians) by his exhortations. Luther's version suggests the same meaning ; Wir ermahen aber euch, als Mithelfer, *as joint-labourers or helpers we exhort you.* Compare 1, 24, where the apostle says, " We are helpers (συνεργοί)

of your joy." This view of the passage is given by many
commentators. It does not, however, so well, as just remarked, agree with the context; and it would require, to
prevent ambiguity, the insertion of ὑμῖν, *with you.* As an
apostle or minister of the gospel, Paul was a co-worker with
God.

That ye receive not the grace of God in vain. What is
it to receive the grace of God in vain? Some say that the
meaning is to accept of the atonement of Christ, or reconciliation with God spoken of in the preceding chapter, and yet to
live in sin. The favour of God is then accepted to no purpose.
But this is an unscriptural idea. Justification and sanctification cannot be thus separated. A man cannot accept of reconciliation with God and live in sin; because the renunciation
of sin is involved in the acceptance of reconciliation. Paul
never assumes that men may accept one benefit of redemption,
and reject another. They cannot take pardon and refuse
sanctification. Others say that the apostle here exhorts his
readers to guard against "falling from grace;" that having
been graciously pardoned they should not, by a relapse into
sin, forfeit the grace or favour which they had received. This
is a very common interpretation. Olshausen says, "It is undeniable that the apostle assumes that grace when once received may be lost; the Scriptures know nothing of the dangerous error of the advocates of predestination, that grace
cannot be lost; and experience stamps it as a lie." But in
the first place, it is no argument in favour of this interpretation that the apostle uses the infinitive aorist (δέξασθαι), *have
received,* because the aorist infinitive is very commonly used
for the present after verbs signifying to command or exhort.
See Rom. 12, 1. 15, 20. 2 Cor. 2, 8. Eph. 4, 1. Winer's Idioms
of the New Testament, p. 386. In the second place, the
"grace of God," here spoken of, does not mean the actual
forgiveness of sin, nor the renewing, sanctifying influence of
the Spirit, but the *favour* of which the apostle spoke in the
preceding chapter. It is the infinite grace or favour of having
made his Son sin for us, so that we may become the righteousness of God in him. This is the grace of God of which the
apostle speaks. He exhorted men not to let it be in vain, as
it regarded them, that a satisfaction for sin sufficient for all,
and appropriate to all, had been made and offered to all who
hear the gospel. In precisely the same sense he says, Gal. 2,
21, "I do not frustrate the grace of God." That is, 'I do

not, by trusting to the works of the law, make it in vain that
God has provided a gratuitous method of salvation.' That
great grace or favour he did not make a thing of naught. In
Gal. 5, 4, he says, "Whosoever of you are justified by the law,
are fallen from grace." That is, 'ye have renounced the gratuitous method of salvation, and are debtors to do the whole
law.' So in Rom. 6, 14, it is said, "We are not under law,
but under grace." In no one of these cases does "grace"
mean either the actual pardon of sin, or inward divine influence. It means the favour of God, and in this connection the
great favour of redemption. The Lord Jesus Christ having
died for our sins and procured eternal redemption for us, the
apostle was most earnest in exhorting men not to allow this
great favour, as regards them, to be in vain. It is the more
evident that such is the meaning of the passage because it is
not so much a direct exhortation to the Corinthians, as a
declaration of the method in which the apostle preached. He
announced the fact that God had made Christ who knew no sin
to be sin for us, and he exhorted all men not to receive the
grace of God in vain, that is, not to reject this great salvation.
And finally, this interpretation is required by the following
verse. "Behold, now is the accepted time; now is the day
of salvation." This is appropriate as a motive to receive the
offer of pardon and acceptance with God, but it is not appropriate as a reason why a renewed and pardoned sinner should
not fall from grace. There is therefore no necessity to assume, contrary to the whole analogy of Scripture, that the
apostle here teaches that those who have once made their
peace with God and experienced his renewing grace can fall
away unto perdition. If reconciled by the death of his Son,
much more shall they be saved by his life. Nothing can ever
separate them from the love of God which is in Christ Jesus.
Whom he calls, them he also glorifies. They are kept by the
mighty power of God through faith unto salvation.

2. (For he saith, I have heard thee in a time accepted, and in the day of salvation have I succoured
thee; behold, now (is) the accepted time; behold, now
(is) the day of salvation.)

The Scriptures contain abundant evidence that inspiration
did not interfere with the natural play of the powers of the

sacred writers. Although they spoke as they were moved by the Holy Ghost, yet they were probably in most cases unconscious of his influence, and acted as spontaneously as the believer does under the power of the Spirit in all his holy exercises. Hence we find that the sacred writings are constructed according to the ordinary laws of mind, and that the writers pass from subject to subject by the usual process of suggestion and association. So here the use of the word δέξασθαι brought up to the apostle's mind the word δεκτῷ, as it occurs in the beautiful passage, Is. 49, 8. Hence the quotation of that passage as it stands in the Greek version of the Old Testament. *I have heard thee in an accepted time.* In the Hebrew it is, *a time of grace;* and to this answers the equivalent expression, *the day of salvation.* It is on these expressions that the appropriateness of the citation rests. The Old Testament speaks of "a time of grace," and of "a day of salvation." That is, of a time and a day in which grace and salvation may be obtained. The apostle adds, by way of comment and application, "Behold, now is the accepted time; behold, now is the day of salvation." The connection between this verse and what precedes is thus clear. 'Receive not the grace of God in vain, *for* there is a time of grace and a day of salvation, and that day is now. Therefore, neglect not this great salvation.' The 49th chapter of Isaiah, whence this passage is taken, is addressed to the Messiah. He it was whom God chose to be his servant to restore Israel and to be a light to the Gentiles. He it was whom man despised and the nation abhorred, to whom kings should rise and princes worship. It was he to whom Jehovah said, "I have heard thee in an accepted time, and in the day of salvation have I succoured thee." This being the case, the use which the apostle makes of the passage may be explained either on the hypothesis adopted by Dr. J. A. Alexander, in his comment on this chapter, that the ideal person addressed is not the Messiah exclusively, but the Messiah and his people as represented in him. Therefore a promise of grace and salvation to the Messiah was at the same time a promise of grace and salvation to his people. This is the view which Bengel adopts. "*He saith,* the Father to Messiah, Is. 49, 8, embracing in him all believers." Or we may assume, in strict accordance with scriptural usage, that the apostle employs the language of the Old Testament to express his own ideas, without regard to its original application. God had in many ways, and on many occasions, promised to save sinners. To this promise the apostle appeals as a reason why men should accept the grace offered to them in Christ Jesus. He clothes this promise in scriptural language. He might have expressed it in any other equivalent form. But the language of the passage in Isaiah being brought to his mind by the principle of association, he adopts the form there given, without any intimation, expressed or implied, that the passage had not in the original a different application. Thus in Rom. 10, 18 he might have expressed the idea of the general proclamation of the gospel in his own words, but he chose to express it in the words of the nineteenth Psalm, "Their sound went into all the earth, and their words unto the ends of the world;" although that Psalm relates to an entirely different subject. We are accustomed, without hesitation and almost unconsciously, to make a similar use of scriptural language.

3. Giving no offence in any thing, that the ministry be not blamed.

The preceding verse is parenthetical, so that the connection is with v. 1. "We beseech—giving, &c." This and the following participles are all connected with the word (παρακαλοῦμεν) we beseech, or exhort, and are designed to show how the apostle discharged the duties of his office. This is his defence. *In nothing he gave offence.* He so acted that no one could fairly make his conduct a ground of rejecting the gospel. The word προσκοπή is properly the act of striking or stumbling; then metonymically, that at which or against which any one stumbles. In the figurative use of the word, as here employed, it means an occasion of unbelief. Paul, in preaching the gospel to those to whom it was previously unknown, and whose principal means of judging of it was the conduct of its preachers, was specially careful to avoid every thing which could prove a stumblingblock to his hearers. Although this motive has peculiar weight where the gospel is new, as among the heathen, yet every one knows that the moral power of a preacher depends almost entirely on the conviction which the people have of his sincerity and of the purity of his motives. This is a source of power for which neither learning nor talents can compensate. *That the ministry be not blamed;* or, as it is in many copies, *our ministry,* which gives the passage a most specific reference to himself, and is well suited to the whole connection.

Although in the following verses the apostle, as is his wont, gives his discourse free scope, allowing it, as it were, to flow on in its own impetuous and majestic course, without any attempt to reduce it to logical arrangement, yet in his mind order was so immanent that a certain method can always be detected even in his most impassioned utterances. So here, he first refers to the manifold trials, vs. 4. 5, then to the graces and gifts, vs. 6. 7, by which his sincerity had been tested and established; and then to the diverse circumstances of evil and of good report, under which he had maintained his integrity, vs. 8. 9. 10. Under these several heads there are the same number of specifications, nine in each. Under the two former, there is a ternary arrangement observable; three divisions, each with three specifications; and under the last, nine pairs of contrasts or antitheses, rising to that highest form of oratorical language, where truth is expressed in seeming contradictions. " Having nothing, yet possessing all things."

4. 5. But in all (things) approving ourselves as the ministers of God, in much patience, in afflictions, in necessities, in distresses, in stripes, in imprisonments, in tumults, in labours, in watchings, in fastings.

So far from causing the ministry to be blamed, Paul *in all things*, (ἐν παντί,) *in every relation, and on every occasion, approved* himself, i. e. commended himself, not by self-laudation, but by so acting as to force the conviction of his sincerity on all men. *As the ministers of God*, i. e. as the ministers of God commend themselves. This interpretation is required, as Paul uses διάκονοι, not διακόνους. It was as a minister he commended himself. *In much patience*, i. e. by patient endurance and constancy. Both ideas are expressed by the word ὑπομονή. Paul proved himself to be a true minister of Christ by the fortitude with which he endured sufferings, and by the constancy with which he adhered to his master under all these trials. In what follows in this and the next verse we have the trials enumerated to which he was subjected. These are arranged, as Bengel remarks, in three classes. The first, are general, *afflictions, necessities, and distresses;* the second are specific, *stripes, imprisonments, and tumults;* the third, voluntary, *labours, watchings, and fastings*. His constancy was exhibited in the cheerful endurance of all these kinds of trials.

As to the first, the terms used are often interchanged and often combined. Θλίψεις, *pressures*, from without or from within; including every thing which presses on the heart or tries the power of endurance or resistance; ανάγκαι, *necessities*, when a man is taxed to the utmost to know what to do or how to bear; στενοχωρίαι, *straits*, when one has no room to stand or turn, and therefore escape seems hopeless. It is opposed to largeness of place. "He brought my feet into a large place," as the Psalmist says. The preposition ἐν is to be rendered *by* before ὑπομονή, and *in* before all the other nouns in these two verses. He commended himself *by* patience, *in* afflictions, *in* necessities, &c., &c. *In stripes.* Paul, as we learn from 11, 24. 25, had already, at this period of his history, been eight times subjected to the ignominy and torture of the lash, five times by the Jews and thrice by the heathen. *In imprisonments.* How often the apostle was in prison we know not, as the Acts contain only a small part of his history. He was a prisoner at Philippi, at Jerusalem, at Cesarea, and at Rome; and when a prisoner his feet were in the stocks, or he was chained. The Holy Ghost testified that in every place "bonds and afflictions" awaited him. *In tumults.* The word is ἀκαταστασίαι, which may mean "tossings to and fro," and refer to Paul's being constantly driven from one place to another, so that he had no quiet abode. This he mentions as one of his sore trials in 1 Cor. 4, 11. The word, however, in the New Testament always elsewhere means either disorder or tumultuous outbreaks. Luke 21, 9. To these violent bursts of popular feeling the apostle was frequently exposed, as at Antioch in Pisidia, Acts 13, 50; at Lystra, 14, 19; at Philippi, 16, 19; at Ephesus, Acts 19, 29; at Jerusalem, 21, 30. Before these manifestations of wrath and power the bravest men often quail. Such tumults can neither be resisted by force, nor be stilled by the voice. What can one man do before an infuriated mob? He could as well resist a tornado. Yet he can be calm and adhere to his purpose. "It is often required," says Calvin, "of ministers of the gospel, that while they strive for peace, they should pass unbroken through tumults, and never deflect from the right course though heaven and earth should be mixed." Besides these trials which came upon the apostle against his will, or without his agency, there were painful sacrifices which he made voluntarily, and which were among the strongest proofs of his sincerity. These were his *labours, watchings, and fastings.* By labours are to be understood not only his working with his own hands to support himself while he made the gospel of no expense, but also the indefatigable exertions which he was constantly called to make, in travelling, and preaching, and in caring for the sick, the poor, and the interests of the church. *Watchings*, the sleepless nights which his constantly travelling, his anxieties and labours caused him to pass. *Fastings ;* this is often understood to refer to his suffering from hunger. But the word νηστεία is never used for involuntary abstinence from food, and as it occurs here in connection with labours and watchings, both of which were voluntary acts of self-denial, it is probably to be taken in its ordinary sense. Perhaps, however, the reference is to those cases of abstinence which were in a measure forced upon him, or which he chose to submit to rather than to omit some duty or to fail to take advantage of some opportunity of usefulness. There is nothing in the connection to demand a reference to religious fasting, as when prayers and fasting are mentioned together. Here it is labours and fastings.

6. 7. By pureness, by knowledge, by long-suffering, by kindness, by the Holy Ghost, by love unfeigned, by the word of truth, by the power of God, by the armour of righteousness on the right hand and on the left.

As the apostle commended himself *in* the various trials enumerated in the two preceding verses, so *by* the graces and gifts here specified, it was made manifest to all that he was a true apostle and faithful minister of God. *By pureness*, both of heart and life. This includes not merely freedom from the pollution of immoral acts, but disinterestedness and singleness of motive. *By knowledge ;* what kind or form of knowledge is here indicated can only be gathered from the context. Some say it is the knowledge of the fitness and propriety of things, which exhibits itself as discretion. But as the apostle is speaking of those things which commended him as a minister of God and preacher of the gospel, and as several of the other specifications in these two verses, refer to gifts as distinguished from graces, it is more probable that the reference is to evangelical knowledge ; that knowledge which he manifested in his teaching. Comp. Eph. 3, 4, where he speaks of his knowledge of the mystery of Christ, as patent to all his readers. And in Gal. 1, 12, *et seq.*, he appeals to his possession of this knowledge, without any human teaching, as an undeniable proof of his divine mission. *By long-suffering,* i. e. patiently submitting to injustice and undeserved injuries. *By kindness,* i. e. χρηστότης (from χρηστός, *useful*) benevolence ; a disposition to do good ; as God is said to be kind to the unthankful and the evil, Luke 6, 35. *By the Holy Ghost ;* that is, by the manifestation of the Holy Ghost as dwelling in me. It is the doctrine of the Scriptures, and specially of Paul's writings, that the Spirit of God dwells in all believers, and that besides those manifestations of his presence common to all, there is given to each one his special gift, whether ordinary or extraordinary ; to one wisdom, to another knowledge, to another the gift of teaching, to another the working of miracles, &c. 1 Cor. 12, 7–11. In proof of his being a true minister of God, Paul appeals to the evidence of the presence of the Spirit in him, which evidence was to be found in those graces and gifts of the Holy Ghost with which he was replenished ; and in the divine power which attended and rendered successful his preaching. He could appeal to his converts and say, " Ye are the seal of my apostleship in the Lord," 1 Cor. 9, 2. *By love unfeigned.* As in the preceding clause he referred to kindness or benevolence, here *love* must be taken in the restricted sense of Christian love—not that affection which is exercised towards the just and the unjust, but that which springs from the peculiar relations of the believer to God and to his brethren. It is brotherly love, or the love of the brethren as such. *By the word of truth,* that is, by the preaching of the truth, or preaching the contents of which is truth. The reference is not to veracity, but to the exhibition of the truth in his preaching. In a previous chapter, 4, 2, he had said, " By the manifestation of the truth I commend myself to every man's conscience in the sight of God." *By the power of God.* The power of God was manifested in various ways in Paul's ministry. " He that wrought in Peter," he says, " to the apostleship of the circumcision, the same was mighty in me towards the Gentiles," Gal. 2, 8. By these various manifestations of divine power in his conversion, in his preparation for his work, and in the exercise of his apostleship, he was proved to be a true servant of God. *By the armour of righteousness.* The word " righteousness " is used in Scripture in two senses. It means either rectitude, uprightness, honesty, in the comprehensive sense of the terms; or it means justifying righteousness, the righteousness of faith, so often called the righteousness of God. Calvin and many others take it in the former sense here, and understand by the "armour of righteousness," that armour which integrity affords, or those arms which are consistent with moral rectitude. Others prefer the latter sense of the word, and understand the armour of righteousness to be that which is secured by our justification before God. This interpretation is not only more in keeping with Paul's usage of the word, but more consistent with the context. It was not Paul's honesty which was his armour, or by which he established his claim to be a minister of God, but the supernatural gifts and graces of the Spirit. In Eph. 6, 14, he compares this righteousness to a breastplate; here to the whole panoply, *on the right hand and on the left*, offensive and defensive, because he who is justified, or clothed with the righteousness of Christ, has every thing at command. He has the shield of faith, and the helmet of salvation, and the sword of the Spirit.

8–10. **By honour and dishonour, by evil report and good report; as deceivers, and (yet) true; as unknown, and (yet) well known; as dying, and behold, we live; as chastened, and not killed; as sorrowful, yet always rejoicing; as poor, yet making many rich; as having nothing, and (yet) possessing all things.**

These verses are intimately connected, forming a distinct division of the apostle's discourse. In vs. 4. 5, we had the preposition *ἐν* in its local sense. Paul commended himself by patience *in* afflictions, *in* necessities, &c. In vs. 6. 7 the same preposition is used in its instrumental sense, *by* pureness, *by* knowledge, &c. Here the preposition *διά* has a local sense, *through, in the midst of*. He maintained his consistency and integrity under all circumstances, through honour and dishonour, through evil report and good report. He was always the same—preached the same doctrine, urged the same duties, maintained the same principles, whether his preaching was approved or disapproved, whether it secured for him admiration or brought down upon him reproach. This is the common and most natural interpretation. Many, however, prefer

the instrumental sense of the preposition. '*By means of*
honour which we receive from the friends of God, and by
means of the dishonour heaped upon us by our enemies.'
That the good honoured him, and the wicked defamed him,
was proof of his integrity. This requires too much to be supplied in order to bring out the sense. The former interpretation is more simple, and gives a meaning quite as pertinent.
The figure which he uses is that of a road, along which he
marches to victory, through all obstacles, disregarding what
is said or thought by others. This last clause serves as the
transition to a new mode of representation. He no longer
speaks of what he did, but of the judgment of others concerning him. *As deceivers, and yet true.* These and the following adjectives and participles, as they are in Greek, though
translated in some cases as substantives, are parallel with
συνιστῶντες in v. 4. 'We beseech you, *commending* ourselves,
&c., and we beseech you, *as deceivers, yet true,* &c.' That is,
we go steadily on in the discharge of our duty whatever men
may think or say. *As deceivers,* (πλάνοι,) not merely false
pretenders, but seducers, men who lead others astray, and
themselves wander from the truth. Matt. 27, 63. 1 Tim. 4, 1.
2 John 7. It is here the opposite of ἀληθεῖς, in the sense of
truthful, loving and speaking the truth. Matt. 22, 16. Mark
12, 14. 'Regarded as seducers, we are the advocates of the
truth.' *As unknown, yet well known,* (ὡς ἀγνοούμενοι, καὶ ἐπιγι-
νωσκόμενοι,) regarded with contempt as obscure and ignoble,
yet recognised and famous. The antithesis is either that expressed in our version, between being unknown and being
well known, or, between being misunderstood and being duly
appreciated. The latter of the two words used by the apostle
may well express that sense, as ἐπιγινώσκω often means to
recognize, or acknowledge one to be what he is, or professes
to be, 1, 13. 14. Matt. 17, 12, and although the former word
does not elsewhere occur precisely in the sense of being misunderstood, yet to be unknown and to be unrecognized are
ideas so nearly related, that it is not unnatural to take the
word in that sense here, if the antithesis and context require
it. Paul was unknown to the mass of the people; he was
taken to be what he was not; and yet he was duly appreciated, and recognized in his true character by others. *As dying,* i. e. regarded by others as certain to perish, *and behold
we live.* This is one interpretation. It is, however, more in
harmony with what follows to understand the apostle to refer

to actual facts. He was, as he says, 4, 11 and 1 Cor. 15, 31, constantly exposed to death. He died daily, and yet he lived. God always interposed to rescue him from destruction when it seemed inevitable, and to sustain him under calamities which to all appearance no man could bear. *As chastened, but not killed.* To chasten (παιδεύειν) is properly to treat as a child, and as children are often made to suffer by their parents for their good, to chasten is to correct by suffering. The word, however, is often used to express simply the idea of infliction of pain without any reference to the end of the infliction. God never punishes his people. That is, their suf ferings are never designed to satisfy justice; nor are they always even chastisements in the proper sense of the word. They are not in all cases sent to correct evils, to repress pride, or to wean from the world. God often afflicts his people and his church simply to enable them the better to glorify his name. It is an unchristian disposition, therefore, which leads us always to ask, when afflictions are sent upon ourselves or others, Why is this? What have we or they done to call forth this expression of parental displeasure or solicitude? What does God mean to rebuke? It may be that our sufferings are chastisements, that is, that they are designed to correct some evil of the heart or life, but this is not to be inferred from the simple fact that they are sufferings. The greater part of Paul's sufferings were not chastisements. They were designed simply to show to all ages the power of the grace of God; to let men see what a man could cheerfully endure, and rejoice that he was called upon to endure, for the sake of the Lord Jesus. In this case *chastened* means simply afflicted. There is no reference to the design of God in sending the sufferings which the apostle was called to endure. There is another view of the meaning of this passage, which supposes the words to be uttered from the stand-point of Paul's enemies. "Chastised, but not killed." 'Regarded as an object of divine displeasure, as smitten of God, (which may be true,) yet I am not killed.' It is, however, more in keeping with what follows to understand the apostle as referring to his actual experience. He was greatly afflicted, but not killed; cast down, as he says in 4, 9, but not destroyed. Compare Ps. 118, 18, "The Lord hath chastened me sore; but he hath not delivered me over unto death." Let believers therefore regard their afflictions, when they can, not as indications of God's disapprobation, but rejoice in them as opportunities graciously afforded them to glorify his name. *As sorrowful, yet always rejoicing.* This again may mean, 'Looked upon as sorrowful, yet in fact always rejoicing;' or, 'Although overwhelmed with sorrow, yet full of joy.' The latter interpretation is to be preferred. This is one of the paradoxes of Christian experience. The believer has more true joy in sorrow, than the world can ever afford. The sense of the love of God, assurance of his support, confidence in future blessedness, and the persuasion that his present light afflictions shall work out for him a far more exceeding and an eternal weight of glory, mingle with his sorrows, and give the suffering child of God a peace which passes all understanding. He would not exchange his lot with that of the most prosperous of the children of this world. *As poor, yet making many rich.* Poor in this world's goods, yet imparting to many the true riches; *as having nothing,* i. e. of earthly treasure, *yet possessing all things,* in the sense in which in 1 Cor. 3, 21, he tells the Corinthians, "All things are yours." The real property in any thing vests in him for whose benefit it is held and used. And as all things, whether the world, or life or death, or things present or things to come, are held and disposed by God for the benefit of his people, for their present good and future glory, they are the real proprietors of all things. Being joint heirs with Christ, Rom. 8, 17, they possess all things.

11. O (ye) Corinthians, our mouth is open unto you, our heart is enlarged.

This and the two following verses are an epilogue to the preceding vindication of himself, and an introduction to the following exhortations. *O Corinthians.* This direct address is unusual with the apostle, and is expressive of strong feeling. Gal. 3, 1. *Our mouth is open* (ἀνέῳγε, 2 perfect, as present and intransitive, see John 1, 52.) To open the mouth is a common scriptural expression, meaning to begin to speak, or, to speak, as in Matt. 5, 2. Acts 8, 32. 35. Here, as the context shows, it is used emphatically, and means, to speak freely and openly. Compare Eph. 6, 19. *Our heart is enlarged.* See 1 Kings 4, 29. Ps. 119, 32. Is. 60, 5. Any joyful, generous feeling is said to enlarge the heart. A large-hearted man is one of generous and warm affections. The apostle had poured out his heart to the Corinthians. He has spoken with the utmost freedom and openness, and in doing so his heart was expanded towards them. He was ready to embrace them all, and to take them to his arms as his dear children.

12. Ye are not straitened in us, but ye are straitened in your own bowels.

The apostle abides by his figure. A large heart is one expanded by love; a straitened heart is one void of generous affections. To be straitened (στενοχωρέω) is to want room; στενοχωρία is want of room, straits, distress, anguish of mind. Hence to enlarge, to give one a wide place, is to deliver, to bless. Ps. 4, 1. 118, 5. *Ye are not straitened in us*, i. e. there is no lack of room for you in our heart; *but ye are straitened in your own bowels*, i. e. your heart is too narrow to admit me. *Straitened in your own bowels*, means, not that you are inwardly afflicted, or that the cause of your trouble is in yourselves, but, as the context requires, 'Your bowels (hearts) are narrow or contracted.' There is not room in them to receive me. Without a figure the meaning is, 'The want of love is on your side, not on mine.'

13. Now for a recompense in the same, (I speak as unto (my) children,) be ye also enlarged.

The exhortation or request is, 'Be ye also enlarged, i. e. open your hearts to receive me, which is only a proper recompense for my love to you. I speak as to children, who are expected to requite the love of their parents with filial affection.' The words τὴν δὲ αὐτὴν ἀντιμισθίαν are explained as a concise expression for τὸ δὲ αὐτό, ὅ ἐστιν ἀντιμισθία, 'as to the same thing, which is a recompense, be ye also enlarged.' The accusative is the accusative absolute.

14. Be ye not unequally yoked together with unbelievers: for what fellowship hath righteousness with unrighteousness? and what communion hath light with darkness?

After the exhortation to requite his love by loving him, he exhorts them to keep aloof from all intimate association with the evil. The exhortation is general, and is not to be confined to partaking of heathen sacrifices, nor to intermarriage with

the heathen, much less to association with the opponents of
the apostle. It no doubt had a special reference or application to the peculiar circumstances of the Corinthians, and was
intended to guard them against those entangling and dangerous associations with the unconverted around them, to which
they were specially exposed. And as we know that their
special danger was from idolaters, (see 1 Cor. ch. 8, and 10,
14–33,) whose festivals they were constantly urged to attend,
it is to be presumed that it was from all association with the
heathen in their worship that the apostle intended to warn
them. But this is only one application of the principle here
laid down, viz., that intimate associations ought not to be
formed by the people of God with those who are not his people. The same remark may be made in reference to the persons here intended by *unbelievers*. It is no doubt true that
by unbelievers (οἱ ἄπιστοι) Paul meant the heathen. (See 1
Cor. 6, 6.) But it does not follow from this that intimate association with the heathen is all that is here forbidden. The
principle applies to all the enemies of God and children of
darkness. It is intimate, voluntary association with the
wicked that is forbidden. The worse a man is, the more
openly he is opposed to Christ and his gospel, the greater the
danger and evil of connection with him. It is not so much
his profession as his real character and influence that is to be
taken into account. If it be asked whether the marriage of
professors of religion with non-professors, in the modern (or
American) sense of those terms, is here expressly prohibited?
The answer must be in the negative. There were no such
classes of persons in the apostolic age, as professing and non-
professing Christians. The distinction was then between
Christians and heathens. Persons born within the pale of the
Christian Church, baptized in the name of Christ, and religiously educated, do not belong to the same category as the
heathen. And the principle which applied to the latter therefore does not apply to the former. Still it is to be remembered that it is the union of incongruous elements, of the
devout and undevout, of the spiritual and the worldly, of the
good and the evil, of the children of God and the children of
the evil one, that the apostle exhorts Christians to avoid. *Be
not unequally yoked.* The word is ἑτεροζυγέω, *to be yoked
heterogeneously*, i. e. with an animal of another kind. The
allusion is evidently to the Mosaic law which forbade the
uniting animals of different kinds in the same yoke. Deut. 22,

10. In Lev. 19, 19, ἑτερόζυγος, in the Septuagint, means an animal of a different kind. It is the union of incongruous, uncongenial elements or persons that is forbidden. *With unbelievers ;* as the dative, ἀπίστοις, cannot depend on the preceding word, it is explained by resolving the concise phrase of the apostle into the full form, μὴ γίνεσθε ἑτερόζυγ. καὶ οὕτως ὁμιζυγοῦντες ἀπίστοις. Winer, p. 252. By unbelievers, as above remarked, are to be understood the heathen, those who did not profess faith in the gospel. The exhortation is enforced by the following questions, which are designed to show the incongruity of such unions. *For what fellowship hath righteousness with unrighteousness ?* This is stronger than asking, What fellowship have the righteous with the unrighteous? because there are many bonds of sympathy between good and bad men, arising from the participation of a common nature, and from the fact that in this life, the good are not wholly good, nor the bad wholly bad. The apostle, therefore, contrasts the characteristic and opposing principles by which the two classes are distinguished. By righteousness as opposed to unrighteousness, (δικαιοσύνη to ἀνομία,) is meant goodness, or moral excellence in general, conformity to the law of God as opposed to opposition to that law. It does not mean justifying righteousness, as though the contrast were, as some explain it, between the justified and the not justified. The opposition intended is that which exists between the righteous and the wicked. What *fellowship*, (μετοχή,) partnership. That is, what have they in common? What bond of union or sympathy is there between them? *And what communion* (κοινωνία), see Acts 2, 42. 1 Cor. 1, 9. 10, 16. Parties are said to be in communion when they are so united that what belongs to the one belongs to the other, or when what is true of the one is true of the other. Believers are in communion, or have fellowship one with another, when they recognize each other as having a joint interest in the benefits of redemption, and are conscious that the inward experience of the one is that of the other. Incongruous elements cannot be thus united, and any attempt to combine them must destroy the character of one or the other. *Hath light with darkness. Light* is the common scriptural emblem of knowledge, holiness and blessedness. Hence Christians are said to be the children of light. Luke 16, 8. 1 Thess. 5, 5. Paul was sent "to turn men from darkness to light," Acts 26, 18. Rom. 13, 12. Eph. 5, 8. 9. *Darkness*, on the other hand, is the emblem of error, sin and

misery. Satan's kingdom is called the kingdom of darkness, and the wicked are the children of darkness; and the state of final perdition is " outer darkness." Nothing can be more incongruous than light and darkness, whether in the literal or figurative meaning of the terms. The attempt, therefore, of Christians to remain Christians and retain their inward state as such, and yet to enter voluntarily into intimate fellowship with the world, is as impossible as to combine light and darkness, holiness and sin, happiness and misery.

15. And what concord hath Christ with Belial? or what part hath he that believeth with an infidel?

What concord, ($\sigma\nu\mu\phi\acute{\omega}\nu\eta\sigma\iota\varsigma,$) " harmony of voice." How discordant or opposite are Christ and Belial? How then can their followers agree? The proper orthography of the word according to the Hebrew is Belial, as here in the received text. Many MSS. read Beliar, (agreeably to a common change of the l for r by the Jews who spoke Greek,) others Beliam. The word is properly an abstract noun signifying *worthlessness,* then *wickedness.* Hence the wicked are called " sons of Belial," i. e. *worthless.* It is used as a concrete noun in 2 Sam. 23, 6. Job 34, 18. " Wicked one," and hence, by way of eminence, for Satan, who is $\acute{o}$ $\pi o\nu\eta\rho\acute{o}\varsigma$, the evil one. Compare 1 Cor. 10, 21, where the impossibility of uniting the service of Christ and the service of Satan is presented in much the same terms as it is here. Christ is God manifest in the flesh; Satan is the prince of darkness. How can they, or their followers agree? *Or what part* ($\mu\epsilon\rho\acute{\iota}\varsigma$, in the sense of *participation, fellowship.* Col. 1, 12) *hath he that believeth with an infidel.* In modern usage an *unbeliever* often means one destitute of saving faith; and an *infidel* one destitute even of speculative faith, one who denies the gospel to be a revelation from God. This is a distinction unknown to the Bible. The word here rendered *infidel* is in v. 14 rendered *unbeliever.* In the apostolic age all who professed faith of any kind were called believers, and unbelievers were infidels. It was assumed that the faith possessed was genuine; and therefore it was assumed that all believers were truly the children of God. A mere speculative believer and an infidel may agree well enough in their tastes, character and pursuits. There is no such incompatibility or antipathy between them, as the apostle assumes to exist between the ($\pi\iota\sigma\tau\acute{o}\varsigma$ and $\check{\alpha}\pi\iota\sigma\tau o\varsigma$) believer and unbeliever. It is taken for granted that faith changes the whole character; that it makes a man move in an entirely different sphere, having different feelings, objects, and principles from those of unbelievers; so that intimate union, communion or sympathy between believers and unbelievers is as impossible as fellowship between light and darkness, Christ and Belial. And it must be so. They may indeed have many things in common; a common country, common kindred, common worldly avocations, common natural affections, but the interior life is entirely different; not only incongruous, but essentially opposed the one to the other. To the one, Christ is God, the object of supreme reverence and love; to the other, he is a mere man. To the one, the great object of life is to promote the glory of Christ and to secure his favour; to the other, these are objects of indifference. Elements so discordant can never be united into a harmonious whole.

16. And what agreement hath the temple of God with idols ? for ye are the temple of the living God ; as God hath said, I will dwell in them, and walk in (them) ; and I will be their God, and they shall be my people.

In this and the following verses we have, 1. The assertion of the incongruity between the temple of God and idols. 2. The reason assigned for presenting this incongruity, '*For* ye are the temple of God.' 3. The proof from Scripture that believers are God's temple. 4. The duty which flows from this intimate relation to God; and 5. The gracious promise made to all those who live in accordance with the relation which they bear to God. *What agreement* (συγκατάθεσις, see Luke 23, 51,) *hath the temple of God with idols ?* A building consecrated to the true God is no place for idols. Men cannot combine the worship of God and the worship of devils. Idolatry is everywhere in Scripture represented as the greatest insult the creature can offer the Creator; and the grossest form of that insult is to erect idols in God's own temple. Such was the indignity which those Corinthians offered to God, who, while professing to be Christians, joined in the religious services of the heathen. And such, in its measure, is the offence committed when the people of God become associated with the wicked in their inward and outward life. It is the introduction of idols into God's temple. *For ye are the temple of the living God.* There would be no propriety in the preceding illustration if believers were not God's temple. This, therefore, the apostle first asserts and then proves. The text is here uncertain. The majority of MSS. read with the common text, ὑμεῖς, *ye;* Lachmann, Meyer and some other editors, on the authority of a few MSS. and of the context, read ἡμεῖς, *we.* The sense is substantially the same. The common text is to be preferred both on external and internal grounds. The apostle is addressing the Corinthians, and properly therefore says, *Ye are the temple of God.* A temple is not a building simply consecrated to God, but one in which he dwells, as he dwelt by the visible manifestation of his glory in the temple of old. Hence heaven, as God's dwelling place, is called his temple. Ps. 11, 2. Habak. 2, 20. Christ's body is called a temple, because in him dwelt the fulness of the Godhead. John 2, 19. Believers collectively, or the church, is God's temple, because inhabited by his Spirit, Eph. 2, 21, and for the same reason every individual believer, and every believer's body is a temple of God. 1 Cor. 3, 16. 6, 19. To prove that they were the temple of God, individually and collectively, he therefore cites the declaration of the Scriptures that God dwells in his people. "I will dwell in them and walk in them." God is said to dwell wherever he specially and permanently manifests his presence. And since he thus specially and permanently manifests his presence in his people collectively and individually, he is said to dwell in all and in each. *To walk in them* is simply a parallelism with the preceding clause, expressing the idea of the divine presence in another form. The nearest approach to the words here cited is Lev. 26, 11. 12, where the same thought is expressed, though in somewhat different words. Instead of, "I will set my tabernacle among you," the apostle expresses the same idea by saying, "I will dwell in them." *In them,* is not simply among them, because the presence of God by his Spirit is always represented as internal, in the heart. "If Christ be in you," says the apostle, "the body is dead, &c." "If the Spirit of Him who raised Christ from the dead dwell in you, &c." Rom. 8, 10. 11. So of every believer our Lord says, "If a man love me, he will keep my words, and my Father will love him; and we will come unto him, and make our abode with him," John 14, 23. Every thing is full of God. An insect, a flower, is a constant manifestation of his presence and power. It is what it is because God is in it. So of the human soul, it is said to be full of God when its inward state, its affections and acts, are determined and controlled by him, so as to be a constant manifestation of the divine presence. Then the soul is pure, and glorious, and free, and blessed. This is what God promises to accomplish in us, when he says, " I will dwell in you and walk in you." It is only a variation of form whem it is added, *I will be their God, and they shall be my people*. This is the great promise of the covenant with Abraham and with all the true Israel. It is one of the most comprehensive and frequently repeated promises of the Scriptures. Gen. 17, 8. Deut. 29, 13. Jerem. 31, 33. Heb. 8, 10, &c., &c. There is unspeakably more in the promises of God than we are able to understand. The promise that the nations should be blessed in the seed of Abraham, as unfolded in the New Testament, is found to comprehend all the blessings of redemption. So the promise, I will be their God, and they shall be my people, contains more than it has ever entered into the heart of man to conceive. How low are our conceptions of God! Of necessity our conceptions of what it is to have a God, and that God, Jehovah, must be entirely inadequate. It is not only to have an infinite protector and benefactor, but an infinite portion; an infinite object of love and confidence; an infinite source of knowledge and holiness. It is for God to be to us what he designed to be when he created us after his image, and filled us with his fulness. *His* people, are those whom he recognizes as his peculiar property, the objects of his love, and the recipients of his favours.

17. Wherefore come out from among them, and be ye separate, saith the Lord, and touch not the unclean (thing) ; and I will receive you.

This is a free citation from Is. 52, 11. 12, where the same exhortation to separate themselves from the wicked, and specially from the heathen, is addressed to the people of God. The words *and I will receive you* have nothing to answer to them in the passage in Isaiah, unless it be the words " God shall be your rere-ward;" literally, " he that gathereth you." In Judges 19, 18 the same word is rendered *to receive*, "There is no one receiveth me to house." It is more probable, however, that they are borrowed from Ezekiel 20, 34, as it is rendered in the Septuagint. The exhortation is founded on the preceding passage. God is most intimately related to his people. They are his temple. He dwells in them. Therefore they are bound to keep themselves unspotted from the world. Their being God's temple, his presence in them, and his regarding them as his people, depends upon their separation from the world. For if any man love the world, the love of the Father is not in him. 1 John 2, 15. In this whole context the apostle clothes his own exhortation to the Corinthians in the language of God himself, that they might see that what he taught was indeed the word of God.

18. And will be a Father unto you, and ye shall be my sons and daughters, saith the Lord Almighty.

This is a continuation of the promise commenced in the preceding verse. God declares that he will not only receive into his favour those who regard themselves as his temple and keep themselves aloof from all contaminating associations with the wicked, but that he will be a father to them. It is not with the favour of a master to a servant that he will regard them, but with the favour which a father exercises to his sons and daughters. This is the language of the Lord Almighty; of the omnipotent God. To be his sons and daughters is a dignity and blessedness before which all earthly honours and all worldly good disappear. It is doubtful what particular passage of the Old Testament the apostle had in his mind in this citation. Some think it was 2 Sam. 7, 14, but there God merely says to David in reference to his promised seed, "I will be his father, and he shall be my son." There is too little similarity in form, and too remote an analogy of sentiment, to render it probable that that passage was the one referred to. Is. 43, 6 is more in point. "Bring my sons from far, and my daughters from the ends of the earth." Here the people of God are said to be his sons and daughters; which is all that the citation of the apostle asserts. The concluding verses of this chapter are an instructive illustration of the way in which the New Testament writers quote the Old. 1. They often quote a translation which does not strictly adhere to the original. 2. They often quote according to the sense and not according to the letter. 3. They often blend together different passages of Scripture, so as to give the sense not of any one passage, but the combined sense of several.

4. They sometimes give the sense not of any particular passage or passages, but, so to speak, the general sense of Scripture. That is, they quote the Scriptures as saying what is nowhere found in so many words, but what nevertheless the Scriptures clearly teach. There is no such passage, for example, as that contained in this verse in the Old Testament, but the sentiment is often and clearly therein expressed. 5. They never quote as of authority any but the canonical books of the Old Testament.

CHAPTER VII.

An exhortation founded on what is said in the preceding chapter, v. 1. Paul's consolation derived from the favourable account which he had received from Corinth, vs. 2–16.

The effect produced on the church in Corinth by the apostle's former letter, and his consequent satisfaction and joy.

AFTER in v. 1 exhorting them to live as became those to whom such precious promises had been given as he had just recited from the word of God, he in vs. 2. 3 repeats his desire before expressed, 6, 13, that they would reciprocate his ardent love. So far as he was concerned there was nothing in the way of this cordial reconciliation. He had not injured them, nor was he alienated from them. He had great confidence in them. His apprehensions and anxiety had been in a great measure removed by the account which he had received from Titus of the feelings of the Corinthians towards him, vs. 4–7. It is true that he did at one time regret having written that letter respecting the incestuous person; but he no longer regretted it, because he found that the sorrow which that letter occasioned was the sorrow of true repentance, redounding not to their injury, but to their good, vs. 8. 9. It was not the sorrow of the world, but true godly sorrow, as was evident from its effects, vs. 10–12. Therefore the apostle was comforted, and delighted to find how much Titus had been gratified by his visit to Corinth. All that the apostle had told him of the good dispositions of the Corinthians had proved to be true, vs. 13–16.

1. Having therefore these promises, dearly beloved, let us cleanse ourselves from all filthiness of the flesh and spirit, perfecting holiness in the fear of God.

This verse properly belongs to the preceding chapter. It is the appropriate conclusion of the exposition there made. The promises referred to are, 1st. Of the indwelling of God, 6, 16.   2d. Of his favour, v. 17.   3d. That they should be his sons and daughters. *Therefore,* says the apostle, having these promises of intimate association with God, and this assurance of his love, *let us purify ourselves ;* i. e. not merely keep ourselves pure by avoiding contamination, but, as already defiled, let us strive to become pure.   Though the work of purification is so often referred to God as its author, Acts 15, 9. Eph. 5, 26, this does not preclude the agency of his people.   They are to work out their own salvation, because it is God who worketh in them both to will and to do.   If God's agency in sanctification does not arouse and direct ours; if it does not create the desire for holiness, and strenuous efforts to attain it, we may be sure that we are not its subjects.   He is leaving us undisturbed in our sins.   *From all filthiness of the flesh and spirit.*   All sin is a pollution.   There are two classes of sin here recognized; those of the flesh, and those of the spirit. By the former we are to understand those sins which defile the body, as drunkenness and debauchery; and by the latter those which affect only the soul, as pride and malice.   By filthiness of the flesh, therefore, is not to be understood mere ceremonial uncleanness, nor the participation of the body in sinful acts, such as bowing down to an idol, or offering incense to false gods, but the desecration of the body as the temple of the Holy Ghost.   See 1 Cor. 6, 19.   *Perfecting holiness.* This expresses or indicates the way in which we are to purify ourselves.   It is by perfecting holiness.   The word ἐπιτελέω does not here mean simply *to practise,* but to complete, to carry on to perfection.   Comp. 8, 6. 11. Phil. 1, 6.   It is only by being completely or perfectly holy that we can attain the purity required of us as the temples of God.   *Holiness* (ἁγιωσύνη, Rom. 1, 3. 1 Thess. 3, 13) includes not only the negative idea of purity, or freedom from all defilement, but also, positively, that of moral excellence.   *In the fear of God.*   This is the motive which is to determine our endeavours to purify ourselves. It is not regard to the good of others, nor our own happiness, but reverence for God. We are to be holy, because he is holy.

2. Receive us; we have wronged no man, we have corrupted no man, we have defrauded no man.

Receive us ; literally, *make room for us,* i. e. in your heart. It is a repetition or resumption of the request, " Be ye also enlarged," contained in 6, 13. Then follow the reasons, at least those of a negative kind, why they should thus receive the apostle. *We have wronged no man,* (ἠδικήσαμεν,) *we have treated no one unjustly.* The expression is perfectly general. It may refer either to his conduct as a man, or to the exercise of his apostolical authority. There is nothing to limit it, or to determine the kind of injustice which had been laid to his charge, or which he here had specially in view. *We have corrupted no man.* The word φθείρω, rendered *to corrupt,* means to injure or destroy, either in a moral or physical sense. It is used in a moral sense, 11, 3. 1 Cor. 15, 33. Eph. 4, 22, and in 1 Cor. 3, 17, it is used first in the one sense and then in the other. " If any defile the temple of God, him shall God destroy." Which sense should be adopted here is uncertain. Paul may mean to say that he had corrupted no one's morals by his example or arts of seduction; or that he had corrupted no man's faith by his false teaching; or that he had ruined no man as to his estate. The only reason for preferring the latter interpretation is that the other words with which it is associated express external injuries. There is no ground for the assumption that Paul refers to his former letter and intends to vindicate himself from the charge of injustice or undue severity in his treatment of the incestuous person. That matter he has not yet adverted to; and the expressions here used are too general, and the last (" we have defrauded no man ") is inapplicable to that case. By *defrauding* he probably means acting unfairly in pecuniary affairs. The word πλεονεκτέω, in the New Testament, means either to have or take advantage of any one, 2, 11, or, *to make gain of, to defraud.* The usage of the word and of its cognates is in favour of the latter sense. 12, 17. 18. 1 Cor. 5, 10. 6, 10. Paul was specially careful to avoid all occasion of suspicion as to the disposition of the money which he raised from the churches for the relief of the poor. 8, 19. 20, and no doubt his enemies were ready enough to insinuate that he appropriated the money to his own use. He had therefore occasion to show that he had never made gain of them, that he had defrauded no man.

3. I speak not (this) to condemn (you): for I have said before, that ye are in our hearts to die and live with (you).

I speak not this to condemn you; i. e. In defending my-self I do not mean to condemn you. This may mean either, 'In saying that I have wronged no man, I do not intend to imply that you have wronged me;' or, 'I do not mean to im-ply that you think of me so unjustly as to suppose that I have wronged, injured or defrauded any one.' In other words, 'I do not mean to question your love.' *For.* What follows as-signs the reason or proof that he had no unkind feeling towards them which would lead him to condemn them. *I said before,* viz., in 6, 12, *that ye are in our hearts.* That is, that I love you. He had said that his heart was enlarged towards them, which was proof enough that he did not now mean to upbraid them. *To die and live with you,* εἰς τὸ συναποθανεῖν καὶ συζῆν, *so as to die and live together.* That is, 'Ye are so rooted in my heart that I would gladly live and die with you,' or, 'so that neither death nor life can separate us.' As remarked above, Paul's love for the Corinthians seems to have been ex-traordinary, having something of the nature of a passion, be-ing more ardent than either their good qualities or their conduct towards him could account for. This is often the case in men of warm and generous feeling, who have frequent-ly to say, 'The more abundantly we love, the less we are loved.'

4. Great (is) my boldness of speech toward you, great (is) my glorying of you: I am filled with com-fort, I am exceeding joyful in all our tribulation.

So far from having any disposition to upbraid or to re-criminate, his heart was overflowing with far different feelings. He had not only confidence in them, he was proud of them; he was not only comforted, he was filled with exceeding joy.

There is a climax here, as Calvin says: Gradatim procedit
amplificando: plus enim est gloriari, quam securo et quieto
esse animo: liberari vero a moerore ex multis afflictionibus
concepto, utroque majus. His boasting of them was more
than having confidence in them; and his rejoicing in the midst
of his afflictions was more than being comforted. *Great is
my boldness of speech towards you.* The word is παρρησία,
which here, as in many other places, Eph. 3, 12. Heb. 3, 6.
1. John 2, 28. 3, 21. 4, 17. 5, 14, instead of its primary sense
of freedom of speech, expresses the idea of joyful confidence;
i. e. the state of mind from which freedom of utterance, or
boldness of speech, flows. Paul means to say that so far from
wishing to condemn the Corinthians he had joyful confidence
in them. And not only that, he adds, but, *Great is my glorying of you,* (καύχησις,) i. e. *my boasting over you.* The accounts which the apostle had just received of the state of
things at Corinth, and especially of the effect produced by his
former letter, had not only obliterated his feelings of anxiety
and doubt concerning them, but made him boast of them.
He gloried on their account. He was disposed to tell every
one how well his dear Corinthians had behaved. He thus, as
it were, unconsciously lays bare the throbbings of his warm
and generous heart. *I am filled with comfort,* literally, ' with
the comfort,' i. e. the comfort to which he afterwards refers;
or the comfort which his situation specially demanded. Such
was the apostle's anxiety about the effect of his former letter
that, as he says, 2, 12, "he had no rest in his spirit," and
therefore left Troas and hastened into Macedonia that he
might meet Titus on his way back from Corinth. This anxiety was now all gone. His mind was at rest. He was full of
consolation. *I am exceedingly joyful,* (ὑπερπερισσεύομαι τῇ
χαρᾷ,) *I more than abound in joy,* or *the* joy. Comp. Rom.
5, 20. He was more than merely comforted, he was overflowing with joy, and that too in spite of all the troubles which
still pressed upon him, for he adds, *in all our tribulation.*
The favourable accounts which Paul had received from Corinth, although they had removed some of the causes of his
anxiety and suffering, left others in their full force. So that
even when he wrote he was in great trouble. He therefore
uses the present tense. 'I am overflowing with joy in the
midst of tribulation.' Another proof that joy and sorrow may
coexist in the mind. The martyr at the stake, in the midst
of his agony, has often been filled with ecstatic joy.

5. For, when we were come into Macedonia, our flesh had no rest, but we were troubled on every side; without (were) fightings, within (were) fears.

The connection is with the last clause of the preceding verse. I was comforted in tribulation, *for also* (καὶ γάρ) *having come into Macedonia, our flesh had no rest.* Paul did not leave his troubles behind him in Troas, 2, 12, but *also* in Macedonia his flesh had no rest. By *flesh* he does not mean his body, for the sufferings, which he immediately specifies, were not corporeal, but mental. It stands for his whole sensitive nature considered as frail. It is equivalent to saying, 'my feeble nature had no rest.' The same idea is expressed in 2, 12 by saying, "I had no rest in my spirit." *But*, so far from having rest, *we were troubled* (θλιβόμενοι, either ἤμεθα is to be supplied, or a slight departure from the regular construction is to be assumed) *on every side,* ἐν παντί, *in every way.* This is amplified and explained by saying, *without* (were) *fightings, within fears.* Calvin and many other commentators understand *within* and *without* to mean within and without the church. Paul's troubles were partly from his contentions with the Jews and heathen, and partly from his anxieties about the conduct and welfare of Christians. It is more common and natural to understand the distinction to be between inward and outward troubles. He had to contend with all kinds of outward difficulties, and was oppressed with an inward load of anxieties. *Fears,* painful apprehensions lest his labours should be vain, lest his enemies should at last prevail, lest his disciples should apostatize and perish, or the peace and purity of the church be disturbed.

6. Nevertheless God, that comforteth those that are cast down, comforted us by the coming of Titus.

The order of the words is inverted in the English version. In the Greek the order is, He who comforteth those who are cast down, comforted us, even God, by the coming of Titus. The fact that it is the characteristic work of God, or, so to speak, his office, to comfort the dejected, is thus made more prominent. All the miserable are thus encouraged, because they are miserable, to look to that God who proclaims himself as the comforter. It is to be remarked that the objects of his compassion, those who call forth the exercise of his power as

a consoler, are described not by a term expressive of moral
excellence, but by a word which simply designates them as
sufferers. The ταπεινοί are properly simply the low, those who
are in depressed circumstances. As, however, it is the tendency of such circumstances to render men fearful, or meek,
or humble, the word often expresses one or the other of these
states of mind. In 10, 1 it means *timid* as opposed to *bold;*
in 1 Pet. 5, 5, it is the opposite of *proud.* Here, however, it
has its simple, proper sense—those who are low, i. e. cast
down by suffering so as to be the proper objects of compassion.
Luke 1, 52. James 1, 9. Ps. 18, 27. Paul says God comforted
him by the coming of Titus, whom he had sent to Corinth to
know the state of the church there.

7. And not by his coming only, but by the consolation wherewith he was comforted in you, when he
told us your earnest desire, your mourning, your fervent mind toward me; so that I rejoiced the more.

It was not the pleasure of seeing Titus, so much as the intelligence which he brought, which comforted the apostle.
By the consolation wherewith he was comforted *in you,* (ἐφ'
ὑμῖν,) in reference to, or, as concerns you. The fact that Titus was comforted in Corinth was a great consolation to the
apostle, and he was made to share in the comfort which Titus
had experienced, as the latter *reported* to him (ἀναγγέλλειν, *to
bring back word, to recount,* Acts 14, 27. 16, 38,) *your earnest
desire,* i. e. either your earnest desire to see me and to secure
my approbation; or, your earnest desire to correct the evils
existing among you. The former is to be preferred, both on
account of the context and the signification of the word ἐπιπό-
θησις, which means strong affection. *Your mourning,* (ὀδυρ-
μός, i. e. *wailing, lamentation,* Matt. 2, 18,) either, mourning
on account of their sins, or on account of having offended and
pained the apostle. The latter is the more probable on account of what follows. *Your fervent mind toward me,* (ζῆλος
ὑπὲρ ἐμοῦ,) *zeal for me,* i. e. the great interest which you took
in me. Gal. 4, 17. 18. As the zeal of which the apostle
speaks is expressly said to be a zeal of which he was the object, it is probable that the preceding words (*earnest desire*
and *mourning*) express their feeling and conduct in reference
to him. What was so specially gratifying to him was that in

a church in which he had met with so much opposition, and in which the false teachers had exerted so great and so evil an influence, the mass of the people proved themselves devoted to him. Devotion to Paul, however, involved devotion to the truth and holiness, just as zeal for the false teachers involved the opposite. *So that I rejoiced the more*, i. e. I had more joy than the mere coming of Titus and the satisfaction which he experienced in Corinth were able to impart.

8. For though I made you sorry with a letter, I do not repent, though I did repent: for I perceive that the same epistle hath made you sorry, though (it were) but for a season.

This and the following verses assign the reason why he rejoiced. It was because the letter which he had written them, although it made them sorry, yet did them good. Though I made you sorry (i. e. caused you grief) *with a letter*, rather, *by the letter*, i. e. the letter which related to the incestuous person. *I do not repent, though I did repent.* That is, he regretted writing as he had done until he learned through Titus the good effect his letter had produced. Calvin says the word μεταμέλομαι must not be taken here to express repentance, for that would imply that his former letter was written under the influence of human feeling, and not by the direction of the Holy Spirit. He thinks that all Paul meant to say is, that he was grieved at having given the Corinthians pain. This, however, is not the meaning of the word. See Matt. 21, 29. 32. We must accommodate our theory of inspiration to the phenomena of Scripture, and not the phenomena to our theory. Inspiration simply rendered its subject infallible in writing and speaking as the messenger of God. Paul might doubt whether he had in a given instance made a wise use of his infallibility, as he might doubt whether he had wisely exercised his power of working miracles. He never doubted as to the truth of what he had written. There is another thing to be taken into consideration. Inspiration did not reveal itself in the consciousness. It is perfectly conceivable that a man might be inspired without knowing it. Paul was no doubt impelled by the Spirit to write his former epistle as well as divinely guided in writing; but all he was conscious of was his own thoughts and feelings. The believer is not conscious of the operations of grace, neither were the apostles conscious of inspiration. As the believer, however, may know that he is the subject of divine influence, so the apostles knew that they were inspired. But as the believer may doubt the wisdom of some of his holiest acts, so the apostles might doubt the wisdom of acts done under divine guidance. Such acts are always wise, but the agent may not always see their wisdom.

For I perceive that the same epistle made you sorry. This gives the reason why he at first regretted having written. He knew that his letter had excited much feeling in Corinth, and until he learned the nature and effects of that feeling, he repented having written. *Though but for a season.* That is, although the sorrow which he had occasioned was only temporary, yet it made him regret his former letter. This interpretation supposes a different punctuation of the passage from that found either in the common editions of the Greek text, or in the English version. It supposes that the proper place for the period or colon is after "I did not repent," and not after the following clause, "I did repent." In this latter case the whole sense is different, and the latter clause of the verse (βλέπω γάρ) is connected with the first clause, and is intended to give the reason why he said he had made them sorry, and not the reason why he regretted having done so. The sense of the whole would then be, 'I made you sorry . . . . . for I perceive from what I hear from Titus, that my former letter did, although only for a while, grieve you.' The next verse then begins a new sentence. But this is an unnatural construction; it requires the verse to be paraphrased in order to bring out the sense; and after all it amounts to little to say, 'I made you sorry, for I see I made you sorry.' The construction is simpler and the sense better if we put a colon or semi-colon after "I do not repent," and make v. 9 a part of the same sentence. 'Though I made you sorry I do not repent: although I did repent, (for I see that my letter made you sorry, though only for a time,) I now rejoice.' The meaning is, 'Though I did repent, I now rejoice.' Thus the passage is printed in the Greek of STIER and THIELE's Polyglott, and, so far as the pointing is concerned, (omitting the marks of parenthesis,) in Tischendorf's Greek Testament. In the Vulgate the same sense is expressed. "Quoniam etsi contristavi vos in epistola, non me pœnitet; et si pœniteret, videns quod epistola illa (etsi ad horam) vos contristavit, nunc gaudeo, &c." So also Luther.

9. Now I rejoice, not that ye were made sorry, but that ye sorrowed to repentance : for ye were made sorry after a godly manner, that ye might receive damage by us in nothing.

He rejoiced, not in their grief, but that their grief led them to repentance. A parent, when he sees a child mourning over his sins, sincerely rejoices, however much he sympathizes in his grief. *Sorrowed unto repentance*, (εἰς μετάνοιαν,) i. e. change of mind, sometimes in the restricted sense of the word mind, (or purpose,) as in Heb. 12, 17; generally, in the comprehensive sense of the word as including the principles and affections, the whole soul, or inward life. Matt. 3, 8. Luke 5, 32. Acts 5, 31. Repentance, therefore, in its religious sense, is not merely a change of purpose, but includes a change of heart which leads to a turning from sin with grief and hatred thereof unto God. Such is the repentance here intended, as appears from what follows. *For* (this shows they sorrowed unto repentance) *they were made sorry* (they grieved) *after a godly sort*, (κατὰ Θεόν,) i. e. in a manner agreeable to the mind and will of God; so that God approved of their sorrow. He saw that it arose from right views of their past conduct. *That*, (ἵνα, *in order that*,) as expressing the design of God in making their sorrow a sorrow unto repentance. *Ye might receive damage by us in nothing.* God had so ordered that Paul's letter, instead of producing any injury, had resulted in the greatest spiritual good.

10. For godly sorrow worketh repentance to salvation not to be repented of; but the sorrow of the world worketh death.

The connection is with the last clause. 'Ye were not injured by us, *for* the sorrow we occasioned worked repentance.' Sorrow in itself is not repentance; neither is remorse, nor self-condemnation, nor self-loathing, nor external reformation. These all are its attendants or consequences; but repentance itself (μετάνοια) is a turning from sin to holiness, from a state of sin to a holy state. It is a real change of heart. It

is a change of views, feelings and purposes, resulting in a
change of life. Godly sorrow *worketh* repentance, i. e. that
sorrow on account of sin, which arises from proper apprehensions of God and of our relation to him, necessarily leads to
that entire change in the inward life which is expressed by
the word repentance, and which is connected with salvation.
It is not the ground of our salvation; but it is a part of it and
a necessary condition of it. Those who repent are saved; the
impenitent perish. Repentance therefore is *unto salvation.*
Comp. Acts 11, 18. It is that inward change in which salvation largely consists. *Never to be repented of.* This may belong either to the *repentance* or to *salvation.* If to the latter,
the word ἀμεταμέλητος may be taken in the sense of *unchange-
able.* See Rom. 11, 29. So the Vulgate explains it, *ad salutem
stabilem ;* or it may mean *not to be regretted.* Repentance
leads to a salvation which no one ever will regret. So Luther
and many of the moderns. The position of the words is in
favour of connecting "not to be repented of" with "salvation." Had Paul intended the other connection, he would
have probably said εἰς μετάνοιαν ἀμετανόητον, and not have
chosen (ἀμεταμέλητον) a word of an entirely different root.
Still, as "not to be repented of" seems to be an unsuitable epithet when applied to salvation, the majority of commentators
prefer the other connection, and consider the apostle as designating true repentance as that which no one will regret notwithstanding the sorrow with which it is attended. *But the
sorrow of the world worketh death.* By the sorrow of the
world is not meant worldly sorrow, i. e. sorrow arising out of
worldly considerations, but the sorrow of men of the world.
In other words, κόσμου is the genitive of the subject, not a
qualifying genitive. "The world" means men, the mass of
mankind as distinguished from the church. 1 Cor. 1, 20. Gal.
4, 3. John 7, 7. 14, 7. &c. What therefore the apostle means
is the sorrow of unrenewed men, the sorrow of the unsanctified
heart. Of this sorrow, as opposed to godly sorrow, he says,
it works death, not physical death, nor specifically eternal
death as opposed to salvation, but evil in the general sense
of the word. The effects of godly sorrow are salutary; the
effects of worldly sorrow (the sorrow of worldly men) are evil.
It is a great mistake to suppose that the natural tendency of
pain and sorrow is to good. They tend rather to excite rebellion against God and all evil feelings. It is only when they
are sanctified, i. e. when they are experienced by the holy, and

are made by the Spirit of God to call into exercise the resignation, patience and faith of the sufferer, that they bring forth fruit unto righteousness. The natural element of holiness is happiness, and misery is the natural element of sin. They stand severally in the relation both of cause and effect. The more miserable you make a bad man, the worse you make him. The wicked are said to curse God while they gnaw their tongues with pain, and they repent not of their deeds. Rev. 16, 10. 11.

11. For behold this self-same thing, that ye sorrowed after a godly sort, what carefulness it wrought in you, yea, (what) clearing of yourselves, yea, (what) indignation, yea, (what) fear, yea, (what) vehement desire, yea, (what) zeal, yea, (what) revenge! In all (things) ye have approved yourselves to be clear in this matter.

The question may be asked whether Paul means here to describe the uniform effects of genuine repentance, so as to furnish a rule by which each one may judge of his own experience. This, to say the least, is not the primary design of the passage. If it affords such a rule it is only incidentally. The passage is historical. It describes the effects which godly sorrow produced in the Corinthian church. It shows how the church felt and acted in reference to a specific offence, when roused to a sense of its enormity. *For, behold!* The connection is with what precedes. 'Godly sorrow is salutary, for, see what effects it wrought for you.' *This self-same thing,* i. e. this very thing, viz., *being sorry after a godly sort.* *What carefulness it wrought in you* (ὑμῖν, *for you,* for your advantage). *Carefulness,* (σπουδήν,) literally, haste; then the inward feeling which leads to haste; then any outward manifestation of that earnestness of feeling. Here it means earnest solicitude as opposed both to indifference and neglect. The Corinthians had strangely allowed a grievous sin, committed by a church-member, to pass unnoticed, as a matter of no importance. The first effect or manifestation of their godly sorrow was an earnest solicitude on the subject, and a desire to have the evil corrected; the very opposite of their former indifference. It is so in all cases of repentance. Sins which had been regarded as of little account, are apprehended in their true character; and deep feeling takes the place of unconcern. *Yea, what clearing of yourselves.* The particle ἀλλά is here and through the verse rendered *yea.* It is used, as in 1, 9, to indicate a gradation—*still more.* 'Not only solicitude, but moreover *clearing of yourselves,*' (ἀπολογίαν.) Their sorrow led them earnestly to apologize for the sin which they had committed. Not to extenuate their guilt, but to acknowledge it and to seek forgiveness. The apology for sin to which repentance leads, includes acknowledgment and deprecation. This apology was addressed to the apostle. They endeavoured to regain his good opinion. Moreover, *indignation,* either at the offence or at themselves that such an offence should have been allowed. They felt angry at themselves for their past misconduct. This is one of the most marked experiences of every sincere penitent. The unreasonableness, the meanness, the wickedness of his conduct rouse his indignation; he desires to seek vengeance on himself. Bengel says the word ἀγανάκτησις is chosen with special propriety, as it denotes a pain of which a man has the cause in himself. *What fear.* Whether fearful apprehension of God's displeasure, or fear of the apostle, depends on the context. The idea is expressed indefinitely. Their repentance was attended by fear of punishment. Doubtless the two sentiments were mingled in the minds of the Corinthians. They had a fear of the wrath of God, and at the same time a fear of the apostle's coming among them displeased and armed with the spiritual power which belonged to his office. The context is in favour of making the latter the prominent idea. *What vehement desire,* either for the correction of the evil complained of, or for the apostle's presence and approbation. In the latter case this clause is a modification of the preceding. It was not so much fear of the apostle as an earnest and affectionate desire towards and for him, that their godly sorrow had produced. As in v. 7 Titus had repeated to the apostle the earnest desire (ἐπιπόθησιν, the same word as here) of the Corinthians for him, it is probable that the same is here meant. *What zeal.* In v. 7 the zeal spoken of is limited or explained by the words (ὑπὲρ ἐμοῦ) *for me.* Without that addition they may be so understood here; zeal or zealous interest in behalf of the apostle manifested by their taking sides with him. The connection, however, with what follows favours the assumption that here the zeal meant is that of which the offender was the object. Zeal for his reformation or punishment *What revenge*, (ἐκδίκησις,) *vindictive justice.* One of the sentiments which godly sorrow had aroused in them was the sense of justice, the moral judgment that sin ought to be punished. This is an instinctive feeling, one belonging to our moral constitution, and therefore a revelation of the nature and will of God. The ground of the punishment of sin is not expediency, nor is it primarily the benefit of the offender, but the satisfaction of justice, or the inherent evil of sin which from its own nature, and apart from the evil consequences of impunity, deserves punishment. Of the six particulars introduced by (ἀλλά) *yea* in this verse, according to Bengel, Meyer and others, " clearing of yourselves " and " indignation " relate to the feelings of the Corinthians towards themselves; " fear " and " vehement desire " to their feelings towards the apostle; and " zeal " and " revenge " to their feelings towards the offender. According to Olshausen, the " apology " relates to their conduct; the " indignation " to their feelings in view of the crime which had been committed; the " fear " to God's displeasure; the " desire " and " zeal " to their feelings towards the apostle, and " revenge " the consequence of all the preceding.

In all things, (ἐν παντί,) in every respect, or, in every point of view. *Ye have proved yourselves,* (συνεστήσατε,) you have set yourselves forth, shown yourselves to be (Gal. 2, 18) *clear,* (ἁγνούς,) *pure,* free from guilt. *In this matter,* or, (without the ἐν, which the older MSS. omit,) *as to the matter.* The Corinthians proved themselves to be free from the sin of approving or in any way countenancing the crime in question. Their sin consisted in not more promptly excluding the offender from their communion. This whole passage, however, is instructive as presenting a clear exhibition of the intimate nature of church fellowship. One member committed an offence. The whole church repents. The godly sorrow which the apostle describes was the sorrow of the church. The effects which that sorrow wrought were common to the church as such. That believers are one body in Christ Jesus, and " every one members one of another," so that " if one member suffers all the members suffer with it," is matter of actual experience.

12. Wherefore, though I wrote unto you, (I did it) not for his cause that had done the wrong, nor for his

cause that suffered wrong, but that our care for you in the sight of God might appear unto you.

Wherefore. That is, because my letter has produced such results. The effects produced by his letter was the end he had in view in writing it. *Though I wrote to you,* i. e. although I interfered with your affairs. His motive in writing he states first negatively and then positively. It was neither for the sake of him who did wrong, nor for him who suffered wrong. His primary object was neither to have the offender punished, nor to secure justice being done to the injured party, viz., the father whose wife the son had married. This is the common and natural interpretation. As, however, nothing is elsewhere said of the father, and as the form of expression in 1 Cor. 5, 1, (γυναῖκα ἔχειν, to marry,) seems to imply that the father of the offender was dead, since otherwise, it is said, there could have been no marriage in the case, various other explanations of this passage have been proposed. Some say that he "who suffered wrong" was the apostle himself; others, as Bengel, say it was the Corinthians, the singular being taken for the plural. Others, as Neander, Billroth, &c., say that ἀδικηθέντος is neuter, *the wrong deed;* so that the meaning is, ' Neither for the offender nor for the offence.' But these explanations are all unnatural and unnecessary. The ordinary interpretation is the only one which the words suggest, and what is said in 1 Cor. 5 is perfectly consistent with the assumption that the father of the offender was still alive. The positive statement of his object in writing is *that our care for you in the sight of God might appear unto you.* The first question concerning this clause relates to the text. Instead of ἡμῶν (*our*), Lachmann, Meyer and others read ὑμῶν (*your*). This latter reading is followed by Calvin and Luther as well as by many of the modern commentators. As the external authorities are nearly equally divided, the decision rests mainly on internal evidence. In favour of the common text is first, the consideration that the manifestation of his love or care for them is elsewhere said to have been his motive in writing his former letter, 2, 4 ; and, secondly, the words πρὸς ὑμᾶς are more easily explained. ' Our care for you might appear unto you,' is plain. But if ὑμῶν is read these words give difficulty. They must be rendered (*apud vos*) "with you." ' Your care for us might be manifest with (i. e. among) you.' That is, that the zeal which you have for us might be brought out so as to be known by yourselves. This, however, would be more naturally expressed by ἐν ὑμῖν or ἐν ἑαυτοῖς, *among yourselves*. Besides, the words "before God," as involving an appeal to the divine omniscience, are more in place if he is speaking of his own zeal, than if speaking of theirs. The immediate context, it must be admitted, is in favour of this latter reading. The apostle had been describing the effects of his letter, dwelling with great satisfaction on the feelings towards himself which that letter had called forth. It was natural for him therefore to say that his object in writing was to bring out this manifestation, and thus reveal themselves to themselves as well as to him. With this also agrees what he says in 4, 9, "To this end also did I write, that I might know the proof of you, whether ye be obedient in all things." Still on the whole the common text gives the better sense. In either case the words πρὸς ὑμᾶς depend on φανερωθῆναι, "might be manifest *towards* (or among) you." So also do the words ἐνώπιον τοῦ θεοῦ, "that our care for you might be manifested *before God*," i. e. in his sight, as what he could approve of. In our version these words are connected with *our care*. "Our care for you in the sight of God." The same sense is expressed by the Vulgate; "ad manifestandam sollicitudinem nostram, quæ habemus pro vobis coram Deo." According to the Greek the natural construction is, "To manifest in the sight of God our care for you."

13. Therefore we were comforted in your comfort : yea, and exceedingly the more joyed we for the joy of Titus, because his spirit was refreshed by you all.

Therefore, i. e. because his letter had led them to repentance. *We were comforted in your comfort*, (ἐπὶ τῇ παρακλήσει ὑμῶν,) on account of your consolation. This, however, does not suit the state of the case. Paul was comforted by their repentance, not by their consolation. To meet this difficulty some make ὑμῶν the genitive of the source; so that the sense would be, 'We were comforted with the consolation derived from you.' The great majority of modern editors read ἡμῶν instead of ὑμῶν, and put a stop after παρακεκλήμεθα. This gives a far better sense. 'Therefore we have been comforted : and besides (ἐπί) our consolation, we have rejoiced exceedingly in the joy of Titus.' Paul had not only the consolation derived from their repentance, but in addition to that, he was delighted to find Titus so full of joy. Compare v. 7. The Vulgate has the same reading and pointing. Ideo consolati sumus. In consolatione autem nostra abundantius magis gavisi sumus super gaudio Titi. *Because his spirit was refreshed by you all.* This is the reason of his joy. Titus rejoiced because his spirit was *refreshed*, (ἀναπέπαυται,) derived rest, according to the comprehensive scriptural sense of the word " rest."

14. For if I have boasted any thing to him of you, I am not ashamed; but as we spake all things to you in truth, even so our boasting, which (I made) before Titus, is found a truth.

This is the reason why Paul was so rejoiced that Titus was satisfied with what he saw in Corinth. Paul had boasted to him of the Corinthians. He had predicted that he would find them obedient, and ready to correct the evils adverted to in his former letter. Had these predictions proved false, he would have been mortified,—ashamed, as he says; but as they were more than fulfilled, he naturally rejoiced. *But as we spake all things to you in truth.* No doubt in allusion to the charge of want of adherence to the truth made against him by the false teachers, to which he refers above, 1, 17. 18. As he spoke the truth to the Corinthians, so he spoke the truth of them. We spake *in truth*, (ἐν ἀληθείᾳ,) *truly. So our boasting before Titus* (ἡ ἐπὶ Τίτου) *is found a truth*, (ἀλήθεια ἐγενήθη,) *has become truth.* Though it is done incidentally, yet the revelation to the Corinthians that Paul had spoken of them in terms of commendation must have convinced them of his love. This was one of the objects, as appears from the whole epistle, he had much at heart.

15. And his inward affection is more abundant toward you, whilst he remembereth the obedience of you all, how with fear and trembling ye received him.

A continuation of the sentence begun in the former verse. Paul informs the Corinthians that Titus's love for them was greater now than when he was with them. The recollection of their good conduct warmed his heart towards them. *His inward affection*, literally, his bowels, which in the Scriptures is a figurative expression for love, compassion, or any other tender affection. *Whilst he remembereth*, literally, *remembering*, i. e. because he remembers. *Your obedience*, viz., towards him, as appears from what follows. *How with fear and trembling ye received him.* "Fear and trembling" is a common scriptural expression for reverence, or solicitous anxiety lest we should fail in doing all that is required of us. 1 Cor. 2, 3. Eph. 6, 5.

16. I rejoice, therefore, that I have confidence in you in all (things).

This is the conclusion of the whole matter. The first seven chapters of the epistle are intimately connected. They all relate to the state of the congregation at Corinth and to Paul's relation to the people there. The eighth and ninth chapters form a distinct division of the epistle. Here, therefore, we have the conclusion of the whole preceding discussion. The result of the long conflict of feeling in reference to the Corinthians as a church, was the full restoration of confidence. I rejoice that I have confidence in you in all things, (ἐν παντί, *in every thing*). *I have confidence in you*, (θαρρῶ ἐν ὑμῖν,) I have good courage, am full of hope and confidence. 5, 6. Heb. 13, 6. As θαρρέω is not elsewhere constructed with ἐν, Meyer says the meaning is, 'I am of good courage, *through* you.' If this objection to the common explanation be considered of weight, ἐν had better be rendered *before*. 'I stand full of confidence before you, i. e. in your presence.' 1 Cor. 14, 11. The sense, however, expressed by the common interpretation is better.

CHAPTER VIII.

Exhortation to liberality to the poor.

To this subject the apostle devotes this and the following chapter. He begins by setting before the Corinthians the liberality of the churches in Macedonia. They, in the midst of great affliction and of extreme poverty, had exceeded their ability in the contributions which they had made for the saints, vs. 1–3. And this not by constraint or in obedience to earnest entreaties on the part of the apostle; but on the contrary, it was they who besought him to receive and take charge of their alms, v. 4. Liberality to the poor was only a part of what they did; they devoted themselves to the Lord, v. 5. The conduct of the Macedonians led the apostle to exhort Titus, as he had already begun the work, to carry it on to completion in Corinth, v. 6.

He begs them, therefore, to add this to all their other graces, v. 7. This was a matter of advice, not of command. He was induced to give this exhortation because others had evinced so much zeal in this matter, and because he desired them to prove the sincerity of their love. What was all they could do for others, compared to what Christ had done for them, vs. 8. 9. The exercise of liberality was a good to them, provided their feelings found expression in corresponding acts, vs. 10. 11. The disposition, not the amount of their contributions, was the main thing, v. 12. What the apostle wished was that there might be some approximation to equality among Christians, that the abundance of one may supply the wants of another, vs. 13–15.

He thanks God who had inspired Titus with so much zeal on this subject, vs. 16. 17. With him he had sent a brother who had not only the approbation of the churches, but had been chosen for the very purpose of taking charge of the contributions in connection with the apostle, vs. 18. 19. Paul was determined to avoid all occasion of reproach, and therefore he associated others with himself in the charge of the money in-

trusted to him, vs. 20. 21. With those already mentioned he
sent another brother of approved character and great zeal, v.
22. Therefore if any one inquired who Titus was, they might
answer, He was Paul's companion and fellow-labourer; or who
those brethren were, they might say, They were the messengers of the churches, and the glory of Christ. Let the church
therefore prove their love and justify his boasting of them,
vs. 23. 24.

1. Moreover, brethren, we do you to wit of the
grace of God bestowed on the churches of Macedonia.

Moreover (δέ) marks the transition to a new subject. *We
do you to wit*, (γνωρίζομεν,) 'we cause you to know.' The
word *to wit*, (Anglo-Saxon, *Witan ;* German, *Wissen*,) to
know, and the cognate words, *Wis* and *Wot*, are nearly obso-
lete, although they occur frequently in our version. The
grace of God, the divine favour. The liberality of the Corinthians was due to the operation of the grace of God. The
sacred writers constantly recognize the fact that the freest
and most spontaneous acts of men, their inward states and
the outward manifestations of those states, when good, are
due to the secret influence of the Spirit of God, which
eludes our consciousness. The believer is most truly self-de-
termined, when determined by the grace of God. *Bestowed
on*, (δεδομένην ἐν,) "given in," i. e. given so that it is in. See
1, 22. "Given the earnest of the Spirit in our hearts." In v.
16 of this chapter, διδόντι ἐν is rendered "*put into*." *The
churches of Macedonia*. Under the Romans Macedonia included the whole of the northern provinces of Greece. The
churches of that region founded by the apostle were those of
Philippi, Thessalonica, and Berœa. Of the extraordinary
liberality of those churches the epistles of Paul furnish numerous intimations. 11, 9. Phil. 2, 25. 4, 15. 18.

2. How that, in a great trial of affliction, the abundance of their joy, and their deep poverty, abounded
unto the riches of their liberality.

A somewhat condensed sentence, meaning, as some say,
that in the midst of their afflictions their joy, and in the midst
of their poverty, their liberality abounded. But this brings
into view two graces, joy in affliction, and liberality in poverty,

whereas the context calls for only one. The meaning rather
is, that notwithstanding their afflictions, their joy and their
poverty abounded to their liberality. This the grammatical
structure of the passage requires. *How that* (ὅτι); the connection is with the verb in the preceding verse, 'I cause you
to know that, &c.' *In a great trial of affliction*, i. e. in afflictions which were a great trial (δοκιμή), i. e. a test of their sincerity and devotion. These afflictions were either those
which they shared in common with their fellow-citizens, arising out of their social condition, or they were peculiar to them
as Christians, arising from persecution. In writing to the
Thessalonians, Paul reminds them that they had received the
word in much affliction. 1, 6. 2, 14. Comp. Acts 16, 20. 17, 5.
The abundance of their joy ; i. e. the joy arising from the
pardon of their sins and the favour of God, which in 1 Thess.
1, 6, he calls the joy of the Holy Ghost, was abundant. That
is, it rose above their sorrows, and produced in them the effect of which he afterwards speaks. *And their deep poverty*,
(ἡ κατὰ βάθους πτωχεία,) their abject poverty, or poverty down
to the depth. *Abounded unto*, i. e. manifested itself as abundant in relation to. The same verb (ἐπερίσσευσεν) belongs to
both the preceding nouns, "joy" and "poverty," but in a
somewhat different sense. Their joy abounded unto their
liberality, because it produced it. The effect proved the joy
to be abundant. Their poverty abounded unto their liberality, because it was seen to be great in relation to it. Their
liberality made their poverty, by contrast, appear the greater.
Unto the riches, (πλοῦτος,) a favourite word with Paul, which
he often uses in the sense of abundance. Rom. 2, 4, "Riches
of his goodness," for abundant goodness. Eph. 1, 7, "Riches
of his grace," for his abundant grace ; 1, 18, "Riches of his
glory," for abundant glory, &c. *Of their liberality*, ἁπλότης,
which is properly the opposite of duplicity, or double-minded-
ness, and, therefore, singleness of heart, simplicity, sincerity.
Eph. 6, 5. Col. 3, 22. The Scriptures, however, often use a
generic term for a specific one, as glory for wisdom, or mercy,
or power, which are different forms of the divine glory. So
here the general term for right-mindedness is put for liberality, which is a specific form or manifestation of the generic
virtue. Comp. 9, 11. Rom. 12, 8. In reference to the poverty of the Macedonian churches, Mr. Stanley, in his Commentary on this Epistle, appropriately quotes a passage from Dr.
Arnold's Roman Commonwealth, in which he says, "The

condition of Greece in the time of Augustus was one of desolation and distress. It had suffered severely by being the
seat of the successive civil wars between Cæsar and Pompey,
between the Triumvirs and Brutus and Cassius, and lastly,
between Augustus and Antonius. Besides, the country had
never recovered from the long series of miseries which had
succeeded and accompanied its conquest by the Romans; and
between those times and the civil contest between Pompey
and Cæsar, it had been again exposed to all the evils of war
when Sylla was disputing the possession of it with the general
of Mithridates. . . . The provinces of Macedonia and Achaia,
when they petitioned for a diminution of their burdens, in the
reign of Tiberius, were considered so deserving of compassion
that they were transferred for a time from the jurisdiction of
the Senate to that of the Emperor, (as involving less heavy
taxation.)"

3–5. For to (their) power, I bear record, yea, and
beyond (their) power, (they were) willing of themselves;
praying us with much entreaty, that we would receive
the gift, and (take upon us) the fellowship of the ministering to the saints. And (this they did,) not as we
hoped, but first gave their own selves to the Lord, and
unto us by the will of God.

These verses must be taken together on account of the
grammatical construction. Wherever the reader of the English version sees the frequent use of words in Italics, he may
conclude there is some difficulty or obscurity in the original,
which the translators endeavour to explain by additions to the
text. In these verses there are no less than five such interpo-
lations; three of which materially affect the sense, viz., the
words, *they were, take upon us,* and, *this they did.* The first
point is to determine the text. The words δέξασθαι ἡμᾶς are
omitted in the great majority of the MSS. versions and
Fathers, and seem very much like an explanatory gloss, or an
interpolation analogous to the explanations in Italics so common in our version. They are, therefore, rejected by Griesbach, and by almost all editors since his time. Their insertion
alters the sense materially. If these words are read, Paul
represents the Macedonian Christians as begging him to re-

ceive their contributions and to take upon him the distribution
of them. If they are omitted, the sense is, they begged to
be permitted to contribute. Granting, however, that these
words should be omitted, the construction of the passage is
doubtful. Stanley says it is " a sentence which has been entirely shattered in passing through the apostle's mind." He
proposes to reduce it to order in the same way that Bengel
does, who, however, thinks that, so far from the sentence being shattered, every thing is smooth and easy. He says the
word ἔδωκαν sustains the structure of the whole passage;
αὐθαίρετοι and δεόμενοι are its nominatives; χάριν, κοινωνίαν and
ἑαυτοὺς are its objects. The sense then is, ' Of their own accord, beyond their ability and with many prayers they gave
not their gifts only as a contribution to the saints, but themselves to the Lord and to us.' Any one, however, who looks
at the Greek sees that it is very unnatural to make χάριν depend on ἔδωκαν; it belongs to δεόμενοι. The construction,
therefore, adopted by Fritzsche, Billroth, Meyer and others is,
at least as to that point, to be preferred. Meyer says that to
ἔδωκαν there are four limiting or qualifying clauses attached.
They gave, 1. Beyond their power; 2. Of their own motion;
3. Praying to be allowed to give; and 4. Not as we expected,
but themselves. De Wette and many others relieve the
harshness of this construction so far as the last clause is concerned by making the sentence end with the fourth verse, and
supplying ἔδωκαν in v. 3. " They gave beyond their power,
of their own accord, begging to be allowed to take part in
the contribution to the saints. And beyond our expectation
they gave themselves to the Lord."

As to the connection, ὅτι is evidently equivalent to γάρ, as
these verses are the proof of what is said in v. 2. The liberality of the Macedonian churches was great, *for to their
power*, (κατὰ δύναμιν,) according to their ability, I bear testimony, and *beyond their power* (ὑπὲρ in the common text, in
the critical editions παρὰ δύναμιν). Here the word ἔδωκαν is
implied. ' They gave beyond their ability,' αὐθαίρετοι, *self-
moved*, i. e. spontaneously, without any suggestion or excitement from me.' From 9, 2, it appears that Paul had boasted
to the Macedonians that Achaia (the Corinthians) was ready
a year ago, and that this had excited their zeal. These two
representations are perfectly consistent. In detailing the success of the gospel in Corinth the apostle would naturally refer
to the liberality of the disciples. It was the simple mention

of this fact which led the Macedonians, without any exhortation from the apostle, but of their own accord, to make the
contribution of which he here speaks. Our translators by the
insertion of the words *they were* alter the sense of this verse.
They make the apostle say, 'They were willing beyond their
power.' Whereas what he says is, 'They gave spontaneously
beyond their power.' The word ἔδωκαν, *they gave*, though
not expressed until the end of the passage, is clearly implied
from the beginning.

Praying us with much entreaty. The thing for which the
Macedonians so earnestly prayed was, according to the received text and our version, that the apostle would receive
their alms and take upon him the distribution of them. But
by common consent the words δέξασθαι ἡμᾶς (*that we would
receive*) should be omitted, and there is nothing in the Greek
to answer to the interpolated words *take upon us*. The
words are, δεόμενοι ἡμῶν τὴν χάριν καὶ τὴν κοινωνίαν, *begging of
us the favour and fellowship*, (or participation,) i. e. the favour
of a participation. The latter word explains the former; the
favour they asked was that of taking part in *the ministry to
the saints*. The word διακονία, *ministry, service*, is often used
in the sense of *aid* or *relief*. 9, 1. 13. Acts 6, 1. 11, 29. Here,
according to some, the sentence ends. The more common
interpretation supposes καὶ οὐ καθὼς ἠλπίσαμεν to be a new
modification of the principal idea, "and not as we expected,"
i. e. a moderate contribution, *but they first gave their own
selves to the Lord and to us.* This does not mean that they
gave themselves before they gave their alms; but they gave
themselves first to the Lord, then to us; πρῶτον belongs to
κυρίῳ and not to ἔδωκαν. *First* does not mean first in time,
but in importance and order. Compare Acts 15, 28. Exodus 14, 31. The offering was immediately and directly
to Christ, and subordinately to the apostle. By giving
themselves to the Lord the apostle means that not content with giving their money they had given themselves;
made an entire dedication of all they had and all they were
to their divine Master. This was far beyond his expectations. To understand this expression as indicating that
devotion to Christ was the motive which determined their
liberality is inconsistent with the context. Their inward devotion to Christ was not a thing to take the apostle by surprise; that was involved in their profession of the gospel.
What surpassed his expectations was, that their liberality led

to the gift not of their money only but of themselves. Some
say that this means that they offered themselves to go to Corinth or elsewhere to collect money for the poor. But the
sense is fuller and simpler as above explained. *By the will
of God.* That is, the will of God was the cause of their giving themselves to the Lord, &c. It is (διὰ θελήματος, not κατὰ
θέλημα) *by*, not *according to*, the will of God.

6. Insomuch that we desired Titus, that as he had
begun, so he would also finish in you the same grace
also.

Insomuch (εἰς τὸ παρακαλ.) so that we were induced to exhort Titus. Paul, 1 Cor. 16, 1, had urged the Corinthians to
make collections for the poor saints. Titus visited Corinth
after that letter was written and made a beginning in this
work. When Paul came to Macedonia and found how liberally
the churches there had contributed, he urged Titus to return
to Corinth and complete what he had so successfully begun.
The exhortation therefore addressed to Titus, of which the
apostle here speaks, was not the exhortation given him before
the visit from which he had just returned, but that which he
gave him in reference to a renewed visit yet to be made.
Instead therefore of the rendering, *I desired Titus*, it would
would be plainer to translate, *I have desired him.   That* (ἵνα,
not *in order that*, according to the usual force of the particle,
but *that*, as expressing the contents of the request), *as he had
begun*, (προενήρξατο, a word which occurs nowhere but in this
chapter,) *had begun before.* This may mean, 'had already
begun,' i. e. begun before the time of Paul's writing; or, had
begun before the Macedonians made their collections. The
latter is the more probable meaning, since, as appears from
v. 10, the Corinthians had commenced this work before the
Macedonian churches had moved in the business. *So he
would also finish*, i. e. either in the sense of bringing a given
work to an end, Heb. 9, 6, or of perfecting an inward grace,
7, 1. *In you*, εἰς ὑμᾶς, in relation to, or, for you. Matt. 10, 10.
This grace also ; χάριν may here mean either *good work*, or,
grace, in the ordinary sense of the word. The connection
with the following verse is in favour of understanding it in
the latter sense. It was a disposition of the mind that Titus
was exhorted to bring into full exercise among the Corinthi-

ans. The grace spoken of was something which belongs to the same category with faith, knowledge, and love.

7. Therefore, as ye abound in every (thing, in) faith, and utterance, and knowledge, and (in) all diligence, and (in) your love to us, (see) that ye abound in this grace also.

From this verse onward to v. 16 the apostle urges on the Corinthians the duty of liberality. 1. Because it was necessary to the completeness and harmony of their Christian character; 2. Because it would be a proof of their sincerity; 3. Because Christ had become poor for their sake; 4. Because it would redound to their own advantage, inasmuch as consistency required that having manifested the disposition, they should carry it out in action; and 5. Because what was required of them was perfectly reasonable. They were asked to give only according to their means; and what they were called upon to do for others, others under like circumstances would be required to do for them. *Therefore* is not a proper translation of ἀλλά (*but*). The word is often used to mark a transition to a new subject, and specially where what follows is an exhortation or command. Mark 16, 7. Acts 9, 6. 10, 20. *As ye abound*, i. e. have in abundance, or, have more than others, i. e. excel. *In every thing*, (ἐν παντί,) limited of course by the context, and explained by what follows, ‘every gift and grace.’ The same testimony is borne in favour of the Corinthians, 1 Cor. 1, 5. 7. That the apostle sometimes speaks so favourably, and sometimes so unfavourably of the church in Corinth, is to be accounted for by the fact that some of the people were very good, probably the majority, and some, especially among the teachers, very much the reverse. *In faith.* To abound in faith is to have a strong, constant, operative faith, sustaining and controlling the whole inward and outward life. *In utterance and knowledge*, (λόγῳ καὶ γνώσει,) the same combination as in 1 Cor. 1, 5. Here and there our translators have rendered λόγος *utterance ;* in both cases it may mean *doctrine*, as it does in so many passages, especially in such cases as "word of truth," "word of salvation," "word of righteousness," "word of Christ." The meaning, therefore, is either that they were enriched with the gifts of utterance and knowledge, or doctrine and knowledge.

Λόγος is the Christian truth as preached, γνῶσις that truth as apprehended or understood. *In diligence,* (σπουδή,) *earnestness,* a general term for the energy or vigour of their spiritual life, of which their love was one manifestation. In *your love to us.* The expression in Greek is peculiar, τῇ ἐξ ὑμῶν ἐν ἡμῖν ἀγάπῃ, *the love which is of you in us,* i. e. your love (to us) which we cherish in our hearts. That is, which we so highly estimate. Or, simply, *amore a vobis profecto et in me collato. That ye may abound.* The ἵνα περισσ. is most naturally explained by supplying some word as in our version, *See* that ye abound. Compare Gal. 2, 10. *In this grace also,* i. e. the grace of liberality. Others here as in the preceding verse make χάρις mean *good work.* But this is not so consistent with the context. Faith, knowledge, and love are not good works so much as divine gifts, and so also is liberality.

8. I speak not by commandment, but by occasion of the forwardness of others, and to prove the sincerity of your love.

The apostle, agreeably to his usual manner, states first negatively, and then affirmatively, his object in what he had said. It was not of the nature of a command. It was not obedience, but spontaneous liberality he desired. The latter may be excited by the exhibition of appropriate motives, but it cannot be yielded to authority. Almsgiving in obedience to a command, or to satisfy conscience, is not an act of liberality. What is not spontaneous is not liberal. Paul, therefore, would not coerce them by a command. His object was to put the genuineness of their love to the test. The nature of the test was suggested by the zeal of the Macedonians. So it was by the occasion of the forwardness of others he was led to put their love to that trial. The real test of the genuineness of any inward affection is not so much the character of the feeling as it reveals itself in our consciousness, as the course of action to which it leads. Many persons, if they judged themselves by their feelings, would regard themselves as truly compassionate; but a judgment founded on their acts would lead to the opposite conclusion. So many suppose they really love God because they are conscious of feelings which they dignify with that name; yet they do not obey him. It is thereby by the fruits of feeling we must judge of its genuineness both in ourselves and others.

9. For ye know the grace of our Lord Jesus Christ, that though he was rich, yet for your sakes he became poor, that ye through his poverty might be rich.

This verse is a parenthesis, the sentence begun in v. 8 being continued in v. 10. Still the connection between this and the preceding verse is intimate and immediate. There are two things indicated and intended in this verse. That self-sacrifice is the proper test of love. And second, that the example of Christ, and the obligation under which we lie to him, should lead us to do good to others. The apostle evidently combines these two thoughts. 'I desire,' he says, 'to put your love to the test of self-sacrifice, *for* ye know that Christ's love was thus manifested;' and, 'You may well be expected to sacrifice yourselves for others, since Christ gave himself for you.' It is not only the example of Christ which is held up for our imitation; but gratitude to Christ for the infinite blessings we receive from him is presented as the motive to liberality. *For ye know.* The fact referred to including the highest mystery of the gospel, viz., the incarnation of the Son of God, or, the manifestation of God in the flesh, and the love therein manifested, is assumed to be known and acknowledged by all who called themselves Christians. Ye know, says Paul, as all Christians must know, *the grace,* i. e. the unmerited, spontaneous love of *our Lord Jesus Christ.* A combination of the most endearing and exalted appellations. *Our Lord,* i. e. the supreme and absolute Lord whom we acknowledge to be our rightful sovereign and possessor, and who is *ours,* belongs to us, in so far as the care, protection, and support of his almighty power are by his love pledged to us. *Jesus Christ.* He who is our Lord is our Saviour and the Christ, God's anointed, invested by Him with supreme dominion. What belongs of right to the Logos in virtue of his divinity, is constantly represented as given to the Theanthropos. See Heb. 1, 2. *That though,* &c. This clause is explanatory of the former. 'Ye know the grace of our Lord Jesus,' that is, 'Ye know that though he was rich, &c.' The grace consisted in, or was manifested by his becoming poor for our sakes. *Being rich, πλούσιος ὢν,* that is, either, as in our version, *Though he was rich,* in the possession of the glory which he had with the Father before the world was, John 17, 5; or, *Being rich* in the actual and constant possession of all divine prerogatives. In the latter case, the idea is

that our blessed Lord while here on earth, although he had
within himself the fulness of the Godhead and the right and
power of possession over all things, yet was poor. He did
not avail himself of his right and power to make himself rich,
but voluntarily submitted to all the privations of poverty.
The former interpretation is commonly and properly preferred.
The reference in ἐπτώχευσε, *he became poor*, is not to what our
Lord did while he was on earth, but to what he did when he
came into the world. The passage is parallel to Phil. 2, 6.
"Being in the form of God, and equal to God, he emptied
(ἐκένωσε) himself." That is, he so far laid aside the glory of
his divine majesty, that he was to all appearance a man, and
even a servant, so that men refused to recognise him as God,
but despised, persecuted, and at last crucified him, as a man.
He who was rich in the plenitude of all divine attributes and
prerogatives thus became poor, δι᾽ ὑμᾶς, *on your account*, out
of love to you. The end to be accomplished by this humiliation of the Son of God, was that, *you through his poverty
might be rich*. Believers are made rich in the possession of
that glory which Christ laid aside, or concealed. They are
made partakers of the divine nature, 2 Pet. 1, 4. That is, of
the divine holiness, exaltation and blessedness. This is divine
not only because of its source as coming from God, but because of its nature. So that our Lord says, "The glory which
thou gavest me, I have given them," John 17, 22. Hence
believers are said to be glorified with Christ and to reign with
him. Rom. 8, 17. The price of this exaltation and everlasting
blessedness of his people was his own poverty. It is by his
poverty that we are made rich. Unless he had submitted to
all the humiliation of his incarnation and death, we should forever have remained poor, destitute of all holiness, happiness
and glory. It should be observed that moral duties, such as
almsgiving, are in the New Testament enforced not so much
on moral grounds as on grounds peculiarly Christian. No
man can enter into the meaning of this verse or feel its power,
without being thereby made willing to sacrifice himself for
others. And the apostle teaches here, what St. John also
teaches, 1 John 3, 17, that it is vain for any man to profess or
to imagine that he loves Christ, if he does not love the brethren and is not liberal in relieving their wants.

10. And herein I give (my) advice : for this is ex-

pedient for you, who have begun before, not only to do, but also to be forward a year ago.

The connection is with v. 8. 'I do not command, I, in this matter, viz., in making collections for the poor, give my mind;' γνώμην, in the sense of opinion. Comp. 1 Cor. 7, 6. *For this is expedient for you.* This admits of two interpretations. 'I advise you to make the collection, for this giving to the poor is profitable to you. It not only promotes your own moral growth, but it is demanded by consistency. Having begun this work it would be an injury to yourselves to leave it unfinished.' This is the common, and on the whole the preferable explanation. It satisfies all the demands of the context; and it makes ἐν τούτῳ and τοῦτο refer to the same thing. 'In this matter (of giving) I express my opinion, for this (giving) is profitable to you.' Meyer, Billroth and many others make τοῦτο refer to the immediately preceding words. 'I give my advice, for advising is better than commanding in your case, seeing ye were willing a year ago.' This, however, is not demanded by the context, and lowers the sense. The former interpretation brings out a higher truth than the second. It is for our own good to do good. *Who, οἵτινες,* (being such as those who.) 'It is expedient for you, *because ye began before not only to do* (τὸ ποιῆσαι), *but to be forward* (τὸ θέλειν) *a year ago.* As the will precedes the deed, many commentators assume an inversion in these words, and reverse their order. 'Ye began not only to will, but to do.' This is arbitrary and unnecessary. Others, as do our translators, take the word θέλειν in an emphatic sense, to be zealous in doing. Luke 20, 46. John 8, 44. 'Ye began not only to do, but to do with zeal.' This, however, does not agree with the following verse, where θέλειν is used in its ordinary sense. Others again understand ποιῆσαι of the beginning of the work, and the θέλειν of the purpose to do more. But this requires much to be supplied which is not in the text. Besides it does not agree with the qualifying clause 'a year ago.' According to this explanation the θέλειν does not express what had occurred a year ago, but to the state of mind now assumed to exist and subsequent to the doing begun the year before. De Wette, Winer, and Meyer give a much more natural interpretation. The word προενήρξασθε, as in v. 6, refers to the Macedonian churches. 'You anticipated the Macedonians not only in the work but in the purpose.' That is, before they had begun to make a collection for the poor saints, you had begun; and before they thought of it, you had determined to do it. 'Having thus been beforehand with them it would be to your disadvantage to leave your work half done, seeing that the mere mention of your purpose, 9, 2, roused them to such self denying liberality.' *A year ago*, (ἀπὸ πέρυσι.) This does not imply that a whole year had intervened, but is analogous to our popular expression *last year*. If Paul, according to the Jewish reckoning, began the year in October, he could properly speak, when writing in November, of an event which happened in the spring, as having occurred last year. An interval of little more than six months, according to this view, from spring to fall, intervened between the date of the first and second epistles of Paul to the Corinthians.

11. Now therefore perform the doing (of it): that as (there was) a readiness to will, so (there may be) a performance also out of that which ye have.

Now therefore, i. e. as there has been the purpose and the commencement, let there be also the completion of the work. Literally, *complete ye also the doing*. *That*, (ὅπως, in order that,) *as the readiness to will, so also the completion*. Consistency required them to carry out their good intentions openly expressed. *Out of that which ye have*, ἐκ τοῦ ἔχειν, according to (your) property. The preposition ἐκ is not here to be rendered *out of*, but it expresses the rule or standard. Compare John 3, 34. The apostle was not desirous to urge them either beyond their inclination, or beyond their ability. What they gave, he wished them to give freely, and with due regard to their resources.

12. For if there be first a willing mind, (it is) accepted according to that a man hath, (and) not according to that he hath not.

The connection is evidently with the last words of v. 11. They were to give according to their property, *for* the standard of judgment with God is the disposition, not the amount given. The same doctrine is taught by our Lord, Mark 12, 42. *If there be first*, literally, *if there be present;* πρόκειται does not mean *prius adest*, but simply *adest*. *A willing mind,* ἡ προθυμία, *the readiness,* or, *disposition. It is;* that is, the προθυμία (the disposition) *is accepted,* εὐπρόσδεκτος, *acceptable.* It is often used in reference to offerings made to God. Rom. 15, 16. 1 Pet. 2, 5. Some of the ancient MSS. introduce the indefinite pronoun τὶς, as the subject of the verbs ἔχῃ and ἔχει, so our translators insert *man,* 'according to that *a man* hath, and not according to that *he* hath not.' The grammatical subject, however, of all the verbs in the verse is προθυμία, which Paul, according to his custom, personifies, and therefore says, It is acceptable *according to that it may have,* (ἐὰν ἔχῃ,) be it more or less; *not according to that it hath not.* This does not mean that the disposition is not acceptable when it exceeds the ability to give, or leads to extravagant gifts. This may be true, but it is not the idea here intended. The meaning is simply that the disposition is what God regards, and that disposition will be judged of according to the resources at its command. A small gift may manifest in one case much greater willingness to give, than a much larger gift in another.

13. For (I mean) not that other men be eased, and you burdened.

The reason why he did not wish them to exceed their ability in giving, is here stated negatively. The positive statement follows in the next verse. The apostle did not wish to throw an unequal burden upon the Corinthians. He did not desire that others should be released from all obligation to give, and they oppressed by it. Not to others ἄνεσις (relief), and to you θλῖψις (oppression), is his concise expression. According to this view, by ἄλλοις, *others,* we are to understand other churches or Christians; and by ἄνεσις, relief from the obligation to give. But this is consistent neither with what precedes nor with what follows. The equality which he aims at, is not the equality of the churches in giving, but that which arises from the deficiency of one class being made up by the abundance of another. By *others,* therefore, we must understand the poor, and in this case, the poor saints at Jerusalem, and by ἄνεσις *release* from the pressure of poverty, and by θλῖψις the burden of indigence. The meaning therefore is, that Paul did not desire that the Corinthians should go beyond their ability in giving, for he had no wish that others should be enriched, and they impoverished. It is

not obligatory on the rich to make themselves poor in order
that the poor may be rich.   That is not the rule.

14. But by an equality, (that) now at this time
your abundance (may be a supply) for their want, that
their abundance also may be (a supply) for your want:
that there may be equality.

The word ἰσότης means here neither reciprocity nor equity,
but equality, as the illustration in v. 15 shows. The ἐκ, as in
v. 11, (ἐκ τοῦ ἔχειν,) expresses the rule or standard in giving.
That rule is equality; we must give so as to produce, or that
there may be, equality. This is not agrarianism, nor community of goods. The New Testament teaches on this subject,
1. That all giving is voluntary. A man's property is his own.
It is in his own power to retain or to give away; and if he
gives, it is his prerogative to decide whether it shall be much
or little. Acts 5, 4. This is the doctrine taught in this whole
connection. Giving must be voluntary. It is the fruit of
love. It is of course obligatory as a moral duty, and the indisposition to give is proof of the absence of the love of God.
1 John 3, 17. Still it is one of those duties the performance
of which others cannot enforce as a right belonging to them.
It must remain at our own discretion. 2. That the end to be
accomplished by giving is relieving the necessities of the poor.
The equality, therefore, aimed at, or intended, is not an
equality as to the amount of property, but equal relief from
the burden of want. This is taught in the remainder of this
verse. 'At the present time,' says the apostle, 'let your
abundance be to (γένηται εἰς, extend to, be imparted to, Gal.
3, 14,) their want, in order that their abundance may be to
your want, that there may be equality;' that is, an equal
relief from want or destitution. 3. A third scriptural principle on this subject is, that while all men are brethren, and the
poor as poor, whether Christians or not, are the proper objects
of charity, yet there is a special obligation resting on the
members of Christ to relieve the wants of their fellow-believers. We are to do good to all men, says the apostle, specially to those who are of the household of faith. Gal. 6, 10. All
the directions in this and the following chapter have reference
to the duty of Christians to their fellow-believers. There are
two reasons for this. The one is the common relation of be-

lievers to Christ as members of his body, so that what is done
to them is done to him; and their consequent intimate relation
to each other as being one body in Christ Jesus. The other
is, the assurance that the good done to them is pure good.
There is no apprehension that the alms bestowed will encourage idleness or vice. 3. A fourth rule is designed to prevent
any abuse of the brotherhood of Christians. The poor have
no right to depend on the benefactions of the rich because
they are brethren. This same apostle says, "This we commanded you, that if any man would not work, neither should
he eat," 2 Thess. 3, 10. Thus do the Scriptures avoid, on the
one hand, the injustice and destructive evils of agrarian com-
munism, by recognising the right of property and making all
almsgiving optional; and on the other, the heartless disregard
of the poor by inculcating the universal brotherhood of believers, and the consequent duty of each to contribute of his
abundance to relieve the necessities of the poor. At the same
time they inculcate on the poor the duty of self-support to the
extent of their ability. They are commanded "with quietness
to work, and to eat their own bread." Could these principles
be carried out there would be among Christians neither idleness nor want.

15. As it is written, He that (had gathered) much
had nothing over; and he that (had gathered) little
had no lack.

The moral lesson taught in Exodus 16, 18, is that which
the apostle had just inculcated. There it is recorded that the
people, by the command of God, gathered of the manna an
omer for each person. Those who gathered more retained
only the allotted portion; and those who gathered less had
their portion increased to the given standard. There was as
to the matter of necessary food an equality. If any one attempted to hoard his portion, it spoiled upon his hands. The
lesson therefore taught in Exodus and by Paul is, that, among
the people of God, the superabundance of one should be employed in relieving the necessities of others; and that any attempt to countervail this law will result in shame and loss.
Property is like manna, it will not bear hoarding.

16. But thanks (be) to God, which put the same
earnest care into the heart of Titus for you.

From this verse to the end of the chapter the apostle commends to the confidence of the Corinthians Titus and the two brethren who were to accompany him on his return to Corinth. The object of Titus's first visit was to ascertain the state of the church, and specially the effect of Paul's former epistle. The object of this mission was to bring to an end the collection for the poor which the Corinthians had so long under consideration. Titus had as much zeal in this matter as Paul, and therefore the apostle thanks God *which put into the heart of Titus ;* τῷ διδόντι ἐν, 'Thanks to God giving in, i. e. giving to be in, the heart of Titus.' *The same earnest care for you ;* τὴν αὐτὴν σπουδήν, the same zeal, i. e. the same zeal which I have for you. Titus felt the same interest in the spiritual welfare of the Corinthians, and the same solicitude that they should act consistently, that Paul had so warmly expressed in the foregoing verses. Often, as the occasion offers, it is still well to notice how uniformly the Scriptures take for granted two great fundamental truths which human philosophy finds it hard to comprehend or to admit. The one is that God can and does control the inward acts and feelings of men without interfering either with their liberty or responsibility. The zeal of Titus was the spontaneous effusion of his own heart and was an index and element of his character. Yet God put that zeal into his heart. This is not a figure of speech. It was a simple and serious truth, a ground of solemn thanksgiving to God. The other great truth is that the believer is dependent on God for the continuance and exercise of spiritual life. The Holy Spirit does not regenerate the soul by implanting in it a new principle of life, and then leave that principle to struggle in its own strength for existence and growth. On the contrary, the new birth is the beginning of a constant indwelling of God in the soul, so that both the continuance and exercise of this new life are due to his presence. Yet so congenial and congruous is this divine influence that the life of God in us is in the highest sense our own life.

17. For indeed he accepted the exhortation ; but being more forward, of his own accord he went unto you.

This is the proof of the zeal of Titus. Some commentators assume that μέν and δέ are here used instead of οὐ μόνον—ἀλλά, 'Not only did he listen to our exhortation, but fulfilled it with

greater zeal as he went forth willingly.' But Meyer gives a
better explanation. 'He accepted indeed our exhortation,
i. e. he modestly submitted himself to my direction, but being
too zealous (σπουδαιότερος) to need an exhortation, he went of
his own accord.' He did not require to be urged to go, although in this, as in other matters, he was willing to do as I
wished. *He went unto you.* Titus was no doubt the bearer
of this epistle, and was with the apostle when it was written.
He had not yet gone forth. In epistolary style the writer
may use the tense suited to his own position, or to that of his
readers. Paul here, and in the following verses, uses the past
tense, because when his epistle came to hand the events referred to would be past.

18. And we have sent with him the brother, whose
praise (is) in the gospel throughout all the churches.

We have sent. The time is from the stand-point of the
reader, as before. *We send with him the brother.* As the
name is not given, and as no data are furnished by which to
determine who the brother here mentioned was, it is useless
to conjecture. It was some one subordinate to Titus sent
with him as a companion, some one well known throughout
the churches, and who had especially the confidence of the
Macedonian Christians, v. 19. But these conditions meet in
so many of the persons mentioned in the Acts or Paul's epistles that they lead to no certain conclusion. Whether, therefore, it was Luke, Mark, Trophimus, or some one else, must be
left undecided. The question is hardly worth the trouble
which commentators have devoted to it. This brother's
praise is said to have been *in the gospel.* He was distinguished by his efforts in that sphere; that is, by his zeal and
labour in promoting the gospel. *Through all the churches.*
If this be taken with the limitation of all the churches of
Macedonia, it still is evidence that the brother referred to was
specially entitled to the confidence of the Corinthians.

19. And not (that) only, but who was also chosen
of the churches to travel with us with this grace, which
is administered by us to the glory of the same Lord,
and (declaration of) your ready mind.

This brother was entitled to confidence, and might safely be intrusted with the contributions of the Corinthians, not only on the ground of his general reputation, but also because he had been elected for the very purpose of taking charge, together with Paul, of the money collected for the saints. *Chosen*, χειροτονηθείς, literally, chosen by the stretching out the hand, therefore popularly. The word, however, is constantly used for selection or appointment without reference to the mode. Thus Josephus speaks of the king as having been ὑπὸ τοῦ θεοῦ κεχειροτονημένος. Ant. vi. 4. 2. See Wetstein. *Of the churches*, probably by the churches of Macedonia. *To travel with us*, συνέκδημος ἡμῶν, i. e. elected our travelling companion. Acts 19, 29. *With this grace.* The word χάρις means either the disposition, or that which is its expression or manifestation, i. e. either kindness or a kindness. Any free gift is therefore a grace. Here the grace intended is the alms collected for the poor. *Which is ministered by us*, i. e. of which we are the administrators. Paul had undertaken to administer the benefactions of the Gentile Christians among the brethren at Jerusalem, and the brother referred to had been chosen to travel with him and assist him in this service or ministry. *To the glory of the same Lord*, i. e. of our common Lord. The natural construction of this clause is with the immediately preceding words. 'This gift is administered by us to the glory of the Lord.' The only objection to this is that it requires the preposition πρός to be taken as expressing different relations in the same sentence. 'Administered πρὸς δόξαν . . . . καὶ προθυμίαν ὑμῶν (or, ἡμῶν), i. e. to promote the glory of the Lord and to prove your readiness.' Meyer and others therefore refer the clause to χειροτονηθείς; 'chosen that by his co-operation Christ may be honoured and my (ἡμῶν) readiness to labour in the gospel, unincumbered by such cares, may have free scope.' But this is unnatural, and supposes too much to be supplied to make out the sense. If the common text, which reads ὑμῶν, be retained, the sense is plain as expressed in our version. 'The ministration of this gift is for the manifestation of the glory of Christ and of your readiness or alacrity (in giving).' The oldest manuscripts as well as the ancient versions, however, read ἡμῶν, which almost all the modern editors adopt. The sense then is, that the gift served to promote the glory of Christ and to prove the apostle's willingness to serve the poor.

20. Avoiding this, that no man should blame us in this abundance which is administered by us.

The participle στελλόμενοι depends on the verb συνεπέμψαμεν of the verse 18. 'We sent the brother with Titus, avoiding this;' that is, in order to avoid. It was not, however, merely the appointment of a brother to accompany Titus, but also the designation of that brother to take part in the distribution of the alms of the churches that Paul had determined upon in order to prevent misrepresentation. The reference is therefore to the whole preceding sentence. The word στέλλειν, literally, to place, means also to set in order, to prepare, a sense which some adopt here. 'Preparing for, taking care with regard to, this.' The word also means to withdraw, to contract, and hence to avoid, which best suits this place as well as 2 Thess. 3, 6, where the word also occurs. *Lest any one should blame us.* He was determined not to give any one the opportunity to call his integrity into question. *In this abundance which is administered by us;* i. e. in the disposition of the large sums of money committed to his charge. The word ἁδρότης means ripeness, fulness, and then abundance; the nature of which is of course determined by the context.

21. Providing for honest things, not only in the sight of the Lord, but also in the sight of men.

This gives the reason for the precaution just mentioned. It was not enough for the apostle to do right, he recognised the importance of appearing right. It is a foolish pride which leads to a disregard of public opinion. We are bound to act in such a way that not only God, who sees the heart and knows all things, may approve our conduct, but also so that men may be constrained to recognise our integrity. It is a general principle regulating his whole life which the apostle here announces. Προνοούμενος, *providing for in one's own behalf.* The apostle says, He took care beforehand that men as well as God should see that he was honest. Compare Rom. 12, 17, and Prov. 3, 4, in the LXX.

22. And we have sent with them our brother, whom we have oftentimes proved diligent in many

things, but now much more diligent, upon the great
confidence which (I have) in you.

Who this second brother was whom Paul sent to accompany Titus and his fellow-traveller, there is no means of determining. The apostle had proved him to be σπουδαῖον, earnest
or diligent, ἐν πολλοῖς πολλάκις, in many things many times.
But now, i. e. on this occasion, *much more diligent* or *earnest*.
His zeal and alacrity was greatly excited *by the confidence
which he has in regard to you.* He was so assured of success
that he entered on his mission with the greatest earnestness.
This interpretation, which most commentators adopt, and
which in our English Bibles is suggested in the margin, is
more natural than that preferred by Calvin, Beza and others.
They connect the word πεποιθήσει with συνεπέμψαμεν, 'We
sent the brother with them; . . . on account of the confidence
we have in you.' This, however, was not the reason for the
mission; nor does it suit the context to say, 'we sent him with
confidence.' The position of the words is in favour of the
explanation first mentioned.

23. Whether (any do inquire) of Titus, (he is) my
partner and fellow-helper concerning you : or our brethren (be inquired of, they are) the messengers of the
churches, (and) the glory of Christ.

This is a recapitulation, or summary commendation. The
language in the original is very concise. *Whether concerning
Titus*, i. e. whether I speak of Titus; or, Whether any do inquire concerning Titus; or, without supplying any thing, 'As
to Titus.' *He is my partner*, κοινωνός, my associate, one who
has a part with me in a common ministry. *And*, specially,
as concerns you my fellow-laborer (συνεργός). *Whether our
brethren*, (they are) *the messengers* (ἀπόστολοι) *of the churches.*
The word apostle is here obviously used in its literal, and not
in its official sense. These men were surely not apostles in
the sense in which Paul was. In like manner, in Phil. 2, 25,
Epaphroditus is called the apostle of the Philippians, because
he was their messenger sent to minister to Paul at Rome.
Both the brethren, therefore, above mentioned, and not only
the one of whom it is said specially that he was chosen by the
churches, were delegated by the people. They are further
said to be *the glory of Christ.* As Christ alone, says Calvin,

is the glory of believers, so he is glorified by them. They reflect his glory. They by their holiness lead men to see the excellence of Christ whose image they bear.

24. Wherefore shew ye to them, and before the churches, the proof of your love, and of our boasting on your behalf.

In conclusion the apostle exhorts the Corinthians to prove to these messengers so worthy of their confidence their love, and the truth of the favourable testimony which he had borne to their liberality. *Show the proof* (τὴν ἔνδειξιν . . ἐνδείξασθε) *of your love.* This may mean, 'your love to me;' or, 'your Christian love;' or, as is most natural, 'your love to them.' Give them evidence of your love, i. e. receive them with affectionate confidence; and let them see that my boasting of you was true. *Before the churches ;* that is, so that the churches, by whom these brethren were sent, may see the proof of your love. Instead of the received text, which has the imperative ἐνδείξασθε, Lachmann, Tischendorf, Meyer and others, after the older MSS., read ἐνδεικνύμενοι. 'Exhibiting the evidence of your love, &c., (do it) in the presence of the churches.' This whole chapter proves how intimately the early Christians were bound together, not only from the intercourse here shown to exist between the several churches, but from the influence which they exerted over each other, from their brotherly love and sympathy, and from the responsibility which each is assumed to owe to the judgment of the others.

CHAPTER IX.

An exhortation to the Corinthians not to falsify his boasting of their liberality, vs. 1–5. An exhortation to give not only liberally but cheerfully, vs. 6–15.

Continuation of the discourse in the preceding chapter on making collections for the saints.

ALTHOUGH aware of their readiness, the apostle sent the brethren to bring the collection for the poor to an end, lest when the Macedonians who were to accompany him to Cor-

inth arrived, they should find them unprepared, not so much
to their disgrace, as to his mortification, vs. 1–4. He sent the
brethren, therefore, that every thing they intended to do
might be done in time, and be done cheerfully, v. 5. It was
not only liberality, but cheerfulness in giving that the Lord
required, vs. 6. 7. God who commanded them to give could
and would supply their wants, and increase their graces.
They would be the richer and the better for what they gave,
vs. 8–10. What he had at heart was not so much that the
temporal sufferings of the poor should be relieved, as that God
might be glorified by the gratitude and mutual love of believers, and by the exhibition of their Christian graces, vs. 10–14.
What are our gifts to the poor compared to the gift of Christ
to us? v. 15.

1. For as touching the ministering to the saints, it
is superfluous for me to write to you.

This is not a new paragraph, much less, as some have conjectured, a separate writing. It is intimately connected with
the preceding. In the last verse of chapter 8, he exhorted them
to receive the brethren with confidence, *for indeed* it is superfluous to write about the collection. He exhorted them to
show their love to the brethren who were to visit them, for
they needed no exhortation to liberality. This is another of
those exhibitions of urbanity and rhetorical skill with which
the epistles of Paul abounds. The δέ answering to the μέν of
this verse is by some said to be found in verse 3. 'It is not
necessary *indeed* to write, *but* I send, &c.' Or, if the connection between vs. 2 and 3 forbid this, the μέν may be taken as
standing alone, as in 1 Cor. 5, 3. 11, 18. So De Wette. Concerning the *ministering* (περὶ τῆς διακονίας.) The word is often
used not only for the ministry of the word, but also for the
service rendered in the collection and distribution of alms.
Acts 6, 1. 12, 25. Rom. 15, 31. *To the saints.* All believers
are called ἅγιοι in the sense of *sacred*, i. e. separated from the
world and consecrated to God, and as inwardly renewed and
purified by the Holy Spirit. 8, 4. Acts 9, 13. Rom. 1, 7. 8, 27.
The saints referred to were of course the poor believers in
Jerusalem for whose benefit Paul instituted this collection in
the several churches which he had founded. 1 Cor. 16, 1–3.
It is superfluous for me (περισσόν μοι ἐστί) *to write* (τὸ γράφειν,
the infinitive has the article because it is the subject of the

sentence) *unto you.* Paul had written and was about to write still further on the subject; so that this is to be understood as only a polite intimation that his writing, so far as they were concerned, was not necessary. They did not need urging.

2. For I know the forwardness of your mind, for which I boast of you to them of Macedonia, that Achaia was ready a year ago; and your zeal hath provoked very many.

The reason why it was superfluous to write to them was that they were disposed to act spontaneously. The apostle says he knew their *forwardness of mind,* ($\pi\rho o\vartheta\upsilon\mu\iota\alpha\nu,$) their readiness or disposition to give. *For which I boast* ($\mathring{\eta}\nu\ \kappa\alpha\nu$-$\chi\mathring{\omega}\mu\alpha\iota,$ see 11, 30 for the same construction) *of you* ($\upsilon\pi\grave{\epsilon}\rho\ \upsilon\mu\mathring{\omega}\nu,$ for you, to your advantage). Their readiness to give was a matter of which Paul at that time boasted to the Macedonians among whom he then was. This does not imply that the apostle regarded their liberal disposition an honour to himself, as though it owed its existence to his agency. We are said to boast of the good qualities of a friend when we proclaim them to his honour and not our own. *That Achaia was ready a year ago.* This was Paul's boast, All the Christians in Achaia belonged to the church in Corinth, although they did not all reside in that city. See 1, 1. *Was ready,* i. e. to take part in a collection for the saints. He does not mean that the collection had already been completed, so that nothing remained to be done. The context does not justify the disparaging supposition that Paul, to excite the emulation of the Macedonian Christians, had overstated the fact as to the Corinthians, representing them as having already a year ago made their collection. *The readiness* to which he here refers is the readiness of purpose. They were fully prepared to take part in the work. Others say the apostle had told the Macedonians that the Corinthians had made their collection and were ready to hand over the money. Those who have sufficient respect for themselves not to speak disrespectfully of the apostle, say that he truly believed this to be the fact, and was now solicitous that the Corinthians should not falsify his assertion by being unprepared. Others, however, as Rückert, (and in a measure De Wette,) represent the apostle as dishonestly telling to the Macedonians that the Corinthians had made

their collection, and now to save his credit, he begged the
latter to finish the work before he and his Macedonian friends
arrived. The whole body of Paul's epistles is a refutation of
this interpretation. No man who is capable of receiving the
true impress of his exalted character can suppose him guilty
of false statement or duplicity. What he told the Macedonians was simply that the Corinthians *were prepared*. What
preparation is meant is plain from the context. It consisted
in their προθυμία, their alacrity of mind to take part in the
work. *A year ago*, 8, 10. *And your zeal*, i. e. your προθυμία,
alacrity, in this business. The words are ὁ ἐξ ὑμῶν ζῆλος, where
the ἐκ may be considered redundant, as our translators have
assumed it to be; or, it may be omitted from the text, as by
Lachmann; or, the meaning is, the zeal which emanated from
you. This last is to be preferred. *Hath provoked*. The
word ἐρεθίζειν means to excite, whether the feeling called into
exercise be good or bad. In Col. 3, 21, fathers are cautioned
not to provoke their children. Here the meaning is that the
zeal of the Corinthians had excited the zeal of others. *Very
many*, τοὺς πλείονας, the majority, the greater number. Acts
19, 32. It was not every individual of the Macedonian Christians, but the majority of them, whom the zeal of the Corinthians had excited.

3. Yet have I sent the brethren, lest our boasting
of you should be in vain in this behalf; that, as I said,
ye may be ready.

If the connection is with v. 1, the δέ here answers to the
μέν there. 'There is no need to write, *but* I send, &c.' The
reference, however, may be to v. 2. 'I boasted of your preparation, *but* lest my boasting be falsified, I send, &c.' *The
brethren*, viz., Titus and his two companions, who were about
to proceed to Corinth to attend to this matter. Lest our
boasting of you *be in vain*, κενωθῇ, be proved unfounded,
1 Cor. 9, 15, i. e. shown to be an empty boast. *In this behalf*.
Paul did not fear that the good account which he had given
of the Corinthians in other matters should be contradicted by
the facts, but only in this one affair of the collection for the
poor. *That, as I said, ye may be ready*. This clause is parallel with the preceding. 'I sent the brethren that my boasting be not found vain, i. e. I sent them that ye may be ready.'

It appears from 8, 10 that the Corinthians had avowed the purpose to make a collection for the poor at Jerusalem, and had actually begun the work a year ago. Paul had mentioned this fact to the Macedonians, telling them that the Corinthians were ready to do their part in this business. He now sends Titus and the brethren that the work may at once be completed, and his boasting of them prove to be true. It is plain that he could not have told the Macedonians that the collection at Corinth had already been made, because he not only knew that such was not the fact, but he in this very passage refers to the work as yet to be accomplished. He could hardly say, 'I told the Macedonians you had made your collection a year ago and had the money all ready to hand over,' at the very moment he was urging them to collect it. The simple fact is that he had said the Corinthians were ready to do their part in this business, and he begged them to do at once what they intended to do, lest his boasting of their readiness (προθυμία) should prove to have been unfounded. There is nothing in this inconsistent with perfect truthfulness and open-hearted fairness.

4. Lest haply if they of Macedonia come with me, and find you unprepared, we (that we say not, ye) should be ashamed in this same confident boasting.

Paul was attended from city to city by travelling companions, who conducted him on his way and ministered to him. 1 Cor. 16, 6. Rom. 15, 24. Acts 17, 14. 15. &c. As he was now in Macedonia it was in accordance with the usual custom that Macedonians should attend him to Corinth. *If they come with me*, ἐὰν ἔλθωσιν, *shall have come*, i. e. 'Lest when they come *and find you unprepared*, i. e. unprepared to do what a year ago you professed your readiness to do, *we (that we say not, you) should be ashamed*. The failure would indeed be a cause of shame to the Corinthians, but he delicately substitutes himself. He appeals to their better feelings when he calls upon them to save him from mortification, instead of exhorting them to save themselves from disgrace. *In this same confident boasting*. The words τῆς καυχήσεως are omitted by almost all the recent editors from Griesbach down. They are not found in the MSS. B, C, D, F, G, or the ancient versions. They probably were added by a transcriber from

11, 17. These words being omitted, the text stands, ἐν τῇ ὑποσ-τάσει ταύτῃ, *in this confidence*, i. e. ashamed in relation to this confidence. Comp. Heb. 3, 14. 11, 1. Others take the word in the sense of *negotium*, "in this thing," which is not only unnecessary, but contrary to usage.

5. Therefore I thought it necessary to exhort the brethren, that they would go before unto you, and make up beforehand your bounty, whereof ye had notice before, that the same might be ready, as (a matter of) bounty, and not as (of) covetousness.

Therefore, i. e. in order to avoid the mortification of his boasting being proved vain. *I thought it necessary to exhort the brethren*, (Titus and his companions,) *that they would go before ;* (παρακαλέσαι—ἵνα, as in 8, 6, and often elsewhere, ἵνα is used after verbs signifying to ask, exhort, &c., in the sense of ὅτι.) *Would go before*, i. e. before Paul and his Macedonian companions. *And make up beforehand*, προκαταρτίσωσι, a word not found in the Greek writers, and occurring in the New Testament only in this passage. The simple verb means, to put fully in order, to complete. This the brethren were to do in reference to the collection, before Paul's arrival. *Your bounty*, τὴν εὐλογίαν ὑμῶν, *your blessing*. The word is used in the sense both of benediction and benefaction. The latter is clearly its meaning here, as perhaps also in Rom. 15, 29 ; see also Eph. 1, 3, and in the LXX. Gen. 33, 11. Judges 1, 15. 1 Sam. 25, 27, &c. So in English, *a blessing* is either a prayer for good, or the good itself. *Whereof ye had notice before.* Here the reading is doubtful. The common text has προκα-τηγγελμένην, *announced beforehand*. Not, however, as our translation has it, announced *to you*, but to others. The benefaction before spoken of, i. e. of which so much has been said. Almost all the critical editions read προεπηγγελμένην, *promised beforehand*, 'your promised benefaction.' And this gives a better sense, as the apostle was urging them to do what they had promised. *That the same might be ready as* a matter of *bounty ;* οὕτως ὡς εὐλογίαν, *so as a blessing*, i. e. as something worthy of the name. This may mean, 'worthy of the name because the fruit of love ;' or, because given freely ; or, because rich, abundant. This last is to be preferred because of the antithesis between εὐλογία and πλεονεξία, because

of the explanation in v. 6, and because cheerfulness in giving
is afterwards enforced. *And not as* of *covetousness;* literally,
not as covetousness, i. e. not such a gift as betrays the avarice
of the giver.

6. But this (I say), He which soweth sparingly,
shall reap also sparingly; and he which soweth bountifully, shall reap also bountifully.

The words τοῦτο δέ, *but this*, are commonly and most naturally explained by supplying some such words as *I say*, or,
consider. Others take them as the accusative absolute; 'as
to this, however.' Meyer unnaturally makes τοῦτο the object
of σπείρων, 'He who sows this sparingly, &c.' That is, in other cases it may be different, but in this spiritual sowing, in
this seed of good deeds, the rule always holds good. Our
version gives a simple and suitable sense. The only question
of doubt in the verse is the meaning of the words ἐπ᾽ εὐλογίαις,
which our translators have rendered adverbially, *bountifully*.
'He that sows bountifully, shall reap also bountifully.' This
undoubtedly is the meaning as determined by the antithesis,
'He that sows φειδομένως *sparingly*, and he that sows ἐπ᾽ εὐλογίαις *bountifully*.' But the question is how to get that sense
out of the words, which literally mean *with blessings*. 'He
that sows *with blessings*, shall reap *with blessings*.' The force
of the preposition ἐπί with the dative in this place may be explained after the analogy of such passages as Rom. 4, 18.
1 Cor. 9, 10; ἐπ᾽ ἐλπίδι, *with hope*, as expressing the condition
under which any thing is done; or after the analogy of such
places as Rom. 5, 14, ἐπὶ τῷ ὁμοιώματι, *after the similitude*, as
expressing the rule according to which it is done. In either
case, the preposition and noun may express an adverbial qualification. In this case therefore, ἐπ᾽ εὐλογίαις, *ad normam bene-
ficiorum*, as Wahl translates it, may, as the context requires,
mean kindly, freely, or bountifully. Here, as just stated, the
antithesis with φειδομένως requires the last, viz., bountifully.
The sentiment here expressed is the same as in Prov. 11, 24,
"There is that scattereth and yet increaseth; and there is that
withholdeth more than is meet, but it tendeth to poverty."
It is comprehended also in the wider truth taught in Gal. 6, 7.
Our Lord teaches the same doctrine, Luke 6, 38, "Give and it
shall be given unto you, &c." Matt. 10, 41, and often else-

where. It is edifying to notice the difference between the divine wisdom and the wisdom of men. As the proper motive to acts of benevolence is a desire for the happiness of others and a regard to the will of God, human wisdom says it is wrong to appeal to any selfish motive. The wisdom of God, while teaching the entire abnegation of self, and requiring a man even to hate his own life when in conflict with the glory of God, tells all who thus deny themselves that they thereby most effectually promote their own interests. He that loses his life shall save it. He that does not seek his own, shall best secure his own. He that humbleth himself shall be exalted. There can, however, be no hypocrisy in this matter. It is not the man who pretends to deny himself, to humble himself, or to seek the good of others rather than his own, while he acts from a regard to self, who is to be thus rewarded. It is only those who sincerely postpone themselves to others, who shall be preferred before them. We may thence learn that it is right to present to men the divinely ordained consequences of their actions as motives to control their conduct. It is right to tell men that obedience to God, devotion to his glory and the good of others, will effectually promote their own welfare.

7. Every man according as he purposeth in his heart, (so let him give;) not grudgingly, or of necessity: for God loveth a cheerful giver.

Though he wished them to give bountifully, he desired them to do it freely. Let each one give *as he purposes in his heart*, i. e. as he cordially, or with the consent of the heart, determines. This stands opposed to what follows, and, therefore, is explained by it. *Not grudgingly*, ἐκ λύπης, not out of sorrow; i. e. let not the gift proceed out of a reluctant state of mind, grieving after what is given as so much lost. *Or of necessity*, i. e. constrained by circumstances to give, when you prefer not to do it. Many gifts are thus given sorrowfully, where the giver is induced to give by a regard to public opinion, or by stress of conscience. This reluctance spoils the gift. It loses all its fragrance when the incense of a free and joyful spirit is wanting. *For God loveth a cheerful giver;* ἱλαρὸν δότην, *a joyful giver*, one to whom giving is a delight, who does it with hilarity. The passage is quoted from Prov. 22, 9, where the Hebrew means, "A good eye shall be

blessed." The LXX. renders the words *quoad sensum*, ἄνδρα
ἱλαρὸν καὶ δότην εὐλογεῖ ὁ θεός; a version which Paul adopts for
substance. God blesses, loves, delights in, the joyous giver.
Let not, therefore, those who give reluctantly, or from stress
of circumstances, or to secure merit, imagine that mere giving
is acceptable to God. Unless we feel it is an honour and a
joy to give, God does not accept the offering.

8. And God (is) able to make all grace abound
toward you ; that ye, always having all sufficiency in
all (things), may abound to every good work.

From this verse to the 11th, the apostle assures them that
the liberal and cheerful giver will always have something to
give. *God is able.* The sacred writers often appeal to the
power of God as a ground of confidence to his people. Rom.
16, 25. Eph. 3, 20. Jude 24. This is done especially when
we are called upon to believe something which is contrary to
the natural course of things. Giving is, to the natural eye,
the way to lessen our store, not to increase it. The Bible
says it is the way to increase it. To believe this it is only
necessary to believe in the power, providence, and promise
of God. God is able to make the paradox, "he that scattereth, increaseth," prove true. *God is able to make all grace
abound ;* χάριν, favour, gift, whether temporal or spiritual, or
both, depends on the context. Here the reference is clearly
to earthly good; that kind of good or favour is intended
which enables those who receive it to give abundantly. The
idea, therefore, obviously is, 'God is able to increase your
wealth.' *That ye, having all sufficiency in all things.* The
expression here is striking, ἐν παντὶ πάντοτε πᾶσαν, *in all things*,
always, all. God is able so to enrich you that you shall have
in every respect, at all times, all kinds of sufficiency. The
word is αὐτάρκειαν, which everywhere else means *contentment*.
This sense Grotius, Meyer and others retain here. 'That having full contentment,' i. e. being fully satisfied and not craving
more, you may, &c. This, however, is not so well suited to
the context, and especially to the qualifying words, ἐν παντί.
It is 'a competency in every thing' of which the apostle
speaks. *That ye may abound*, περισσεύητε, *may have abundance.* Phil. 4, 18. The word is used transitively in the first
clause of the verse and intransitively in the last. ' God is able

to cause your riches to abound, that ye may have abundance *to every good work ;'* εἰς πᾶν ἔργον ἀγαθόν, in reference to, so as to be able to perform every good work. The logical connection is not with the intermediate participial clause, 'that having sufficiency, ye may have abundance,' but with the first clause, 'God is able to cause your resources to abound, that ye may have abundance.' The participial clause expresses simply what, notwithstanding their liberality, would be the result. Having (i. e. still having) a competency for yourselves, ye will have abundance for every good work. There is another interpretation of this passage which the English version naturally suggests. 'That ye may abound in every good work.' But this the Greek will not admit ; because it is εἰς πᾶν, κ.τ.λ., and not ἐν παντί, κ.τ.λ. See 1 Cor. 15, 58. Besides, the other interpretation is better suited to the context.

9. As it is written, He hath dispersed abroad ; he hath given to the poor : his righteousness remaineth forever.

The connection is with the last clause of the preceding verse. Paul had said that he who gives shall have abundance to give. This is precisely what is said in Psalm 112. Of the man who fears God it is there said, "Wealth and riches shall be in his house." "He showeth favour, and lendeth." "He hath dispersed, he hath given to the poor ; his righteousness endureth forever." The main idea the apostle designs to present as having the sanction of the word of God is, that he who is liberal, who disperses, scatters abroad his gifts with free-handed generosity, as a man scatters seed, shall always have abundance. And this the Psalmist expressly asserts. It may be said that this is not in accordance with experience. We do not always see liberality attended by riches. This is a difficulty not peculiar to this case. The Bible is full of declarations concerning the blessedness of the righteous, and of the providential favours which attend their lot. This Psalm says, "Wealth and riches," or, as the LXX. and Vulgate have it, "Glory and riches shall be in their house;" and our Lord says, that those who forsake all for him shall in this life receive an hundred-fold, houses, lands, &c. Mark 10, 30. These passages were not designed to be taken literally or applied universally. They teach three things. 1st. The tendency of things. It is the tendency of righteousness to produce bless-

edness, as it is the tendency of evil to produce misery. 2d.
The general course of divine providence. God in his providence does as a general rule prosper the diligent and bless
the righteous. Honesty is the best policy, is a maxim even
of worldly wisdom. 3d. Even in this life righteousness produces a hundred-fold more good than unrighteousness does.
A righteous man is a hundred-fold more happy than a wicked
man, other things being equal. A good man is a hundred-fold
more happy in sickness, in poverty, in bereavement, than a
wicked man in the same circumstances. It is, therefore, according to Scripture, a general law, that he that scattereth,
increaseth; he that gives shall have wherewith to give.

His righteousness (i. e. the righteousness of the man who
gives to the poor) *endureth forever.* The word δικαιοσύνη,
righteousness, in Scripture, is often used in a comprehensive
sense, including all moral excellence; and of,en in a restricted
sense for rectitude or justice. When used in the comprehensive sense, it depends on the context what particular form of
goodness is intended. To return a poor man's pledge is an
act of δικαιοσύνη, Deut. 24, 13; so is giving alms, Matt. 6, 1
(where the true reading is δικαιοσύνην, and not ἐλεημοσύνην).
In like manner the "glory of God" may mean the sum of his
divine perfections, or his wisdom, power, or mercy, as special
forms of his glory, as the context requires. In this passage it
is plain that righteousness means general excellence or virtue,
as manifested in beneficence. And when it is said that his
beneficence shall continue forever, the implication is that he
shall always have wherewith to be beneficent. And this is
here the main idea. He shall always be prosperous; or, as it
is expressed at the close of v. 8, he shall have abundance for
every good work. *Forever* is equivalent to *always,* as εἰς τὸν
αἰῶνα is often used for indefinite duration. Whether the
duration be absolutely without limit, or whether the limit be
unknown or undetermined, depends in each case on the nature
of the thing spoken of, and on the analogy of Scripture.

10. Now, he that ministereth seed to the sower,
both minister bread for (your) food, and multiply your
seed sown, and increase the fruits of your righteousness.

Now; δέ is continuative. God is able to give you abund

ance, *and* he will do it. This verse is a declaration, and not a
wish. Our translation, which makes it a prayer, is founded
on the Elzevir, or common text, which reads χορηγήσαι, πληθύ-
ναι, αὐξήσαι in the optative, instead of the futures χορηγήσει,
πληθυνεῖ, αὐξήσει, which are supported by a great preponder-
ance of authorities, and are adopted by Griesbach, Lachmann,
Tischendorf, and by the great majority of editors. The sense
expressed by the future forms is also better suited to the context. Paul's desire was to produce the conviction in the
minds of the Corinthians, which he himself so strongly felt,
that no man is the poorer for being liberal. The ground of
this conviction was twofold; the explicit promise of God, and
his character and general mode of dealing with men. *He that
ministereth seed to the sower ;* ὁ ἐπιχορηγῶν, he whose prerogative and wont it is to supply seed to the sower. Such being
the character and, so to speak, the office of God, Paul was
sure he would supply the necessities of his giving people.
The words καὶ ἄρτον εἰς βρῶσιν our translators, after Calvin and
others, connect with the following clause, and render καί *both*.
"Shall both minister bread for food, and multiply, &c." The
obviously natural construction is with the preceding clause,
'He that ministereth seed to the sower, and bread for eating.'
(The word is βρῶσις, *eating*, and not βρῶμα, *food*.) This connection is also in accordance with the passage in Is. 55, 10, which
was evidently in the apostle's mind, and where the words are,
"Seed to the sower, and bread to the eater." This bountiful
God *will give and increase your seed*. Your seed means your
resources, your wealth, that which you can scatter abroad in
acts of beneficence, as a sower scatters seed. He who furnishes the husbandman seed for his harvest, will abundantly
supply you with seed for your harvest. *And increase the
fruits of your righteousness*. This is parallel with the preceding clause, and means the same thing. 'The fruits of your
righteousness,' are not the rewards of your righteousness,
either here or hereafter. But 'your works of righteousness,'
i. e. of beneficence ; the word δικαιοσύνη having the same sense
here as in the preceding clause. As in v. 9, the words "his
righteousness remaineth forever" mean that the righteous
shall always have the means of being beneficent; so here to
increase "the fruits of your righteousness," means, 'will increase your means of doing good.' This sense the context
demands, and the words, in their scriptural sense, readily admit. The other interpretation, however, according to which

"the fruits of your righteousness" mean the reward of your righteousness, amounts substantially to the same thing; for the reward of beneficence is, according to the context, the increase of the means wherewith to be beneficent.

11. Being enriched in every thing to all bountifulness, which causeth through us thanksgiving to God.

In our version vs. 9 and 10 are regarded as a parenthesis, and this verse is connected with v. 8. "That ye may have abundance for every good work—being enriched, &c." But this is unnecessary and forbidden by the regular connection of vs. 9 and 10 with v. 8. Others supply the substantive verb "ye shall be enriched." Almost all the modern commentators assume the irregular construction of the participle of which so many examples occur both in the New Testament and in the classics. See Eph. 4, 2. 3, 17. Col. 2, 2. 3, 16. Acts 15, 22, &c. The connection is therefore with what immediately precedes. 'God will increase the fruits of your righteousness, (i. e. your resources,) being enriched, i. e. so that you shall be enriched, &c.' The reference is not to inward or spiritual riches, but, as the whole context demands, to worldly riches. 'If you are liberal, God will give you abundance, so that you shall be rich *to all bountifulness*, εἰς πᾶσαν ἁπλότητα. The preposition (εἰς) expresses the design or end for which they shall be enriched. *Bountifulness* or liberality; the word is ἁπλότης, which means sincerity, rightmindedness. Another example of a general term used in a specific sense. See 8, 2. Rom. 15, 12. *Which causes through us*, i. e. by our ministry. Paul had been instrumental in exciting the liberality of the Corinthians and in effecting the contribution for the poor in Jerusalem, and therefore he could say that the *thanksgiving to God* which was thus called forth was *through him*. The good effect of the liberality of Christians was not limited to the relief of the temporal necessities of their brethren; it had the higher effect of promoting gratitude to God. On this idea the apostle enlarges in the following verses.

12. For the administration of this service not only supplieth the want of the saints, but is abundant also by many thanksgivings unto God.

Your liberality produces gratitude, *for* (ὅτι), because, *the*

administration of this service, ἡ διακονία τῆς λειτουργίας ταύτης.
This may mean, 'The administration by me of this service of
yours, i. e. this benefaction of yours, which is a service rendered to God and his people.' It is a λειτουργία; properly a
public service, but always in the New Testament (except perhaps Phil. 2, 30) a religious service such as was rendered by
the priests in the temple, Luke 1, 23. Heb. 8, 6. 9, 21; or by
the Christian ministry, Phil. 2, 17. Comp. Rom. 1, 9. Or, it
may mean, 'The service which you render by this benefaction.'
The διακονία, ministry, or service, consisted in the λειτουργία,
the contribution. This suits better with v. 13, where διακονία
is used for what the Corinthians did, not for what Paul did.
Not only supplieth. The Greek is somewhat peculiar; ἐστὶ
προσαναπληροῦσα, it is not only fully compensatory . . . but it is
(περισσεύουσα) *overflowing;* the participles being used as adjectives expressing the quality of the thing spoken of. *The
want of the saints.* Their necessities are not only supplied,
but your service overflows, or is abundantly productive of
good; *by means of many thanksgivings to God;* τῷ θεῷ depending on εὐχαριστιῶν as in verse 11.

**13. While by the experiment of this ministration
they glorify God for your professed subjection unto the
gospel of Christ, and for (your) liberal distribution unto
them, and unto all (men).**

There is the same irregularity of grammatical construction
in this verse as in v. 11; the participle δοξάζοντες here referring
to πολλῶν, as there πλουτιζόμενοι to ὑμῶν. The sense is, 'Many
thank God, *glorifying* him (διὰ τῆς δοκιμῆς τῆς διακονίας ταύτης)
on the occasion of the evidence offered by this service.' The
preposition διά here expresses the occasional, not the instrumental, or rational cause. It is neither *through,* nor, *on account of,* but simply *by,* i. e. occasioned by. The simplest
explanation of δοκιμή, in this passage, is proof, or evidence;
and the genitive, διακονίας, is the genitive of apposition. The
service was the proof. The thing proved by the service rendered by the Corinthians to their poor brethren, is what is
mentioned in the sequel, viz., their obedience and their fellowship with the saints. Meyer makes δοκιμή mean *indoles spec-
tata,* the nature, or internal character. "From the nature of
this service," whereby it proved itself to be genuine, or what

the Christian spirit demanded. Calvin's explanation is, Specimen idoneum probandæ Corinthiorum caritati, quod erga fratres procul remotos tam liberales erant; which amounts very much to what is implied in the first interpretation mentioned. They glorify God *for your professed subjection.* The words are, ἐπὶ τῇ ὑποταγῇ τῆς ὁμολογίας ὑμῶν; on account of obedience to your confession. Ὁμολογία is always in the New Testament used for the profession, or confession, of Christianity. 1 Tim. 6, 12. Heb. 3, 1. 4, 14. 10, 23. Beza, whom our translators follow, gives the genitive the force of the participle, *professed obedience,* i. e. obedience which you profess. Others make it the genitive of the source, "the obedience which flows from your confession;" others again make it the genitive of the object, "obedience to your confession." This gives the best sense, and agrees best with the analogous expression, "obedience of Christ," 10, 5. *To the gospel of Christ,* εἰς εὐαγ. These words, it is said, cannot properly be constructed either with ὑποταγῇ or with ὁμολογίας, because neither ὑποτάσσω nor ὁμολογέω is followed by εἰς. On this account Meyer connects the clause in question with δοξάζοντες, 'they praise God—in reference to the gospel.' But this is forced, and does not agree with the following clause; as there, εἰς πάντας, if connected with δοξάζοντες, gives no definite sense. De Wette connects εἰς εὐαγ. with what precedes, 'Your confession—as it concerns the gospel.' *And for your liberal distribution unto them, and unto all.* This is the second ground of praise to God. The words are ἁπλότητι τῆς κοινωνίας, *the sincerity of your fellowship.* These general terms may, if the context required, be taken in the specific sense, "liberality of your contribution," as is done by our translators; or they may be understood in their wider and more natural sense. The ground on which the saints at Jerusalem would praise God was the manifestation of the Christian fellowship which the Corinthians cherished not only for them, but for all believers. It was the consciousness of the communion of saints—the assurance that believers, however separated, or however distinguished as Jews and Gentiles, bond or free, are one body in Christ, that called forth their praise to God. And, therefore, the apostle says it was the (κοινωνία) fellowship of the Corinthians not only towards them, (the saints in Jerusalem,) but towards *all* believers, that was the ground of their praise. See Phil. 1, 5, for an example of κοινωνία followed by εἰς, as it is in this verse.

14. And by their prayer for you, which long after you, for the exceeding grace of God in you.

This verse admits of a threefold construction. It may be connected with v. 12, δεήσει being parallel with διὰ πολλῶν εὐχ. 'Your liberality is abundant, or overflowing, (περισσεύουσα,) through many thanksgivings—and by their prayer for you.' That is, our liberality is productive of abundant good, not only by calling forth thanksgiving to God, but also by leading the objects of your kindness to pray for you. This is a full compensation. The prayers and blessings of the poor are their benefactions to the rich, descending on them as the dew on Hermon. Or the connection may be with δοξάζοντες in v. 13. 'They glorify God for your obedience, ... and by their prayer.' But in this case, the natural meaning would be, (δεήσει being co-ordinate with ὑποταγῇ), 'They glorify God for your subjection—and for their prayer.' This does not give a good sense. Believers do not glorify God *for* their prayers. Others, as Meyer, take αὐτῶν ἐπιποθούντων together as the genitive absolute, and καί, not as *and*, but *also*. 'You (Corinthians) manifest your fellowship for them—they also with prayer for you earnestly longing for you.' This gives a pertinent sense. The first mentioned explanation is, however, generally preferred. *For the exceeding grace of God in you.* That is, *on account of*, (διὰ τὴν χάριν,) the surpassing grace, or favour of God manifested towards or upon you (ἐφ᾽ ὑμῖν); in that he had rendered them so liberal, and so filled them with a Christian spirit.

15. Thanks (be) unto God for his unspeakable gift.

According to Calvin, and perhaps the majority of commentators, the gift to which Paul refers, is that spoken of in the context, viz., the grace bestowed on the Corinthians, or the good effect anticipated from their liberality. Confident that the Corinthians would be liberal, and that their liberality would excite the gratitude of their suffering brethren, and cement the union between the Jewish and Gentile converts, the apostle breaks forth in this expression of thanksgiving to God, for bringing about so happy a consummation. But the language is too strong for this. God's unspeakable gift is his Son. This, according to the analogy of Scripture, is that one

great, supreme, all-comprehending gift, which is here intended. This is the more natural, because it is Paul's wont, when
speaking either of the feeble love, or trivial gifts of believers,
one to another, to refer in contrast to the infinite love and
unspeakable gift of God in Christ to us. 8, 9. Eph. 5, 1. It is
his habit also to introduce ejaculations of adoration or thanksgiving into the midst, or at the close of his teachings or exhortations. Rom. 1, 25. 9, 5. 1 Cor. 15, 17. 1 Tim. 1, 17. The
passage, therefore, ought to stand, as we doubt not the vast
majority of the readers of the Bible understand it, as an outburst of gratitude to God for the gift of his Son.

CHAPTER X.

Paul deprecates the necessity of asserting his authority and of exercising his
power to punish the disobedient, vs. 1–6. He confronts his opposers
with the assertion of divinely derived power, vs. 9–11. He shows that
he claims authority only over those who were committed to his care,
vs. 12–18.

*Paul's assertion of his authority and vindication of his
apostolic prerogatives.*

THE remarkable change in the whole tone and style of this
portion of the epistle, from the beginning of the 10th chapter
to near the end of the 13th, has attracted the attention of
every careful reader. The contrast between this and the preceding portions of the epistle is so great, that some have concluded that they are separate letters, written at different
times and under different circumstances. There is no external authority for this conjecture, and it is not only unnecessary, but inconsistent with the facts of the case. The same
topics are presented, and there is in 12, 18 reference to the
mission of Titus, spoken of in the earlier chapters. It is an
adequate explanation of the change in question, that in chs.
1–9, Paul had in his mind, and was really addressing, the
faithful and obedient portion of the church, whereas he has
here in view the unreasonable and wicked false teachers and
their adherents, who not only made light of his authority, but

corrupted the gospel, which he was appointed to propagate and defend. He therefore naturally assumes a tone of authority and severity. Satisfied of his divine mission, and conscious of supernatural power, he cautioned them not to rely too much on his forbearance. He was indeed as a man humble, and, if they chose, insignificant ; but there was slumbering in his arm an energy which they would do well not to provoke. He had no desire to exercise in Corinth the authority with which Christ had invested him for the purpose of bringing down all opposition. He would give them a fair trial, and wait to see how far they would be obedient, before he punished their disobedience, vs. 1–6. They should not judge by appearance, or set themselves up on the ground of their fancied advantages, because whatever they had, he had in larger measure, vs. 7. 8. He had no intention to frighten them by his epistles —which they said were written in a tone he would not dare to assume when present— for they would find that, when occasion called for it, he could be as bold when present as when he was absent, vs. 9–11. They were subject to his apostolic authority. He usurped nothing in exercising the powers of his office over the churches which he had himself founded. He did not interfere with the jurisdiction of the other apostles, or undertake the special oversight of churches founded by others. Macedonia and Achaia were within the sphere of his operations, and he hoped to preach the gospel far beyond those limits in regions where it had never been heard, vs. 12–16. His confidence was not self-confidence, but confidence in God. His self-commendation amounted to nothing, unless the Lord commended him. Paul constantly felt that in himself he could do nothing, but in the Lord he could do all things, vs. 17. 18.

1. Now I Paul myself beseech you, by the meekness and gentleness of Christ, who in presence (am) base among you, but being absent am bold toward you.

He enters without any preamble or circumlocution on his new subject, and places himself face to face with his unscrupulous opponents. He says, *I Paul myself.* He usually employs the first person plural when speaking of himself. Here, and throughout this context, he makes his individuality prominent, in saying I. This is rendered the more emphatic by the addition of the word *myself;* αὐτὸς ἐγώ, *I myself,* the man whom you so despise and calumniate. Comp. Gal. 5, 2. Eph. 3, 1. Philemon, 19. In this case the expression is so emphatic that many suppose that Paul here began to write with his own hand; as though he were so excited, that he seized the pen from his amanuensis, and says, 'I Paul myself now write to you.' This, however, is unnecessary, and unsustained by any thing in the context. *Beseech you by the meekness and gentleness of Christ.* That is, the meekness and gentleness which belonged to Christ, and which, therefore, his disciples are bound to imitate. To beseech *by* (διά), is to beseech on account of, or out of regard to. The request is enforced by a reference to the obligation of Christians to be meek and gentle as was their Lord. Matt. 11, 29. Is. 42, 2. In Rom. 12, 1, we have a similar expression, "I beseech you by the mercies of God." See Phil. 2, 1. The words πραότης and ἐπιείκεια differ very much as our words meekness and gentleness do; the former referring more to the inward virtue, the latter to its outward expression. As Christians are bound to be meek and gentle, Paul begged the Corinthians not to force him to be severe. He describes himself as his opposers described him, as craven when present, and a braggart when absent. *Who in presence am base among you.* In presence, κατὰ πρόσωπον, *coram,* before, towards the face of any one, here opposed to ἀπών, *absent.* The word ταπεινός, literally, *low;* then lowly, humble. It is commonly used in a good sense. Our Lord says of himself that he was, ταπεινὸς τῇ καρδίᾳ, *lowly in heart,* and his followers are always described as *the lowly.* But the word also means *downcast,* as in 7, 6, and thence it sometimes expresses depression when it is the effect of the want of courage. This is its meaning here. *But being absent am bold towards you.* Bold, in the sense opposite to base, or craven. This word also (θαρρέω) is commonly used in a good sense, 5, 6. It is only the context which gives it a different shade of meaning. Paul was regarded by his enemies as in heart a coward, and his boldness as merely assumed when there was no danger to confront. No one (except Rückert) now believes this. True heroism was never more fully exemplified than in the life of this apostle, who against numbers, wealth and power, always was true to his convictions; who encountered all manner of dangers and sufferings in the service of Christ, and whose whole conduct showed that he was ready not only to be bound, but to die for the name of the Lord Jesus. Acts 21, 13.

2. But I beseech (you), that I may not be bold when I am present with that confidence, wherewith I think to be bold against some, which think of us as if we walked according to the flesh.

The particle (δέ), *but*, serves to resume the exhortation in the first clause of v. 1. There it is (παρακαλῶ ὑμᾶς) *I exhort you*, here it is (δέομαι) *I beseech*. This shows that ὑμᾶς and not Ͽεόν is to be supplied as the object of the verb. The sense is, 'I beseech *you*,' not, 'I pray *God*.' What Paul beseeches of them is, that they would not force him to have recourse to severity. This he expresses by saying, τὸ μὴ παρὼν Ͽαῤῥῆσαι, *that I may not be bold when present*. The article (τό) serves to render the object of the verb more prominent; and παρών is in the nominative because the subject of both verbs is the same. *To be bold*, i. e. to act with decision and courage; to exhibit the character which the opponents of the apostle said he assumed only when absent. *With the confidence*, i. e. with the conviction of his right to exercise the authority which he claimed, and with the consciousness of power to carry his decisions into effect. *Wherewith I think ;* λογίζομαι, which means to reckon, to reason, and then, as here, to purpose. Paul had determined in his own mind that if persuasion failed to bring his opponents to a right state of mind, he would resort to that power with which God had armed him to put down all opposition. The Vulgate gives the word λογίζομαι a passive sense, *qua existimor*, 'which I am thought, or supposed to assume.' So Luther, "die man mir zumisset," *which men ascribe to me*. Bengel and many other commentators adopt the same interpretation. This has the advantage of giving λογίζομαι and the following participle λογιζομένους the same sense. But it is objected to this interpretation that it would require ἀπών to be used. 'The confidence wherewith I am thought *when absent* to assume.' The common interpretation, therefore, is to be preferred. *To be bold*. The word is here not Ͽαῤῥῆσαι as before, but τολμῆσαι, *to dare ;* to act without fear and without regard to consequences. Paul had determined, if forced to it, to set his opponents at defiance and to act with utter disregard of all they could say or do.

The persons against whom he had determined to exercise this severity, were those who *think of us*, he says, *as if we walked according to the flesh*. The word *flesh* sometimes means the body, sometimes it expresses the secondary idea of weakness, sometimes, and most frequently in Paul's epistles, our corrupt nature. Beza gives it here the second of these meanings. He understands Paul as describing his opponents as those who regarded him as weak and cowardly, or, as invested with nothing more than human powers (non alio præsidio freti, quam quod præ nobis ferimus), so that, as Bengel says, "they may despise us with impunity." But this is not only inconsistent with the scriptural use of the word "to walk," which, in its figurative sense, refers to moral deportment, but also with the familiar use of the phrase (κατὰ σάρκα), *after the flesh*. See the next verse, and Rom. 8, 1. 4. 5. 13. The persons referred to were those who regarded the apostle not only as an ordinary man, but as acting under the control of his corrupt nature, governed by selfish or malicious feelings, and relying on himself.

3. For though we walk in the flesh, we do not war after the flesh.

There is here, so to speak, a play on the word *flesh*, which is used in somewhat different senses. Paul did indeed walk in the flesh, he was a man, and a mere man, not only invested with a body, but subject to all the infirmities of human nature; but he did not war after the flesh. What was human and worldly neither determined his conduct, nor was the ground of his confidence. The phrase to be *in the flesh* has various meanings according to the connection in which it is used. In 1 Tim. 3, 16, it is said, "God was manifested in the flesh," i. e. in human nature. In Rom. 8, 8. 9, to be "in the flesh," means to be in an unrenewed state. In Phil. 1, 22. 24, "to live," or, "to abide in the flesh," means to live, or abide, in the body. Here the phrase has substantially the same meaning, but with the accessory idea of weakness and exposure to temptation. 'Though he was a man, and therefore compassed with the infirmities incident to humanity, yet, &c.' "Hic," says Calvin, "*Ambulare in carne* significat in mundo versari : quod alibi dicit, habitare in corpore (supra 5, 6). Erat enim inclusus in corporis sui ergastulo : sed hoc non impediebat quominus Spiritus sancti virtus mirifice se exsereret in ejus infirmitate."

Instead of the general expression " to walk," Paul uses, in the second clause, the more specific term, " to war." *We war not ;* οὐ στρατευόμεϑα. Στρατεύω means, to go to war, to make a campaign ; στρατεύομαι means, to serve as a soldier, to fight. The war here referred to, is that which the apostle waged against error and every thing opposed to the gospel. This war, he says, he did not conduct (κατὰ σάρκα) *after the flesh ;* that is, governed by the flesh, or relying on it. He was not guided by the principles of ordinary men, who act under the influence of their corrupt nature ; neither did he depend for success on any thing the flesh (i. e. human nature) could afford. He was governed by the Spirit and relied upon the Spirit. "What Paul says of himself, is true of all the faithful ministers of Christ. They bear about an incomparable treasure in earthen vessels. Therefore, although they are compassed with infirmities, nevertheless the spiritual power of God is resplendent in them."—CALVIN. The connection of this verse, as indicated by the particle γάρ (*for*), is either with the middle clause of the preceding verse, 'I am determined to be bold towards the opponents of the truth, *for* though I walk in the flesh, I do not war after the flesh ;' or, as is often the case in Paul's epistles, the γάρ refers to a thought omitted. 'Some think that I walk after the flesh—*that is not true*—for though I walk in the flesh, I do not war after it.' The latter seems the more natural and forcible.

4. (For the weapons of our warfare (are) not carnal, but mighty through God to the pulling down of strong holds).

This proves that the main idea intended by warring *after the flesh*, is warring with human weapons, relying on human resources. In the war in which Paul was engaged, his confidence was not in himself, not in human reason, not in the power of argument or eloquence, not in the resources of cunning or management, but simply and only in the supernatural power of God. 'We war not after the flesh, for our weapons are not carnal.' That is, such as the flesh, or human nature, furnishes, and which therefore in their own nature are carnal, or human. By *weapons* is, of course, to be understood all the means which the apostle employed in the defence and propagation of the truth. Those means, he says, were *mighty through God.* The words are δυνατὰ τῷ Θεῷ, which are variously explained. Some, as Beza, Grotius and others, give the dative the force of the ablative—mighty by God—*afflatu Dei,* as Erasmus expresses it. Others regard the expression as a Hebraic superlative. Others say the meaning is, mighty *for* God, i. e. for his use, weapons which are powerful in his hand. The common explanation is, 'mighty to God,' i. e. such means as even God himself regards as mighty; mighty in his estimation. Of Nineveh it is said it was, πόλις μεγάλη τῷ Θεῷ, a city great to God, a version which strictly answers to the Hebrew. Reference is also made to Acts 7, 20, where Moses is said to have been ἀστεῖος τῷ Θεῷ, *beautiful to God,* i. e. in his sight; and 2 Peter 3, 14. These weapons were divinely powerful *to the pulling down of strong holds,* πρὸς καθαίρεσιν ὀχυρωμάτων. The last word is most appropriately rendered strong holds, as it is from ὀχυρός (from ἔχω), *haltbar,* what may be held, what is secure from assault. The opposers of the gospel felt that they were so entrenched, so protected by the fortresses which they occupied, that they despised the ministers of Christ and derided their efforts. What these strong-holds were the apostle tells us in what follows. This verse is properly marked as a parenthesis, not only in our version, but in almost all the critical editions of the Greek Testament, because the grammatical construction of v. 5 connects it immediately with v. 3.

5. Casting down imaginations, and every high thing that exalteth itself against the knowledge of God, and bringing into captivity every thought to the obedience of Christ.

As just intimated, the participle καθαιροῦντες (*pulling down*) depends on the verb στρατευόμεθα at the end of v. 3. 'We war—pulling down, &c.' According to this view v. 3 is parenthetical. Rückert, De Wette and others, however, on the ground that v. 4 contains the main idea, which is carried out in v. 8, prefer considering the construction of the passage as irregular, the participle being used here as in 9, 11. 13. They therefore connect this verse with what immediately precedes. 'Our weapons are mighty—in that we pull down, &c.'

What the apostle was thus confident he could cast down were
imaginations (λογισμούς), *thoughts*, i. e. the opinions, or convictions of those who set themselves and the deductions of
their own reason against the truth of God. Compare 1 Cor.
1, 17–31, and Rom. 1, 21–23. *And every high thing* (ὕψωμα),
every tower, or fortress; the same as ὀχύρωμα in v. 4. Not
persons, but thoughts, are intended by this figure. It is every
thing which the pride of human reason exalts against *the
knowledge of God;* i. e. that revelation of himself which God
has made in the gospel. 1 Cor. 3, 18–20. The conflict to
which the apostle here refers is that between truth and error,
between the wisdom of God and the wisdom of the world.
When the gospel was first proclaimed it found itself in conflict
with all the forms of religion and philosophy then prevailing
among men. To the wise of this world the gospel appeared
as foolishness. It was, however, the wisdom and power of
God. The conflict then begun has continued ever since, and
is now as deadly as at any former period. Men of science
and philosophers are as confident in their conclusions, and as
much disposed to exalt themselves, or their opinions against
the knowledge of God as ever. There is no doubt as to the
issue of this contest. It is a contest between God and man,
in which, of course, God must prevail. The instructive lesson
which the apostle designs here to inculcate is, that this warfare must not be conducted on the part of the advocates of
the gospel, with carnal weapons. They must not rely upon
their own resources and attempt to overcome their enemies
by argument. They must not become philosophers and turn
the gospel into a philosophy. This would be to make it a human conflict on both sides. It would be human reason against
human reason, the intellect of one man against the intellect of
another man. Paul told the Corinthians in his former epistle,
that he did not appear among them as a philosopher, but as a
witness; he came not with the words of man's wisdom; he
did not rely for success on his powers of argument or of persuasion, but on the demonstration of the Spirit. The faith,
which he laboured to secure, was not to be founded on the
wisdom of men, but on the power of God; not on arguments
addressed to the understanding, but on the testimony of God.
That testimony has the same effect which intuition has. It
reveals the truth to the mind and conscience as self-evident;
and therefore it cannot be resisted. A rationalistic Christian,
a philosophizing theologian, therefore, lays aside the divine

for the human, the wisdom of God for the wisdom of men, the infinite and infallible for the finite and fallible. The success of the gospel depends on its being presented, not as the word of man, but as the word of God; not as something to be proved, but as something to be believed. It was on this principle Paul acted, and hence he was in no degree intimidated by the number, the authority, the ability, or the learning of his opponents. He was confident that he could cast down all their proud imaginations, because he relied not on himself but on God whose messenger he was.

And bringing into captivity every thought, πᾶν νόημα. This word means either *thought*, or *the mind*, that which thinks. 3, 14. 4, 4. Phil. 4, 7. Hence it may be translated *thought*, as it is in our version; or as in the Vulgate, "omnem intellectum," *every understanding*, and by Luther, "alle Vernunft." Although the modern commentators make an outcry against this latter translation, it really differs little from the former. It does not matter much whether we say that human reason must be subjected, or that all the products of human reason (every thought) must be subjected. It amounts to the same thing. Both forms of statement are equally true. It is the indispensable condition of salvation that our understanding should be brought into captivity, led submissive, as though bound, *into the obedience of Christ*, εἰς τὴν ὑπακοὴν τοῦ Χριστοῦ. Agreeably to the figure in the context, the obedience of Christ is conceived of as a place, or fortress, into which the captive is led. The sense is the same as the dative, τῇ ὑπακοῇ τοῦ Χριστοῦ, would have expressed. We must renounce dependence on our own understanding and submit implicitly, as obedient children, to the teaching of Christ. He who would be wise, must become a fool. 1 Cor. 3, 18.

6. And having in a readiness to revenge all disobedience, when your obedience is fulfilled.

And having in a readiness ; ἐν ἑτοίμῳ ἔχοντες, holding ourselves ready, i. e. being ready. He had the ability and the determination to do what he declares he would do. Compare ἑτοίμως ἔχω, 12, 14. The participle ἔχοντες is connected by καί with καθαιροῦντες of the preceding verse. 'We war— casting down all that opposes itself—and ready, &c.' *To avenge all disobedience ;* ἐκδικῆσαι, to maintain, or to exact justice, or satisfaction, to punish. *All disobedience*, i. e. every case of disobedience. The gospel, being the word of God, is divinely efficacious, and is certain ultimately to triumph over all opposition. This, however, does not imply that all will obey it. In the apostolic churches, there were those who corrupted the word of God, Judaizing or philosophizing teachers and their followers, who refused to obey the truth. Such persons Paul announced his ability and his determination to punish. They were in the church, for what, he said in his former epistle, have I to do to judge them that are without? 1 Cor. 5, 12. They had voluntarily submitted themselves to his jurisdiction, and he therefore had a legitimate authority over them. What was the nature of the punishment which he threatened, he does not intimate. It may be that he purposed nothing more than excommunication. The fact, however, that the apostles were armed with supernatural power, that they exercised that power for the punishment of offenders, 1 Cor. 5, 5. 1 Tim. 1, 20, and the whole tone of the passage are in favour of the assumption that Paul was determined to use all the means at his command to suppress the insolence, and to destroy the power of the corrupters of the truth in Corinth. He gives what he had said a special application by adding, *when your obedience is fulfilled.* That is, he would not resort to severity until all other means had failed, and until it had become fully manifest who among the Corinthians would submit to God, and who would persist in their disobedience.

7. Do ye look on things after the outward appearance? If any man trust to himself that he is Christ's, let him of himself think this again, that, as he (is) Christ's, even so (are) we Christ's.

Abrupt transitions are characteristic of this epistle. Paul having in the preceding verses so strongly asserted his apostolic authority and supernatural power, turns to those who denied the validity of his claims, and calls upon them to give a reason for skepticism. He was thus led to vindicate his title to the apostolic office and to his special jurisdiction over the church of Corinth. This vindication extends to 12, 18. After which he resumes the subject broached in the preceding verses of this chapter, viz., what he purposed to do when he again visited Corinth.

Do ye look on things after the outward appearance? τὰ κατὰ πρόσωπον βλέπετε. This clause may be taken interrogatively, as by most commentators, or imperatively, or declaratively. If interrogatively, the sense may be, 'Do ye regard, or take into view, only what is external? Do you judge of me from my personal appearance, manner, and speech?' It would seem that a judgment founded on such grounds as these, led the false teachers to regard the apostle with contempt. Or, the meaning is, 'Do you regard only external advantages? Such as being a minister of Christ, being a Hebrew, an Israelite, of the seed of Abraham, &c.' 11, 22. In favour of this view is the use of πρόσωπον in this epistle, 5, 12. 11, 1. See also Matt. 22, 16. Mark 12, 14; the parallel passage in 11, 18 (where κατὰ τὴν σάρκα answers to κατὰ πρόσωπον here); and the context, which goes to show that the things which Paul's opponents regarded, and on which they prided themselves, were their supposed external advantages. Those who take βλέπετε as imperative understand the passage thus: 'Look at what is before your eyes, i. e. at what is evident to all. If you are thus and so, so am I.' Calvin and others take the verb as in the indicative. 'Ye do regard what is external —and therefore despise me.' The first interpretation, for the reasons stated, is to be preferred. *If any man trust to himself.* The use of τίς (any one), in this passage, and of the singular number in vs. 10 and 11, and in 11, 4, has led to the conjecture that there was in Corinth one particular opponent of the apostle to whom in this whole context he refers. But it is evident from the general drift of the epistle that it was a whole class of persons who had arrayed themselves against Paul's authority. *Trust to himself*, πέποιθεν ἑαυτῷ, is persuaded concerning himself, *that he is Christ's.* What that means is somewhat doubtful. It may be taken in the most general sense, 'If any thinks that he is a Christian,' i. e. belongs to Christ as every believer does; or, 'If any man thinks that he is a minister of Christ;' or, 'If any man thinks that he stands in a peculiar relation to Christ.' It is probable from 1 Cor. 1, 10 that there were certain persons in Corinth who said, 'We are of Christ,' as claiming some nearer connection with him than that which belonged to other believers or to other ministers. Whether this claim rested on their having seen Christ in the flesh, or on relationship to his kinsmen, is mere matter of conjecture. Still as the claim existed, it is most likely referred to here. *Let him of himself,* i. e. without its being suggested by others. The fact was so plain that it needed not to be asserted. Let him think *this again*, i. e. let him consider the matter again. The last reflection will convince him that as he is *Christ's, so are we.* There was no relationship which these false teachers could rightfully claim to Christ to which Paul was not equally entitled. They were in no respect his superiors. They had no advantage which did not belong equally to him.

8. For though I should boast somewhat more of our authority, which the Lord hath given us for edification, and not for your destruction, I should not be ashamed.

Paul might have said much more than he had said in what precedes. He was not only all that his opponents claimed to be, but more. He had an authority and power to which they could make no pretensions. He therefore here says that if he had set forth higher claims, he should not be ashamed—facts would not prove those claims to be unfounded. *For though*, ἐάν τε γὰρ καί, *for even in case*, &c. The connection is with the words "we are Christ's." 'We are Christ's, in all the senses in which you can claim to be, *for* we have received more from him.' The greater includes the less. *Somewhat more*, περισσότερόν τι, i. e. somewhat more than was claimed in vs. 3–6, or more than 'being in Christ,' which might be said of others as well as of the apostle. Paul had an *authority* which extended beyond the limits of any claim which he had yet advanced. Εξουσία includes the ideas of power and authority. The apostle had authority (i. e. the right to rule) and he had ability, inherent power, to enforce that authority. *Which the Lord hath given* (or rather, *gave*) *to us.* The authority in question was given when he was constituted an apostle, with not only a commission to exercise dominion, but a grace, or inward gift of the Spirit, rendering him infallible as a teacher and investing him with supernatural power. The giver of this authority and power was the Lord, i. e. Christ. Christ, therefore, as the author of supernatural gifts, is a divine person, for to give such gifts is a prerogative of God. The design for which Paul was not endowed, was not his own exaltation, not the accomplishment of any worldly end, not, as he says, "for your destruction," i. e. not that he might be able to put down his personal enemies, but *for edification*, i. e. the building up of the church in holiness and peace. Power in the church comes not from the civil magistrate, nor from the people, but from Christ only. He is, as Calvin says, Solus Dominus et Magister. And this power can be legitimately exercised only for the edification of the church. When exercised for other objects, or for the destruction of the church, then it should be disowned and resisted. Even an apostle, or an angel from heaven, who should preach any other gospel—teach or require any thing contrary to the word of God—would be accursed. And of this contrariety, from the necessity of the case, and from the authority of Scripture, the people, i. e. those who are required to believe and obey, are (at their peril) to be the judges. If they reject a true apostle, their sin is as great as if they gave ear to false teachers. Having the inward teaching of the Spirit, they know of the doctrine whether it be of God.

9. That I may not seem as if I would terrify you by letters.

The connection of this clause (ἵνα μὴ δόκω) is somewhat doubtful. If it belongs immediately to the preceding words, the sense is, ' I should not be ashamed—in order that I should seem,' i. e. God would so order it that I should not appear as an empty boaster. But this is evidently unnatural. The design of God in sustaining the apostle, and giving him a victory over the enemies of the truth, was something higher than preserving him from being regarded as a boaster. A very large number of commentators connect this verse with the 11th, throwing the 10th into a parenthesis. ' That I may not seem to terrify you—let such an one think, &c.' But neither in this way is the connection natural or logical; and v. 11 evidently refers to v. 10, and would not be intelligible if that verse were omitted; verse 11, therefore, is not a parenthesis. A clause with ἵνα, as we have seen before in this epistle, (compare also Gal. 2, 10,) often depends on some word or words omitted but easily supplied from the context. In this case we may supply, ' *This I say*.' ' This I say in order that I may not appear, &c.' So Luther ("Das sage ich aber "), Beza, and many others. *As if I would terrify*, ὡς ἂν ἐκφοβεῖν. This is the only instance in the New Testament where ἄν after a conjunction is used with the infinitive. Winer resolves it into ὡς ἂν ἐκφοβοῖμι ὑμᾶς, *tanquam velim vos terrere*, which agrees with our translation. These particles serve to soften the expression, and are equivalent to *as if perhaps*, or, *so to speak*. There is evident allusion to the false representations made by the false teachers, that Paul wrote in the authoritative tone which he assumed merely to frighten his readers, having neither the power nor the purpose to carry his threats into execution. *By letters*, or, *by the letters*, i. e. the letters which he had already written or intended to write.

10. For (his) letters, say they, (are) weighty and powerful; but (his) bodily presence (is) weak, and (his) speech contemptible.

There was reason for his not wishing to appear as assuming a tone of threatening in his letters, *for* this was the very reproach cast upon him. *His letters, they say*, (φησί, here, as often, used impersonally, ' one says,' *sagt man*,) *are weighty* (βαρεῖαι, i. e. impressive) *and powerful*, (ἰσχυραί,) including the ideas of vigour, authority and severity. *But his bodily presence is weak*. This passage, probably more than any other, has given rise to the impression, in accordance with a tradition neither very ancient nor well sustained, that Paul was small in stature, weak and unattractive in his personal appearance. The words here used, however, even supposing that this language of his enemies expressed the truth, do not necessarily imply this. The phrase ἡ παρουσία τοῦ σώματος probably refers not to his personal appearance, but to his deportment. He wrote boldly, but acted feebly. There was not that energy and decision in his acts which one would expect from his language. This was the representation of his enemies; the truth of which, however, the apostle denies. The same remark applies to the next clause, *his speech contemptible*. This does not refer to feebleness of voice, but to the impression made by his oral instructions and addresses. He dared not assume any such authority in speaking to the people that he did in writing to them. The whole history of the apostle, his unceasing labours, his constant journeyings, his innumerable sufferings which he sustained so heroically, prove that he was not physically a man of feeble constitution. And his own declarations, as well as his clearly revealed character, prove that there was no such want of correspondence between his

letters and his actions as the false teachers in Corinth, to whom
he was probably personally unknown, endeavoured to make
the people believe.

11. Let such an one think this, that such as we are
in word by letters when we are absent, such (will we
be) also in deed when we are present.

Let such an one, i. e. any one, not necessarily implying
that there was only one person who had set himself up in opposition to the apostle. *That such as we are in word*, &c.
It was admitted that his letters were energetic. He assures
them that, when present, his deeds would correspond to his
words. His denunciations would not prove idle threats.

12. For we dare not make ourselves of the number,
or compare ourselves with some that commend themselves : but they, measuring themselves by themselves,
and comparing themselves among themselves, are not
wise.

In confirmation of his declaration that his acts would be
found to correspond with his words, he adds, 'For I am not
like those, who having nothing to recommend them, commend
themselves.' *We dare not* (οὐ τολμῶμεν, we cannot bring ourselves to, or, we cannot prevail on ourselves to. Rom. 5, 7.
1 Cor. 6, 1) *make ourselves of the number, or compare ourselves ;* (ἐγκρῖναι ἢ συγκρῖναι, enrol ourselves among, or place
ourselves by,) *some who commend themselves.* The reference
is obviously to the false teachers, whose only reliance was self-
laudation. So far this verse is plain. The latter part of the
passage is exceedingly difficult, and has been very variously
explained. There are three classes of interpretation, two of
which proceed on the assumption of the correctness of the
common text, and the third is founded on a different reading.
According to the first general view, the αὐτοί refers to the
apostle himself. He is assumed to contrast himself, in this
verse, with his opponents. The sense, according to some
then is, 'They commend themselves, but we, measuring ourselves by ourselves, (i. e. we do not overestimate ourselves,
but determine our importance by our performances) and

comparing ourselves with ourselves, not with these wise men.'
According to this view, συνιοῦσιν, at the end of the verse, is a
participle, and is used ironically in reference to the false teachers. To this interpretation it is objected, 1. That συνιοῦσιν
would require the article in order to express the meaning
given to it; and 2. That it is plainly inconsistent with the
ἡμεῖς δέ of the next verse, which are antithetical to the αὐτοί
of this verse. 'They do so—but we do so.' Others, who
make the latter part of this verse refer to the apostle, refer
συνιοῦσιν also to him. 'We measure ourselves by ourselves,
and compare ourselves with ourselves, we who, as they say,
are unwise.' Then the ἡμεῖς δέ of verse 13th refers to this last
clause. 'They say we are unwise, but we, &c.' This, however, is liable to the same objections, and gives a sense unsuited to the context. According to the second interpretation, αὐτοί in this verse refers to the false teachers, with whom,
in the next verse, Paul contrasts himself, (ἡμεῖς δέ,) and συνιοῦσιν is the third person plural, as from the verb συνιέω, as in
Matt. 13, 13. 'They measuring themselves by themselves,
and comparing themselves with themselves, are not wise; but
we, &c.' This is the view of the passage adopted by our
translators, after Chrysostom, Calvin, and Luther. It is also
sanctioned by De Wette, Meyer, and Rückert, and many others. These false teachers commended themselves, confined
their views to themselves, despised or disregarded all others,
intruding into other men's labours. Paul, on the contrary,
boasted not of himself; he relied only on God and his grace,
and he kept himself within his own limits, not appropriating
to himself the fruits of the labours of other men. The third
mode of interpreting this passage assumes that the text afforded by the Western, as distinguished from the Eastern manuscripts, is correct. Those authorities omit οὐ συνιοῦσι, ἡμεῖς δέ,
so that αὐτοί (ἡμεῖς) is the nominative to καυχησόμεθα in v. 13,
if that verb be retained. 'They commend themselves; but
we, measuring ourselves by ourselves, and comparing ourselves with ourselves, will not boast as to things beyond our
measure.' Fritsche and Billroth, on the authority of the Co-
dex Clarom., omit also καυχησόμεθα, and connect the participles
μετζοῦντες and συγκρίνοντες with καυχώμενοι of v. 15, thus bringing out substantially the same sense, but rendering the sentence longer and more complicated. The meaning afforded
by this new reading is simple and pertinent. Since, however,
the critical authorities by which it is supported are compara-

tively few and of a secondary class, the great body of editors
adhere to the common text. If that text is correct, then the
interpretation given in our English version is the most natural
and suitable. Calvin applies this whole passage, with his
usual vigour, to the monks of his day. Hujus loci expositio
non aliunde petenda est quam a monachis: nam quum sint
omnes fere indoctissimi asini, et tamen oblongæ vestis et cuculli causa docti censeantur: si quis tenuem modo gustum ele-
gantioris literaturæ habeat, plumas suas instar pavonis fastuose
extendit: spargitur de eo mirabilis fama, adoratur inter
sodales. At si seposita cuculli larva ventum fuerit ad justum
examen, deprehenditur vanitas. Cur hoc? Verum quidem
est vetus proverbium: Audax inscitia: sed inde praecipue
monachalis insolentissimus ille fastus, quod se metiuntur ex se
ipsis: nam quum in eorum claustris nihil sit praeter barbari-
em, illic nihil mirum, si regnet luscus inter cæcos.

13. But we will not boast of things without (our)
measure, but according to the measure of the rule
which God hath distributed to us, a measure to reach
even unto you.

The words εἰς τὰ ἄμετρα may be taken adverbially, equivalent to ἀμέτρως, *immoderately*, beyond what is proper; or,
since in the latter part of the verse μέτρον is used literally, they
may be explained as in our version, in reference to things beyond our measure, i. e. beyond the limits of my apostolic labours. This idea is clearly presented in the following verses;
but here the contrast with the preceding verse favours the
former explanation. The false teachers set no limits to their
boasting—self-conceit and not facts determined the character
and amount of their assumptions, and therefore their claims
were inordinate. Paul expresses his determination to limit
his claims to his actual gifts and labours. *According to the
measure of the rule*, κατὰ τὸ μέτρον τοῦ κανόνος, i. e. according
to the measure determined by the rule, or line, that is, the
measure allotted to him. The κανών is the rule, or measuring
line, which, so to speak, God used in determining the apostle's
gifts and sphere of activity. Paul's boasting, therefore, was
not immoderate, but confined to just limits. According to
Beza κανών is used metonymically for that which is measured;
certum et definitum spatium; the district or diocese measured

off to him.   But this is not consistent with the ordinary meaning of the word, or with the context.   *Which God hath distributed to us ;* οὗ ἐμέρισεν ἡμῖν ὁ θεὸς μέτρου, for μέτρου ὁ ἐμέρισεν ὁ θεός, by attraction.   This clause is in apposition with
κανόνος, and explains what was the rule or line which determined the sphere of his activity.   It was not something self-
assumed, or self-applied, but something which God had
appointed ; *a measure,* he adds, *to reach even unto you.*   It is
agreeable to Paul's manner to include two or more related
ideas in the same form of expression.   *To boast according to
the measure assigned him,* may mean to regulate his boasting
according to his gifts; or, to boast in reference to what was
done within the limits assigned him in preaching the gospel.
Both ideas are here united.   In opposition to the false teachers, who not only boasted of gifts which they did not possess,
but appropriated to themselves the fruits of other men's labours by intruding into churches which they had not founded,
Paul says he did neither one nor the other.   His boasting was
neither immoderate, nor was it founded on what others had
done.   He invaded no man's sphere of labour.   It was his settled purpose to preach the gospel where Christ had not been
named, and not to build on another man's foundation.   Rom.
15, 20.   Acting on this principle he had the right to regard
Corinth as legitimately within his field.   His assigned limit of
labour reached at least that far.   He had founded the church
in that city; others had built thereon.   1 Cor. 3, 10.   The
Corinthians were his work in the Lord.   1 Cor. 9, 1.   Over
them, therefore, if over no others, he had the authority of an
apostle.   It is plain, on the one hand, from the New Testament that the apostles had a general agreement among themselves as to their several fields of labour.   Paul was to go to
the Gentiles ; Peter, James and John to the Jews.   Gal. 2, 9.
But it is no less plain that they were not confined to any prescribed limits.   They had not, as modern bishops or pastors,
each his particular diocese or parish.   As their authority did
not arise from their election or appointment to a particular
church or district, but from their plenary knowledge, infallibility, and supernatural power, it was the same everywhere,
and in relation to all churches.   Hence we find Paul writing
to the church in Rome which he had never visited, as well as
to others who had never seen his face in the flesh, with the
same authority with which he addressed churches which he
had himself planted.   Peter addressed his epistles to churches

within Paul's sphere of labour; and, according to all tradition, St. John presided during the latter years of his life over the churches in Asia Minor, founded by the apostle to the Gentiles. Still it was a matter of courtesy that one apostle should not intrude unnecessarily upon the sphere already occupied by another. Paul, at least, determined that he would not build upon another man's foundation.

14. For we stretch not ourselves beyond (our) measure), as though we reached not unto you; for we are come as far as to you also in (preaching) the gospel of Christ.

This verse is generally regarded as a parenthesis, although some commentators make it the beginning of a new sentence. It is logically connected with the last clause of v. 13. 'God assigned us a measure extending to you, *for* not, as not reaching to you, do we unduly stretch ourselves out;' ὑπερεκτείνο-μεν ἑαυτούς, *do we overstretch ourselves.* The present tense is used, because the reference is to the sphere of the apostle's authority. *For we have come as far as you,* (ἐφθάσαμεν.) 'Our authority extends to you, *for* we have come to you in preaching the gospel.' That is, Corinth was included in the region throughout which he had been the first to preach Christ. The word φθάνω properly means, to come, or be, beforehand; to anticipate; and then, in the aorist, to have come already. See Matt. 12, 28. Phil. 3, 16. 1 Thess. 2, 16. This sense may be retained here. 'We have already come even unto you.' He had already reached them and expected soon to reach beyond them; see v. 16.

15. Not boasting of things without (our) measure, (that is), of other men's labours; but having hope, when your faith is increased, that we shall be enlarged by you, according to our rule abundantly.

If verse 14 is parenthetical, then this verse is connected with the 13th. 'We will boast according to our measure—not boasting immoderately.' *Of other men's labours.* This is explanatory of the εἰς τὰ ἄμετρα. He did not boast of what other men had done. If the connection is with the 14th verse, the participle καυχώμενοι most naturally depends on οὐ ὑπερεκτείνομεν. 'We do not stretch ourselves unduly—not boasting, &c.' The reproach to the false teachers here implied is of course obvious. They had done what Paul refused to do. They came to Corinth after the church had been gathered, assumed an authority to which they were not entitled, and endeavoured to destroy the influence of the apostle to whom the church owed its existence, and the people their hope of salvation. Jam, says Calvin, liberius pungit pseudo-apostolos, qui quum in alienam messem manus intulissent, audebant tamen iis obtrectare, qui sudore ac industria locum illis paraverant.

But having hope, when your faith is increased. This clause the Vulgate renders, 'Habentes spem crescentis fidei vestræ.' This interpretation the words αὐξανομένης τῆς πίστεως (*your faith being increased*) do not admit. Corinth was not the limit which Paul had fixed for his field of labour. He had the purpose, as soon as the state of the Corinthians would allow of his leaving them, to press forward to preach the gospel in regions beyond them. *That we shall be enlarged by you,* ἐν ὑμῖν μεγαλυνθῆναι. Luther, Calvin, Beza, and others, connect ἐν ὑμῖν with the preceding clause—'Your faith being increased among you.' Beza says this is required by the opposite clause, as the advantage was mutual. They were to grow in faith among themselves, he was to enlarge his boundaries. But in this case the words ἐν ὑμῖν are redundant. They belong to the following word, and are to be rendered either *by you,* or, *among you.* This depends on the sense given to μεγαλυνθῆναι. This word is used either literally, as in Matt. 23, 5, "They make broad their phylacteries;" or figuratively, as in Luke 1, 58, "The Lord hath made great his mercy toward her." In every other case where it occurs in the New Testament it means to praise, to declare great. Luke 1, 46, "My soul doth magnify the Lord." So in Acts 5, 13. 10, 46. 19, 17. Phil. 1, 20. This meaning of the word is very commonly retained here. 'I hope to be honoured by you abundantly.' But the object of the apostle's hope was neither to be glorified by them, nor among them. Besides, the following clause ('according to our rule') does not agree with this interpretation. The word, therefore, is to be taken in its more literal sense—'He hoped to be enlarged abundantly (εἰς περισσείαν) according to his rule.' That is, he hoped to preach the gospel far beyond Corinth, agreeably to the line of action marked out for him. The ἐν ὑμῖν may then be rendered, vobis adjuvantibus. They would aid Paul in his future labours. The same idea is brought out by rendering the clause thus, 'To become great among you as to that which is beyond.'

16. To preach the gospel in the (regions) beyond you, (and) not to boast in another man's line of things made ready to our hand.

This infinitive (to preach) is either exegetical, 'We hope to be enlarged, that is, we hope to preach beyond you;' or it is the infinitive of the object, 'We hope to become great among you, in order to preach, &c.' The choice between these explanations depends on the interpretation of the preceding verse. *To preach the gospel in the regions beyond you;* εἰς ὑπερέκεινα (an adverb, *beyond*), *parts beyond,* and with ὑμῶν, *parts beyond you.* Εἰς is not here for ἐν, but means *unto,* as expressing the extent to which. *Not to boast in another man's line;* ἐν ἀλλοτρίῳ κανόνι, within another's line. That is, within the field of labour occupied by another man. *Made ready to our hand.* This is not a literal translation of εἰς τὰ ἕτοιμα. These words belong to καυχήσασθαι, 'Not to boast in reference to things prepared.' The sense is plain; he would not appropriate to himself the fruits of other men's labours.

17. 18. But he that glorieth, let him glory in the Lord. For not he that commendeth himself is approved, but whom the Lord commendeth.

'To glory in the Lord,' is either to regard God as the ground of confidence and source of all good, and to ascribe every thing we have, are, and hope to his grace; or, it is to exult in his approbation. Instead of comforting ourselves with our own high estimate of our attainments and efficiency, or allowing ourselves to be inflated by the applause of men, we should be satisfied with nothing short of the divine approbation. The connection is here in favour of the latter view. 'He that glories should glory in the Lord, i. e. he that rejoices should rejoice in the approbation of God, (not in his own good opinion of himself, nor in the praises of others,) *for* not he who commendeth himself is approved, i. e. is really worthy of approbation, but he whom the Lord commendeth. Paul did not commend himself; his claims were not founded on the suggestions of self-conceit; neither did he rely on the commendation of others, his eye was fixed on God. If he could secure his favour, it was to him a small matter to be judged by man's judgment. 1 Cor. 4, 3.

CHAPTER XI.

The apostle apologizes for the self-commendation which was forced upon him, vs. 1–15. He contrasts himself and his labours with the assumptions of the false teachers, vs. 15–33.

Reasons for his self-commendation, vs. 1–15.

HE had just condemned all self-commendation, yet he was forced to do what had the appearance of self-laudation. The Corinthians were in danger of being turned away from Christ by having their confidence in Paul undermined by the misrepresentations of his enemies. It was therefore necessary for him to present the grounds which he had for claiming authority over them, and for asserting his superiority over his opponents. Yet so repugnant was this task to his feelings, that he not only humbly apologizes for thus speaking of himself, but he finds it difficult to do what he felt must be done. He over and over begins what he calls his boasting, and immediately turns aside to something else. He begs them to bear with him while he proceeds to praise himself, v. 1, for his doing so sprang from the purest motive, love for them and anxiety for their welfare, vs. 2. 3. An anxiety justified by the readiness with which they bore with those who preached another gospel, v. 4. He thus spoke because he was on a par with the chief apostles, and not behind those who among them claimed to be his superiors, v. 5. They might have higher pretensions as orators, but in knowledge and in every thing that really pertained to the apostolic office he was abundantly manifest among them, v. 6. His refusal to avail himself of his right to be supported by those to whom he preached was no offence to them, and no renunciation of his

apostleship, vs. 7–9. He was determined to refuse any pecuniary aid from the Christians in Achaia, not because he did
not love them, but because he wished to cut off all occasion
to question his sincerity from those who sought such occasion,
and because he desired to put the false teachers to the same
test of disinterestedness, vs. 10–12. These teachers claimed
to be apostles, though they had no more right to the office,
than Satan had to be regarded as an angel of light, vs. 13–15.

1. Would to God ye could bear with me a little in
(my) folly : and indeed bear with me.

The self-commendation of the false teachers was the fruit
of conceit and vanity ; with the apostle it was self-vindication.
Although so different in character and design, they had one
element in common. Both included self-laudation. Both,
therefore, are designated by the same word, boasting ; and
both, therefore, he calls ἀφροσύνη, a want of sense. *Would to
God*, in the Greek simply, ὄφελον, *oh that, I would.* In fact,
however, every such exclamation is, in the pious mind, a
prayer ; and, therefore, the rendering, 'I would to God,' is
neither irreverent nor inaccurate. Oh that *ye could bear with
me*, (ἀνείχεσθε, Hellenistic form, instead of ἠνείχεσθε.) The
pronoun μοῦ properly belongs to the verb, and not to the following μικρόν τι, as if the sense were, *a little of my folly.* The
meaning is, 'Bear with me (μικρόν τι ἀφροσύνης), *as to a little
of folly.*' This reading is, on the authority of the majority of MSS., adopted by the later editors. Knapp and others
read, μικρὸν τῇ ἀφροσύνῃ, *a little as to folly ;* which amounts to
the same thing. *And indeed bear with me.* So Calvin, Beza,
and many others, who take ἀνέχεσθε as the imperative. This
clause is then a repetition of the first, only more vehemently
expressed. The former is a wish, the latter a supplication or
demand. But the context does not require this vehemence.
A more appropriate sense is afforded by taking the word in
the indicative, 'But indeed ye do bear with me ;' i. e. the
request is not necessary, I know you are disposed to suffer
me to speak as I see fit.

2. For I am jealous over you with godly jealousy :
for I have espoused you to one husband, that I may
present (you as) a chaste virgin to Christ.

This is the reason either why they should bear with him, or why he was assured that they would do so. That is, the connection is either with the first and principal clause of v. 1, or with the latter clause. It makes but little difference. The sense is better if the connection is with the first clause. 'Bear with my folly—for I am jealous over you.' Ζηλῶ γὰρ ὑμᾶς. The word ζηλόω may mean, I ardently love, or more specifically, I am jealous. The latter, as the figure of marriage is used, is probably the sense in which the apostle uses the word. *With godly jealousy;* ζῆλος θεοῦ may mean a zeal of which God is the object, as in Rom. 10, 2; comp. John 2, 17. In that case Paul intends to say that the feeling which he had for the Corinthians was a pious feeling. It was no selfish or mercenary interest, but such as arose from his desire to promote the honour of God. Or, the meaning is, a zeal of which God is the author; or, a zeal which God approves; or, the zeal which God has. As the people of God are so often represented in the Bible as standing to God in a relation analogous to that of a wife to a husband, so God is represented as being jealous, i. e. moved to deep displeasure when they transfer their love to another object. Is. 54, 5. 62, 5. Ez. 16. Hos. 2. In this view, the apostle means to say, that he shares in the feeling which God is represented as entertaining towards his church. The translation given in the English version includes all the meanings above mentioned; for a godly jealousy (or zeal) is a pious zeal, it is a zeal of which God is both the object and the author, and it is such a zeal as he has. *For I have espoused you to one husband.* It was natural for the apostle to feel this jealousy over them, *for* he stood in a most intimate relation to them. Their union with Christ was his work. 1 Cor. 4, 15. 9, 1. He may compare himself in this verse to a father who gives his daughter to the bridegroom. To this it is objected that Paul became the father of the Corinthians by their conversion; whereas the relation here referred to subsisted before their conversion or espousal to Christ. It is commonly assumed that the allusion is to the office of "the friend of the bridegroom," John 3, 29, (παρανύμφιος,) whose business it was to select the bride, to be responsible for her conduct, and to present her to the bridegroom. In this sense Moses was called παρανύμφιος by the Rabbis, as it was through him the people entered into covenant with God. In either way the sense is the same. Paul's relation was so intimate with the Corinthians as the author of their espousals to Christ, that he could not fail to feel the deepest interest in their fidelity. *I have espoused you.* The verb ἁρμόζω in the active voice is used of the father who betroths his daughter; in the passive of the bride who is betrothed; in the middle voice it is generally used of the man who pledges himself to a woman. The middle form, however, is sometimes used, as in this verse, (ἡρμοσάμην,) in the active sense. *To one husband.* The marriage relation from its nature is exclusive. It can be sustained only to one man. So the relation of the church, or of the believer, to Christ is in like manner exclusive. We can have but one God and Saviour. Love to him of necessity excludes all love of the same kind to every other being. Hence the apostle says he had espoused (betrothed) them to *one* man. This was done in order, in due time, *to present them as a chaste virgin unto Christ.* As in Eph. 5, 27, this presentation of the church to Christ as his bride, is said to take place at his second coming, this passage is commonly understood to refer to that event. Paul's desire was that the Corinthians should remain faithful to their vows, so as to be presented to Christ a glorious church, without spot or wrinkle, on that great day. He dreaded lest they should, in that day, be rejected and contemned as a woman unfaithful to her vows.

3. But I fear, lest by any means, as the serpent beguiled Eve through his subtilty, so your minds should be corrupted from the simplicity that is in Christ.

The apostle adheres to his figure. Though they were betrothed to Christ, he feared that their affections might be seduced from him and fixed on some other object. Men are not jealous until their apprehensions are excited. They must have some reason, either real or imaginary, for suspecting the fidelity of those they love. The ground of the apostle's jealousy was his fear. He feared (μήπως) *lest peradventure.* They had not yet turned aside, but there was great danger that they might yield to the seductions to which they were exposed. There was one standing example and warning both of the inconstancy of the human heart, and of the fearful consequences of forsaking God. Eve was created holy, she stood in paradise in the perfection of her nature, with every conceivable motive

to secure her fidelity. Yet by the subtilty of Satan she fell.
What reason then have we to fear who are exposed to the
machinations of the same great seducer. *As the serpent beguiled Eve ;* i. e. Satan in the form of a serpent. *The* serpent,
i. e. the well-known serpent of which Moses speaks. The
New Testament writers thus assume, and thereby sanction,
the historical verity of the Old Testament record. The account of the temptation as recorded in Genesis is regarded by
the inspired writers of the New Testament not as a myth, or
as an allegory, but as a true history. Comp. 1 Tim. 2, 14.
Rev. 12, 9. 15. *Beguiled,* ἐξηπάτησεν, *thoroughly deceived.*
All seduction is by means of deception. Sin is in its nature
deceit. The imagination is filled with false images, and the
foolish heart is darkened. Eve was thus deceived by the subtilty of Satan. She was made to disbelieve what was true, and
to believe what was false. Man's belief, in a very large sphere,
is determined by his feelings. The heart controls the understanding. The good believe the true; the evil believe the
untrue. This is the reason why men are accountable for their
faith, and why the wicked are led captive by Satan into all
manner of error. Eve was deceived by exciting unholy feelings in her heart. Paul's apprehension was lest the Corinthians, surrounded by false teachers, the ministers of Satan,
should in like manner be beguiled. What he feared was that
their *minds should be corrupted.* It was a moral perversion,
or corruption, that he apprehended. *Your minds,* τὰ νοήματα
ὑμῶν. The word νόημα means first *thought ;* then that which
thinks, the understanding; and then, the affections or dispositions. Phil. 4, 7. Our translation, "your minds," as including the idea both of thought and feeling, is the most appropriate rendering. *Corrupted from,* is a pregnant expression,
meaning corrupted so as to be turned from. *The simplicity
that is in Christ ;* ἀπὸ τῆς ἁπλότητος τῆς εἰς τὸν Χριστόν, 'from
singleness of mind towards Christ.' That is, the undivided
affection and devotion to Christ which is due from a bride to
her spouse. The allusion to the marriage relation is kept up.
Paul had compared the Corinthians to a virgin espoused to
one man, and he feared lest their affections might be seduced
from Christ and transferred to another.

4. For if he that cometh preacheth another Jesus,
whom we have not preached, or (if) ye receive another

spirit, which ye have not received, or another gospel, which ye have not accepted, ye might well bear with (him).

There are two entirely different views of the meaning of this verse, depending on the view taken of the connection. If the association of ideas is with the preceding verse, so that this passage assigns the reason of the fear there expressed, the meaning is, 'I am afraid concerning you, for if a false teacher comes and preaches another gospel, you readily bear with him.' It is a reproof of their credulity and easiness of persuasion to forsake the truth, analogous to that administered to the Galatians. Gal. 4, 6–8. 5, 8. But if this verse is connected with the main subject as presented in v. 1, then the sense is, 'Bear with me, for if a false teacher preaches another gospel you bear with him.' This is to be preferred, not only because the sense is better as more consistent with the context, but also because ἀνέχομαι means to *endure, to put up with*, and supposes that the thing endured is in itself repulsive. In this sense the word is used twice in v. 1, and should be so taken here. 'If a man preaches a new Christ ye would put up with his self-laudation, therefore, you should put up with mine.' The proper force of the verb (ἀνέχομαι) is also against the interpretation given by Chrysostom and followed by many later commentators. 'If any one really preached another gospel (i. e. communicated to you another method of salvation), you would do well to bear with him and receive him gladly.' But all this is foreign to the context. The thing to be endured, was something hard to put up with. It was what the apostle calls folly.

For if he that cometh, ὁ ἐρχόμενος, *the comer*, any one who happens to come. The reference is not to any one well known false teacher, but to a whole class. *Preaches another Jesus ;* not another Saviour, but another person than the son of Mary whom we preached. That is, if he sets forth some other individual as the true deliverer from sin. *Or if ye receive another spirit, which ye have not received.* The gift of the Holy Ghost was secured by the work of Christ. He redeemed us from the curse of the law—in order that we might receive the promise of the Spirit. Gal. 3, 13. 14. The indwelling of the Spirit, therefore, as manifested by his sanctifying and miraculous power, was the great evidence of the truth of the gospel. Hence the apostle, to convince the Galatians of the folly of

apostasy to Judaism, says, "This only would I learn of you
Received ye the Spirit by the works of the law, or by the
hearing of faith?" Gal. 3, 2; and in Heb. 2, 4, he says, God
bore witness to the gospel by the gifts of the Holy Ghost.
The apostle here supposes the impossible case that a like confirmation had attended the preaching of the false teachers.
'If,' he says, 'they preach another (ἄλλος) Jesus, and in proof
that he is truly a Saviour, ye receive a different (ἕτερος) spirit,
i. e. a spirit whose manifestations were of a different kind
from those of the Spirit who attests my preaching,' &c. *Or
another* (ἕτερος, a different) *gospel, which ye have not accepted.*
In the former clause the verb is ἐλάβετε (ye received), in the
latter ἐδέξασθε (ye accepted), because, as Bengel says, Non
concurrit voluntas hominis in accipiendo Spiritu, ut in recipi-
endo evangelio. That is, man is passive in receiving the
spirit, and active in accepting the gospel. *Ye might well
bear with* him. The word is ἀνείχεσθε, in the imperfect. The
tense which the context would seem to demand is the present,
ἀνέχεσθε, a reading which Lachmann and Rückert, on the authority of the MS. B, have introduced into the text. The
other leading verbs of the verse are in the present, 'If one
preaches another Jesus, and ye receive another Spirit, and
accept another gospel, (in that case,) ye do bear with him.'
Instead, however, of saying, 'ye do bear with him,' the apostle
is supposed purposely to soften the expression by saying, 'ye
might well bear with him;' the particle ἄν being, as often,
understood. In this way he avoids the direct charge of tolerating the conceited boasting of the false teachers. Others,
as Meyer and Winer, assume an irregularity, or change of
construction.

5. For I suppose I was not a whit behind the very chiefest apostles.

The sense here again depends on the connection. If the
γάρ refers to v. 4, the reference must be (as so often occurs in
Paul's writings) to a thought omitted. 'Ye are wrong in
thus bearing with the false teachers, *for* I am equal to the
chief apostles.' This, however, is not in harmony with the
context. Paul's design is not so much to reprove the Corinthians for tolerating the folly of the false teachers, as to induce
them to bear with his. He felt it to be necessary to vindicate
himself, and he therefore prays them to bear with him a little

in his folly. To this point every thing here refers. They should thus bear with him, 1. Because he was jealous over them with a godly jealousy. 2. Because they would bear with any who really preached another gospel, were that possible. 3. Because he was on a par with the chief apostles. The connection, therefore, is not with v. 4, but with the main subject as presented in v. 1. This also determines the question, Who are meant by the chiefest apostles? If the connection is with v. 4, then the expression is to be understood ironically in reference to the false teachers. 'Ye do wrong to tolerate them, for I am in no respect behind those superlative apostles.' So Beza, Billroth, Olshausen, Meyer, and the majority of the moderns. The reason given for this is, that there is no controversy with the true apostles in this connection, and therefore nothing to call for such an assertion of his equality with them as we find in Gal. 2, 6–11. There is, however, no force in this reason if the connection is with v. 1. 'Bear with me in my boasting, for I am not behind the chiefest apostles.' In this view the reference to the true apostles is pertinent and natural. Paul says, μηδὲν ὑστερηκέναι, that *as to nothing*, in no one respect, had he fallen short, or was he left behind by the chiefest apostles; neither in gifts, nor in labours, nor in success had any one of them been more highly favoured, nor more clearly authenticated as the messenger of Christ. He was therefore fully entitled to all the deference and obedience which were due to the chiefest apostles. The expression τῶν ὑπερλίαν ἀποστόλων, is not in itself bitter or ironical. This is a force which must be given by the connection; it does not lie in the words themselves. It is not equivalent to the ψευδαπόστολοι of v. 13, and therefore there is no more reason why the true apostles should not be called οἱ ὑπερλίαν ἀπόστολοι than οἱ δοκοῦντες εἶναί τι in Gal. 2, 6. The argument, therefore, which the Reformers derived from this passage against the primacy of Peter is perfectly legitimate. Paul was Peter's equal in every respect, and so far from being under his authority, he not only refused to follow his example but reproved him to his face. Gal. 2, 11.

6. But though (I be) rude in speech, yet not in knowledge; but we have been thoroughly made manifest among you in all things.

In Corinth, where Grecian culture was at its height, it had

been urged as an objection to Paul that he did not speak with
the wisdom of words. 1 Cor. 1, 17. He was no rhetorician,
and did not appear in the character of an orator. This he
here, as in the former epistle, concedes. If that were an objection, he had no answer to make other than that his dependence was on the demonstration of the Spirit, and not the persuasive words of man's wisdom. 1 Cor. 2, 4. Εἰ δὲ καί is
concessive. 'But if, as is true, I am rude in speech;' ἰδιώτης
τῷ λόγῳ, untrained, or unskilful in speech. The word ἰδιώτης
means a private person as opposed to those in official station;
a commoner as opposed to a patrician; an uneducated, or
unskilful man, as opposed to those who were specially trained
for any service or work, corporeal or mental. What Paul
concedes is not the want of eloquence, of which his writings
afford abundant evidence, but of the special training of a
Grecian. He spoke Greek as a Jew. It is not improbable
that some of his opponents in Corinth, although themselves
of Hebrew origin, prided themselves on their skill in the use
of the Greek language, and made the apostle's deficiency in
that respect a ground of disparagement. *But not in knowledge.* He was no ἰδιώτης τῇ γνώσει. Having been taught the
gospel by immediate revelation from Christ, Gal. 2, 12, he had
complete possession of that system of truth which it was the
object of the apostleship to communicate to men. He therefore everywhere asserts his competency as a teacher instructed
of God and entitled to full credence and implicit confidence.
1 Cor. 2, 6–11. Eph. 3, 4. 5. *But we have been thoroughly
made manifest among you in all things.* In this clause,
after φανερωθέντες, ἐσμέν is to be supplied; ἐν παντί, rendered
thoroughly, is in every point, or in every respect; ἐν πᾶσιν, *in
all things,* so that in every point in all departments he was
manifest, i. e. clearly known; εἰς ὑμᾶς, as it concerns you, (not
among you, which would require ἐν ὑμῖν). So far from being
deficient in knowledge, he stood clearly revealed before them
as thoroughly furnished in every respect and in all things as
an apostle of Jesus Christ. In nothing did he fall behind the
very chief of the apostles. Luther's translation of this clause
is, Doch ich bin bei euch allenthalben wohl bekannt. It is in
this view a correction of what goes before. 'I am not deficient in knowledge. Yet I am in all respects perfectly
known by you; there is no need to tell you what I am.'
Beza and Olshausen give the same explanation. This, however, does not agree with what follows in the next verse.

Others again, understand the apostle as here asserting his well established character for purity of purpose and conduct. 'My whole conduct is perfectly open and straightforward for you to see.' There is, however, no impeachment of his conduct referred to in the context, and therefore no call for this general assertion of integrity. It is better to restrict the passage to the point immediately in hand. 'He was not behind the chief apostles; but although rude in speech, he was not deficient in knowledge, and was manifest before them in all things, i. e. in all things pertaining to the apostolic office.' Instead of φανερωθέντες the MSS. B, F, G, 17, read φανερώσαντες, which Lachmann, Rückert and Tischendorf adopt. This alters the whole sense. The meaning most naturally then is, 'I am not deficient in knowledge, but have manifested it in every point in all things.' The majority of critical editors retain the common text, which gives a sense equally well suited to the connection.

7. Have I committed an offence in abasing myself that ye might be exalted, because I have preached to you the gospel of God freely?

Our version omits the particle ἤ (*or*), which is necessary to indicate the connection. Paul was clearly manifested as an apostle. '*Or*,' he asks, 'is it an objection to my apostleship that I have not availed myself of the right of an apostle to be supported by those to whom I preach? Have I sinned in this respect?' Comp. 1 Cor. 9, 4–15. *Have I committed an offence in abasing myself;* ἐμαυτὸν ταπεινῶν, *humbling myself* by renouncing a privilege which was my due. Comp. Phil. 4, 12. It was an act of self-humiliation that Paul, though entitled to be supported by the people, sustained himself in great measure by the labour of his own hands. I humbled myself, he says, *that ye might be exalted,* that is, for your good. It was to promote their spiritual interests that he wrought at the trade of a tent-maker. *Because I preached unto you the gospel of God freely?* This clause, beginning with ὅτι, is exegetical of the preceding. 'Have I sinned humbling myself, i. e. have I sinned because I preached freely?' (δωρεάν, gratuitously). It is clearly intimated in 1 Cor. 9, that Paul's refusing to be supported by the Corinthians was represented by his enemies as arising from the consciousness of the invalidity of his claim to the apostleship. As they had no other objection to him, he asks whether they were disposed to urge that.

8. I robbed other churches, taking wages (of them), to do you service.

To rob is to take with violence what does not belong to us. It is therefore only in a figurative sense the word is here used. What Paul received from other (i. e. the Macedonian) churches, he was fully entitled to, and it was freely given. The only point of comparison or analogy was that he took from them what the Corinthians ought to have contributed. *Taking wages* (λαβὼν ὀψώνιον), or a stipend. *To do you service*, πρὸς τὴν ὑμῶν διακονίαν, *for your ministry*. This expresses the object of his receiving assistance from others. It was that he might minister gratuitously to them.

9. And when I was present with you, and wanted, I was chargeable to no man : for that which was lacking to me the brethren which came from Macedonia supplied : and in all (things) I have kept myself from being burdensome unto you, and (so) will I keep (myself).

It is plain from this verse that when Paul went to Corinth, he took with him a supply of money derived from other churches, which he supplemented by the proceeds of his own labour; and when his stock was exhausted the deficiency was supplied by the brethren from Macedonia. *And when I was present* (παρὼν πρὸς ὑμᾶς), 'being present with you;' (καὶ ὑστερηθείς), 'and being reduced to want;' (οὐ κατενάρκησα οὐδενός), *I was chargeable to no man*, literally, 'I pressed as a dead weight upon no one,' i. e. I was burdensome to no one. The verb here used is derived from νάρκη, *torpor*, hence ναρκάω, *to be torpid*. The compound καταναρκάω, *to be torpid against* any one, (to press heavily upon him,) is found only here and in 12, 13. 14. In confirmation of the assertion that he had been chargeable to no man he adds, *for that which was lacking to me* (τὸ ὑστέρημά μου, *my deficiency*,) *the brethren which*

came from Macedonia (rather, 'the brethren having come
from Macedonia,') *supplied ;* προσανεπλήρωσαν, a double compound verb, to supply in addition.   The contribution of the
churches were added to what Paul earned by his labour, or,
to his diminished stock which he had brought with him to
Corinth.   The point on which he here dwells is not that he
laboured for his own support, but that he received assistance
from other churches, while he refused to receive any thing
from the Corinthians.   His conduct in reference to receiving
aid varied with circumstances.   From some churches he received it without hesitation ; from others he would not receive
it at all.   He said to the Ephesians, "I coveted no man's silver, or gold, or apparel.   Yea, ye yourselves know, that these
hands have ministered unto my necessities, and to them that
were with me," Acts 20, 34. 35.   So also to the Thessalonians
he said, "Ye remember, brethren, our labour and travail : for
labouring night and day, because we would not be chargeable
unto any of you, we preached unto you the gospel of God,"
1 Thess. 2, 9. 2 Thess. 3, 8.   Among the Corinthians he adopted the same course. Acts 18, 3. 1 Cor. 9, 15–18.   Whereas
from the Philippians he received repeated contributions, not
only while labouring among them, but as he reminds them,
"Even in Thessalonica ye sent once and again unto my necessity," Phil. 4, 16 ; and when a prisoner in Rome they sent by
the hands of Epaphroditus an abundant supply, so that he
said, "I have all, and abound," Phil. 4, 18.   It was therefore
from no unwillingness to receive what he knew to be due by
the ordinance of Christ, (viz., an adequate support,) 1 Cor. 9,
14, but simply, as he says, to cut off occasion from those who
sought occasion.   He was unwilling that his enemies should
have the opportunity of imputing to him any mercenary motive in preaching the gospel.   This was specially necessary in
Corinth, and therefore the apostle says, 'In all things (ἐν παντί,
in every thing, not only in pecuniary matters, but in every
thing else,) I have kept myself from being burdensome unto
you, and will keep myself.' He would receive no obligation
at their hands. He was determined to assume towards them
a position of entire independence. This was doubtless very
painful to the faithful in Corinth. They could not but regard
it as a proof either of the want of love or of the want of confidence on his part. Still his determination as to this point
was settled, and he therefore adds solemnly in the next
verse :

10. As the truth of Christ is in me, no man shall stop me of this boasting in the regions of Achaia.

Calvin, Beza, and others, understand this as an oath, or asseveration. Our translators adopted the same view, and therefore supply the word *as*, which is not in the Greek. This interpretation is not required by the text or context. The words are simply, 'The truth (ἀλήθεια, the veracity, truthfulness) of Christ, (i. e. the veracity which pertains to Christ, and which Christ produces,) is in me.' That is, in virtue of the veracity which Christ has produced in me, I declare, *that* (ὅτι, which our translators omit,) *no man shall stop me of this boasting.* Literally, 'This boasting shall not be stopped as to me.' The word is φραγήσεται, which in the New Testament is only used in reference to the mouth. Rom. 3, 19. Heb. 11, 33. 'This boasting as to me shall not have its mouth stopped.' *In all the regions of Achaia ;* not in Corinth only, but in all that part of Greece not included in Macedonia. From the Macedonians he was willing to receive aid ; from the Christians of Achaia he would not. The reason for this distinction he states negatively and affirmatively in the following verses.

11. 12. Wherefore? because I love you not? God knoweth. But what I do, that I will do, that I may cut off occasion from them which desire occasion ; that wherein they glory, they may be found even as we.

That his purpose not to receive aid from the Corinthians did not, as it might seem, arise from want of love to them he solemnly declares. The expression "God knows" in the lips of the apostle, it need not be remarked, implies no irreverence. It is a pious recognition of the omniscience of God, the searcher of all hearts, to whom he appeals as the witness of the strength of his affection for his people. The true reason for his determination to continue to do as he had already done, was, as he says, *That I may cut off occasion from them that desire occasion.* That is, that I may avoid giving those who desire to impeach my motives any pretence for the charge that I preach the gospel for the sake of gain. It is plain from 1 Cor. 9, 15–18, that this was his motive in refusing to receive aid from the Corinthians; and that his special καύχημα, or ground of boasting, was that he preached the gospel gratuitously. He said he would rather die than that any man should take from him that ground of confidence. This of course implies that the purity of his motives had been assailed, and that his object in making "the gospel of Christ without charge" was to stop the mouths of his accusers. *That wherein they glory.* This clause (with ἵνα) depends on the immediately preceding one. He desired to cut off occasion from those seeking it, in order that, if they chose to boast, *they may be found even as we.* That is, he wished to force them to be as disinterested as he was. According to this interpretation, ἐν ᾧ, in the phrase ἐν ᾧ καυχῶνται, does not refer to any special ground of boasting, but to the general disposition. 'Inasmuch as they are so fond of boasting and of setting themselves up as apostles, they may be forced to give over making gain of the gospel.'

Calvin, Grotius, Rückert, and others, assume that the false teachers in Corinth preached gratuitously, and that the reason why the apostle did the same, was that he might not give them occasion to glory over him. In this view the second clause with ἵνα is co-ordinate with the first, and ἐν ᾧ in the last clause refers to their special ground of boasting, and the sense of the whole is, 'I will do as I have done in order that these false teachers shall have no occasion to exalt themselves over me; that is, in order that they be found, when they boast of their disinterestedness, to be no better than I am.' But to this it may be objected, 1. That it is evident from v. 20 of this chapter, and from the whole character of these false teachers as depicted by the apostle, that so far from preaching gratuitously, they robbed the churches. 2. It is clear from what is said in the former epistle that Paul's object was not to prevent his opponents setting themselves forth as his superiors, but to make undeniably manifest the purity of his own motives in preaching the gospel. Others again, admitting that the false teachers received money from the Corinthians, understand the apostle to say, that he refused aid in order that he might take away from the false teachers all occasion for boasting that they were as he was. This, however, was not their boast. They did not claim to be what the apostle was, for they denounced him as an impostor. The first interpretation suits both the words and the context.

13. For such (are) false apostles, deceitful workers, transforming themselves into the apostles of Christ.

The reason assigned in this verse for the determination expressed in the preceding, to cut off occasion from those who sought to degrade the apostle, is, the unworthy character of his opponents. They were so unprincipled and unscrupulous that Paul was determined they should have no advantage over him. The words οἱ τοιοῦτοι ψευδαπόστολοι may be rendered either, Such false apostles *are*, &c., or, Such *are* false apostles. The Vulgate, Luther, Calvin, and the majority of the earlier commentators, give the former interpretation; most of the later writers the latter. The latter is to be preferred because the emphasis is on the word *false apostles ;* and because *such* false apostles would imply that there were other false apostles who were not deceitful workers. *False apostles* are those who falsely claimed to be apostles, as false Christs, Matt. 24, 24, and false prophets, Matt. 11, 15, are those who falsely claimed to be Christ or prophets. An apostle was commissioned by Christ, endowed with the gifts of plenary inspiration and knowledge, and invested with supernatural powers. Those in that age, and those who now claim to be apostles without this commission, these gifts, and these signs of the apostleship, are false apostles. They claim to be what they are not, and usurp an authority which does not belong to them. The fundamental idea of Romanism is the perpetuity of the apostolic office. Bishops are assumed to be apostles, and therefore claim infallibility in teaching, and supreme authority in ruling. If we admit them to be apostles, we must admit the validity of their claims to unquestioning faith and obedience. *Deceitful workers*, i. e. workers who use deceit. They were workers in so far as they were preachers or teachers; but they were not honest; they availed themselves of every means to deceive and pervert the people. To the same persons the apostle refers in Phil. 3, 2, "as evil workers." *Transforming themselves into*, i. e. assuming the character of, *the apostles of Christ*. Though their real object was not to advance the kingdom and glory of Christ, and although they were never commissioned for that work, they gave themselves out as Christ's messengers and servants, and even claimed to have a more intimate relation to him, and to be more devoted to his service than Paul himself.

14. And no marvel; for Satan himself is transformed into an angel of light.

It is not wonderful that false apostles should put themselves forward under the guise of apostles of Christ, and appear and be received as such, for Satan himself, the most evil of all beings, assumes the form of the highest and purest of created intelligences. *An angel of light*, i. e. a bright, pure, happy angel. Light is always the symbol of excellence and blessedness, hence the expressions kingdom of light, children of light, &c. And hence God is said to dwell in light, and the saints are said to have their inheritance in light. It is by no means clear that the apostle refers either to the history of the fall or to Satan's appearing with the sons of God as mentioned in Job 1, 6. It is more probable that the statement rests on the general doctrine of the Bible concerning the great adversary. He is everywhere represented as the deceiver, assuming false guises, and making false representations.

15. Therefore (it is) no great thing if his ministers also be transformed as the ministers of righteousness; whose end shall be according to their works.

If Satan can be thus changed, it is no great thing if his ministers undergo a similar transformation. If a bad angel can assume the appearance of a good angel, a bad man may put on the semblance of a good man. The false teachers are called *ministers of Satan*, that is, they are his servants, 1. In so far as they are instigated and controlled in their labours by him. 2. And in so far that their labours tend to advance his kingdom, i. e. error and evil. All wicked men and all teachers of false doctrine are, in this sense the servants of Satan. He is their master. The false teachers assumed to be *ministers of righteousness*. This may mean, righteous, upright ministers; or, promoters of righteousness in the sense of general excellence. They pretended to be the promoters of all that is good. Or, righteousness may be taken in its peculiar New Testament and Pauline sense, as in 3, 9, where the the phrase "ministry of righteousness" occurs; see also Eph. 6, 15. In these and many other places the word righteousness refers to "the righteousness of God," or, as it is also called "the righteousness of faith." These false teachers professed to be the preachers of that righteousness which is of God and which avails to the justification of sinners in his sight. Satan does not come to us as Satan; neither does sin present itself as sin, but in the guise of virtue; and the teachers of error set themselves forth as the special advocates of truth. *Whose end shall be according to their works.* Satan is none the less Satan when he appears as an angel of light, and evil is evil when called by the name of good. God's judgments are according to the truth. He does not pass sentence on the (σχῆμα) the external fashion which we assume, but on our real character; not on the mask, but on the man. The end, i. e. the recompense of every man, shall be not according to his professions, not according to his own convictions or judgment of his character or conduct, not according to appearances or the estimate of men, but according to his works. If men really promote the kingdom of Christ, they will be regarded and treated as his servants; if they increase the dominion of sin and error, they will be regarded and treated as the ministers of Satan.

16. I say again, Let no man think me a fool; if otherwise, yet as a fool receive me, that I may boast myself a little.

After the foregoing outburst of feeling against the false teachers, the apostle resumes his purpose of self-vindication. He therefore says again what he had in substance said in v. 1. *Let no man think me a fool,* that is, a boaster. Self-laudation is folly; and self-vindication, when it involves the necessity of self-praise, has the appearance of folly. Therefore the apostle was pained and humbled by being obliged to praise himself. He was no boaster, and no one could rightfully so regard him, *but if otherwise* (εἰ δὲ μήγε, the negative is used because although the preceding clause is negative, the idea is, 'I would that no man should regard me as a fool, but if you do not think of me as I would wish, still, &c.') *Receive me,* (i. e. bear with me,) *that I may boast myself a little.* The words are κἀγώ, *I also,* i. e. I as well as others. 'You allow my enemies to boast of what they do, permit me to say a little of what I have done and suffered.'

17. That which I speak, I speak (it) not after the

Lord, but as it were foolishly, in this confidence of boasting.

That which I speak, ὃ λαλῶ. The apostle uses λαλῶ and not λέγω, because the reference is not to any definite words which he had uttered, but general—my talk, or language. Is not *after the Lord*, i. e. is not such as characterized Christ, or becomes his disciples. Our Lord was no boaster, and his Spirit does not lead any one to boast. This is very commonly regarded as a denial of inspiration, or divine guidance in these utterances. Even Bengel says, "Whatever Paul wrote without this express exception, was inspired and spoken after the Lord;" and Meyer says, οὐ λαλῶ κατὰ κύριον, negirt allerdings den theopneusten Charakter der Rede. This arises from a misconception of the nature and design of inspiration. The simple end of inspiration is to secure infallibility in the communication of truth. It is not designed to sanctify; it does not preclude the natural play of the intellect or of the feelings. When Paul called the High Priest a "whited wall," Acts 23, 3, although he apologized for it, he was as much inspired as when he wrote his epistle to the Ephesians. Even supposing therefore that there was something of human weakness in his boasting, that would not prove that he was not under the inspiration of God in saying that he boasted, or in saying that boasting was folly. But this assumption is unnecessary. There was nothing wrong in his self-laudation. He never appears more truly humble than when these references to his labour and sufferings were wrung from him, filling him with a feeling of self-contempt. Alas! how few of the holiest of men does it pain and mortify to speak of their own greatness or success. How often are the writings even of good men coals on which they sprinkle incense to their own pride. When Paul said that his boasting was not *after the Lord*, he said no more than when he called it folly. All that the expression implies is that self-praise in itself considered, is not the work of a Christian; it is not a work to which the Spirit of Christ impels the believer. But, when it is necessary to the vindication of the truth or the honor of religion, it becomes a duty. *But as it were foolishly*, (ἐν ἀφροσύνῃ, *in folly*.) That is, speaking boastfully was not religious but foolish. *In this confidence of boasting*, ἐν ταύτῃ τῇ ὑποστάσει τῆς καυχήσεως. Ὑπόστασις may mean *matter*, or *confidence*. 'In this particular matter, or case of boasting.' In this sense

it is a limitation of what precedes. He was justified in boasting in this particular matter. It is, however, more consistent
with the common use of the word in the New Testament, that
here, as in 9, 4, it should be taken in the sense of *confidence*,
and *ἐν* be rendered *with*. 'I speak with this confidence of
boasting.'

18. Seeing that many glory after the flesh, I will glory also.

The apostle here assigns the reason of his glorying. His
opponents so magnified themselves and their services, and so
depreciated him and his labours, that he was forced, in order
to maintain his influence as the advocate of a pure gospel, to
set forth his claims to the confidence of the people. *Seeing
that* (*ἐπεί, since, because*) *many glory.* From this, as well as
from other intimations abounding in this epistle, it is evident
that the opposition to Paul was headed not by one man, but
by a body or class of false teachers, all of whom were Judaizers. They gloried *after the flesh* (*κατὰ τὴν σάρκα*). This
may mean, 'they gloried *as to* the flesh.' Then flesh means
what is external and adventitious, such as their Hebrew descent, their circumcision, &c. See v. 22, where these false
teachers are represented as boasting of their external advantages. Compare also Gal. 6, 13 and Phil. 3, 4, where the
apostle says in reference to the same class of opponents, " If
any other man thinketh that he hath whereof he might trust
in the flesh, I more." The sense in this case is good and appropriate, but it would require *ἐν* and not *κατά*. See 10, 17.
11, 12. 12, 9, &c., &c. *Κατὰ σάρκα* more properly means *according to the flesh*, i. e. according to corrupt human nature,
as opposed to *κατὰ κύριον* in the preceding verse. These men
were influenced in their boasting by unworthy motives. *I
will glory also.* Does Paul mean, 'As others glory after the
flesh, I also will glory after the flesh'? i. e. as others give
way to their selfish feelings, I will do the same. This is the
view which many commentators take. They say that *κατὰ
σάρκα* is necessarily implied after *κἀγὼ καυχήσομαι*, because the
apostle had just said that in boasting he did not act *κατὰ κύριον*,
which implies that he did act *κατὰ σάρκα*; and because in the
following verse he makes himself one of *ἄφρονες* of whose glorying the Corinthians were so tolerant. But the sense thus
expressed is neither true nor consistent with the character of

the apostle. It is not true that he was influenced in boasting by corrupt feelings; that self-conceit and the desire of applause were in him, as in the false teachers, the motives which governed him in this matter. There is no necessity for supplying κατὰ σάρκα after the last clause. What Paul says is, 'As many boast from unworthy motives, I also will boast.' If they did it from bad motives, he might well do it from good ones.

19. For ye suffer fools gladly, seeing ye (yourselves) are wise.

That is, 'I will indulge in the folly of boasting, for ye are tolerant of fools.' The Corinthians had, to a degree disgraceful to themselves, allowed the boasting Judaizing teachers to gain an ascendency over them, and they could not, therefore, with any consistency object to the self-vindication of Paul. *Seeing ye are wise.* As it is the part of the wise to bear with fools, so the Corinthians in their wisdom might bear with the apostle. Of course this is said ironically and as a reproof. In the same spirit and with the same purpose he had said to them in his former epistle, 4, 8, "We are fools, but ye are wise."

20. For ye suffer, if a man bring you into bondage, if a man devour (you), if a man take (of you), if a man exalt himself, if a man smite you on the face.

They might well bear with Paul since they bore with the tyranny, the rapacity, the insolence, and the violence of the false teachers. The character of these troublers of the church was everywhere the same; see Gal. 1, 7. They were lords over God's heritage, 1 Pet. 5, 3, not only as they endeavoured to reduce the Christians under the bondage of the law, as appears from the epistle to the Galatians, but as they exercised a tyrannical authority over the people. To this the apostle here refers when he says, *If any man bring you into bondage* (καταδουλοῖ), i. e. makes slaves of you. That this is not to be limited to subjection to the Jewish law, is evident from what follows, which is an amplification of the idea here expressed. These men were tyrants, and therefore they devoured, insulted and maltreated the people. *If any man devour (you),* i. e. rapaciously consumes your substance, as our Lord de-

scribes the Pharisees as devouring widows' houses, Matt.
23, 14. *If any take* (of you); εἴ τις λαμβάνει; ὑμᾶς is to be
supplied as after κατεσθίει in the preceding clause. "*If any
take you,*" i. e. capture you or ensnare you, as a huntsman his
prey.   Our version by supplying *of you* alters the sense, and
makes this clause express less than the preceding; devouring
is a stronger expression for rapacity than 'taking of you.'
If any man exalt himself (ἐπαίρεται, sc. καθ' ὑμῶν), i. e. if any
one proudly and insolently lifts himself up against you.   And
as the climax, *If any one smite you on the face.*   To smite
the face or mouth was the highest indignity; as such it was
offered to our Lord, Luke 22, 64, and to Paul, Acts 23, 2;
see also 1 Kings 22, 24. Matt. 5, 39.   Such was the treatment
to which the Corinthians submitted from the hands of the
false teachers; and such is ever the tendency of unscriptural
church-authority.   It assumes an absolute dependence of the
people on the clergy—an inherent, as well as official superiority of the latter over the former, and therefore false teachers
have, as a general rule, been tyrants.   The gospel, and of
course the evangelical, as opposed to the high-church system
of doctrine, is incompatible with all undue authority, because
it teaches the essential equality of believers and opens the
way to grace and salvation to the people without the intervention of a priest.

21. I speak as concerning reproach, as though we
had been weak. Howbeit, whereinsoever any is bold,
(I speak foolishly) I am bold also.

I speak as concerning reproach. Κατὰ ἀτιμίαν λέγω means
simply *I reproach.* After ἀτιμίαν may be supplied ἐμήν. The
sense would then be, 'I say to my own shame, that, &c.;'
λέγω being understood as referring to what follows. 'I say
to my shame that I was weak.' The Greek is, κατὰ ἀτιμίαν
(ἐμὴν) ὡς ὅτι ἡμεῖς ἠσθενήσαμεν; where ὡς ὅτι may, as Winer,
§ 67, 1, says, be a redundancy for simply ὅτι (5, 19. 2 Thess.
2, 2.) 'I say *that.*' This would be a direct assertion on the part
of Paul that he was weak in the sense intended.   It is better,
with Meyer and others, to give ὡς its proper force, *as, as if.*
His being weak was not a fact, but an opinion entertained concerning him. 'I say that (as people think) I was weak.'   One
class of the Corinthians regarded Paul as weak in bodily pres-

ence and contemptible in speech, 10, 10. In reference to this
judgment of his opponents he says, 'I acknowledge to my shame
that, when present with you (the aorist, ἠσθενήσαμεν, is used),
I was weak.' In 1 Cor. 2, 3 he told the Corinthians that he
came among them in weakness and fear and much trembling.
There was a sense in which he admitted and professed himself
to be weak. He had no self confidence. He did not believe
in his own ability to persuade or convert men. He felt the
responsibility of his office, and he relied both for knowledge
and success entirely on the Spirit of God. His conceited and
arrogant opposers were strong in their own estimation; they
contemned the mean-spirited apostle, and considered him destitute of all sources of power. The weakness of which Paul
here speaks is that which was attributed to him by his enemies. The whole preceding context is ironical, and so is this
clause. 'Your teachers are great men, I am nothing compared to them. They are strong, but, I say it to my shame,
I am weak. *But*, as opposed to this imputed weakness, I
am equal to any of them, I speak in folly.' *Howbeit whereinsoever any is bold* (ἐν ᾧ δ᾽ ἄν τις τολμᾷ), 'But whatever they
dare, I dare. Whatever claims they put forth, I can assert
the same. If they boast, I can outboast them. If they are
Hebrews, so am I, &c.'

The foregoing interpretation of this passage, which assumes that λέγω in the first clause refers to what follows, and
that the reproach mentioned had Paul for its object, is given
by Storr, Flatt, Meyer, and many others. The great majority
of commentators, however, understand λέγω as referring to
what precedes and the Corinthians and not Paul to be the object of the reproach. 'I say this to *your* shame.' Compare
1 Cor. 6, 5, πρὸς ἐντροπὴν ὑμῖν λέγω. (In this latter passage,
however, it will be remarked that the preposition is πρός and
not κατά, as in the passage before us, and that ὑμῖν is in the
text, whereas here there is no pronoun used.) The two principal objections to this interpretation are, 1. That if λέγω refers to the preceding verses the sense must be, 'I make this
exhibition of the character of your teachers in order to shame
you.' This would do very well if what follows carried out
that idea; but instead of speaking of the Corinthians, and endeavouring to convince them of their folly in adhering to such
men as teachers, he immediately speaks of himself, and shows
how he was despised as weak. 2. According to this interpretation there is great difficulty in explaining the following

clause. It would not do to say, 'I speak to shame you that I was weak;' or, if ὅτι be made causal, 'I speak to shame you because I was weak,' still the sense is not good. The former interpretation of this difficult passage is therefore to be preferred.

22. Are they Hebrews? so (am) I. Are they Israelites? so (am) I. Are they the seed of Abraham? so (am) I.

In this verse the apostle begins his boasting by showing that in no point did he come behind his opponents. The three designations here used belonged to the chosen people. The Hebrews were Israelites, and the Israelites were the seed of Abraham. The first, as Meyer remarks, is the national designation of the people of God; the second their theocratic appellation; and the third marked them as the heirs of Abraham and expectants of the Messianic kingdom. Or, as Bengel remarks with no less justice, the first refers to their national, and the two others to their religious or spiritual relation. A Hebrew was not a Jew of Palestine as distinguished from the Hellenists, or Jews born out of Palestine and speaking the Greek language. For Paul himself was born in Tarsus, and yet was a Hebrew of the Hebrews, that is, a man of pure Hebrew descent. In Acts 6, 1 the word is used for the Jews of Palestine in distinction from other Jews, but it is obviously not so either here or in Phil. 3, 5.

23. Are they ministers of Christ? (I speak as a fool) I (am) more; in labours more abundant, in stripes above measure, in prisons more frequent, in deaths oft.

In all that related to the privileges of birth, as belonging to the chosen seed, Paul stood on a level with the chief of his opposers; in all that related to Christ and his service he stood far above them. *Are they the ministers of Christ?* Such they were by profession, and such for the moment he admits them to be, although in truth they were the ministers of Satan, as he had said in v. 15. *I more* (ὑπὲρ ἐγώ, where ὑπέρ is used as an adverb). This may mean either, I am more than a (διάκονος) minister of Christ; or, I am a minister or servant of

Christ in a higher measure than they. That is, I am more devoted, laborious and suffering than they. The latter is the true explanation as is clear from what follows, and because in Paul's language and estimation there was no higher title or service than that of minister of Christ. *I speak as a fool,* παραφονῶν λαλῶ. This is a strong expression, 'I speak as one beside himself.' This is said out of the consciousness of ill-desert and utter insufficiency. Feeling himself to be in himself both impotent and unworthy, this self-laudation, though having reference only to his infirmities and to what God had done in him and by him, was in the highest degree painful and humiliating to the apostle. It is Paul's judgment of himself, not the judgment which others are presumed to pass upon him. *In labours more abundant,* ἐν κόποις περισσοτέρως. There are three ways of explaining this and the following clauses, 1. In (or, *by*) labours I am more abundantly the servant of Christ. 2. Or, (supplying ἦν or γέγονα,) I have been more abundant in labours. 3. Or, connecting, as De Wette and Meyer do, the adverbs with the substantives with the sense of adjectives, *by more abundant labours.* This latter explanation can better be carried through, and expresses the sense clearly. *In stripes above measure,* ἐν πληγαῖς ὑπερβαλλόντως, i. e. *by stripes exceeding measure* (in frequency and severity). *In prisons more frequent,* either, as before, 'I have been more frequently imprisoned,' or, 'By more frequent prisons.' The sense remains the same. *In deaths oft,* ἐν θανάτοις πολλάκις, *by manifold deaths.* Paul, in accordance with common usage, elsewhere says, "I die daily." He suffered a thousand deaths, in the sense of being constantly in imminent danger of death and of enduring its terrors.

24. 25. Of the Jews five times received I forty (stripes) save one. Thrice was I beaten with rods, once was I stoned, thrice I suffered shipwreck, a night and a day I have been in the deep.

These verses are a parenthesis designed to confirm the preceding assertion that he had laboured and suffered more in the service of Christ than any of his opponents. In v. 26 the construction is resumed. The apostle had at this period of his history been scourged eight times; five times by the Jews and thrice by the Romans. Of this cruel ill-treatment at the hands of his own countrymen, the Acts of the Apostles contain no record; and of the three occasions on which he was beaten with rods, that mentioned in Acts 16, 22 as having occurred at Philippi is the only one of which we have elsewhere any account. In the law of Moses, Deut. 25, 3, it was forbidden to inflict more than forty stripes on an offender, and it appears that the Jews, in their punctilious observance of the letter of the law, were in the habit of inflicting only thirty-nine so as to be sure not to transgress the prescribed limit. From the distinction which the apostle makes between receiving stripes at the hands of the Jews and being beaten with rods, it is probable that the Jews were at that period accustomed to use a lash. The later Rabbis say that the scourge was made with three thongs, so that each blow inflicted three stripes; and that only thirteen strokes were given to make up the prescribed number of thirty-nine lashes. *Once was I stoned.* Acts 14, 19. On this occasion his enemies supposed he was dead. He must therefore have been rendered for the time insensible. *Thrice I suffered shipwreck* Of this we have no mention in the Acts. The *shipwreck in which Paul was involved on his journey to Rome, was at a much later period. *A night and a day have I been in the deep.* That is, for that length of time he was tossed about by the waves, clinging to a fragment of a wreck. *A night and day* (νυχϑήμερον), i. e. a whole day of twenty-four hours. The Jews commenced the day at sunset.

26. (In) journeyings often, (in) perils of waters, (in) perils of robbers, (in) perils by (mine own) countrymen, (in) perils by the heathen, (in) perils in the city, (in) perils in the wilderness, (in) perils in the sea, (in) perils among false brethren.

Our translators have throughout this passage supplied the preposition *in.* But as ἐν in the preceding verse is used instrumentally, so here we have the instrumental dative, *by journeyings, by perils,* &c. It was by voluntarily exposing himself to these dangers, and by the endurance of these sufferings the apostle proved his superior claim to be regarded as a devoted minister of Christ. *Perils of water*, literally, *of rivers ;* as distinguished from the dangers of the sea mentioned afterwards. History shows that in the country traversed in

Paul's journeys great danger was often encountered in passing the rivers which crossed his path. *Perils of robbers,* to which all travellers were exposed. Perils from my own countrymen (ἐκ γένους as opposed to ἐξ ἐθνῶν). The Jews were, at least in most cases, the first to stir up opposition and to excite the mob against the apostle. This was the case at Damascus, Acts 9, 23; at Jerusalem, Acts 9, 29; at Antioch in Pisidia, Acts 13, 50; at Iconium, 14, 5; at Lystra, 14, 19; at Thessalonica, Acts 17, 5; at Berea, Acts 17, 13; at Corinth, 18, 12. *From the Gentiles,* as at Philippi and Ephesus. *In the city,* as in Damascus, Jerusalem and Ephesus. *In the desert.* The dangers of the desert are proverbial. Paul traversed Arabia, as well as the mountainous regions of Asia Minor, and was doubtless often exposed in these journeys to the dangers of robbers, as well as those arising from exposure, and hunger and thirst. *Of the sea,* not only in the case of shipwreck before mentioned, but to other and lesser perils. *Perils among false brethren,* referring probably to the treachery of those who falsely professed to be his brethren in Christ, and yet endeavoured to deliver him into the power of his enemies.

27. In weariness and painfulness, in watchings often, in hunger and thirst, in fastings often, in cold and nakedness.

Here the preposition ἐν is again used, but in its instrumental sense *by.* It was *by* these trials and sufferings he proved himself to be what he claimed to be. *By weariness and painfulness,* ἐν κόπῳ καὶ μόχθῳ. These words are thus associated in 1 Thess. 2, 9, and 2 Thess. 3, 8, in both of which places they are rendered "labour and travail." They both express the idea of wearisome toil and the consequent exhaustion and suffering. *By watchings often,* referring to the sleepless nights which he was often compelled by business or suffering to pass. *In hunger and thirst, in fastings often.* The common meaning of the word νηστεία, and its connection with the words "hunger and thirst," implying involuntary abstinence from food, are urged as reasons for understanding it to mean voluntary fasting. But the context is in favour of the common interpretation which makes it refer to involuntary abstinence. Every other particular here mentioned belongs to the class of sufferings; and it would therefore be incongruous to introduce into this enumeration any thing so insignificant and so common as religious fasting. In this the Pharisees were his equals and probably far his superior. They fasted twice in the week. Paul was no ascetic, and certainly did not deny himself food to the extent of making that denial an act of heroism. It is remarkable that we have no record of Paul's ever having fasted at all, unless Acts 13, 3. *By cold and nakedness.* This completes the picture. The greatest of the apostles here appears before us, his back lacerated by frequent scourgings, his body worn by hunger, thirst, and exposure; cold and naked, persecuted by Jews and Gentiles, driven from place to place without any certain dwelling. This passage, more perhaps than any other, makes even the most laborious of the modern ministers of Christ hide their face in shame. What have they ever done or suffered to compare with what this apostle did? It is a consolation to know that Paul is now as pre-eminent in glory, as he was here in suffering.

28. Besides those things that are without, that which cometh upon me daily, the care of all the churches.

This verse is variously interpreted. The first clause, *Besides those things which are without,* is rendered in the same way in the Vulgate. Praeter illa, quae extrinsecus sunt. So also Calvin, Beza, and others. But this is contrary to the usage of the words τὰ παρεκτός, which mean, *the things besides,* i. e. other things; so that the sense of the clause χωρὶς τῶν παρεκτός is, 'Not to mention other things.' The preceding enumeration, copious as it is, was not exhaustive. There were other things of a like nature which the apostle would not stop to mention, but proceeded to another class of trials. That class included his exhausting official duties. *That which cometh on me daily,* viz., *the care of all the churches.* The latter clause is, according to this explanation, assumed to be explanatory of the former. The same view is taken of the relation of the two clauses by Meyer, who renders the passage thus: "My daily attention, the care of all the churches." This latter interpretation assumes that instead of ἐπισύστασις, which is in the common text, the true reading is ἐπίστασις, a reading adopted by Lachmann, Tischendorf, Meyer, Rückert, and others. Both words are used in the sense of concourse, tumult, as of the people, see Acts 24, 12, but the former has also the sense of care, or attention. If the corrected text be adopted, then the interpretation just mentioned is to be preferred. 'Without mentioning other things, (ἡ ἐπίστασίς μου ἡ καθ' ἡμέραν) my daily oversight, the care of all the church.' If the common text, although not so well sustained, be adhered to, the meaning probably is, 'My daily concourse' (*quotidiani hominum impetus*). That is, the crowding upon him every day of people demanding his attention. This is the sense expressed by Luther; "Dass ich täglich werde angelaufen, und trage Sorge für alle Gemeinen." The solicitude which the apostle felt for the churches which he had founded, is apparent from all his epistles; and it may be easily imagined how various and constant must have been the causes and occasions of anxiety and trouble on their account.

29. Who is weak, and I am not weak? who is offended, and I burn not?

That is, he sympathized with his fellow Christians, who were his children in the faith, so that their sorrows and sufferings were his own. This was the consequence not only of the communion of saints, in virtue of which, "if one member suffer, all the members suffer with it; or one member be honoured, all the members rejoice with it," 1 Cor. 12, 26; but also of the peculiar relation which Paul sustained to the churches, which he had himself planted. *Who is weak;* i. e. in faith, or scrupulous through want of knowledge, compare 1 Cor. 9, 22, *and I am not weak?* That is, with whose infirmities of faith and knowledge do I not sympathize? He pitied their infirmities and bore with their prejudices. To the weak, he became as weak. There are men, says Calvin, who either despise the infirmities of their brethren, or trample them under their feet. Such men know little of their own hearts, and have little of the spirit of Paul or of Paul's master. God never quenches the smoking flax. *Who is offended* (σκανδαλίζεται), i. e. caused to stumble, or led into sin; and *I burn not.* That is, *and I am not indignant?* It was not to Paul a matter of indifference when any of the brethren, by the force of evil example, or by the seductions of false teachers, were led to depart from the truth or to act inconsistently with their profession. Such events filled him not only with grief at the fall of the weak, but with indignation at the authors of their fall. Thus his mind was kept in a state of constant agitation by his numerous anxieties and his wide-hearted sympathy.

30. If I must needs glory, I will glory of the things which concern mine infirmities.

Paul's boasting was not like that of the false teachers. They boasted not only of their descent, but of their learning, eloquence, and personal advantages; he boasted only of the things which implied weakness, his sufferings and privations. The future, καυχήσομαι, expresses a general purpose, illustrated in the past, and not having reference merely to what was to come. The persecutions, the poverty, the scourgings, the hunger and nakedness of which Paul had boasted, were not things in which men of the world pride themselves, or which commonly attract human applause.

31. The God and Father of our Lord Jesus Christ, which is blessed for evermore, knoweth that I lie not.

This is a peculiarly solemn asseveration. An oath is the act of calling God to witness the truth of what we say. Here the appeal is not simply to God as God, but to God in his peculiar covenant relation to believers. When the Israelite called on Jehovah as the God of Abraham, Isaac, and Jacob, he recognized him not only as the creator and moral governor of the world, but as the covenant God of his nation. So the Christian when he calls God "The God and Father of our Lord Jesus Christ," recognizes him not only as his Creator, but as the author of redemption through his eternal Son. Jesus Christ is a designation of the Theanthropos, the historical person so named and known, to whom God stood in the relation at once of God and Father. Our Lord had a dependent nature to which God stood in the relation of God, and a divine nature to which He stood in the relation of Father, and therefore to the complex person Jesus Christ God bore the relation of both God and Father.

There is a difference of opinion as to the reference of this passage. Some suppose that the apostle intended by this oath to confirm the truth of the whole preceding exhibition of his labours and sufferings; others, that it is to be confined to the assertion in v. 30, viz., that he would boast only of his infirmities; others, as Calvin and many others, refer it to what follows, i. e., to the account which he was about to give of his escape from Damascus. To give this explanation the more plausibility, Meyer assumes that Paul had intended to introduce an extended narrative of his escape and sufferings, beginning with the incident at Damascus, but was interrupted and did not carry out his intention. As, however, there is no intimation of this in the context, it is probable that the reference is to the whole of the preceding narrative. He intended to satisfy his readers that he had not exaggerated or overstated his sufferings. God knew that all he had said was true.

32. In Damascus the governor under Aretas the king kept the city of the Damascenes with a garrison, desirous to apprehend me.

It is useless to inquire why Paul introduces, as it were, as an after-thought, this disconnected account of his escape from Damascus. It is enough that the fact occurred to him when writing, and that he saw fit to record it. The account here given agrees with that found in Acts 9, 24. 25, except that there the attempt to apprehend the apostle is attributed to the Jews, and here to the governor of the city. There is no inconsistency between the two. The governor acted no doubt at the instigation of the Jews. He had no grievance of his own to redress or avenge. The governor, or *ethnarch*, a term applied to a vassal prince, or ruler appointed by a sovereign over a city or province. Governor *under*, literally, *of* Aretas the king. Aretas was a common name of Arabian kings, as Pharaoh of the kings of Egypt. A king of that name is mentioned as contemporary with the high-priest Jason, and with the king Antiochus Epiphanes. The one here referred to was the father-in-law of Herod Antipas. Herod having repudiated the daughter of Aretas, the latter declared war against him and totally defeated his army. Vitellius, proconsul of Syria, undertook to punish him for this assault on a Roman vassal, but was arrested on his march by the death of the emperor Tiberius. It is commonly supposed that it was during this respite that Aretas, who was king of Petra, gained temporary possession of Damascus. *Kept the city of the Damascenes,* not, *besieged the city,* but as it is expressed in Acts, watched the gates.   The words *of the Damascenes* (τὴν Δαμασκηνῶν πόλιν) are omitted in the original edition of 1611 of King James's version, but are now found in all the copies.   *With a garrison.*   The word is simply ἐφρούρει, *he kept*, or *guarded.*   *Desirous to apprehend me.*   The governor set a guard at the gates to seize the apostle should he attempt to leave the city.

33. And through a window in a basket was I let down by the wall, and escaped his hands.

Through a window, *θυρίς, a little door,* or *aperture.*   This was either an aperture in the wall itself, or, as is more probable, a window of a house built upon the walls of the city.   A representation of these overhanging houses as still to be seen on the walls of Damascus, may be found in Conybeare and Howson's life of St. Paul, p. 98 of the 8vo. edition.   The same mode of escape was adopted by the spies mentioned in Joshua 2, 15, and by David, 1 Sam. 19, 12.

CHAPTER XII.

The account of a remarkable vision granted to the apostle, vs. 1–6.   The other evidences of his apostleship and his conduct and purposes in the exercise of his office, vs. 7–21.

Paul's revelations and visions.

HE would give over boasting, and refer not to what he had done, but to what God had done; not to scenes in which he was the agent, but to those in which he was merely the subject—to revelations and visions.   He had been caught up to the third heavens, and received communications and revelations which he was not permitted to make known.   This was to him, and to all who believed his word, a more reliable evidence of the favour of God to him as an apostle than any thing he had yet mentioned, vs. 1–6.   With this extraordinary proof of the divine favour there was given him some painful bodily affection, from which he could not be delivered, in order to keep him duly humble, vs. 7–10. This reference to his personal experience was exceedingly painful to him. He had been forced by their unreasonable opposition to speak of himself as he had done; for the external signs of his apostleship should have convinced them that he was the immediate messenger of Christ, vs. 11. 12. They themselves were a standing proof that he was truly an apostle. They were not less richly endowed than other churches founded by other apostles. If inferior at all, it was only that he had refused to be supported by them. This he could not help. He was determined to pursue in the future the course in that matter which he had hitherto adopted; neither by himself nor by others, neither mediately nor immediately, would he receive any thing at their hands, vs. 13–18. All this self-vindication was of little account. It was a small matter what they thought of him. God is the only competent and final judge. His fear was that when he reached Corinth he would be forced to appear as a judge; that not finding them what he desired them to be, he should be obliged to assume the aspect of a reprover, vs. 19–21.

1. It is not expedient for me doubtless to glory. I will come to visions and revelations of the Lord.

The authorities differ much as to the text in this verse. The common text has δή (*indeed, doubtless*) with few MSS. or versions in its support. Many of the oldest MSS. read δεῖ, *it is necessary ;* some few δέ, which is adopted by Meyer as the original reading. The difference is only as to the shades of the thought. The idea is that boasting is not expedient; he will pass to something else, or at least to things which implied no agency or superior power on his part. *Is not expedient.* Here again some MSS. read with the common text, οὐ συμφέρει μοι, ἐλεύσομαι γάρ, (*is not expedient for me, for I will come;*) others with Lachmann, Tischendorf, and Rückert, οὐ συμφέροι μὲν, ἐλεύσομαι δέ, (*it is not expedient indeed, but I will come.*) The common text is on the whole to be preferred. Boasting, the apostle says, *is not expedient for me,* either in the sense that it does not become me, is not a seemly or proper thing; or, is not profitable; does not contribute to set my apostleship in a clear light. There is a better way of proving my divine mission than by boasting. The former explanation is better suited to the apostle's mode of representation. He had repeatedly spoken of boasting as a kind of folly, something derogatory and painful. He expresses the same feeling here when he says it is not expedient. *I will come.* Our translators omit the γάρ, *for I will come.* The connection is with a thought omitted. Boasting is not expedient, (therefore I desist,) *for* I will pass to something else. What follows in the relation of the revelations made to him, was no self-laudation, but a recital of God's goodness. *Visions and revelations.* The latter term is, on the one hand, more general than the former, as there might be revelations where there were no visions; and, on the other, the latter is higher than the former, as implying a disclosure of the import of the things seen. *Of the Lord;* not visions of which the Lord was the object; it was not seeing the Lord that he here speaks of, but visions and revelations of which the Lord is the author. By *Lord* is obviously to be understood Christ, whose continued existence and divine power over the thoughts and states of the soul is hereby recognized.

2. I knew a man in Christ above fourteen years ago, (whether in the body, I cannot tell; or whether out of the body, I cannot tell: God knoweth;) such an one caught up to the third heaven.

He speaks of himself in the third person, "I knew a man." Why he does this is not clear. He narrates what had happened as though he had been a spectator of the scene, perhaps because his own activity was so completely in abeyance. *A man in Christ;* a man who was in Christ; the scriptural designation of a Christian, because union with Christ makes a man a Christian. It is the one only indispensable condition of salvation; so that all who are in Christ are saved, and all who are out of Christ perish. It is also the plain doctrine of the Bible that, so far as adults are concerned, this saving union with Christ is conditioned, not on any thing external, not on union with this or that external church, but on a personal appropriating act of faith, by which we receive and rest on Christ alone for salvation. And still further, it is no less clearly taught that holiness of heart and life is the certain fruit and therefore the only satisfactory evidence of the genuineness of that faith. *Above fourteen years ago.* The event referred to in this verse is not the same as that which occurred at the time of Paul's conversion. That was a vision of Christ to the apostle here on earth, this was a translation of the apostle into heaven; that occurred twenty years before the probable date of this epistle. So that the two agree neither in nature, nor in the time of their occurrence. *Whether in the body or out of the body, I cannot tell.* The point as to which Paul was in doubt, was not the nature of the event, not as to whether it was a mere exaltation of his consciousness and perceptions or a real translation, but simply whether that translation was of the soul separated from the body, or of the body and soul together. Though heaven is a state, it is also a place. According to the scriptural representation, more is necessary to our introduction into heaven than merely opening the eyes to what is now about us and around us. The glorified body of our Lord is somewhere, and not everywhere. *Such an one caught up;* ἁρπαγέντα, *carried away,* the proper term to express a removal from one place to another without the agency of the subject. Paul was entirely passive in the translation of which he here speaks. Comp. Acts 8, 39. 1 Thess. 4, 17, "Caught up to meet the Lord in the air." *To the third heaven.* This means either the highest heavens; or, on the assumption that Paul used the language and intended to conform to the ideas of the Rabbins who taught that there were seven heavens, it means the air, the region of the clouds. He was caught up into the air, and then still further raised to Paradise. The former explanation is to be preferred, 1. Because there is no evidence that the opinions of the Jewish writers, whose works are still extant, were prevalent at the time of the apostle. 2. Because there is no evidence in the New Testament that the sacred writers adopted those opinions. 3. Because if Paul believed and taught that there were seven heavens, that is, if he sanctioned the Rabbinical doctrine on that subject, it would be a part of Christian doctrine, which it is not. It is no part of the faith of the Christian church. 4. Because it is plain that the "third heaven" and "paradise" are synonymous terms; and paradise, as is admitted, at least by those who suppose that Paul here speaks as a Jew, means heaven.

3. 4. And I knew such a man, (whether in the body, or out of the body, I cannot tell: God knoweth ;) how that he was caught up into paradise, and heard

unspeakable words, which it is not lawful for a man to utter.

This is a repetition of v. 2, with the exception of the substitution of the word "paradise" for the phrase "the third heaven." *Paradise* is a word of Sanscrit origin, and signifies a park, or garden. It is used in the Septuagint, Gen. 2, 8, in the description of Eden, which was a paradise or garden. The word was early used among the Jews as a designation of heaven, or the abode of the blessed after death, as appears from Luke 23, 43, (compare Ecclesiasticus 40, 17. 28.) In Rev. 2, 7, it occurs in the same sense. *And heard unspeakable words*, ἄρρητα ῥήματα, literally, unspoken words; here obviously the meaning is words not to be spoken, as explained by what follows. *Which it is not lawful for a man to utter.* The communications made to the apostle he was not allowed to make known to others. The veil which conceals the mysteries and glories of heaven God has not permitted to be raised. It is enough that we know that in that world the saints shall be made perfectly holy and perfectly blessed in the full enjoyment of God forever.

5. Of such an one will I glory : yet of myself I will not glory, but in mine infirmities.

Of such a one, ὑπὲρ τοῦ τοιούτου, *for* such a one, i. e. in his behalf; or, ὑπέρ being taken in the sense of περί, *about,* or concerning. This latter gives the better sense. 'Concerning such a person I will glory.' This is equivalent to saying, 'Such an event is a just ground of glorying.' But τοιούτου is not to be taken as neuter, (of such a thing,) as is plain from the antithetical ἐμαυτοῦ. 'Of such a one, but not of myself.' The translation which he had experienced was a proper ground of boasting, because it was a gratuitous favour. It implied no superiority on the part of the subject of this act of divine goodness, and therefore might be gloried in without assuming any special merit to himself. *Of myself I will not glory ;* that is, he would not boast of his personal qualities as entitling him to admiration. *But* (εἰ μή, *except*) *in my infirmities.* That is, 'I will boast concerning myself only of those things which prove or imply my own weakness.'

6. For though I would desire to glory, I shall not

be a fool; for I will say the truth: but (now) I forbear, lest any man should think of me above that
which he seeth me (to be), or (that) he heareth of me.

The connection as indicated by (γάρ) *for*, is not immediately with what is expressed in the preceding verse, but with
a thought obviously implied. Paul had said he would not
glory concerning himself. The reason for this determination
was not the want of grounds of boasting. 'I could do it, *for*
if I chose to boast, *I should not be a fool* ; i. e. an empty
boaster—for I would speak the truth.' *But I forbear* (φείδο-
μαι δέ sc. τοῦ καυχᾶσθαι). Abundant as were the materials for
boasting at the apostle's command, justly as he could refer to
the extraordinary gifts with which he was endowed, and the
extraordinary success which had attended his labours, he did
not dwell on these things. The reason which he assigns for
this forbearance is that others might not be led to think of
him too highly. He did not wish to be judged of by what
he said of himself or of his experiences. He preferred that
men should judge of him by what they saw or heard.

7. And lest I should be exalted above measure
through the abundance of the revelations, there was
given to me a thorn in the flesh, the messenger of
Satan to buffet me, lest I should be exalted above
measure.

As Paul determined not to give occasion to others to
think too highly of him, he here tells us that God provided
against his being unduly elated even in his own mind. It is a
familiar matter of experience that men are as much exalted
in their own estimation by the distinguishing favour of their
superiors, as by the possession of personal advantages. Therefore the apostle, although he would not boast of himself, was
still in danger of being unduly elated by the extraordinary
manifestations of the divine favour. The order of the words
is inverted. "And by the excess of revelations lest I should
be exalted above measure;" ὑπεραίρωμαι, be lifted up above
what is meet or right. The expression *excess*, or exceeding
abundance, *of revelations* seems to refer not exclusively to the
event above mentioned, but to other similar communications
made to him at other times. That was not the only occasion

on which God had unveiled to the apostle the treasures of divine knowledge. *There was given to me,* i. e. by God. It was God who sent the trial here referred to, and from God the apostle sought deliverance. *A thorn in the flesh,* σκόλοψ τῇ σαρκί. The word σκόλοψ properly means a sharpened stake, a palisade, then any piece of sharpened wood, and specifically a thorn. This last is the meaning best suited to this passage, and is the one commonly adopted. Others say the meaning is, "a goad for the flesh," borrowing a figure from oxen, metaphora a bobus sumpta, as Calvin says; others again understand σκολόψ to refer to a stake on which offenders were impaled, or the cross on which they were suspended. A stake, or cross, for the flesh, would be a figurative expression for bodily torture. *Flesh* may be taken literally for the body, or figuratively for the corrupt nature. Calvin and many others take the latter view. But there is no reason for departing from the literal meaning, which should in all cases be preferred, other things being equal. The dative σαρκί may be rendered either, *for* the flesh, or *pertaining to* the flesh, i. e. in the flesh. This last is to be preferred, as it suits the context and is sustained by the parallel passage, Gal. 4, 14, τὸν πειρασμόν μου τὸν ἐν τῇ σαρκί μου. If this is the true interpretation of the word σάρξ, it goes far to determine the nature of the thorn of which the apostle here speaks. It cannot be the evil suggestions, or fiery darts of Satan, as Luther, Calvin, and others, understand it; nor some prominent adversary, as many of the ancients suppose; it was doubtless some painful bodily affection. *A messenger of Satan.* In the Bible the idea is often presented that bodily diseases are at times produced by the direct agency of Satan, so that they may be regarded as his messengers, something sent by him. The word Σατᾶν is used here probably as an indeclinable noun, as in the Septuagint in one or two places, but in the New Testament it is always, except in this instance, declined, nom. Σατανᾶς, gen. Σατανᾶ. On this account many are disposed to take the word here as in the nominative, and translate the phrase *angel Satan,* i. e. an angel (or messenger) who is Satan. But inasmuch as Σατᾶν is at times indeclinable, and as Satan is never in the New Testament called an angel, the great majority of commentators give the same exposition as that given in the English version. *To buffet me,* ἵνα με κολαφίζῃ, *in order that he* (i. e. the angel or messenger) *may buffet me.* The use of the present tense seems to imply that "the thorn in the flesh" was a permanent affection under which the apostle continued to suffer. *Lest I should be exalted above measure.* This last clause expresses the design of God in permitting the apostle to be thus afflicted. He carried about with him a continued evidence of his weakness. However much he was exalted, although raised to the third heaven, he could not extract this rankling thorn. And the experience of God's people shows that bodily pain has a special office to perform in the work of sanctification. In the unrenewed its tendency is to exasperate; when self-inflicted its tendency is to debase and fill the soul with grovelling ideas of God and religion, and with low self-conceit. But when inflicted by God on his own children, it more than any thing teaches them their weakness and dependence, and calls upon them to submit when submission is most difficult. Though he slay me, I will trust in him, is the expression of the highest form of faith.

8. 9. For this thing I besought the Lord thrice, that it might depart from me. And he said unto me, My grace is sufficient for thee: for my strength is made perfect in weakness. Most gladly therefore will I rather glory in my infirmities, that the power of Christ may rest upon me.

For this thing, ὑπὲρ τούτου, *in reference to this; ὑπέρ* is here used in the sense of περί. Τούτου may be neuter, *for this thing,* i. e. this affliction; or masculine referring to ἄγγελος, "about this angel or messenger of Satan," &c. This is generally preferred on account of the following clause, ἵνα ἀποστῇ, *that he might depart from me.* I besought the Lord, says the apostle, *thrice.* So our blessed Lord prayed "the third time saying, Let this cup pass from me." Paul was therefore importunate in his petition for deliverance from this sore trial. He says, I besought *the Lord,* that is, Christ, as is clear not only from the general usage of Scripture, but from what follows in v. 9, where he speaks of the "power of Christ." *And he said unto me,* εἴρηκέ μοι. The perfect is used either for the aorist, or in its proper force connecting the past with the present. The answer was not simply something past, but something which continued in its consoling power. Winer, § 41. "He has said;" the answer was ever sounding in the apostle's ears, and not in his ears only, but in those of all his suffering people from that day to this. Each hears the Lord say, *My grace is sufficient for thee*, ἀρκεῖ σοι ἡ χάρις μου. These words should be engraven on the palm of every believer's hand. *My grace*, either, 'my love,' or metonymically, 'the aid of the Holy Spirit,' which is so often meant by the word *grace*. The connection is in favour of the common meaning of the term. 'My love is enough for thee.' These are the words of Christ. He says, to those who seek deliverance from pain and sorrow, 'It is enough that I love you.' This secures and implies all other good. His favour is life; his loving-kindness is better than life. *For my strength is perfected in weakness*. This is given as the reason why the grace or favour of Christ is all-sufficient. That reason is, that his strength is perfected, i. e. clearly revealed as accomplishing its end, in weakness. 'Weakness, in other words, says our Lord, is the condition of my manifesting my strength. The weaker my people are, the more conspicuous is my strength in sustaining and delivering them.' *Most gladly therefore will I rather glory in my infirmities*. The sense is not, 'I will glory in infirmities rather than in other things,' as though Paul had written μᾶλλον ἐν ταῖς ἀσθενείαις, but, 'I will rather glory in infirmities than seek deliverance.' If Paul's sufferings were to be the occasion of the manifestation of Christ's glory, he rejoiced in suffering. This he did ἥδιστα, *most sweetly*, with an acquiescence delightful to himself. His sufferings thus became the source of the purest and highest pleasure. Καυχάομαι ἐν ταῖς ἀσθενείαις does not mean *I glory in the midst of infirmities*, but *on account of* them. See 5, 12. 10, 15. Rom. 2, 23, &c., &c. This rejoicing on account of his sufferings, or those things which implied his weakness and dependence, was not a fanatical feeling, it had a rational and sufficient basis, viz., *that the power of Christ may rest upon me*. The word is ἐπισκηνώσῃ, *may pitch its tent upon me;* i. e. dwell in me as in a tent, as the shechinah dwelt of old in the tabernacle. To be made thus the dwelling-place of the power of Christ, where he reveals his glory, was a rational ground of rejoicing in those infirmities which were the condition of his presence and the occasion for the manifestation of his power. Most Christians are satisfied in trying to be resigned under suffering. They think it a great thing if they can bring themselves to submit to be the dwelling-place of Christ's power. To rejoice in their afflictions because thereby Christ is glorified, is more than they aspire to. Paul's experience was far above that standard. The power of Christ is not only thus manifested in the weakness of his people, but in the means which he employs for the accomplishment of his purposes. These are in all cases in themselves utterly inadequate and disproportionate to the results to be obtained. The treasure is in earthly vessels that the excellency of the power may be of God. By the foolishness of preaching he saves those who believe. By twelve illiterate men the church was established and extended over the civilized world. By a few missionaries heathen lands are converted into Christian countries. So in all cases, the power of Christ is perfected in weakness. We have in this passage a clear exhibition of the religious life of the apostle, and the most convincing proof that he lived in communion with Christ as God. To him he looked as to his supreme, omnipresent, all-sufficient Lord for deliverance from "the thorn in the flesh," from the buffetings of the messenger of Satan, under which he had so grievously suffered. To him he prayed. From him he received the answer to his prayer. That answer was the answer of God; it implies divine perfection in him who gave it. To what sufferer would the favour of a creature be sufficient? Who but God can say, "My grace is sufficient for thee?" To Paul it was sufficient. It gave him perfect peace. It not only made him resigned under his afflictions, but enabled him to rejoice in them. That Christ should be glorified was to him an end for which any human being might feel it an honour to suffer. It is therefore most evident that the piety of the apostle, his inward spiritual life, had Christ for its object. It was on him his religious affections terminated; to him the homage of his supreme love, confidence and devotion was rendered. Christianity is not merely the religion which Christ taught; but it is, subjectively considered, the religion of which Christ is the source and the object.

10. Therefore I take pleasure in infirmities, in reproaches, in necessities, in persecutions, in distresses for Christ's sake: for when I am weak, then am I strong.

The difference between glorying in infirmities and taking pleasure in them, is that the former phrase expresses the outward manifestation of the feeling expressed by the latter.

He gloried in infirmities when he boasted of them, that is, referred to them as things which reflected honour on him and
were to him a source of joy. As they were thus the occasions of manifesting the power of Christ, Paul was pleased
with them and was glad that he was subjected to them. *Infirmities* is a general term, including every thing in our condition, whether moral or physical, which is an evidence or
manifestation of weakness. From the context it is plain that
the reference is here to sufferings, of which reproaches, necessities, persecutions and distresses were different forms. *For
Christ's sake.* These words belong to all the preceding
terms. It was in the sufferings, whether reproaches, necessities, persecutions or distresses, endured for Christ's sake, that
the apostle took pleasure. Not in suffering in itself considered, not in self-inflicted sufferings, nor in those which were
the consequences of his own folly or evil dispositions, but in
sufferings endured for Christ's sake, or considered as the condition of the manifestation of his power. *For when I am
weak, then am I strong.* When really weak in ourselves, and
conscious of that weakness, we are in the state suited to the
manifestation of the power of God. When emptied of ourselves we are filled with God. Those who think they can
change their own hearts, atone for their own sins, subdue the
power of evil in their own souls or in the souls of others, who
feel able to sustain themselves under affliction, God leaves to
their own resources. But when they feel and acknowledge
their weakness he communicates to them divine strength.

11. I am become a fool in glorying ; ye have compelled me : for I ought to have been commended of
you : for in nothing am I behind the very chiefest
apostles, though I be nothing.

I am become a fool, &c. This some understand as ironically said, because the self-vindication contained in what precedes was not an act of folly, although it might be so regarded
by Paul's opposers. It is more natural, and more in keeping
with the whole context, to understand the words as expressing the apostle's own feelings. Self-laudation is folly. It was
derogatory to the apostle's dignity, and painful to his feelings,
but he was forced to submit to it. And, therefore, in his case
and under the circumstances, although humiliating, it was

right. *Ye have compelled me.* It was their conduct which made it necessary for the apostle to commend himself. This is explained in the following clause. *For I ought to have been commended of you.* If they had done their duty in vindicating him from the aspersions of the false teachers, there would have been no necessity for him to vindicate himself. They were bound thus to vindicate him, *for in nothing was he behind the very chiefest apostles.* It is an imperative duty resting on all who have the opportunity to vindicate the righteous. For us to sit silent when aspersions are cast upon good men, or when their character and services are undervalued, is to make ourselves partakers of the guilt of detraction. The Corinthians were thus guilty under aggravating circumstances; because the evidences of Paul's apostleship and of his fidelity were abundant. He came behind in no one respect the very chief of the apostles. Besides this they were not only the witnesses of the signs of his divine mission, but they were the recipients of the blessings of that mission. For them therefore to fail to vindicate his claims and services was an ungrateful and cowardly dereliction of duty. By the chief of the apostles, still more clearly here than in 11, 5, are to be understood the most prominent among the true apostles, as Peter, James, and John, who in Gal. 2, 9 are called pillars. Neither here nor in 11, 5 is it an ironical designation of the false teachers. *Though I be nothing.* The apostle felt that what was the effect of the grace, or free gift of God, was no ground of self-complacency or self-exaltation. 1 Cor. 4, 7. 15, 8–10. There were therefore united in him a deep sense of his own unworthiness and impotence, with the conviction and consciousness of being full of knowledge, grace and power, by the indwelling of the Holy Ghost.

12. Truly the signs of an apostle were wrought among you in all patience, in signs, and wonders, and mighty deeds.

This is the proof that he did not come behind the chief apostles. *Truly ; μέν,* to which no δέ answers. The opposition is plain from the connection. 'The signs *indeed* of an apostle were wrought among you, *but* you did not acknowledge them.' So Rückert, De Wette, and others. *The signs of an apostle* were the insignia of the apostleship; those

things which by divine appointment were made the evidence
of a mission from God. When these were present an obligation rested on all who witnessed them to acknowledge the
authority of those who bore those insignia. When they were
absent, it was, on the one hand, an act of sacrilege to claim
the apostleship; and, on the other, an act of apostacy from
God to admit its possession. To acknowledge the claims of
those who said they were apostles and were not, was (and is)
to turn from God to the creature, to receive as divine what
was in fact human or Satanic. This is evidently Paul's view
of the matter, as appears from 11, 13–15, where he speaks of
those who were the ministers of Satan and yet claimed to be
the apostles of Christ. Comp. Rev. 2, 2. These signs of an
apostle, as we learn from Scripture, were of different kinds.
Some consisted in the manifestations of the inward gifts of the
apostleship (i. e. of those gifts the possession of which constituted a man an apostle); such as plenary knowledge of the
gospel derived by immediate revelation from Jesus Christ,
Gal. 1, 12. 1 Cor. 15, 3; inspiration, or that influence of the
Holy Spirit which rendered its possessor infallible in the communication of the truth, 1 Cor. 2, 10–13. 12, 8, in connection
with 12, 29 and 14, 37. Others of these signs consisted in the
external manifestations of God's favour sanctioning the claim
to the apostleship, Gal. 2, 8. To this class belongs fidelity in
teaching the truth, or conformity to the authenticated standard of faith, Gal. 1, 8. 9. Unless a man was thus kept faithful
to the gospel, no matter what other evidence of being an
apostle he might be able to adduce, he was to be·regarded as
accursed. Gal. 1, 8. To this class also belong, success in
preaching the gospel, 1 Cor. 9, 2. 2 Cor. 3, 2. 3; the power
of communicating the Holy Ghost by the imposition of hands,
Acts 8, 18. 19, 6; the power of working miracles, as appears
from the passage under consideration, from Rom. 15, 18. 19,
and many other passages, as Heb. 2, 4. Mark 14, 20. Acts 5,
12. 14, 3; and a holy walk and conversation, 2 Cor. 6, 4.
Without these signs no man can be recognized and obeyed as
an apostle without apostacy from God; without turning from
the true apostles to those who are the ministers of Satan.
In all patience, or constancy. This does not mean that the
patient endurance of severe trials was one of the signs of his
apostleship, but that those signs were wrought out under ad-
verse circumstances requiring the exercise of the greatest
constancy. *In signs, and wonders, and mighty deeds.* These

are different designations for the same thing. Miracles are
called *signs* in reference to their design, which is to confirm
the divine mission of those who perform them; *wonders* because of the effect which they produced; and *mighty deeds*
(δυνάμεις) because they are manifestations of divine power.

13. For what is it wherein ye were inferior to other churches, except (it be) that I myself was not burdensome to you? forgive me this wrong.

For. The connection indicated by this particle is with
the assertion in v. 12. 'I am not inferior to the chief apostles,
for you are not behind other churches.' The fact that the
churches founded by Paul were as numerous, as well furnished
with gifts and graces, as those founded by the other apostles,
was a proof that he was their equal. In other words, as it is
said Gal. 2, 8, "He that wrought effectually in Peter to the
apostleship of the circumcision, the same was mighty in me
towards the gentiles." Comp. 1 Cor. 1, 5–7. *Were ye inferior to other churches*, literally, less, or weaker than. The
verb ἡττάομαι (from ἥττων, *less*) has a comparative sense, and
therefore is followed by ὑπέρ, *beyond;* 'weak beyond other
churches.' The only distinction to the disadvantage of the
Corinthians was, that the apostle had refused to accept aid
from them. This is not to be regarded as a sarcasm, or as a
reproach. It was said in a tone of tenderness, as is plain from
what follows. *Forgive me this wrong.* It was, apparently, a
reflection on the Corinthians; it seemed to imply a want of
confidence in their liberality or love, that Paul refused to
receive from them what he willingly received from other
churches. In the preceding chapter he endeavoured to convince them that his doing so was no proof of his want of affection to them, or of his want of confidence in their love to him.
His conduct in this matter had other and sufficient reasons,
reasons which constrained him to persist in this course of conduct, however painful to him and to them.

14. Behold, the third time I am ready to come to
you; and I will not be burdensome to you: for I seek
not yours, but you. For the children ought not to lay
up for the parents, but the parents for the children.

The Acts of the Apostles mention but one visit of Paul to Corinth prior to the date of this epistle. From this passage, as well as from 2, 1 and 13, 1. 2, it is plain that he had already been twice in that city. The words, therefore, *the third time*, in this verse, belong to the word *come*, and not to *I am ready*. The sense is not, ' I am the third time ready,' but, ' I am ready to come the third time.' His purpose was to act on this third visit on the same principle which had controlled his conduct on the two preceding occasions. *I will not be bur-densome to you*, I will receive nothing from you. For this he gives two reasons, both not only consistent with his love for them, but proofs of his love. *For I seek not yours, but you*. This is the first reason. He had no mercenary or selfish ends to accomplish. It was not their money, but their souls he desired to win. *For the children ought not to lay up for the parents, but the parents for the children*. This was the second reason. He stood to them in the relation of a parent. In the course of nature, it was the parent's office to provide for the children, and not the children for the parent. You must al-low me, says Paul, a parent's privilege. Thus gracefully and tenderly does the apostle reconcile a seemingly ungracious act with the kind feelings which he cherished in himself and de-sired to excite in them.

15. And I will very gladly spend and be spent for you; though the more abundantly I love you, the less I be loved.

As I am your father, I will gladly act as such, spend and be spent for you; even though I forfeit your love by acting in a way which love forces me to act. This is the strongest expression of disinterested affection. Paul was willing not only to give his property but himself, his life and strength, for them (literally, *for your souls*, ὑπέρ τῶν ψυχῶν ὑμῶν), not only without a recompense, but at the cost of their love.

16. But be it so, I did not burden you: neverthe-less, being crafty, I caught you with guile.

Be it so ; that is, admitted that I did not personally bur-den you, yet (you may say) I craftily did it through others. This was designed to meet the ungenerous objection which the false teachers might be disposed to make. They might insinuate that although he refused to receive any thing himself, he quartered his friends upon them, or spoiled them through others. *I caught you with guile*, δόλῳ ὑμᾶς ἔλαβον, i. e. I despoiled you by artifice, as an animal is taken by being deceived. This shows the character of the opponents of the apostle in Corinth. That he should think it necessary to guard against insinuations so ungenerous and so unfounded, is proof of his wisdom in refusing to give such antagonists the least occasion to question the purity of his motives.

17. 18. Did I make a gain of you by any of them whom I sent unto you? I desired Titus, and with (him) I sent a brother. Did Titus make a gain of you? walked we not in the same spirit? (walked we) not in the same steps?

The best refutation of the insinuation that Paul did in an underhand way by others what he refused to do openly and in his own person, was an appeal to facts. The Corinthians knew the charge to be unfounded. They knew that no one of those whom Paul had sent to Corinth received any compensation at their hands. This was specially true in the case of Titus, his immediate representative. All his messengers followed the example, and doubtless the injunctions of Paul, in bearing their own expenses. The mission of Titus to Corinth here referred to, is not that mentioned in chap. 8, which was not yet accomplished, but that mentioned in chap. 7, designed to ascertain the effect produced by Paul's previous letter. *In the same spirit;* either the same inward disposition of mind, or *with* the same Holy Spirit, i. e. imbued and guided by the same divine agent, who controls the conduct of the people of God. *In the same steps.* Paul and his messengers walked in the same footsteps. That is, they all followed Christ, whose steps mark the way in which his followers are to tread.

19. Again, think ye that we excuse ourselves unto you? we speak before God in Christ: but (we do) all things, dearly beloved, for your edifying.

There were two false impressions which the apostle here

designs to correct. First, that he felt himself accountable to the Corinthians, or that they were the judges at whose bar he was defending himself. Second, that his object was in any respect personal or selfish. He spoke before God, not before them; for their edification, not for his own reputation.

Again think ye. Do you again think, as you have thought before. Instead of πάλιν, *again,* the MSS. D, E, J, K read πάλαι, *formerly, long.* This reading is adopted by the majority of modern editors. The sense then is, 'Ye are long of the opinion,' or, 'Ye have long thought.' Comp. εἰ πάλαι ἐπέθανεν, *whether he had been long dead,* in Mark 15, 44. The common reading has so much MSS. authority in its favour, and it gives so good a sense, that it is generally by the older editors and commentators retained. With πάλιν the passage is best read interrogatively. Do ye again think? as they had before done. See 3, 1. 5, 12. They were too much disposed to think that the apostle, like the false teachers, was anxious to commend himself to their favour, and to appeal to them as his judges. He on more occasions than one gives them to understand that he was not under their authority, his office was not received from their hands, and he was not accountable to them for the manner in which he exercised it. See 1 Cor. 4, 3. *Excuse ourselves unto you ; ὑμῖν, before you as judges. Excuse,* ἀπολογέομαι, *to talk oneself off, to plead,* or *answer for oneself.* This was not the position which the apostle occupied. He was not an offender, real or supposed, arraigned at their bar. On the contrary, as he says, *we speak before God ;* i. e. as responsible to him, and as in his presence; *in Christ,* i. e. as it becomes one conscious of his union with the Lord Jesus. In all his self-vindication he considers himself as a Christian speaking in the presence of God, to whom alone he was, as a divinely commissioned messenger, answerable for what he said. *All things, dearly beloved, for your edification.* This is the second point. His apology, or self-vindication, had their good, not his reputation or advantage, for its object.

20. For I fear, lest, when I come, I shall not find you such as I would, and (that) I shall be found unto you such as ye would not : lest (there be) debates, envyings, wraths, strifes, backbitings, whisperings, swellings, tumults.

He aimed at their edification, *for* he feared their state was not what he could desire. He feared lest they would not be acceptable to him, nor he to them. What he feared was that the evils to which frequent reference had already been made, should be found still to exist. Those evils were, ἔρεις, *contentions*, such as existed between the different factions into which the church was divided, some saying we are of Paul, others, we are of Cephas, &c., see 1 Cor. 1, 11; *envyings*, ζῆλοι, those feelings of jealousy and alienation which generally attend contentions; θυμοί, *outbreaks of anger;* ἐριθεῖαι, *cabals.* The word is from ἔριθος, *a hireling*, and is often used of a factious spirit of party; καταλαλιαὶ and ψιθυρισμοί, backbiting and whisperings, i. e. open detractions and secret calumnies; φυσιώσεις, *swellings*, i. e. manifestations of pride and insolence; ἀκαταστασίαι, *tumults*, i. e. those disorders which necessarily follow the state of things above described. This is a formidable list of evils, and it seems hard to reconcile what is here said with the glowing description of the repentance and obedience of the church found in the preceding part of this epistle, especially in chapter 7. To account for this discrepancy some suppose, as before mentioned, that the latter part of this epistle, from ch. 10 to the end, formed a distinct letter written at a different time and under different circumstances from those under which the former part was written. Others, admitting that the two portions are one and the same epistle sent at the same time, still assume that a considerable interval of time elapsed between the writing of the former and latter parts of the letter; and that during that interval intelligence had reached the apostle that the evils prevailing in the church had not been so thoroughly corrected as he had hoped. The common and sufficient explanation of the difficulty is, that part of the congregation, probably the majority, were penitent and obedient, while another part were just the opposite. When the apostle had the one class in view he used the language of commendation; when the other, the language of censure. Examples of this kind are abundant in his epistles. The first part of his first epistle to the Corinthians is full of the strongest expressions of praise, but in what follows severe reproof fills most of its pages.

21. (And) lest, when I come again, my God will humble me among you, and (that) I shall bewail many

which have sinned already, and have not repented of
the uncleanness, and fornication, and lasciviousness,
which they have committed.

The same apprehension expressed under a different form.
The word *again* may belong to *coming*, "me coming again;"
or with *will humble*, "God will humble me again." This implies that during his second unrecorded visit, Paul was humbled
by what he saw in Corinth, and grieved, as he says, 2, 1, in
having to use severity in suppressing prevalent disorders. He
feared lest his third should prove like that painful second
visit. The more obvious and natural connection, however, of
πάλιν is with ἐλθόντα, as in our version. 'Lest God will humble me when I come again.' Nothing filled the apostles with
greater delight than to see the churches of their care steadfast in faith and in obedience to the truth; and nothing so
pained and humbled them as the departure of their disciples
from the paths of truth and holiness. Humble me *among
you ;* πρὸς ὑμᾶς, *in relation to you.*

And that I shall bewail, πενθήσω. The word πενθέω is
here used transitively; to mourn any one, to grieve for him.
Many suppose that the sorrow here intended was that which
arises from the necessity of punishing; so that the idea really
intended is, 'I fear I shall have to discipline (or excommunicate) some, &c.' But this, to say the least, is not necessary.
All that the words or context requires is, that Paul dreaded
having to mourn over many impenitent members of the
church. *Many which have sinned already and have not repented,* πολλοὺς τῶν προημαρτηκότων καὶ μὴ μετανοησάντων, *many
of those who having sinned shall not have repented.* The προ
in προημαρτηκότων is probably not to be pressed, so as to make
the word refer to those who had sinned *before* some specific
time,—as their profession of Christianity, or Paul's previous
visit. The force of the preposition is sufficiently expressed by
the word *heretofore.* 'Those who have heretofore sinned.'
What Paul feared, was, that when he got to Corinth he should
find that many of those who had sinned, had not joined in the
repentance for which he commended the congregation as a
whole. *Of the uncleanness, &c., which they committed.* According to Meyer, ἐπὶ τῇ ἀκαθαρσία, κ.τ.λ., are to be connected
with πενθήσω, 'I shall lament many on account of the uncleanness, &c.' The position of the words is evidently in favour
of the common construction. 'Who have not repented con-

cerning the uncleanness they have committed.' The classes
of sins most prevalent in Corinth were those referred to in v.
20, arising out of the collisions of the different classes or parties in the church; and those here mentioned, arising out of
the corruptions of the age and of the community. To make
a holy church out of heathen, and in the midst of heathenism,
was impossible to any but an almighty arm. And we know
that in the work of sanctification of the individual or of a
community, even Omnipotence works gradually. The early
Christians were babes in Christ, much like the converts from
among the heathen in modern times.

CHAPTER XIII.

Threatening of punishment to impenitent offenders; exhortation to self-examination and amendment; conclusion of the epistle.

Paul's warnings and exhortations.

HAVING previously admonished and warned, he now distinctly
announces his purpose to exercise his apostolic power in the
punishment of offenders, vs. 1. 2. As they sought evidence
of his apostleship, he would show that although weak in himself, he was invested with supernatural power by Christ. As
Christ appeared as weak in dying, but was none the less imbued with divine power, as was proved by his resurrection
from the dead; so the apostle in one sense was weak, in another full of power, vs. 3. 4. Instead of exposing themselves
to this exercise of judicial authority, he exhorts them to try
themselves, since Christ lived in them unless they were reprobates, v. 5. He trusted that they would acknowledge him as
an apostle, as he sought their good, vs. 6. 7. His power was
given, and could be exercised, only for the truth. He rejoiced in his own weakness and in the prosperity of the Corinthians. The object in thus warning them was to avoid the
necessity of exercising the power of judgment with which
Christ had invested him, vs. 8–10. Concluding exhortation
and benediction, vs. 11–13.

1. This is the third (time) I am coming to you: In the mouth of two or three witnesses shall every word be established.

From this it is evident that Paul had already been twice in Corinth. He was about to make his third visit. Those who do not admit that he went to Corinth during the interval between the writing the first and second epistle, say that all that is proved by this verse, is that "once he had been there; a second time he had intended to come; now the third time he was actually coming." Others, still more unnaturally, say he refers to his presence by letter, as Beza explains it: Binas suas epistolas pro tolidem profectionibus recenset. There is no necessity for departing from the obvious meaning of the words. The Acts of the Apostles do not contain a full record of all the journeys, labours and sufferings of the apostle. He may have visited Corinth repeatedly without its coming within the design of that book to mention the fact. *In the mouth of two or three witnesses, &c.* It was expressly enjoined in the Old Testament that no one should be condemned unless on the testimony of two or three witnesses. Num. 35, 30. Deut. 17, 6. 19, 15. In this latter passage, the very words used by the apostle are to be found: "One man shall not rise up against any man for any iniquity, or for any sin, in any sin that he sinneth; at the mouth of two witnesses, or at the mouth of three witnesses, shall the matter be established." This principle of justice was transferred by our Lord to the New Dispensation. In his directions for dealing with offenders he says, "Take with thee one or two more, that in the mouth of two or three witnesses every word shall be established," Matt. 18, 16; see also John 8, 17. Heb. 10, 28. In 1 Tim. 5, 19 the apostle applies the rule specially to the case of elders: "Against an elder receive not an accusation, but before two or three witnesses." In the judgment of God, therefore, it is better that many offenders should go unpunished through lack of testimony, than that the security of reputation and life should be endangered by allowing a single witness to establish a charge against any man. This principle, although thus plainly and repeatedly sanctioned both in the Old and New Testaments, is not held sacred in civil courts. Even in criminal cases the testimony of one witness is often considered sufficient to establish the guilt of an accused person, no matter how pure his previous reputation may have been. Paul here announces his determination to adhere, in the administration of discipline, strictly to the rule relating to testimony laid down in the Scriptures. There are two explanations, however, given of this passage. Some suppose that Paul merely alludes to the prescription in the Law, and says that his three visits answers the spirit of the divine injunction by being equivalent to the testimony of three witnesses. *Tres mei adventus trium testimoniorum loco erunt*, says Calvin. This interpretation is adopted by a great many commentators, ancient and modern. But the formality with which the principle is announced, the importance of the principle itself, and his own recognition of it elsewhere, show that he intended to adhere to it in Corinth. Three visits are not the testimony of three witnesses. *Every word*, πᾶν ῥῆμα, *every accusation*, a sense which, agreeably to the usage of the corresponding Hebrew word, the Greek word ῥῆμα has here in virtue of the context, as in Matt. 5, 11. 18, 16. 27, 14. *Shall be established*, i. e. legally and conclusively proved.

2. I told you before, and foretell you, as if I were present, the second time; and being absent now I write to them which heretofore have sinned, and to all other, that, if I come again, I will not spare.

The meaning of this verse is doubtful. The words *second time* (τὸ δεύτερον,) may be connected with *being present* (ὡς παρών,) or with *I foretell* (προλέγω). If the former, the sense may be, "I foretold (i. e. when in Corinth), and I foretell, as though present the second time, although yet absent, to those who heretofore have sinned, &c." If the latter connection be preferred, the sense is, "I foretold you, and foretell you the second time, as if present, although now absent, &c." This is not consistent with the natural order of the words. Assuming Paul to have been already twice in Corinth, the simplest explanation of this verse is that given by Calvin, Meyer, Rückert, and others, "I have said before, and say before, as when present the second time, so now when absent, to those who have sinned, I will not spare." Paul gives now when absent the same warning that he gave during his second visit. The words προεῖπον and προλέγω are combined here as in Gal. 5, 21 and 1 Thess. 3, 4. "I said before, and I forewarn." *Those who heretofore have sinned;* προημαρτηκόσι, to those who sinned before, not before Paul's second visit, but those who heretofore have sinned, i. e. those who already stand in the category of known sinners, and *to all other*, i. e. to those who were not thus known, who had not as yet offended. *If I come again* (εἰς τὸ πάλιν), *I will not spare.* Paul had forborne long enough, and he was now determined to try the effect of discipline on those whom his arguments and exhortations failed to render obedient. From this, as well as from other passages of Paul's epistles, two things are abundantly manifest. First, the right of excommunication in the church. It is only in established churches controlled by the state, or thoroughly imbued with Erastian principles, that this right is seriously questioned, or its exercise precluded. In his former epistle, chap. 5, the apostle had enjoined on the Corinthians the duty of casting out of their communion those who openly violated the law of Christ. The second thing here rendered manifest, is, that the apostle as an individual possessed the right of excommunication. The apostolic churches were not independent democratic communities, vested with supreme authority over their own members. Paul could cast out of their communion whom he would. He was indeed clothed with supernatural power which enabled him to deliver offenders "unto Satan for the destruction of the flesh," 1 Cor. 5, 5, but this was not all. This presupposed the power of excommunication. It was the ability miraculously to punish with corporeal evils those whom he cut off from the church. This right to discipline, as it is not to be merged into the supernatural gift just referred to, so it is not to be referred to the inspiration and consequent infallibility of the apostles. The apostles were infallible as teachers, but not as men or as disciplinarians. They received unrenewed men into the church, as in the case of Simon Magus. They did not pretend to read the heart, much less to be omniscient. Paul proposed to arrive at the knowledge of offences by judicial examination. He avowed his purpose to condemn no one on his own judgment or knowledge, but only on the testimony of two or three witnesses. This right to exercise discipline which Paul claimed was not founded on his miraculous gifts, but on his ministerial office.

3. Since ye seek a proof of Christ speaking in me, which to you-ward is not weak, but is mighty in you.

This is part of the sentence begun in v. 2. 'I will not spare since ye seek a proof of Christ speaking in me.' Olshausen says the sense of the context is, 'Since they wished to put the apostle to the test and see whether Christ was in him, they had better try themselves and see whether Christ was in them. If Christ was in them, they would recognize the power of God in the apostle's weakness.' This supposes v. 4 to be a parenthesis, and connects ἐπεὶ δοκιμὴν ζητεῖτε of v. 3, with ἑαυτοὺς δοκιμάζετε of v. 5. But this is arbitrary and unnatural, as it is unnecessary, there being no indication of want of continuity in the connection. *A proof of Christ*, may mean, 'a proof which Christ gives,' or, 'a proof that Christ speaks in me.' De Wette and Meyer prefer the former, on account of the following, 'who is not weak,' which agrees better with the assumption that Χριστοῦ is the genitive of the subject. 'Since ye seek a proof or manifestation of Christ who speaks in me, who is not weak.' Calvin's idea is that it was not Paul, but Christ, that the Corinthians were questioning. "It is Christ who speaks in me; when therefore you question my doctrine, it is not me, but him whom you offend." He refers to Num. 16, 11, where murmuring against Moses and Aaron is represented as murmuring against God. Compare also Isaiah 7, 13. The common interpretation, however, is more in keeping with the drift of the whole context. What the false teachers and their adherents denied, was Paul's apostleship; what they demanded was proof that Christ spoke in him, or that he was a messenger of Christ. Since the evidence which he had already given in word and deed had not satisfied them, he was about to give them a proof which they would find it difficult to resist. *Who is not weak as concerns you, but is mighty among you.* The messenger and organ of Christ was not to be rejected or offended with impunity, since Christ was not weak, but powerful. His power had been proved among them not only in the conversion of multitudes, but by signs and wonders, and by divers manifestations of omnipotence.

4. For though he was crucified through weakness, yet he liveth by the power of God. For we also are weak in him, but we shall live with him by the power of God toward you.

Christ is divinely powerful, for though he died as a man, he lives as God. He had a feeble human nature, but also an omnipotent divine nature. So we his apostles, though in one aspect weak, in another are strong. We are associated with Christ both in his weakness and in his power; in his death and in his life. *For though.* The text is doubtful. The common edition has καὶ γὰρ εἰ, *for even if,* which the Vulgate renders *etsi* and the English version *although,* taking καὶ εἰ (*even if*) as equivalent to εἰ καί, *if even.* Many MSS. and editors omit the εἰ. The sense then is, 'For he was even crucified through weakness.' The common text gives a clear meaning, 'For *even if* he were crucified through weakness.' The case is hypothetically presented. *Through weakness,* ἐκ ἀσθενείας. His weakness was the cause or necessary condition and evidence of his death; not of course as implying that his death was not voluntary, for our Lord said he laid down his life of himself; but the assumption of a weak human nature liable to death, was of course necessary, in order that the eternal Son of God should be capable of death. Comp. Phil. 2, 9. Heb. 2, 14, 15. His death, therefore, was the evidence of weakness, in the sense of having a weak, or mortal nature. *Yet he liveth by the power of God.* The same person who died, now lives. That complex person, having a perfect human and a true divine nature hypostatically united, rose from the dead, and lives forever, and therefore can manifest the divine power which the apostle attributed to him. The resurrection of Christ is sometimes referred to God, as in Rom. 6, 4. Eph. 1, 20. Phil. 2, 9; sometimes to himself, as in Matt. 26, 61. Mark 14, 58. John 2, 19. 10, 18. This is done on the same principle that the works of creation and providence are referred sometimes to the Father and sometimes to the Son. That principle is the unity of the divine nature, or the identity of the persons of the Trinity as to essence. They are the same in substance, and therefore the works *ad extra* of the one are the works of the others also. It is not, however, the fact that the resurrection of Christ was effected by the power of God, but the fact that he is now alive and clothed with divine power, that the apostle urges as pertinent to his object. *For we also,* &c. The connection of this clause may be with the immediately preceding one, 'Christ liveth by the power of God, *for* we live.' The life which the apostle possessed and manifested being derived from Christ, was proof that Christ still lived. Or the connection is with the close of the preceding verse. 'Christ is powerful among you, 1. Because though he died as a man, he lives; and 2. Because though we are weak, we are strong in him.' In either way the sense is substantially the same. In what sense does the apostle here speak of himself as weak? It is not a moral weakness, for it is conditioned by his communion with Christ; *we are weak in him.* It is not subjection to those sufferings which were a proof of weakness and are therefore called *infirmities;* because the context does not call for any reference to the apostle's sufferings. Nor does it mean a weakness in the estimation of others, i. e. that he was despised. It is obviously antithetical to the strength or power of which he was a partaker; and as the power which he threatened to exercise and demonstrate was the power to punish, so the weakness of which he speaks was the absence of the manifestation of that power. He in Christ, that is, in virtue of his fellowship with Christ, was when in Corinth weak and forbearing, as though he had no power to vindicate his authority; just as Christ was weak in the hands of his enemies when they led him away to be crucified. But as Christ's weakness was voluntary, as there rested latent in the suffering Lamb of God the resources of almighty power; so in the meek, forbearing apostle was the plenitude of supernatural power which he derived from his ascended master. *We shall live with him.* "Vitam," says Calvin, "opponit infirmitati: ideoque hoc nomine florentem et plenum dignitatis statum intelligit." As the life of Christ subsequent to his resurrection was a state in which he assumed the exercise and manifestation of the power inherent in him as the Son of God, so the life of which Paul here speaks, was the state in which he manifested the apostolic power with which he was invested. There is no reference to the future or eternal life of which Paul, as a believer, was hereafter to partake. He is vindicating the propriety of his denunciation of chastisement to the disobedient in Corinth. Though he had been among them as weak and forbearing, yet he would manifest that he was alive in the sense of having power to enforce his commands. *By the power of God.* Paul's power was a manifestation of the power of God. It was derived from God. It was not his own either in its source or in its exercise. He could do nothing, as he afterwards says, against the truth. *Toward you;* i. e. *we shall live toward you.* We shall exercise our authority, or manifest our apostolic life and power in relation to you.

5. Examine yourselves, whether ye be in the faith; prove your own selves. Know ye not your own selves, how that Jesus Christ is in you, except ye be reprobates?

There are two links of association between this verse and what precedes. They had been trying the apostle, seeking proof of Christ speaking in him. He tells them they had better examine themselves and see whether Christ was in them. Hence the antithesis between ἑαυτοὺς (yourselves) placed before the verb for the sake of emphasis, and δοκιμὴν ζητεῖτε (ye seek a proof, &c.) of v. 3. 'Ye would prove me—prove yourselves.' Another idea, however, and perhaps a more important one is this, ' Ye seek a proof of Christ speaking in me, seek it in yourselves. Know ye not that Christ is in you (unless you be reprobates), and if he is in you, if you are really members of his body, ye will know that he is in me.' The passage in this view is analogous to those in which the apostle appeals to the people as seals of his ministry, 1 Cor. 9, 1, and as his letters of commendation, 3, 2. *To examine* and *to prove* mean the same thing. Both express the idea of trying or putting to the test to ascertain the nature or character of the person or thing tried. *Whether ye be in the faith*, that is, whether you really have faith, or are Christians only in name. This exhortation to self-examination supposes, on the one hand, that faith is self-manifesting, that it reveals itself in the consciousness and by its fruits; and, on the other hand, that it may exist and be genuine and yet not be known as true faith by the believer himself. Only what is doubtful needs to be determined by examination. The fact, therefore, that we are commanded to examine ourselves to see whether we are in the faith, proves that a true believer may doubt of his good estate. In other words, it proves that assurance is not essential to faith. Calvin, in his antagonism to the Romish doctrine that assurance is unattainable in this life, and that all claims to it are unscriptural and fanatical, draws the directly opposite conclusion from this passage. Hic locus, he says, valet ad probandam fidei certitudinem, quam nobis Sorbonici sophistæ labefactarunt, imo penitus exterminarunt ex hominum animis: temeritatis damnant, quotquot persuasi sunt se esse Christi membra, et illum habere in se manentem; nam morali quam vocant, conjectura, hoc est, sola opinione contentos esse nos jubent, ut conscientiæ perpetuo suspensæ hæreant ac perplexæ. Quid autem hic Paulus? reprobos esse testatur quicunque dubitant an possideant Christum, et sint ex illius corpore. Quare sit nobis hæc sola recta fides, quæ facit ut tuto, neque dubia opinione, sed stabili constantique certitudine, in gratia Dei acquiescamus. Elsewhere, however, Calvin teaches a different doctrine, in so far as he admits that true believers are often disturbed by serious doubts and inward conflicts. See his Institutes, Lib. iii. cap. ii. 17, and Lib. iv. cap. xiv. 7. 8.

Know ye not your own selves how that Christ is in you. This version overlooks the connecting particle ἤ (*or*), the force of which indeed it is not easy to see. It may be that the apostle designed in these words to shame or to rouse them. 'Examine yourselves, *or* are you so besotted or ignorant as not to know that Christ is in you; that some thing is to be discovered by self-examination, unless ye are no Christians at all.' It may, however, be a direct appeal to the consciousness of his readers. 'Do you not recognize in yourselves, that is, are ye not conscious, that Christ is in you.' The construction in this clause is analogous to that in 1 Cor. 14, 37 and 16, 15. 'Know yourselves that, &c.,' equivalent to 'know that.' Winer 63, 3. The expression *Christ is in you*, does not mean 'Christ is among you as a people.' It refers to an indwelling of Christ in the individual believer, as is plain from such passages as Gal. 2, 20, "Christ liveth in me," and Gal. 4, 19. Rom. 8, 10. Christ dwells in his people by his Spirit. The presence of the Spirit is the presence of Christ. This is not a mere figurative expression, as when we say we have a friend in our heart—but a real truth. The Spirit of Christ, the Holy Ghost, is in the people of God collectively and individually, the ever-present source of a new kind of life, so that if any man have not the Spirit of Christ he is none of his. Rom. 8, 9. *Unless ye be reprobates.* The word *reprobate*, in its theological sense, means one who is judicially abandoned to everlasting perdition. Such is obviously not its sense here, otherwise all those not now converted would perish forever. The word is to be taken in its ordinary meaning, *disapproved, unworthy of approbation.* Any person or thing which cannot stand the test is ἀδόκιμος. Those therefore in whom Christ does not dwell cannot stand the test, and are proved to be Christians, if at all, only in name.

6. But I trust that ye shall know that we are not reprobates.

In v. 3 Paul had said that the Corinthians sought δοκιμήν (evidence) that Christ was in him as an apostle. He exhorted them to seek evidence that he was in them as believers. If they should prove to be (ἀδόκιμος) without evidence, he was satisfied that they would find that he was not ἀδόκιμος. The δοκιμή (or evidence) of Christ speaking in him which he proposed or threatened to give, was the exercise of the apostolic power which resulted from the indwelling of Christ, and therefore proved his presence. He was loath, however, to give that evidence; he would rather be (ἀδόκιμος) without that evidence; and he therefore adds,

7. Now I pray to God that ye do no evil; not that we should appear approved, but that ye should do that which is honest, though we be as reprobates.

Now I pray God that ye do no evil; that is, I pray that ye may not give occasion for me to give the evidence of Christ speaking in me, which I have threatened to give, in case of your continued disobedience. So far from desiring an opportunity of exhibiting my supernatural power, I earnestly desire that there may be no occasion for its exercise. The interpretation which Grotius, and after him Flatt, Billroth, and others give of this clause, 'I pray God that I may do you no evil,' is possible so far as the words are concerned, as ποιῆσαι ὑμᾶς κακόν may mean either, *to do you evil*, or, *that you do evil*. But to do evil is not to punish. And had Paul intended to say, 'I pray God that I may not punish you,' he certainly would have chosen some more suitable expression. Besides, ποιῆσαι κακόν is the opposite of ποιῆτε τὸ καλόν (*ye may do right*) in this same verse. *Not that we should appear approved,* &c. This and the following clause give the reason of the prayer just uttered. The negative statement of that reason comes first. He did not desire their good estate for the selfish reason that he might appear, i. e. stand forth apparent, as δόκιμος (approved), as one concerning whom there could be no doubt that Christ dwelt in him. There were different kinds of evidence of the validity of Paul's claims as a believer and as an apostle; his holy life and multiform labours; signs and wonders; the apostolic power with which he was clothed; his success in preaching, or the number and character of his converts. The good state of the Corinthian church was therefore an evidence that he was approved, i. e. could stand the test. This, however, as he says, was not the reason why he prayed that they might do no evil. That reason, as stated positively, was, *that ye should do that which is honest.* That is, it was their good, and not his own recognition, that he had at heart. *Do what is honest,* τὸ καλὸν ποιῆτε, that ye may do the good, the beautiful, what is at once right and pleasing. *Though we be as reprobates,* ἀδόκιμοι, *without approbation.* Paul was earnestly desirous that the Corinthians should do what was right, although the consequence was that he should have no opportunity of giving that δοκιμήν (evidence) of Christ speaking in him which he had threatened to give, and thus, in that respect, be ἀδόκιμος, *without evidence.* There is such a play on words in this whole connection that the sense of the passage is much plainer in the Greek than it is in the English version. This view of the passage is simple and suited to the connection, and is commonly adopted. Calvin and others interpret it more generally and without specific reference to the connection. "Concerning myself," he makes the apostle say, "I am not solicitous; I only fear lest ye should offend God. I am ready to appear as reprobate, if you are free of offence. Reprobate, I mean, in the judgment of men, who often reject those who are worthy of special honour." This is the general sense, but the peculiar colouring of the passage is thus lost.

8. For we can do nothing against the truth, but for the truth.

This verse is connected with the last clause of the preceding. 'We shall, in one sense, be ἀδόκιμοι (without evidence) if you do what is right, *for* we can do nothing against the truth, but are powerful only for the truth.' That is, 'We can exercise the apostolic and supernatural power which is the evidence of Christ speaking in us, only in behalf of the truth.' By *the truth* is not to be understood moral excellence, or rectitude—a sense indeed which the word ἀλήθεια often has when antithetical to unrighteousness; nor does it mean judicial rectitude specifically, i. e. that standard to which a judge should be conformed, or, as Bengel explains it, "the exact authority to be exercised over the Corinthians;" but it means truth in its religious, scriptural sense; that revelation which God has made in his word as the rule of our faith and practice. This passage is of special interest as fixing the limits of all ecclesiastical power, whether ordinary or miraculous. The decision of the apostle, if against the truth, availed nothing in the sight of God; the supernatural power with which he was invested forsook his arm, if raised against God's own people. The promise of our Lord, that what the church binds on earth shall be bound in heaven, is limited by the condition that her decisions be in accordance with the truth. The doctrine of the extreme Romish party that acts of discipline are effectual in cutting off from the true church and the communion of God, even *clave errante*, i. e. when the church errs in her knowledge of the facts, is utterly inconsistent with Paul's doctrine. He claimed no such power.

9. For we are glad, when we are weak, and ye are strong : and this also we wish, (even) your perfection.

If connected with the preceding clause the sense of this verse is, 'We can act only for the truth, *for* we have no desire to exercise our power to punish; we are glad when we are weak.' The meaning is better if this verse is regarded as coordinate with verse 8, and subordinate to v. 7. 'We desire that you should do right, though we appear as ἀδόκιμοι (without evidence), for we are glad when we are weak.' That is, we are glad when we have no occasion to exercise or manifest our power to punish. This is evidently the sense in which the word *weak* is to be here taken. It does not mean weak in the estimation of men, that is, despised as unworthy of respect. *And ye are strong*, i. e. such as cannot be overcome. They were strong when they were good. Their goodness was a sure protection from the disciplinary power of the apostle. *This also we wish*, viz. *your perfection*. That is, we are not only glad when you are strong, but we pray for your complete establishment. *Perfection*, κατάρτισις, from καταρτίζω, in the sense *to put in complete order*. Paul prayed that they might be perfectly restored from the state of confusion, contention, and evil into which they had fallen.

10. Therefore I write these things being absent,

lest being present I should use sharpness, according to
the power which the Lord hath given me to edification,
and not to destruction.

Therefore, i. e. because I desire your good, and because I
prefer to appear ἀδόκιμος, *without proof*, so far as the proof of
my apostleship consists in the exercise of my power to punish.
This is the reason why the apostle wrote these exhortations
and warnings, *lest being present I should use sharpness*, i. e.
be obliged to exercise severity in dealing with offenders.
The expression is ἀποτόμως χρήσωμαι, where ὑμῖν must be supplied, 'lest I should use *you* sharply.' *According to the
power*. The word is ἐξουσίαν, which includes the ideas of
ability and authority or right. Paul was invested both with
the authority to punish offenders and with the power to carry
his judgments into effect. *Which the Lord hath given me.*
His authority was not self-assumed, and his power was not
derived from himself. They were the gifts of the Lord, the
only source of either in the church. *The Lord* is of course
Christ, whose divine power and omnipresence are taken for
granted. Paul everywhere as much assumes that the Lord
Jesus is invested with divine attributes and entitled to divine
worship, as God himself. Nothing can be more foreign to
the whole spirit of the New Testament than the idea, that
Christ, having finished his work on earth as a teacher and
witness, has passed away so as to be no longer present with
his people. The whole Scriptures, on the contrary, assume
that he is everywhere present in knowledge and power, the
source of all grace, strength and consolation, the object of the
religious affections, and of the acts of religious worship. *For
edification, and not for destruction.* This not only expresses
the design with which Paul was invested and endowed with
apostolic power, but it teaches that the power itself could be
exercised only for good. Christ would not sanction an unjust
decision, or clothe the arm of man with supernatural power to
inflict unmerited punishment. The apostles could not strike
a saint with blindness nor deliver a child of God unto Satan.
The church and its ministers are in the same predicament still.
They are powerful only for good. Their mistaken decisions
or unrighteous judgments are of no avail. They affect the
standing of the true believer in the sight of God no more
than the judgments of the Jewish synagogues when they cast
out the early disciples as evil. Truth and holiness are a sure

defence against all ecclesiastical power. No one can harm us, if we be followers of that which is good. 1 Peter 3, 13.

11. Finally, brethren, farewell. Be perfect, be of good comfort, be of one mind, live in peace ; and the God of love and peace shall be with you.

The severe rebukes contained in the preceding chapters, are softened down by the parental and apostolic tone assumed in these concluding verses. He addresses them as brethren, members of the family of God and of the body of Christ. *Farewell*, χαίρετε; literally, *rejoice*, or, *joy to you.* It is used often in salutations, as Hail! On account of what follows it is better to take it as an exhortation to spiritual joy. *Rejoice*, i. e. in the Lord. In Phil. 3, 1 and 4, 4 we have the same exhortation, χαίρετε ἐν κυρίῳ. Joy in redemption, rejoicing in our union and communion with the Lord is one of our highest duties. Blessings so infinite as these should not be received with indifference. Joy is the atmosphere of heaven, and the more we have of it on earth, the more heavenly shall we be in character and temper. *Be perfect*, καρτίζεσθε, *reform yourselves ;* correct the evils which prevail within and among you. *Be of good comfort*, παρακαλεῖσθε, which may be rendered, *exhort one another.* This latter interpretation is perhaps preferable, because more distinct from the preceding command. The exhortation to rejoice includes that to be of good comfort. *Be of one mind*, τὸ αὐτὸ φρονεῖτε, be united in faith, in feeling, and in object. Cognate with this is the exhortation, *Live in peace.* One of the greatest evils prevailing in Corinth, as we learn from 1 Cor. 1, 10–12, was the contentions of the various parties into which the church was divided. *And the God of love and peace*, i. e. God is the author of love and of peace, *shall be with you.* The existence of love and peace is the condition of the presence of the God of peace. He withdraws the manifestations of his presence from the soul disturbed by angry passions, and from a community torn by dissensions. We have here the familiar Christian paradox. God's presence produces love and peace, and we must have love and peace in order to have his presence. God gives what he commands. God gives, but we must cherish his gifts. His agency does not supersede ours, but mingles with it and becomes one with it in our consciousness. We work out our own salvation, while God works in us. Our duty is to yield ourselves to the operation of God, and to exert our faculties as though the effect desired were in our own power, and leave to his almighty, mystic co-operation its own gracious office. The man with the withered hand, did something when he stretched it forth, although the power to move was divinely given. It is vain for us to pray for the presence of the God of love and peace, unless we strive to free our hearts from all evil passions. *Shall be with you;* shall manifest his .presence, his glory and his love. This gives perfect peace, and fills the soul with joy unspeakable and full of glory. It is the restoration of the original and normal relation between God and the soul, and secures at once its purification and blessedness. He who has the presence of God can feel no want.

12. Greet one another with a holy kiss.

The kiss was the expression of fellowship and affection. It was and is in the East the common mode of salutation among friends. A *holy* kiss, is a kiss which expresses Christian communion and love. It was the usage in Christian assemblies for the men to kiss the minister and each other, especially at the celebration of the Lord's supper. It did not go out of use in the Western churches until about the thirteenth century, and is still observed among some eastern sects. It is not a command of perpetual obligation, as the spirit of the command is that Christians should express their mutual love in the way sanctioned by the age and community in which they live.

13. All the saints salute you.

The saints, in scriptural usage, are not those who are complete in glory, but believers, separated from the world, consecrated to God, and inwardly purified. This term, therefore, expresses the character and the relations, not of a class among God's people, but of the disciples of Christ as such. They are all, if sincere, separated from the world, distinguished from men of the world as to their objects of desire and pursuit, and as to the rules by which they are governed; they are consecrated to the service and worship of God, as a holy people; and they are cleansed from the guilt and controlling power of sin. They are therefore bound to live in accordance with this character. *All* the saints, i. e. all those in the place in which Paul then was. The communion of saints includes all believers who feel themselves to be one body in Christ. *Salute you*, that is, wish you salvation, which includes all good.

14. The grace of the Lord Jesus Christ, and the love of God, and the communion of the Holy Ghost, (be) with you all. Amen.

This comprehensive benediction closes the epistle. It includes all the benefits of redemption. First, *the grace*, or *favour*, of the Lord Jesus Christ. This is the theanthropical designation of our blessed Saviour. It includes or indicates his divine nature, he is our Lord; his human nature, he is Jesus; his office, he is the Christ, the Messiah, the long-promised Redeemer. It is the favour, the unmerited love and all that springs from it, of this divine person clothed in our nature, and who as the theanthropos is invested with the office of Messiah, the headship over his own people and all power in heaven and earth, that the apostle invokes for all his believing readers. Every one feels that this is precisely what he, as a guilty, polluted, helpless sinner, needs. If this glorious, mysteriously constituted, exalted Saviour, Son of God and Son of man, makes us the objects of his favour, then is our present security and ultimate salvation rendered certain. *The love of God.* In one view the love of God is the source of redemption. God manifested his love in giving his Son for us, Rom. 5, 8. But in another view the love of God to us is due to the grace and work of Christ. That is, the manifestation of that love in the pardon, sanctification and salvation of men, was conditional on the work of Christ. We are reconciled to God by the death of his Son. His death as a satisfaction for our sins was necessary in order to our being actually introduced into the fellowship of God and made partakers of his love. Therefore the apostle puts the grace of Christ before the love of God, as, in the sense mentioned, the necessary condition of its manifestation. *And the communion* (κοινωνία, the participation) *of the Holy Ghost.* The primary object of the death of Christ was the communication of the Holy Spirit. He redeemed us from the curse of the law, that we might receive the promise of the Spirit, Gal. 3, 13. 14. It is the gift of the Holy Ghost secured in the covenant of redemption by the death of Christ that applies to us the benefits of his mediation. As the gift of the Spirit is secured to all the people of God, they are κοινωνοί, joint partakers, of the Holy Ghost, and thereby made one body. This is the ground of the communion of saints in which the church universal professes her faith.

The distinct personality and the divinity of the Son, the Father, and the Holy Spirit, to each of whom prayer is addressed, is here taken for granted. And therefore this passage is a clear recognition of the doctrine of the Trinity, which is the fundamental doctrine of Christianity. For a Christian is one who seeks and enjoys the grace of the Lord Jesus, the love of God, and the communion of the Holy Ghost.

THE END.